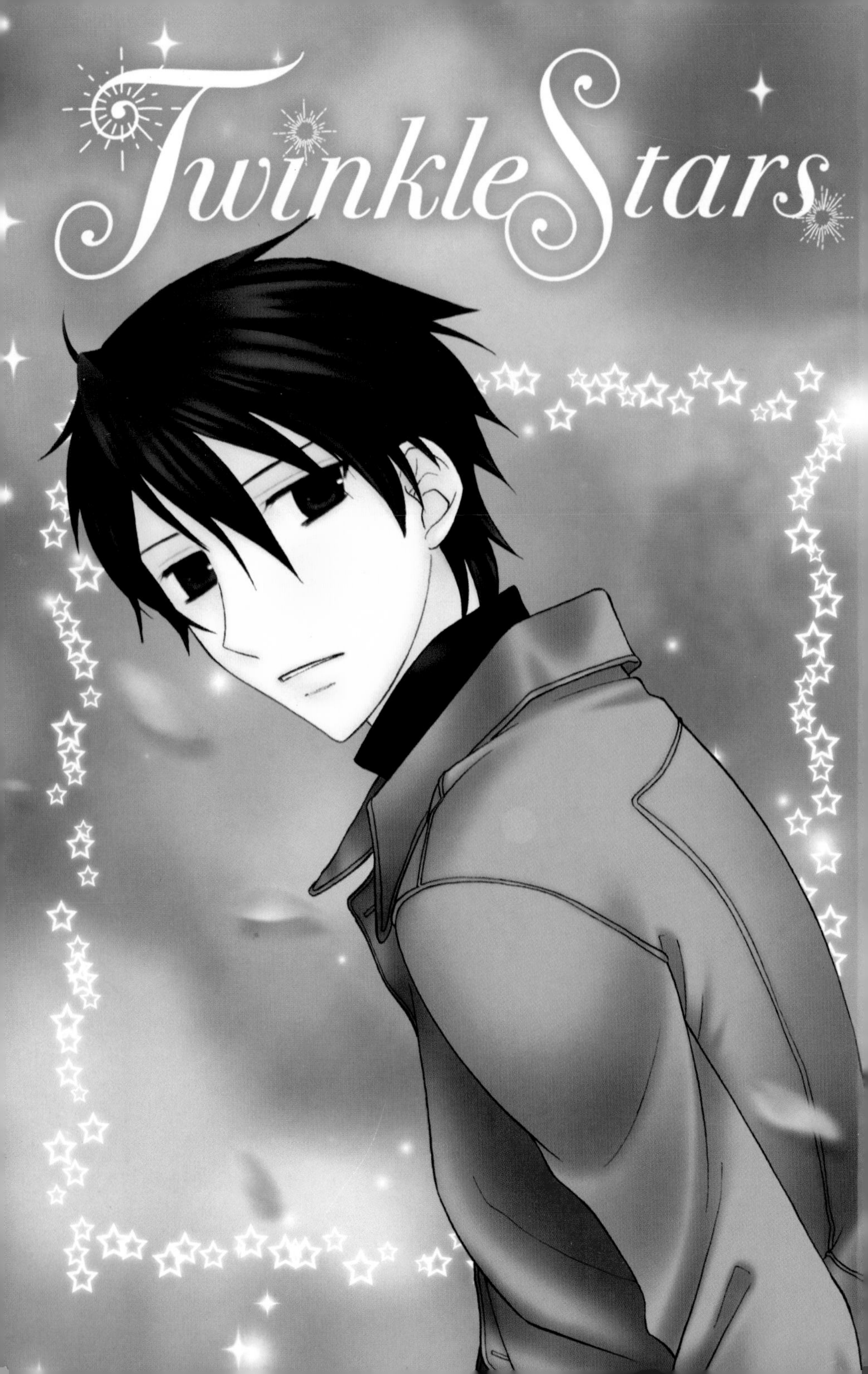
Twinkle Stars

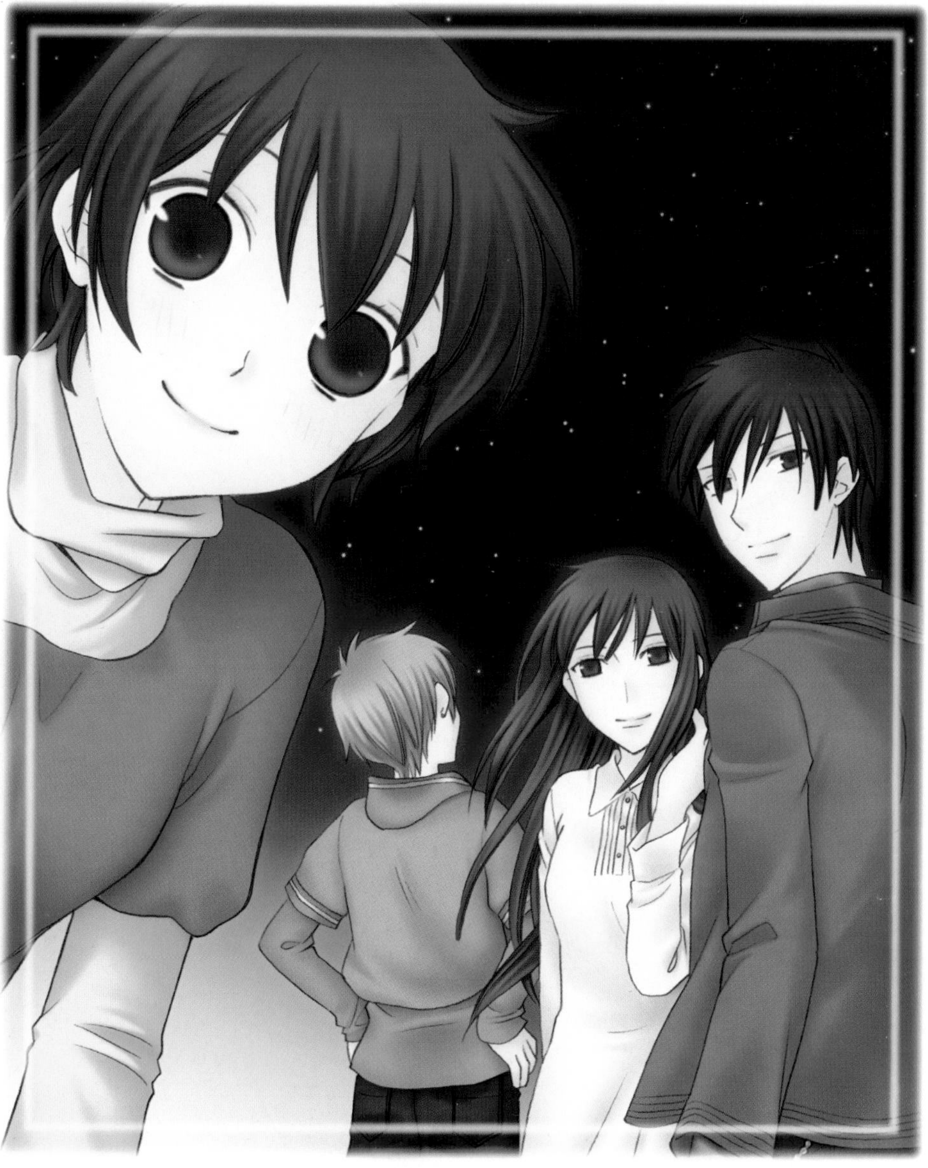

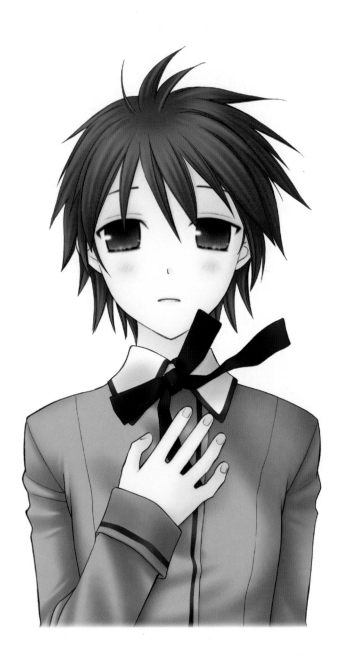

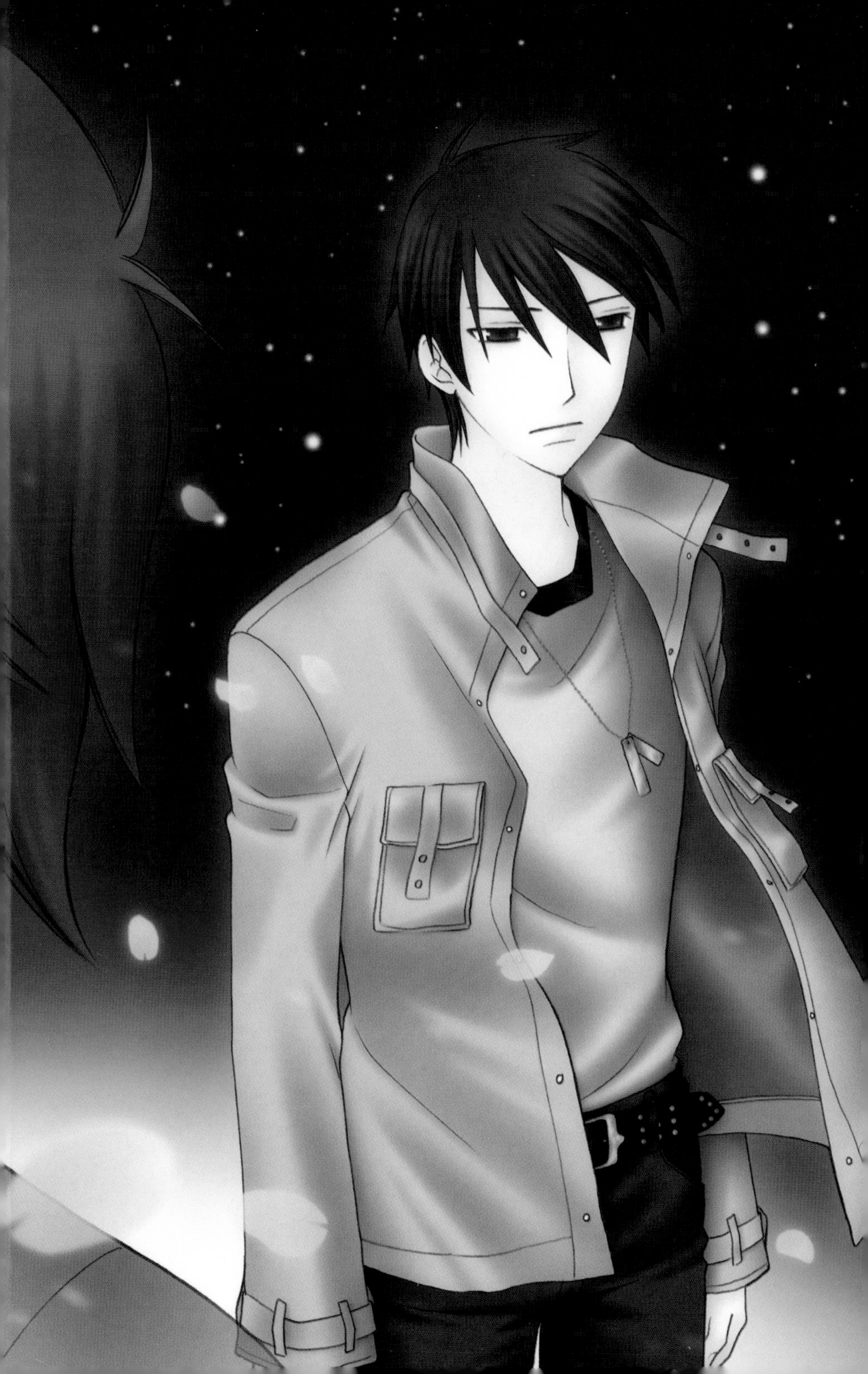

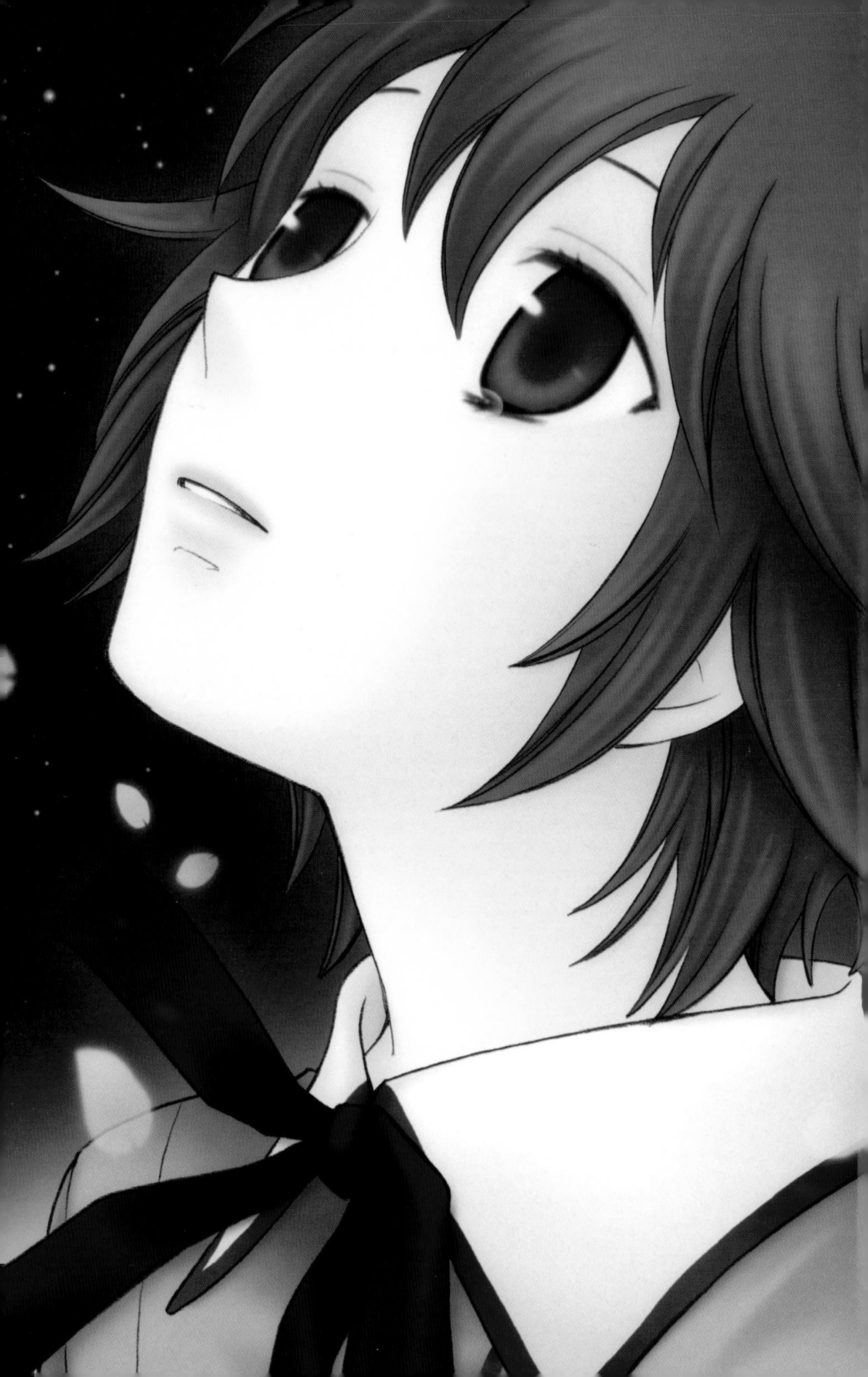

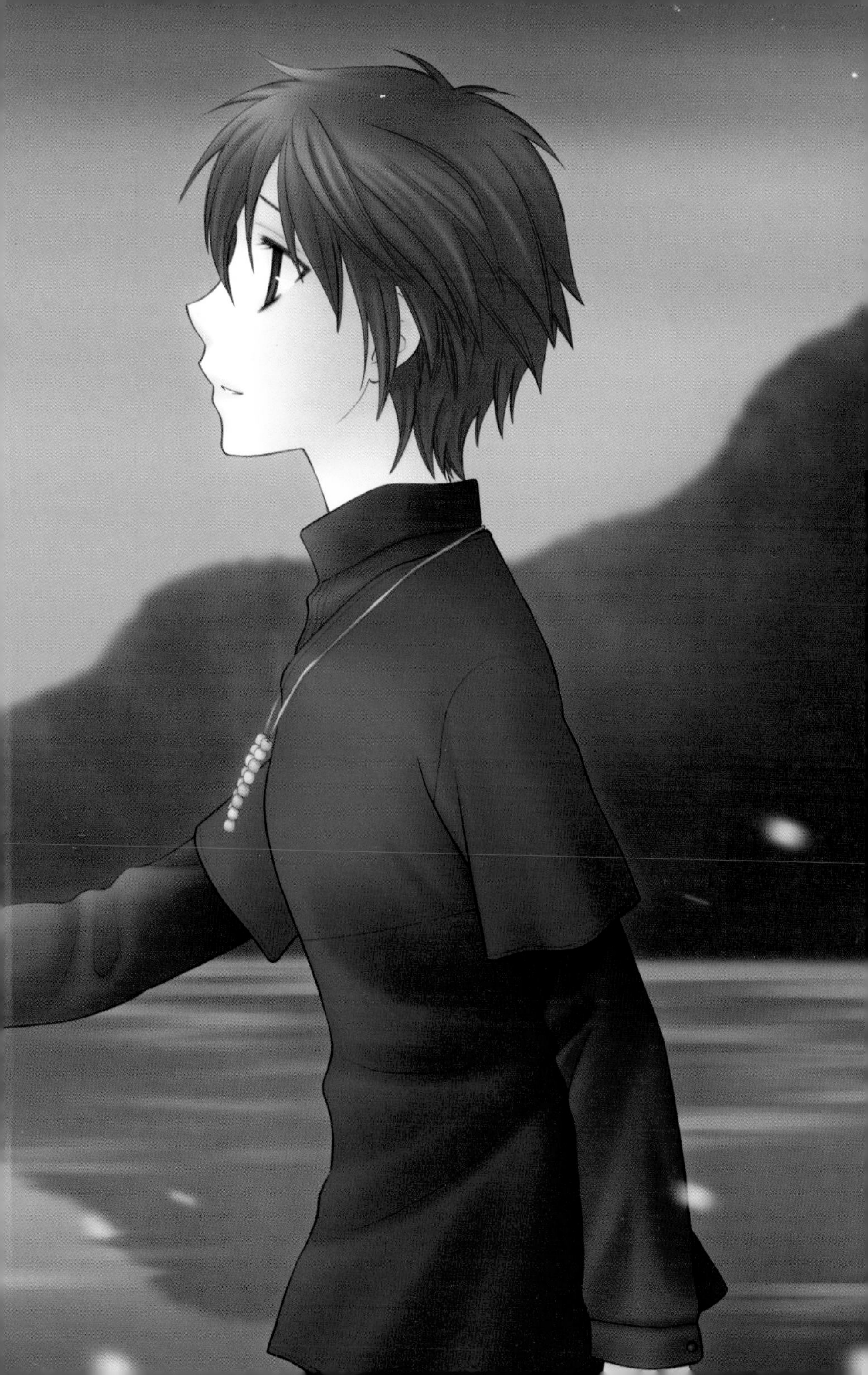

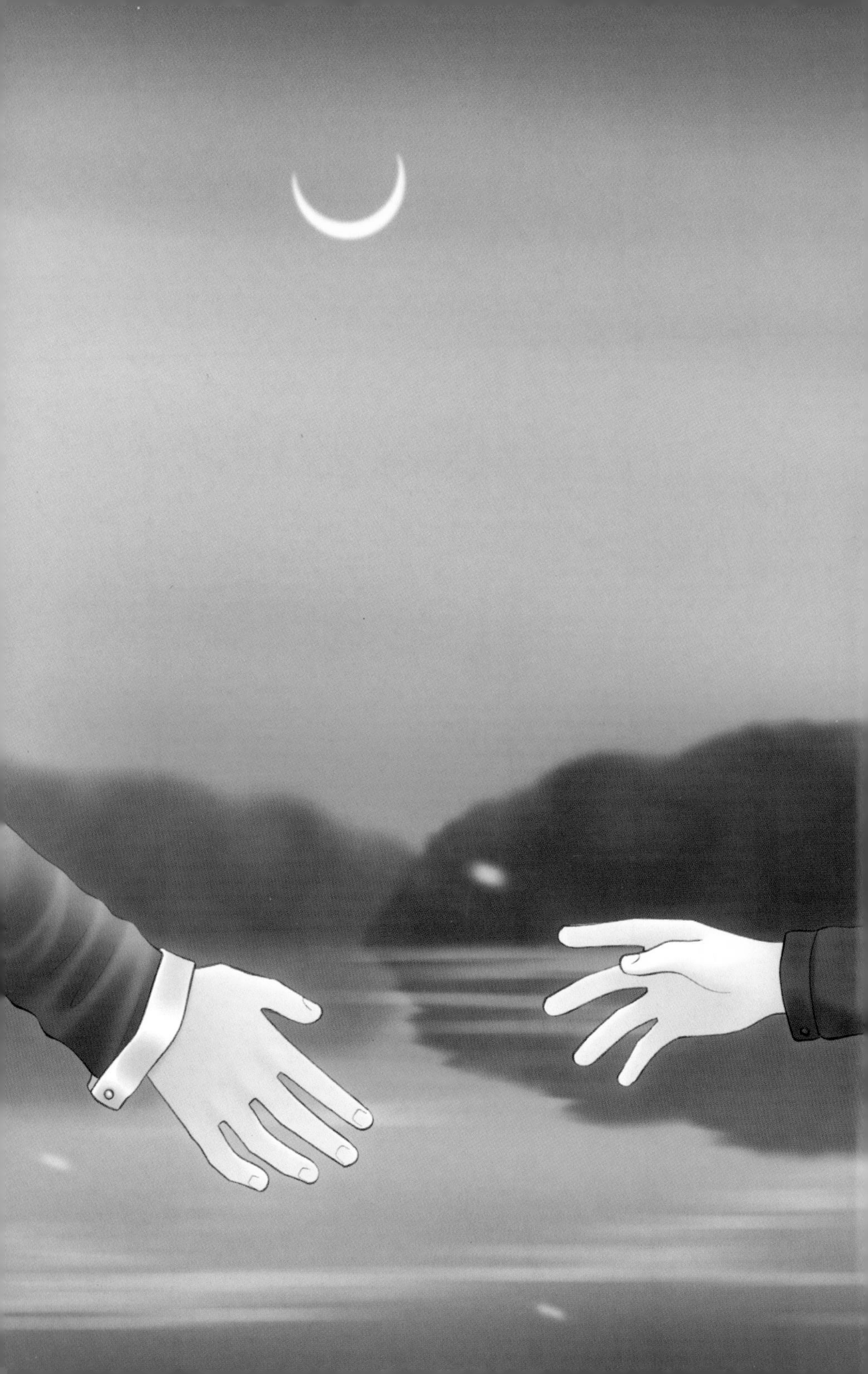

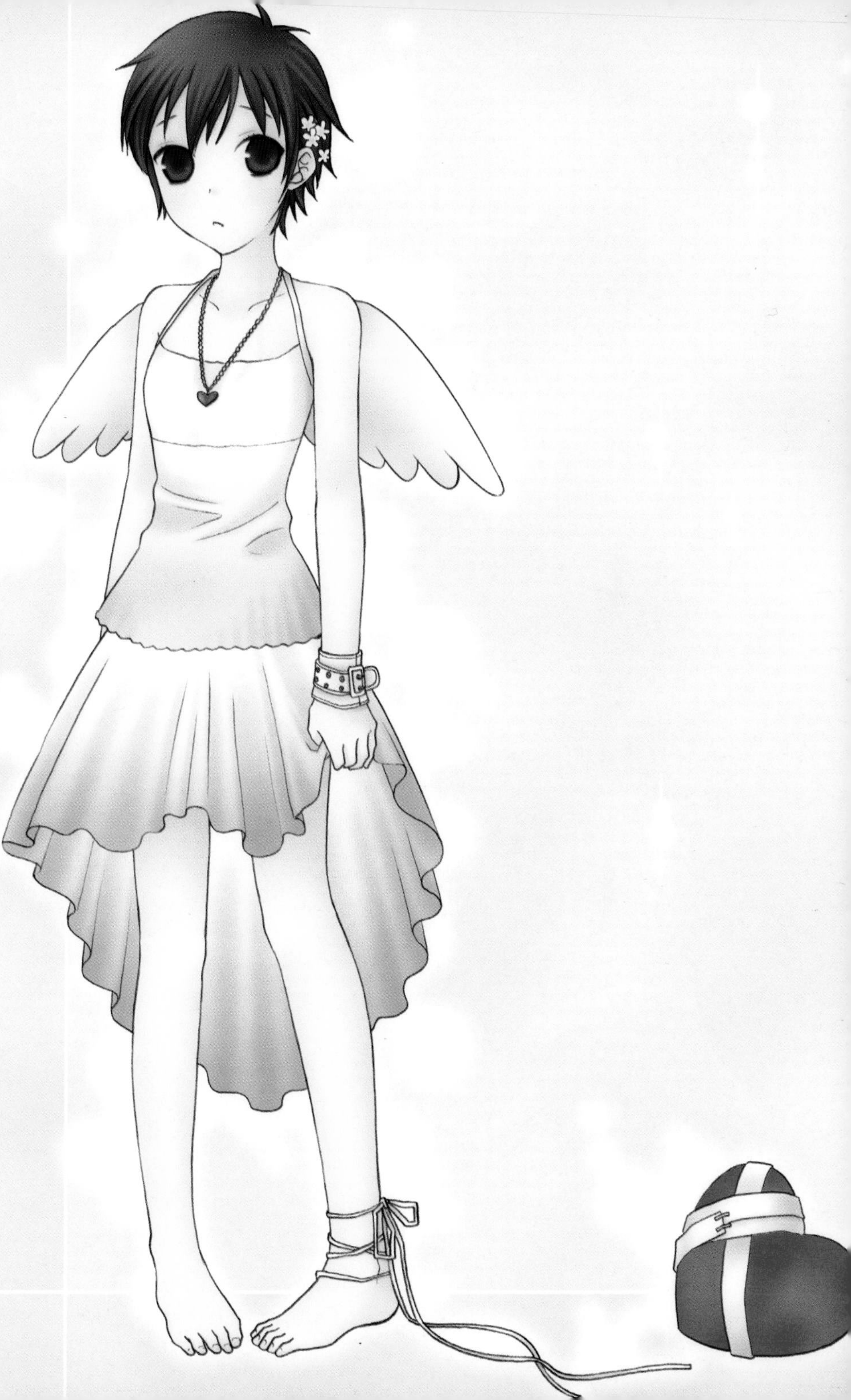

Twinkle Stars

Volume 1

NATSUKI TAKAYA

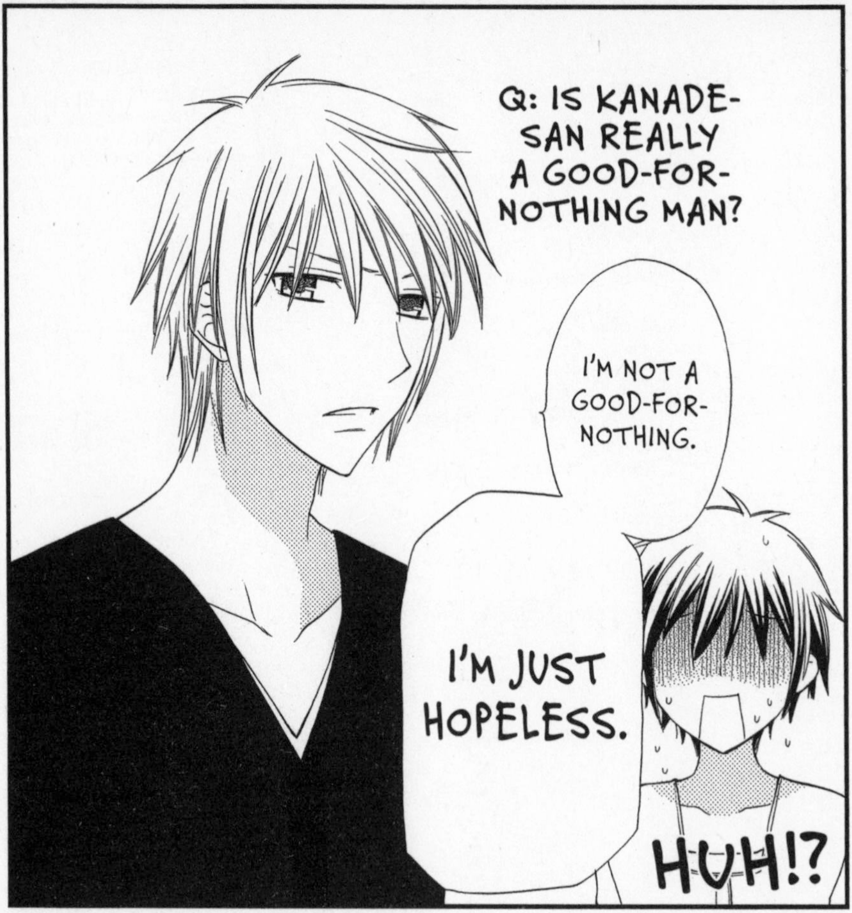
Q: IS KANADE-SAN REALLY A GOOD-FOR-NOTHING MAN?
I'M NOT A GOOD-FOR-NOTHING.
I'M JUST HOPELESS.
HUH!?

TwinkleStars

EVEN IF I'D KNOWN,

I STILL WOULD'VE FALLEN IN LOVE.

I WOULD'VE BEEN IN LOVE.

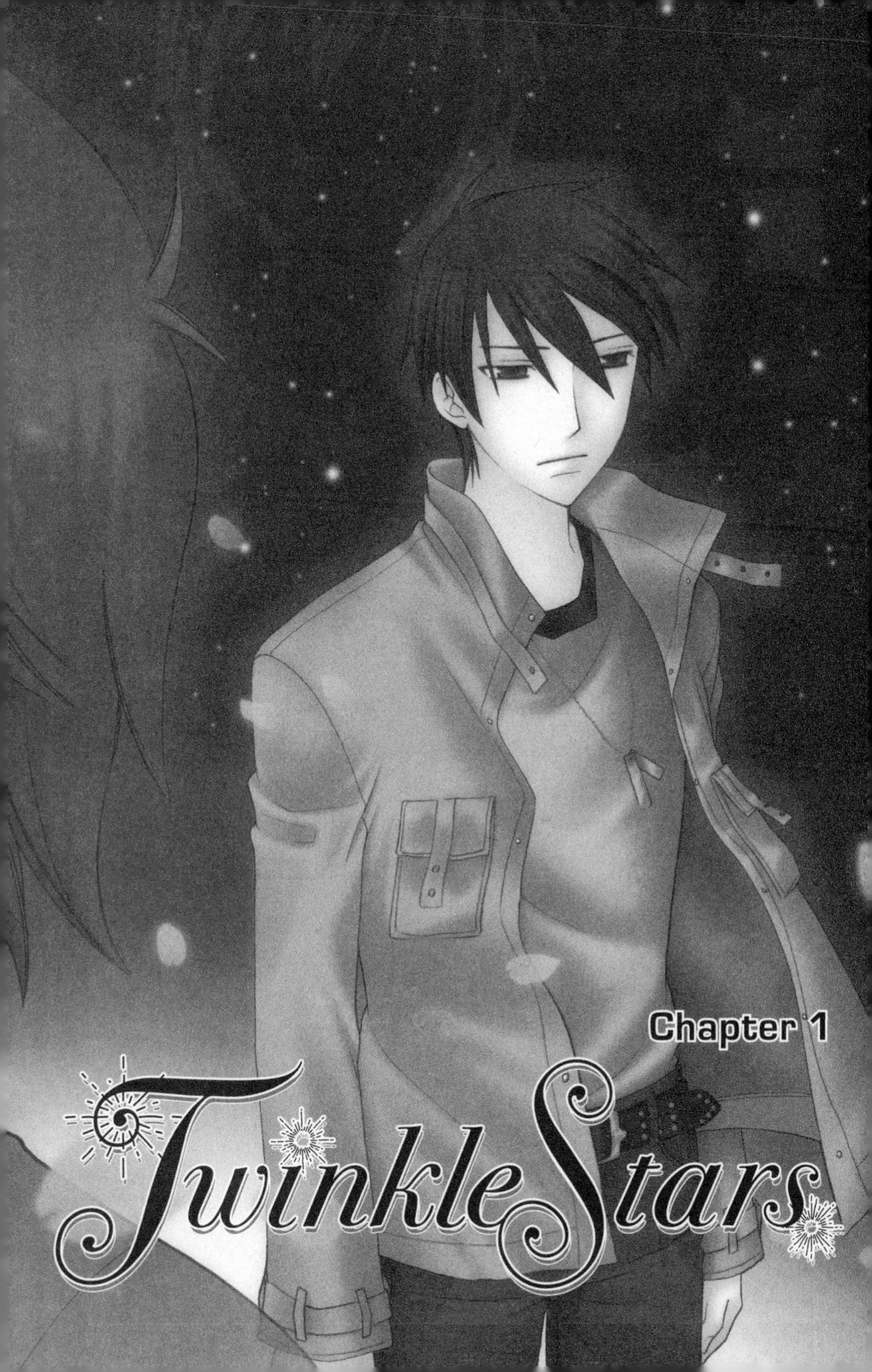
Chapter 1
Twinkle Stars

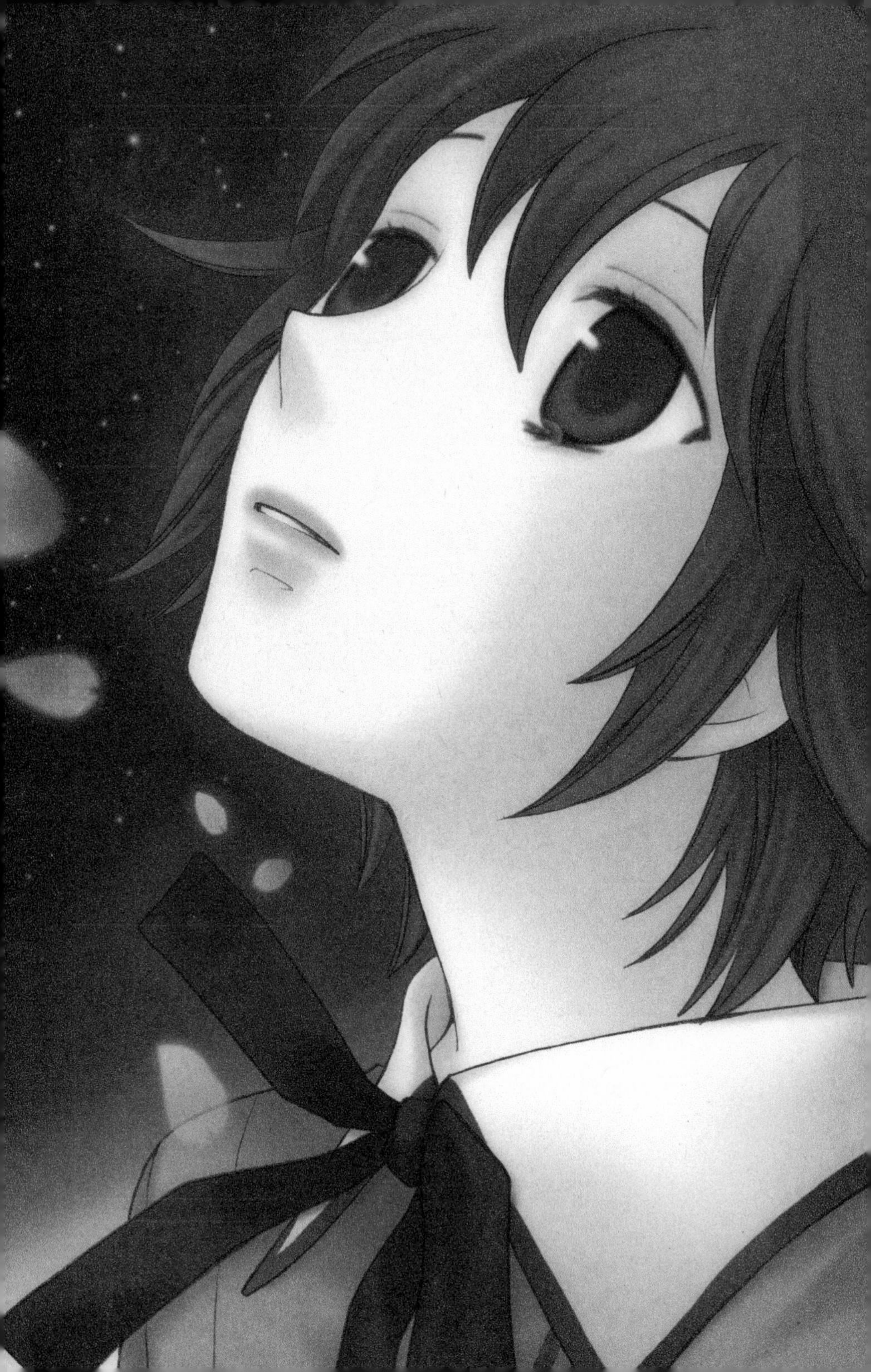

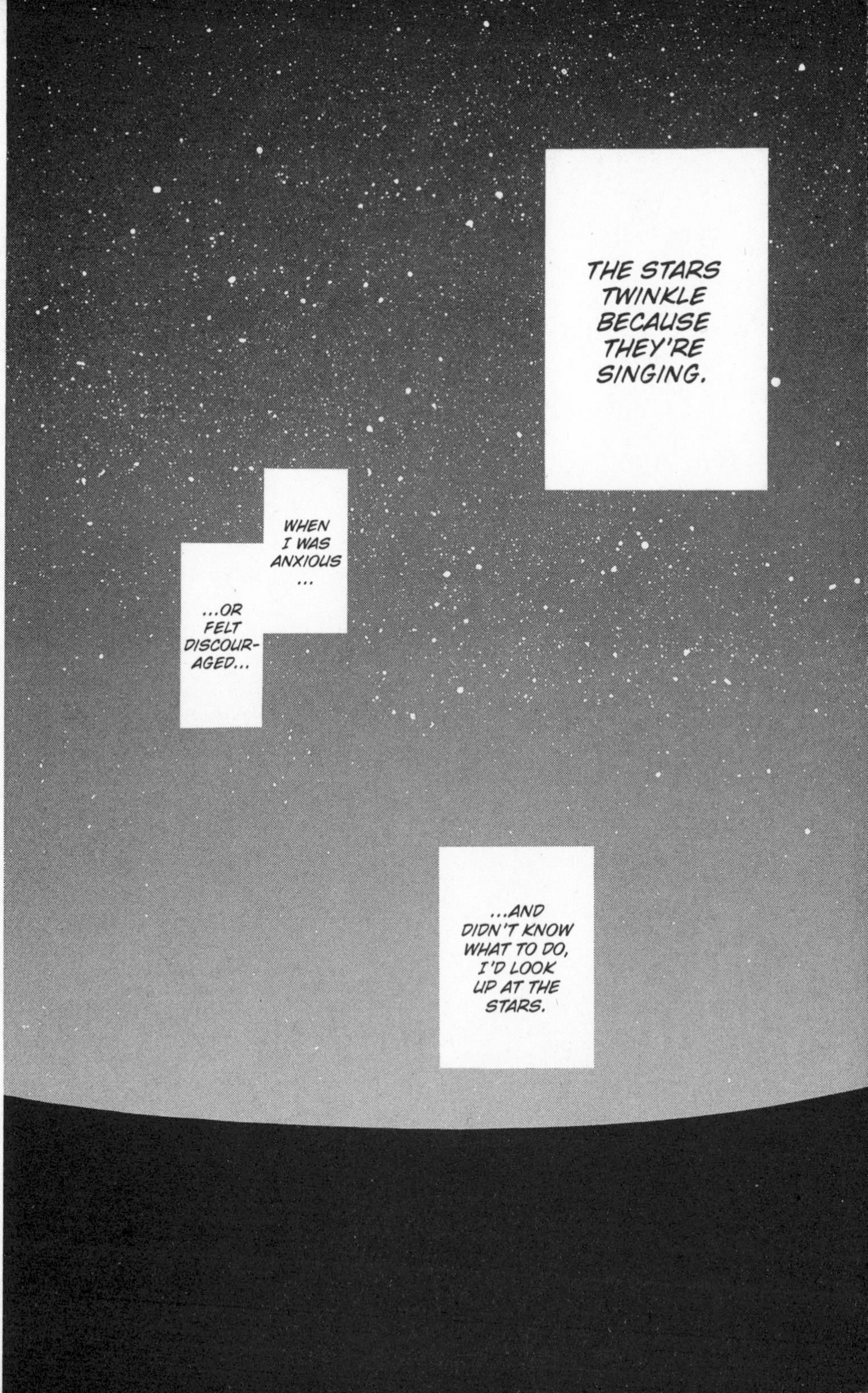
THE STARS TWINKLE BECAUSE THEY'RE SINGING.
WHEN I WAS ANXIOUS...
...OR FELT DISCOUR-AGED...
...AND DIDN'T KNOW WHAT TO DO, I'D LOOK UP AT THE STARS.

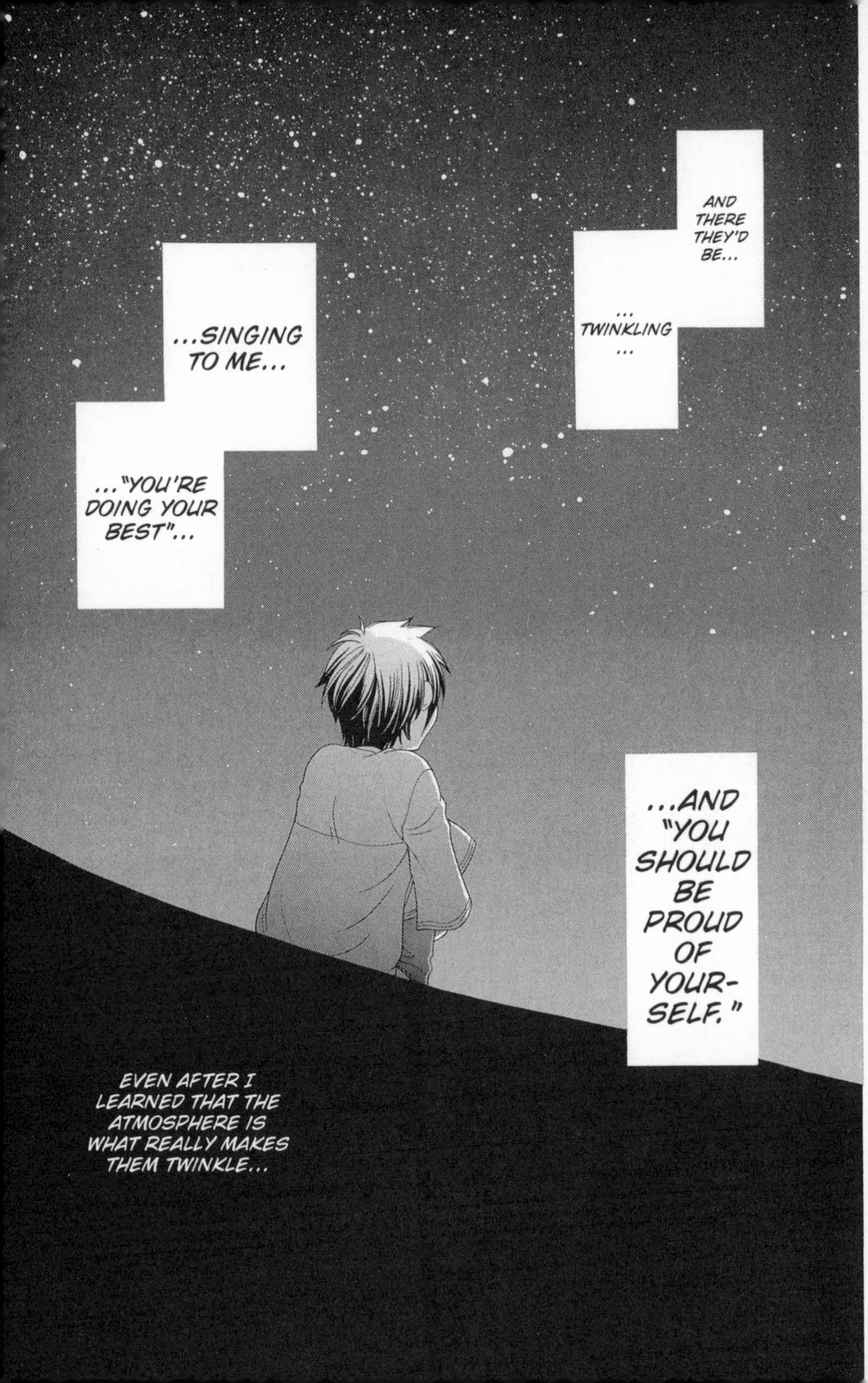
AND THERE THEY'D BE...
...TWINKLING...
...SINGING TO ME...
..."YOU'RE DOING YOUR BEST"...
...AND "YOU SHOULD BE PROUD OF YOUR-SELF."
EVEN AFTER I LEARNED THAT THE ATMOSPHERE IS WHAT REALLY MAKES THEM TWINKLE...

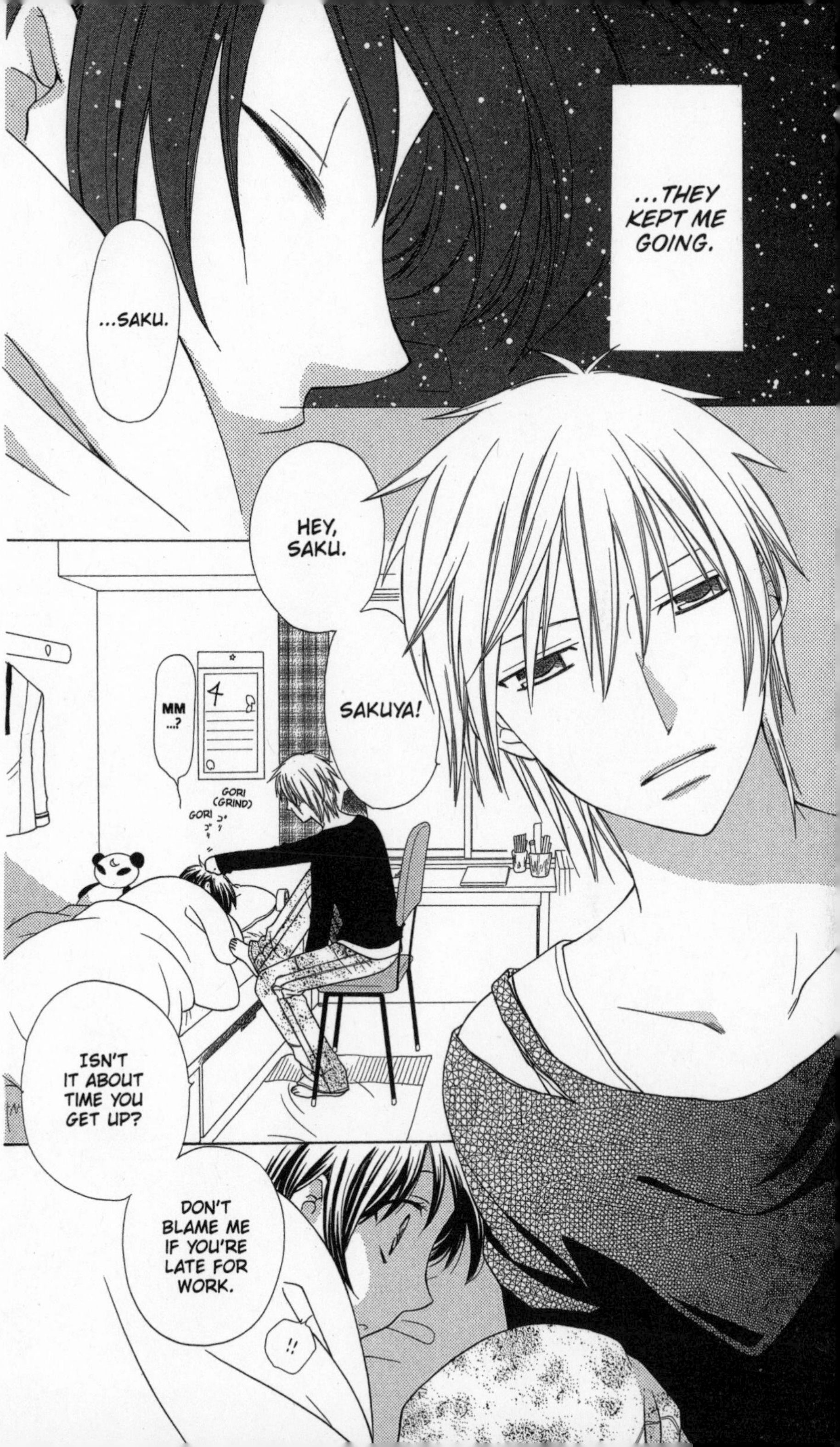
...THEY KEPT ME GOING.
...SAKU.
HEY, SAKU.
SAKUYA!
MM ...?
GORI (GRIND)
GORI
ISN'T IT ABOUT TIME YOU GET UP?
DON'T BLAME ME IF YOU'RE LATE FOR WORK.
!!

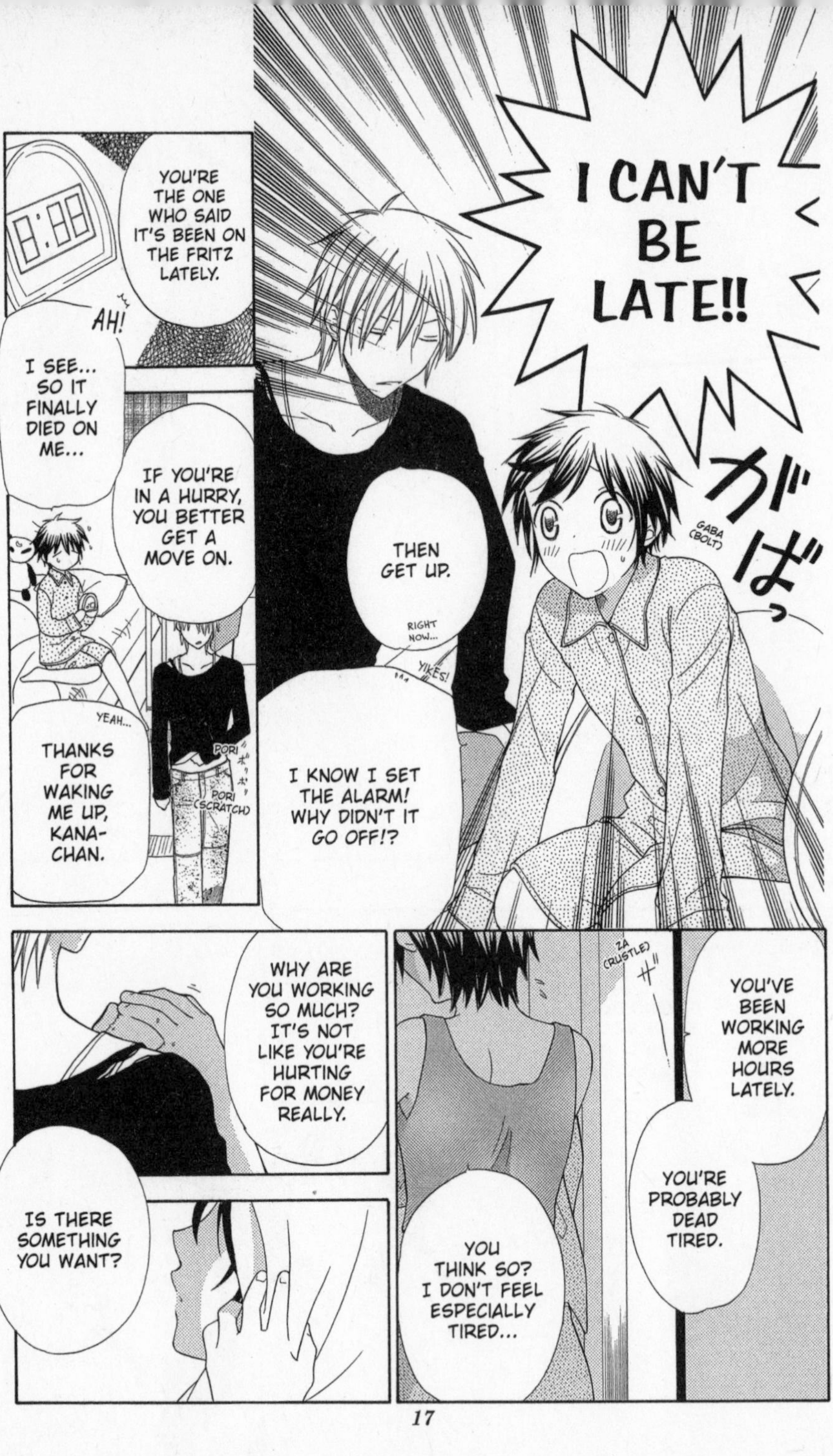
I CAN'T BE LATE!!
がばっ
GABA (BOLT)
THEN GET UP.
RIGHT NOW...
YIKES!
I KNOW I SET THE ALARM! WHY DIDN'T IT GO OFF!?
YOU'RE THE ONE WHO SAID IT'S BEEN ON THE FRITZ LATELY.
AH!
I SEE... SO IT FINALLY DIED ON ME...
IF YOU'RE IN A HURRY, YOU BETTER GET A MOVE ON.
PORI PORI (SCRATCH)
YEAH...
THANKS FOR WAKING ME UP, KANA-CHAN.
ZA (RUSTLE)
YOU'VE BEEN WORKING MORE HOURS LATELY.
YOU'RE PROBABLY DEAD TIRED.
YOU THINK SO? I DON'T FEEL ESPECIALLY TIRED...
WHY ARE YOU WORKING SO MUCH? IT'S NOT LIKE YOU'RE HURTING FOR MONEY REALLY.
IS THERE SOMETHING YOU WANT?

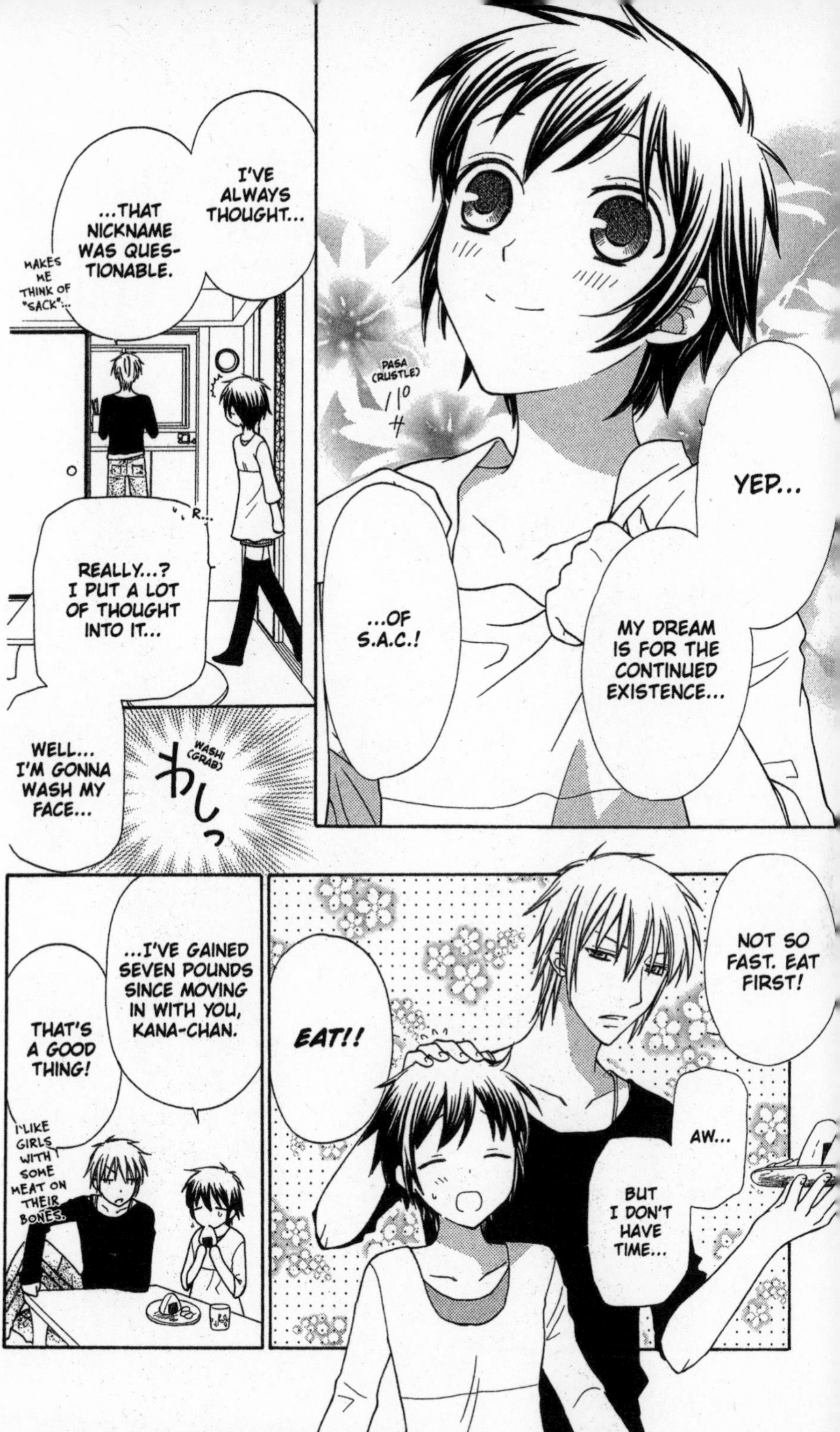
YEP...
MY DREAM IS FOR THE CONTINUED EXISTENCE...
...OF S.A.C.!
PASA (RUSTLE)
I'VE ALWAYS THOUGHT...
...THAT NICKNAME WAS QUES-TIONABLE.
MAKES ME THINK OF "SACK"...
...R...
REALLY...? I PUT A LOT OF THOUGHT INTO IT...
WASHI (GRAB)
WELL... I'M GONNA WASH MY FACE...
NOT SO FAST. EAT FIRST!
EAT!!
AW...
BUT I DON'T HAVE TIME...
...I'VE GAINED SEVEN POUNDS SINCE MOVING IN WITH YOU, KANA-CHAN.
THAT'S A GOOD THING!
I LIKE GIRLS WITH SOME MEAT ON THEIR BONES.

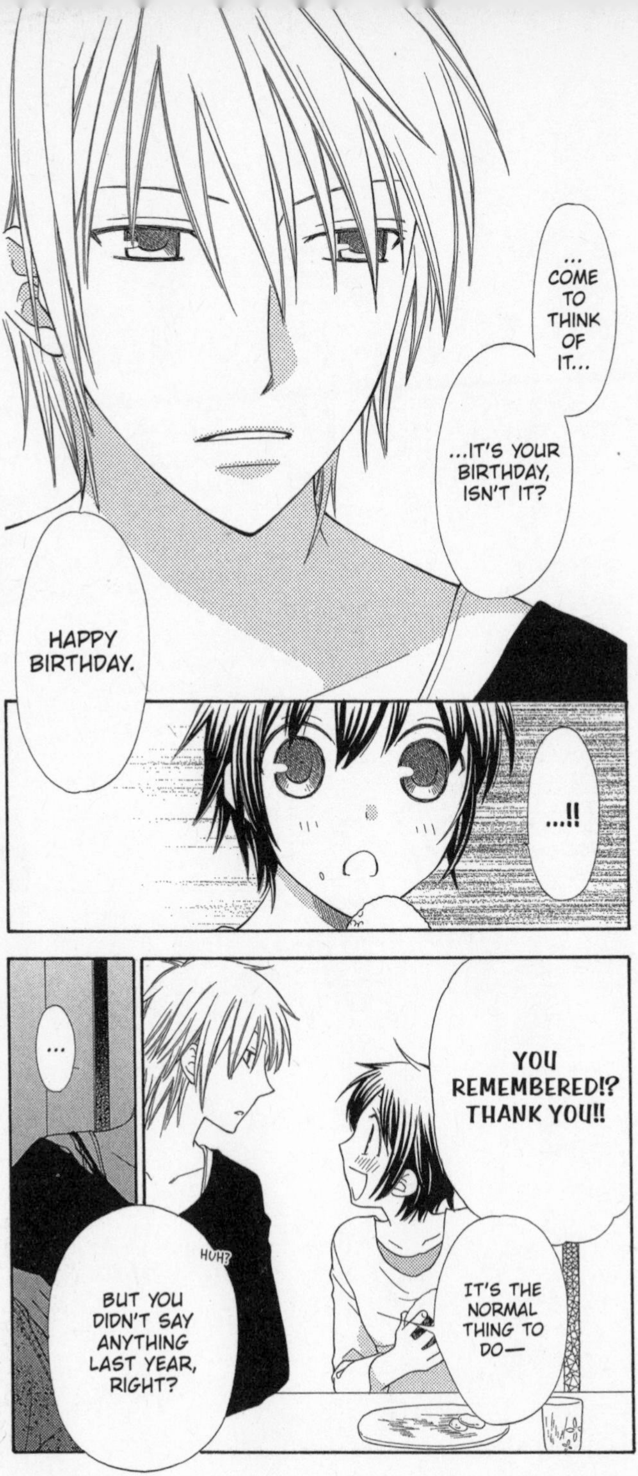
...COME TO THINK OF IT...
...IT'S YOUR BIRTHDAY, ISN'T IT?
HAPPY BIRTHDAY.
...!!
YOU REMEMBERED!? THANK YOU!!
IT'S THE NORMAL THING TO DO—
HUH?
BUT YOU DIDN'T SAY ANYTHING LAST YEAR, RIGHT?
...

Twinkle Stars

Nice to meet you and hello. I'm Takaya. This is Volume 1 of Twinkle Stars.

Clap, clap.

As I work on this manga, I sometimes think back on the times I felt hopeless, when my heart felt like it was chewed up and spit out. I would go up to the top of the apartment building (where I was living at the time) and just gaze up at the sky by myself. I apologize to those readers who expected this to be more of a technical story about stars.

And so we begin Volume 1!

It's been a while since I've written by hand, so I bet this is hard for you to read, huh?

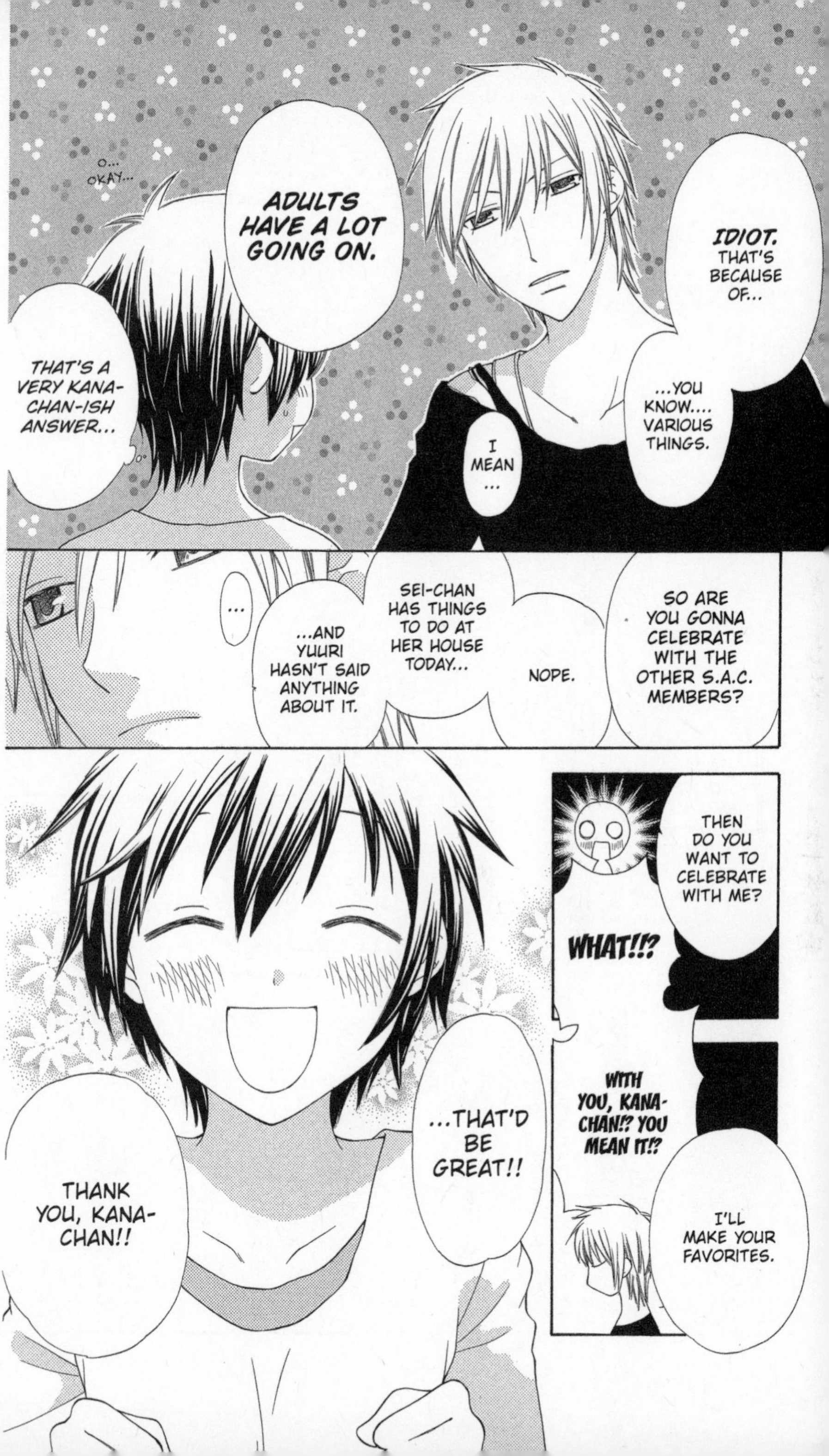
IDIOT. THAT'S BECAUSE OF...
...YOU KNOW.... VARIOUS THINGS.
I MEAN ...
ADULTS HAVE A LOT GOING ON.
O... OKAY...
THAT'S A VERY KANA-CHAN-ISH ANSWER...
SO ARE YOU GONNA CELEBRATE WITH THE OTHER S.A.C. MEMBERS?
NOPE.
SEI-CHAN HAS THINGS TO DO AT HER HOUSE TODAY...
...AND YUURI HASN'T SAID ANYTHING ABOUT IT.
...
THEN DO YOU WANT TO CELEBRATE WITH ME?
WHAT!!?
WITH YOU, KANA-CHAN!? YOU MEAN IT!?
I'LL MAKE YOUR FAVORITES.
...THAT'D BE GREAT!!
THANK YOU, KANA-CHAN!!

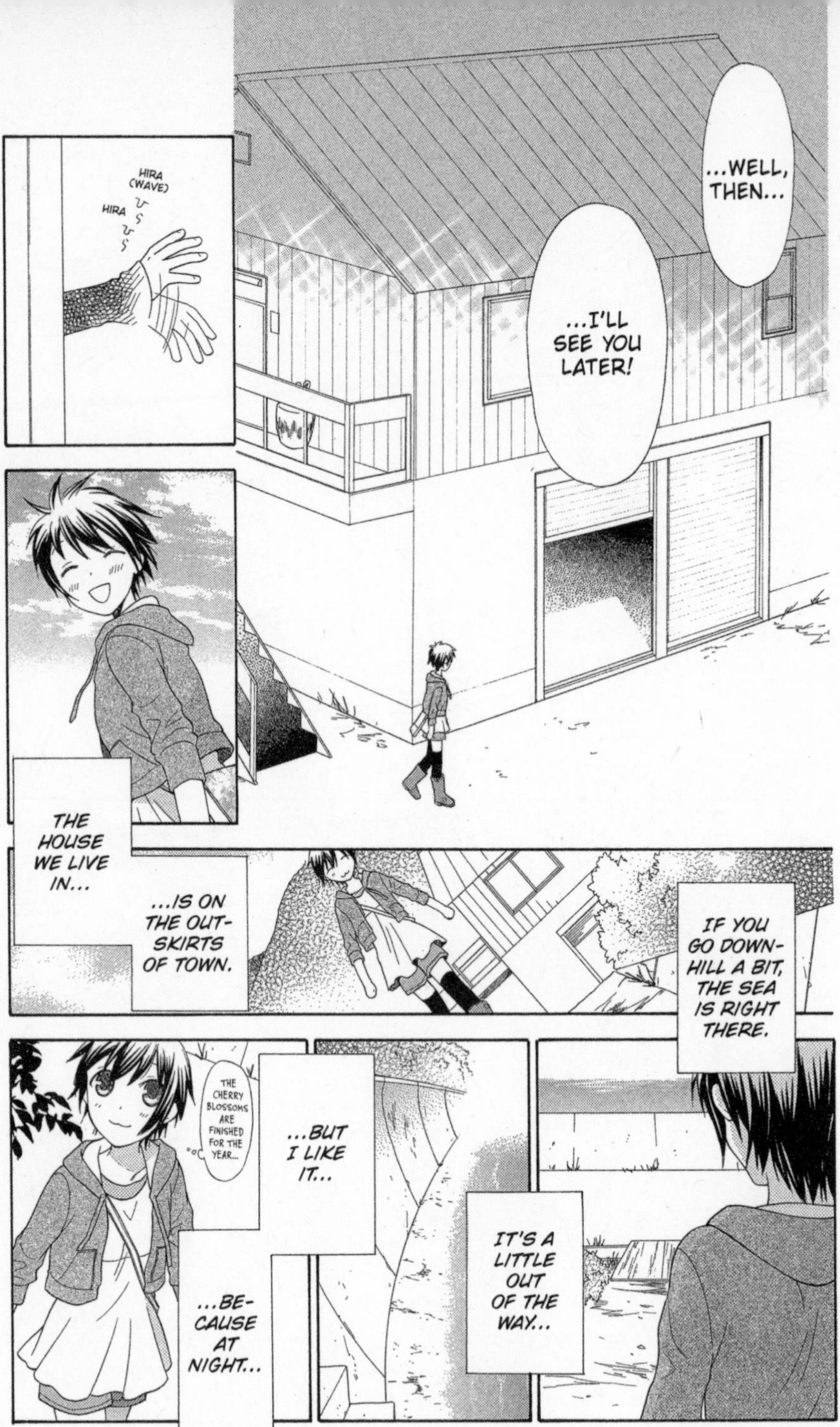
...WELL, THEN...
...I'LL SEE YOU LATER!
HIRA (WAVE) HIRA
ひらひら
THE HOUSE WE LIVE IN...
...IS ON THE OUT-SKIRTS OF TOWN.
IF YOU GO DOWN-HILL A BIT, THE SEA IS RIGHT THERE.
IT'S A LITTLE OUT OF THE WAY...
...BUT I LIKE IT...
THE CHERRY BLOSSOMS ARE FINISHED FOR THE YEAR...
...BE-CAUSE AT NIGHT...

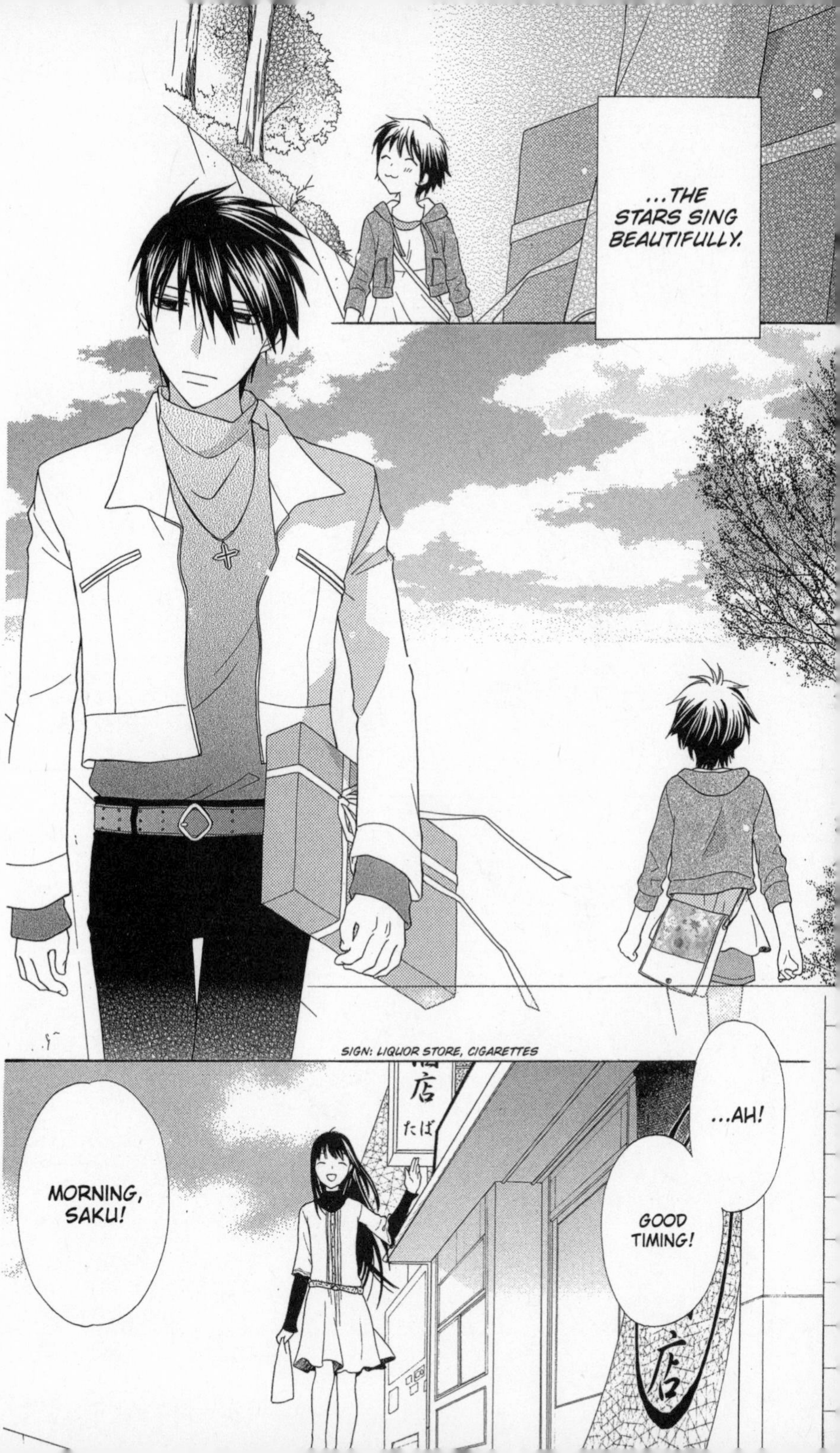
...THE STARS SING BEAUTIFULLY.
SIGN: LIQUOR STORE, CIGARETTES
店
たば
...AH!
GOOD TIMING!
MORNING, SAKU!
店

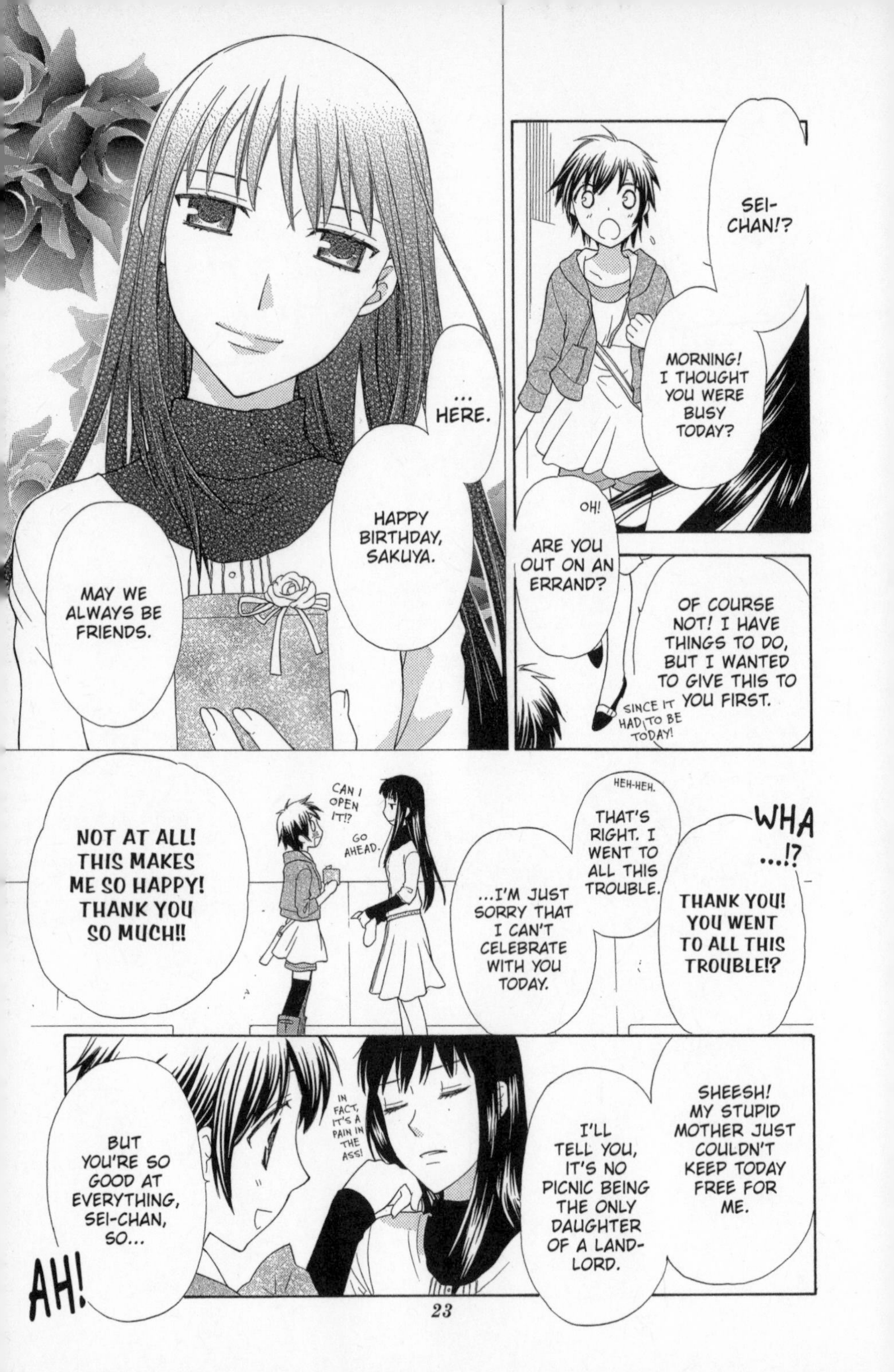
SEI-CHAN!?
MORNING! I THOUGHT YOU WERE BUSY TODAY?
OH!
ARE YOU OUT ON AN ERRAND?
OF COURSE NOT! I HAVE THINGS TO DO, BUT I WANTED TO GIVE THIS TO YOU FIRST.
SINCE IT HAD TO BE TODAY!
...HERE.
HAPPY BIRTHDAY, SAKUYA.
MAY WE ALWAYS BE FRIENDS.
WHA ...!?
THANK YOU! YOU WENT TO ALL THIS TROUBLE!?
HEH-HEH.
THAT'S RIGHT. I WENT TO ALL THIS TROUBLE.
...I'M JUST SORRY THAT I CAN'T CELEBRATE WITH YOU TODAY.
CAN I OPEN IT!?
GO AHEAD.
NOT AT ALL! THIS MAKES ME SO HAPPY! THANK YOU SO MUCH!!
SHEESH! MY STUPID MOTHER JUST COULDN'T KEEP TODAY FREE FOR ME.
I'LL TELL YOU, IT'S NO PICNIC BEING THE ONLY DAUGHTER OF A LAND-LORD.
IN FACT, IT'S A PAIN IN THE ASS!
BUT YOU'RE SO GOOD AT EVERYTHING, SEI-CHAN, SO...
AH!

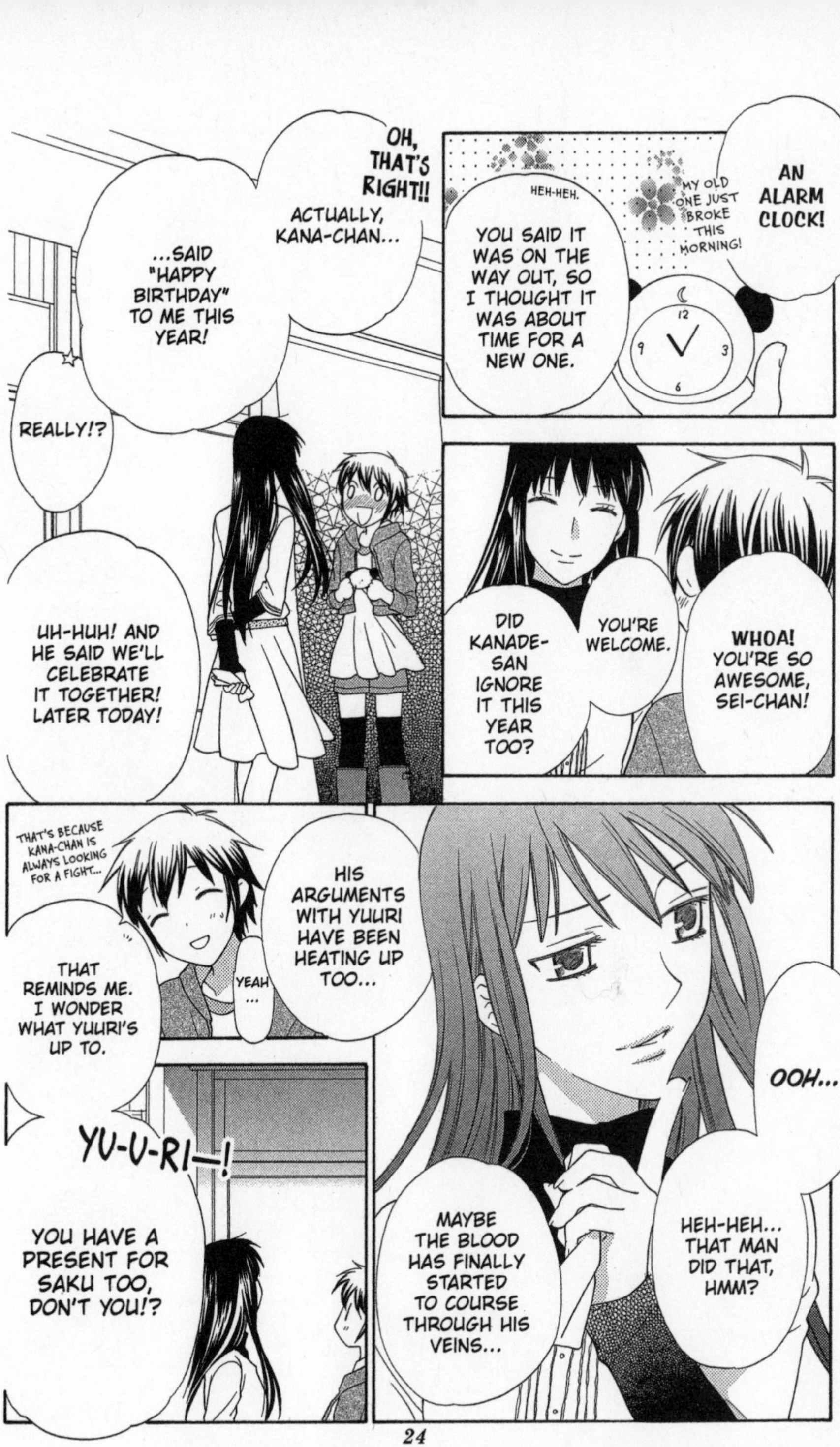
AN ALARM CLOCK!
MY OLD ONE JUST BROKE THIS MORNING!
HEH-HEH.
YOU SAID IT WAS ON THE WAY OUT, SO I THOUGHT IT WAS ABOUT TIME FOR A NEW ONE.
WHOA! YOU'RE SO AWESOME, SEI-CHAN!
YOU'RE WELCOME.
DID KANADE-SAN IGNORE IT THIS YEAR TOO?
OH, THAT'S RIGHT!!
ACTUALLY, KANA-CHAN...
...SAID "HAPPY BIRTHDAY" TO ME THIS YEAR!
REALLY!?
UH-HUH! AND HE SAID WE'LL CELEBRATE IT TOGETHER! LATER TODAY!
OOH...?
HEH-HEH... THAT MAN DID THAT, HMM?
MAYBE THE BLOOD HAS FINALLY STARTED TO COURSE THROUGH HIS VEINS...
HIS ARGUMENTS WITH YUURI HAVE BEEN HEATING UP TOO...
THAT'S BECAUSE KANA-CHAN IS ALWAYS LOOKING FOR A FIGHT...
YEAH...
THAT REMINDS ME. I WONDER WHAT YUURI'S UP TO.
YU-U-RI—!
YOU HAVE A PRESENT FOR SAKU TOO, DON'T YOU!?

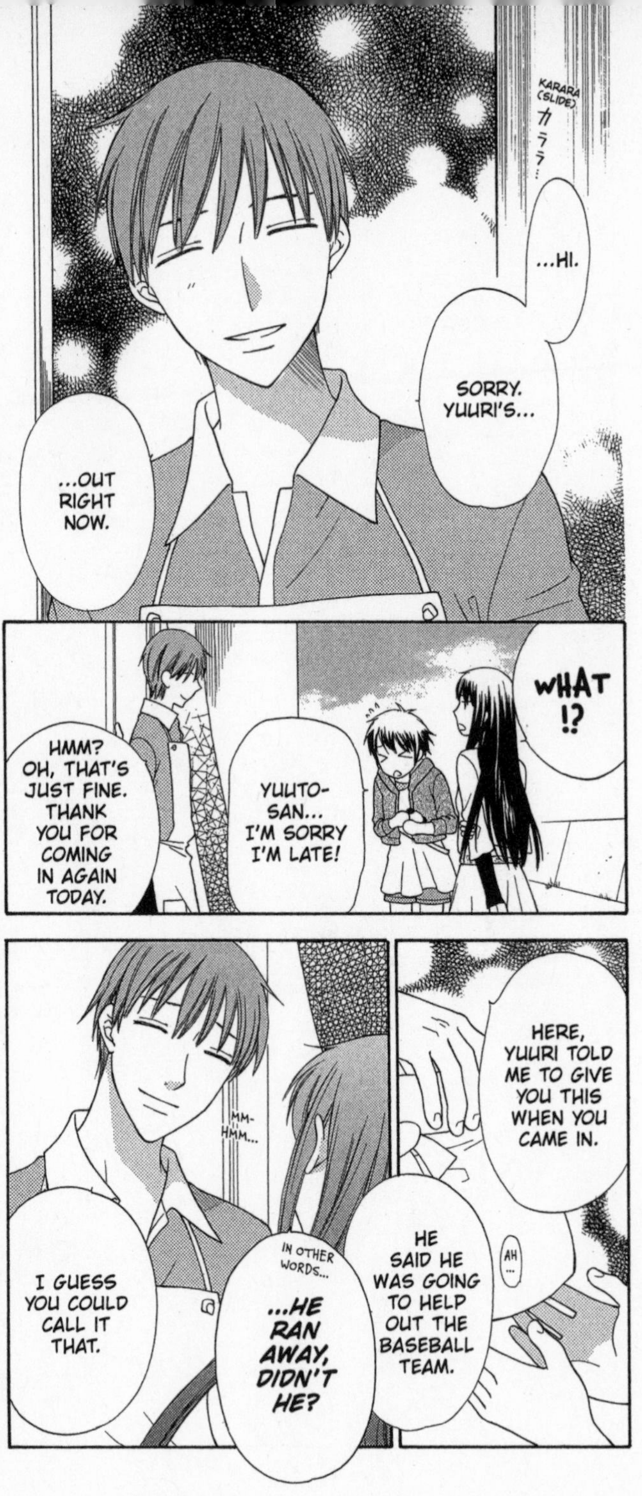
KARARA (SLIDE)
カララ…
...HI.
SORRY. YUURI'S...
...OUT RIGHT NOW.
WHAT!?
YUUTO-SAN... I'M SORRY I'M LATE!
HMM? OH, THAT'S JUST FINE. THANK YOU FOR COMING IN AGAIN TODAY.
HERE, YUURI TOLD ME TO GIVE YOU THIS WHEN YOU CAME IN.
AH...
HE SAID HE WAS GOING TO HELP OUT THE BASEBALL TEAM.
MM-HMM...
IN OTHER WORDS...
...HE RAN AWAY, DIDN'T HE?
I GUESS YOU COULD CALL IT THAT.

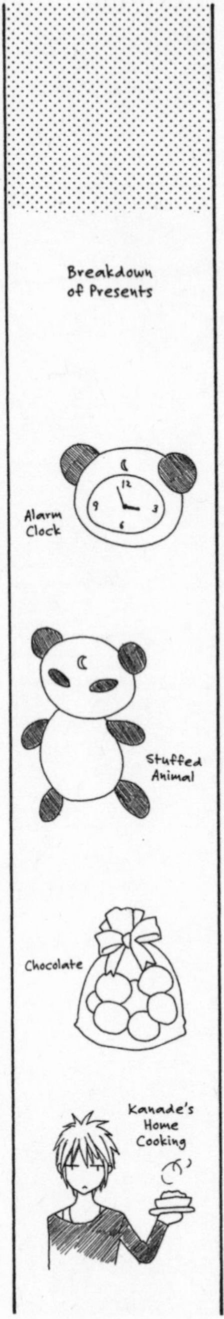
Breakdown of Presents
Alarm Clock
Stuffed Animal
Chocolate
Kanade's Home Cooking

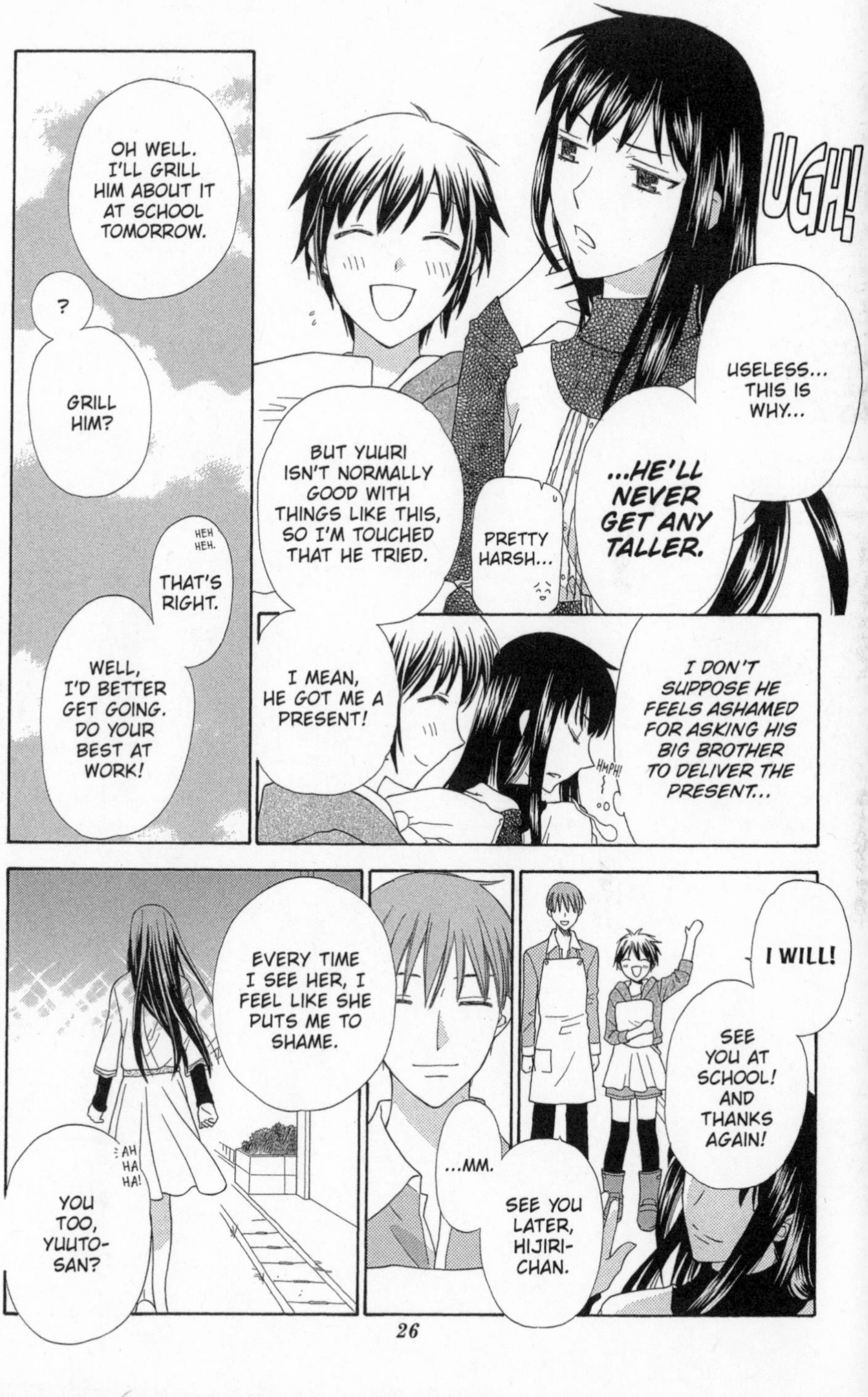
UGH!
USELESS... THIS IS WHY...
...HE'LL NEVER GET ANY TALLER.
PRETTY HARSH...
BUT YUURI ISN'T NORMALLY GOOD WITH THINGS LIKE THIS, SO I'M TOUCHED THAT HE TRIED.
I DON'T SUPPOSE HE FEELS ASHAMED FOR ASKING HIS BIG BROTHER TO DELIVER THE PRESENT...
HMPH!
I MEAN, HE GOT ME A PRESENT!
OH WELL. I'LL GRILL HIM ABOUT IT AT SCHOOL TOMORROW.
?
GRILL HIM?
HEH HEH.
THAT'S RIGHT.
WELL, I'D BETTER GET GOING. DO YOUR BEST AT WORK!
I WILL!
SEE YOU AT SCHOOL! AND THANKS AGAIN!
SEE YOU LATER, HIJIRI-CHAN.
EVERY TIME I SEE HER, I FEEL LIKE SHE PUTS ME TO SHAME.
...MM.
AH HA HA!
YOU TOO, YUUTO-SAN?

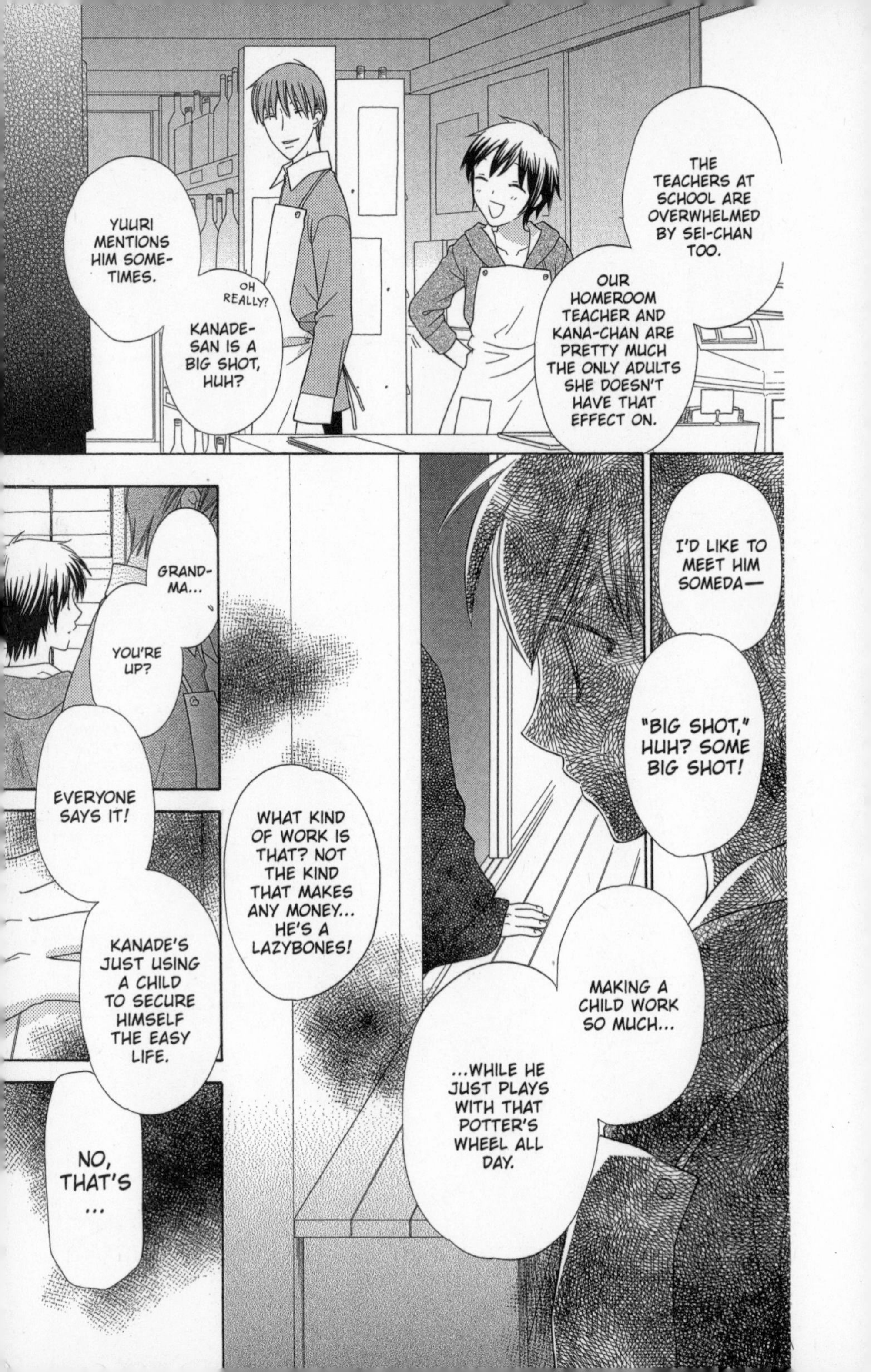
THE TEACHERS AT SCHOOL ARE OVERWHELMED BY SEI-CHAN TOO.
OUR HOMEROOM TEACHER AND KANA-CHAN ARE PRETTY MUCH THE ONLY ADULTS SHE DOESN'T HAVE THAT EFFECT ON.
OH REALLY?
KANADE-SAN IS A BIG SHOT, HUH?
YUURI MENTIONS HIM SOME-TIMES.
I'D LIKE TO MEET HIM SOMEDA—
"BIG SHOT," HUH? SOME BIG SHOT!
MAKING A CHILD WORK SO MUCH...
...WHILE HE JUST PLAYS WITH THAT POTTER'S WHEEL ALL DAY.
WHAT KIND OF WORK IS THAT? NOT THE KIND THAT MAKES ANY MONEY... HE'S A LAZYBONES!
GRAND-MA...
YOU'RE UP?
EVERYONE SAYS IT!
KANADE'S JUST USING A CHILD TO SECURE HIMSELF THE EASY LIFE.
NO, THAT'S ...

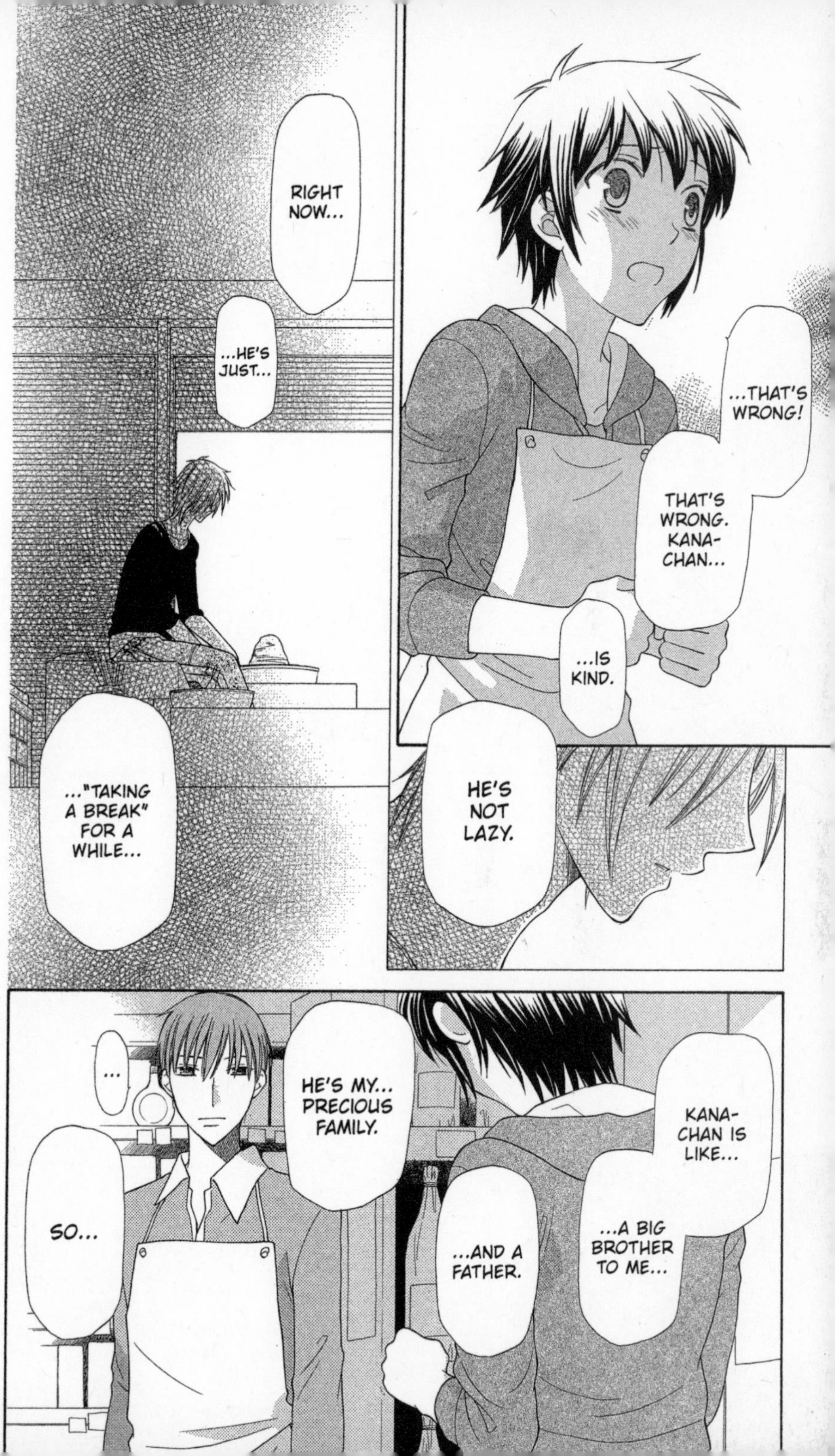
...THAT'S WRONG!
THAT'S WRONG. KANA-CHAN...
...IS KIND.
HE'S NOT LAZY.
RIGHT NOW...
...HE'S JUST...
..."TAKING A BREAK" FOR A WHILE...
KANA-CHAN IS LIKE...
...A BIG BROTHER TO ME...
...AND A FATHER.
HE'S MY... PRECIOUS FAMILY.
...
SO...

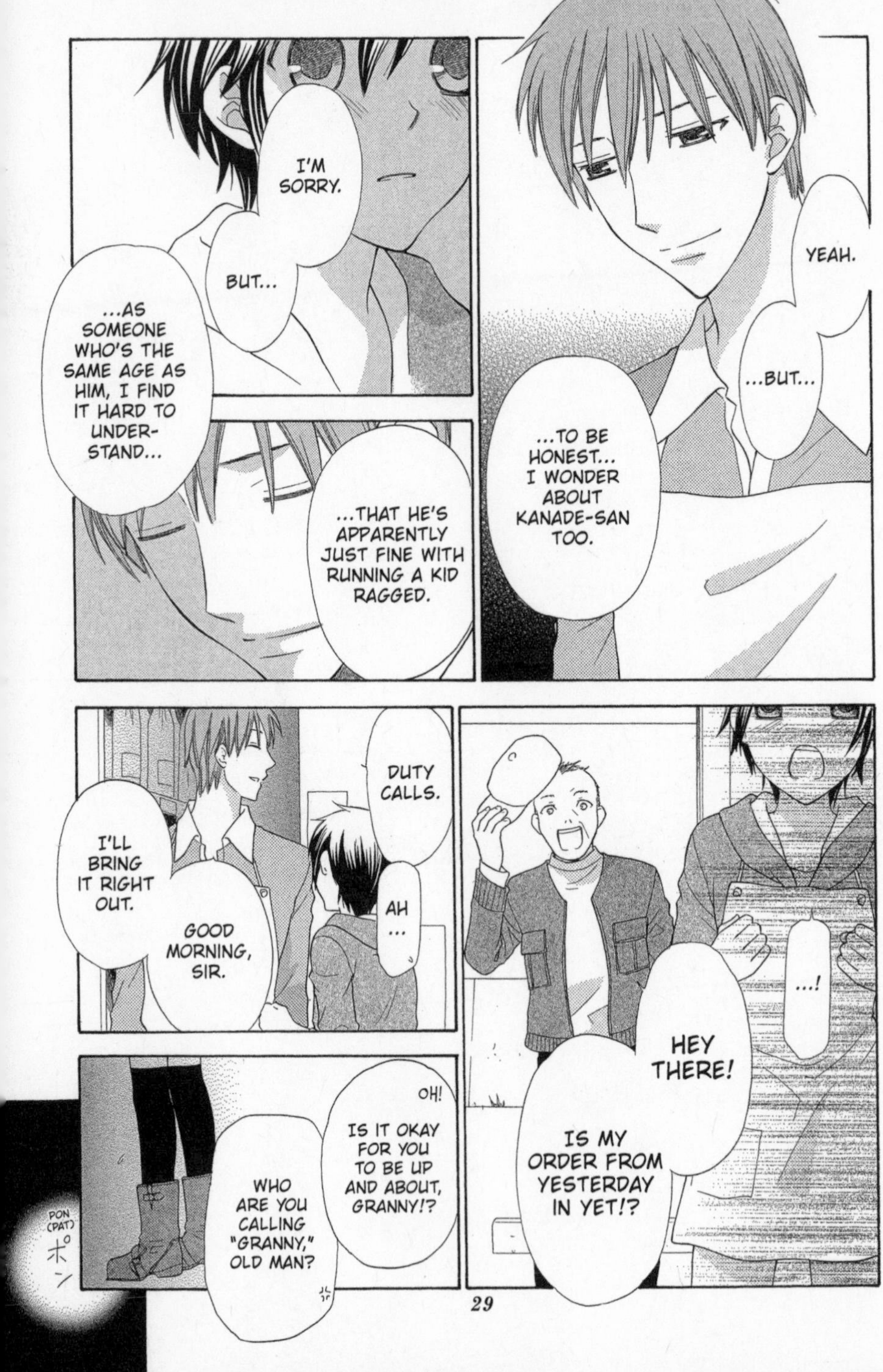
YEAH.
...BUT...
...TO BE HONEST... I WONDER ABOUT KANADE-SAN TOO.
I'M SORRY.
BUT...
...AS SOMEONE WHO'S THE SAME AGE AS HIM, I FIND IT HARD TO UNDERSTAND...
...THAT HE'S APPARENTLY JUST FINE WITH RUNNING A KID RAGGED.
...!
HEY THERE!
IS MY ORDER FROM YESTERDAY IN YET!?
DUTY CALLS.
AH...
I'LL BRING IT RIGHT OUT.
GOOD MORNING, SIR.
OH!
IS IT OKAY FOR YOU TO BE UP AND ABOUT, GRANNY!?
WHO ARE YOU CALLING "GRANNY," OLD MAN?
PON (PAT) ポン

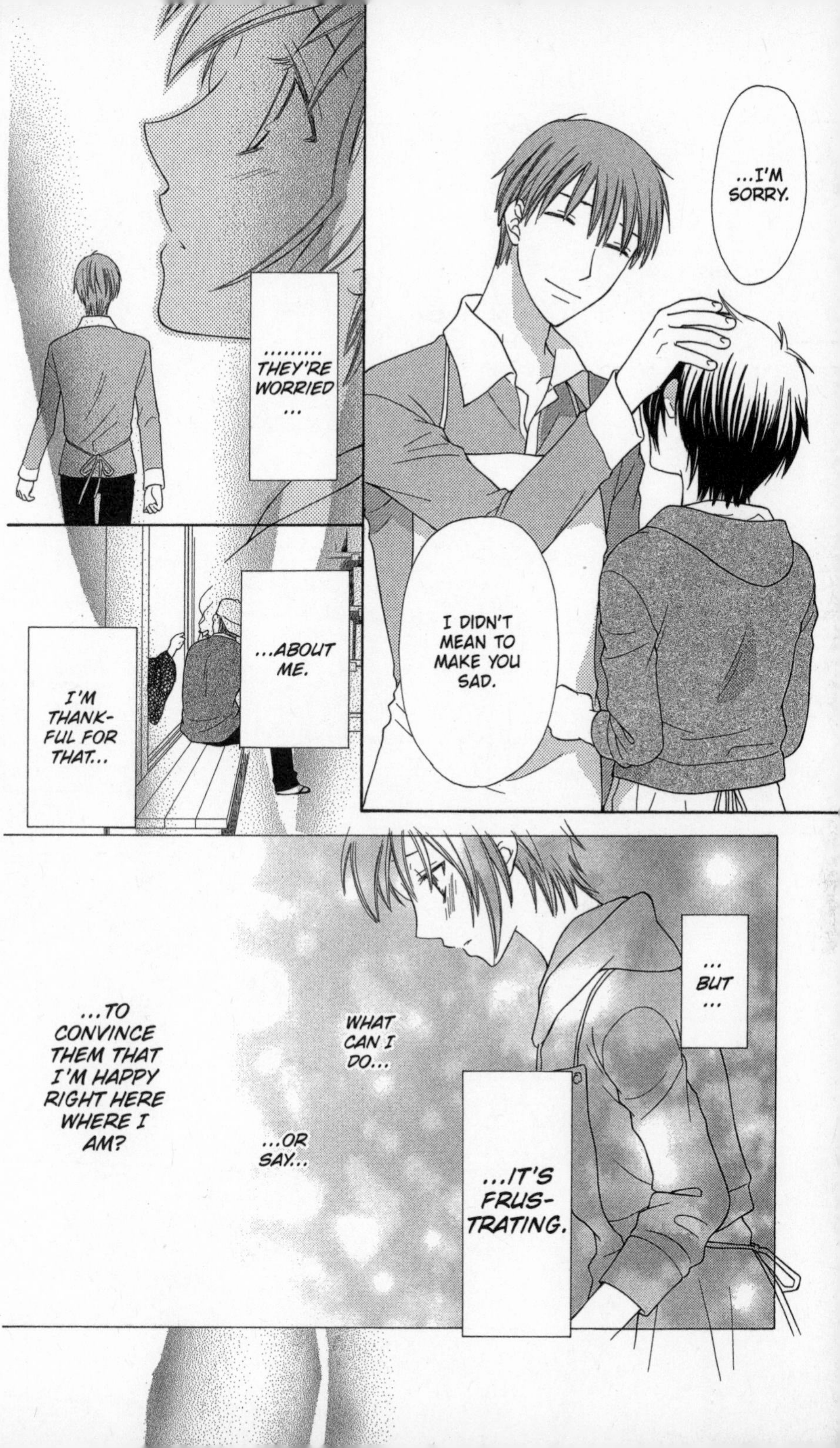
...I'M SORRY.
I DIDN'T MEAN TO MAKE YOU SAD.
....
THEY'RE WORRIED ...
...ABOUT ME.
I'M THANK-FUL FOR THAT...
... BUT ...
...IT'S FRUS-TRATING.
WHAT CAN I DO...
...OR SAY...
...TO CONVINCE THEM THAT I'M HAPPY RIGHT HERE WHERE I AM?

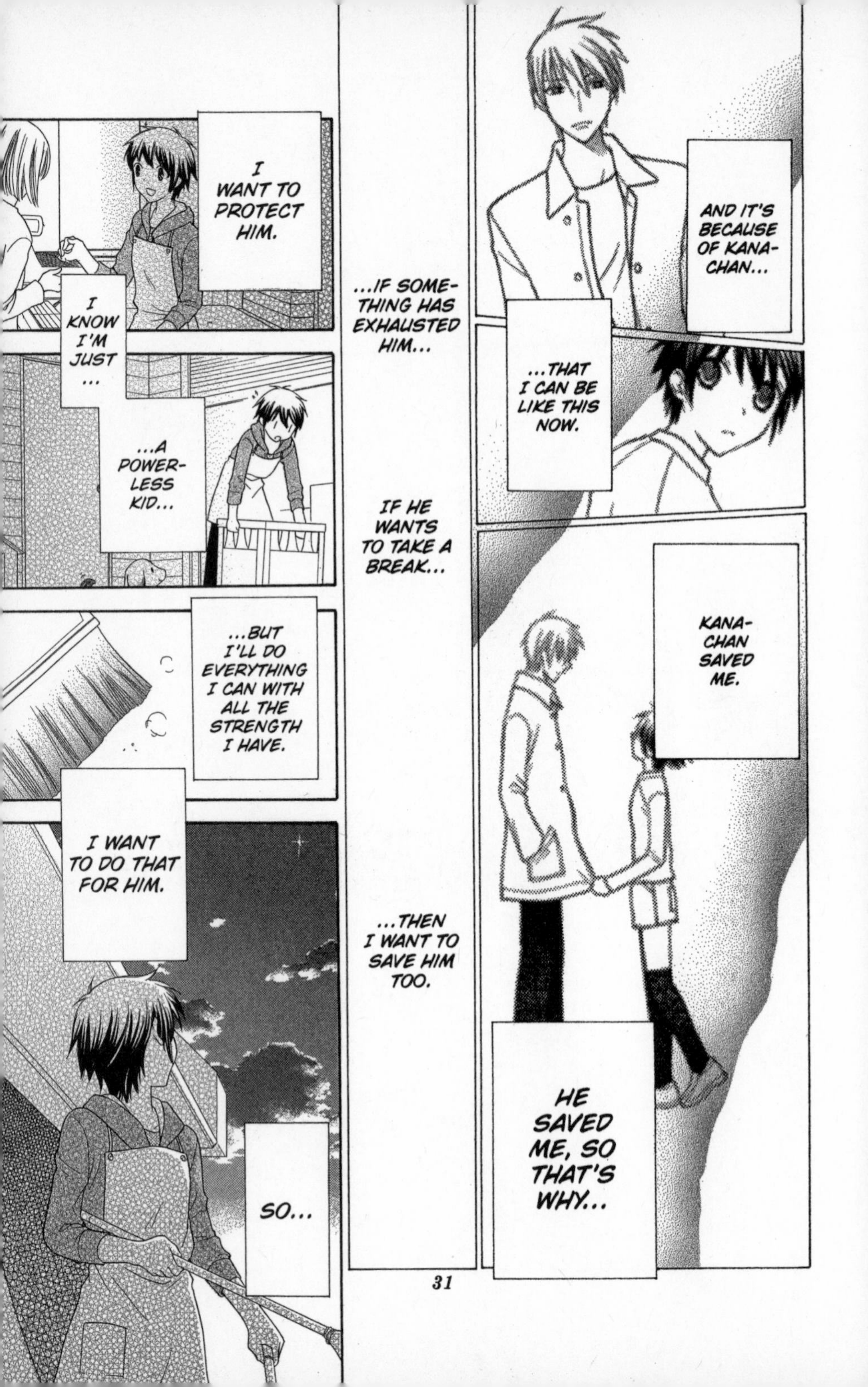
AND IT'S BECAUSE OF KANA-CHAN...
...THAT I CAN BE LIKE THIS NOW.
KANA-CHAN SAVED ME.
HE SAVED ME, SO THAT'S WHY...
...IF SOME-THING HAS EXHAUSTED HIM...
IF HE WANTS TO TAKE A BREAK...
...THEN I WANT TO SAVE HIM TOO.
I WANT TO PROTECT HIM.
I KNOW I'M JUST...
...A POWER-LESS KID...
...BUT I'LL DO EVERYTHING I CAN WITH ALL THE STRENGTH I HAVE.
I WANT TO DO THAT FOR HIM.
SO...

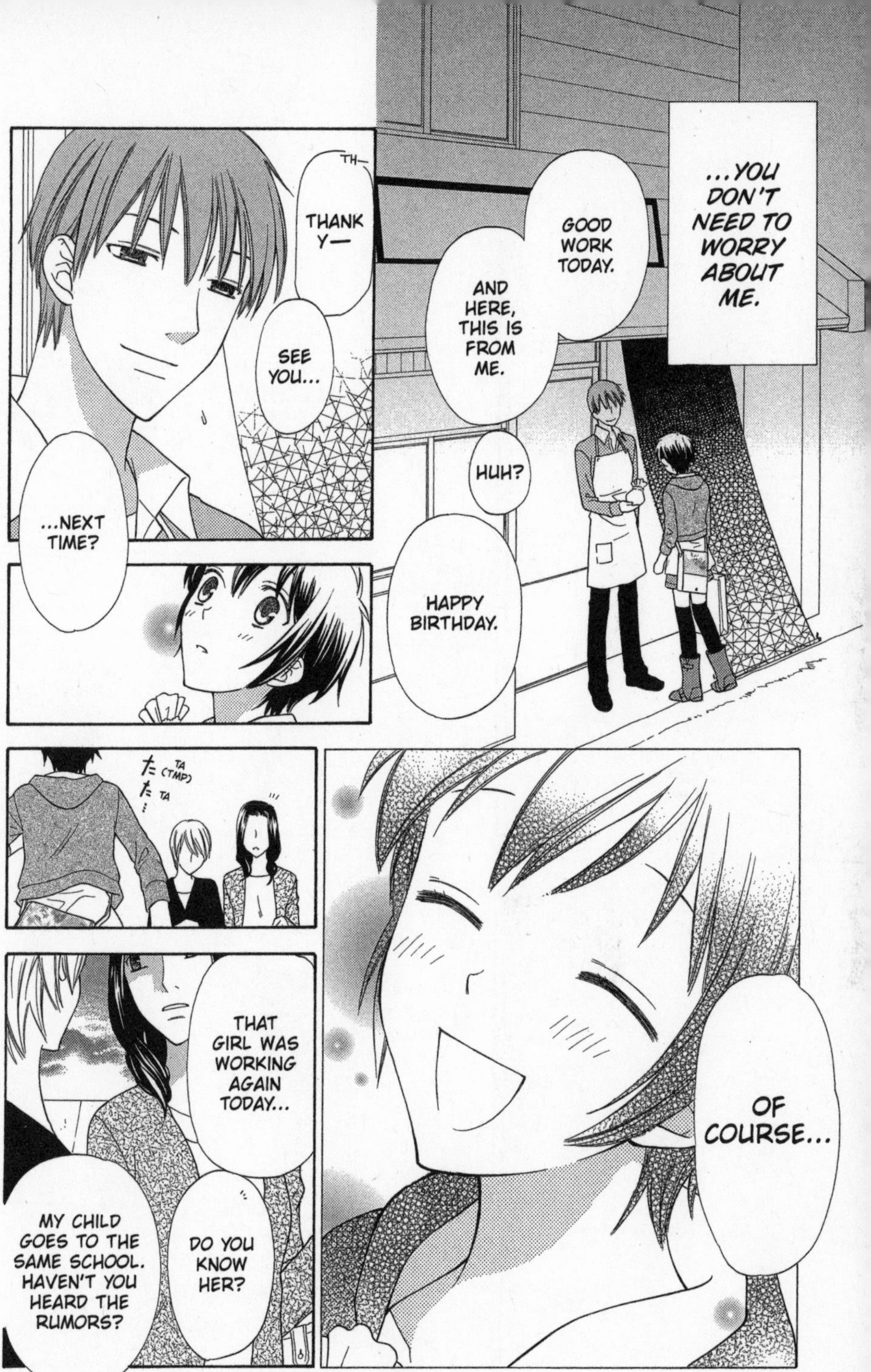
...YOU DON'T NEED TO WORRY ABOUT ME.
GOOD WORK TODAY.
AND HERE, THIS IS FROM ME.
HUH?
HAPPY BIRTHDAY.
TH— THANK Y—
SEE YOU...
...NEXT TIME?
OF COURSE...
た TA (TMP)
た TA
THAT GIRL WAS WORKING AGAIN TODAY...
DO YOU KNOW HER?
MY CHILD GOES TO THE SAME SCHOOL. HAVEN'T YOU HEARD THE RUMORS?

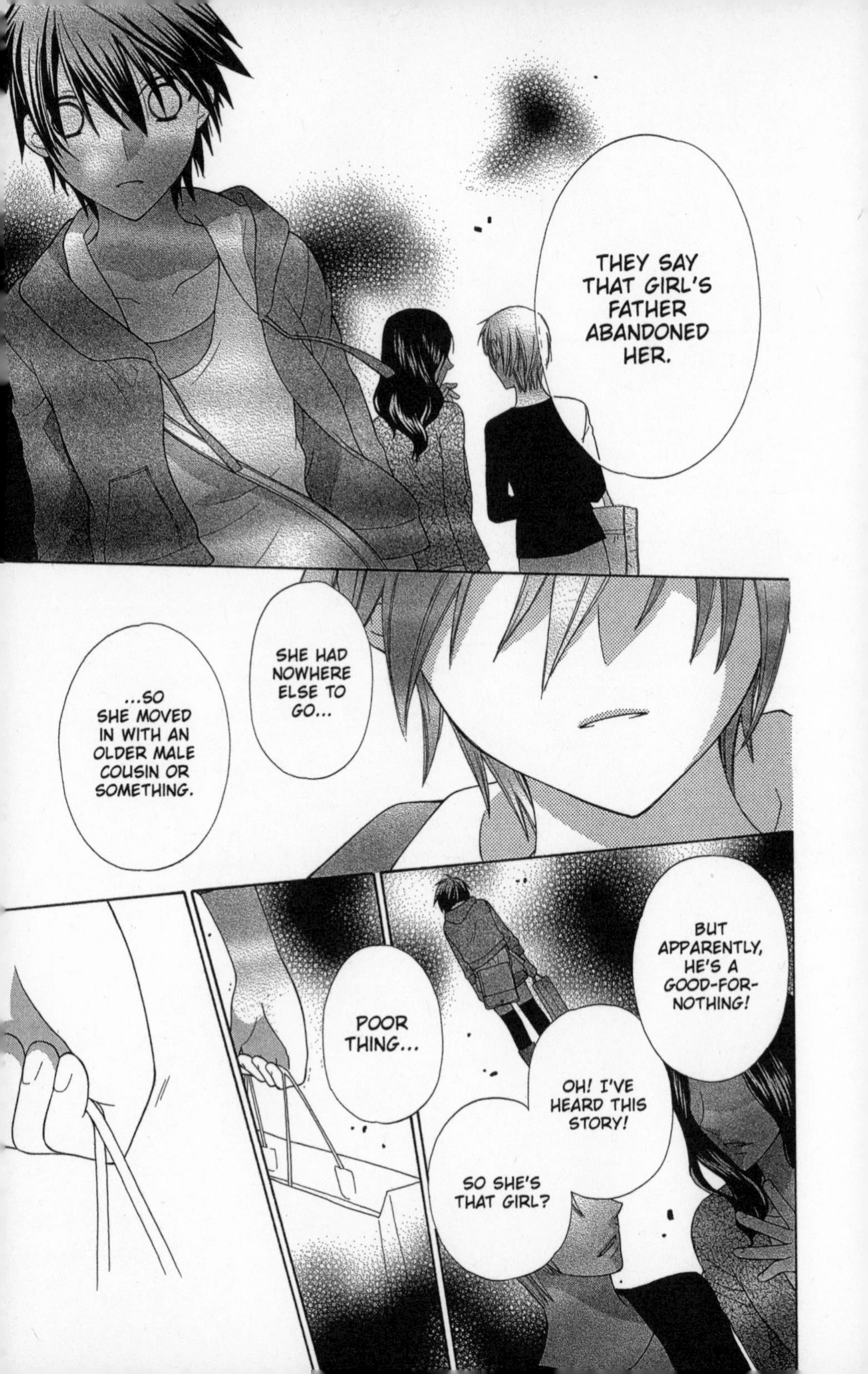
THEY SAY THAT GIRL'S FATHER ABANDONED HER.
SHE HAD NOWHERE ELSE TO GO...
...SO SHE MOVED IN WITH AN OLDER MALE COUSIN OR SOMETHING.
BUT APPARENTLY, HE'S A GOOD-FOR-NOTHING!
OH! I'VE HEARD THIS STORY!
SO SHE'S THAT GIRL?
POOR THING...

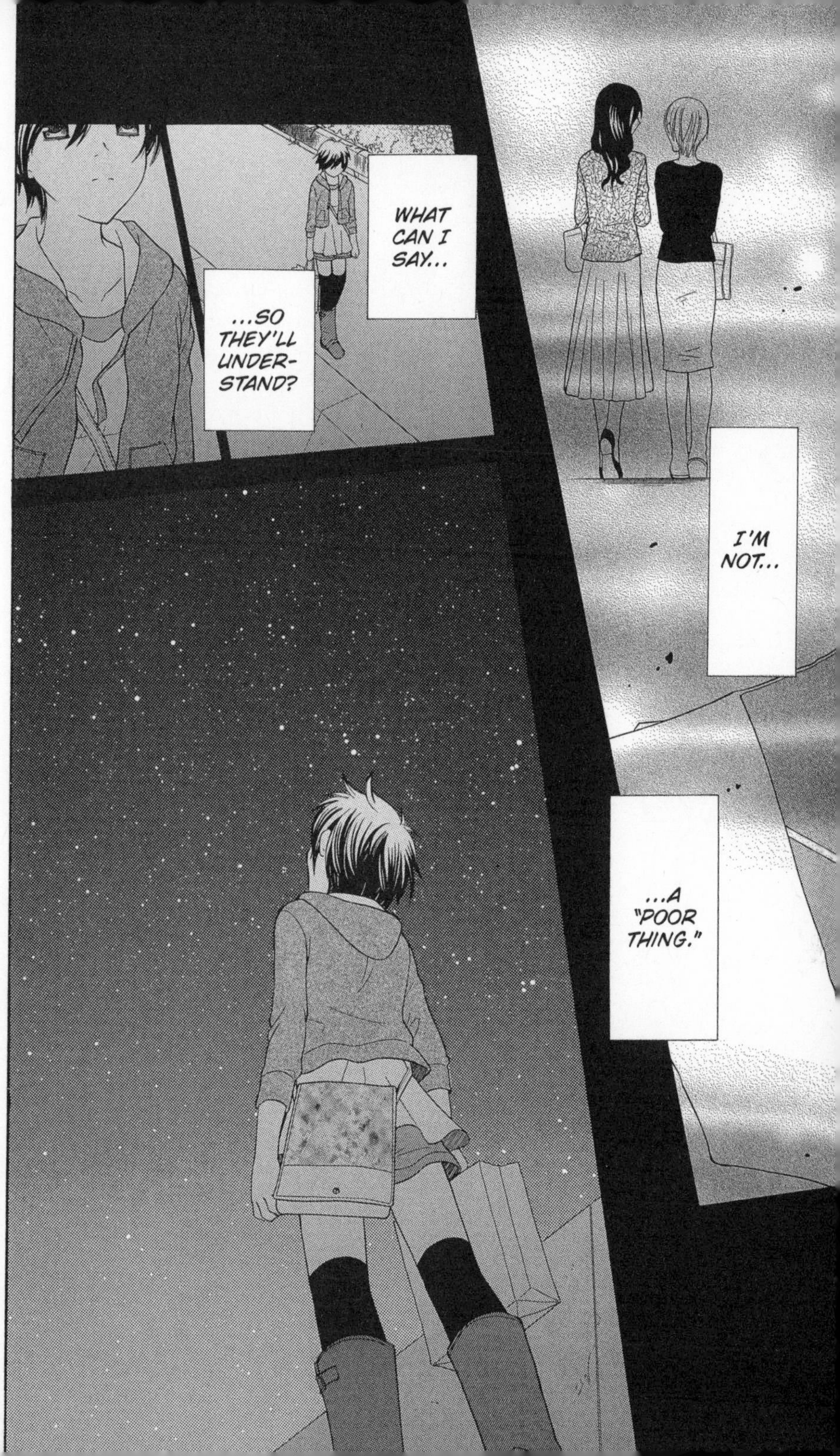
I'M NOT...
...A "POOR THING."
WHAT CAN I SAY...
...SO THEY'LL UNDER-STAND?

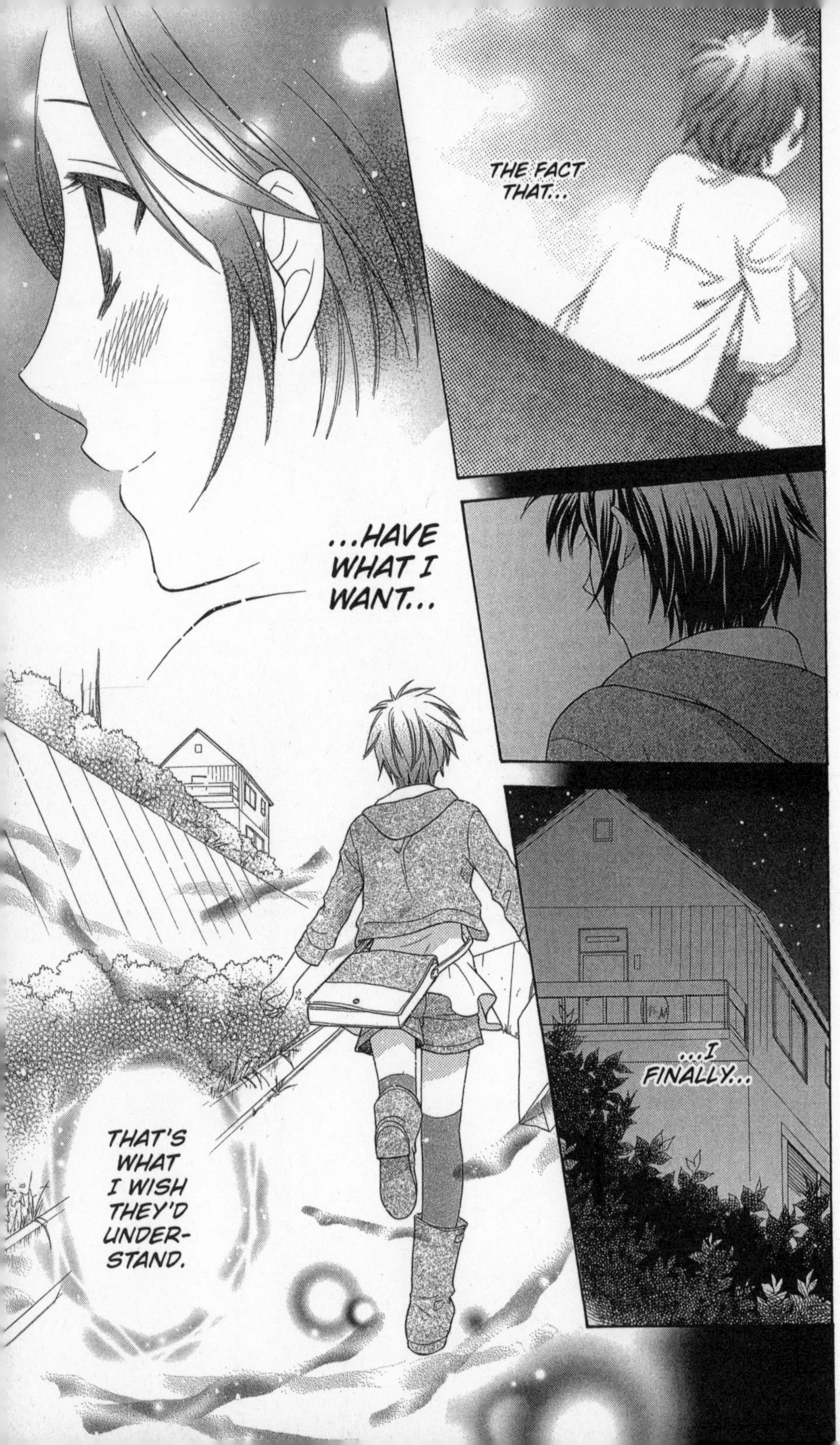
THE FACT THAT...
...I FINALLY...
...HAVE WHAT I WANT...
THAT'S WHAT I WISH THEY'D UNDER-STAND.

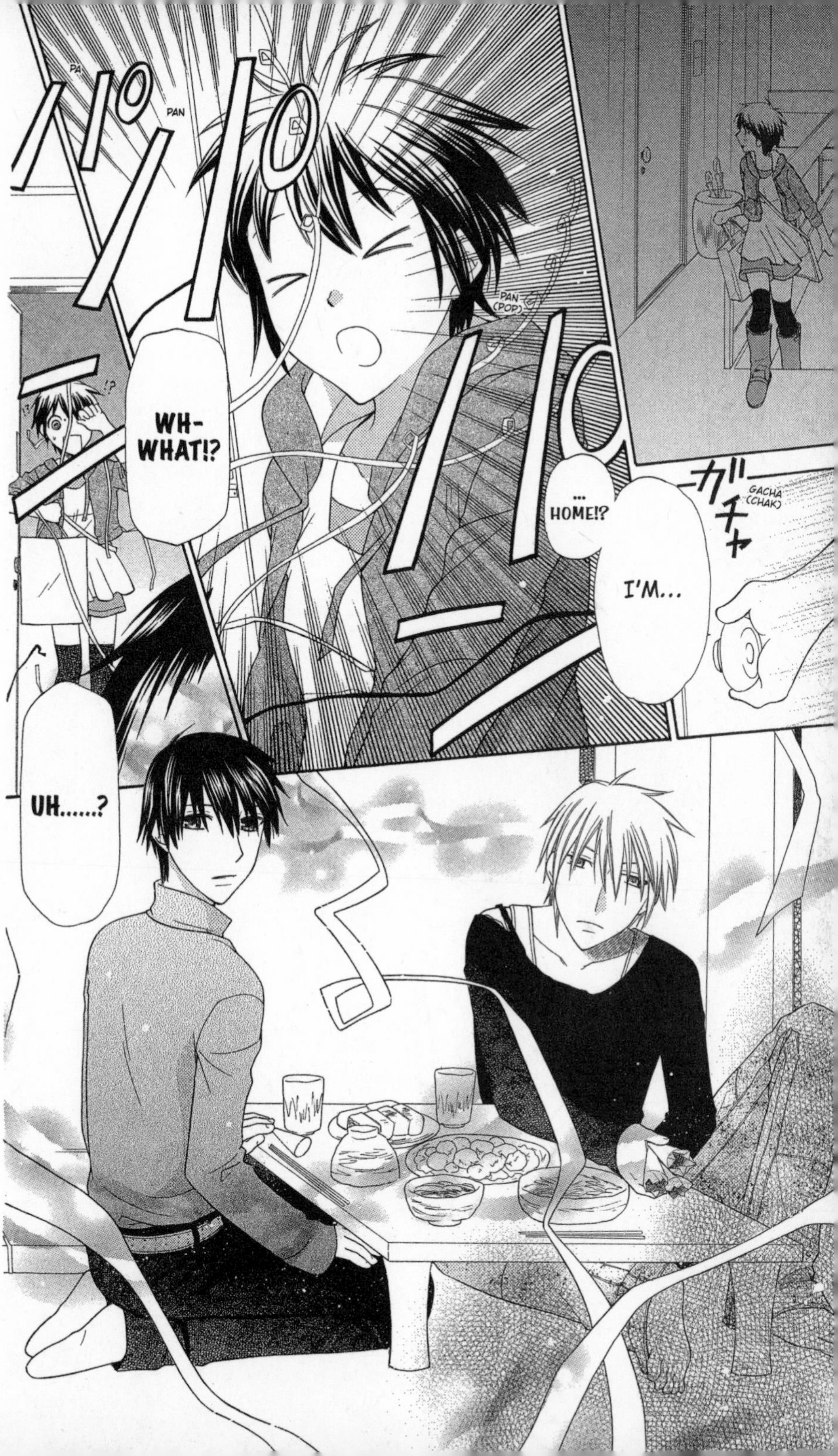
ガチャ
GACHA (CHAK)
I'M...
...HOME!?
パパパン
PA
PAN
PAN (POP)
!?
WH-WHAT!?
UH......?

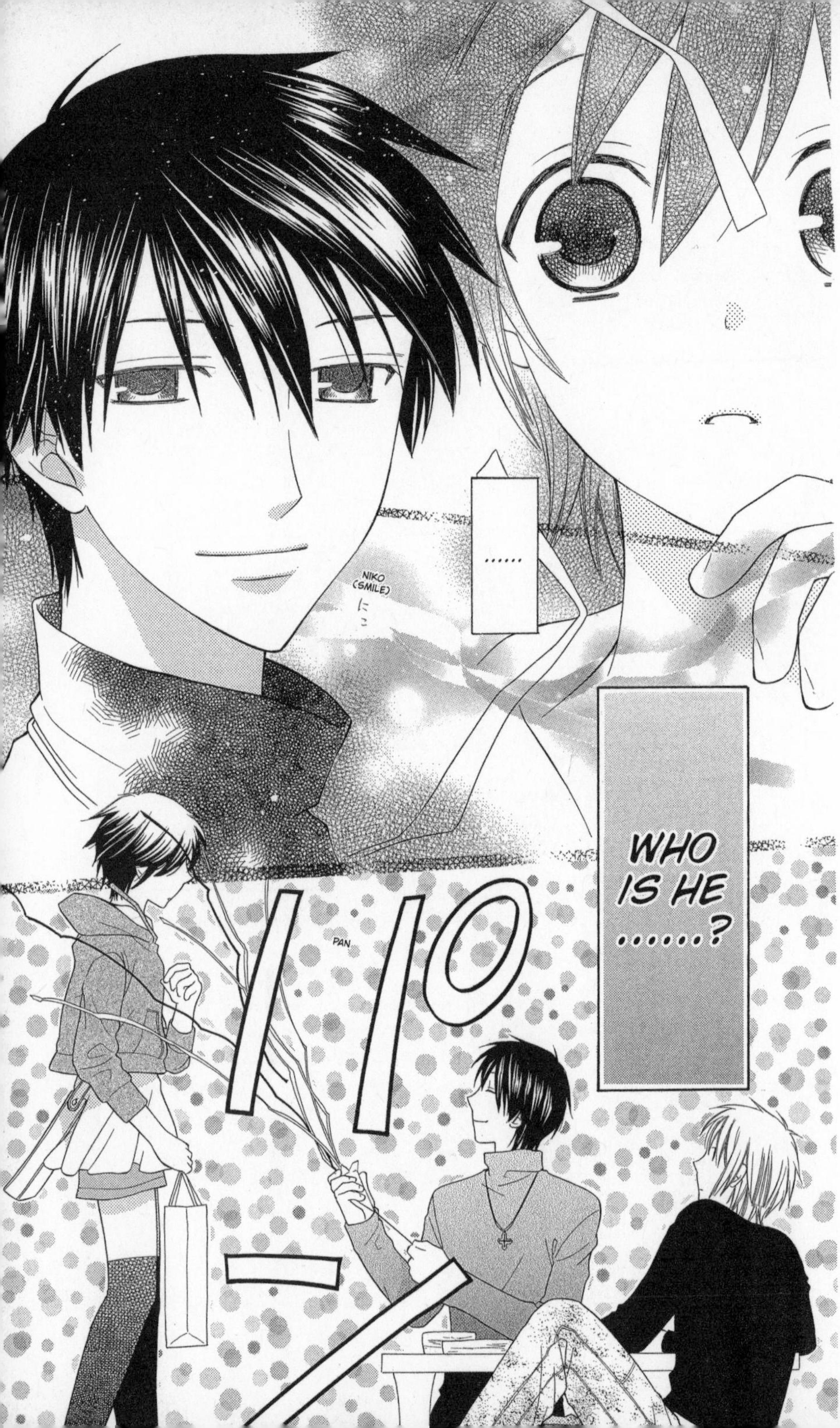
......
NIKO (SMILE)
にこ
WHO IS HE ......?
PAN

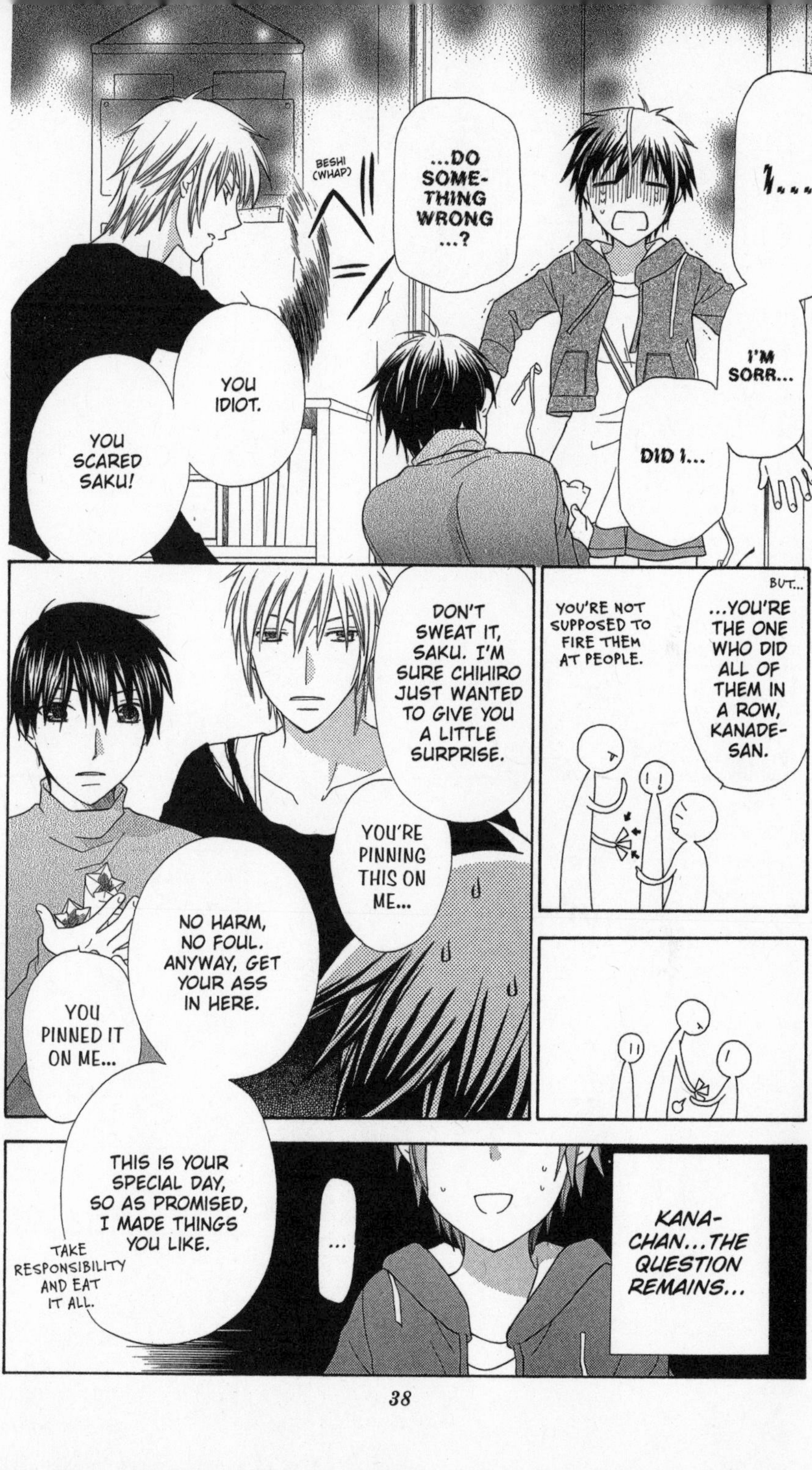
I...
I'M SORR...
DID I...
...DO SOMETHING WRONG ...?
BESHI (WHAP)
YOU IDIOT.
YOU SCARED SAKU!
BUT...
...YOU'RE THE ONE WHO DID ALL OF THEM IN A ROW, KANADE-SAN.
YOU'RE NOT SUPPOSED TO FIRE THEM AT PEOPLE.
DON'T SWEAT IT, SAKU. I'M SURE CHIHIRO JUST WANTED TO GIVE YOU A LITTLE SURPRISE.
YOU'RE PINNING THIS ON ME...
NO HARM, NO FOUL. ANYWAY, GET YOUR ASS IN HERE.
YOU PINNED IT ON ME...
KANA-CHAN...THE QUESTION REMAINS...
...
THIS IS YOUR SPECIAL DAY, SO AS PROMISED, I MADE THINGS YOU LIKE.
TAKE RESPONSIBILITY AND EAT IT ALL.

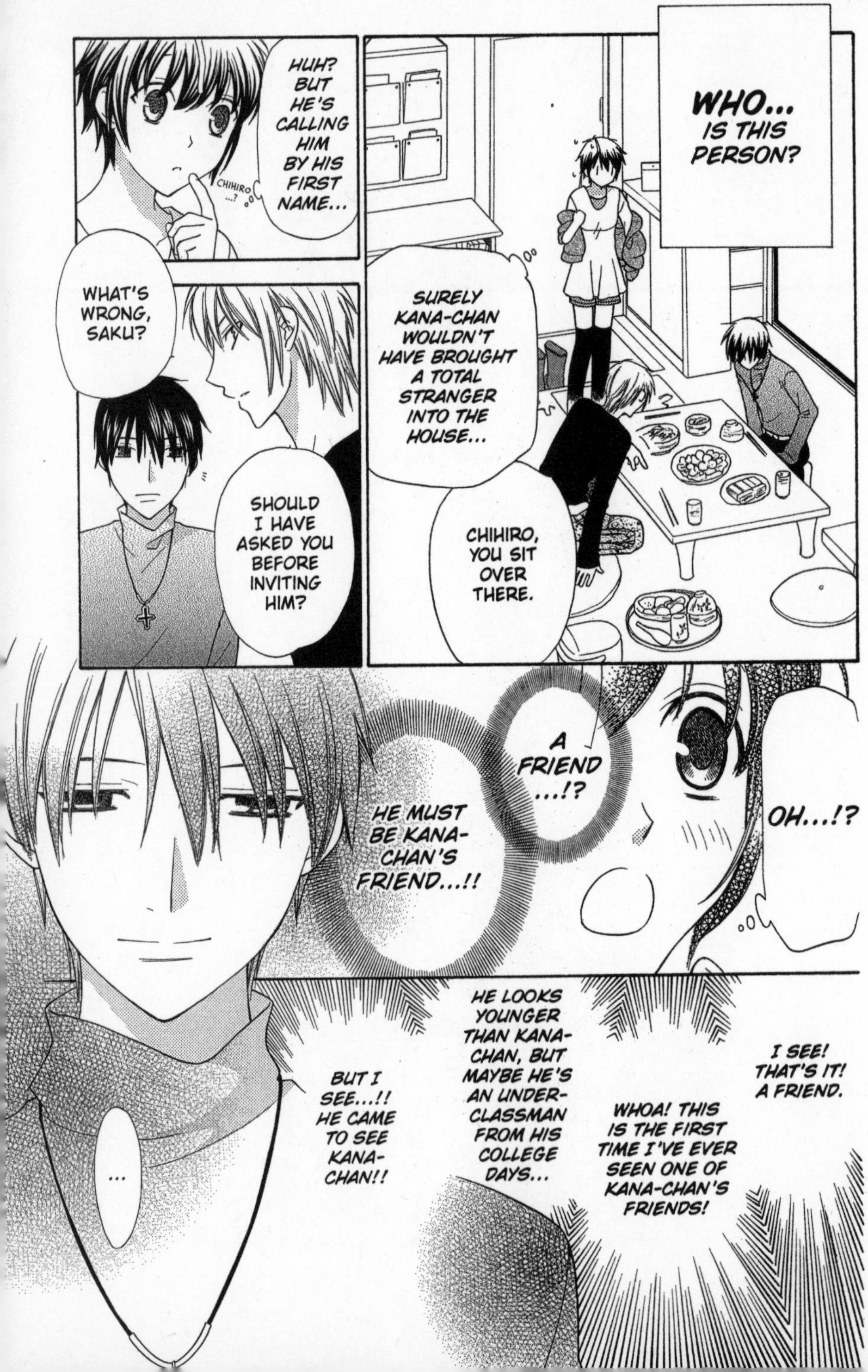
WHO... IS THIS PERSON?
SURELY KANA-CHAN WOULDN'T HAVE BROUGHT A TOTAL STRANGER INTO THE HOUSE...
CHIHIRO, YOU SIT OVER THERE.
HUH? BUT HE'S CALLING HIM BY HIS FIRST NAME...
CHIHIRO ...?
WHAT'S WRONG, SAKU?
SHOULD I HAVE ASKED YOU BEFORE INVITING HIM?
OH...!?
A FRIEND ...!?
HE MUST BE KANA-CHAN'S FRIEND...!!
I SEE! THAT'S IT! A FRIEND.
WHOA! THIS IS THE FIRST TIME I'VE EVER SEEN ONE OF KANA-CHAN'S FRIENDS!
HE LOOKS YOUNGER THAN KANA-CHAN, BUT MAYBE HE'S AN UNDER-CLASSMAN FROM HIS COLLEGE DAYS...
BUT I SEE...!! HE CAME TO SEE KANA-CHAN!!
...

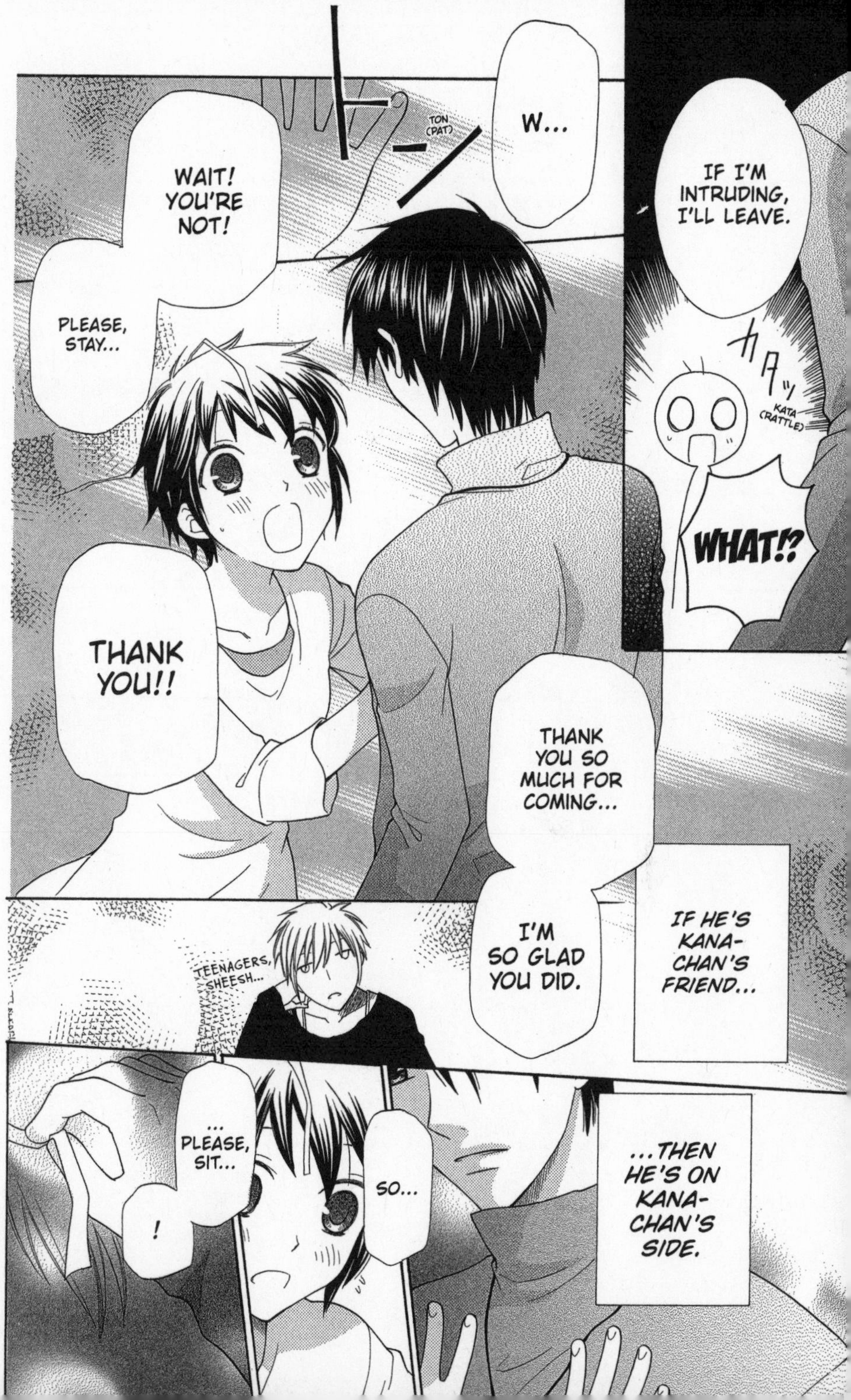
IF I'M INTRUDING, I'LL LEAVE.
KATA (RATTLE)
WHAT!?
W...
TON (PAT)
WAIT! YOU'RE NOT!
PLEASE, STAY...
THANK YOU!!
THANK YOU SO MUCH FOR COMING...
IF HE'S KANA-CHAN'S FRIEND...
I'M SO GLAD YOU DID.
TEENAGERS, SHEESH...
...THEN HE'S ON KANA-CHAN'S SIDE.
SO...
!
...PLEASE, SIT...

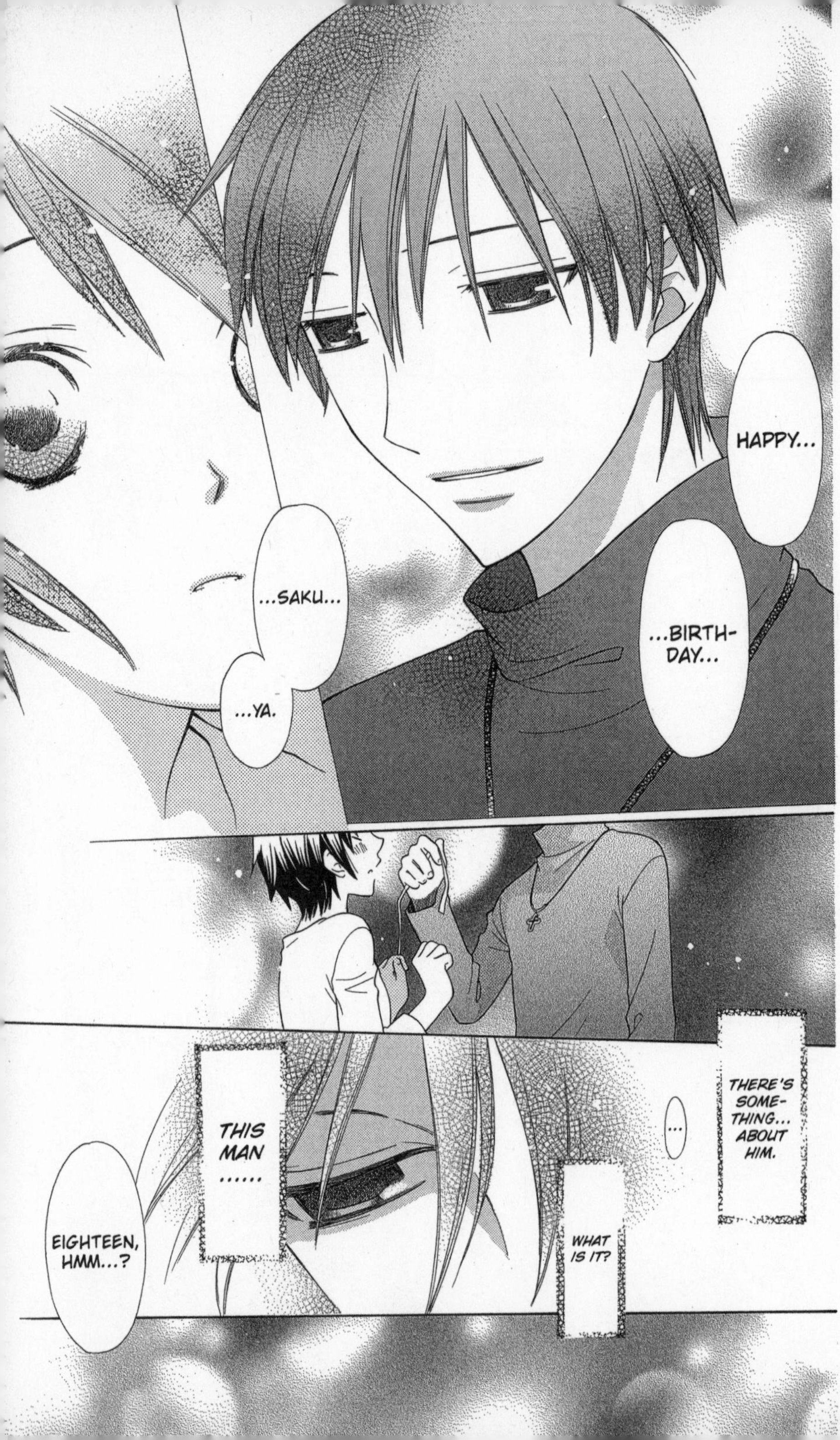
HAPPY...
...BIRTH-DAY...
...SAKU...
...YA.
THERE'S SOME-THING... ABOUT HIM.
...
WHAT IS IT?
THIS MAN ......
EIGHTEEN, HMM...?

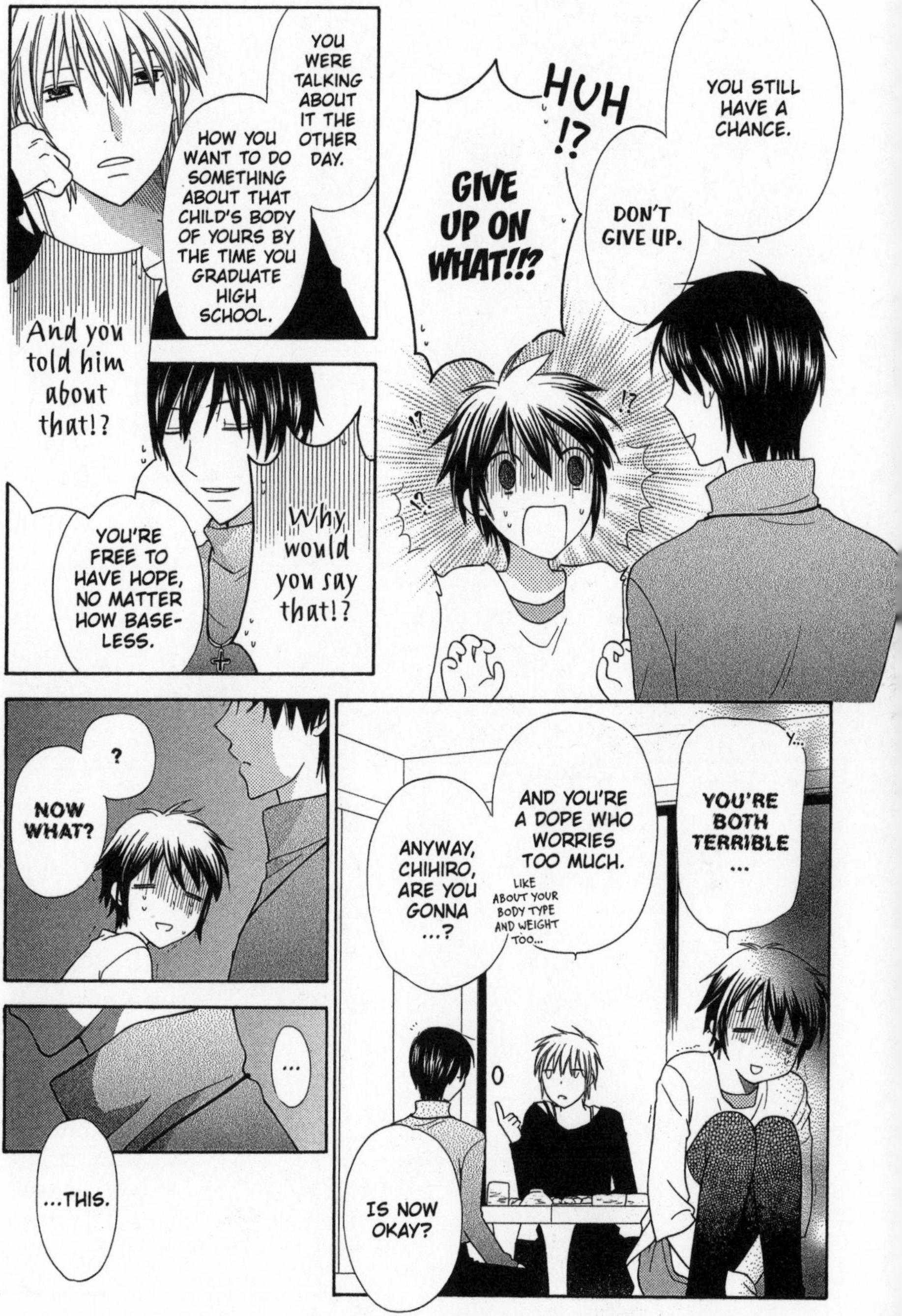
YOU STILL HAVE A CHANCE.
DON'T GIVE UP.
HUH!?
GIVE UP ON WHAT!!?
YOU WERE TALKING ABOUT IT THE OTHER DAY.
HOW YOU WANT TO DO SOMETHING ABOUT THAT CHILD'S BODY OF YOURS BY THE TIME YOU GRADUATE HIGH SCHOOL.
And you told him about that!?
Why would you say that!?
YOU'RE FREE TO HAVE HOPE, NO MATTER HOW BASE-LESS.
Y...
YOU'RE BOTH TERRIBLE...
AND YOU'RE A DOPE WHO WORRIES TOO MUCH.
LIKE ABOUT YOUR BODY TYPE AND WEIGHT TOO...
ANYWAY, CHIHIRO, ARE YOU GONNA...?
IS NOW OKAY?
?
NOW WHAT?
...
...THIS.

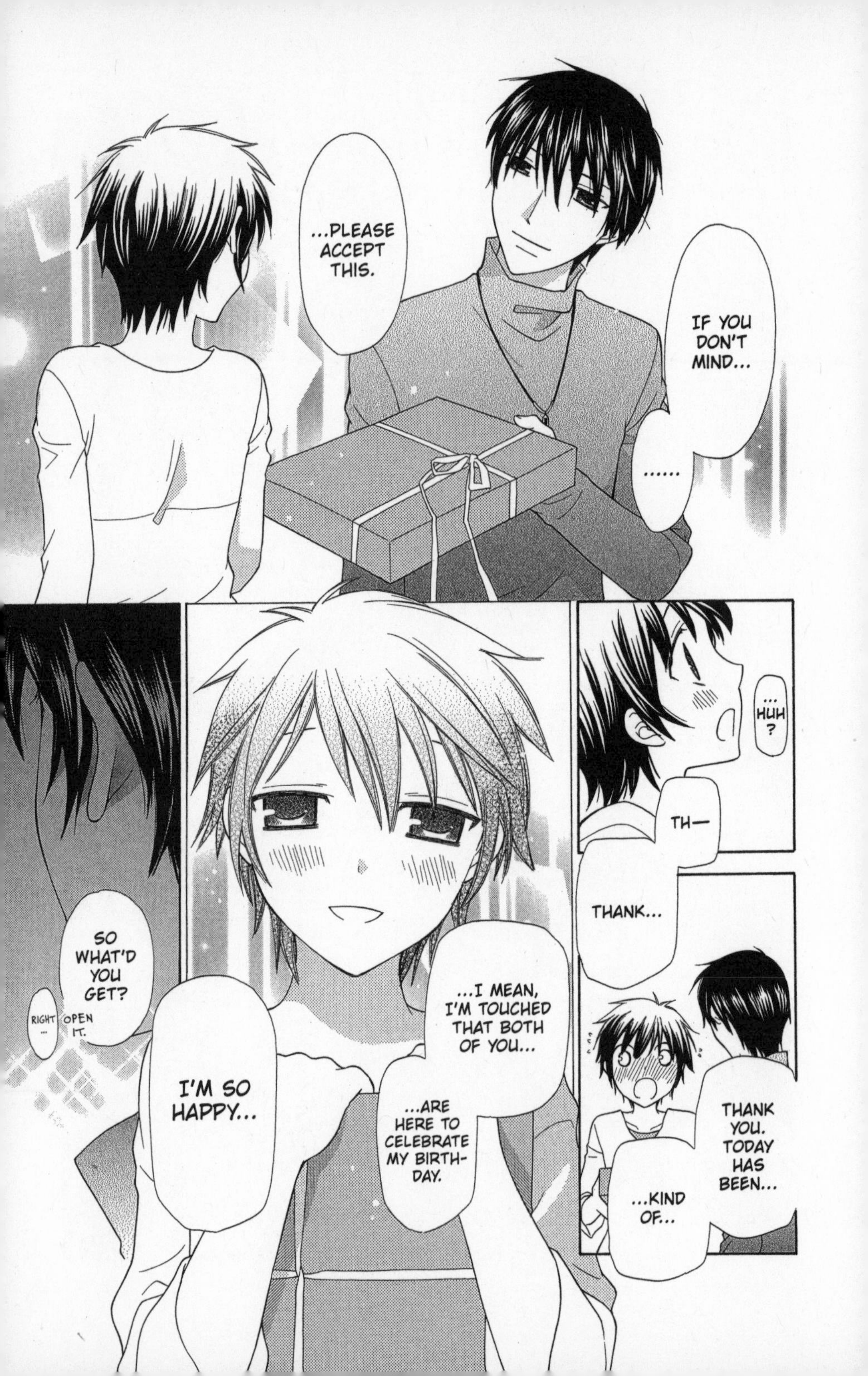
IF YOU DON'T MIND...
......
...PLEASE ACCEPT THIS.
...HUH?
TH—
THANK...
THANK YOU. TODAY HAS BEEN...
...KIND OF...
...I MEAN, I'M TOUCHED THAT BOTH OF YOU...
...ARE HERE TO CELEBRATE MY BIRTH-DAY.
I'M SO HAPPY...
SO WHAT'D YOU GET?
OPEN IT.
RIGHT...

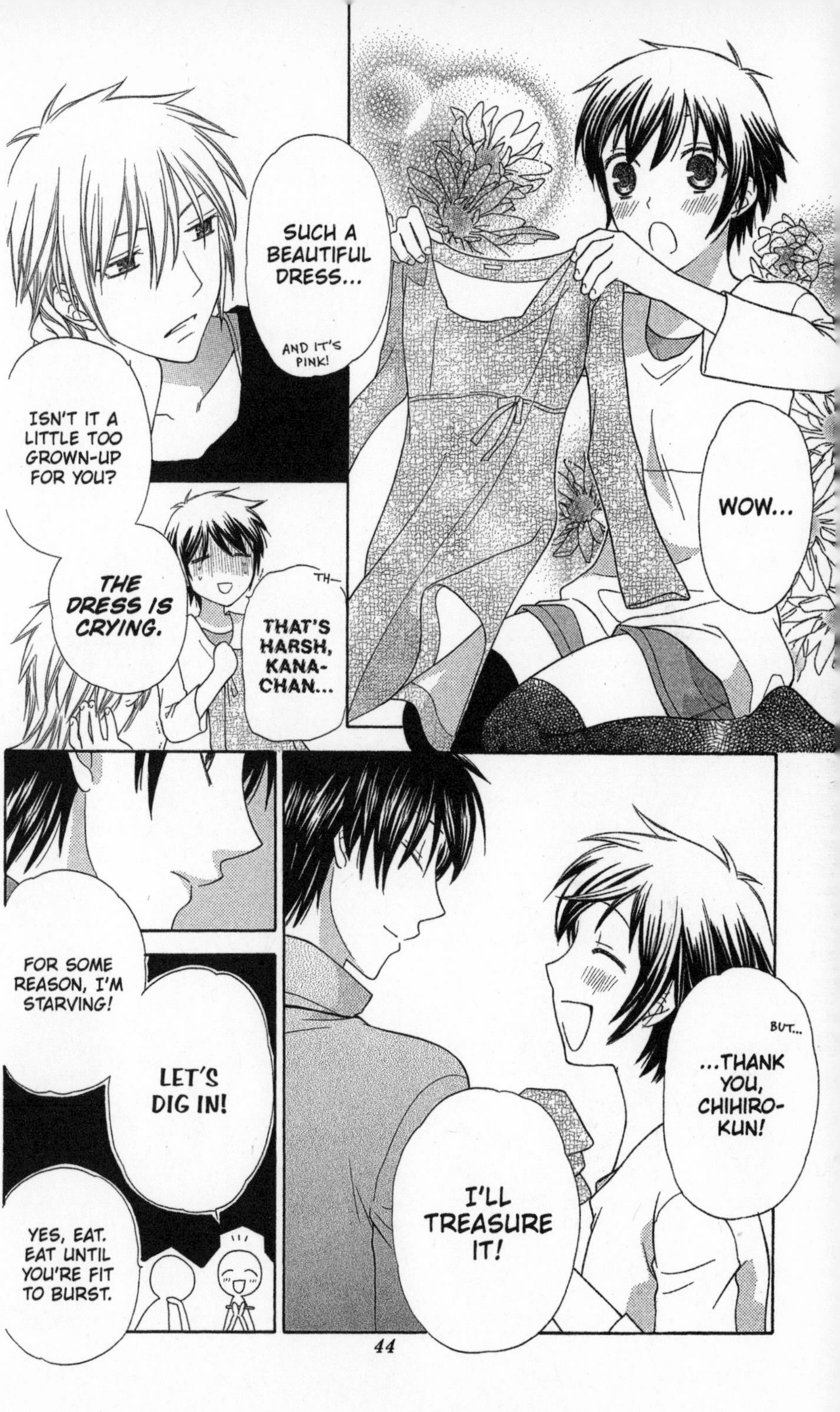
WOW...
SUCH A BEAUTIFUL DRESS...
AND IT'S PINK!
ISN'T IT A LITTLE TOO GROWN-UP FOR YOU?
THE DRESS IS CRYING.
TH— THAT'S HARSH, KANA-CHAN...
BUT... ...THANK YOU, CHIHIRO-KUN!
I'LL TREASURE IT!
FOR SOME REASON, I'M STARVING!
LET'S DIG IN!
YES, EAT. EAT UNTIL YOU'RE FIT TO BURST.

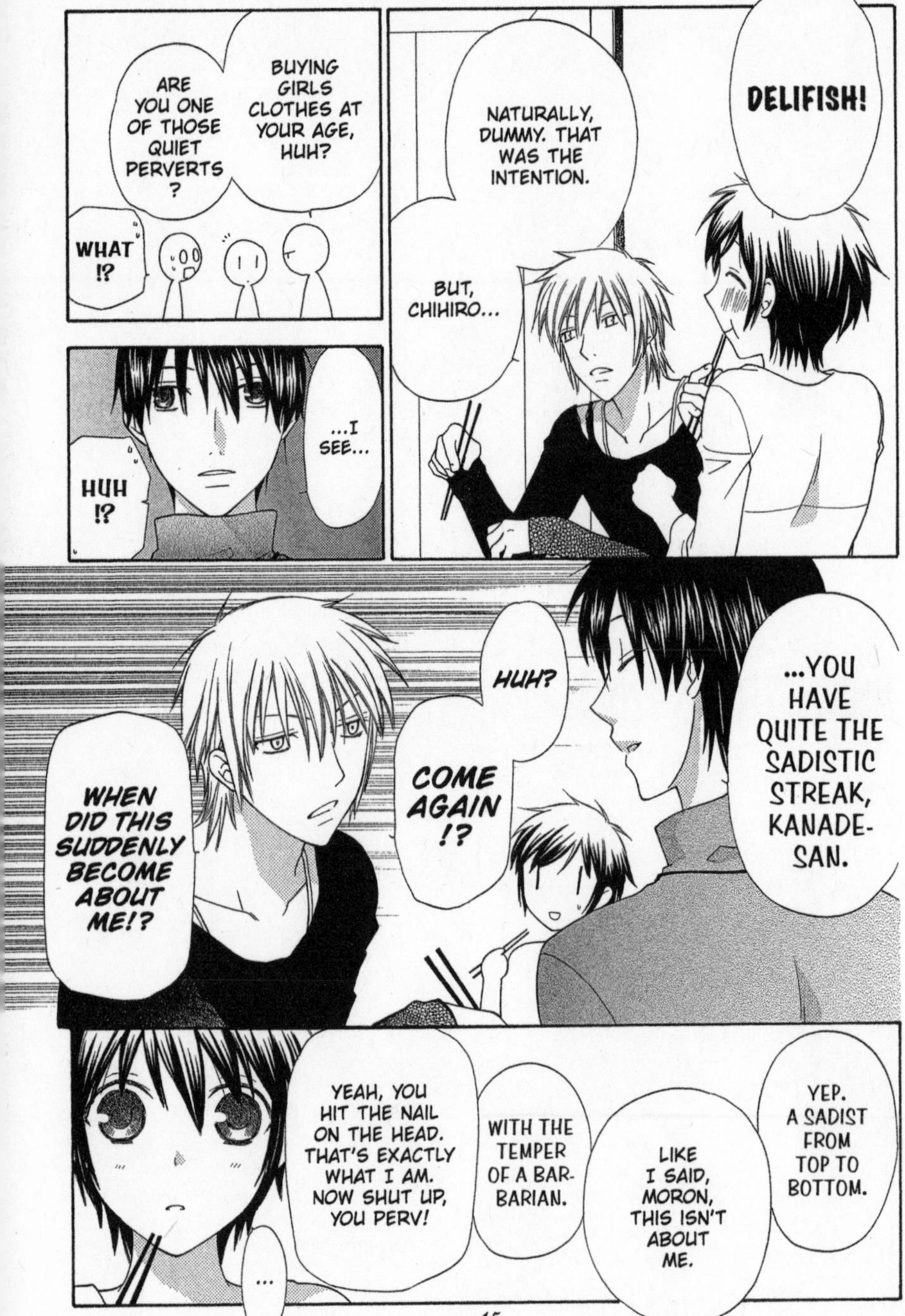
DELIFISH!
NATURALLY, DUMMY. THAT WAS THE INTENTION.
BUT, CHIHIRO...
BUYING GIRLS CLOTHES AT YOUR AGE, HUH?
ARE YOU ONE OF THOSE QUIET PERVERTS?
WHAT!?
...I SEE...
HUH!?
...YOU HAVE QUITE THE SADISTIC STREAK, KANADE-SAN.
HUH?
COME AGAIN!?
WHEN DID THIS SUDDENLY BECOME ABOUT ME!?
YEP. A SADIST FROM TOP TO BOTTOM.
LIKE I SAID, MORON, THIS ISN'T ABOUT ME.
WITH THE TEMPER OF A BAR-BARIAN.
YEAH, YOU HIT THE NAIL ON THE HEAD. THAT'S EXACTLY WHAT I AM. NOW SHUT UP, YOU PERV!
...

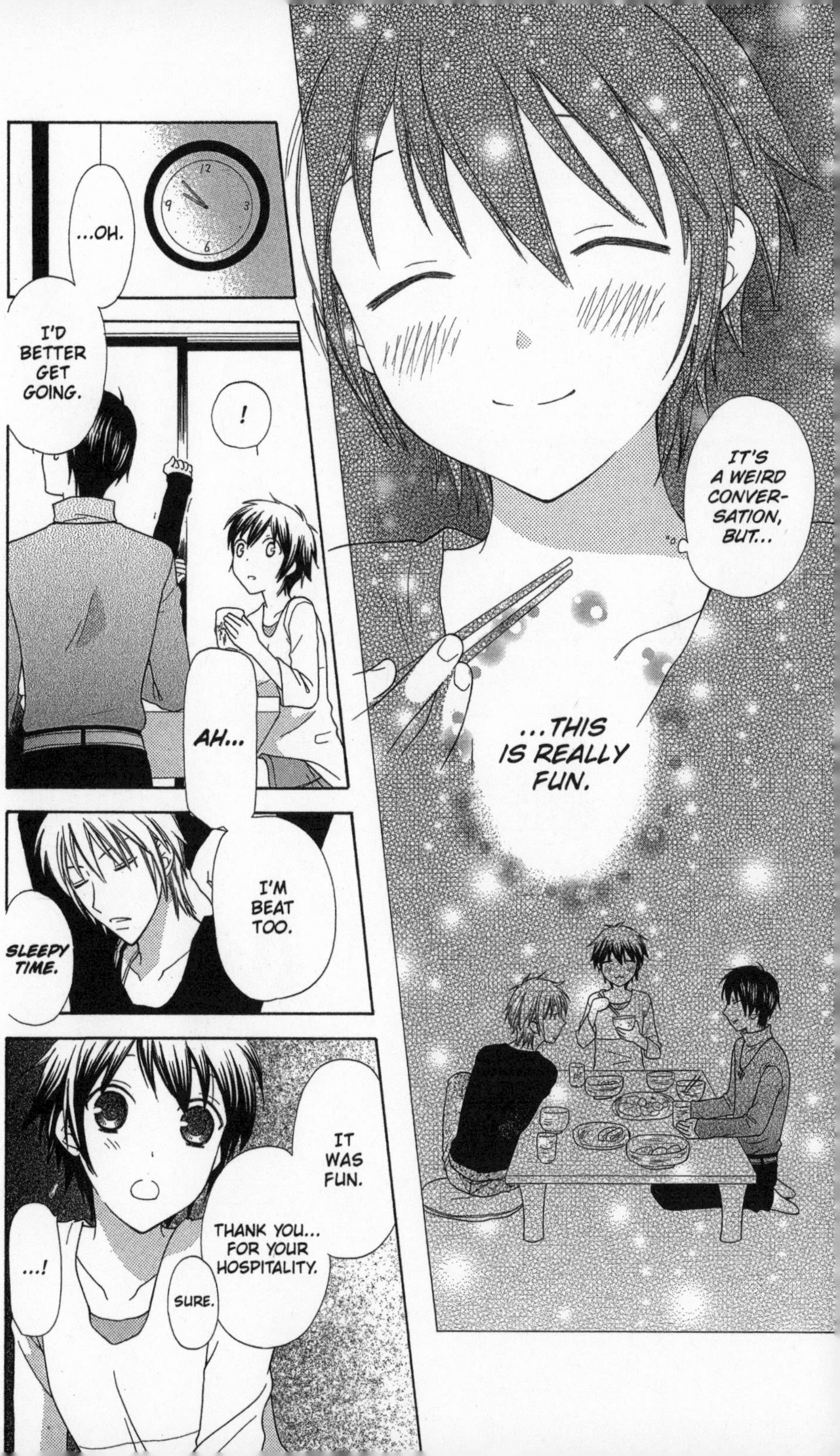
IT'S A WEIRD CONVERSATION, BUT...
...THIS IS REALLY FUN.
...OH.
I'D BETTER GET GOING.
!
AH...
I'M BEAT TOO.
SLEEPY TIME.
IT WAS FUN.
THANK YOU... FOR YOUR HOSPITALITY.
...!
SURE.

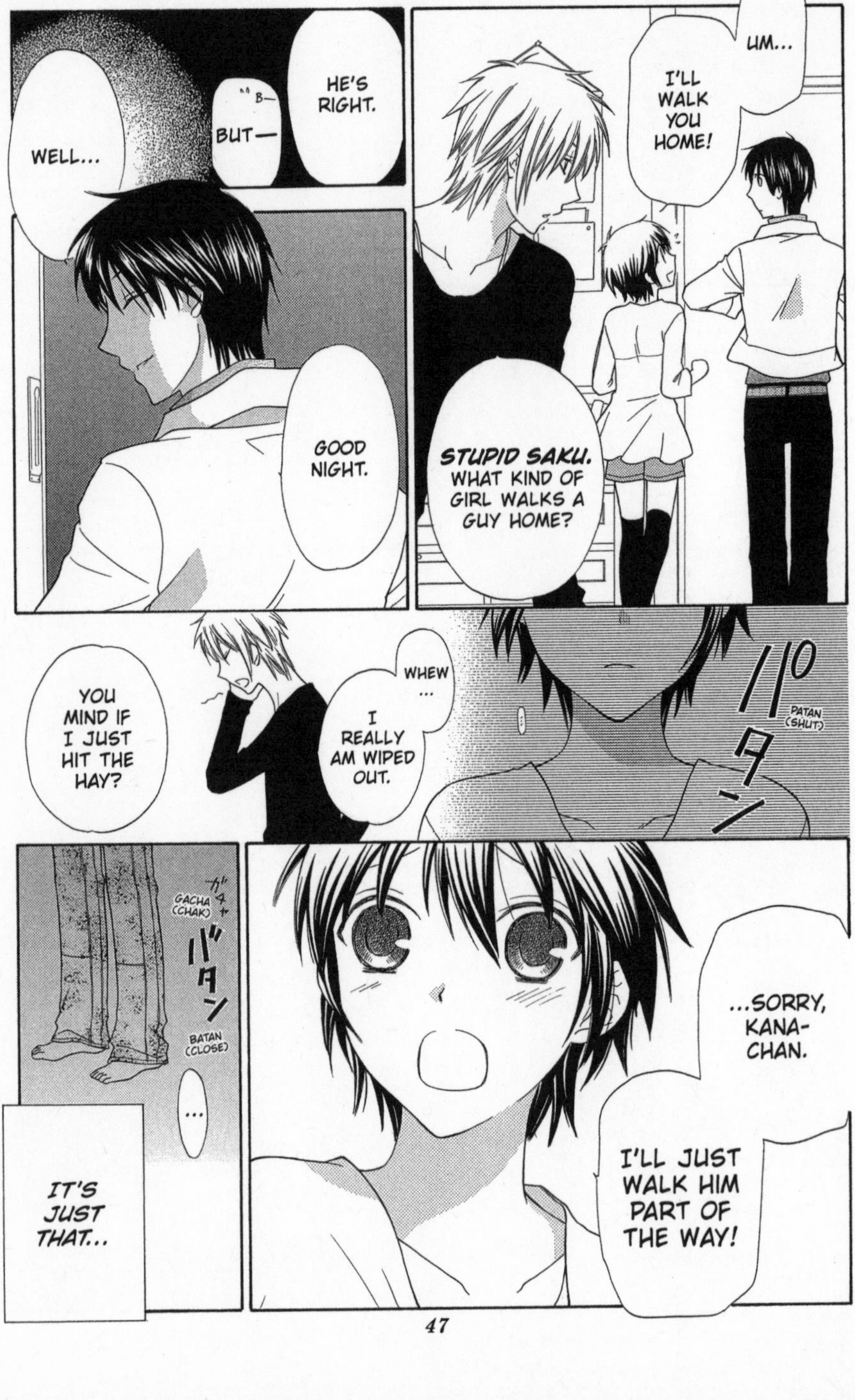
UM...
I'LL WALK YOU HOME!
STUPID SAKU. WHAT KIND OF GIRL WALKS A GUY HOME?
HE'S RIGHT.
B— BUT—
WELL...
GOOD NIGHT.
パタン
PATAN (SHUT)
...
WHEW ... I REALLY AM WIPED OUT.
YOU MIND IF I JUST HIT THE HAY?
...SORRY, KANA-CHAN.
I'LL JUST WALK HIM PART OF THE WAY!
ガチャ
GACHA (CHAK)
バタン
BATAN (CLOSE)
...
IT'S JUST THAT...

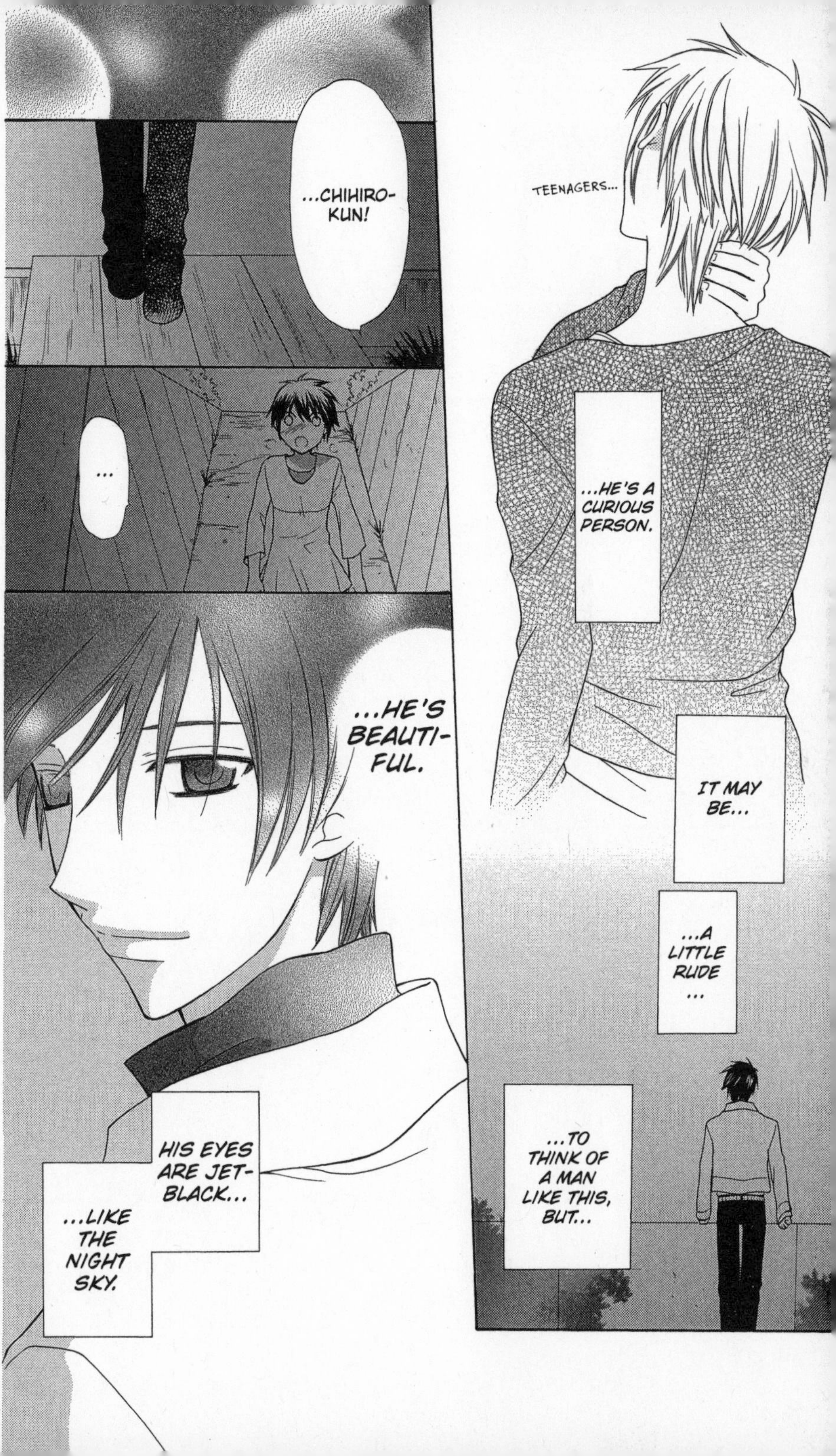
TEENAGERS...
...HE'S A CURIOUS PERSON.
IT MAY BE...
...A LITTLE RUDE ...
...TO THINK OF A MAN LIKE THIS, BUT...
...CHIHIRO-KUN!
...
...HE'S BEAUTIFUL.
HIS EYES ARE JET-BLACK...
...LIKE THE NIGHT SKY.

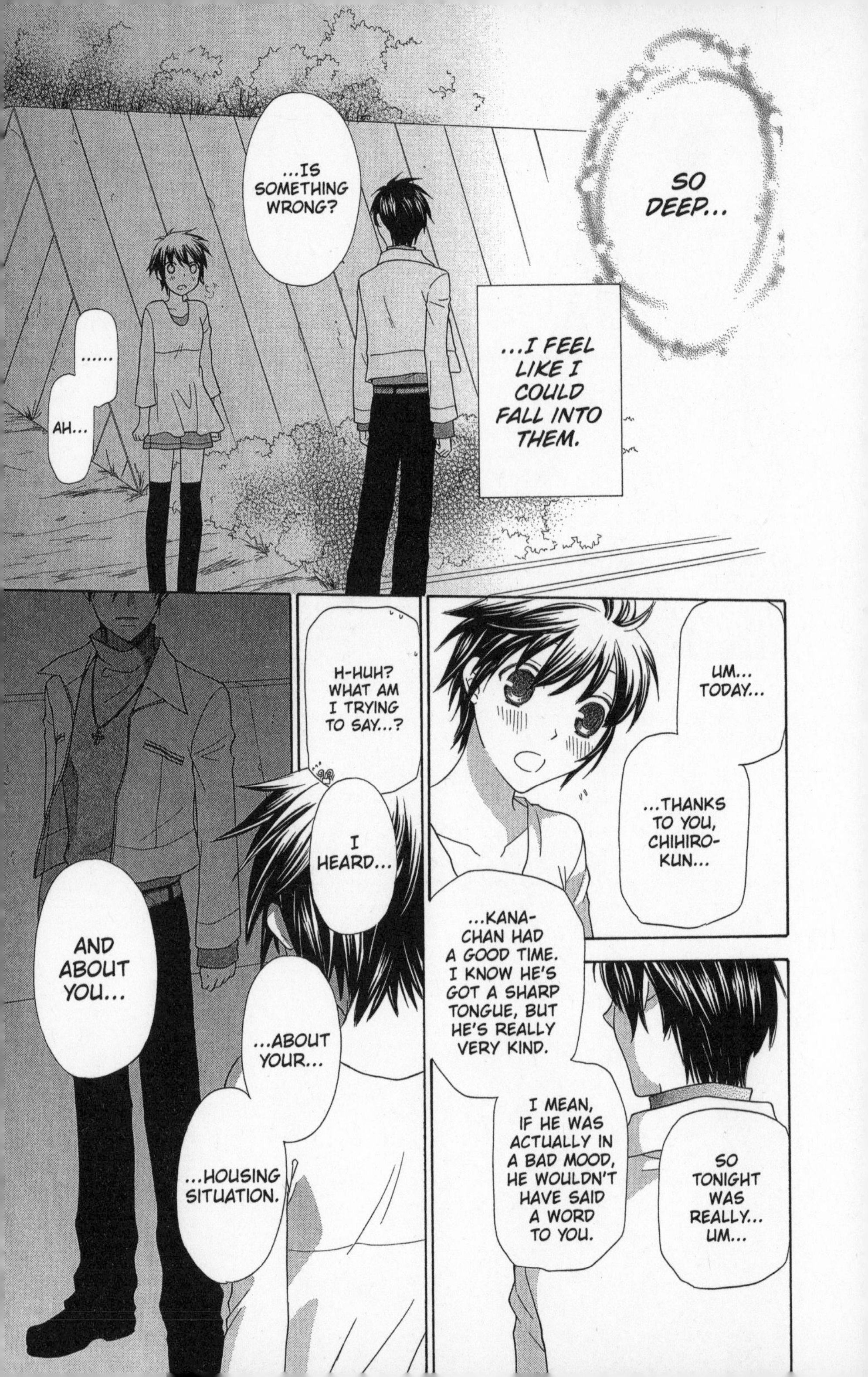
SO DEEP...
...I FEEL LIKE I COULD FALL INTO THEM.
...IS SOMETHING WRONG?
......
AH...
UM... TODAY...
...THANKS TO YOU, CHIHIRO-KUN...
H-HUH? WHAT AM I TRYING TO SAY...?
...KANA-CHAN HAD A GOOD TIME. I KNOW HE'S GOT A SHARP TONGUE, BUT HE'S REALLY VERY KIND.
I MEAN, IF HE WAS ACTUALLY IN A BAD MOOD, HE WOULDN'T HAVE SAID A WORD TO YOU.
SO TONIGHT WAS REALLY... UM...
I HEARD...
AND ABOUT YOU...
...ABOUT YOUR...
...HOUSING SITUATION.

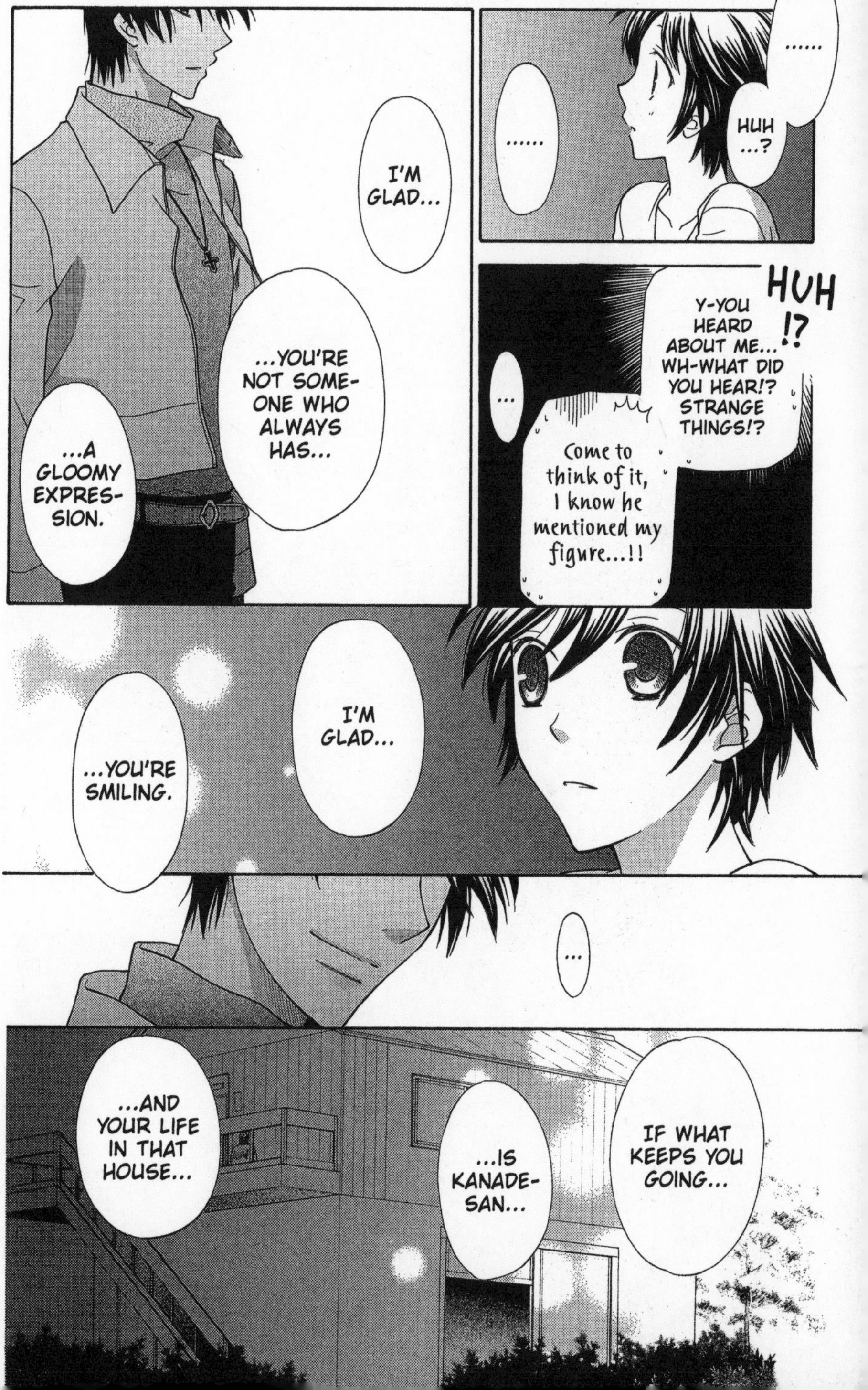
......
HUH ...?
......
HUH !?
Y-YOU HEARD ABOUT ME... WH-WHAT DID YOU HEAR!? STRANGE THINGS!?
...
Come to think of it, I know he mentioned my figure...!!
I'M GLAD...
...YOU'RE NOT SOME-ONE WHO ALWAYS HAS...
...A GLOOMY EXPRES-SION.
I'M GLAD...
...YOU'RE SMILING.
...
IF WHAT KEEPS YOU GOING...
...IS KANADE-SAN...
...AND YOUR LIFE IN THAT HOUSE...

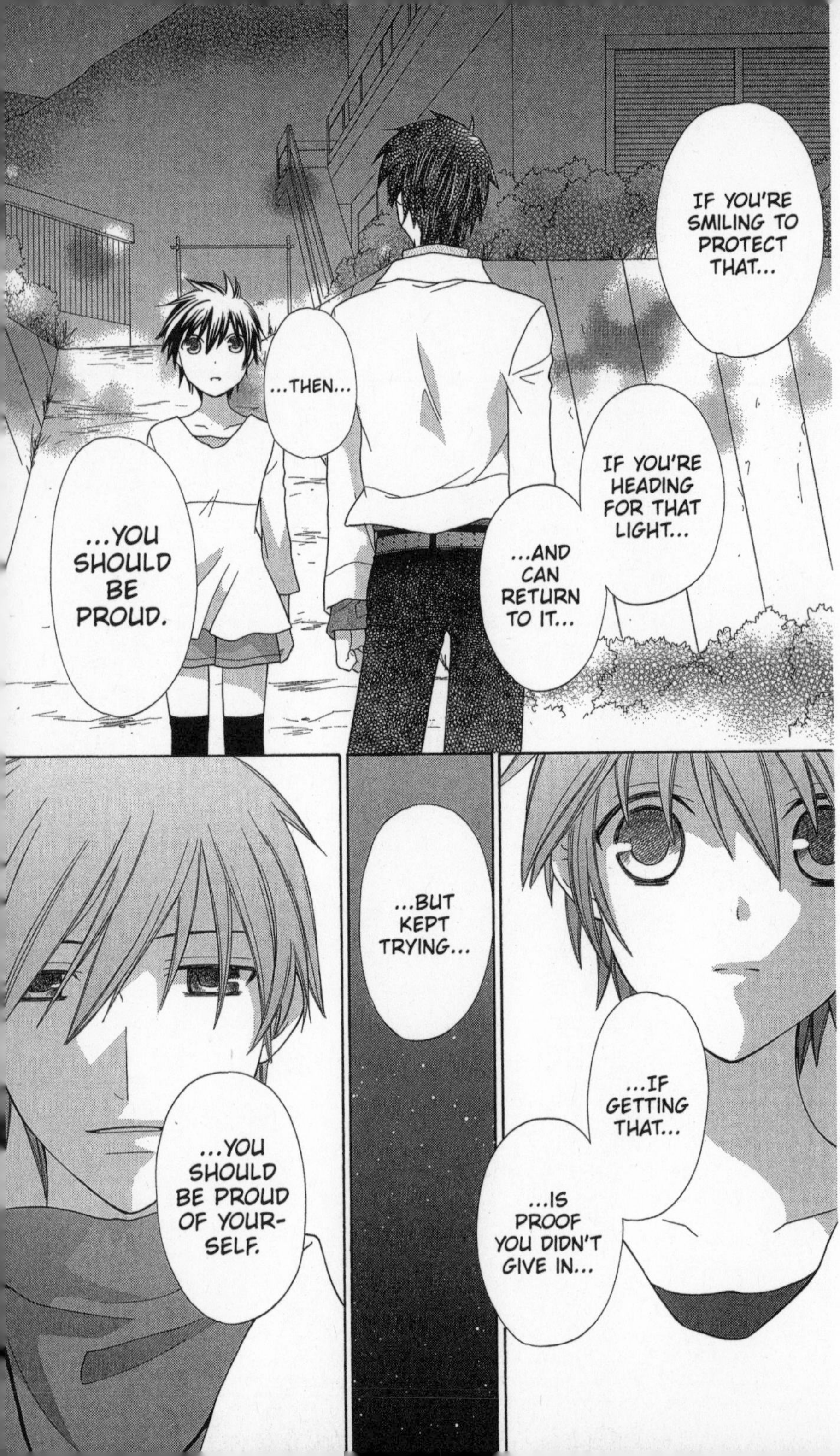
IF YOU'RE SMILING TO PROTECT THAT...
IF YOU'RE HEADING FOR THAT LIGHT...
...AND CAN RETURN TO IT...
...THEN...
...YOU SHOULD BE PROUD.
...IF GETTING THAT...
...IS PROOF YOU DIDN'T GIVE IN...
...BUT KEPT TRYING...
...YOU SHOULD BE PROUD OF YOUR-SELF.

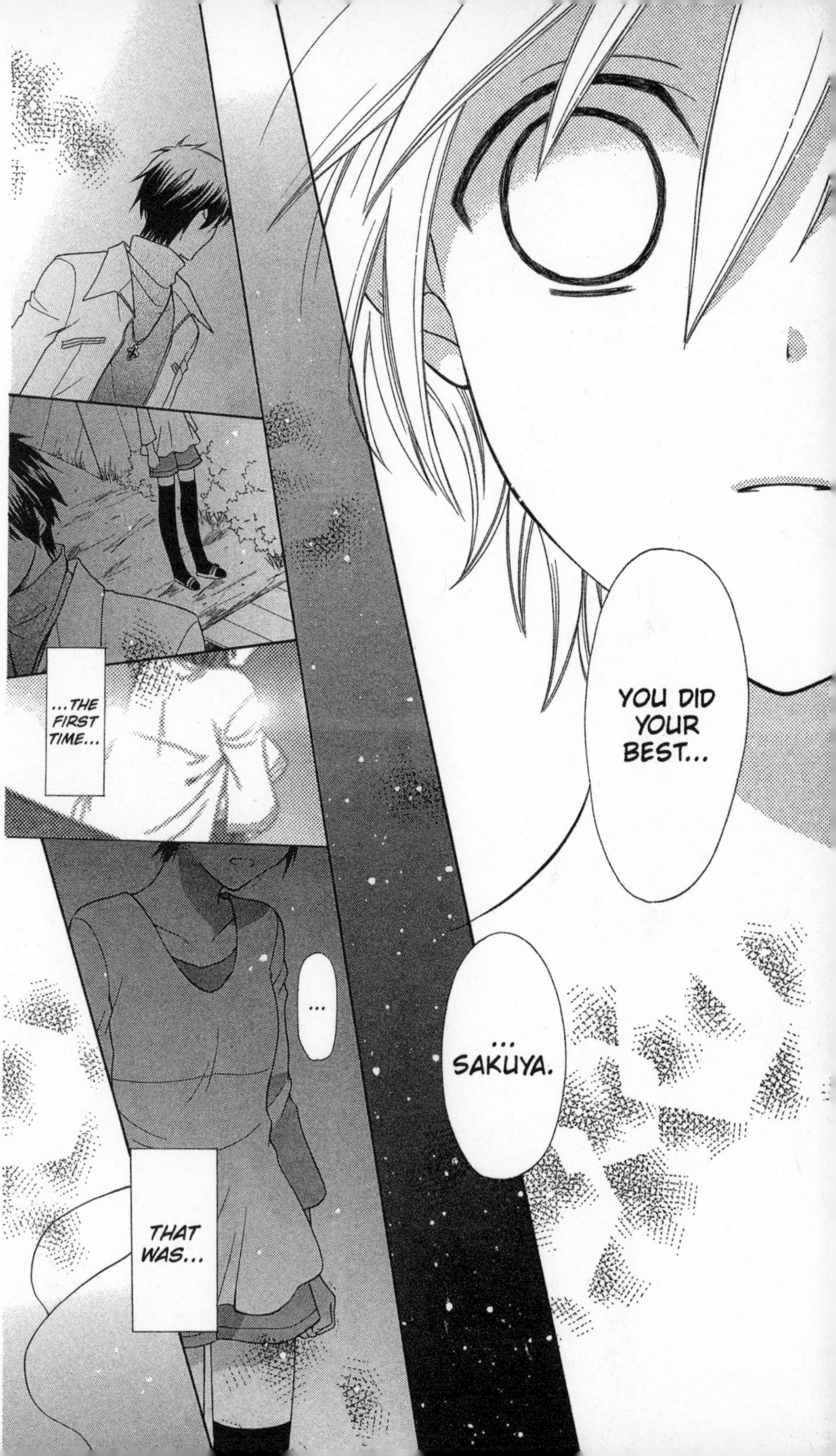
YOU DID YOUR BEST...
...SAKUYA.
...THE FIRST TIME...
...
THAT WAS...

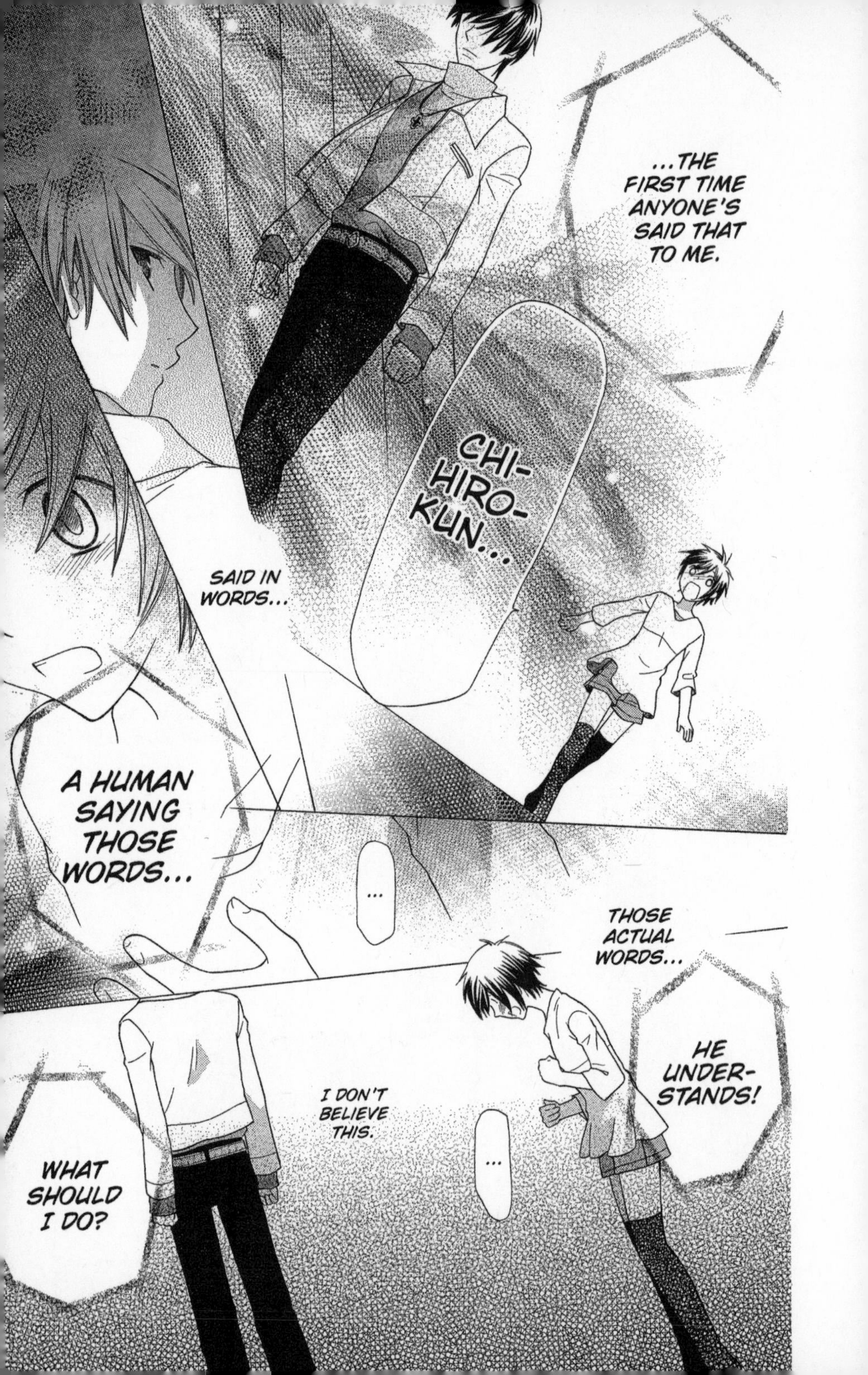
...THE FIRST TIME ANYONE'S SAID THAT TO ME.
CHI-HIRO-KUN...
SAID IN WORDS...
A HUMAN SAYING THOSE WORDS...
THOSE ACTUAL WORDS...
...
HE UNDER-STANDS!
...
I DON'T BELIEVE THIS.
WHAT SHOULD I DO?

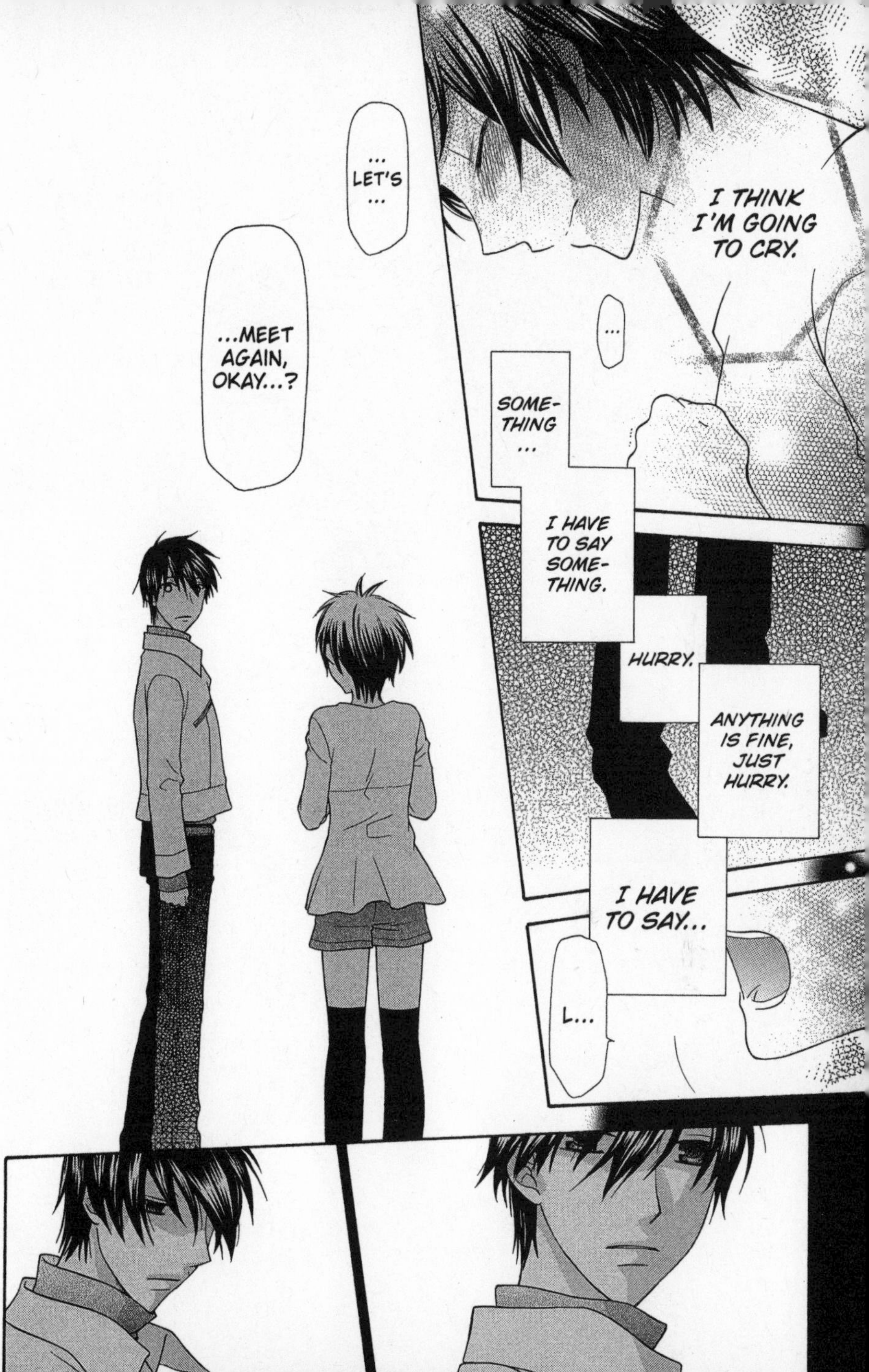
I THINK I'M GOING TO CRY.
...
SOME-THING...
I HAVE TO SAY SOME-THING.
HURRY.
ANYTHING IS FINE, JUST HURRY.
I HAVE TO SAY...
L...
...LET'S...
...MEET AGAIN, OKAY...?

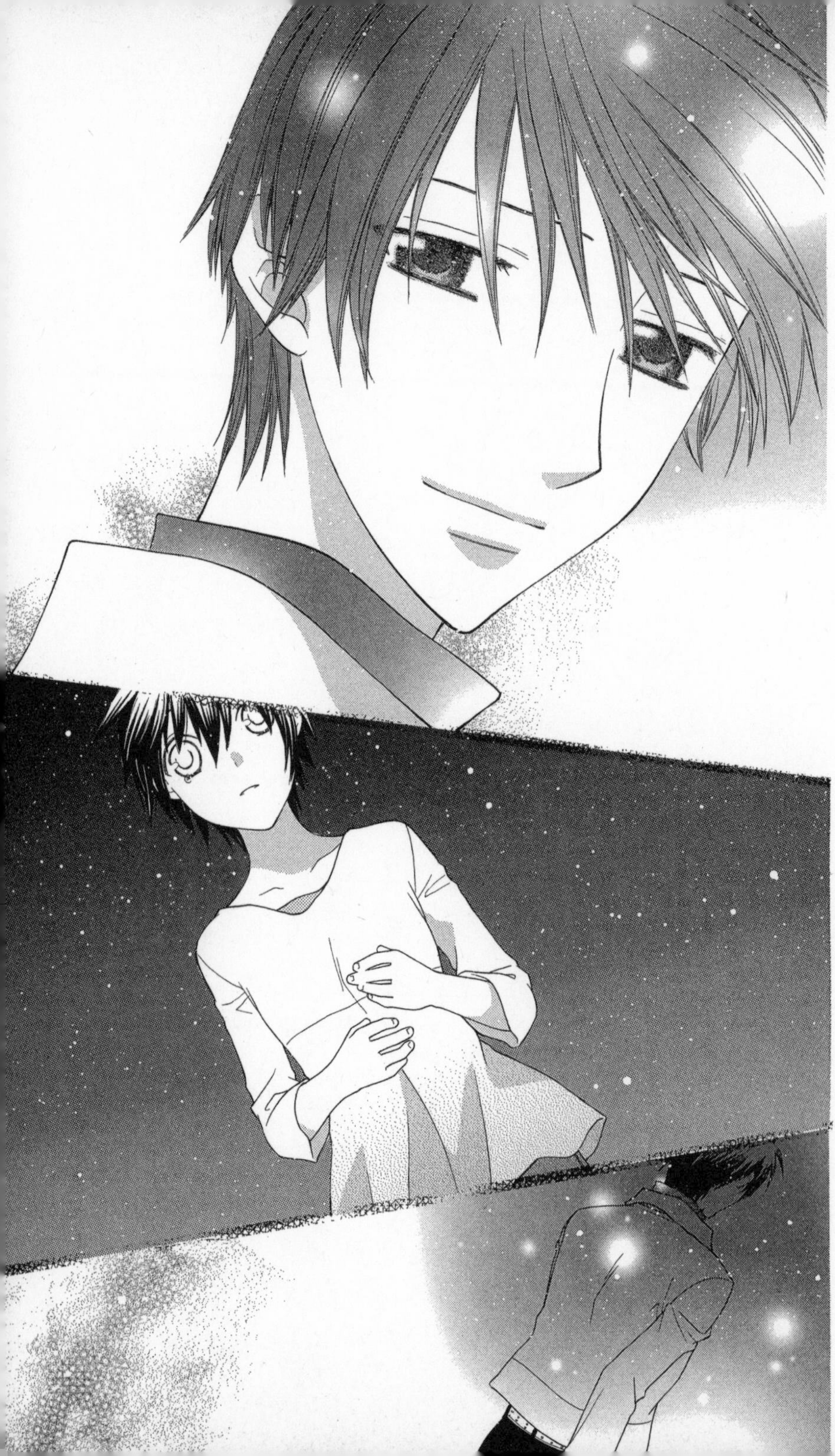

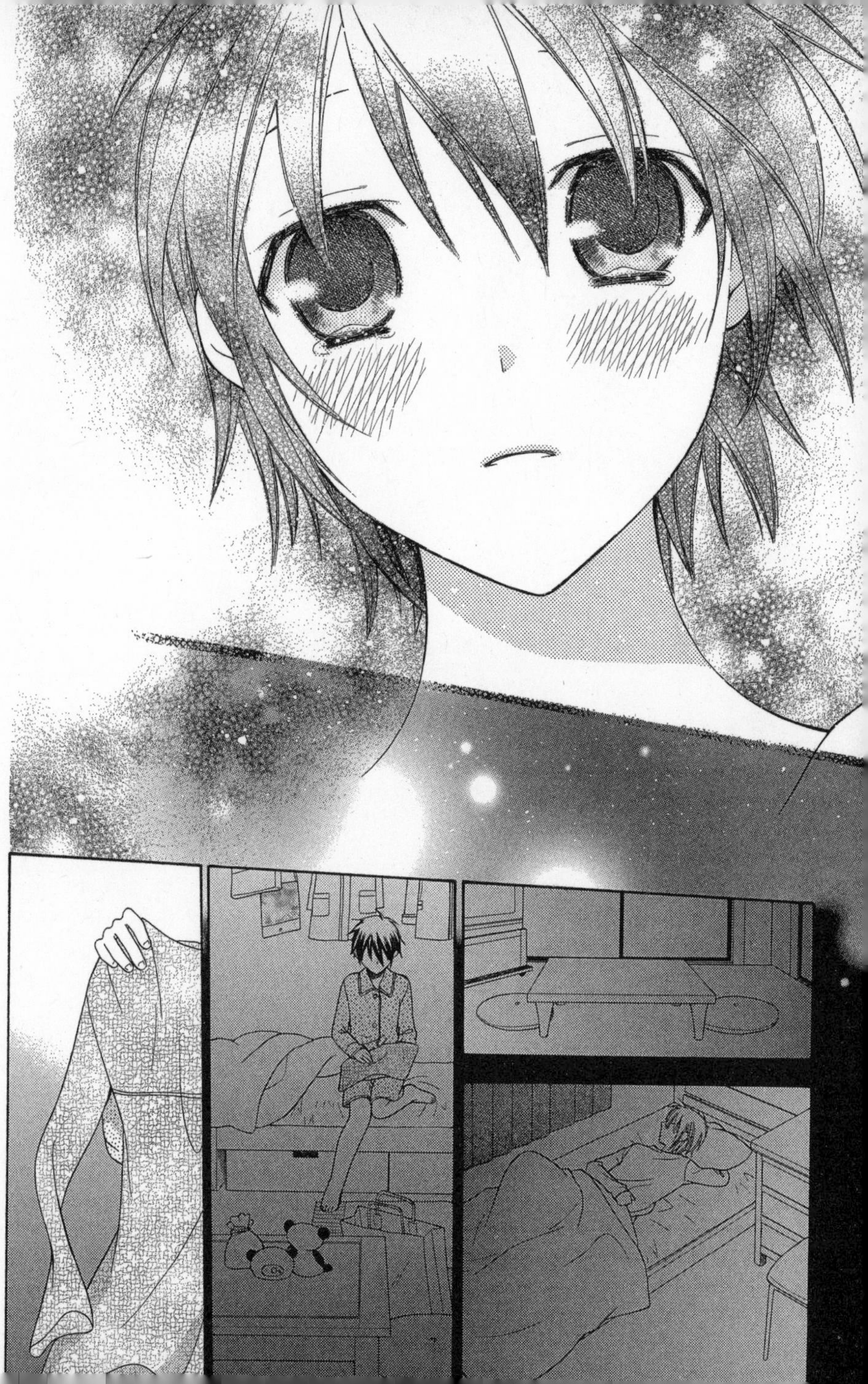

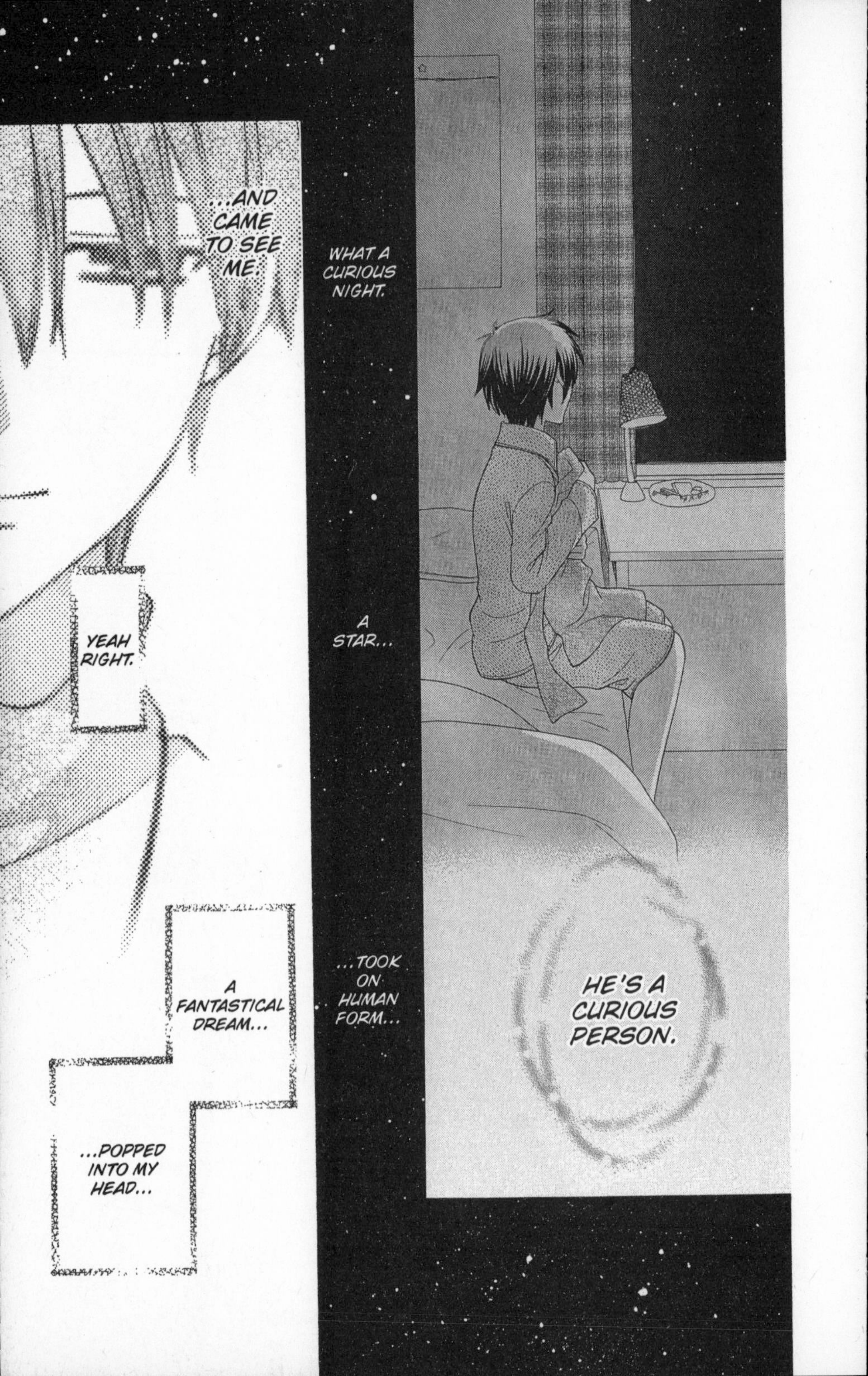
HE'S A CURIOUS PERSON.
WHAT A CURIOUS NIGHT.
A STAR...
...TOOK ON HUMAN FORM...
...AND CAME TO SEE ME.
YEAH RIGHT.
A FANTASTICAL DREAM...
...POPPED INTO MY HEAD...

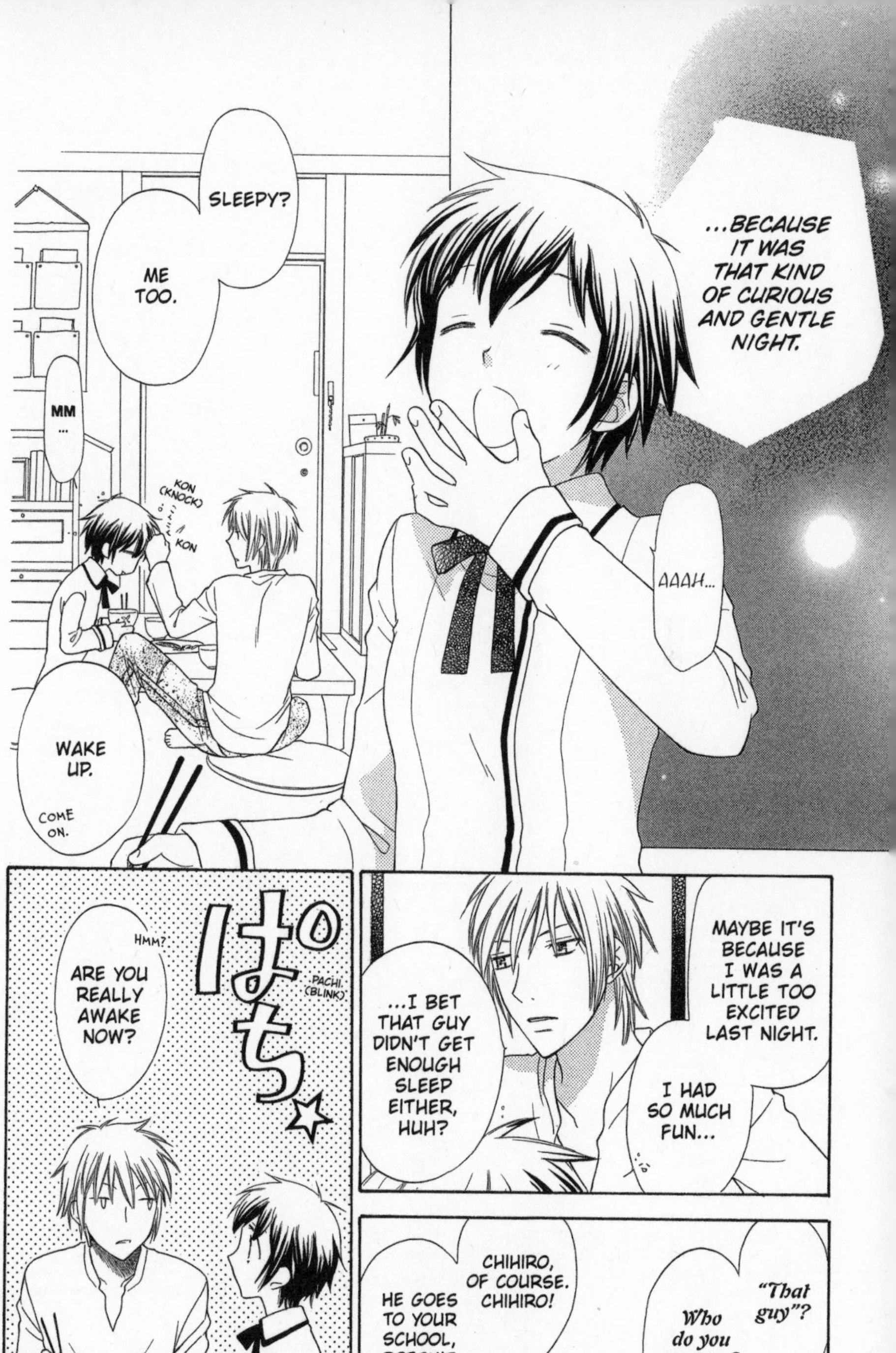
...BECAUSE IT WAS THAT KIND OF CURIOUS AND GENTLE NIGHT.
AAAH...
SLEEPY?
ME TOO.
MM ...
KON (KNOCK)
KON
WAKE UP.
COME ON.
MAYBE IT'S BECAUSE I WAS A LITTLE TOO EXCITED LAST NIGHT.
I HAD SO MUCH FUN...
...I BET THAT GUY DIDN'T GET ENOUGH SLEEP EITHER, HUH?
"That guy"?
Who do you mean...?
CHIHIRO, OF COURSE. CHIHIRO!
HE GOES TO YOUR SCHOOL, DOESN'T HE?
ぱち☆
PACHI (BLINK)
HMM?
ARE YOU REALLY AWAKE NOW?

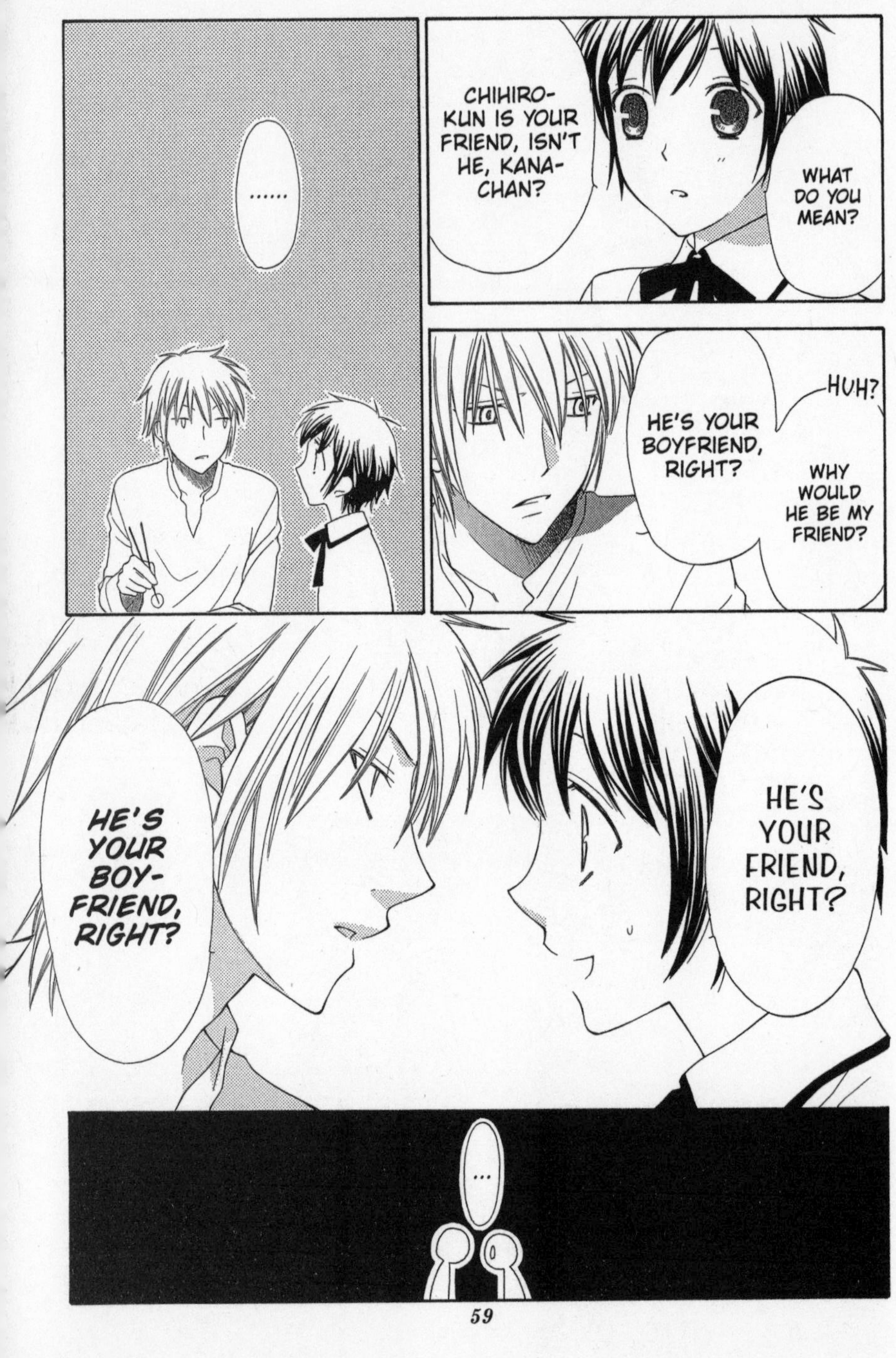
CHIHIRO-KUN IS YOUR FRIEND, ISN'T HE, KANA-CHAN?
WHAT DO YOU MEAN?
HUH?
WHY WOULD HE BE MY FRIEND?
HE'S YOUR BOYFRIEND, RIGHT?
......
HE'S YOUR FRIEND, RIGHT?
HE'S YOUR BOY-FRIEND, RIGHT?
...

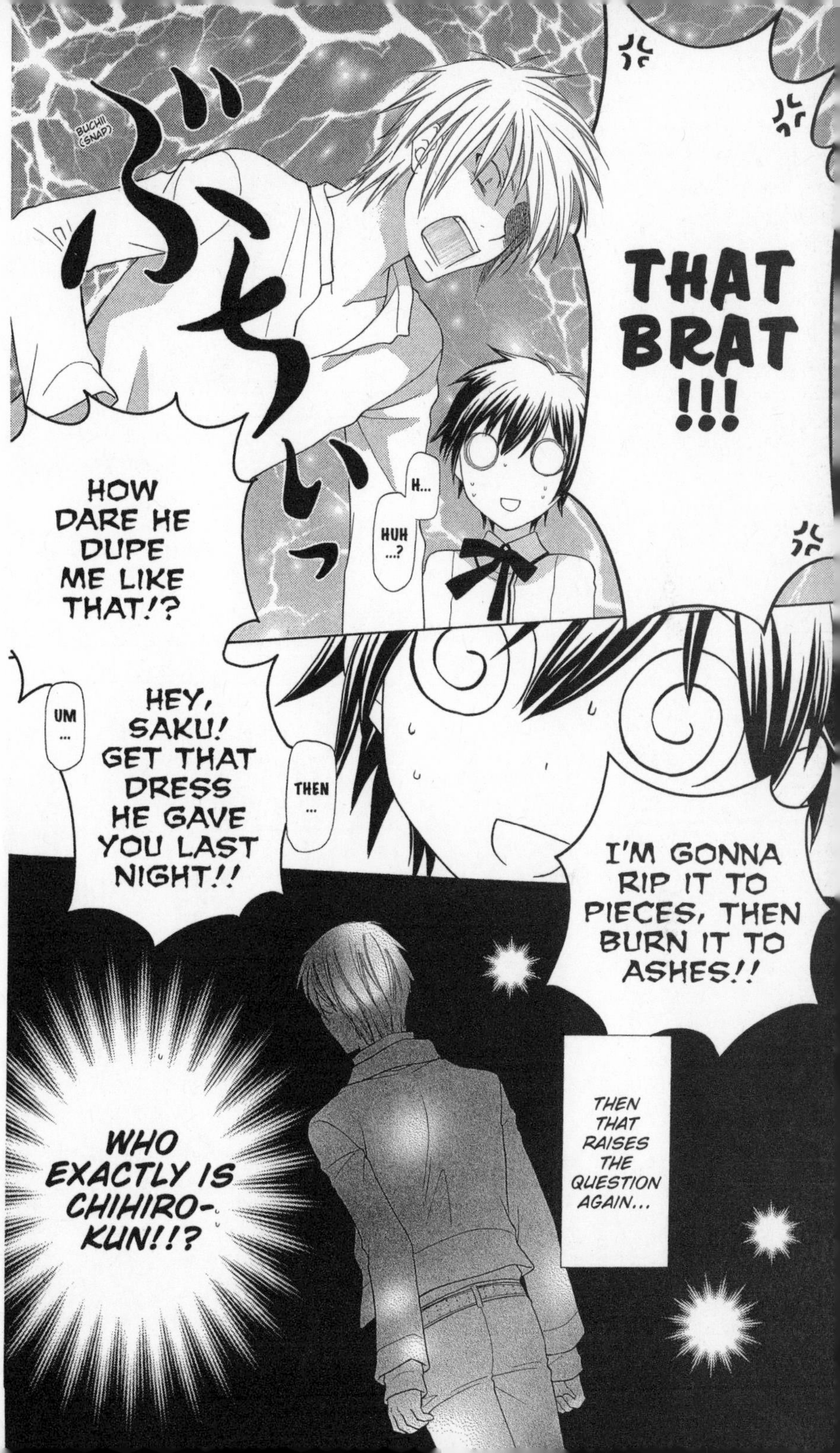
THAT BRAT!!!
HOW DARE HE DUPE ME LIKE THAT!?
BUCHII (SNAP)
H...
HUH...?
HEY, SAKU! GET THAT DRESS HE GAVE YOU LAST NIGHT!!
I'M GONNA RIP IT TO PIECES, THEN BURN IT TO ASHES!!
THEN...
UM...
THEN THAT RAISES THE QUESTION AGAIN...
WHO EXACTLY IS CHIHIRO-KUN!!?

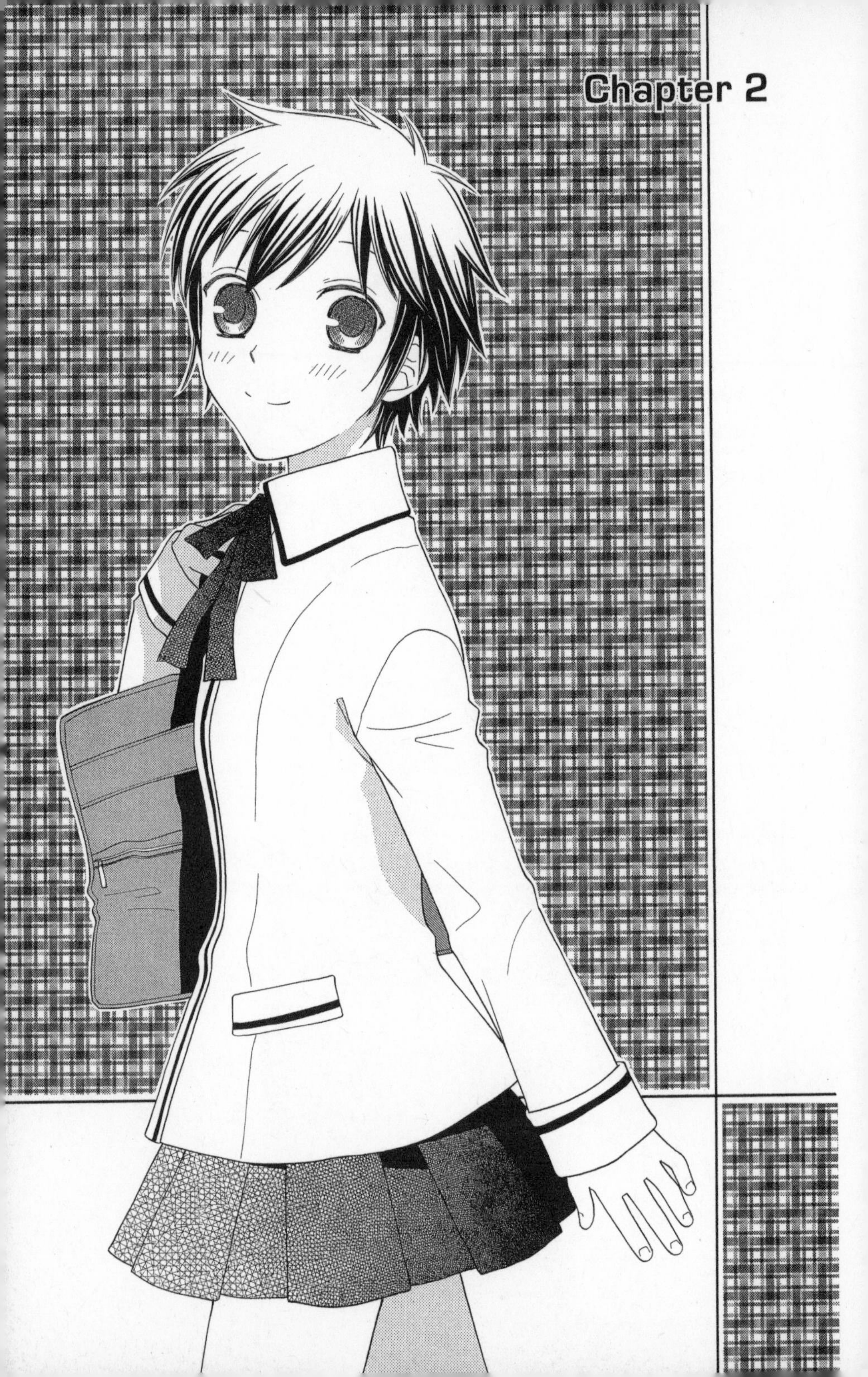
Chapter 2

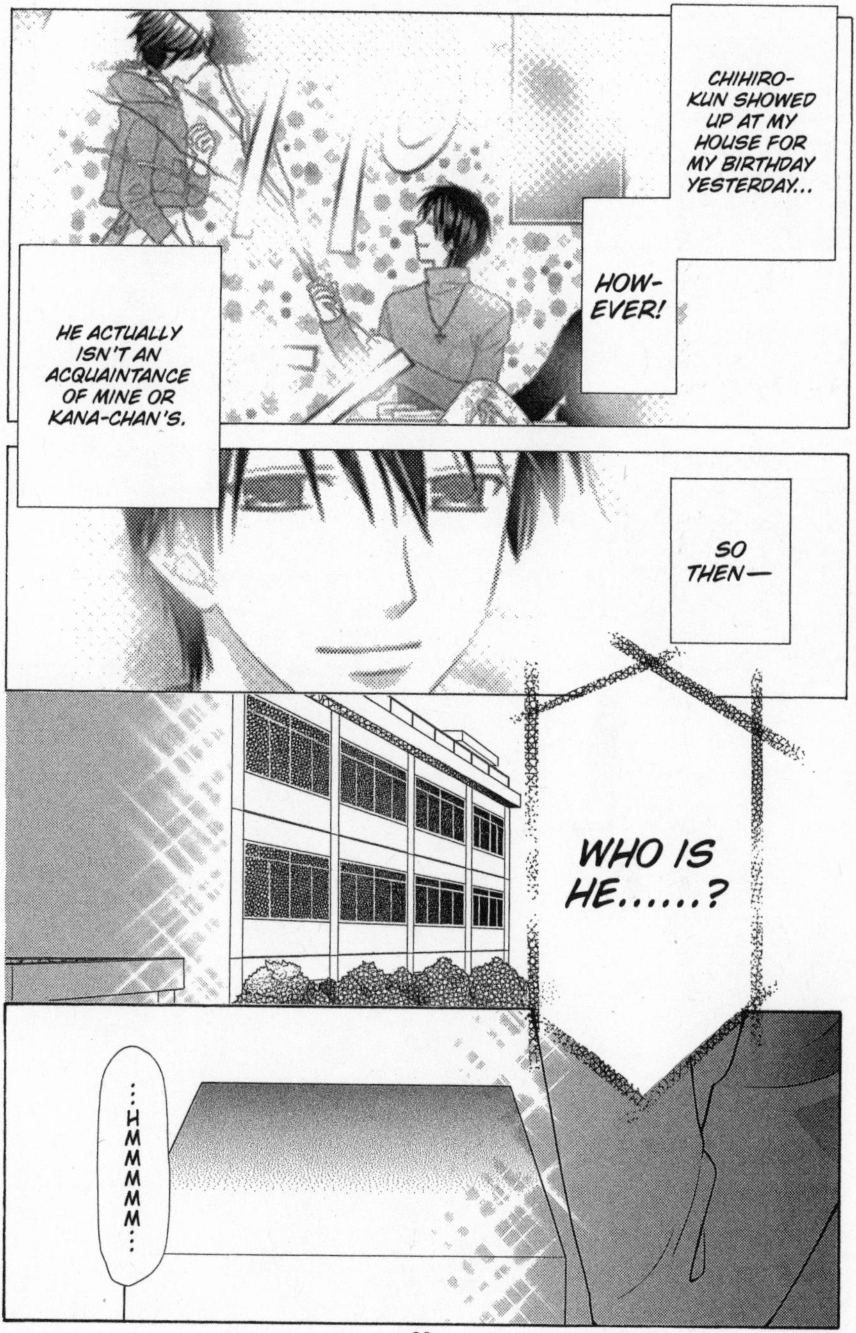
CHIHIRO-KUN SHOWED UP AT MY HOUSE FOR MY BIRTHDAY YESTERDAY...
HOW-EVER!
HE ACTUALLY ISN'T AN ACQUAINTANCE OF MINE OR KANA-CHAN'S.
SO THEN—
WHO IS HE......?
...HMMMMM...

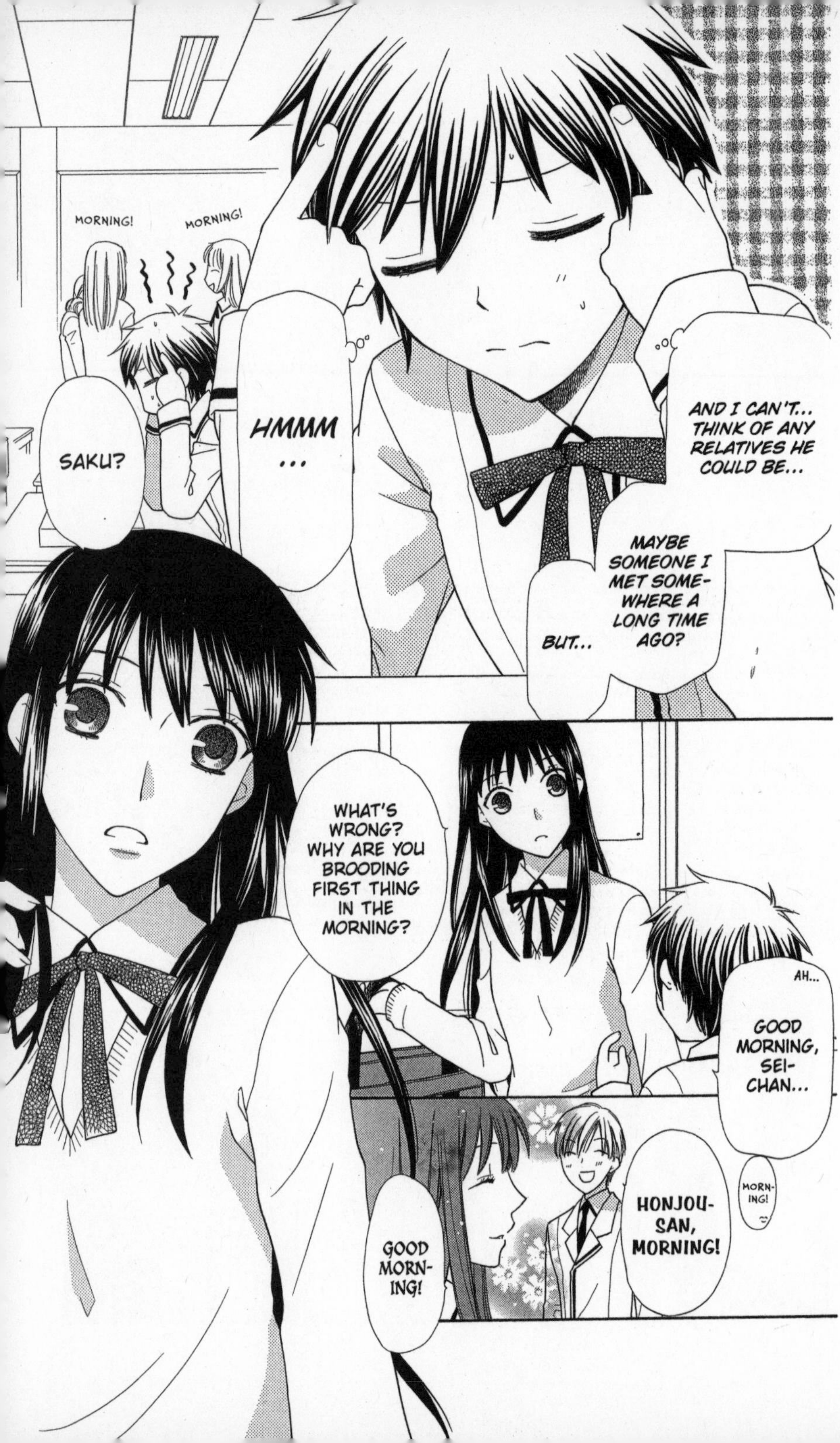
AND I CAN'T... THINK OF ANY RELATIVES HE COULD BE...
MAYBE SOMEONE I MET SOME-WHERE A LONG TIME AGO?
BUT...
HMMM ...
MORNING!
MORNING!
SAKU?
AH...
GOOD MORNING, SEI-CHAN...
WHAT'S WRONG? WHY ARE YOU BROODING FIRST THING IN THE MORNING?
MORN-ING!
HONJOU-SAN, MORNING!
GOOD MORN-ING!

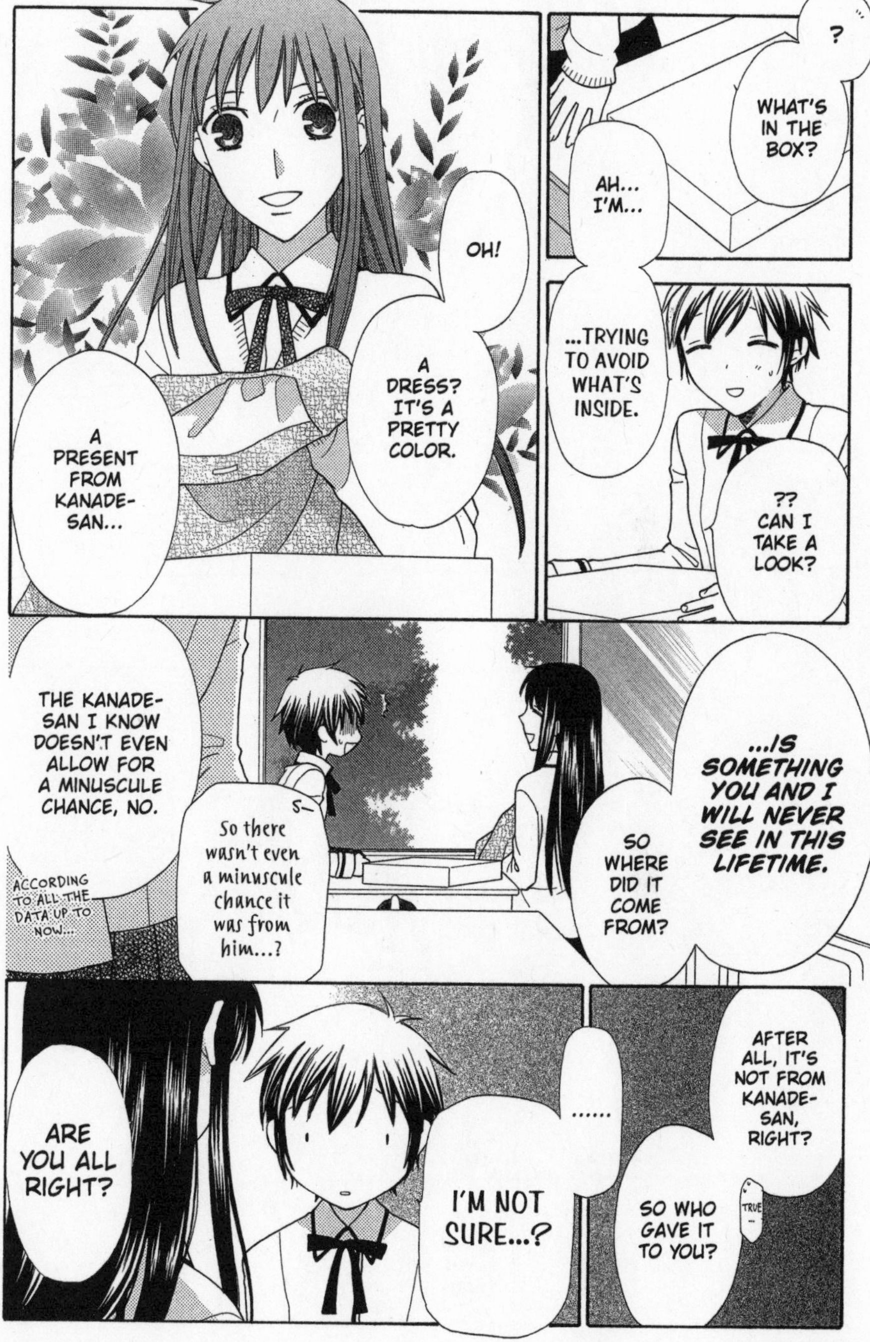
?
WHAT'S IN THE BOX?
AH... I'M...
...TRYING TO AVOID WHAT'S INSIDE.
?? CAN I TAKE A LOOK?
OH!
A DRESS? IT'S A PRETTY COLOR.
A PRESENT FROM KANADE-SAN...
...IS SOMETHING YOU AND I WILL NEVER SEE IN THIS LIFETIME.
SO WHERE DID IT COME FROM?
S—
So there wasn't even a minuscule chance it was from him...?
THE KANADE-SAN I KNOW DOESN'T EVEN ALLOW FOR A MINUSCULE CHANCE, NO.
ACCORDING TO ALL THE DATA UP TO NOW...
AFTER ALL, IT'S NOT FROM KANADE-SAN, RIGHT?
TRUE...
SO WHO GAVE IT TO YOU?
......
I'M NOT SURE...?
ARE YOU ALL RIGHT?

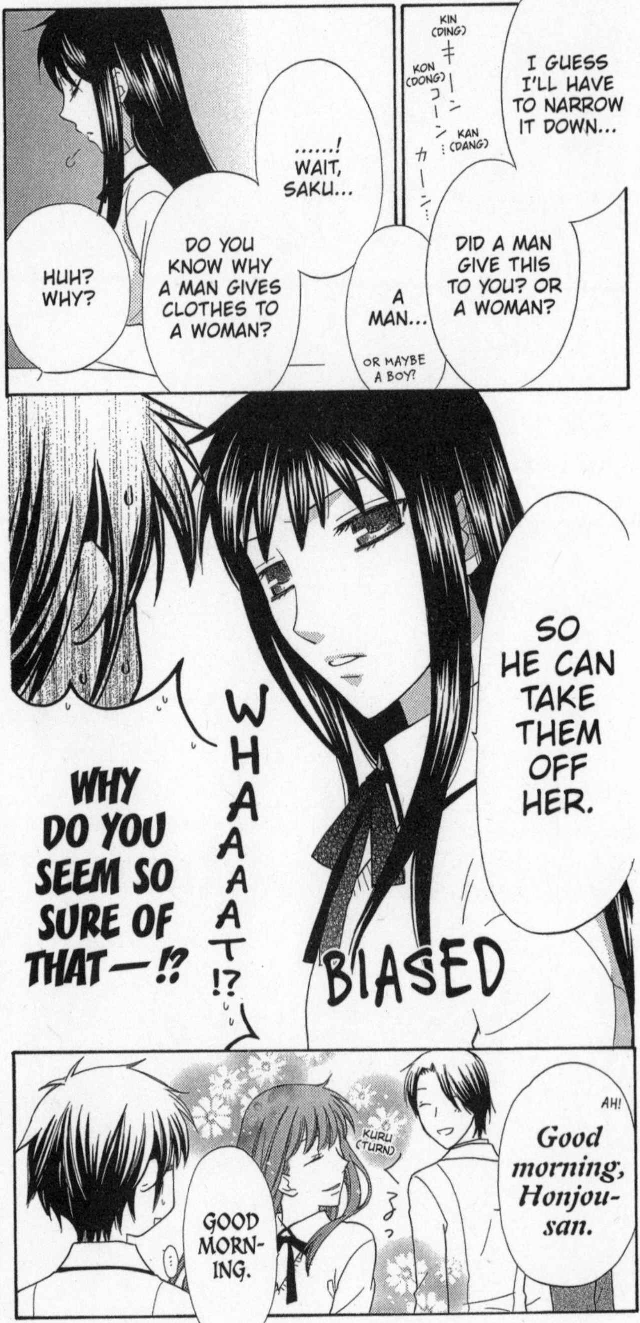
I GUESS I'LL HAVE TO NARROW IT DOWN...
KIN (DING) KON (DONG) KAN (DANG)
DID A MAN GIVE THIS TO YOU? OR A WOMAN?
A MAN...
OR MAYBE A BOY?
......! WAIT, SAKU...
DO YOU KNOW WHY A MAN GIVES CLOTHES TO A WOMAN?
HUH? WHY?
SO HE CAN TAKE THEM OFF HER.
BIASED
WHAAAAAT!?
WHY DO YOU SEEM SO SURE OF THAT—!?
AH!
Good morning, Honjou-san.
KURU (TURN)
GOOD MORN-ING.

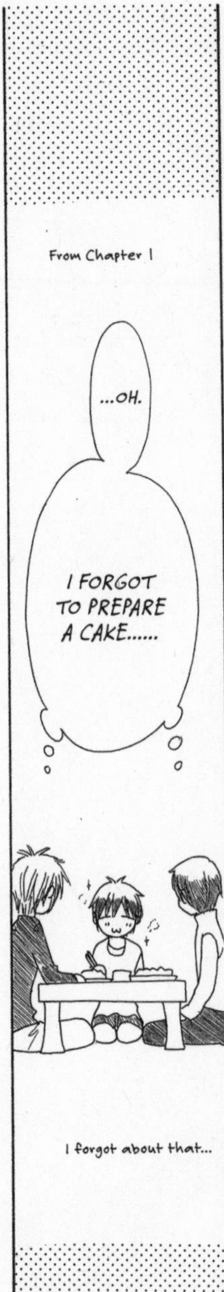
From Chapter 1
...OH.
I FORGOT TO PREPARE A CAKE......
I forgot about that...

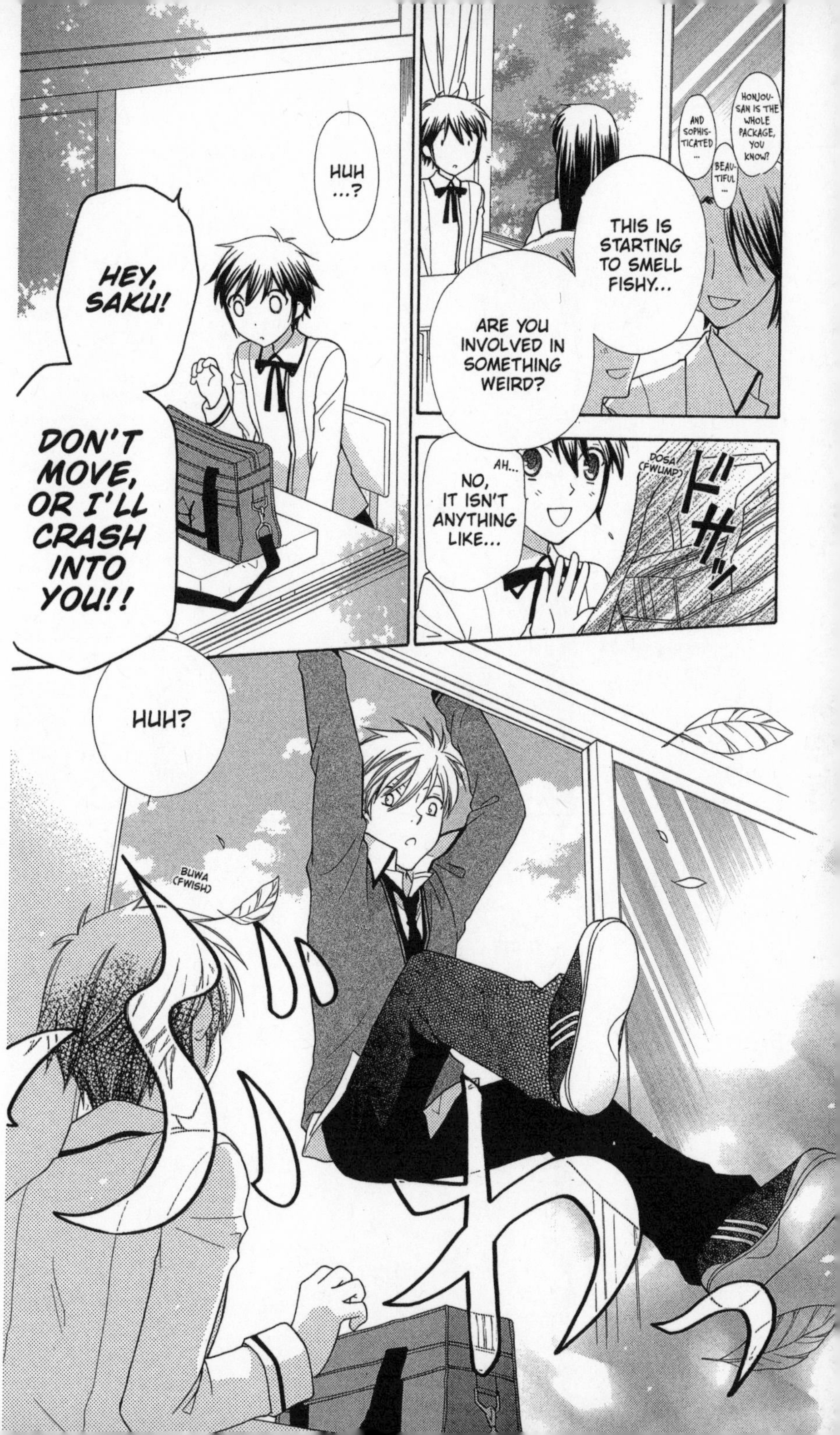
HONJOU-SAN IS THE WHOLE PACKAGE, YOU KNOW?
BEAU-TIFUL...
AND SOPHIS-TICATED...
THIS IS STARTING TO SMELL FISHY...
ARE YOU INVOLVED IN SOMETHING WEIRD?
DOSA (FWUMP)
AH...
NO, IT ISN'T ANYTHING LIKE...
HUH ...?
HEY, SAKU!
DON'T MOVE, OR I'LL CRASH INTO YOU!!
HUH?
BUWA (FWISH)

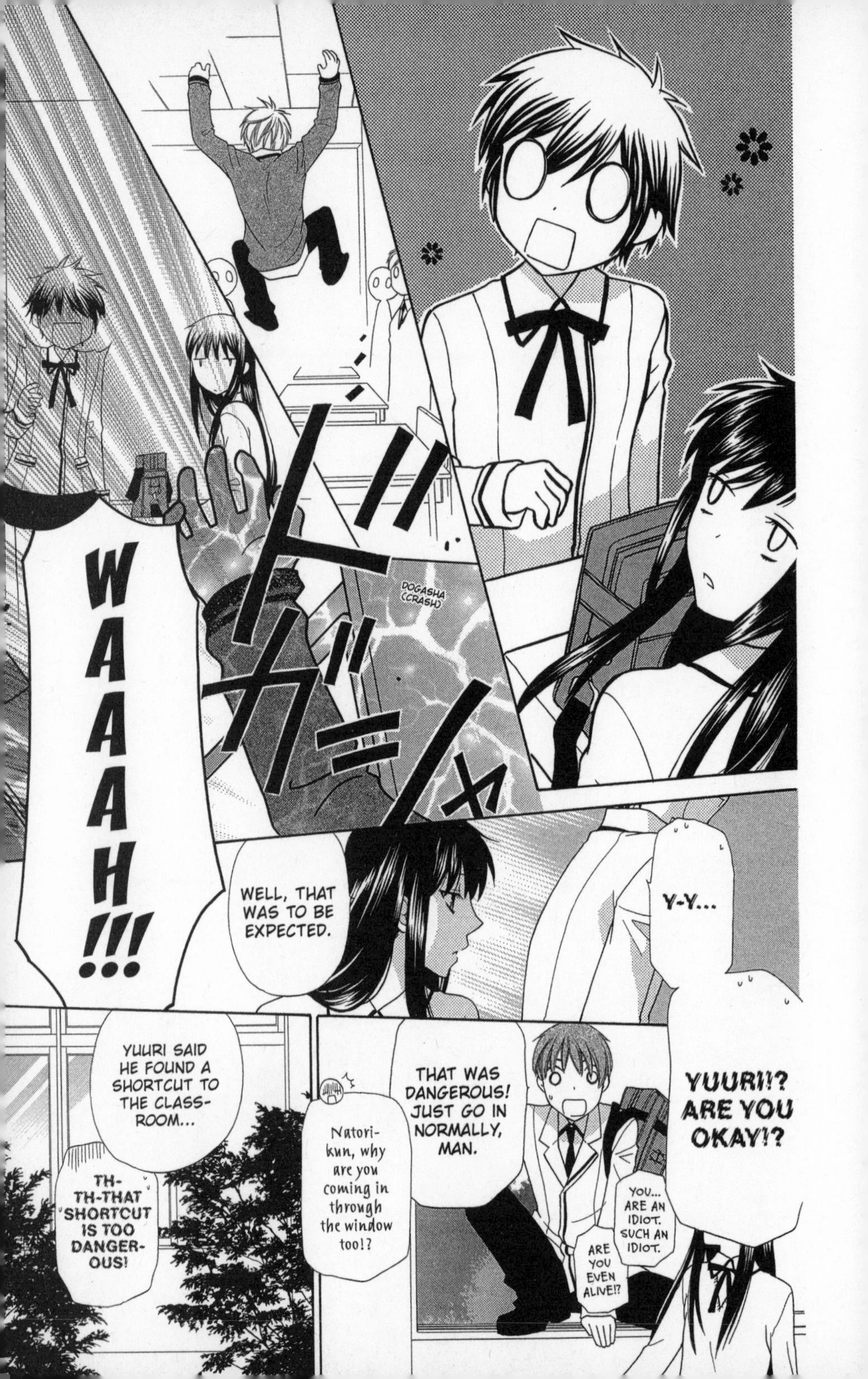
DOGASHA (CRASH)
WAAAAAH!!!
Y-Y...
WELL, THAT WAS TO BE EXPECTED.
YUURI!? ARE YOU OKAY!?
YOU... ARE AN IDIOT. SUCH AN IDIOT.
ARE YOU EVEN ALIVE!?
THAT WAS DANGEROUS! JUST GO IN NORMALLY, MAN.
Natori-kun, why are you coming in through the window too!?
YUURI SAID HE FOUND A SHORTCUT TO THE CLASS-ROOM...
TH-TH-THAT SHORTCUT IS TOO DANGER-OUS!

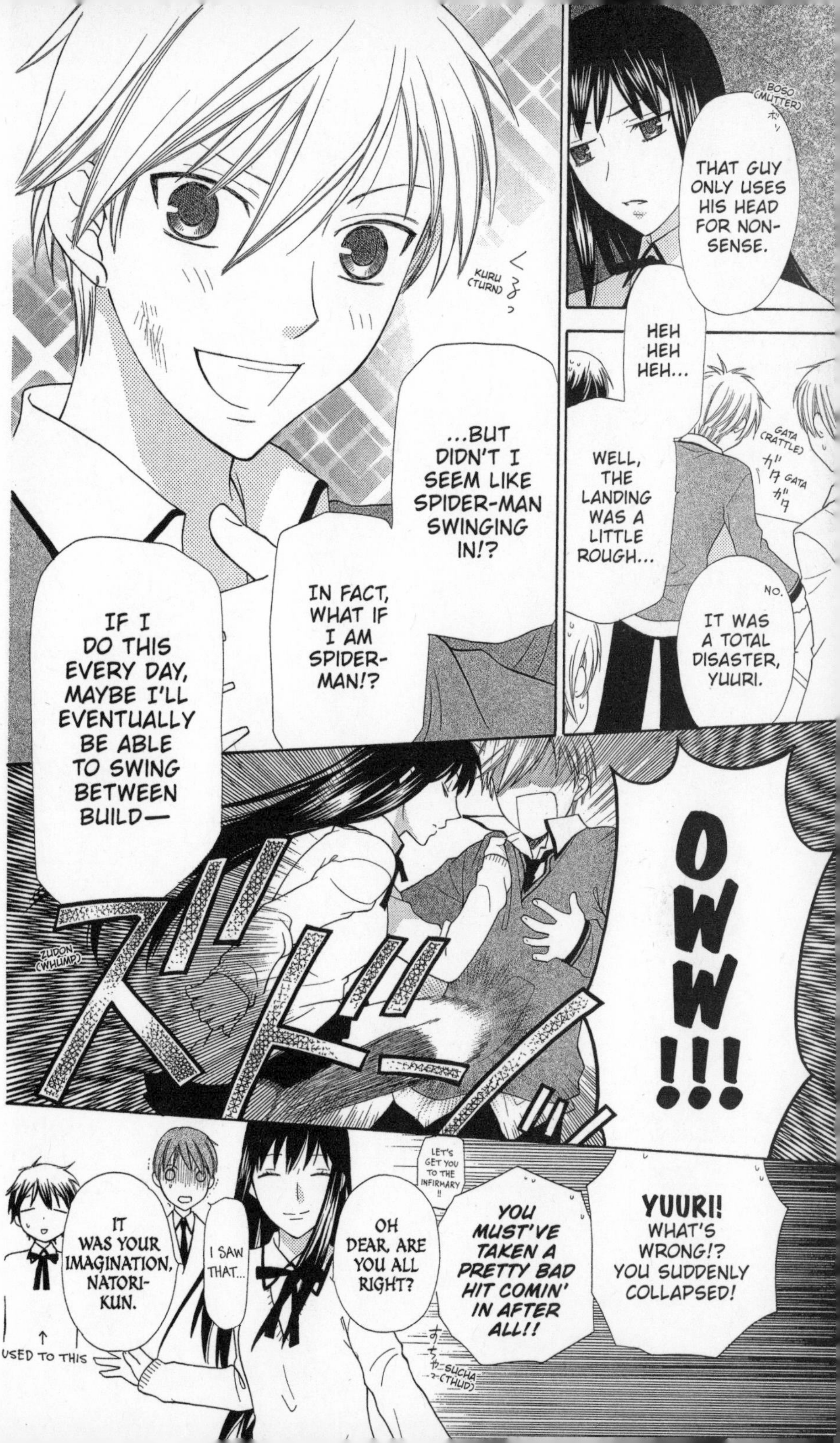
BOSO (MUTTER)
THAT GUY ONLY USES HIS HEAD FOR NON-SENSE.
HEH HEH HEH...
WELL, THE LANDING WAS A LITTLE ROUGH...
GATA (RATTLE)
GATA
NO.
IT WAS A TOTAL DISASTER, YUURI.
KURU (TURN)
...BUT DIDN'T I SEEM LIKE SPIDER-MAN SWINGING IN!?
IN FACT, WHAT IF I AM SPIDER-MAN!?
IF I DO THIS EVERY DAY, MAYBE I'LL EVENTUALLY BE ABLE TO SWING BETWEEN BUILD—
OWW!!!
ZUDON (WHUMP)
YUURI! WHAT'S WRONG!? YOU SUDDENLY COLLAPSED!
YOU MUST'VE TAKEN A PRETTY BAD HIT COMIN' IN AFTER ALL!!
LET'S GET YOU TO THE INFIRMARY!!
SUCHA (THUD)
OH DEAR, ARE YOU ALL RIGHT?
I SAW THAT...
IT WAS YOUR IMAGINATION, NATORI-KUN.
↑ USED TO THIS

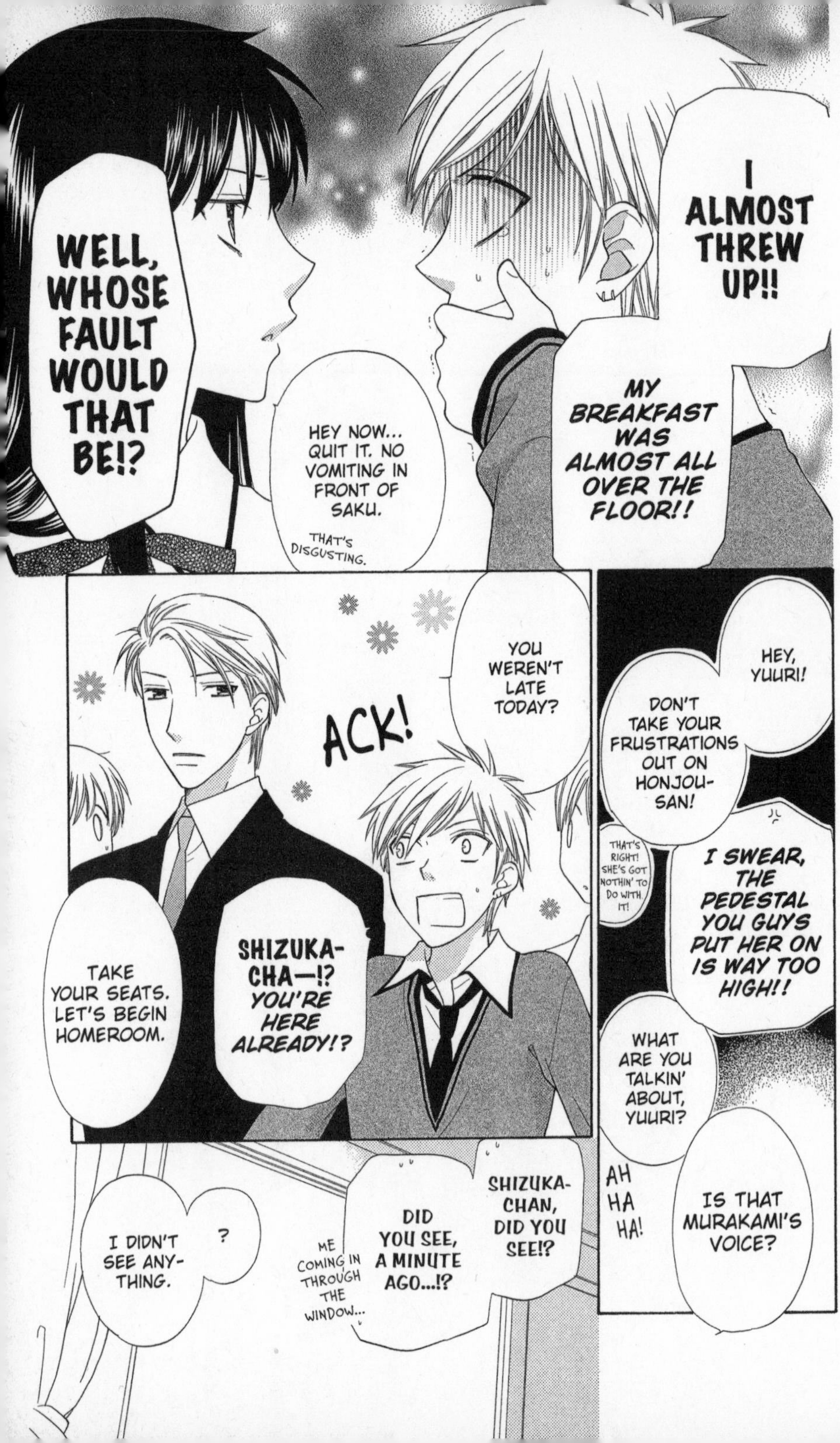
I ALMOST THREW UP!!
MY BREAKFAST WAS ALMOST ALL OVER THE FLOOR!!
HEY NOW... QUIT IT. NO VOMITING IN FRONT OF SAKU.
THAT'S DISGUSTING.
WELL, WHOSE FAULT WOULD THAT BE!?
HEY, YUURI!
DON'T TAKE YOUR FRUSTRATIONS OUT ON HONJOU-SAN!
THAT'S RIGHT! SHE'S GOT NOTHIN' TO DO WITH IT!
I SWEAR, THE PEDESTAL YOU GUYS PUT HER ON IS WAY TOO HIGH!!
WHAT ARE YOU TALKIN' ABOUT, YUURI?
IS THAT MURAKAMI'S VOICE?
AH HA HA!
YOU WEREN'T LATE TODAY?
ACK!
SHIZUKA-CHA—!? YOU'RE HERE ALREADY!?
TAKE YOUR SEATS. LET'S BEGIN HOMEROOM.
SHIZUKA-CHAN, DID YOU SEE!?
DID YOU SEE, A MINUTE AGO...!?
ME COMING IN THROUGH THE WINDOW...
?
I DIDN'T SEE ANY-THING.

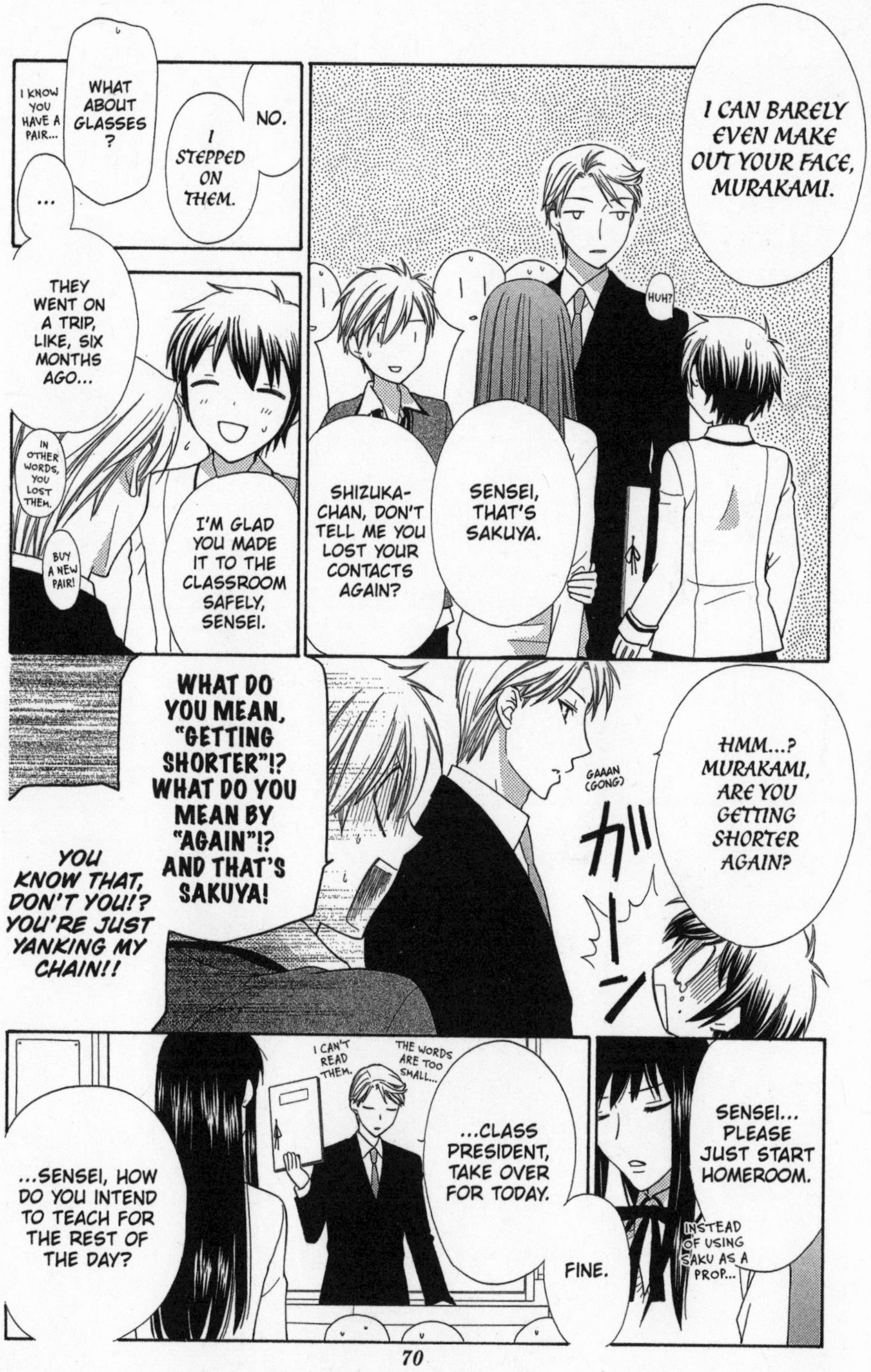
I CAN BARELY EVEN MAKE OUT YOUR FACE, MURAKAMI.
HUH?
SENSEI, THAT'S SAKUYA.
SHIZUKA-CHAN, DON'T TELL ME YOU LOST YOUR CONTACTS AGAIN?
WHAT ABOUT GLASSES?
I KNOW YOU HAVE A PAIR...
NO.
I STEPPED ON THEM.
...
I'M GLAD YOU MADE IT TO THE CLASSROOM SAFELY, SENSEI.
THEY WENT ON A TRIP, LIKE, SIX MONTHS AGO...
IN OTHER WORDS, YOU LOST THEM.
BUY A NEW PAIR!
HMM...? MURAKAMI, ARE YOU GETTING SHORTER AGAIN?
GAAAN (GONG)
ガーン
WHAT DO YOU MEAN, "GETTING SHORTER"!? WHAT DO YOU MEAN BY "AGAIN"!? AND THAT'S SAKUYA!
YOU KNOW THAT, DON'T YOU!? YOU'RE JUST YANKING MY CHAIN!!
SENSEI... PLEASE JUST START HOMEROOM.
INSTEAD OF USING SAKU AS A PROP...
...CLASS PRESIDENT, TAKE OVER FOR TODAY.
THE WORDS ARE TOO SMALL...
I CAN'T READ THEM.
FINE.
...SENSEI, HOW DO YOU INTEND TO TEACH FOR THE REST OF THE DAY?

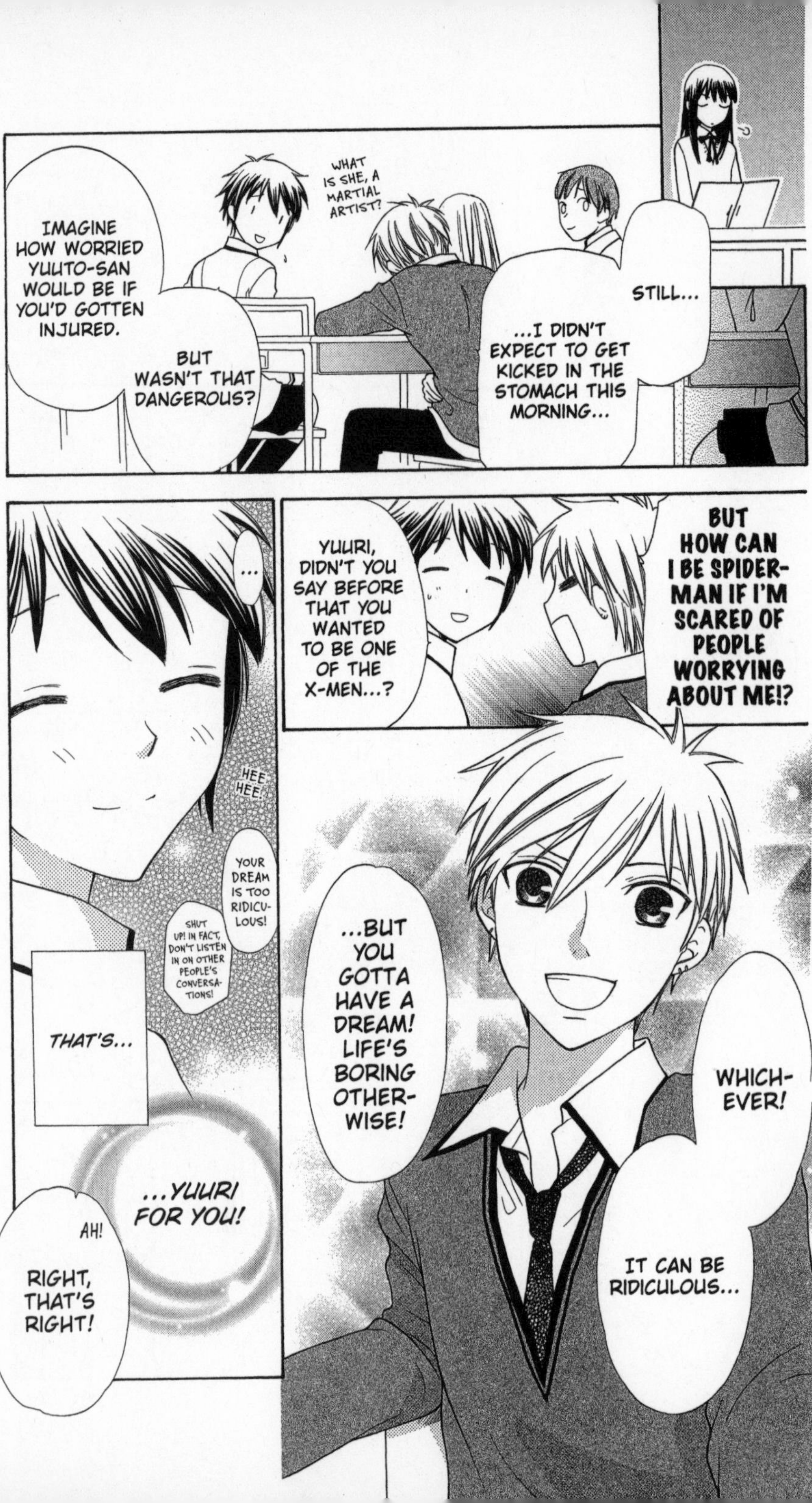
STILL...
...I DIDN'T EXPECT TO GET KICKED IN THE STOMACH THIS MORNING...
WHAT IS SHE, A MARTIAL ARTIST?
BUT WASN'T THAT DANGEROUS?
IMAGINE HOW WORRIED YUUTO-SAN WOULD BE IF YOU'D GOTTEN INJURED.
BUT HOW CAN I BE SPIDER-MAN IF I'M SCARED OF PEOPLE WORRYING ABOUT ME!?
YUURI, DIDN'T YOU SAY BEFORE THAT YOU WANTED TO BE ONE OF THE X-MEN...?
WHICH-EVER!
IT CAN BE RIDICULOUS...
...BUT YOU GOTTA HAVE A DREAM! LIFE'S BORING OTHER-WISE!
...
HEE HEE.
YOUR DREAM IS TOO RIDICU-LOUS!
SHUT UP! IN FACT, DON'T LISTEN IN ON OTHER PEOPLE'S CONVERSA-TIONS!
THAT'S...
...YUURI FOR YOU!
AH!
RIGHT, THAT'S RIGHT!

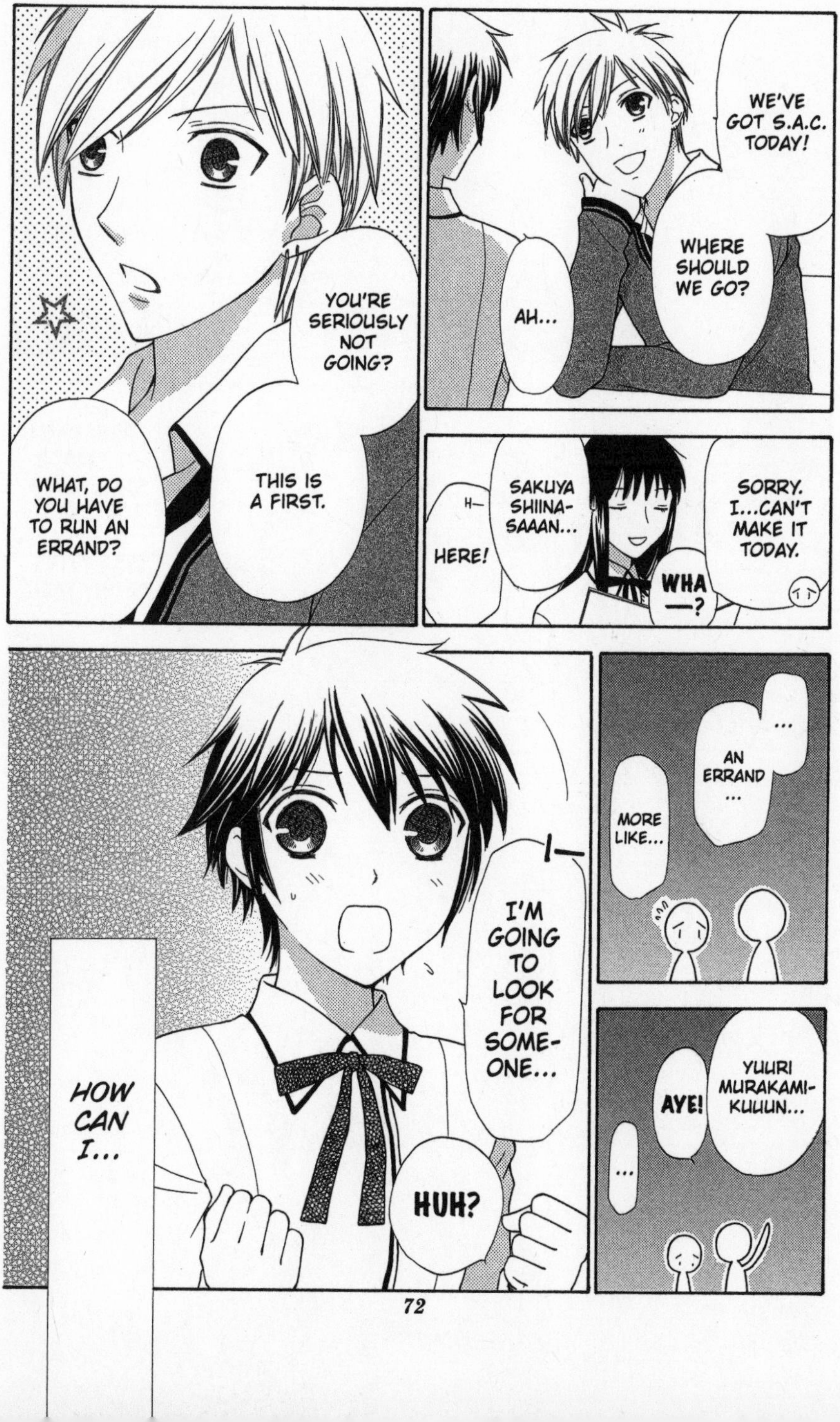
WE'VE GOT S.A.C. TODAY!
WHERE SHOULD WE GO?
AH...
SORRY. I...CAN'T MAKE IT TODAY.
WHA—?
SAKUYA SHIINA-SAAAN...
H— HERE!
YOU'RE SERIOUSLY NOT GOING?
THIS IS A FIRST.
WHAT, DO YOU HAVE TO RUN AN ERRAND?
...
AN ERRAND ...
MORE LIKE...
YUURI MURAKAMI-KUUUN...
AYE!
...
I—
I'M GOING TO LOOK FOR SOME-ONE...
HUH?
HOW CAN I...

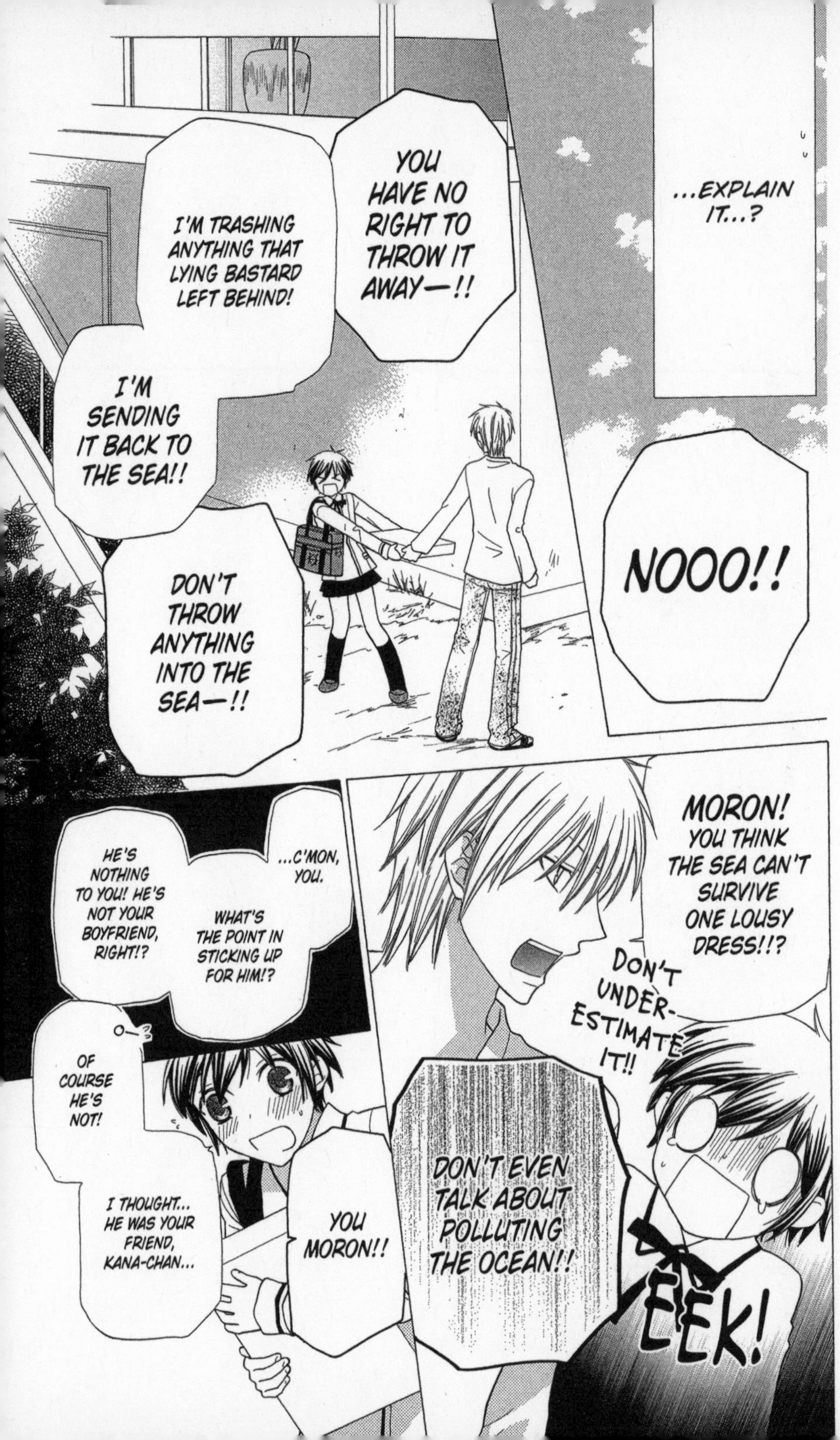
...EXPLAIN IT...?
NOOO!!
YOU HAVE NO RIGHT TO THROW IT AWAY—!!
I'M TRASHING ANYTHING THAT LYING BASTARD LEFT BEHIND!
I'M SENDING IT BACK TO THE SEA!!
DON'T THROW ANYTHING INTO THE SEA—!!
MORON! YOU THINK THE SEA CAN'T SURVIVE ONE LOUSY DRESS!!?
DON'T UNDER-ESTIMATE IT!!
DON'T EVEN TALK ABOUT POLLUTING THE OCEAN!!
EEK!
...C'MON, YOU.
WHAT'S THE POINT IN STICKING UP FOR HIM!?
HE'S NOTHING TO YOU! HE'S NOT YOUR BOYFRIEND, RIGHT!?
OF COURSE HE'S NOT!
YOU MORON!!
I THOUGHT... HE WAS YOUR FRIEND, KANA-CHAN...

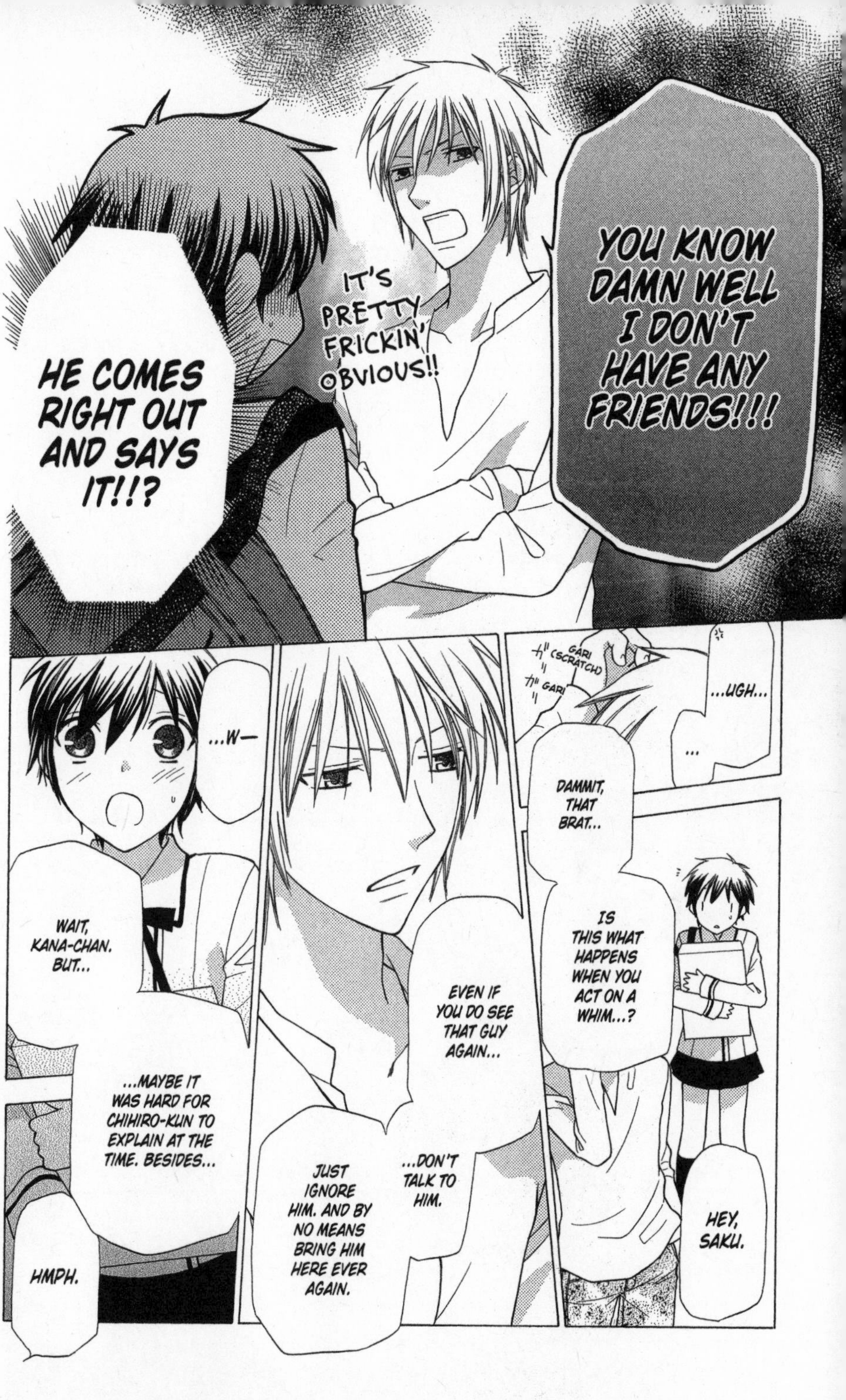
YOU KNOW DAMN WELL I DON'T HAVE ANY FRIENDS!!!
IT'S PRETTY FRICKIN' OBVIOUS!!
HE COMES RIGHT OUT AND SAYS IT!!?
...UGH...
ガリ GARI (SCRATCH)
ガリ GARI
...
DAMMIT, THAT BRAT...
IS THIS WHAT HAPPENS WHEN YOU ACT ON A WHIM...?
HEY, SAKU.
EVEN IF YOU DO SEE THAT GUY AGAIN...
...DON'T TALK TO HIM.
JUST IGNORE HIM. AND BY NO MEANS BRING HIM HERE EVER AGAIN.
...W—
WAIT, KANA-CHAN. BUT...
...MAYBE IT WAS HARD FOR CHIHIRO-KUN TO EXPLAIN AT THE TIME. BESIDES...
HMPH.

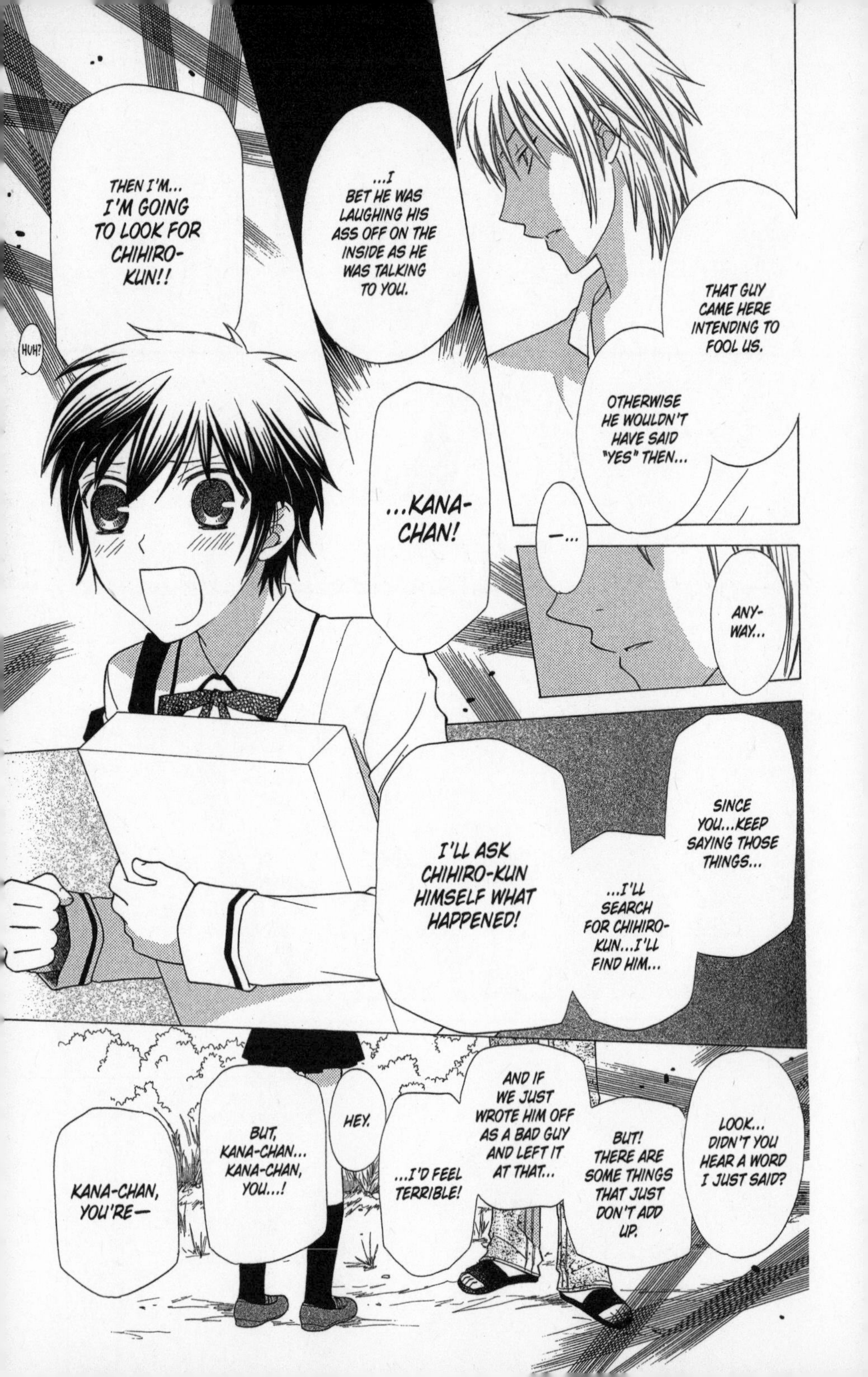
THAT GUY CAME HERE INTENDING TO FOOL US.
OTHERWISE HE WOULDN'T HAVE SAID "YES" THEN...
...I BET HE WAS LAUGHING HIS ASS OFF ON THE INSIDE AS HE WAS TALKING TO YOU.
—...
ANY-WAY...
...KANA-CHAN!
THEN I'M... I'M GOING TO LOOK FOR CHIHIRO-KUN!!
HUH?
SINCE YOU...KEEP SAYING THOSE THINGS...
...I'LL SEARCH FOR CHIHIRO-KUN...I'LL FIND HIM...
I'LL ASK CHIHIRO-KUN HIMSELF WHAT HAPPENED!
LOOK... DIDN'T YOU HEAR A WORD I JUST SAID?
BUT! THERE ARE SOME THINGS THAT JUST DON'T ADD UP.
AND IF WE JUST WROTE HIM OFF AS A BAD GUY AND LEFT IT AT THAT...
...I'D FEEL TERRIBLE!
HEY.
BUT, KANA-CHAN... KANA-CHAN, YOU...!
KANA-CHAN, YOU'RE—

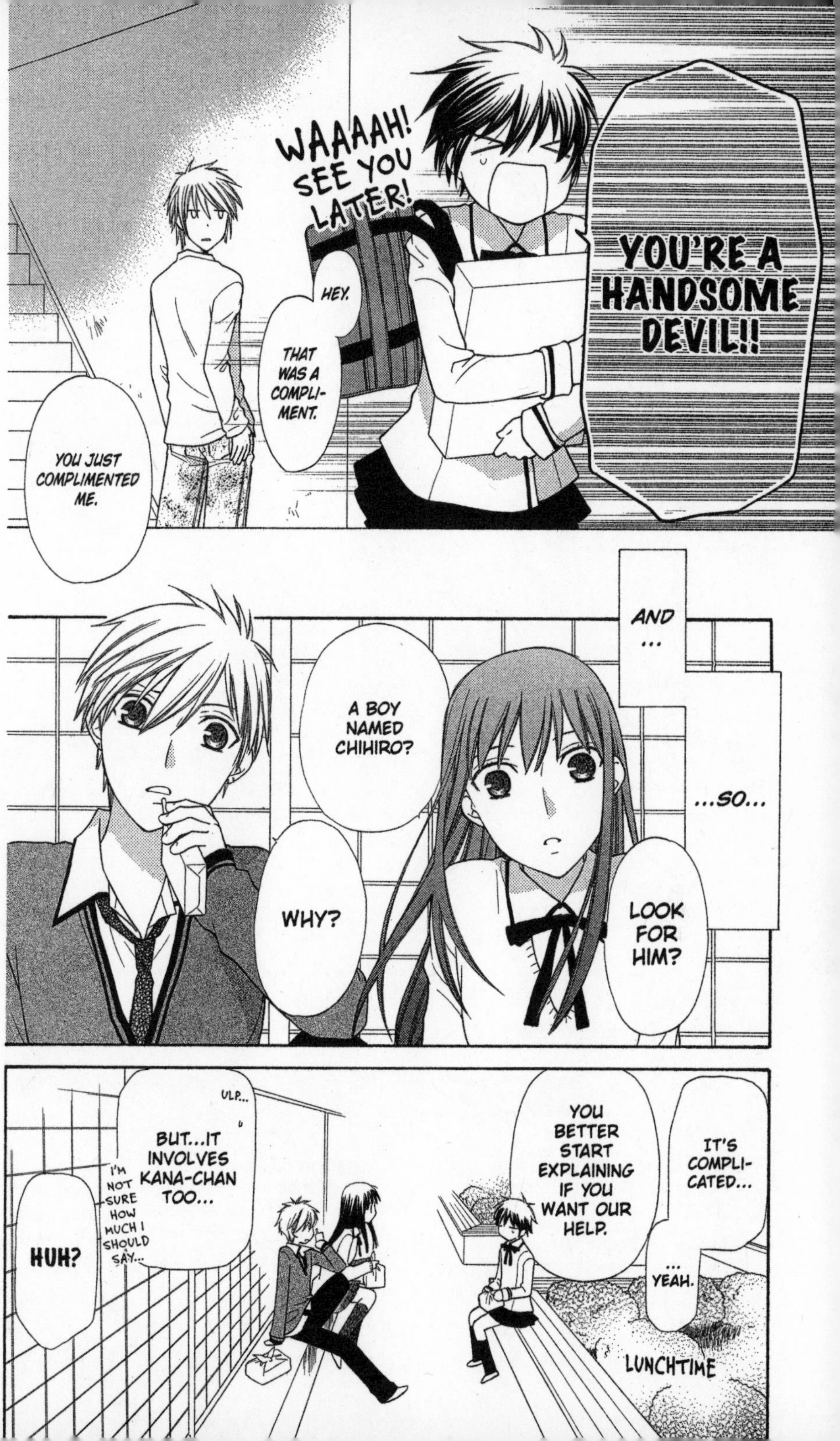
YOU'RE A HANDSOME DEVIL!!
WAAAAH! SEE YOU LATER!
HEY.
THAT WAS A COMPLIMENT.
YOU JUST COMPLIMENTED ME.
AND ...
...SO...
LOOK FOR HIM?
A BOY NAMED CHIHIRO?
WHY?
IT'S COMPLICATED...
LUNCHTIME
... YEAH.
YOU BETTER START EXPLAINING IF YOU WANT OUR HELP.
ULP...
BUT...IT INVOLVES KANA-CHAN TOO...
I'M NOT SURE HOW MUCH I SHOULD SAY...
HUH?

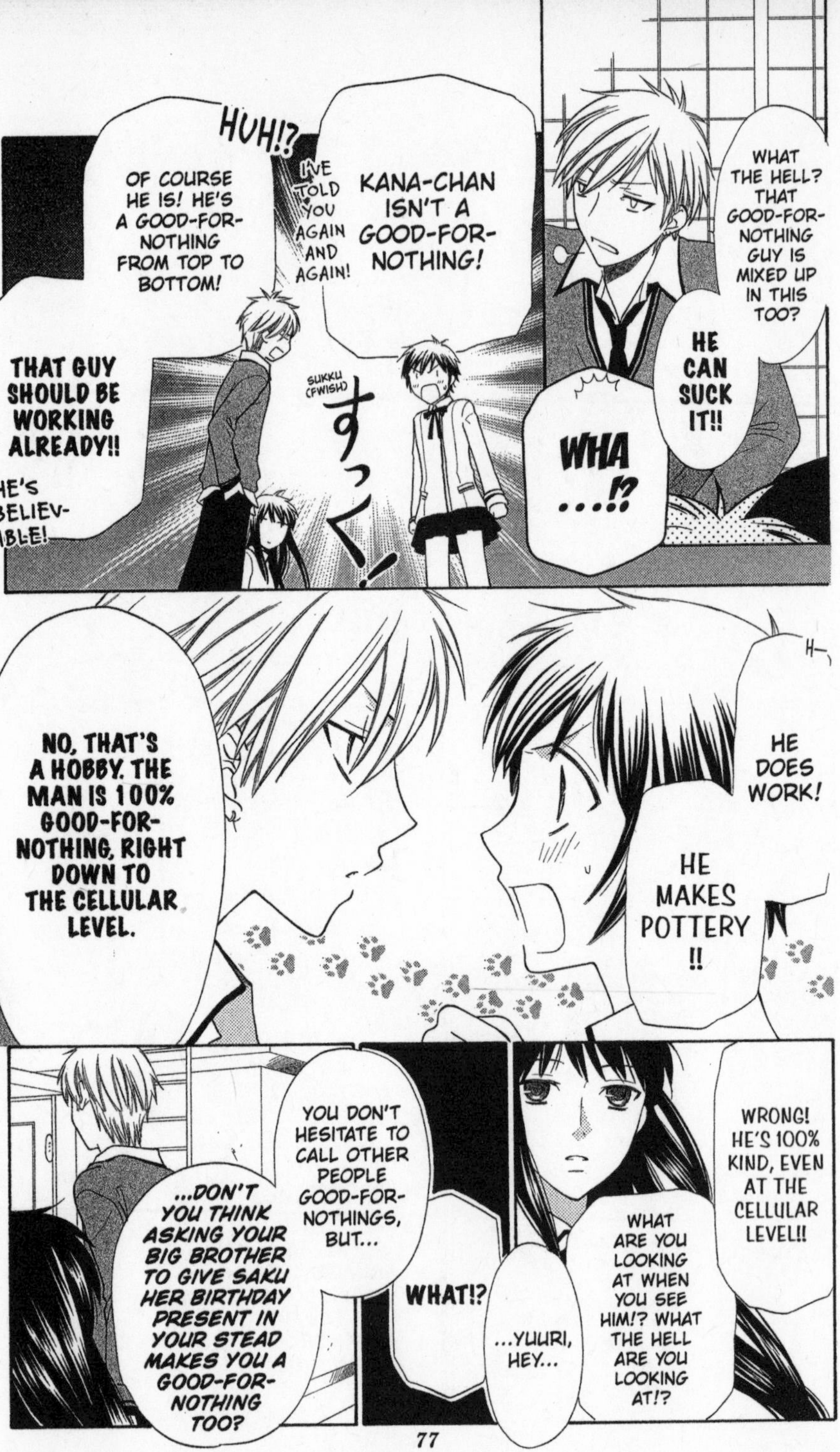
WHAT THE HELL? THAT GOOD-FOR-NOTHING GUY IS MIXED UP IN THIS TOO?
HE CAN SUCK IT!!
WHA...!?
KANA-CHAN ISN'T A GOOD-FOR-NOTHING!
I'VE TOLD YOU AGAIN AND AGAIN!
SUKKU (FWISH)
すっく!
HUH!?
OF COURSE HE IS! HE'S A GOOD-FOR-NOTHING FROM TOP TO BOTTOM!
THAT GUY SHOULD BE WORKING ALREADY!!
HE'S UNBELIEV-ABLE!
H—
HE DOES WORK!
HE MAKES POTTERY!!
NO, THAT'S A HOBBY. THE MAN IS 100% GOOD-FOR-NOTHING, RIGHT DOWN TO THE CELLULAR LEVEL.
WRONG! HE'S 100% KIND, EVEN AT THE CELLULAR LEVEL!!
WHAT ARE YOU LOOKING AT WHEN YOU SEE HIM!? WHAT THE HELL ARE YOU LOOKING AT!?
...YUURI, HEY...
WHAT!?
YOU DON'T HESITATE TO CALL OTHER PEOPLE GOOD-FOR-NOTHINGS, BUT...
...DON'T YOU THINK ASKING YOUR BIG BROTHER TO GIVE SAKU HER BIRTHDAY PRESENT IN YOUR STEAD MAKES YOU A GOOD-FOR-NOTHING TOO?

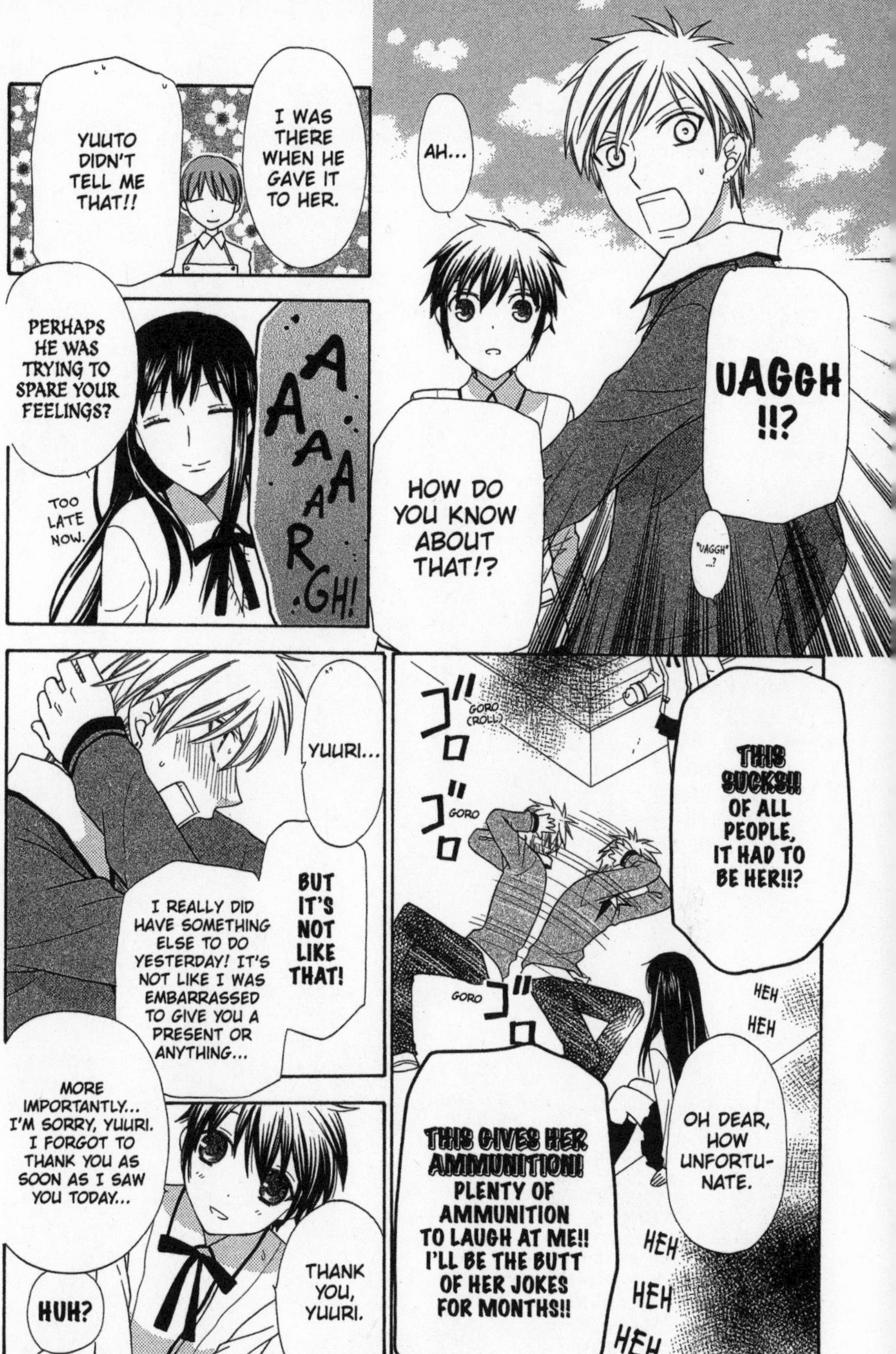
AH...
UAGGH !!?
"UAGGH" ...?
HOW DO YOU KNOW ABOUT THAT!?
I WAS THERE WHEN HE GAVE IT TO HER.
YUUTO DIDN'T TELL ME THAT!!
AAAARGH!
PERHAPS HE WAS TRYING TO SPARE YOUR FEELINGS?
TOO LATE NOW.
GORO (ROLL)
THIS SUCKS!! OF ALL PEOPLE, IT HAD TO BE HER!!?
GORO
GORO
HEH HEH
OH DEAR, HOW UNFORTU-NATE.
THIS GIVES HER AMMUNITION! PLENTY OF AMMUNITION TO LAUGH AT ME!! I'LL BE THE BUTT OF HER JOKES FOR MONTHS!!
HEH HEH HEH.
YUURI...
BUT IT'S NOT LIKE THAT!
I REALLY DID HAVE SOMETHING ELSE TO DO YESTERDAY! IT'S NOT LIKE I WAS EMBARRASSED TO GIVE YOU A PRESENT OR ANYTHING...
MORE IMPORTANTLY... I'M SORRY, YUURI. I FORGOT TO THANK YOU AS SOON AS I SAW YOU TODAY...
THANK YOU, YUURI.
HUH?

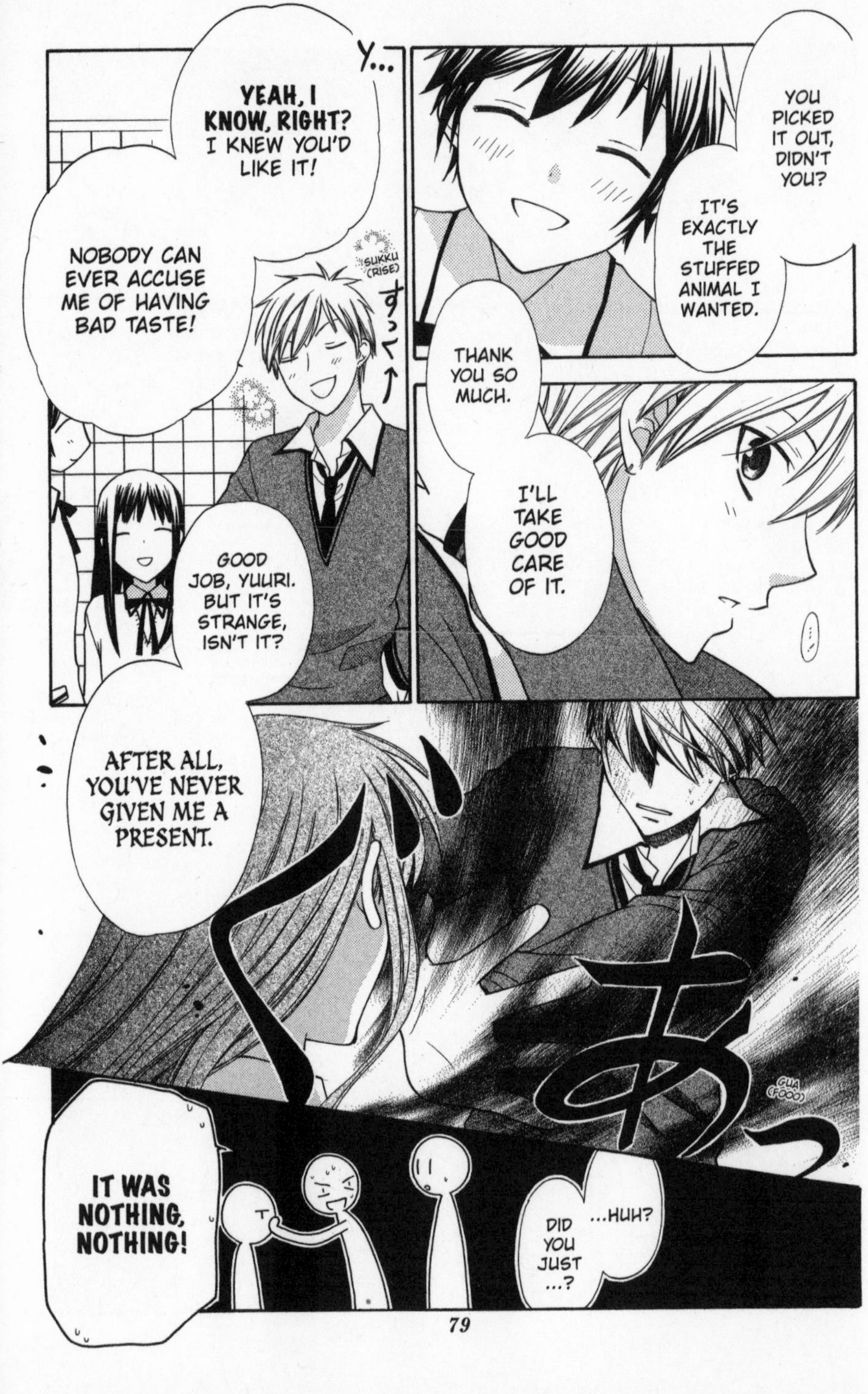
YOU PICKED IT OUT, DIDN'T YOU?
IT'S EXACTLY THE STUFFED ANIMAL I WANTED.
THANK YOU SO MUCH.
I'LL TAKE GOOD CARE OF IT.
...
Y...
YEAH, I KNOW, RIGHT? I KNEW YOU'D LIKE IT!
NOBODY CAN EVER ACCUSE ME OF HAVING BAD TASTE!
SUKKU (RISE)
GOOD JOB, YUURI. BUT IT'S STRANGE, ISN'T IT?
AFTER ALL, YOU'VE NEVER GIVEN ME A PRESENT.
GUA (FOOO)
...HUH?
DID YOU JUST ...?
IT WAS NOTHING, NOTHING!

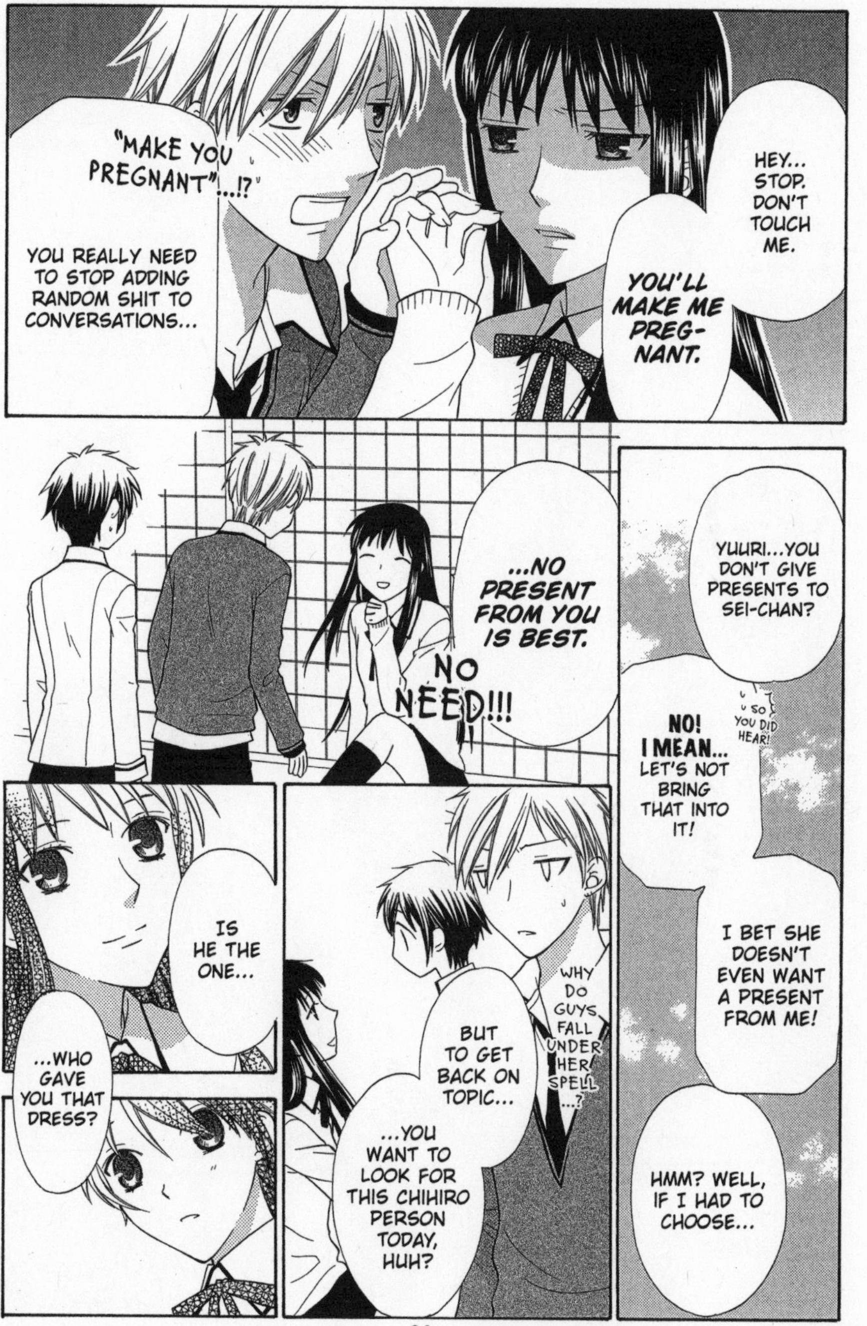
HEY... STOP. DON'T TOUCH ME.
YOU'LL MAKE ME PREG-NANT.
"MAKE YOU PREGNANT"...!?
YOU REALLY NEED TO STOP ADDING RANDOM SHIT TO CONVERSATIONS...
YUURI...YOU DON'T GIVE PRESENTS TO SEI-CHAN?
NO! I MEAN... LET'S NOT BRING THAT INTO IT!
SO YOU DID HEAR!
I BET SHE DOESN'T EVEN WANT A PRESENT FROM ME!
HMM? WELL, IF I HAD TO CHOOSE...
...NO PRESENT FROM YOU IS BEST.
NO NEED!!!
WHY DO GUYS FALL UNDER HER SPELL...?
BUT TO GET BACK ON TOPIC...
...YOU WANT TO LOOK FOR THIS CHIHIRO PERSON TODAY, HUH?
IS HE THE ONE...
...WHO GAVE YOU THAT DRESS?

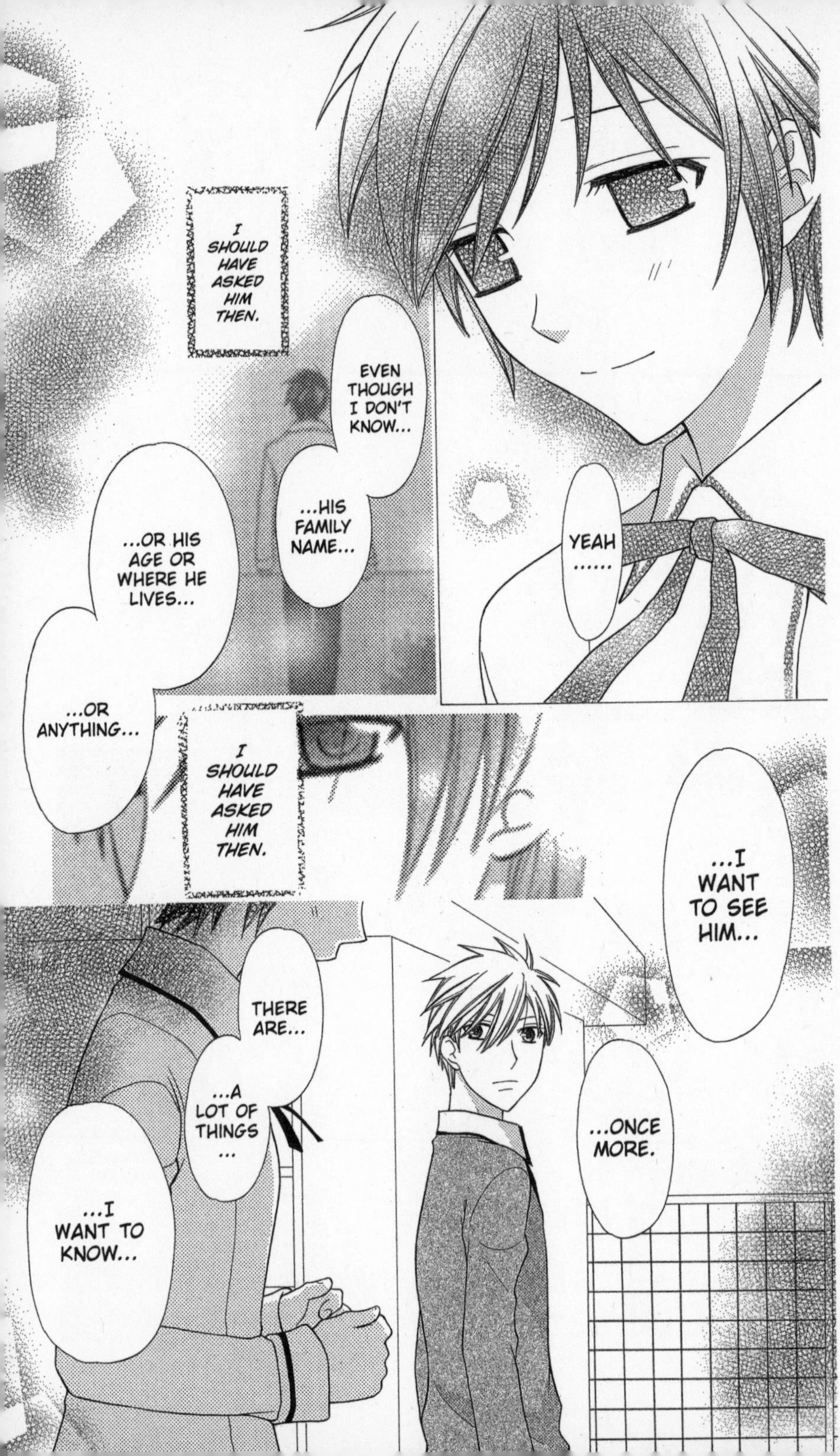
YEAH......
I SHOULD HAVE ASKED HIM THEN.
EVEN THOUGH I DON'T KNOW...
...HIS FAMILY NAME...
...OR HIS AGE OR WHERE HE LIVES...
...OR ANYTHING...
I SHOULD HAVE ASKED HIM THEN.
...I WANT TO SEE HIM...
...ONCE MORE.
THERE ARE...
...A LOT OF THINGS ...
...I WANT TO KNOW...

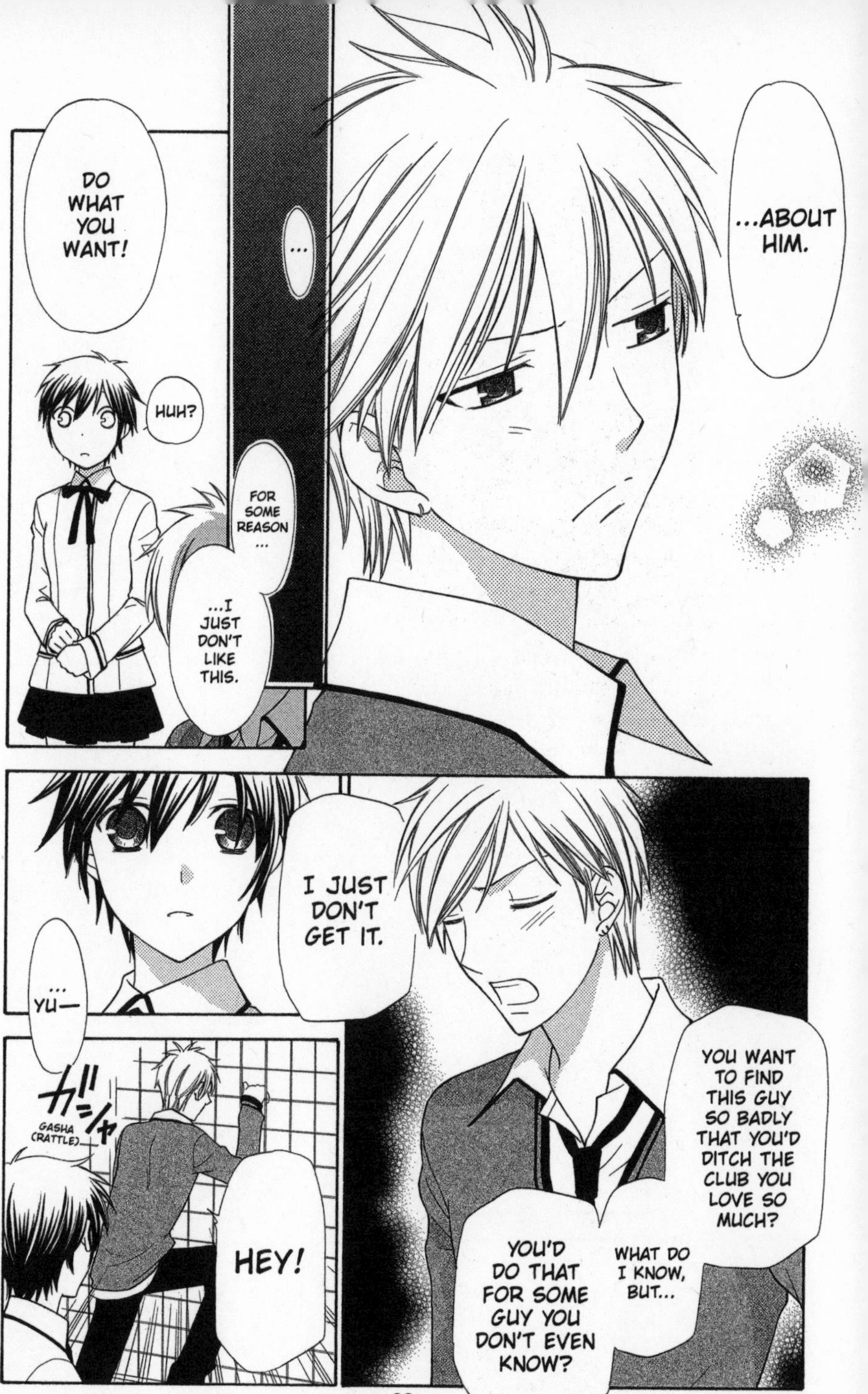
...ABOUT HIM.
...
DO WHAT YOU WANT!
HUH?
FOR SOME REASON...
...I JUST DON'T LIKE THIS.
I JUST DON'T GET IT.
YOU WANT TO FIND THIS GUY SO BADLY THAT YOU'D DITCH THE CLUB YOU LOVE SO MUCH?
WHAT DO I KNOW, BUT...
YOU'D DO THAT FOR SOME GUY YOU DON'T EVEN KNOW?
...YU—
ガシャ
GASHA (RATTLE)
HEY!

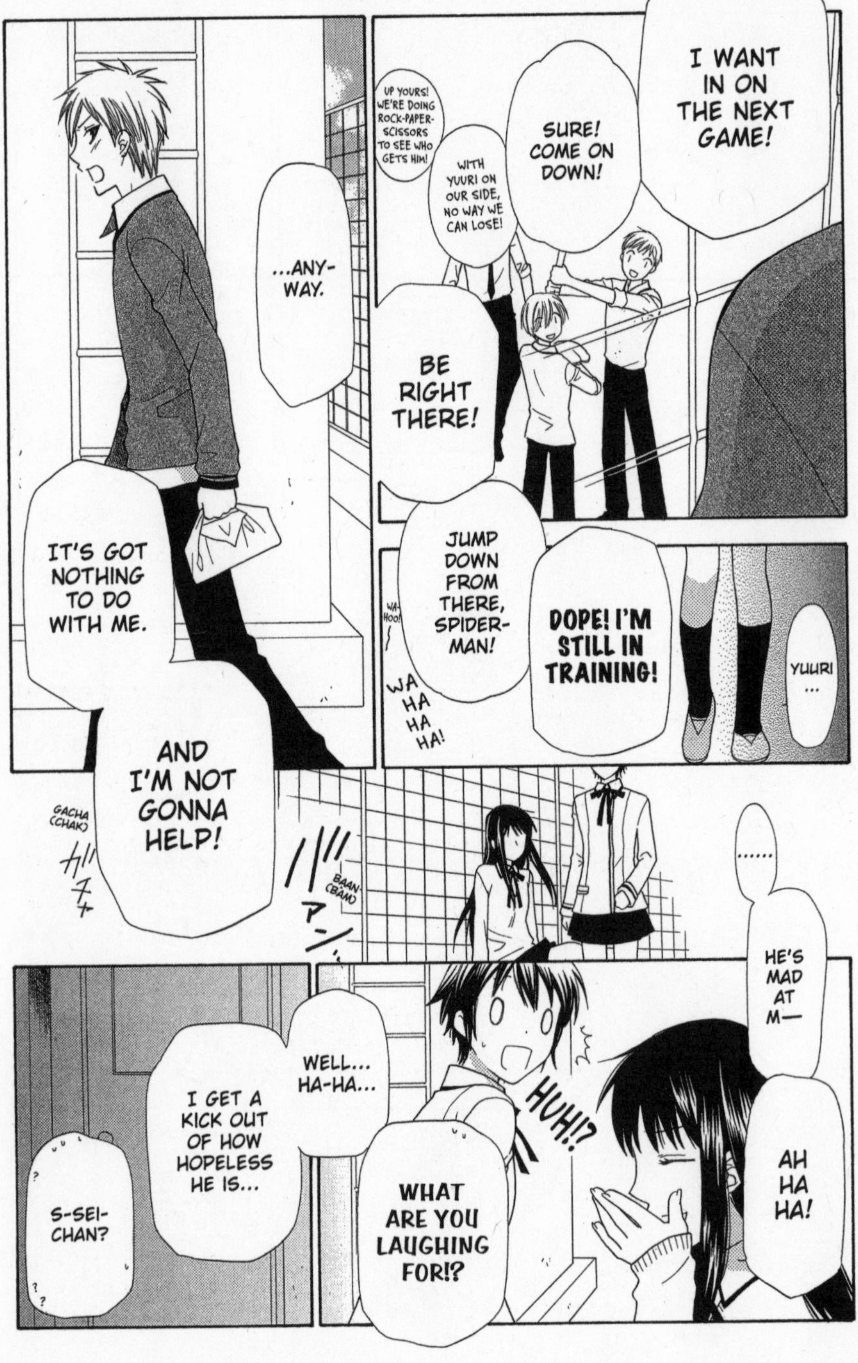
I WANT IN ON THE NEXT GAME!
SURE! COME ON DOWN!
WITH YUURI ON OUR SIDE, NO WAY WE CAN LOSE!
UP YOURS! WE'RE DOING ROCK-PAPER-SCISSORS TO SEE WHO GETS HIM!
BE RIGHT THERE!
YUURI...
DOPE! I'M STILL IN TRAINING!
JUMP DOWN FROM THERE, SPIDER-MAN!
WA-HOO!
WA HA HA HA!
...ANYWAY.
IT'S GOT NOTHING TO DO WITH ME.
AND I'M NOT GONNA HELP!
GACHA (CHAK)
BAAN (BAM)
......
HE'S MAD AT M—
AH HA HA!
HUH!?
WHAT ARE YOU LAUGHING FOR!?
WELL... HA-HA...
I GET A KICK OUT OF HOW HOPELESS HE IS...
S-SEI-CHAN?

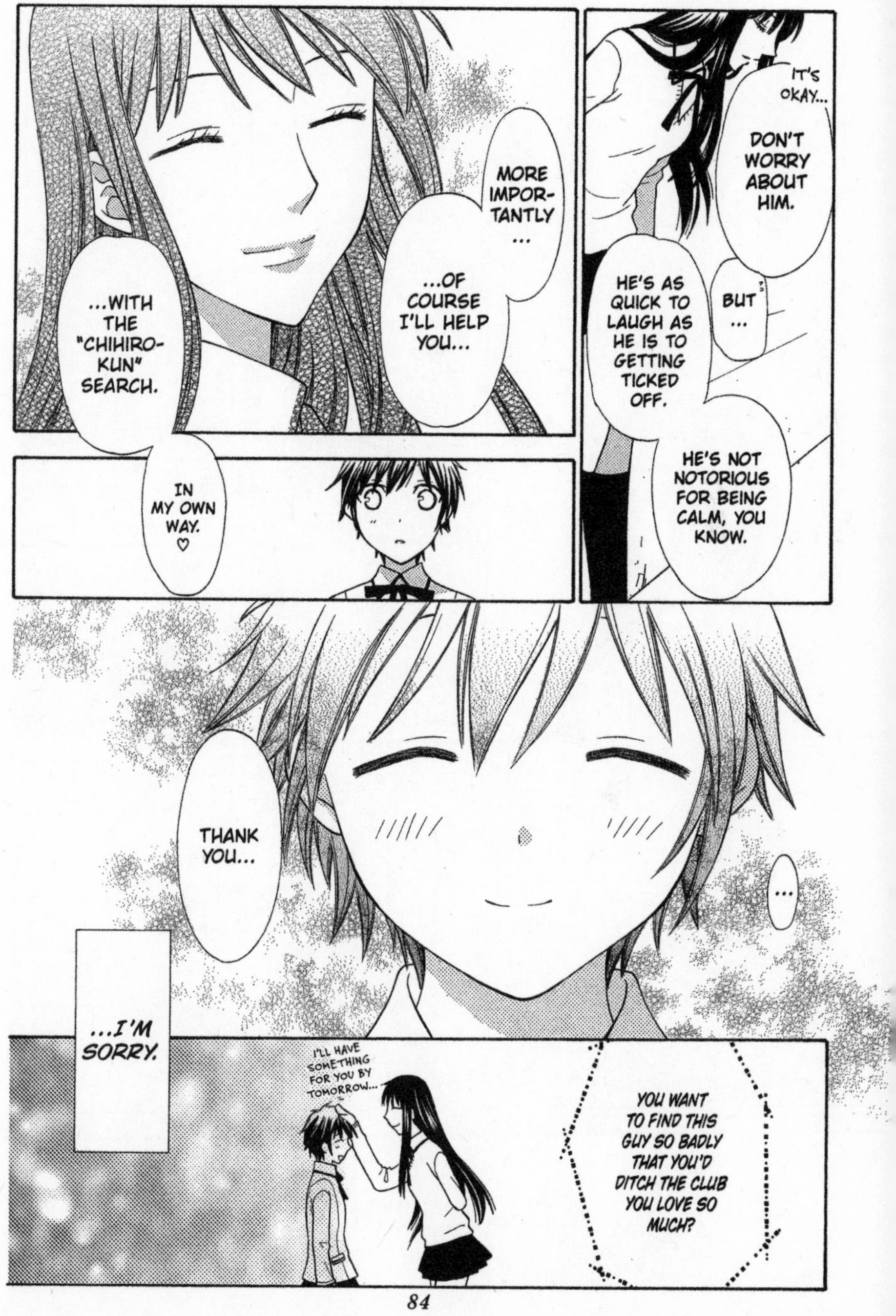
IT'S OKAY... DON'T WORRY ABOUT HIM.
BUT...
HE'S AS QUICK TO LAUGH AS HE IS TO GETTING TICKED OFF.
HE'S NOT NOTORIOUS FOR BEING CALM, YOU KNOW.
MORE IMPORTANTLY...
...OF COURSE I'LL HELP YOU...
...WITH THE "CHIHIRO-KUN" SEARCH.
IN MY OWN WAY. ♡
...
THANK YOU...
...I'M SORRY.
YOU WANT TO FIND THIS GUY SO BADLY THAT YOU'D DITCH THE CLUB YOU LOVE SO MUCH?
I'LL HAVE SOMETHING FOR YOU BY TOMORROW...

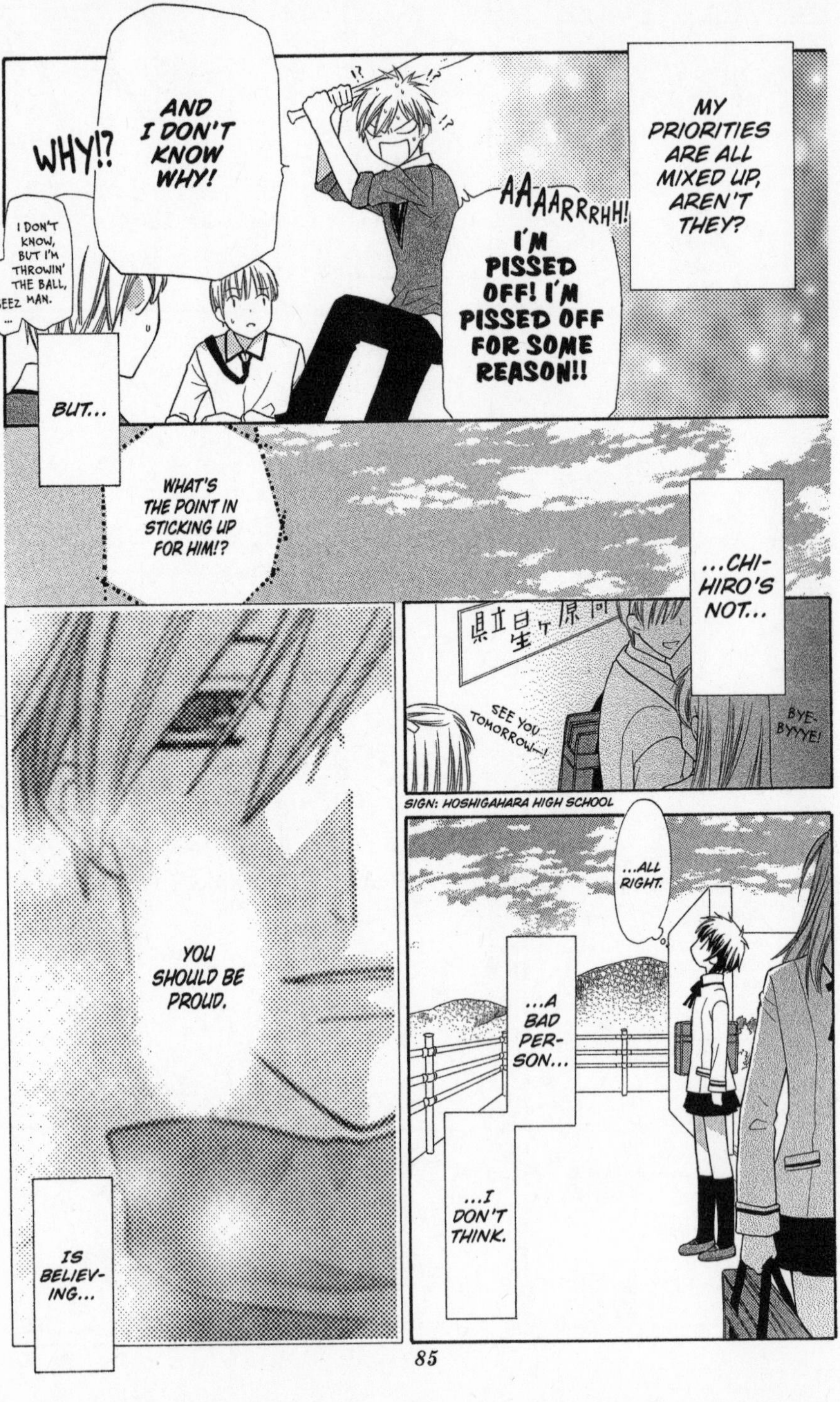
MY PRIORITIES ARE ALL MIXED UP, AREN'T THEY?
AAAARRRHH!
I'M PISSED OFF! I'M PISSED OFF FOR SOME REASON!!
!?
AND I DON'T KNOW WHY!
WHY!?
I DON'T KNOW, BUT I'M THROWIN' THE BALL, GEEZ MAN. ...
BUT...
WHAT'S THE POINT IN STICKING UP FOR HIM!?
...CHI-HIRO'S NOT...
BYE-BYYYE!
県立星ヶ原高
SEE YOU TOMORROW—!
SIGN: HOSHIGAHARA HIGH SCHOOL
...ALL RIGHT.
...A BAD PER-SON...
...I DON'T THINK.
YOU SHOULD BE PROUD.
IS BELIEV-ING...

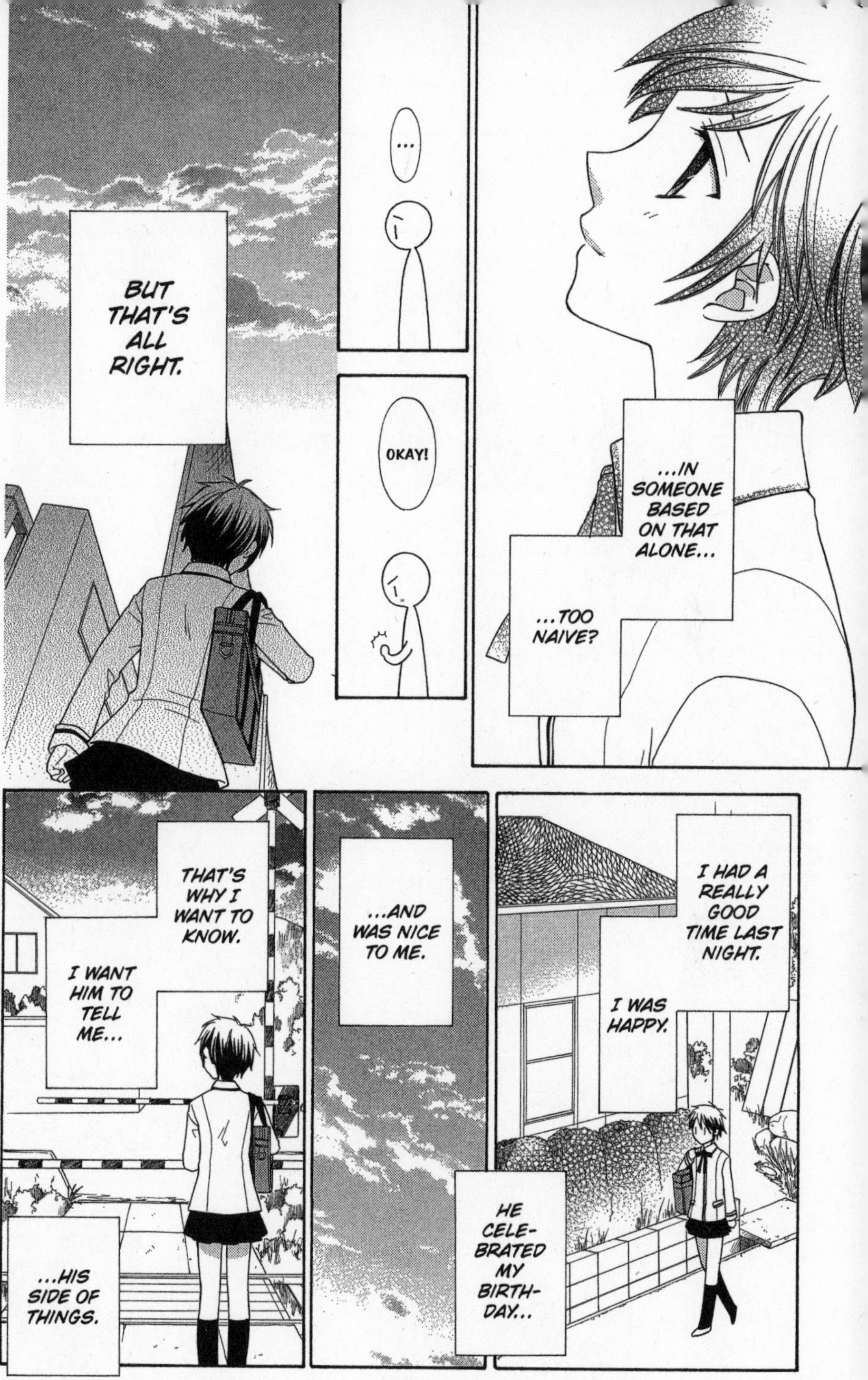
...IN SOMEONE BASED ON THAT ALONE...
...TOO NAIVE?
...
OKAY!
BUT THAT'S ALL RIGHT.
I HAD A REALLY GOOD TIME LAST NIGHT.
I WAS HAPPY.
HE CELE-BRATED MY BIRTH-DAY...
...AND WAS NICE TO ME.
THAT'S WHY I WANT TO KNOW.
I WANT HIM TO TELL ME...
...HIS SIDE OF THINGS.

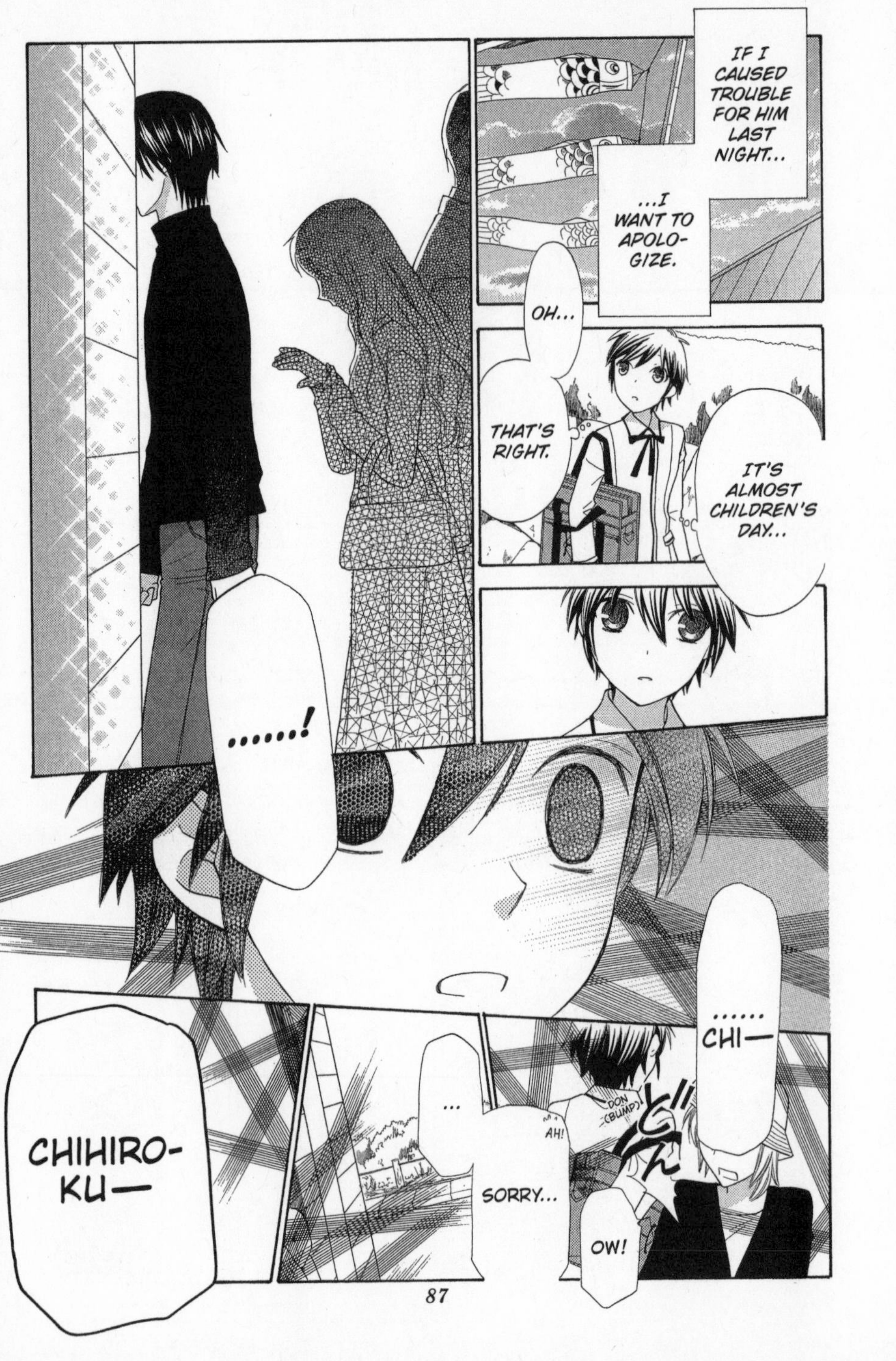
IF I CAUSED TROUBLE FOR HIM LAST NIGHT...
...I WANT TO APOLOGIZE.
IT'S ALMOST CHILDREN'S DAY...
OH...
THAT'S RIGHT.
......!
......
CHI—
DON (BUMP)
AH!
OW!
SORRY...
...
CHIHIRO-KU—

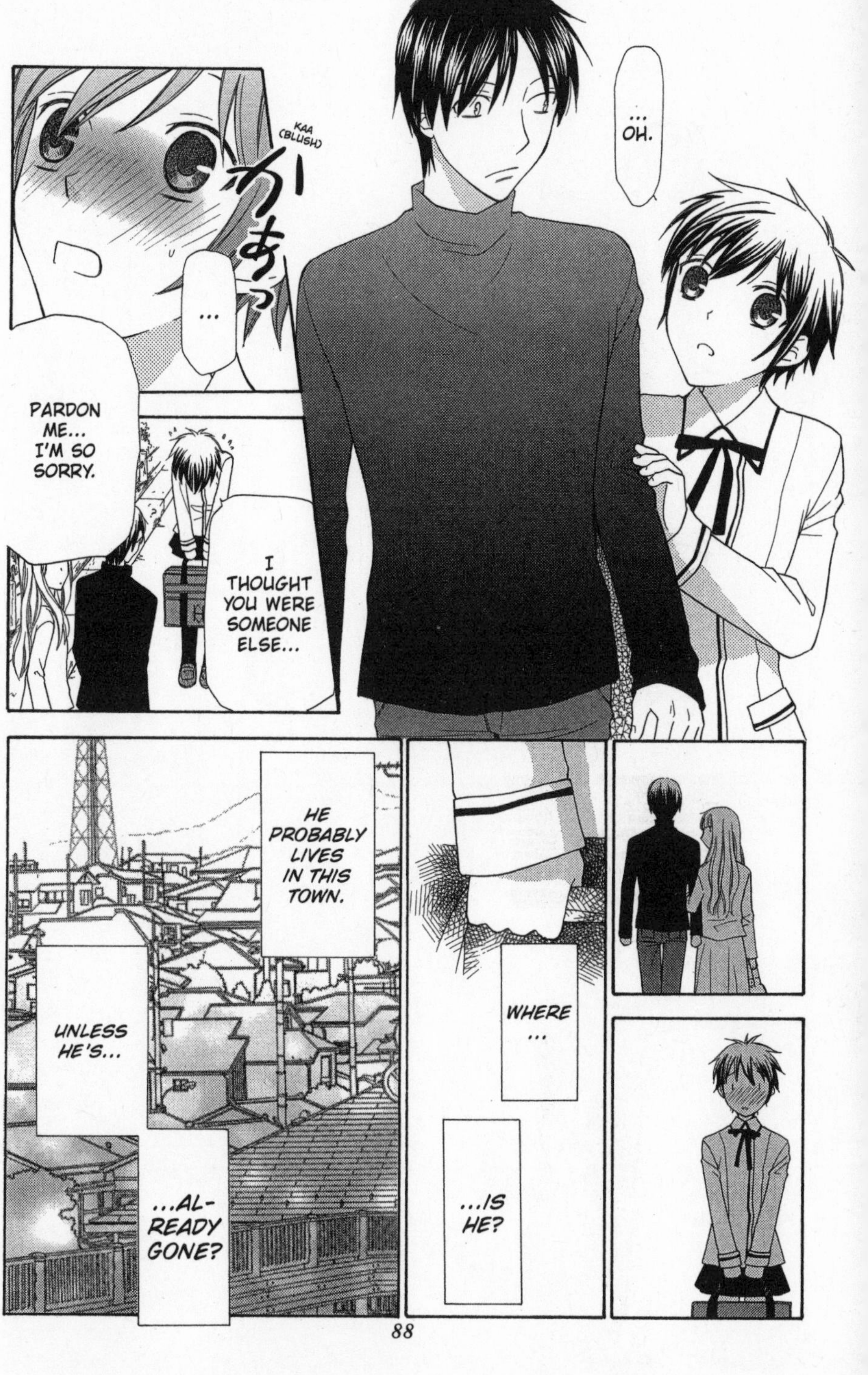
...OH.
KAA (BLUSH)
...
PARDON ME... I'M SO SORRY.
I THOUGHT YOU WERE SOMEONE ELSE...
WHERE ...
...IS HE?
HE PROBABLY LIVES IN THIS TOWN.
UNLESS HE'S...
...AL-READY GONE?

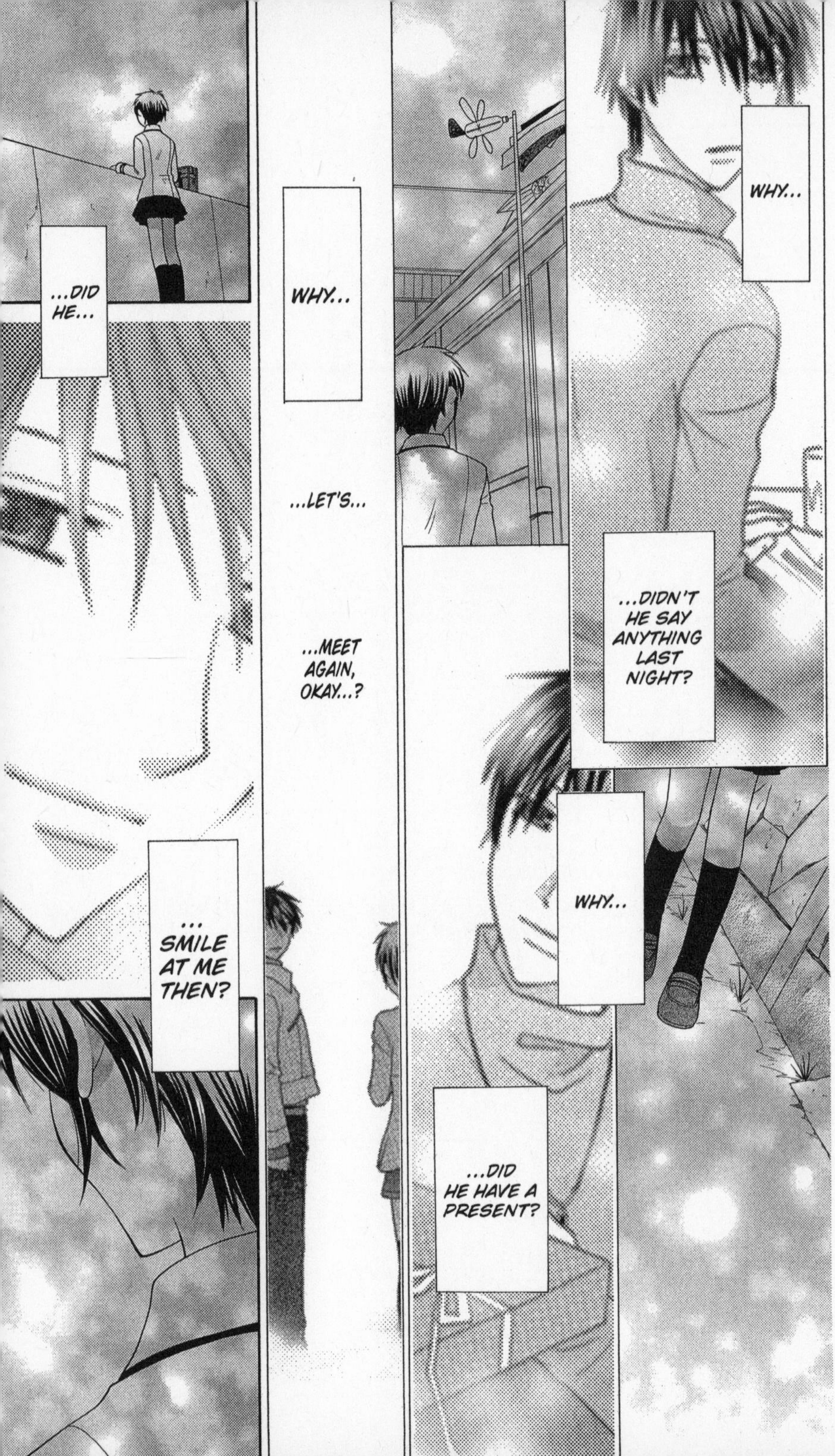
WHY...
...DIDN'T HE SAY ANYTHING LAST NIGHT?
WHY...
...DID HE HAVE A PRESENT?
WHY...
...LET'S...
...MEET AGAIN, OKAY...?
...DID HE...
...SMILE AT ME THEN?

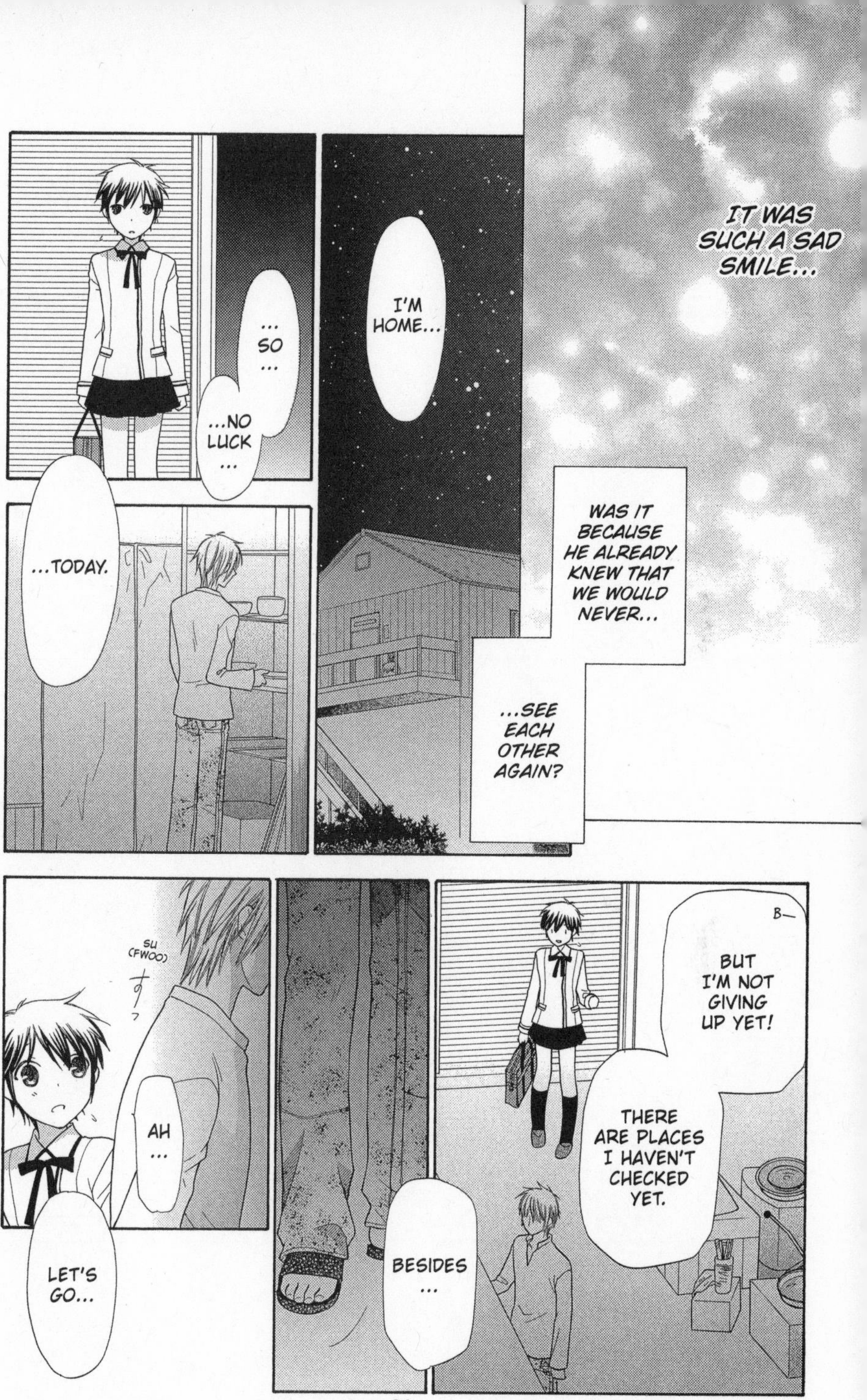
IT WAS SUCH A SAD SMILE...
WAS IT BECAUSE HE ALREADY KNEW THAT WE WOULD NEVER...
...SEE EACH OTHER AGAIN?
I'M HOME...
...SO...
...NO LUCK...
...TODAY.
B—
BUT I'M NOT GIVING UP YET!
THERE ARE PLACES I HAVEN'T CHECKED YET.
BESIDES...
SU (FWOO)
すっ
AH...
LET'S GO...

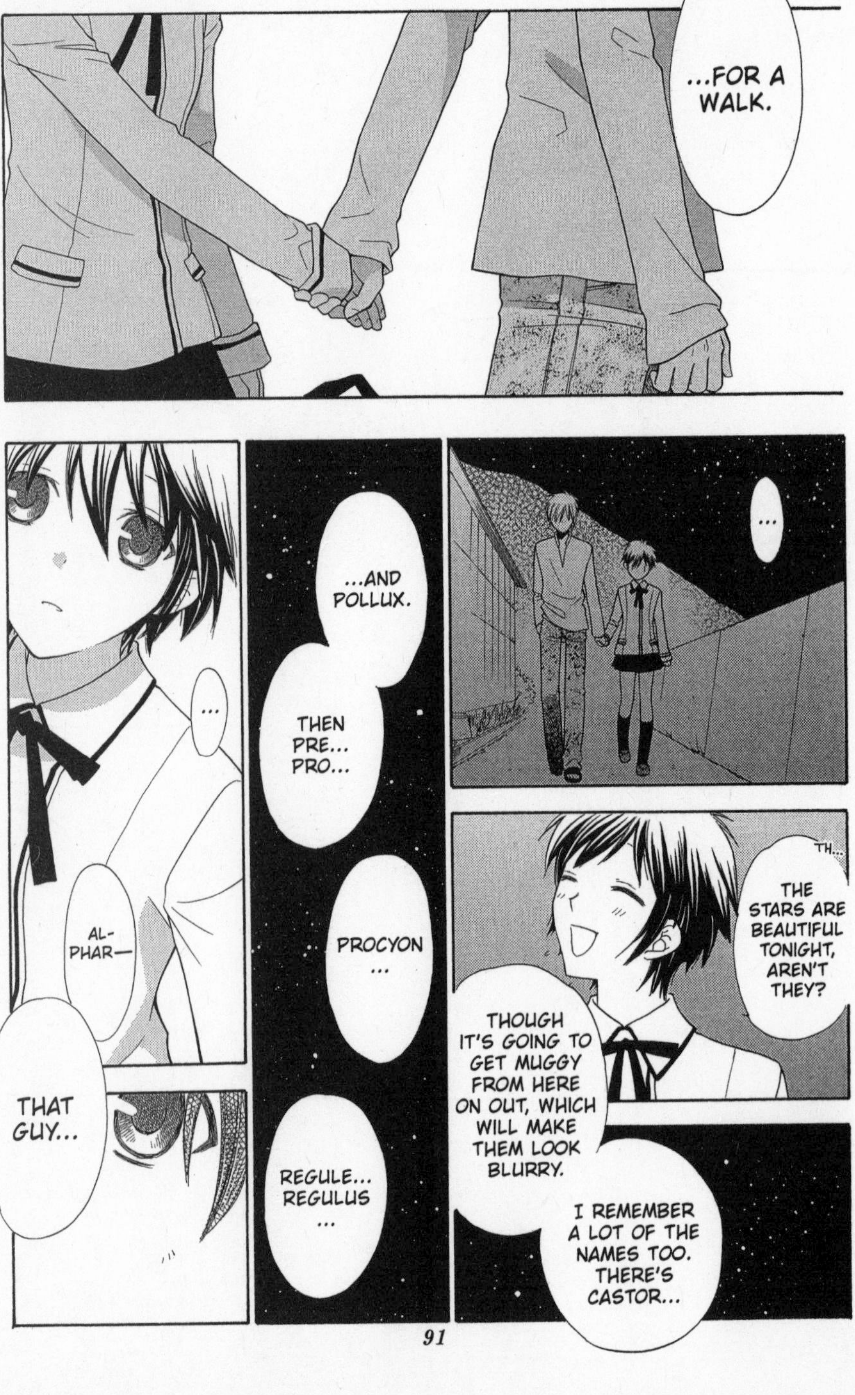
...FOR A WALK.
...
TH...
THE STARS ARE BEAUTIFUL TONIGHT, AREN'T THEY?
THOUGH IT'S GOING TO GET MUGGY FROM HERE ON OUT, WHICH WILL MAKE THEM LOOK BLURRY.
I REMEMBER A LOT OF THE NAMES TOO. THERE'S CASTOR...
...AND POLLUX.
THEN PRE... PRO...
PROCYON ...
REGULE... REGULUS ...
...
AL-PHAR—
THAT GUY...

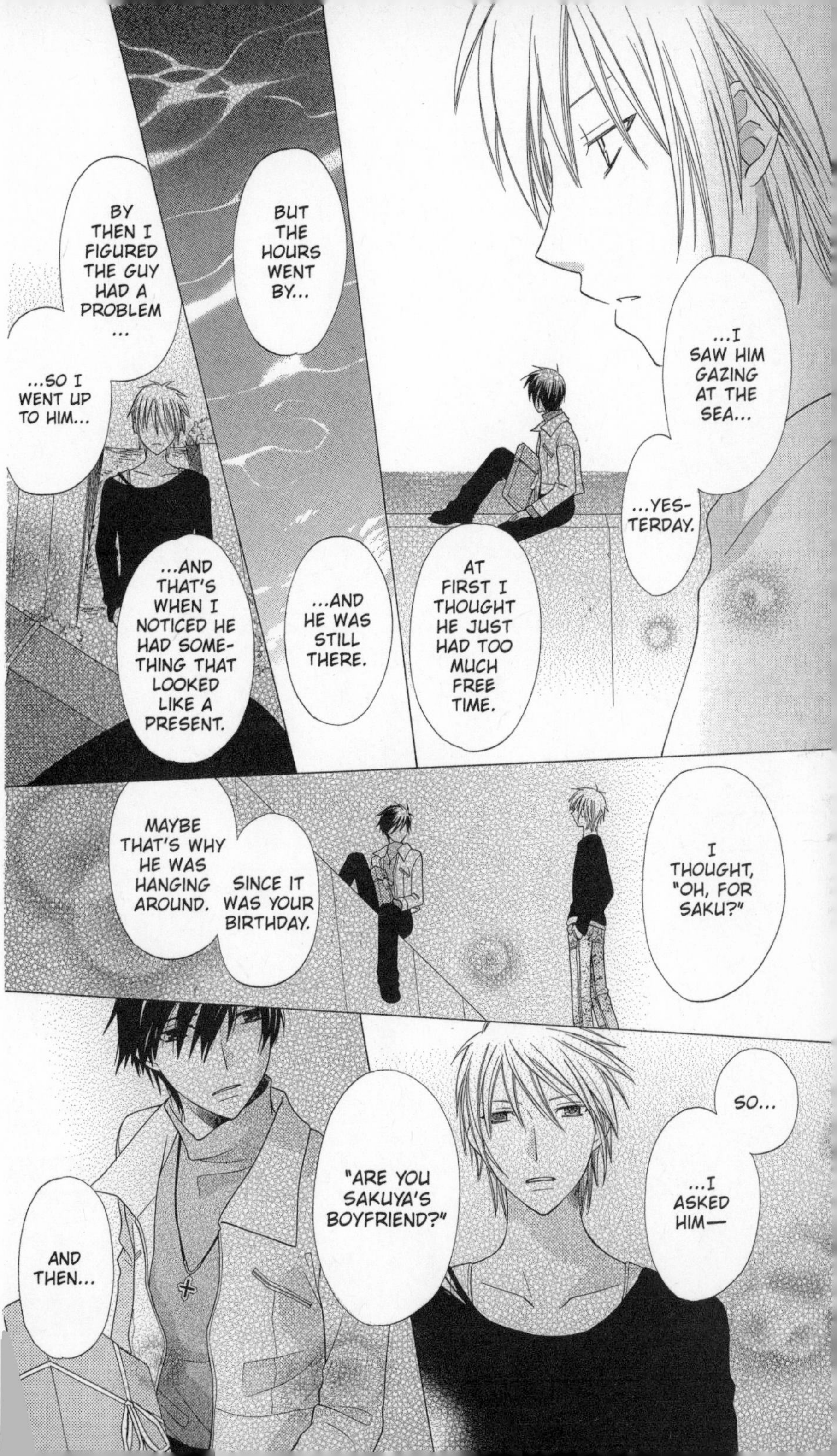
...I SAW HIM GAZING AT THE SEA...
...YES-TERDAY.
AT FIRST I THOUGHT HE JUST HAD TOO MUCH FREE TIME.
BUT THE HOURS WENT BY...
...AND HE WAS STILL THERE.
BY THEN I FIGURED THE GUY HAD A PROBLEM ...
...SO I WENT UP TO HIM...
...AND THAT'S WHEN I NOTICED HE HAD SOME-THING THAT LOOKED LIKE A PRESENT.
I THOUGHT, "OH, FOR SAKU?"
MAYBE THAT'S WHY HE WAS HANGING AROUND.
SINCE IT WAS YOUR BIRTHDAY.
SO...
...I ASKED HIM—
"ARE YOU SAKUYA'S BOYFRIEND?"
AND THEN...

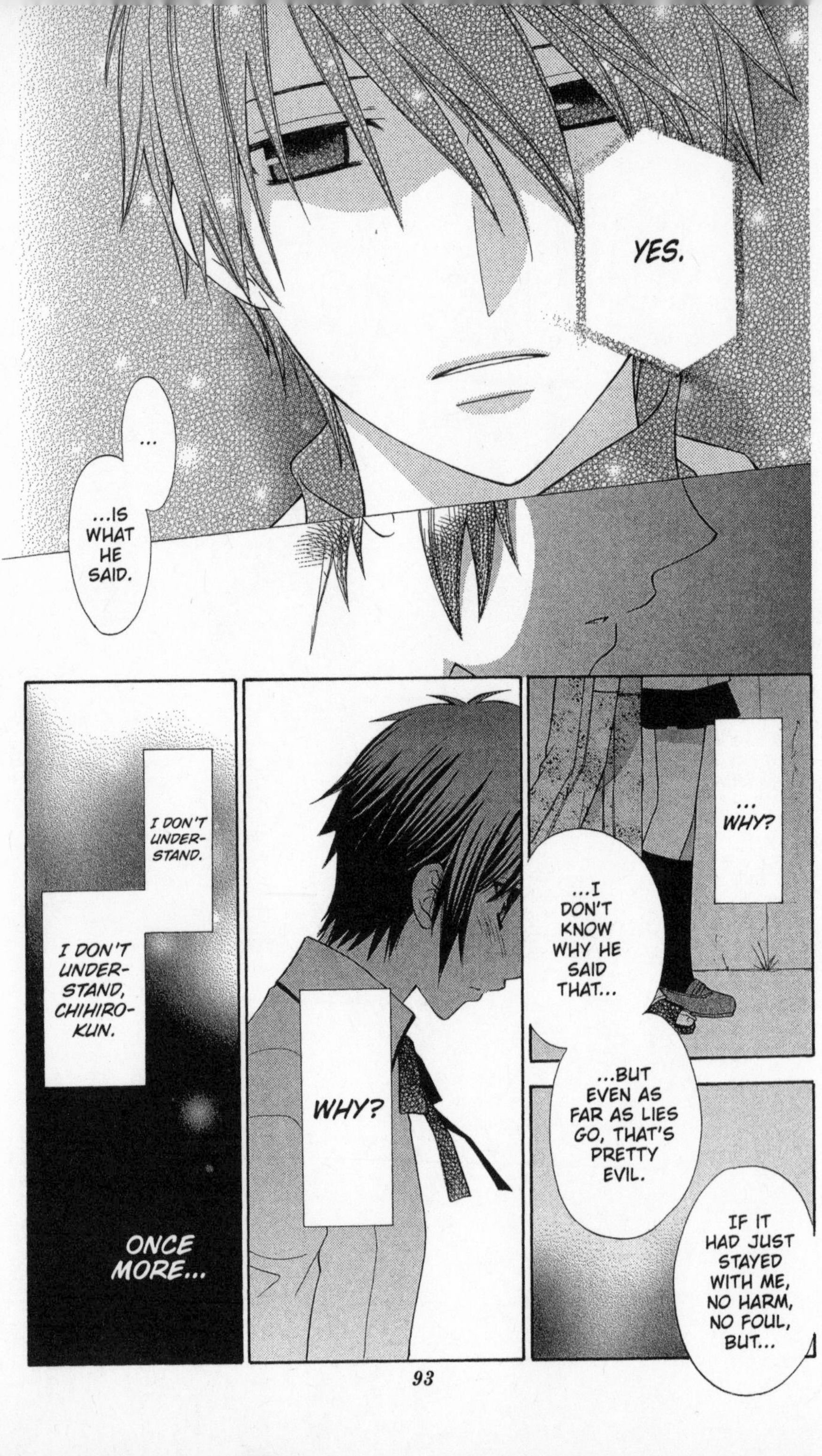
YES.
...
...IS WHAT HE SAID.
... WHY?
...I DON'T KNOW WHY HE SAID THAT...
...BUT EVEN AS FAR AS LIES GO, THAT'S PRETTY EVIL.
IF IT HAD JUST STAYED WITH ME, NO HARM, NO FOUL, BUT...
WHY?
I DON'T UNDER-STAND.
I DON'T UNDER-STAND, CHIHIRO-KUN.
ONCE MORE...

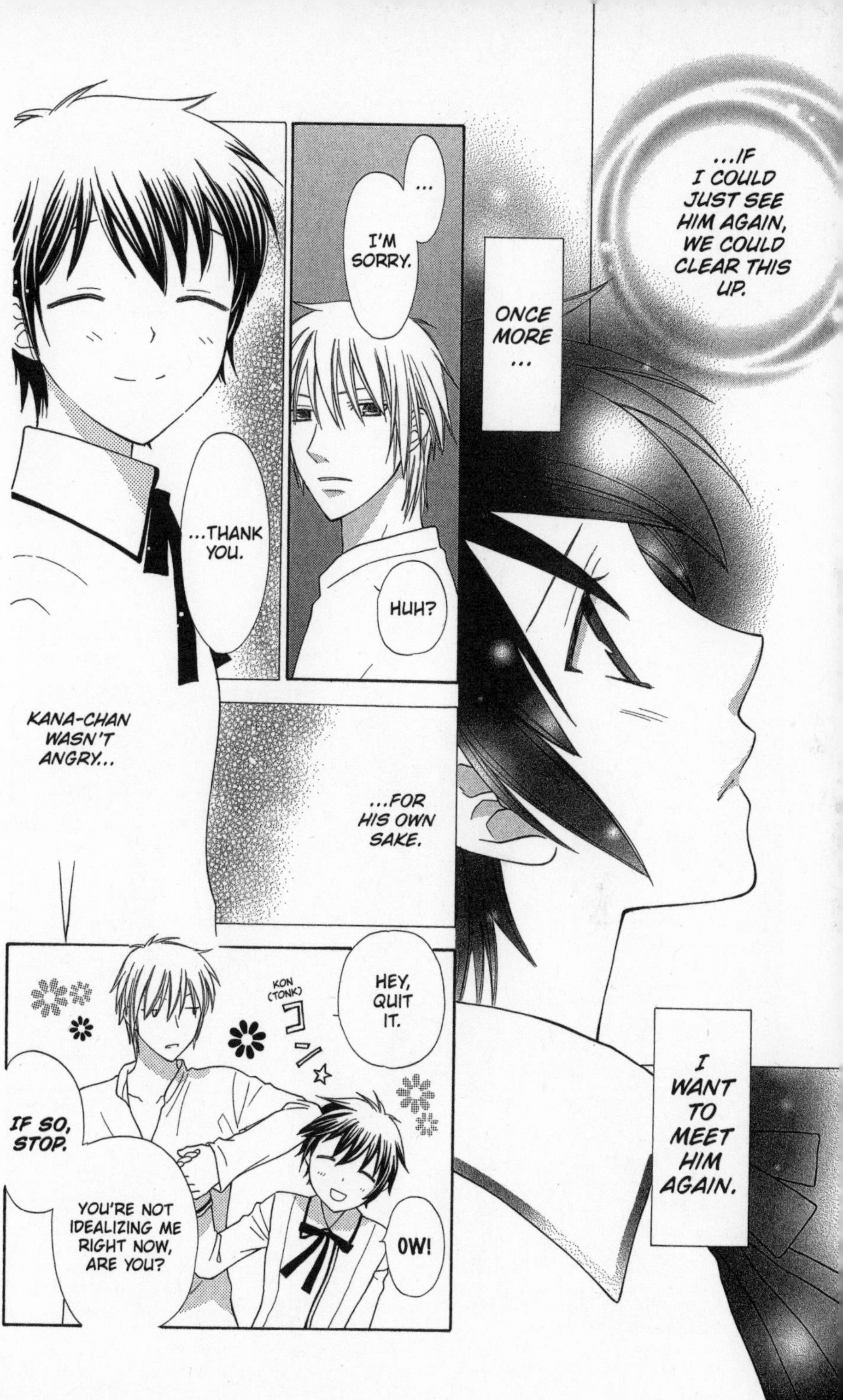
...IF I COULD JUST SEE HIM AGAIN, WE COULD CLEAR THIS UP.
ONCE MORE...
I WANT TO MEET HIM AGAIN.
...
I'M SORRY.
HUH?
...THANK YOU.
KANA-CHAN WASN'T ANGRY...
...FOR HIS OWN SAKE.
HEY, QUIT IT.
KON (TONK)
OW!
YOU'RE NOT IDEALIZING ME RIGHT NOW, ARE YOU?
IF SO, STOP.

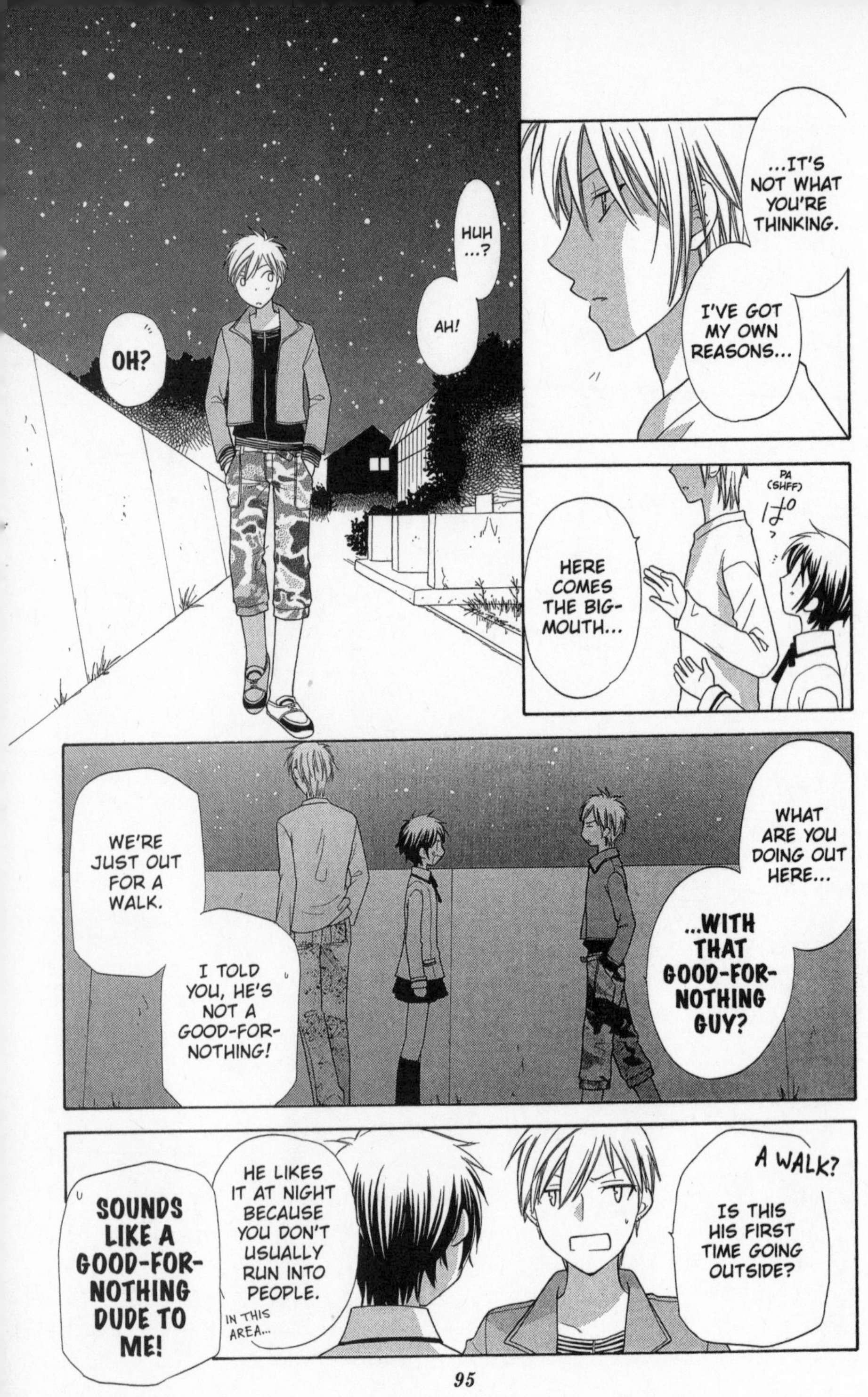
...IT'S NOT WHAT YOU'RE THINKING.
I'VE GOT MY OWN REASONS...
PA (SHFF)
HERE COMES THE BIG-MOUTH...
HUH ...?
AH!
OH?
WHAT ARE YOU DOING OUT HERE...
...WITH THAT GOOD-FOR-NOTHING GUY?
WE'RE JUST OUT FOR A WALK.
I TOLD YOU, HE'S NOT A GOOD-FOR-NOTHING!
A WALK?
IS THIS HIS FIRST TIME GOING OUTSIDE?
HE LIKES IT AT NIGHT BECAUSE YOU DON'T USUALLY RUN INTO PEOPLE.
IN THIS AREA...
SOUNDS LIKE A GOOD-FOR-NOTHING DUDE TO ME!

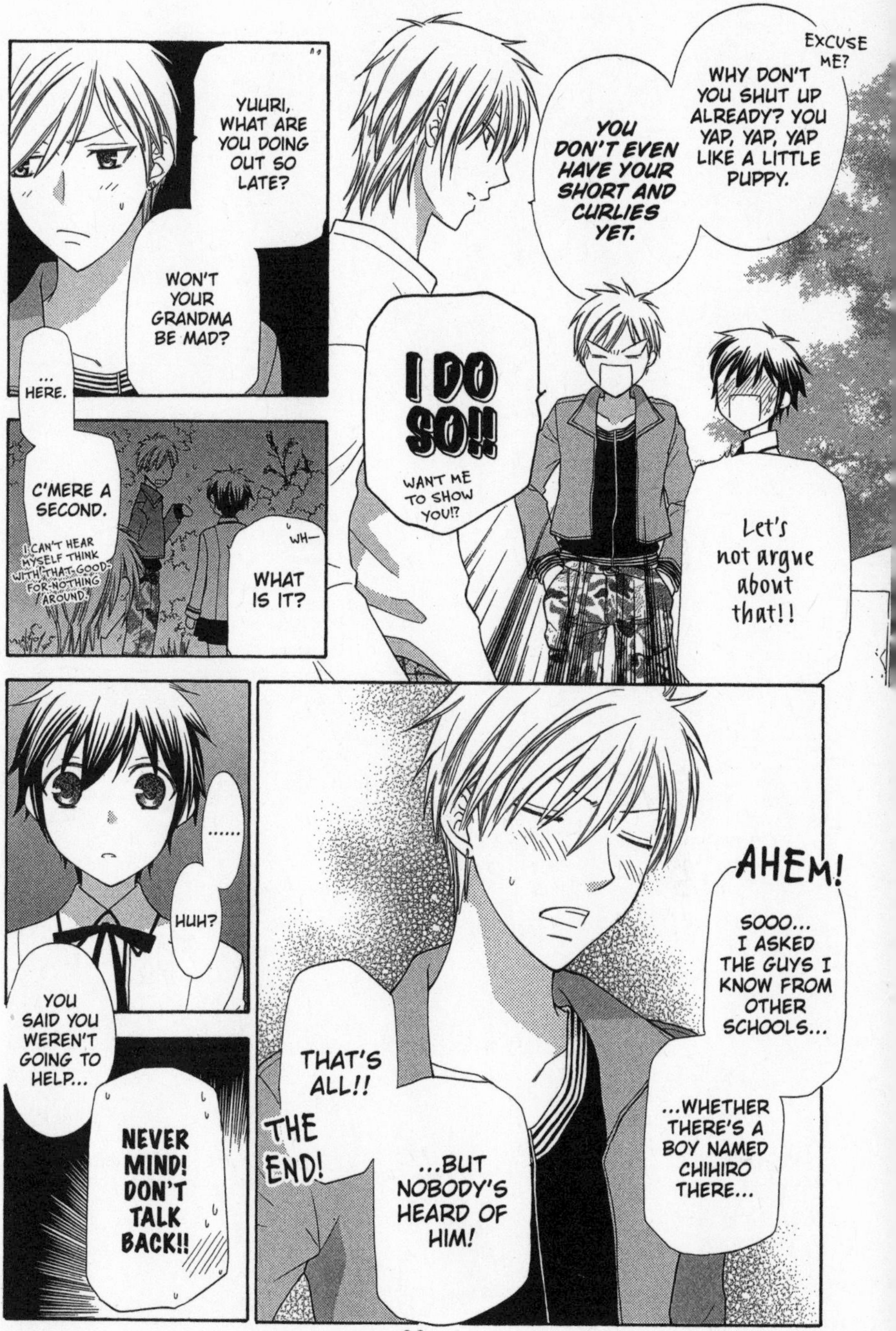

EXCUSE ME?
WHY DON'T YOU SHUT UP ALREADY? YOU YAP, YAP, YAP LIKE A LITTLE PUPPY.
YOU DON'T EVEN HAVE YOUR SHORT AND CURLIES YET.
I DO SO!!
WANT ME TO SHOW YOU!?
Let's not argue about that!!
YUURI, WHAT ARE YOU DOING OUT SO LATE?
WON'T YOUR GRANDMA BE MAD?
...HERE.
C'MERE A SECOND.
I CAN'T HEAR MYSELF THINK WITH THAT GOOD-FOR-NOTHING AROUND.
WH—
WHAT IS IT?
AHEM!
SOOO... I ASKED THE GUYS I KNOW FROM OTHER SCHOOLS...
...WHETHER THERE'S A BOY NAMED CHIHIRO THERE...
...BUT NOBODY'S HEARD OF HIM!
THAT'S ALL!!
THE END!
......
HUH?
YOU SAID YOU WEREN'T GOING TO HELP...
NEVER MIND! DON'T TALK BACK!!

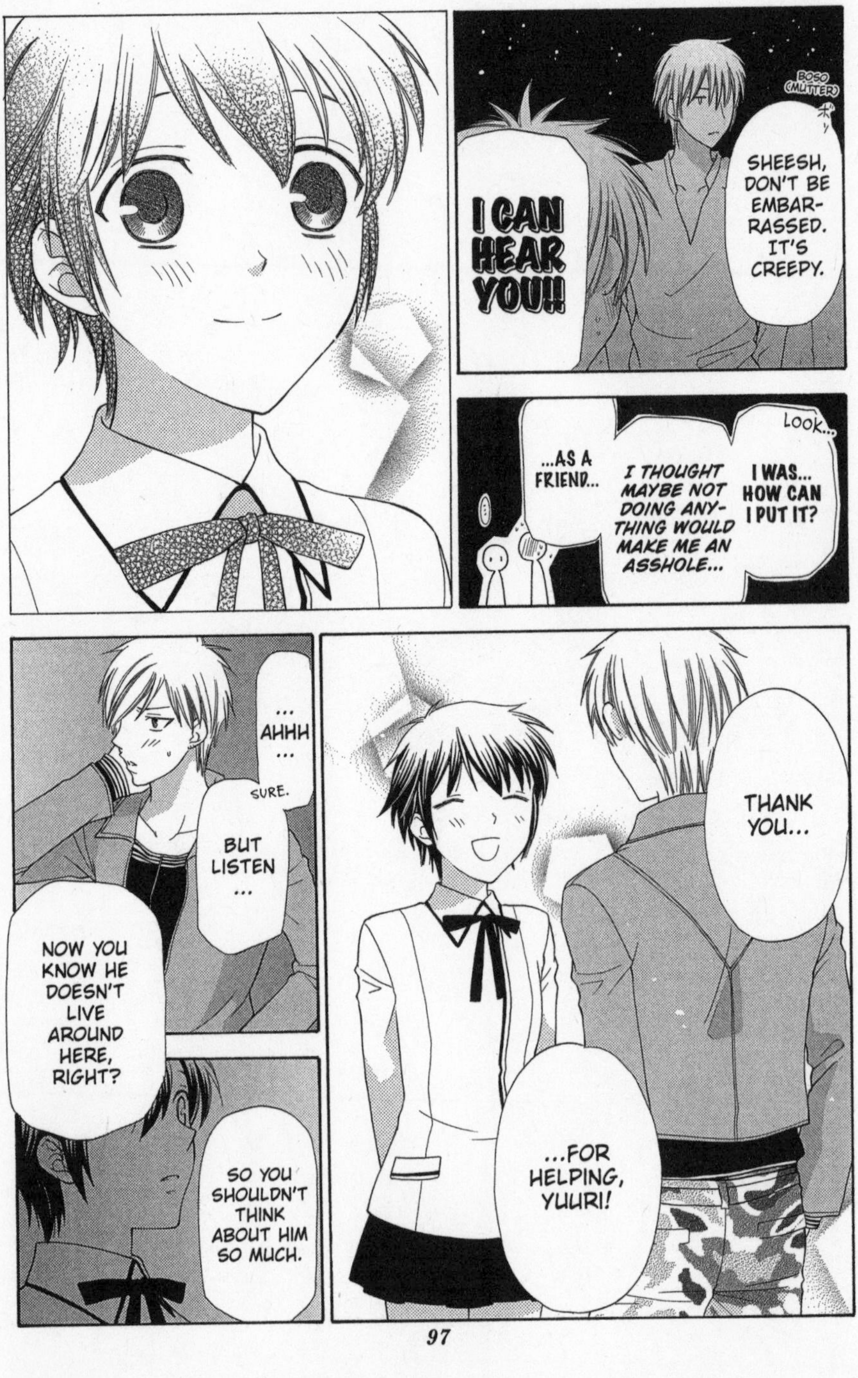
BOSO (MUTTER)
SHEESH, DON'T BE EMBAR-RASSED. IT'S CREEPY.
I CAN HEAR YOU!!
LOOK...
I WAS... HOW CAN I PUT IT?
I THOUGHT MAYBE NOT DOING ANY-THING WOULD MAKE ME AN ASSHOLE...
...AS A FRIEND...
THANK YOU...
...FOR HELPING, YUURI!
... AHHH ...
SURE.
BUT LISTEN ...
NOW YOU KNOW HE DOESN'T LIVE AROUND HERE, RIGHT?
SO YOU SHOULDN'T THINK ABOUT HIM SO MUCH.

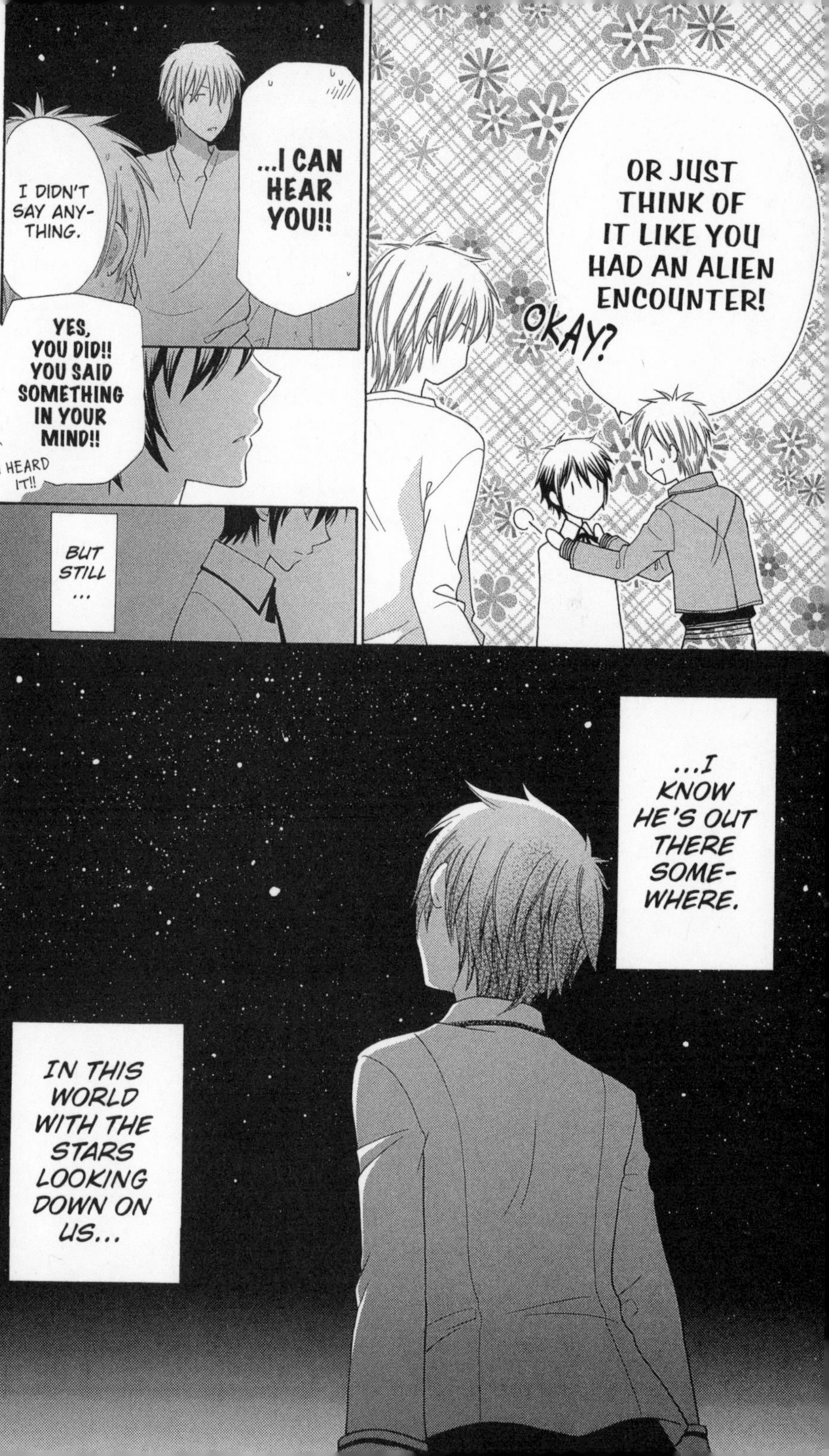
OR JUST THINK OF IT LIKE YOU HAD AN ALIEN ENCOUNTER!
OKAY?
...I CAN HEAR YOU!!
I DIDN'T SAY ANYTHING.
YES, YOU DID!! YOU SAID SOMETHING IN YOUR MIND!!
I HEARD IT!!
BUT STILL...
...I KNOW HE'S OUT THERE SOMEWHERE.
IN THIS WORLD WITH THE STARS LOOKING DOWN ON US...

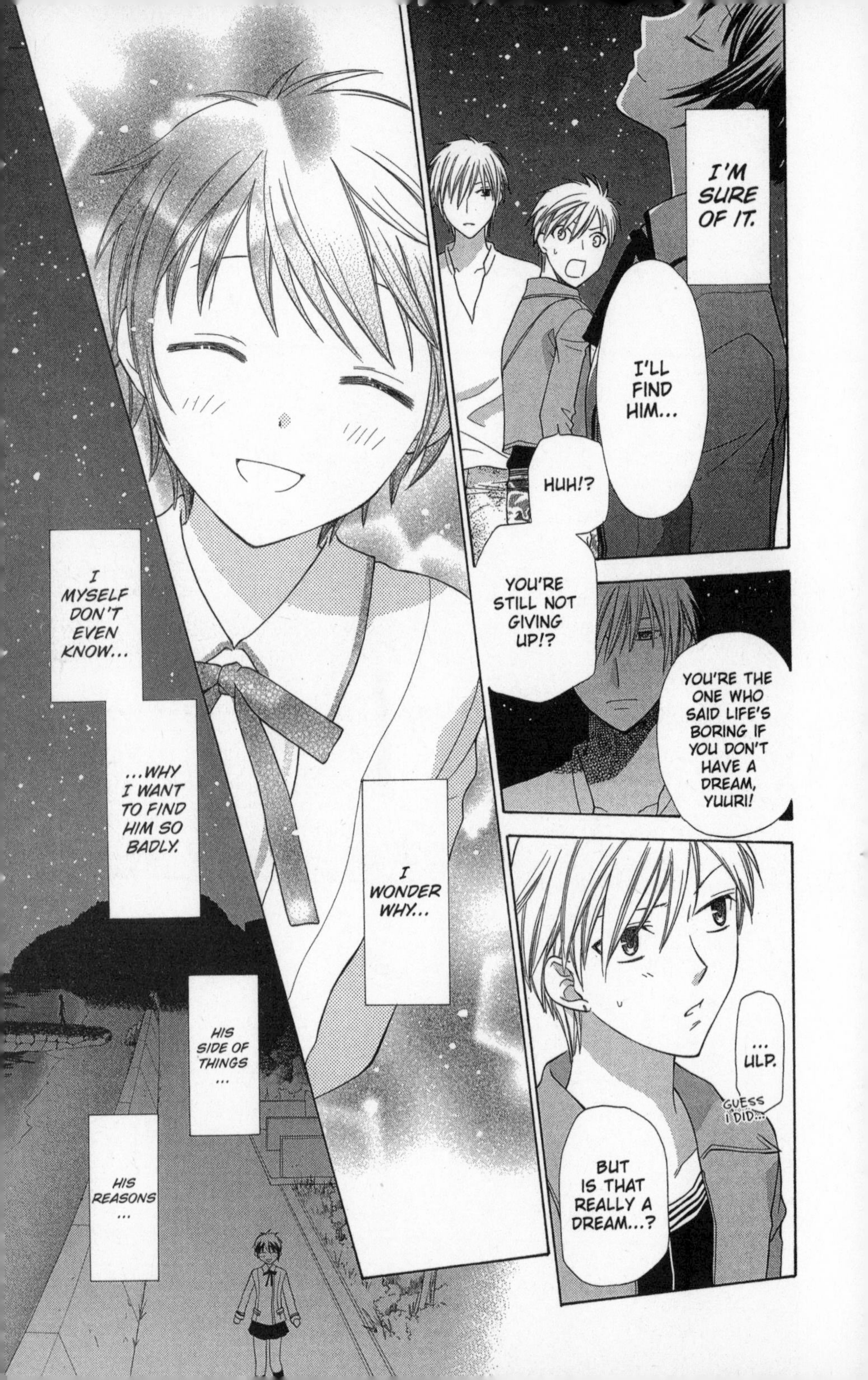
I'M SURE OF IT.
I'LL FIND HIM...
HUH!?
YOU'RE STILL NOT GIVING UP!?
YOU'RE THE ONE WHO SAID LIFE'S BORING IF YOU DON'T HAVE A DREAM, YUURI!
...ULP.
GUESS I DID...
BUT IS THAT REALLY A DREAM...?
I WONDER WHY...
I MYSELF DON'T EVEN KNOW...
...WHY I WANT TO FIND HIM SO BADLY.
HIS SIDE OF THINGS...
HIS REASONS...

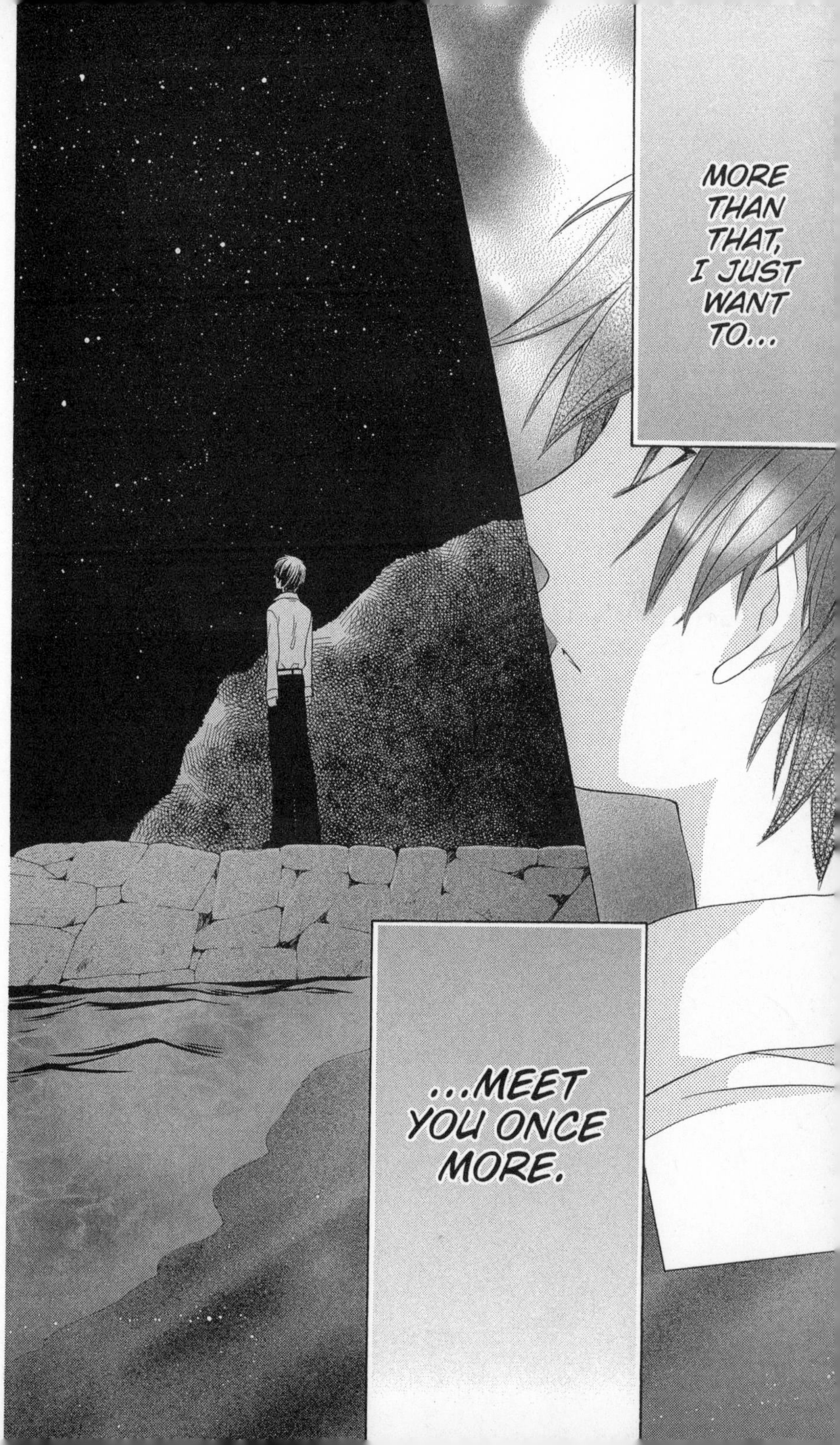
MORE THAN THAT, I JUST WANT TO...
...MEET YOU ONCE MORE.

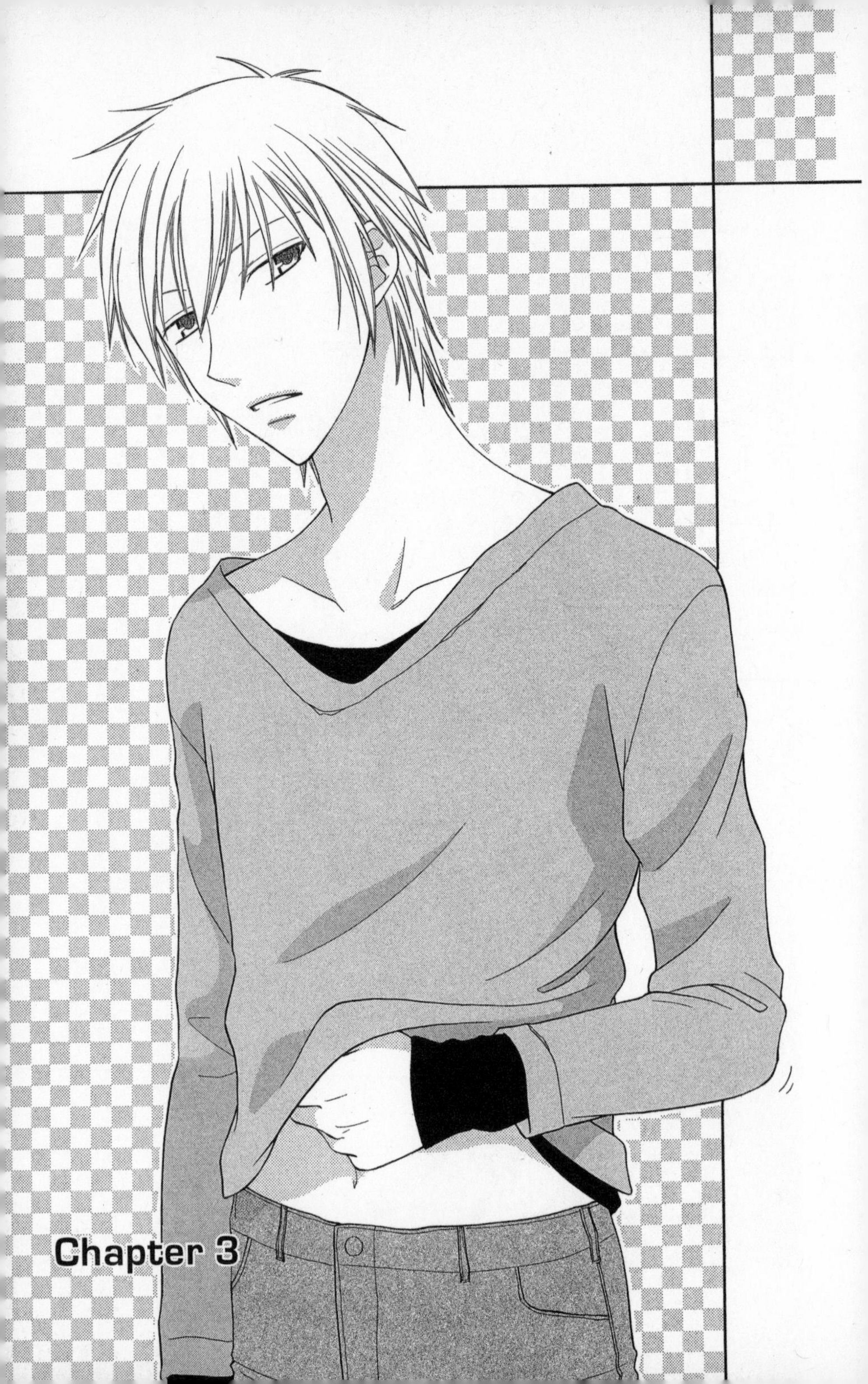
Chapter 3

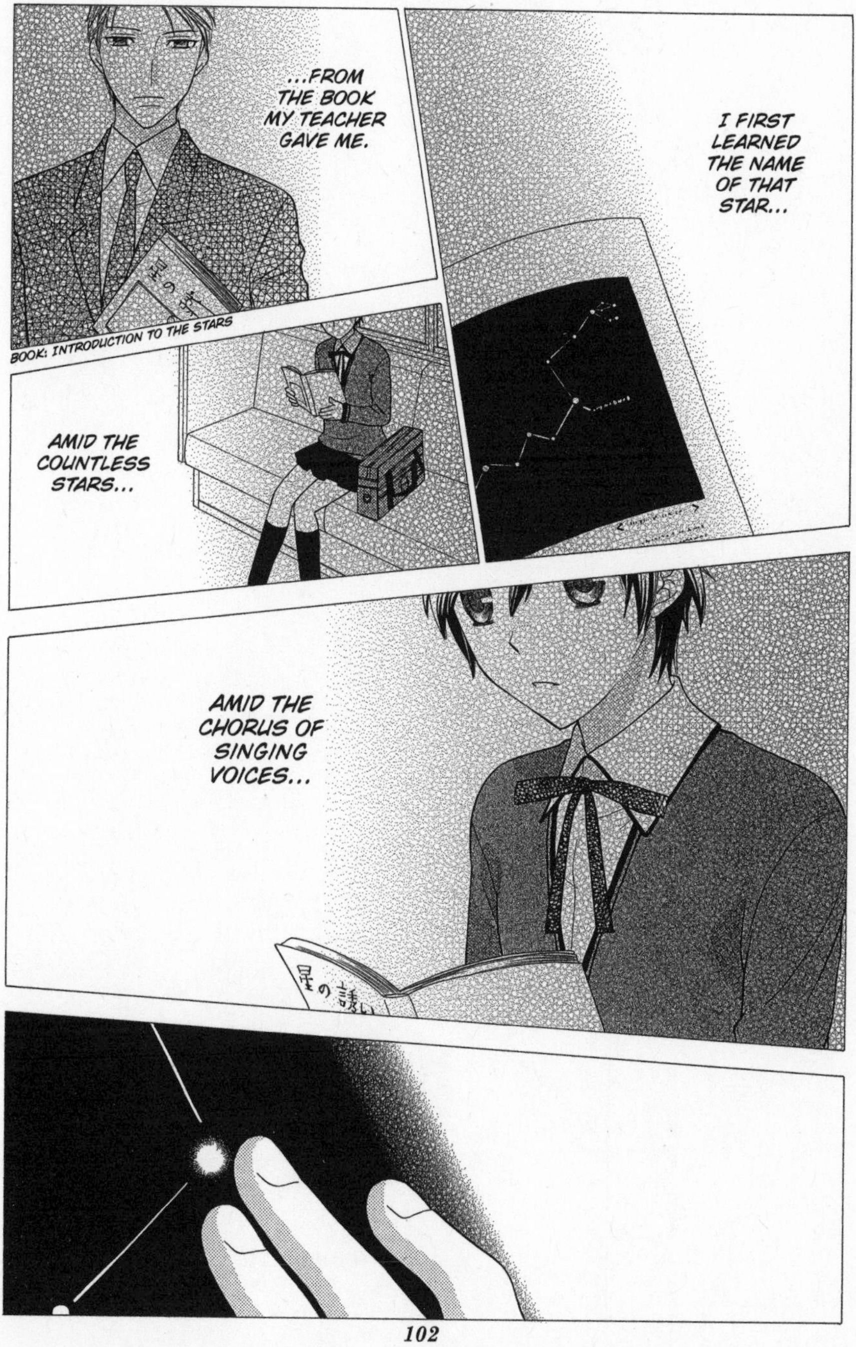
I FIRST LEARNED THE NAME OF THAT STAR...
...FROM THE BOOK MY TEACHER GAVE ME.
BOOK: INTRODUCTION TO THE STARS
AMID THE COUNTLESS STARS...
AMID THE CHORUS OF SINGING VOICES...

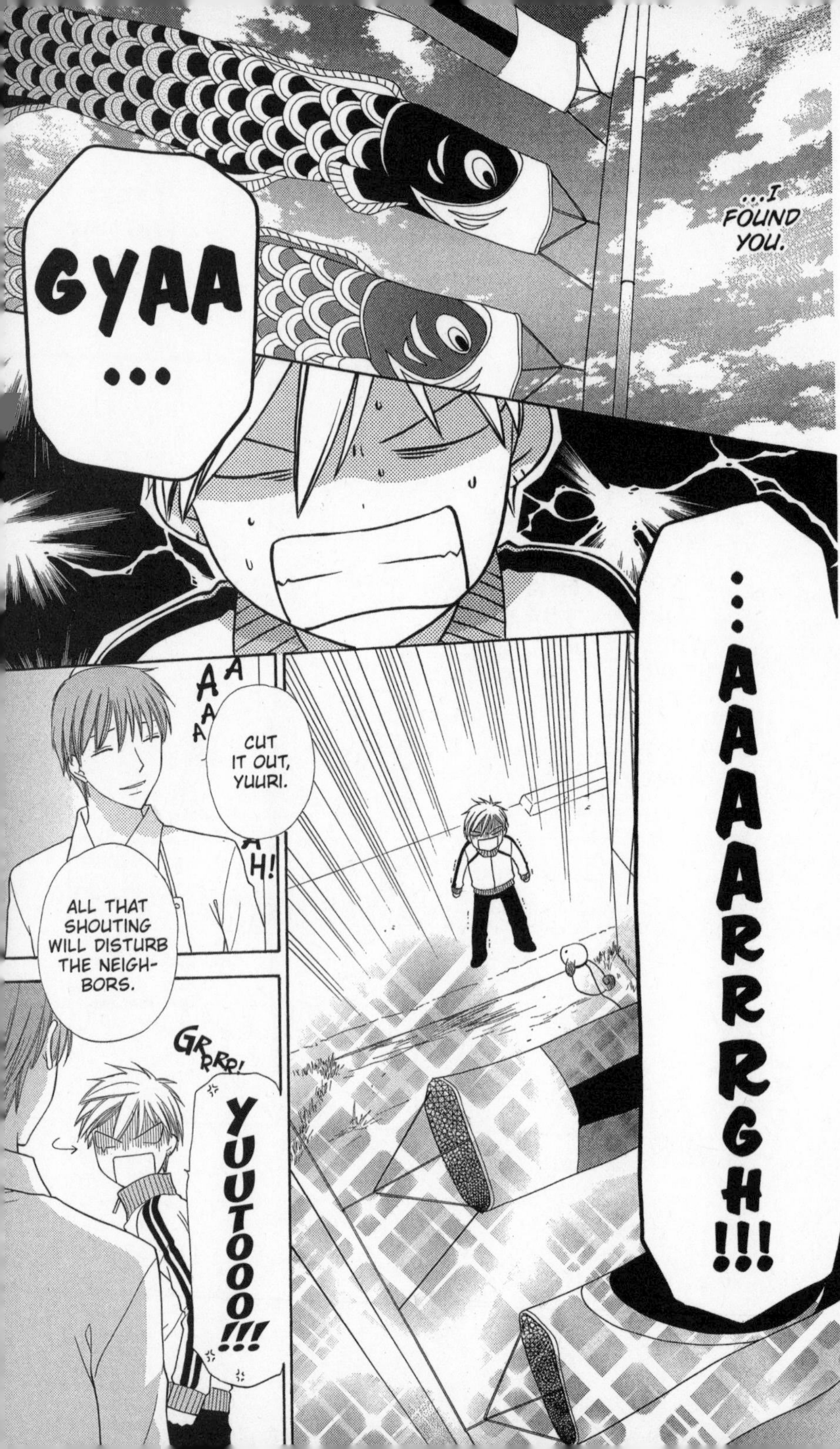
...I FOUND YOU.
GYAA...
...AAAAARRRGH!!!
AAAA
CUT IT OUT, YUURI.
AH!
ALL THAT SHOUTING WILL DISTURB THE NEIGHBORS.
GRRRR!
YUUTOOOO!!!

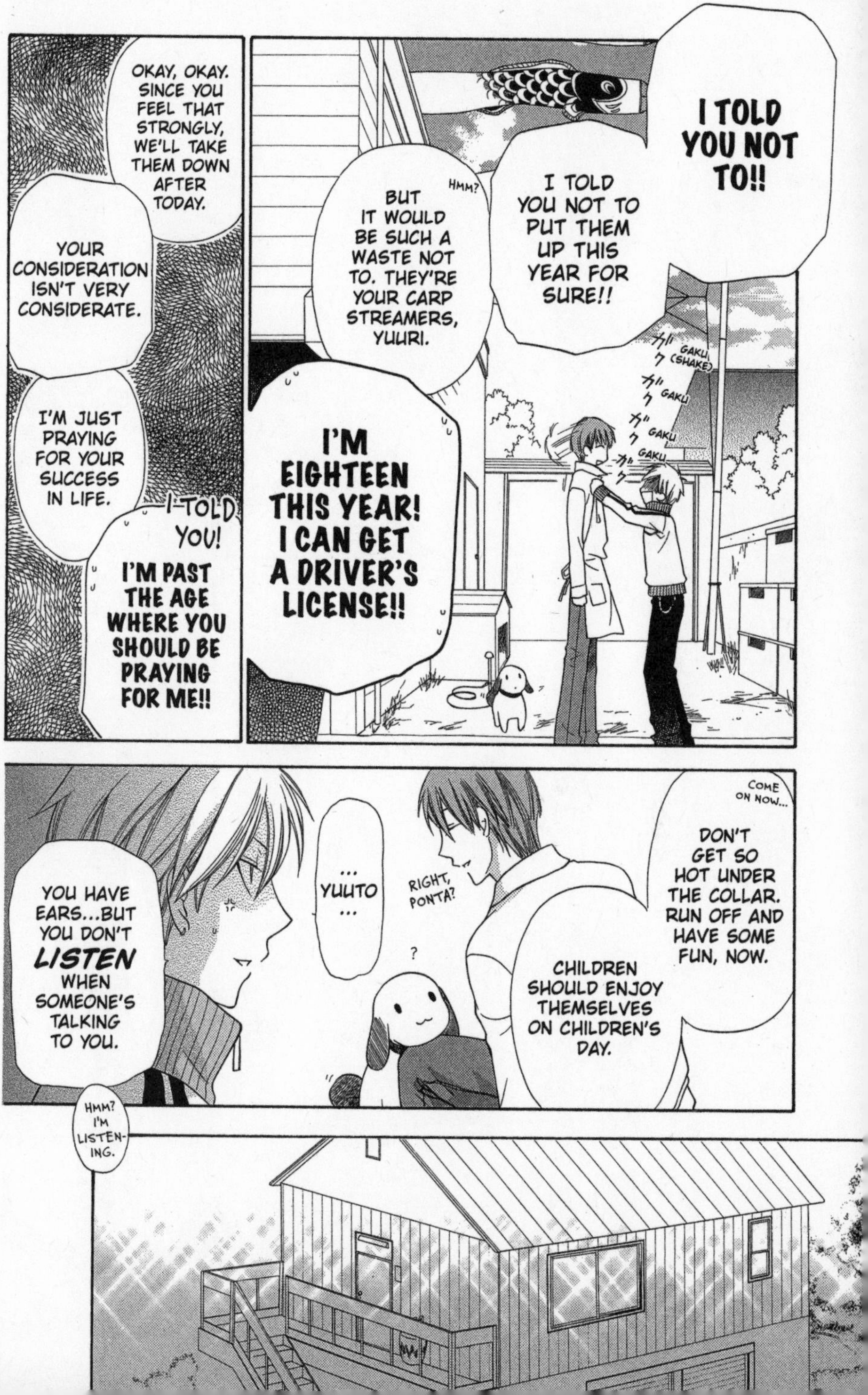
I TOLD YOU NOT TO!!
I TOLD YOU NOT TO PUT THEM UP THIS YEAR FOR SURE!!
HMM?
BUT IT WOULD BE SUCH A WASTE NOT TO. THEY'RE YOUR CARP STREAMERS, YUURI.
GAKU (SHAKE)
GAKU
GAKU
GAKU
I'M EIGHTEEN THIS YEAR! I CAN GET A DRIVER'S LICENSE!!
OKAY, OKAY. SINCE YOU FEEL THAT STRONGLY, WE'LL TAKE THEM DOWN AFTER TODAY.
YOUR CONSIDERATION ISN'T VERY CONSIDERATE.
I'M JUST PRAYING FOR YOUR SUCCESS IN LIFE.
I TOLD YOU!
I'M PAST THE AGE WHERE YOU SHOULD BE PRAYING FOR ME!!
COME ON NOW...
DON'T GET SO HOT UNDER THE COLLAR. RUN OFF AND HAVE SOME FUN, NOW.
CHILDREN SHOULD ENJOY THEMSELVES ON CHILDREN'S DAY.
RIGHT, PONTA?
?
...YUUTO...
YOU HAVE EARS...BUT YOU DON'T LISTEN WHEN SOMEONE'S TALKING TO YOU.
HMM? I'M LISTENING.

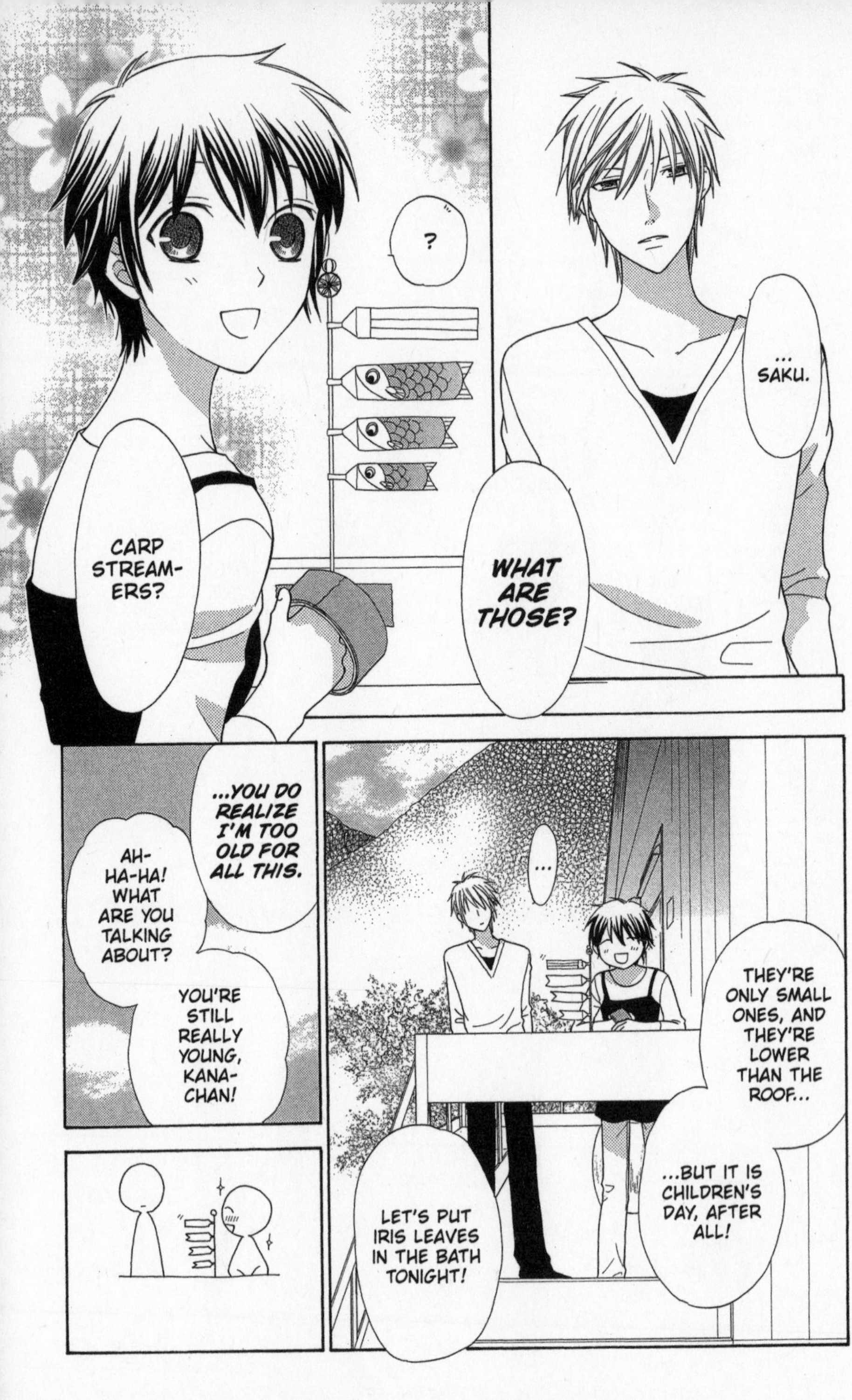

... SAKU.
WHAT ARE THOSE?
?
CARP STREAMERS?
...
THEY'RE ONLY SMALL ONES, AND THEY'RE LOWER THAN THE ROOF...
...BUT IT IS CHILDREN'S DAY, AFTER ALL!
LET'S PUT IRIS LEAVES IN THE BATH TONIGHT!
...YOU DO REALIZE I'M TOO OLD FOR ALL THIS.
AH-HA-HA! WHAT ARE YOU TALKING ABOUT?
YOU'RE STILL REALLY YOUNG, KANA-CHAN!

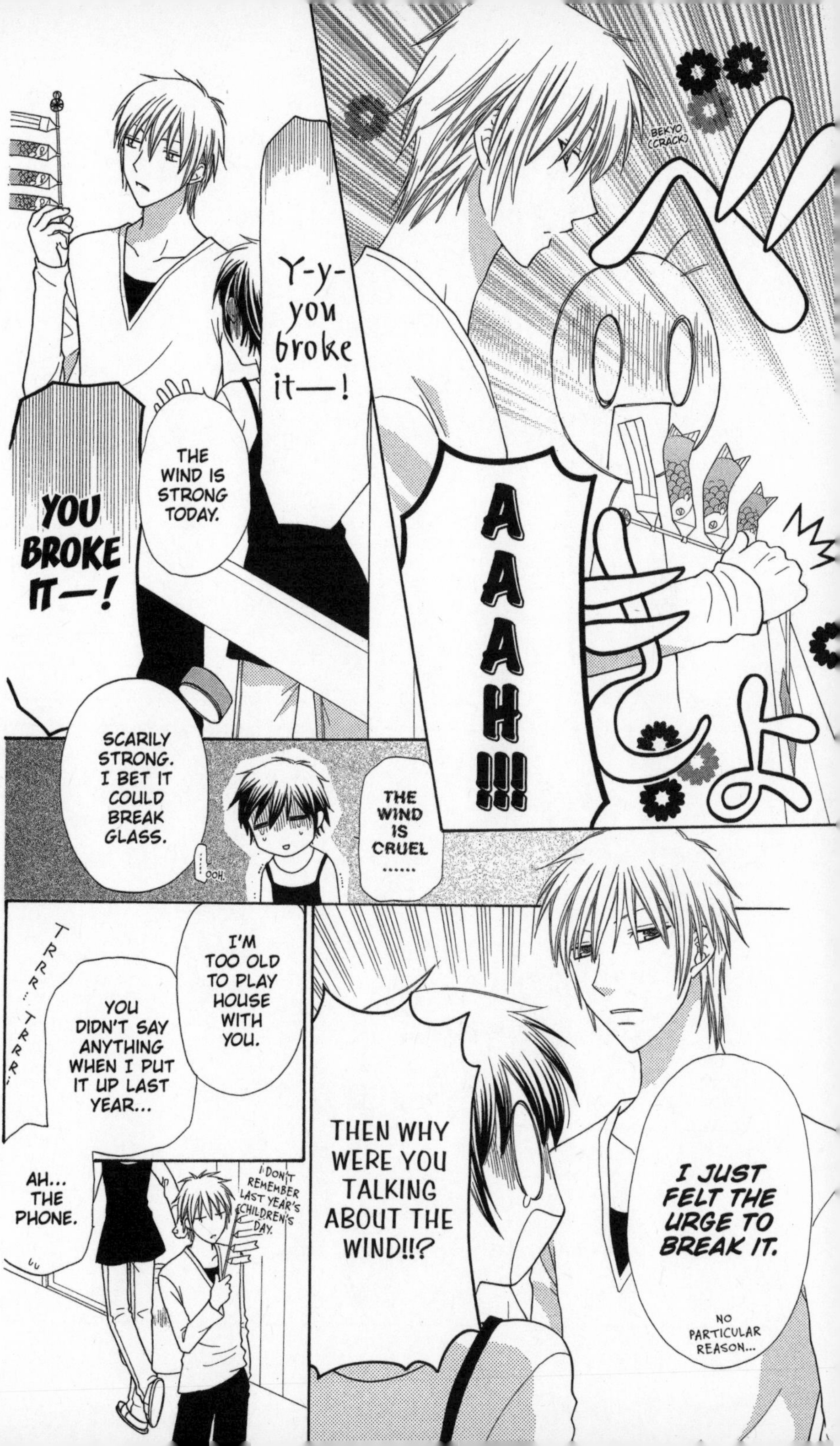

BEKYO (CRACK)
AAAAH!!!
Y-y-you broke it—!
THE WIND IS STRONG TODAY.
YOU BROKE IT—!
THE WIND IS CRUEL ......
...OOH.
SCARILY STRONG. I BET IT COULD BREAK GLASS.
I JUST FELT THE URGE TO BREAK IT.
NO PARTICULAR REASON...
THEN WHY WERE YOU TALKING ABOUT THE WIND!!?
I'M TOO OLD TO PLAY HOUSE WITH YOU.
YOU DIDN'T SAY ANYTHING WHEN I PUT IT UP LAST YEAR...
TRRR... TRRR...
I DON'T REMEMBER LAST YEAR'S CHILDREN'S DAY.
AH... THE PHONE.

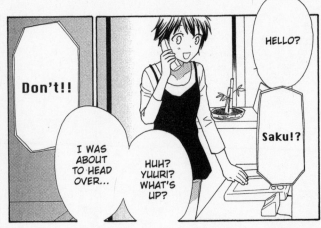

HELLO?
Saku!?
HUH? YUURI? WHAT'S UP?
I WAS ABOUT TO HEAD OVER...
Don't!!
ANOTHER NICE DAY...
Huh!?
DON'T COME TO MY PLACE! LET'S JUST MEET THERE.
CHANGE OF PLANS, GOT IT!?
I'LL CALL HIJIRI TO TELL HER TOO!
Then I'll see you later!!
GACHAN (CLICK)
......?
AH!
WHAT WAS THAT?
A PRANK CALL?

The left and right side of Yuuri-kun's hair are different lengths, so to me it feels like he gives off a slightly different impression when facing left or facing right. Hmmm?

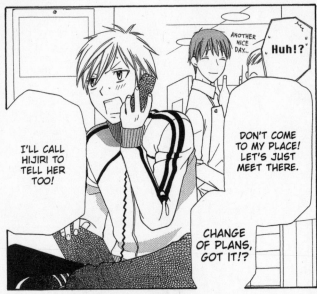

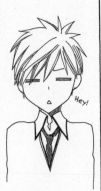

Hey!

I bet it's hard to get his hair under control in the morning. That's probably why he's late to school so often. (LOL)

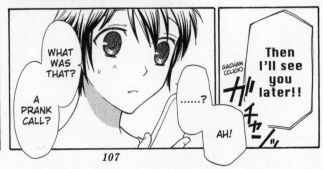

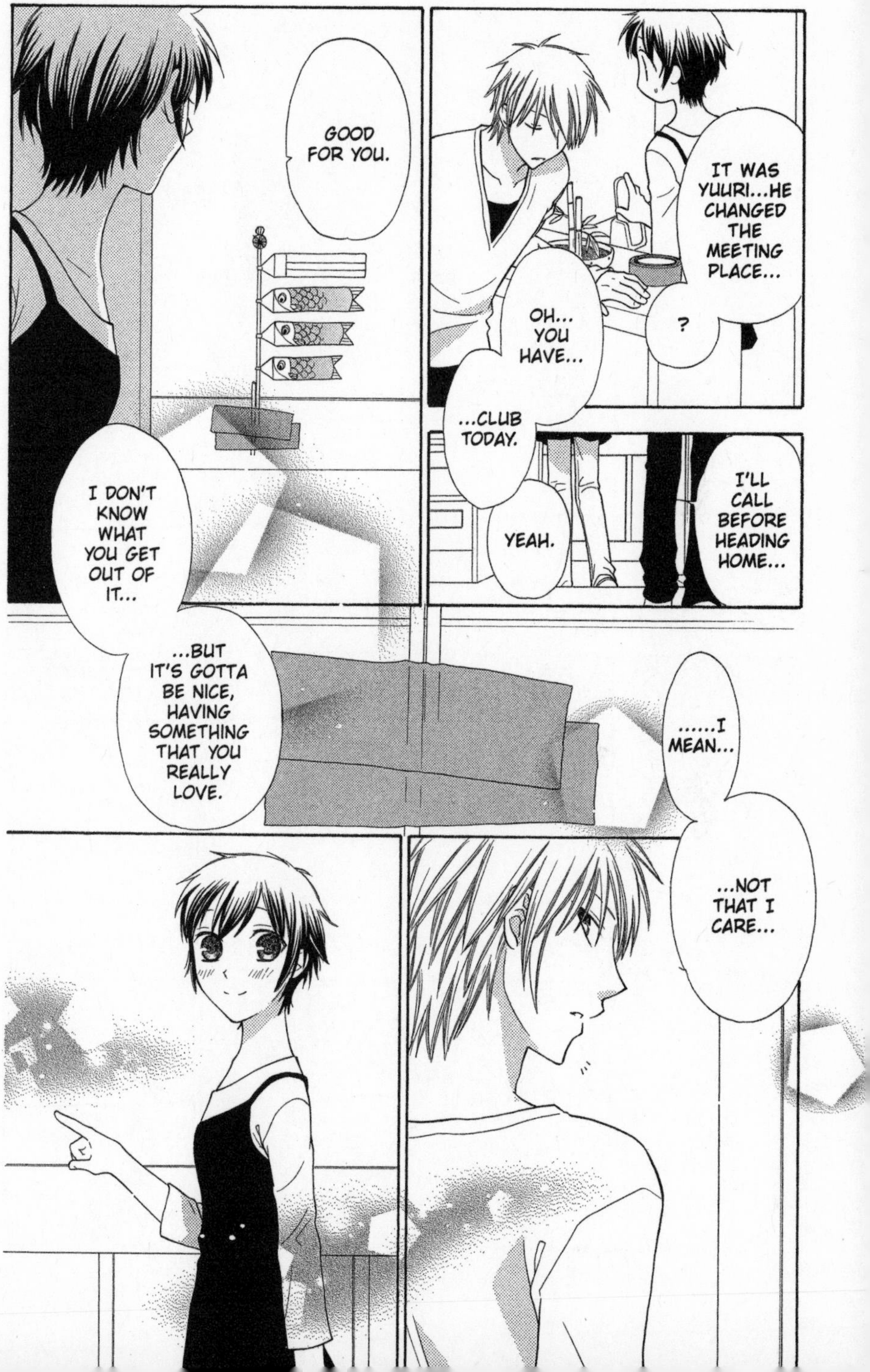
IT WAS YUURI...HE CHANGED THE MEETING PLACE...
?
OH... YOU HAVE...
...CLUB TODAY.
I'LL CALL BEFORE HEADING HOME...
YEAH.
GOOD FOR YOU.
I DON'T KNOW WHAT YOU GET OUT OF IT...
...BUT IT'S GOTTA BE NICE, HAVING SOMETHING THAT YOU REALLY LOVE.
......I MEAN...
...NOT THAT I CARE...

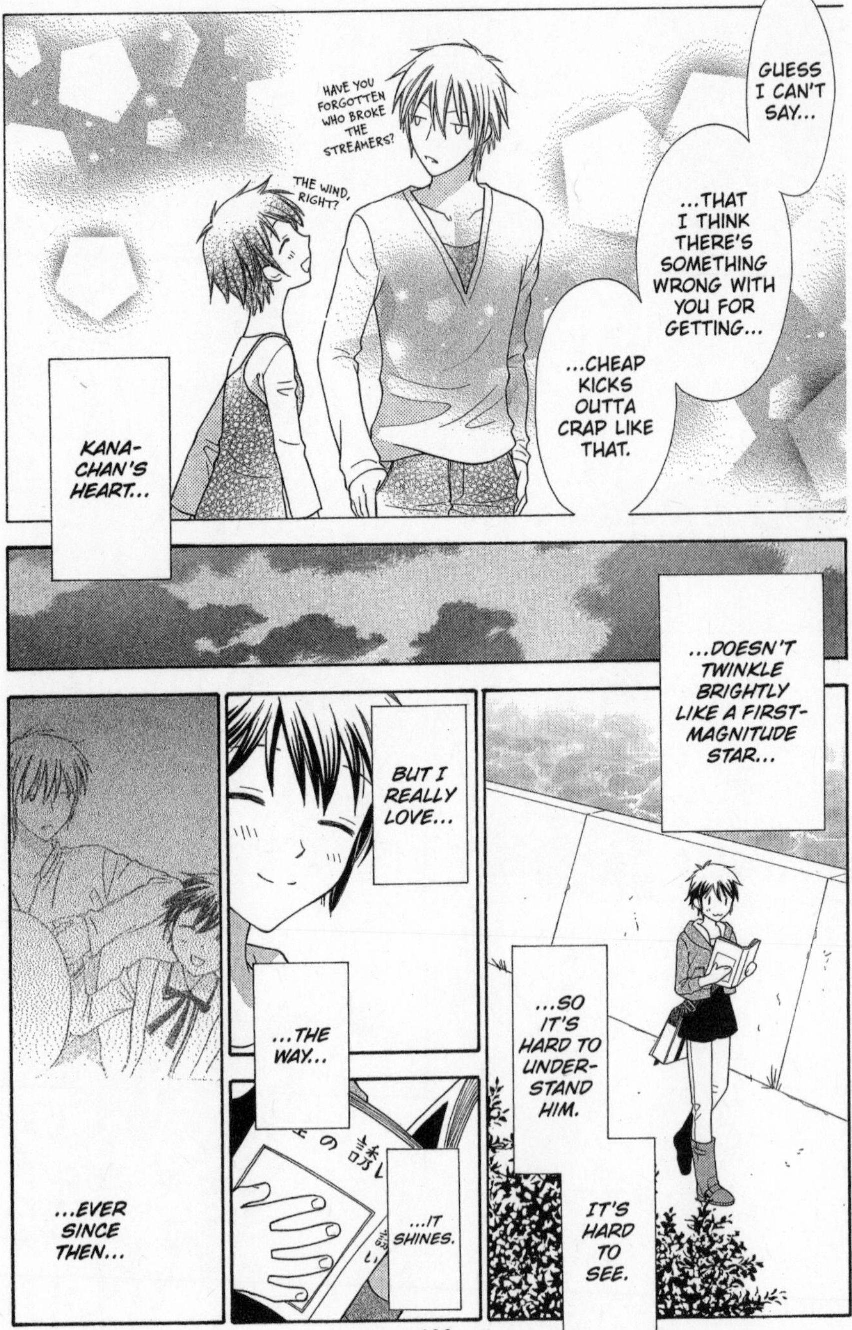
GUESS I CAN'T SAY...
...THAT I THINK THERE'S SOMETHING WRONG WITH YOU FOR GETTING...
...CHEAP KICKS OUTTA CRAP LIKE THAT.
HAVE YOU FORGOTTEN WHO BROKE THE STREAMERS?
THE WIND, RIGHT?
KANA-CHAN'S HEART...
...DOESN'T TWINKLE BRIGHTLY LIKE A FIRST-MAGNITUDE STAR...
...SO IT'S HARD TO UNDER-STAND HIM.
IT'S HARD TO SEE.
BUT I REALLY LOVE...
...THE WAY...
...IT SHINES.
...EVER SINCE THEN...

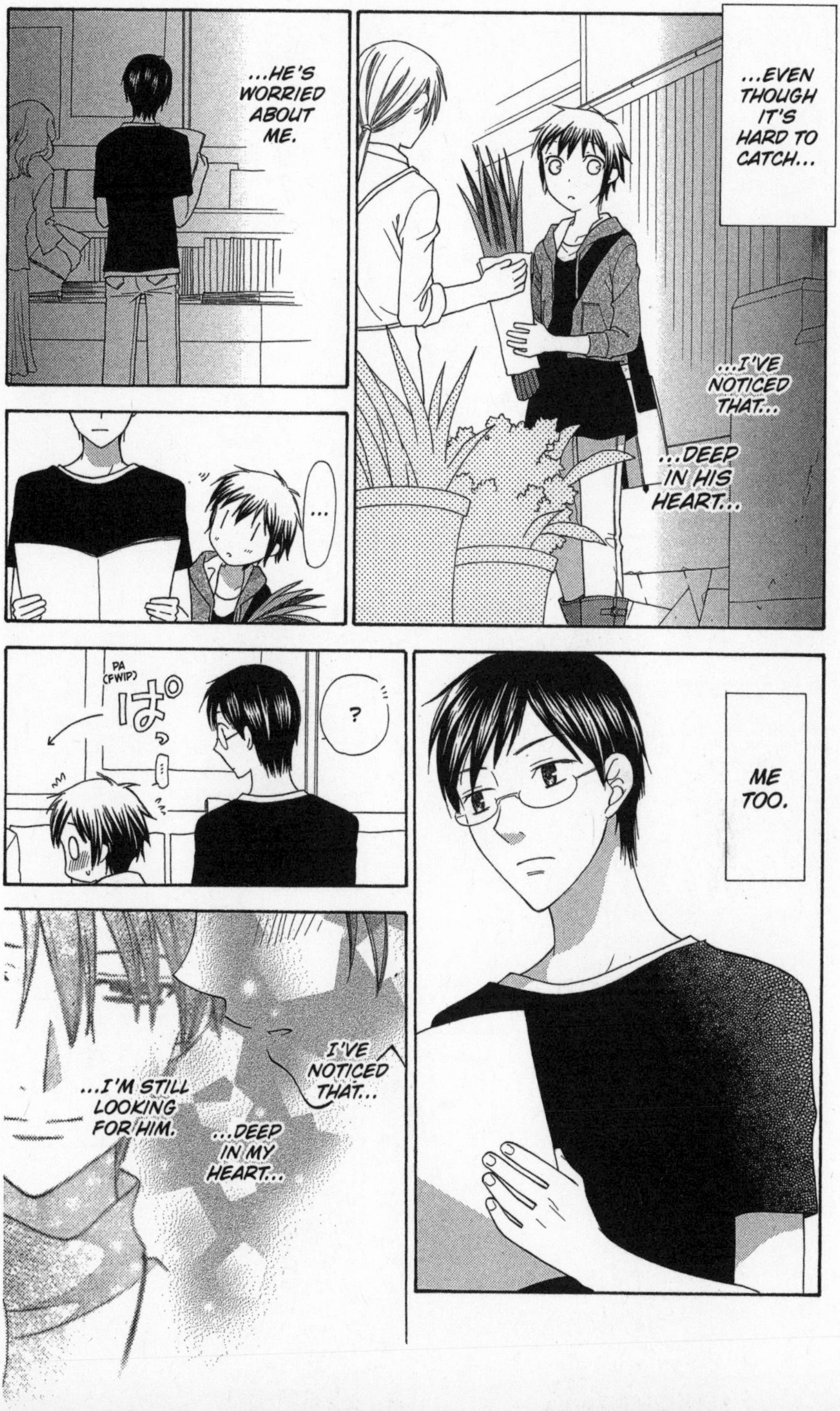
…EVEN THOUGH IT'S HARD TO CATCH…
…I'VE NOTICED THAT…
…DEEP IN HIS HEART…
…HE'S WORRIED ABOUT ME.
…
ME TOO.
?
PA (FWIP)
ぱっ
!
I'VE NOTICED THAT…
…DEEP IN MY HEART…
…I'M STILL LOOKING FOR HIM.

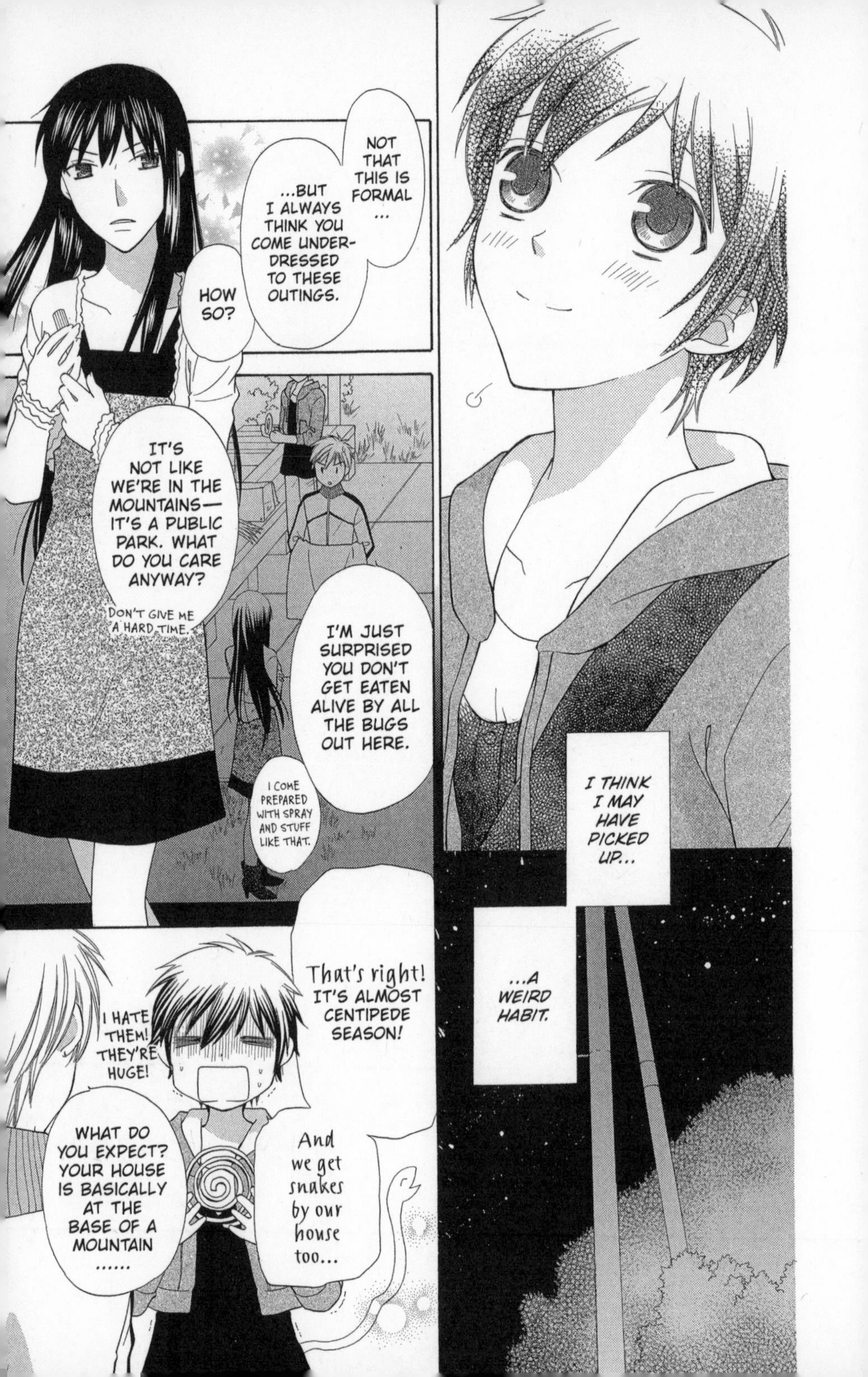
I THINK I MAY HAVE PICKED UP...
...A WEIRD HABIT.
NOT THAT THIS IS FORMAL...
...BUT I ALWAYS THINK YOU COME UNDER-DRESSED TO THESE OUTINGS.
HOW SO?
IT'S NOT LIKE WE'RE IN THE MOUNTAINS—IT'S A PUBLIC PARK. WHAT DO YOU CARE ANYWAY?
DON'T GIVE ME A HARD TIME.
I'M JUST SURPRISED YOU DON'T GET EATEN ALIVE BY ALL THE BUGS OUT HERE.
I COME PREPARED WITH SPRAY AND STUFF LIKE THAT.
That's right! IT'S ALMOST CENTIPEDE SEASON!
I HATE THEM! THEY'RE HUGE!
And we get snakes by our house too...
WHAT DO YOU EXPECT? YOUR HOUSE IS BASICALLY AT THE BASE OF A MOUNTAIN ......

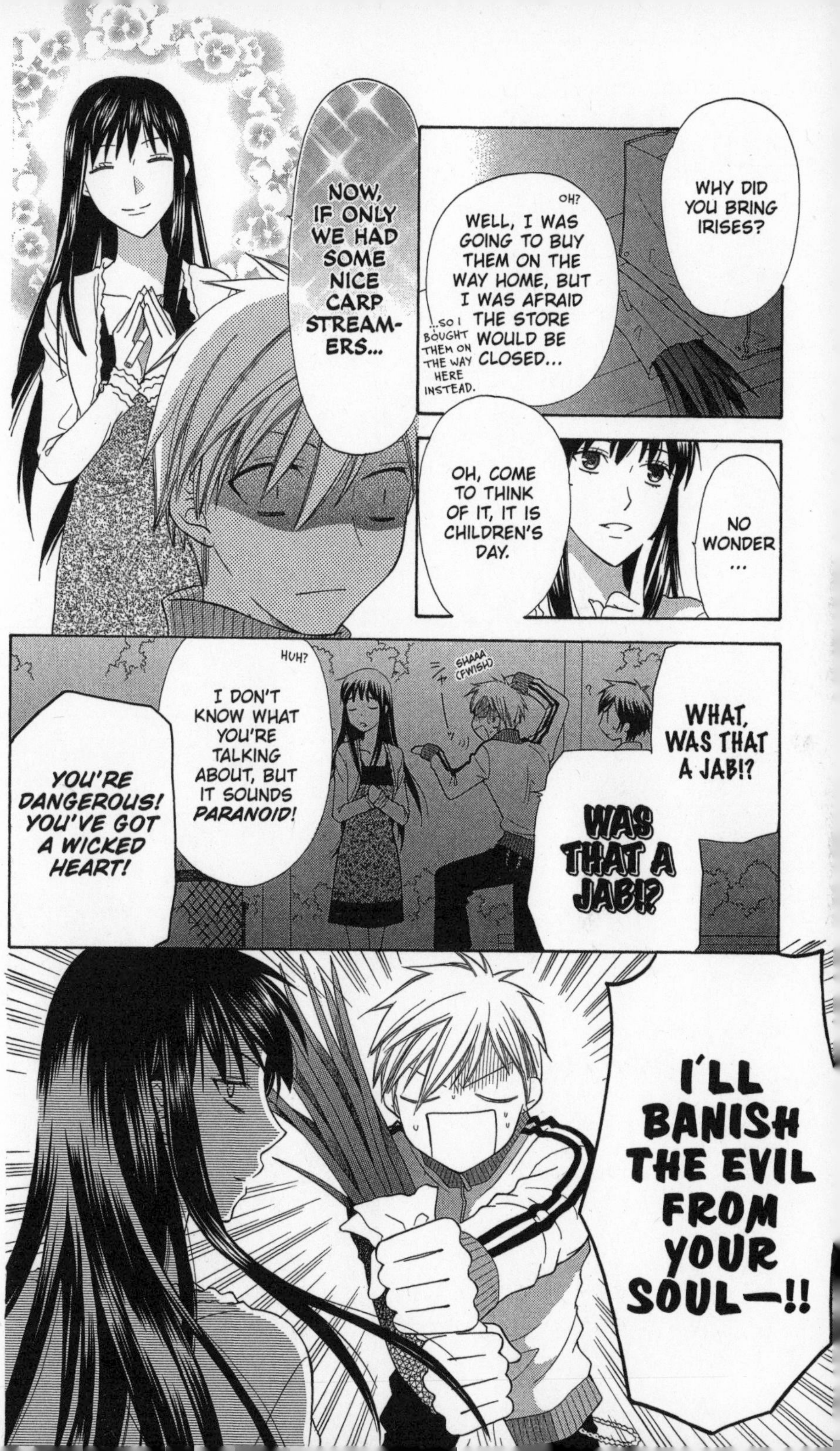
WHY DID YOU BRING IRISES?
OH?
WELL, I WAS GOING TO BUY THEM ON THE WAY HOME, BUT I WAS AFRAID THE STORE WOULD BE CLOSED...
...SO I BOUGHT THEM ON THE WAY HERE INSTEAD.
NO WONDER...
OH, COME TO THINK OF IT, IT IS CHILDREN'S DAY.
NOW, IF ONLY WE HAD SOME NICE CARP STREAMERS...
WHAT, WAS THAT A JAB!?
WAS THAT A JAB!?
SHAAA (FWISH)
HUH?
I DON'T KNOW WHAT YOU'RE TALKING ABOUT, BUT IT SOUNDS PARANOID!
YOU'RE DANGEROUS! YOU'VE GOT A WICKED HEART!
I'LL BANISH THE EVIL FROM YOUR SOUL—!!

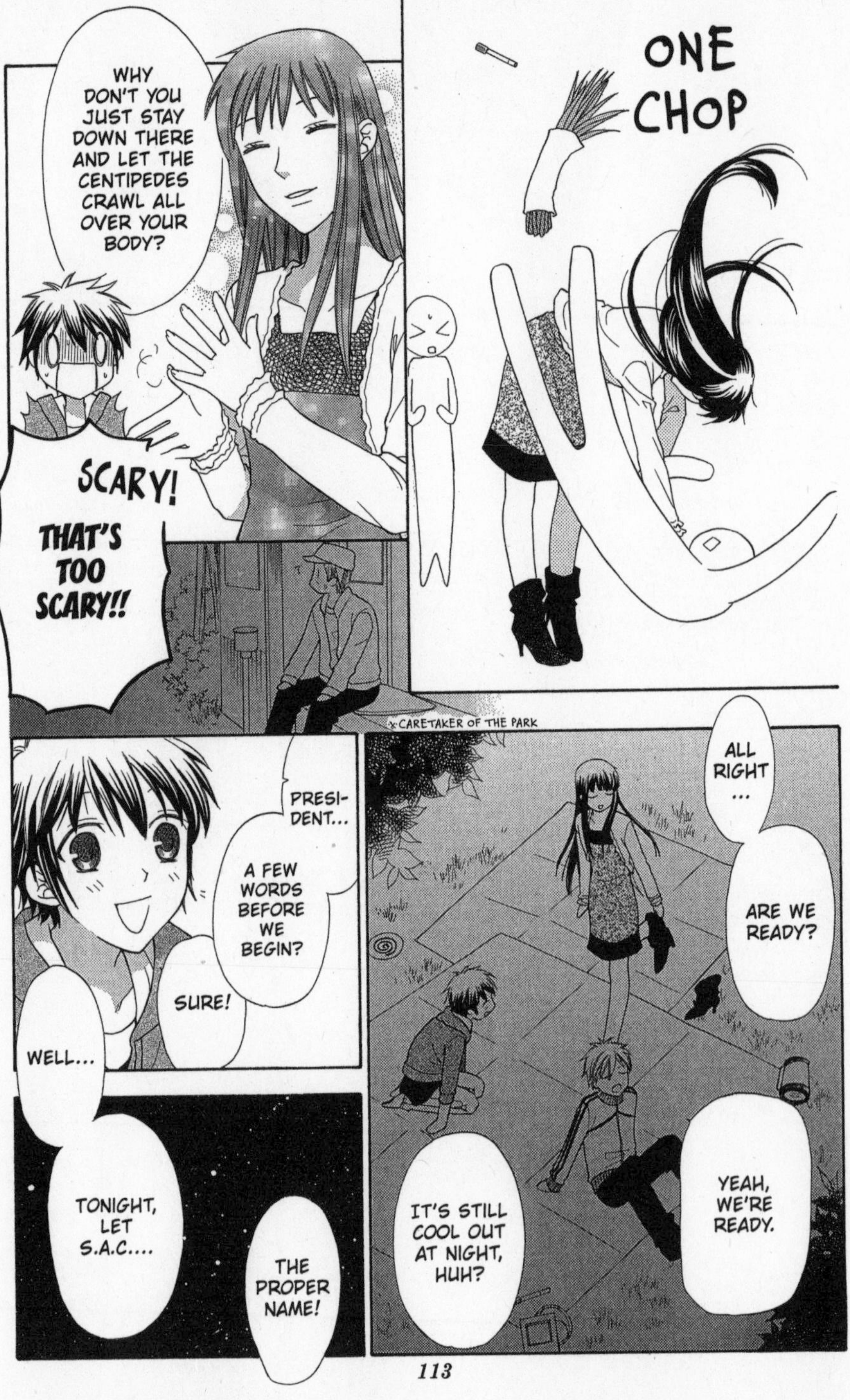
ONE CHOP
WHY DON'T YOU JUST STAY DOWN THERE AND LET THE CENTIPEDES CRAWL ALL OVER YOUR BODY?
SCARY!
THAT'S TOO SCARY!!
※CARETAKER OF THE PARK
ALL RIGHT...
ARE WE READY?
YEAH, WE'RE READY.
IT'S STILL COOL OUT AT NIGHT, HUH?
PRESIDENT...
A FEW WORDS BEFORE WE BEGIN?
SURE!
WELL...
TONIGHT, LET S.A.C....
THE PROPER NAME!

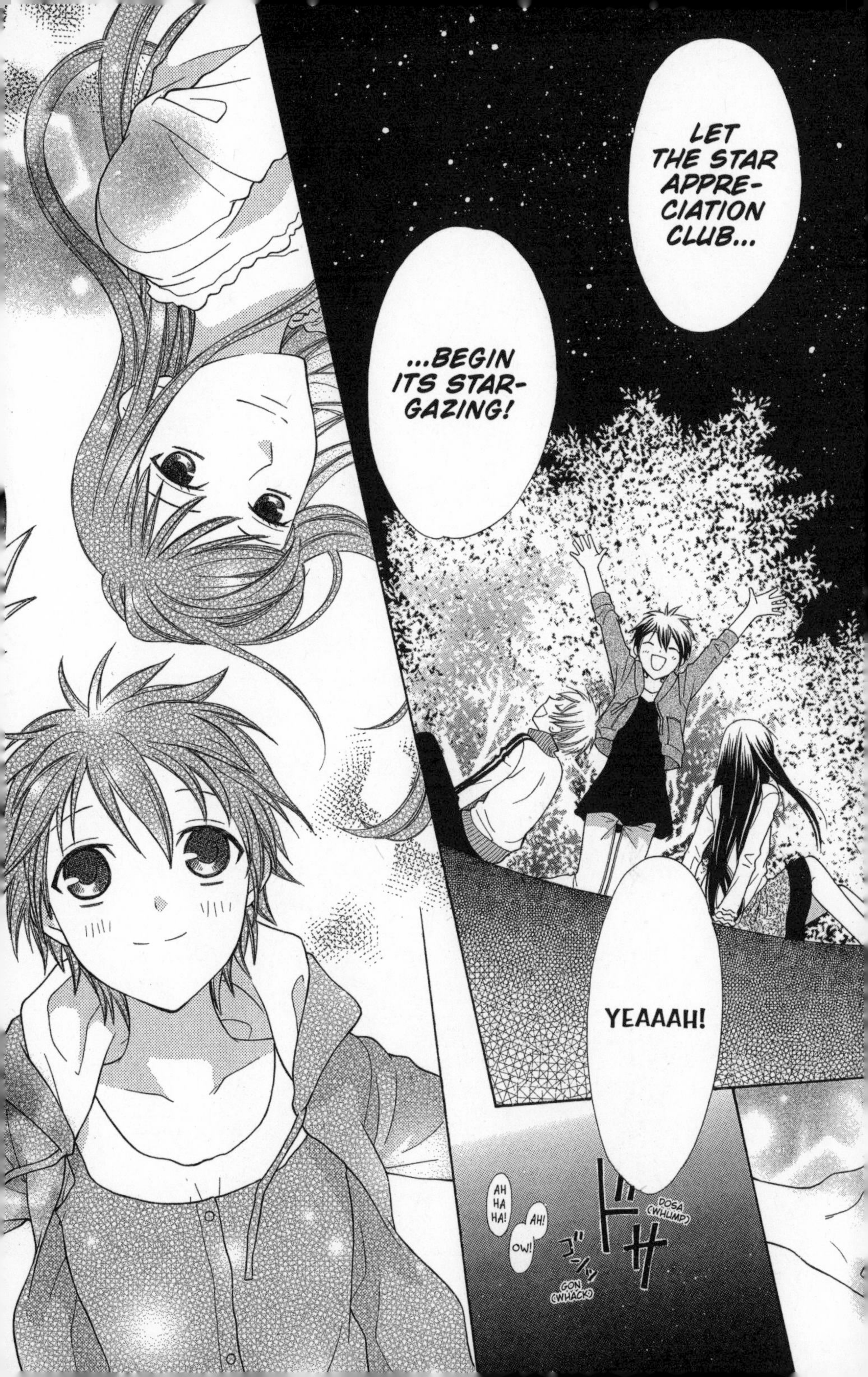
LET THE STAR APPRE-CIATION CLUB...
...BEGIN ITS STAR-GAZING!
YEAAAH!
DOSA (WHUMP)
GON (WHACK)
AH!
OW!
AH HA HA!

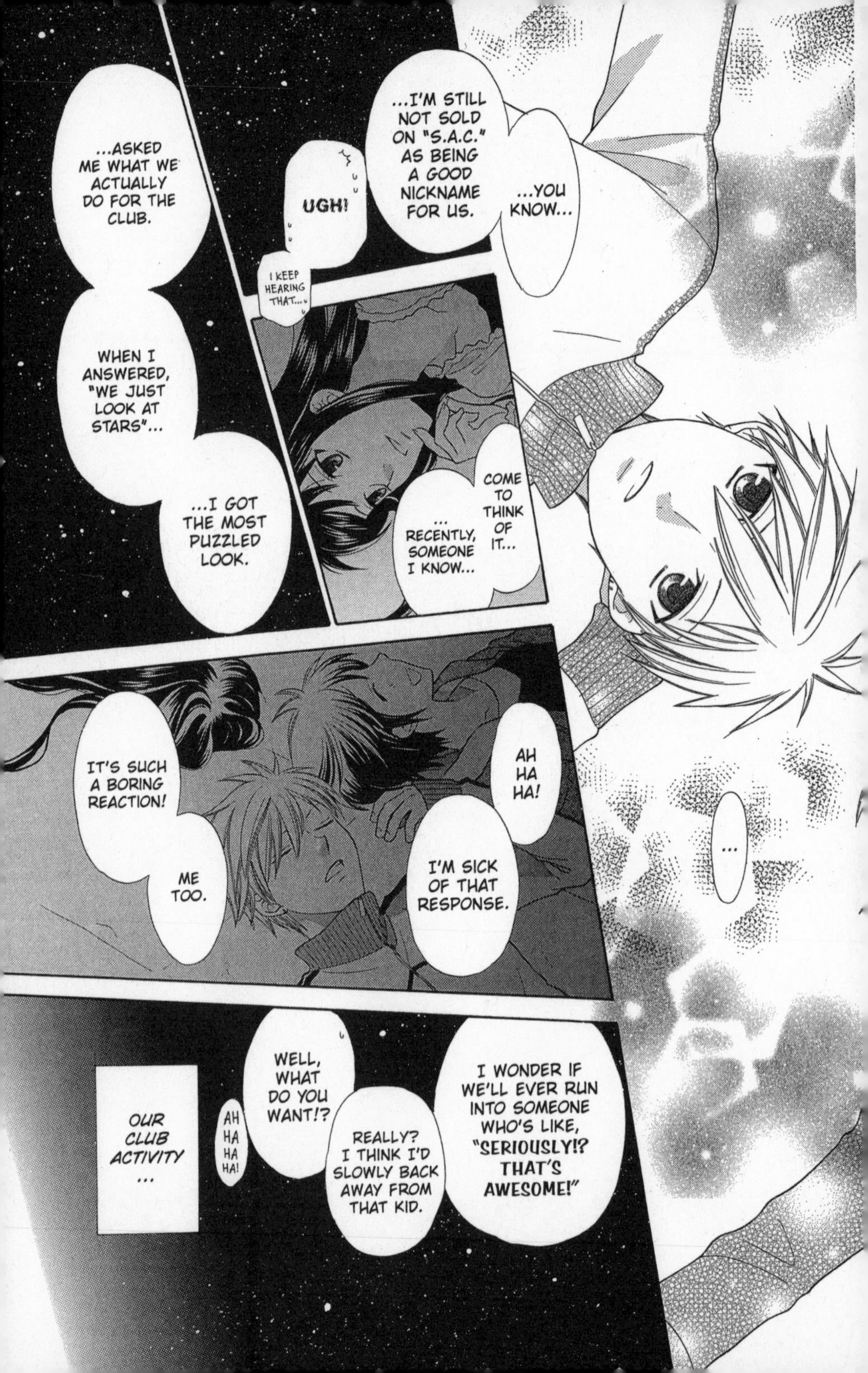
...YOU KNOW...
...I'M STILL NOT SOLD ON "S.A.C." AS BEING A GOOD NICKNAME FOR US.
UGH!
I KEEP HEARING THAT...
COME TO THINK OF IT...
...RECENTLY, SOMEONE I KNOW...
...ASKED ME WHAT WE ACTUALLY DO FOR THE CLUB.
WHEN I ANSWERED, "WE JUST LOOK AT STARS"...
...I GOT THE MOST PUZZLED LOOK.
AH HA HA!
I'M SICK OF THAT RESPONSE.
IT'S SUCH A BORING REACTION!
ME TOO.
...
I WONDER IF WE'LL EVER RUN INTO SOMEONE WHO'S LIKE, "SERIOUSLY!? THAT'S AWESOME!"
REALLY? I THINK I'D SLOWLY BACK AWAY FROM THAT KID.
WELL, WHAT DO YOU WANT!?
AH HA HA HA!
OUR CLUB ACTIVITY ...

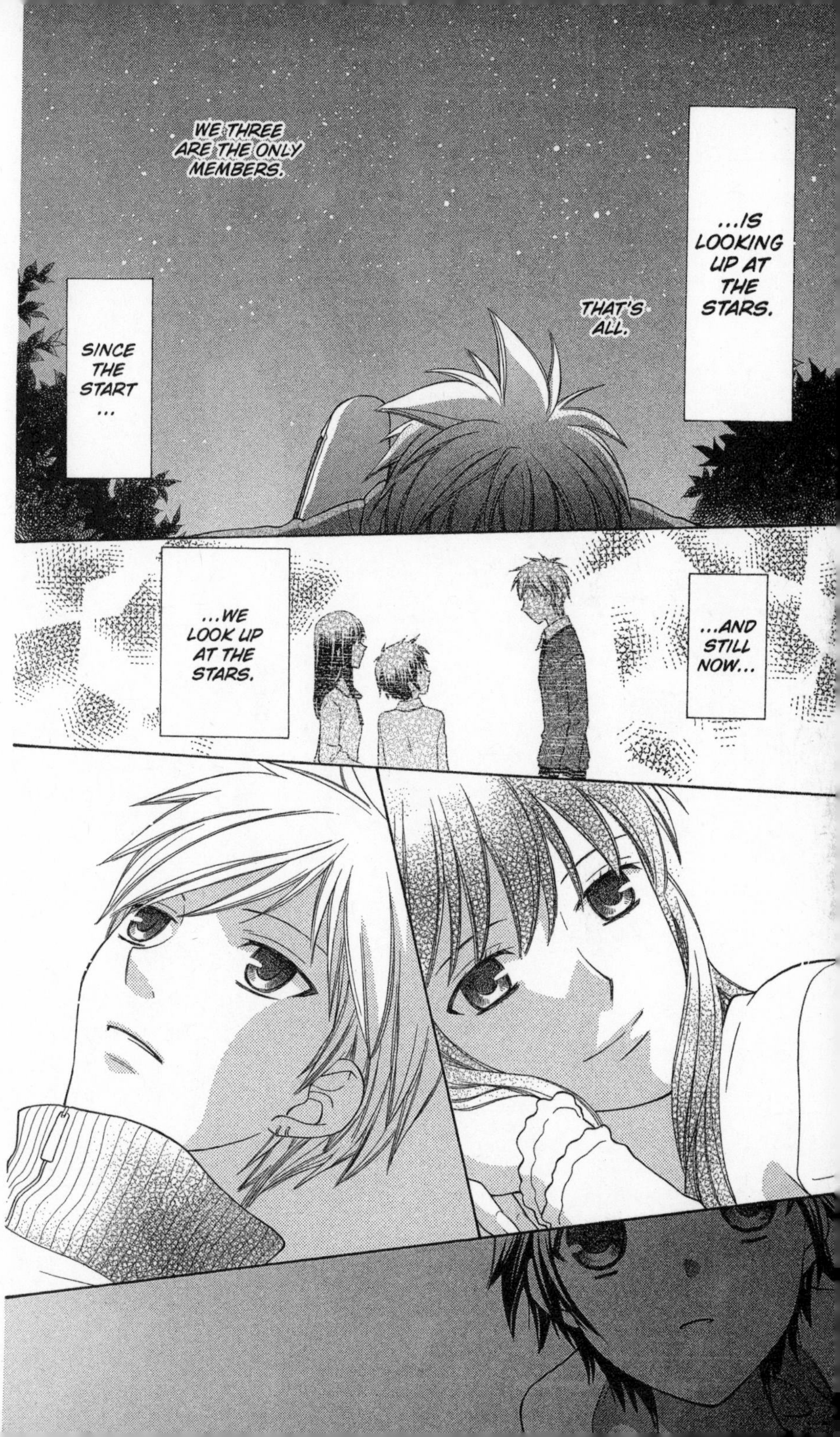
...IS LOOKING UP AT THE STARS.
THAT'S ALL.
WE THREE ARE THE ONLY MEMBERS.
SINCE THE START ...
...AND STILL NOW...
...WE LOOK UP AT THE STARS.

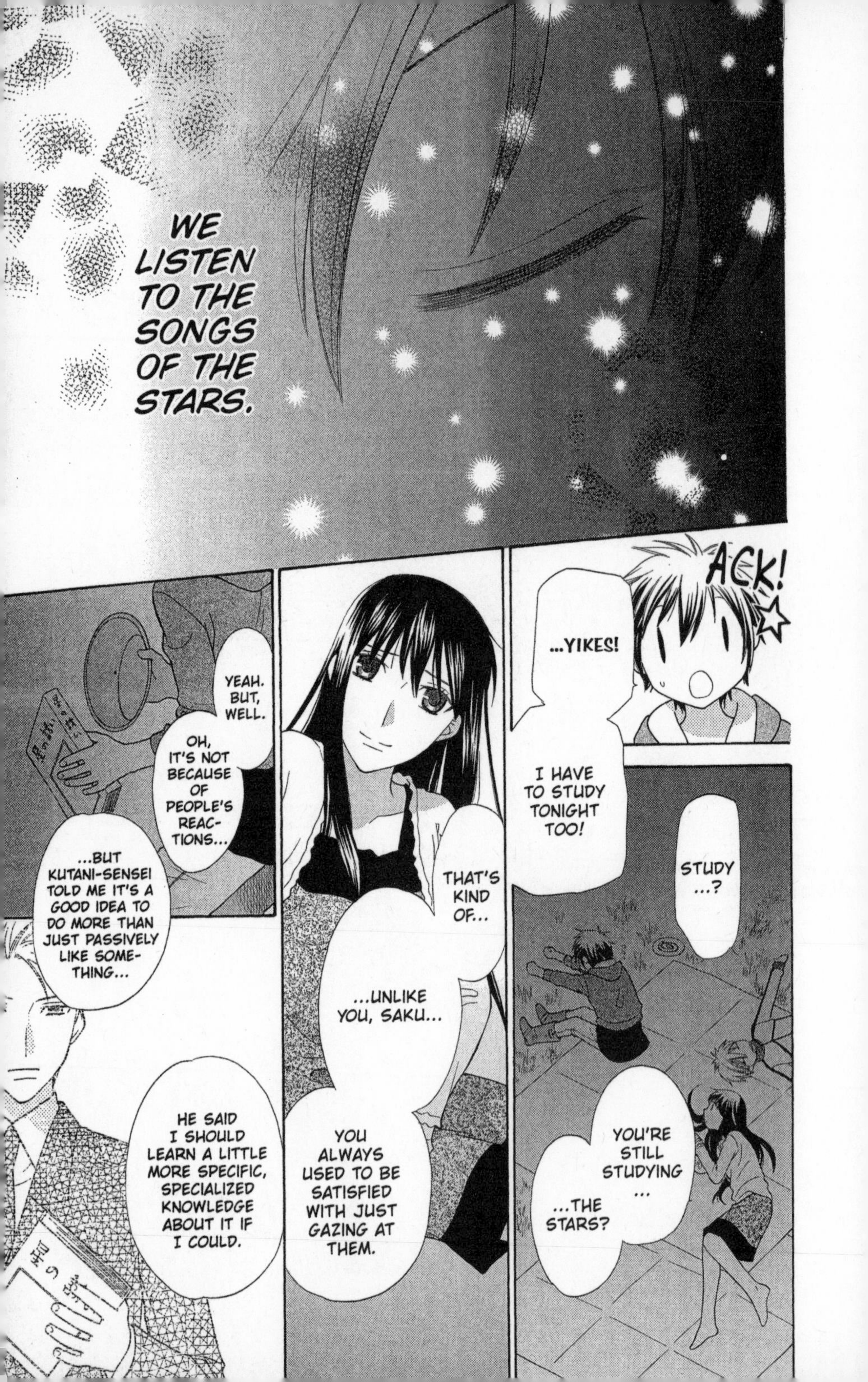
WE LISTEN TO THE SONGS OF THE STARS.
ACK!
...YIKES!
I HAVE TO STUDY TONIGHT TOO!
STUDY ...?
YOU'RE STILL STUDYING ...
...THE STARS?
THAT'S KIND OF...
...UNLIKE YOU, SAKU...
YOU ALWAYS USED TO BE SATISFIED WITH JUST GAZING AT THEM.
YEAH. BUT, WELL.
OH, IT'S NOT BECAUSE OF PEOPLE'S REAC-TIONS...
...BUT KUTANI-SENSEI TOLD ME IT'S A GOOD IDEA TO DO MORE THAN JUST PASSIVELY LIKE SOME-THING...
HE SAID I SHOULD LEARN A LITTLE MORE SPECIFIC, SPECIALIZED KNOWLEDGE ABOUT IT IF I COULD.

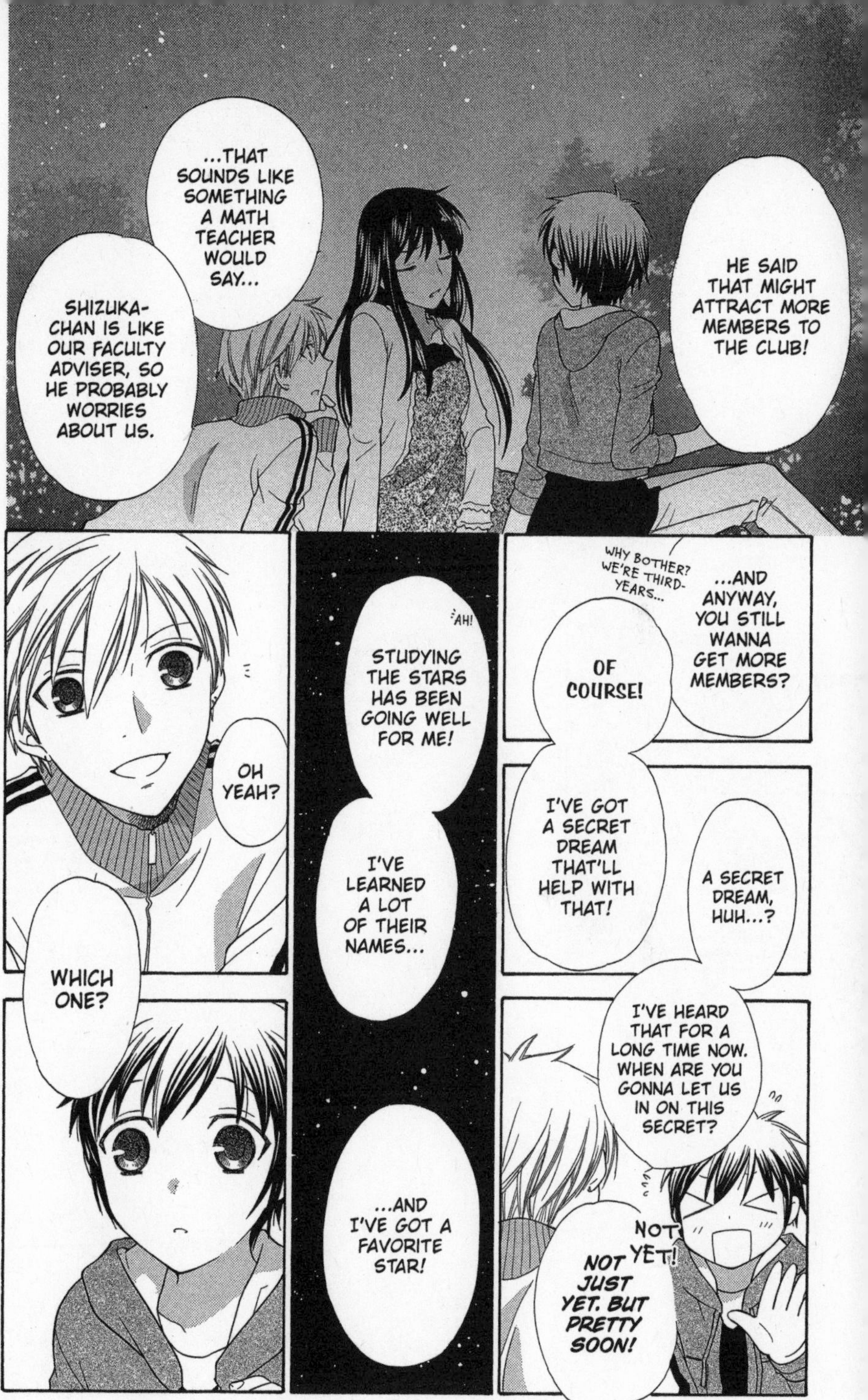
HE SAID THAT MIGHT ATTRACT MORE MEMBERS TO THE CLUB!
...THAT SOUNDS LIKE SOMETHING A MATH TEACHER WOULD SAY...
SHIZUKA-CHAN IS LIKE OUR FACULTY ADVISER, SO HE PROBABLY WORRIES ABOUT US.
...AND ANYWAY, YOU STILL WANNA GET MORE MEMBERS?
WHY BOTHER? WE'RE THIRD-YEARS...
OF COURSE!
I'VE GOT A SECRET DREAM THAT'LL HELP WITH THAT!
A SECRET DREAM, HUH...?
I'VE HEARD THAT FOR A LONG TIME NOW. WHEN ARE YOU GONNA LET US IN ON THIS SECRET?
NOT YET!
NOT JUST YET. BUT PRETTY SOON!
AH!
STUDYING THE STARS HAS BEEN GOING WELL FOR ME!
I'VE LEARNED A LOT OF THEIR NAMES...
...AND I'VE GOT A FAVORITE STAR!
OH YEAH?
WHICH ONE?

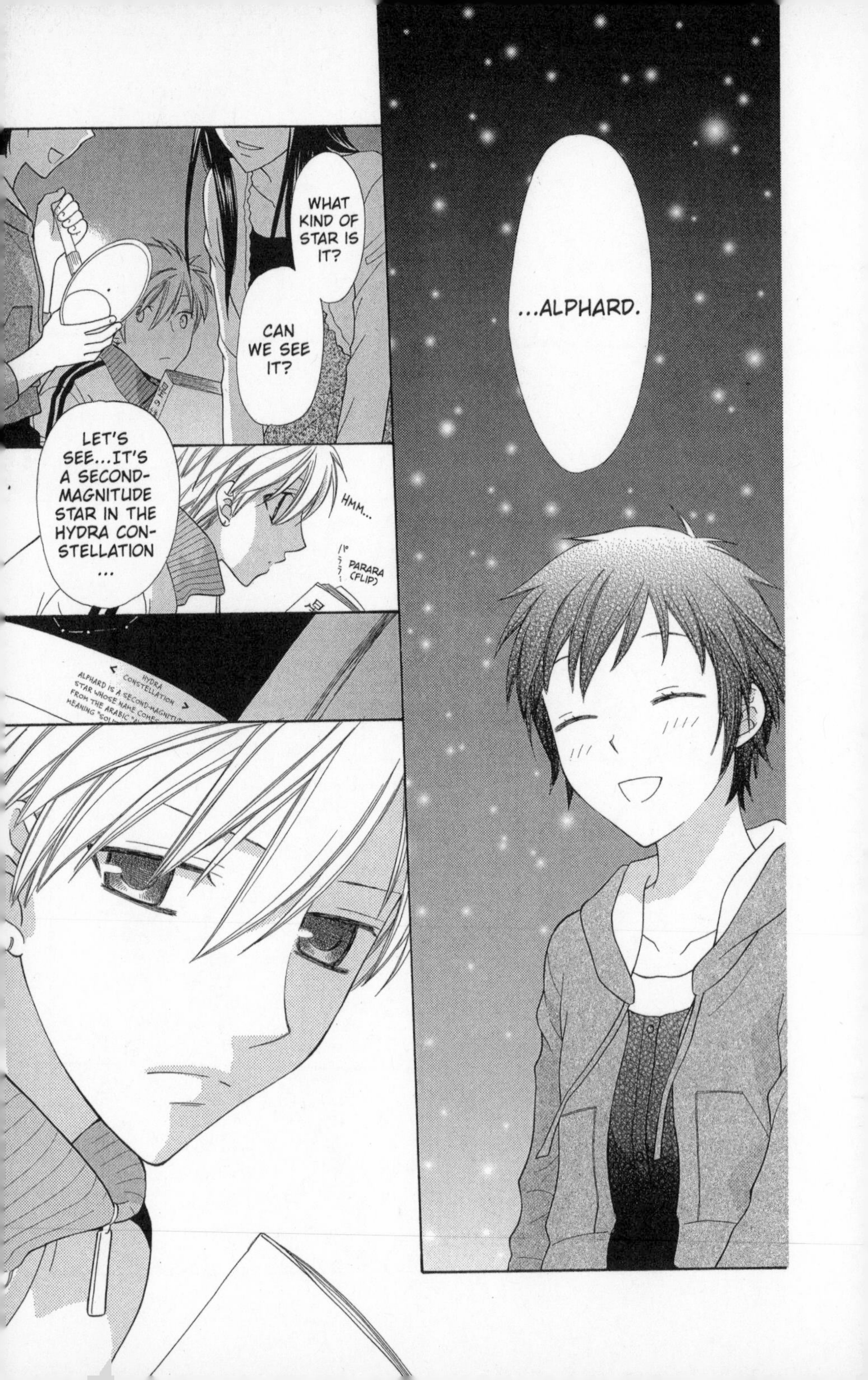
...ALPHARD.
WHAT KIND OF STAR IS IT?
CAN WE SEE IT?
LET'S SEE...IT'S A SECOND-MAGNITUDE STAR IN THE HYDRA CONSTELLATION ...
HMM...
PARARA (FLIP)
HYDRA CONSTELLATION

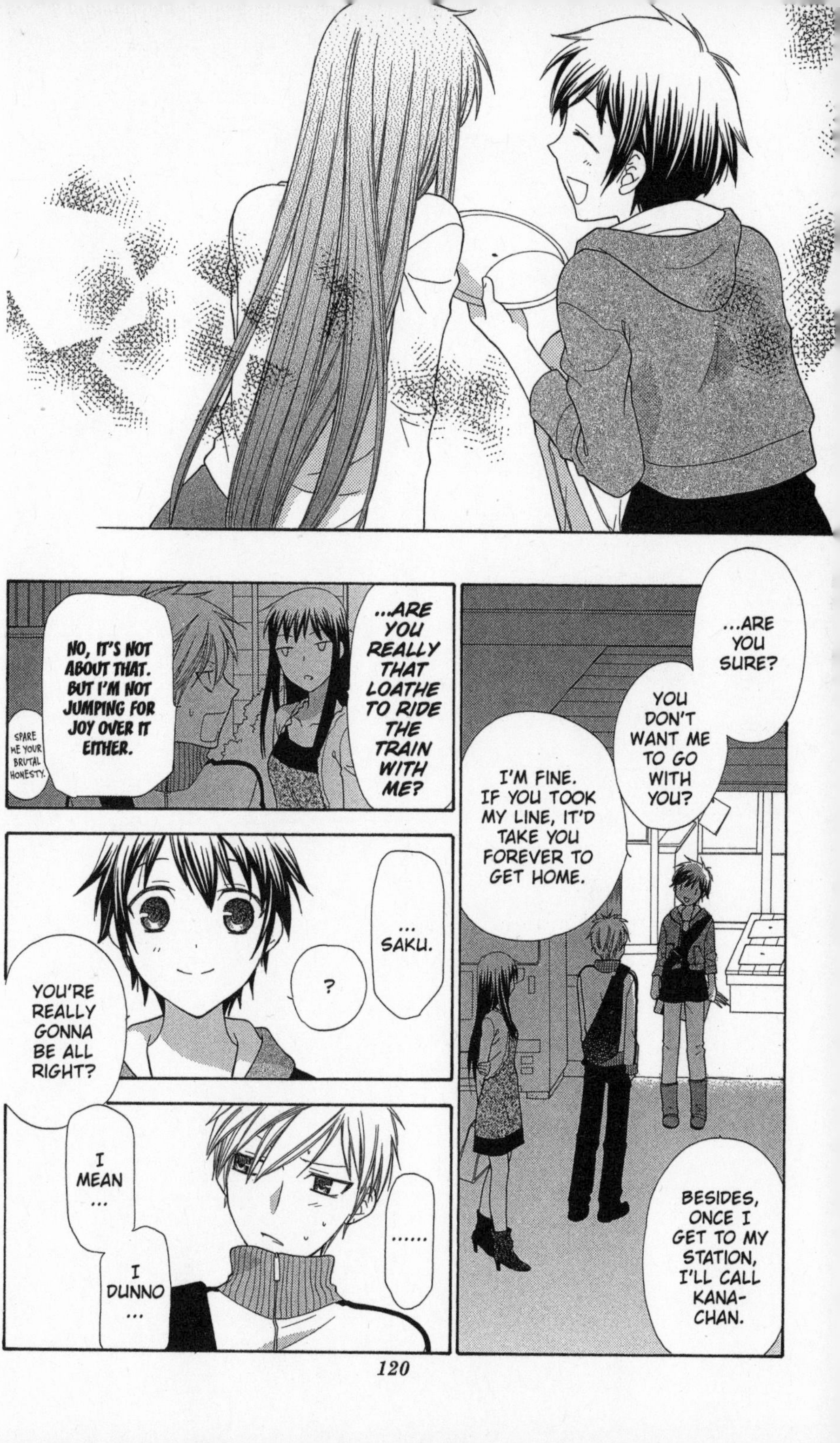
...ARE YOU SURE?
YOU DON'T WANT ME TO GO WITH YOU?
I'M FINE. IF YOU TOOK MY LINE, IT'D TAKE YOU FOREVER TO GET HOME.
BESIDES, ONCE I GET TO MY STATION, I'LL CALL KANA-CHAN.
...ARE YOU REALLY THAT LOATHE TO RIDE THE TRAIN WITH ME?
NO, IT'S NOT ABOUT THAT. BUT I'M NOT JUMPING FOR JOY OVER IT EITHER.
SPARE ME YOUR BRUTAL HONESTY.
... SAKU.
?
YOU'RE REALLY GONNA BE ALL RIGHT?
......
I MEAN ...
I DUNNO ...

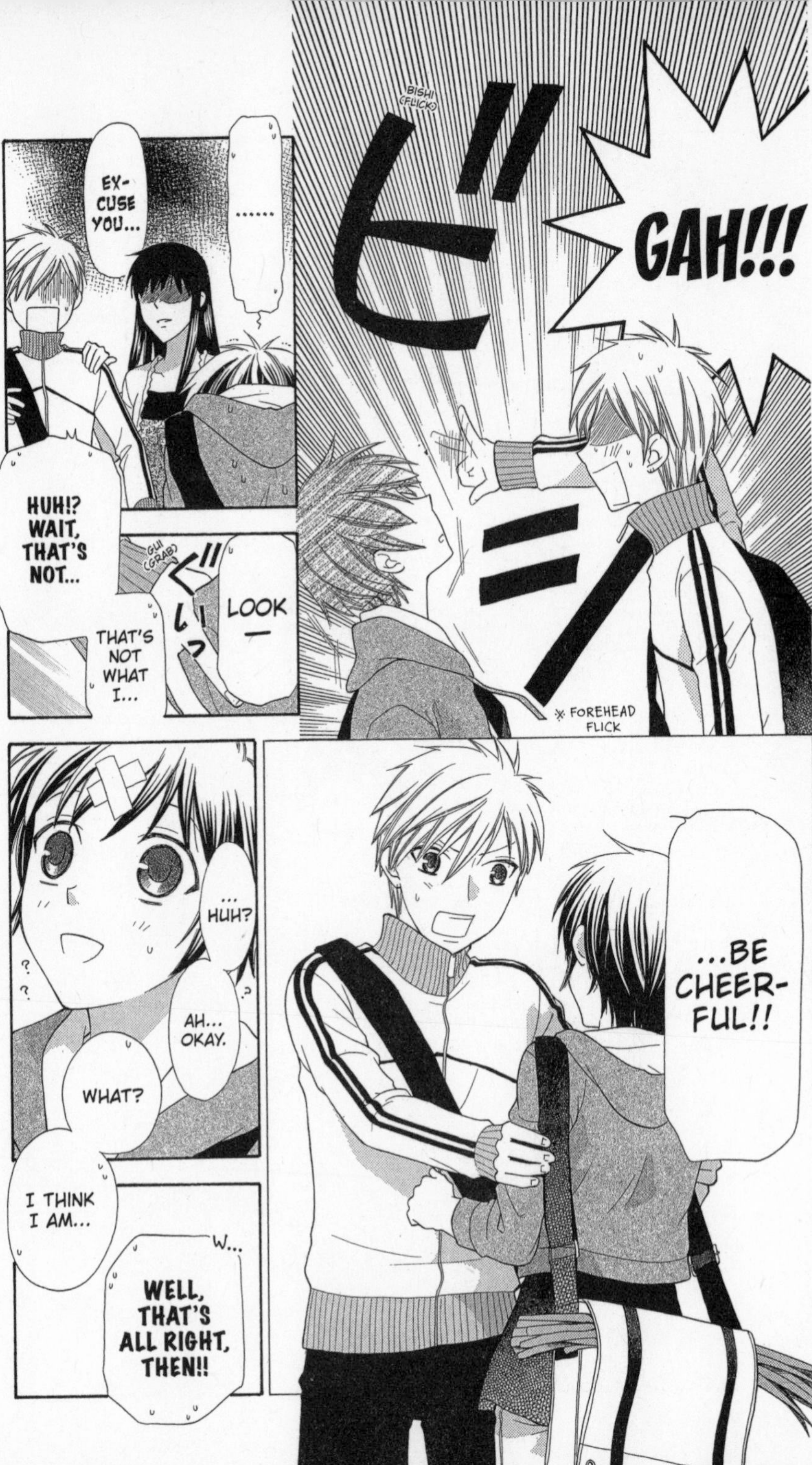
BISHI (FLICK)
GAH!!!
※ FOREHEAD FLICK
......
EX-CUSE YOU...
HUH!? WAIT, THAT'S NOT...
GUI (GRAB)
LOOK—
THAT'S NOT WHAT I...
...BE CHEERFUL!!
... HUH?
AH... OKAY.
WHAT?
I THINK I AM...
W...
WELL, THAT'S ALL RIGHT, THEN!!

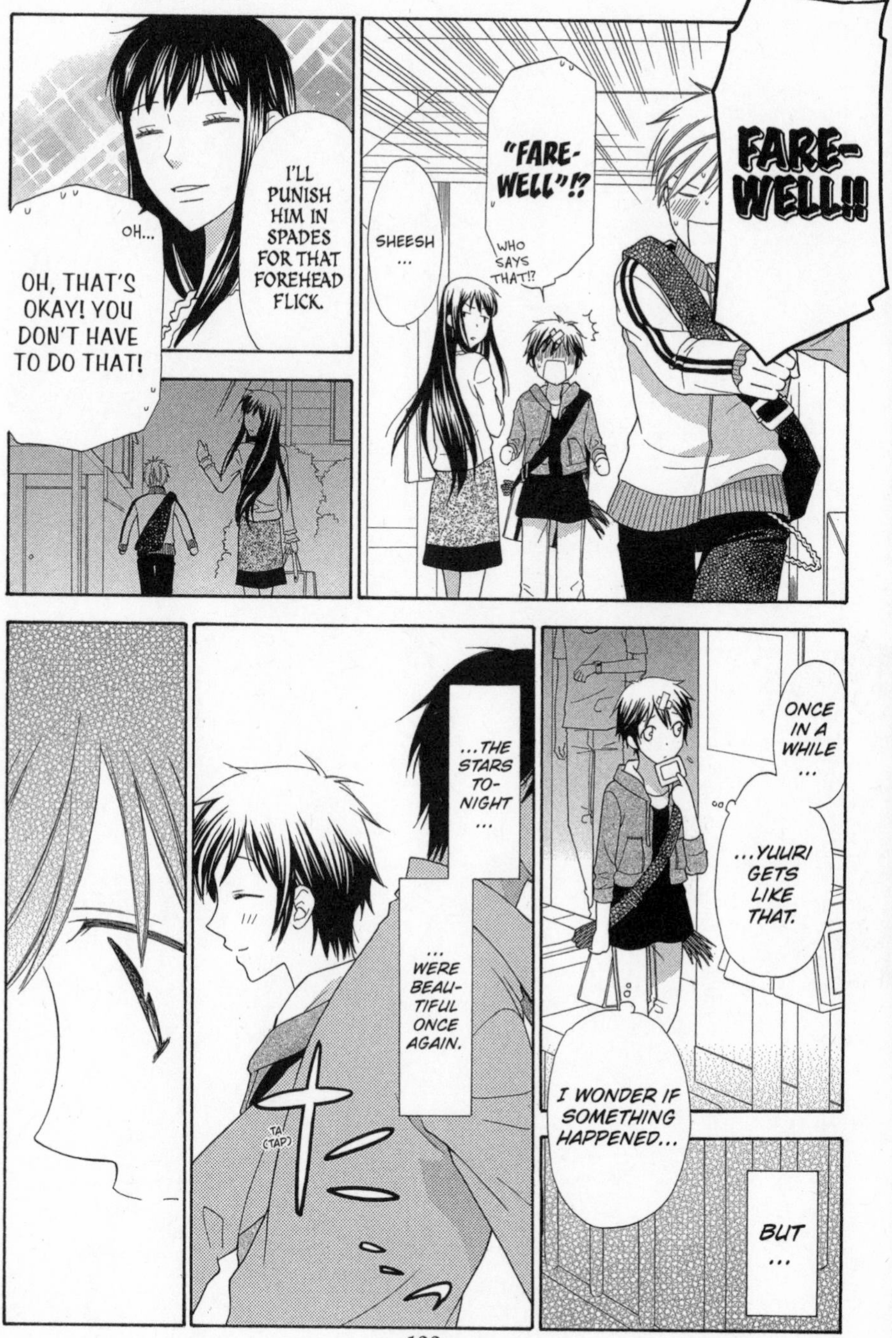
FARE-WELL!!
"FARE-WELL"!?
WHO SAYS THAT!?
SHEESH...
I'LL PUNISH HIM IN SPADES FOR THAT FOREHEAD FLICK.
OH...
OH, THAT'S OKAY! YOU DON'T HAVE TO DO THAT!
ONCE IN A WHILE...
...YUURI GETS LIKE THAT.
I WONDER IF SOMETHING HAPPENED...
BUT...
...THE STARS TO-NIGHT...
...WERE BEAU-TIFUL ONCE AGAIN.
TA (TAP)

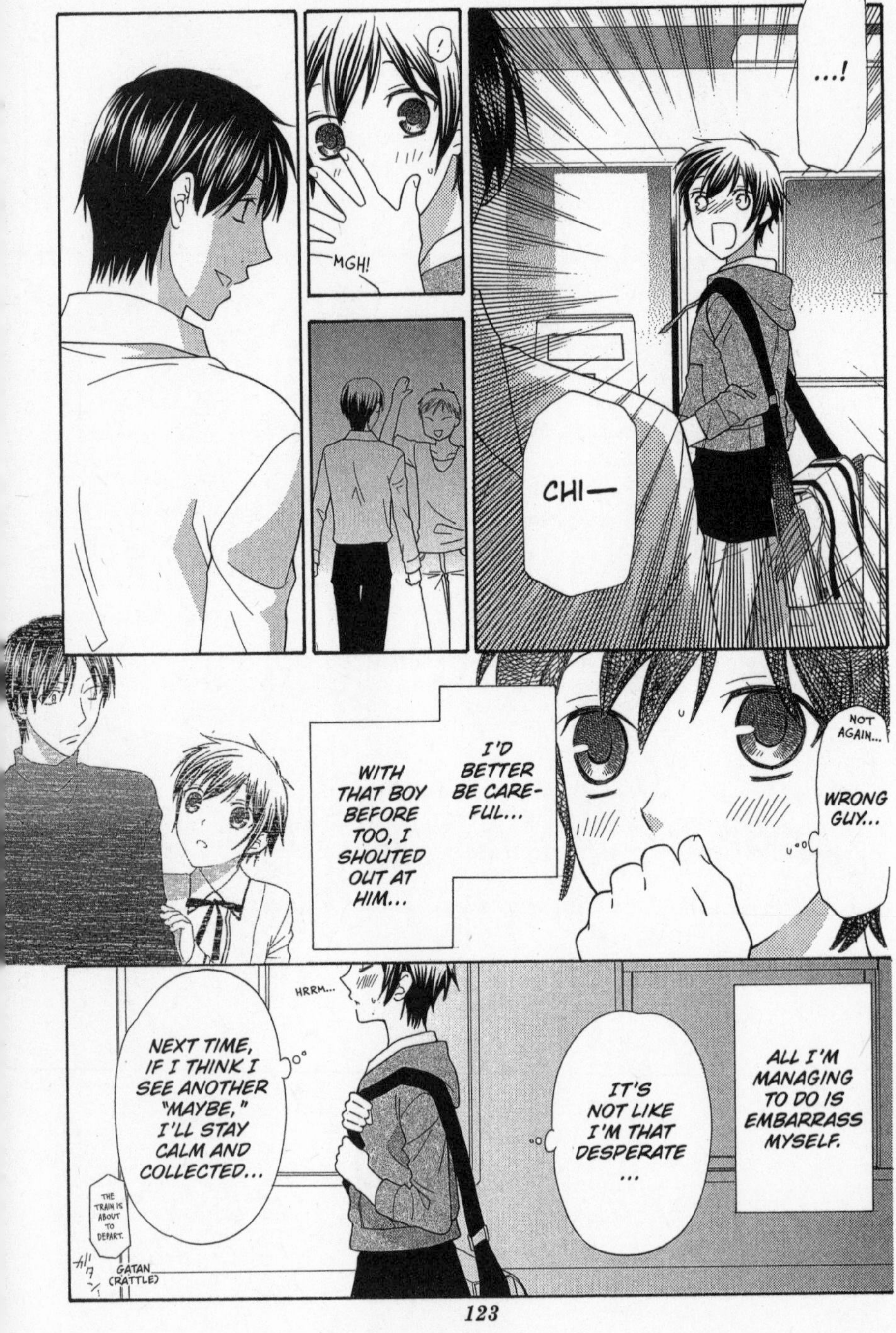
...!
CHI—
!
MGH!
NOT AGAIN...
WRONG GUY...
WITH THAT BOY BEFORE TOO, I SHOUTED OUT AT HIM...
I'D BETTER BE CARE-FUL...
ALL I'M MANAGING TO DO IS EMBARRASS MYSELF.
IT'S NOT LIKE I'M THAT DESPERATE...
HRRM...
NEXT TIME, IF I THINK I SEE ANOTHER "MAYBE," I'LL STAY CALM AND COLLECTED...
THE TRAIN IS ABOUT TO DEPART.
GATAN (RATTLE)

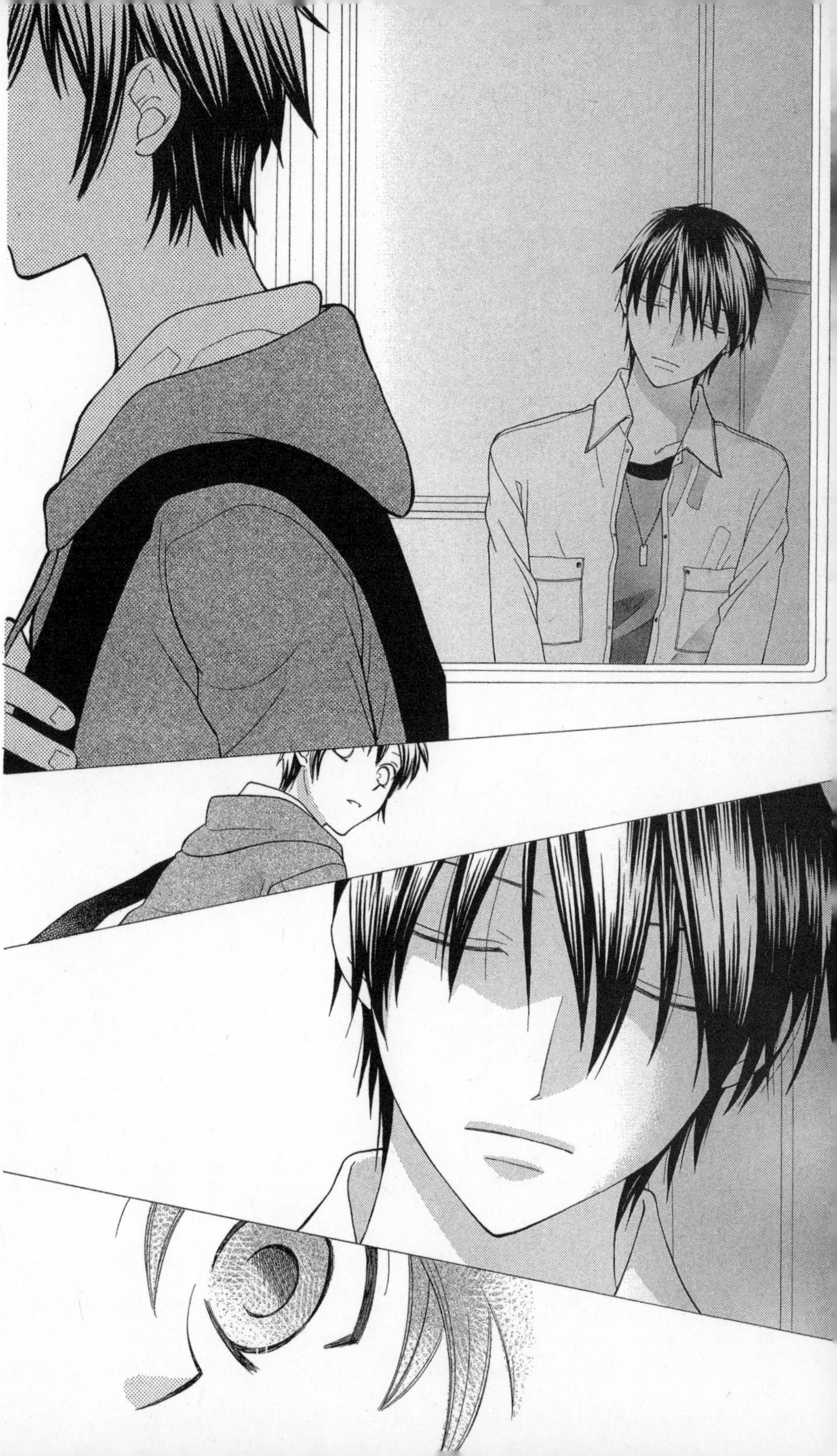

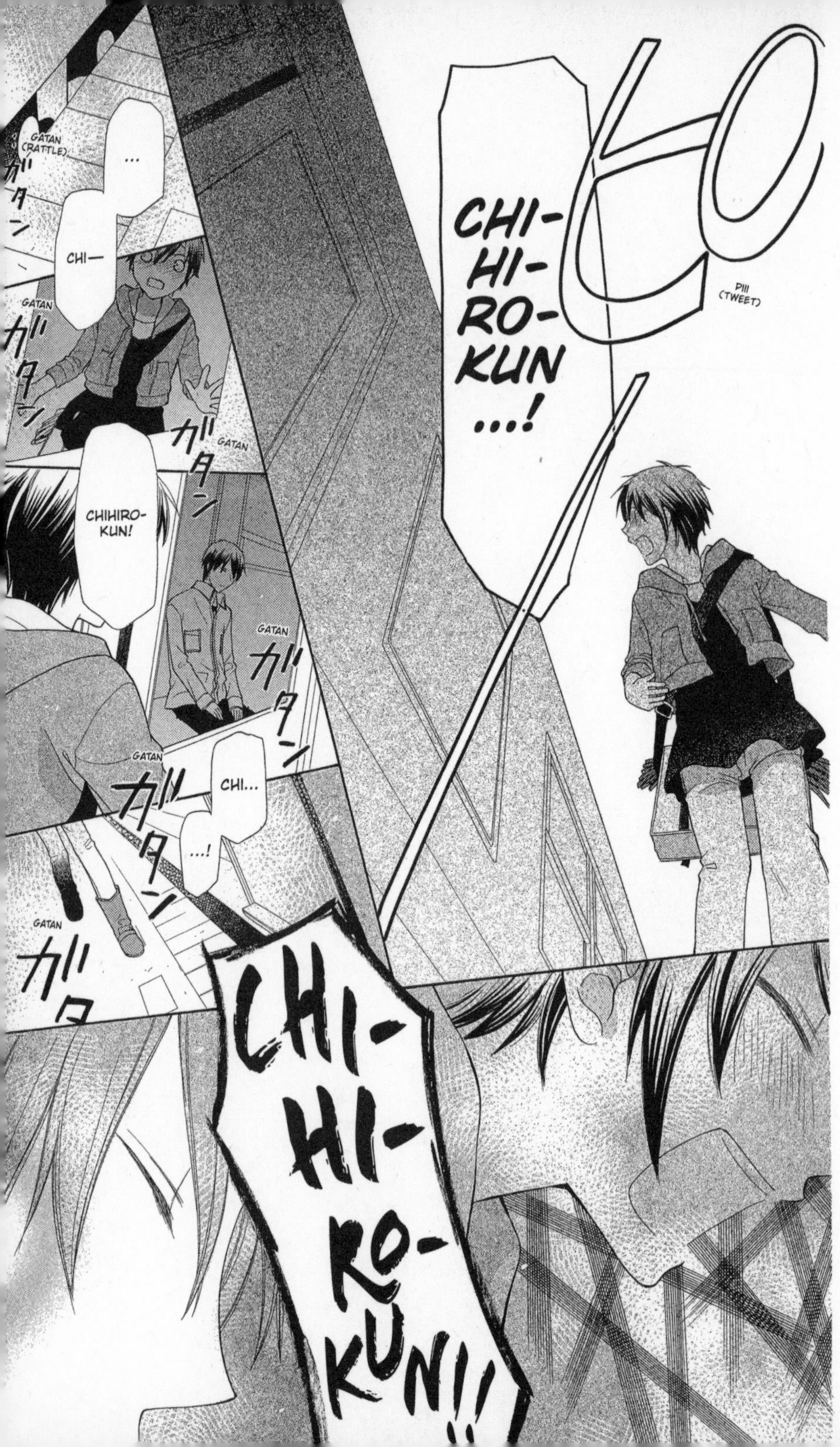
CHI-HI-RO-KUN...!
PIII (TWEET)
GATAN (RATTLE)
...
CHI—
GATAN
GATAN
CHIHIRO-KUN!
GATAN
GATAN
CHI...
...!
GATAN
CHI-HI-RO-KUN!!

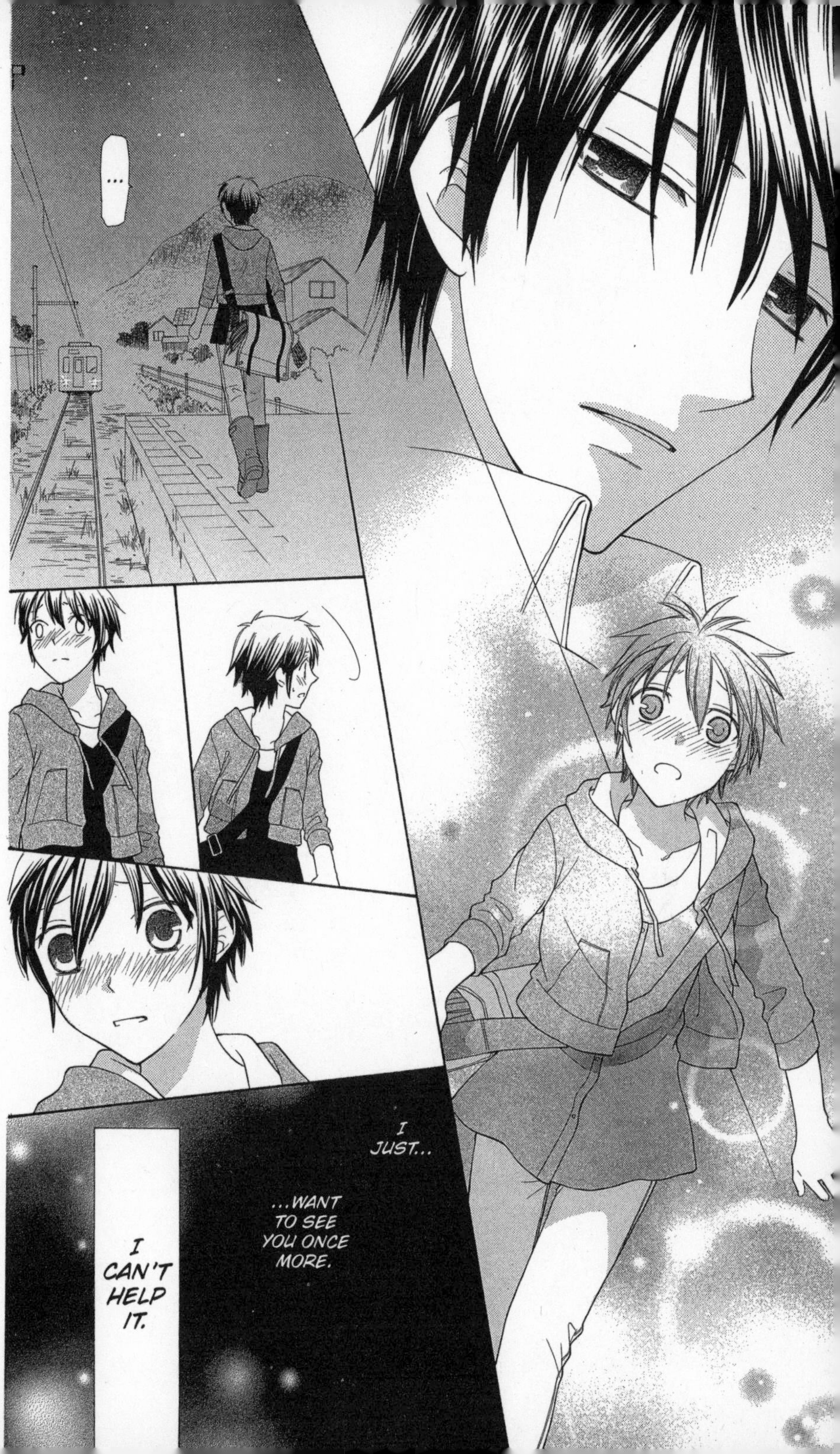
I JUST...
...WANT TO SEE YOU ONCE MORE.
...
I CAN'T HELP IT.

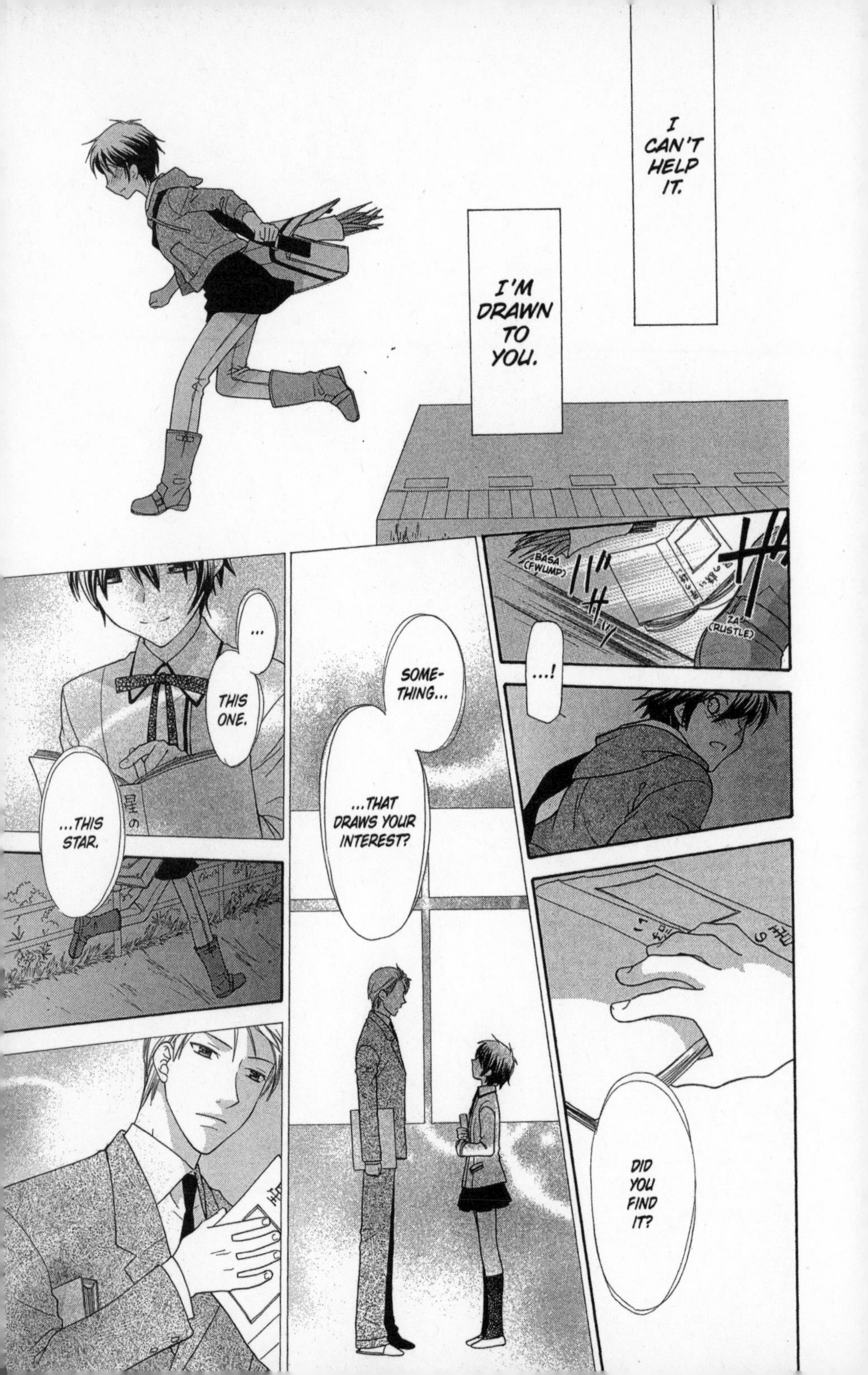
I CAN'T HELP IT.
I'M DRAWN TO YOU.
ZA (RUSTLE)
BASA (FWUMP)
...!
DID YOU FIND IT?
SOMETHING...
...THAT DRAWS YOUR INTEREST?
...
THIS ONE.
...THIS STAR.

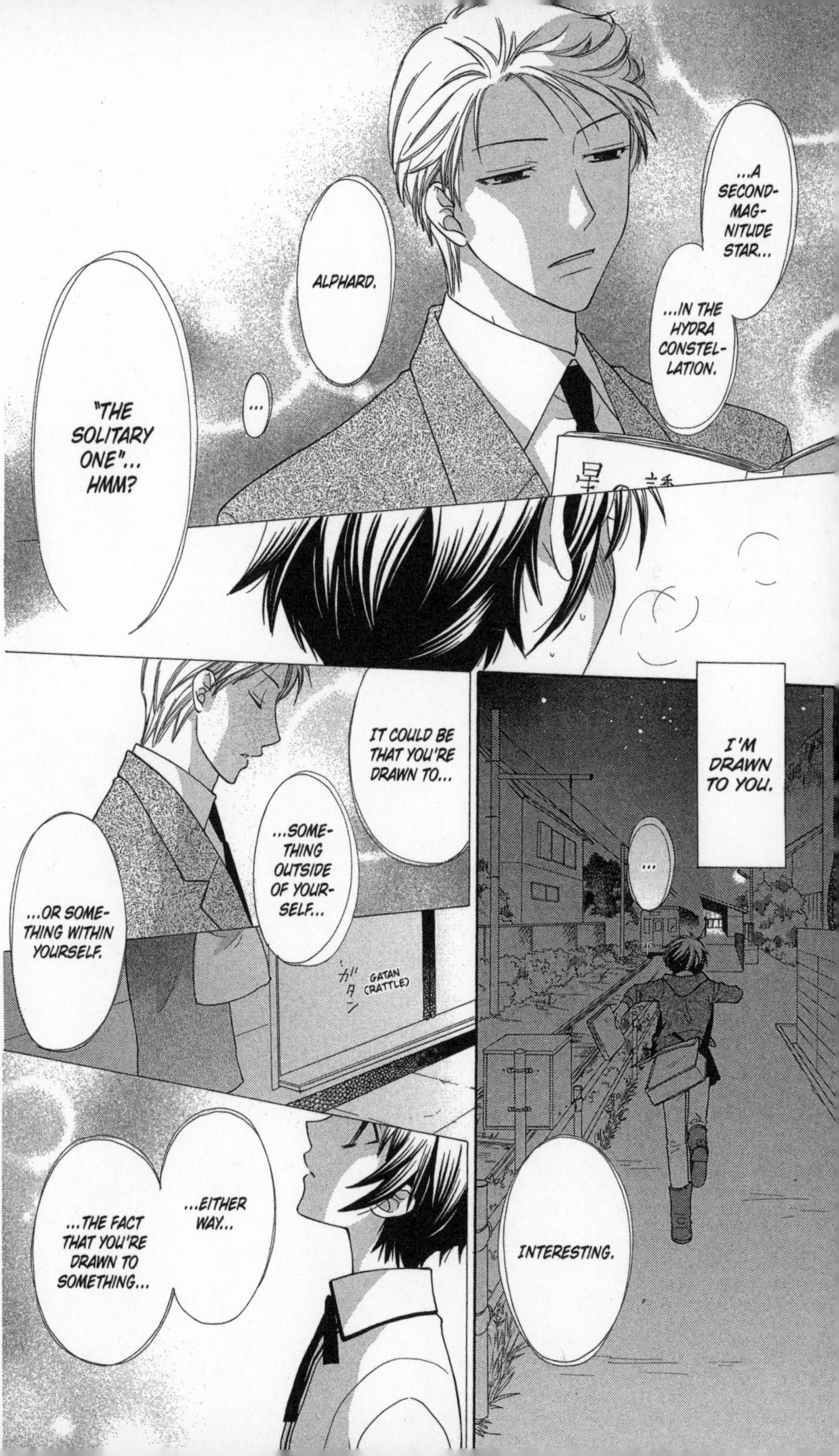
...A SECOND-MAGNITUDE STAR...
...IN THE HYDRA CONSTELLATION.
ALPHARD.
...
"THE SOLITARY ONE"... HMM?
I'M DRAWN TO YOU.
...
INTERESTING.
IT COULD BE THAT YOU'RE DRAWN TO...
...SOMETHING OUTSIDE OF YOURSELF...
...OR SOMETHING WITHIN YOURSELF.
GATAN (RATTLE)
...EITHER WAY...
...THE FACT THAT YOU'RE DRAWN TO SOMETHING...

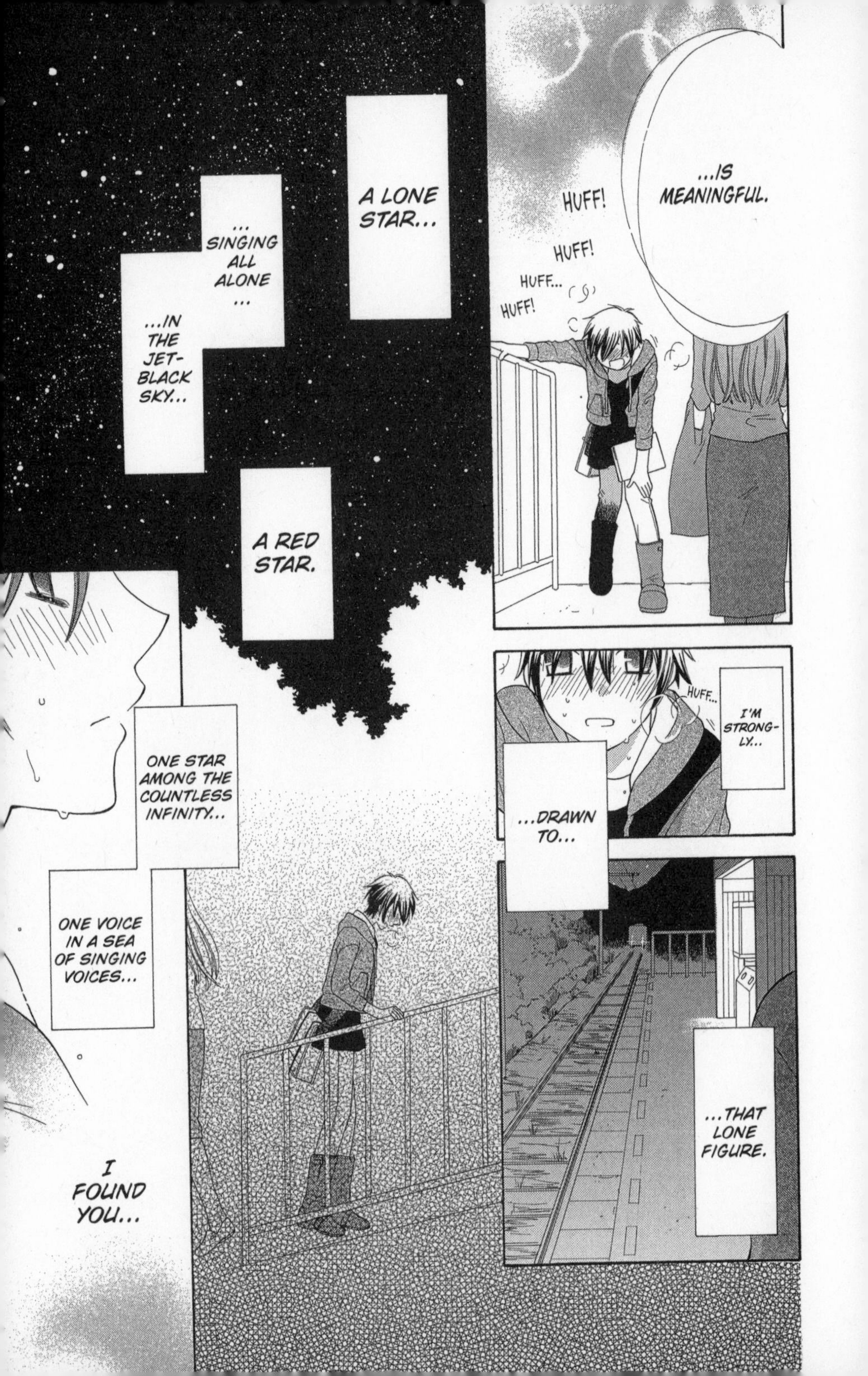
...IS MEANINGFUL.
HUFF!
HUFF!
HUFF...
HUFF!
A LONE STAR...
...SINGING ALL ALONE...
...IN THE JET-BLACK SKY...
A RED STAR.
HUFF...
I'M STRONGLY...
...DRAWN TO...
...THAT LONE FIGURE.
ONE STAR AMONG THE COUNTLESS INFINITY...
ONE VOICE IN A SEA OF SINGING VOICES...
I FOUND YOU...

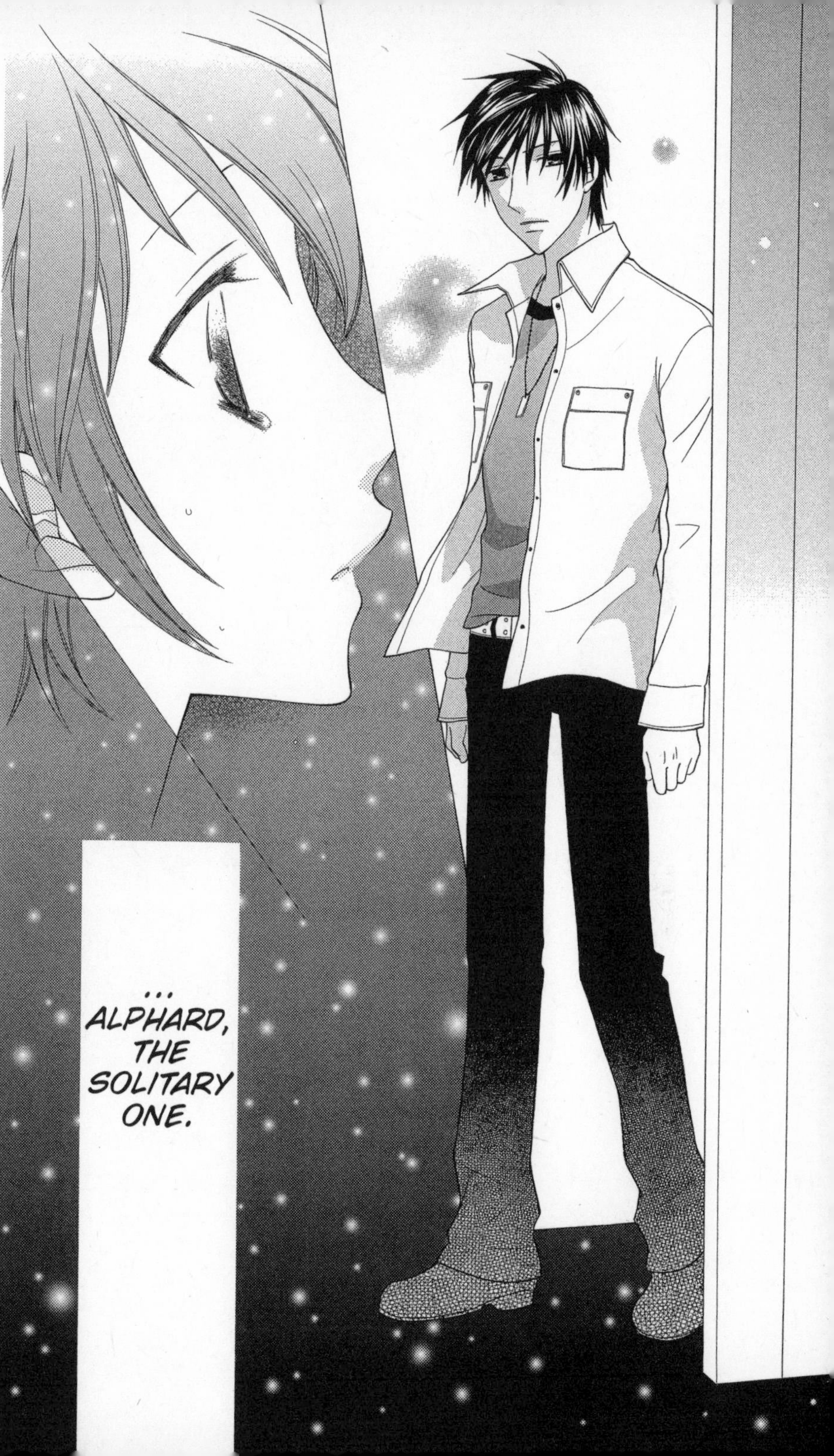
...
ALPHARD, THE SOLITARY ONE.

Chapter 4

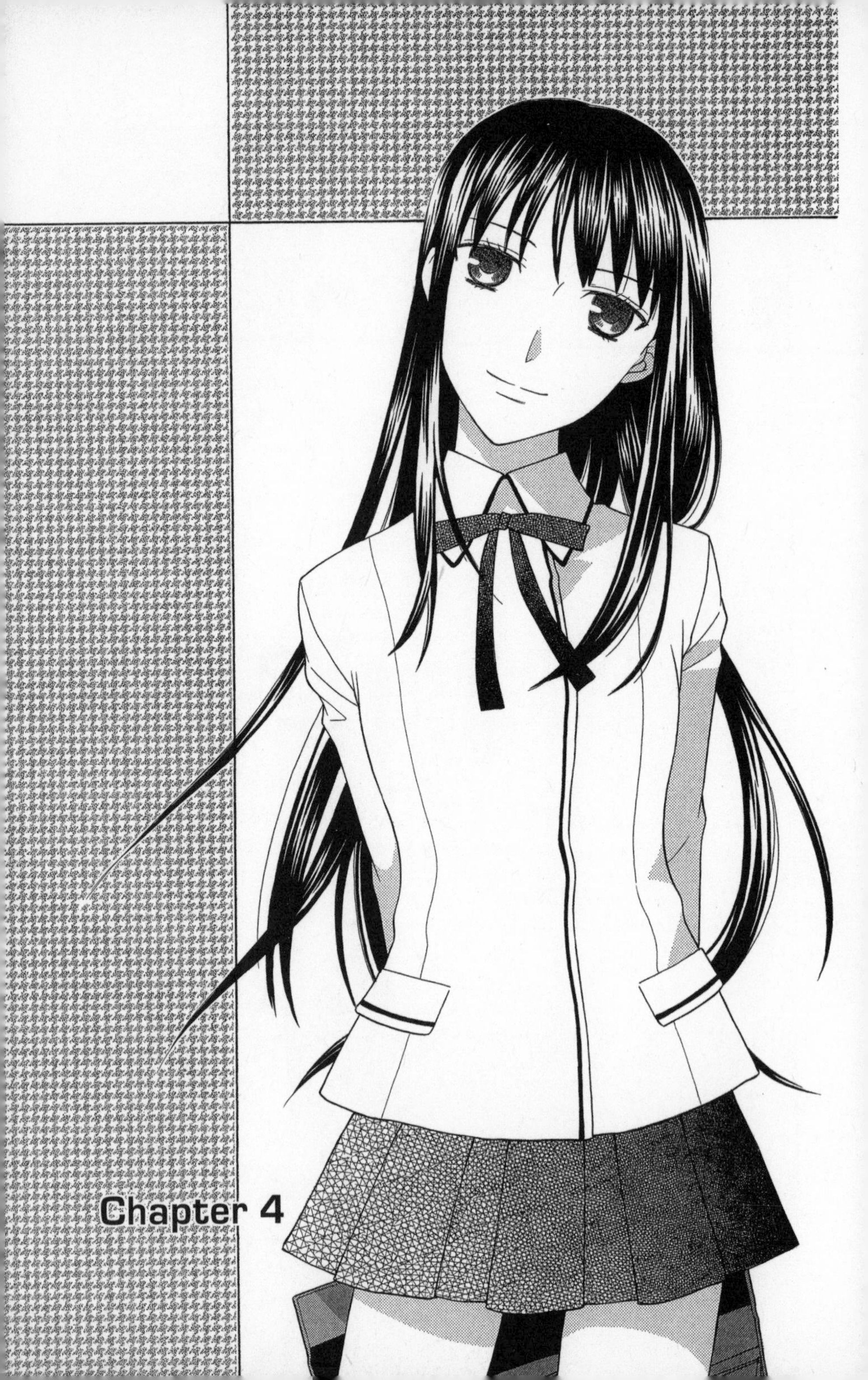

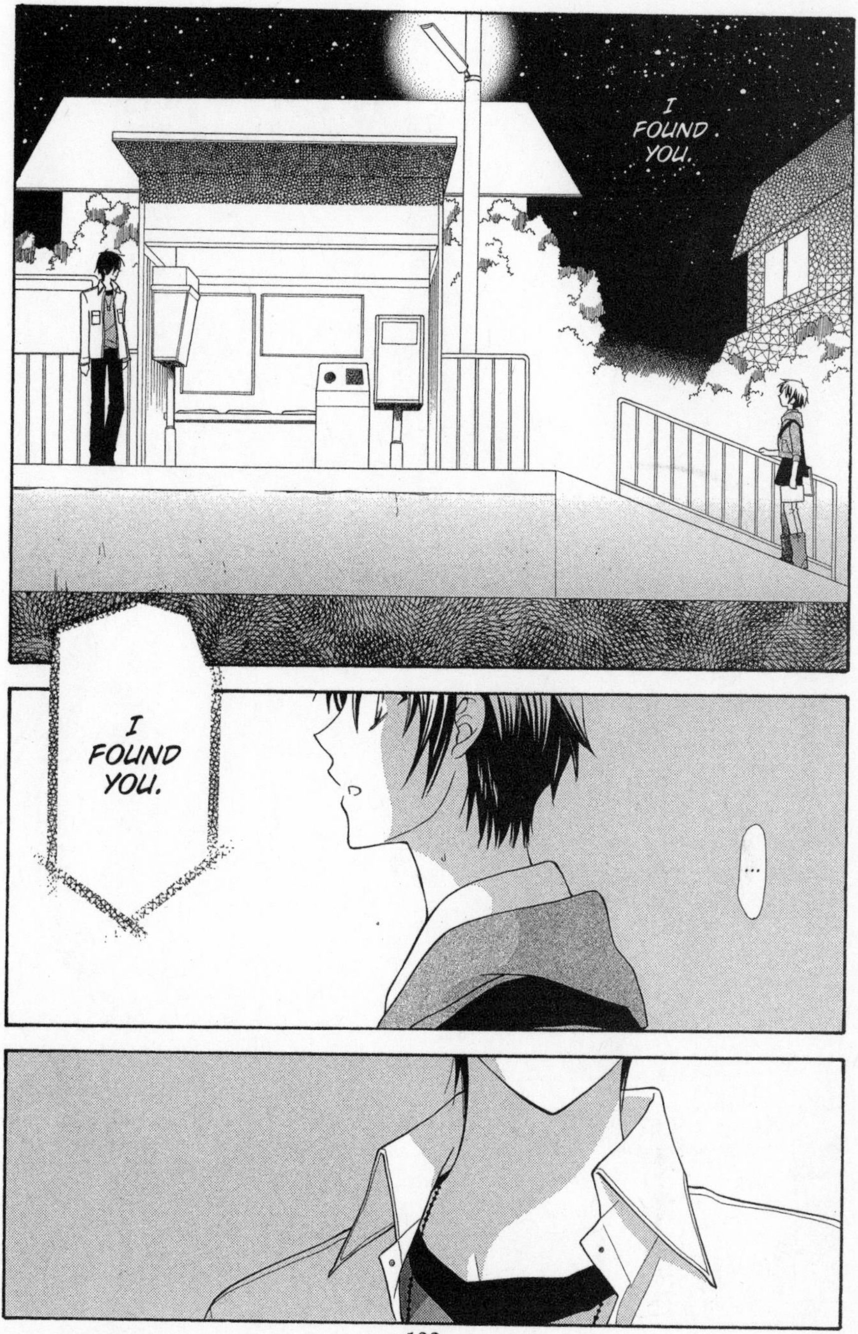
I FOUND YOU.
I FOUND YOU.
...

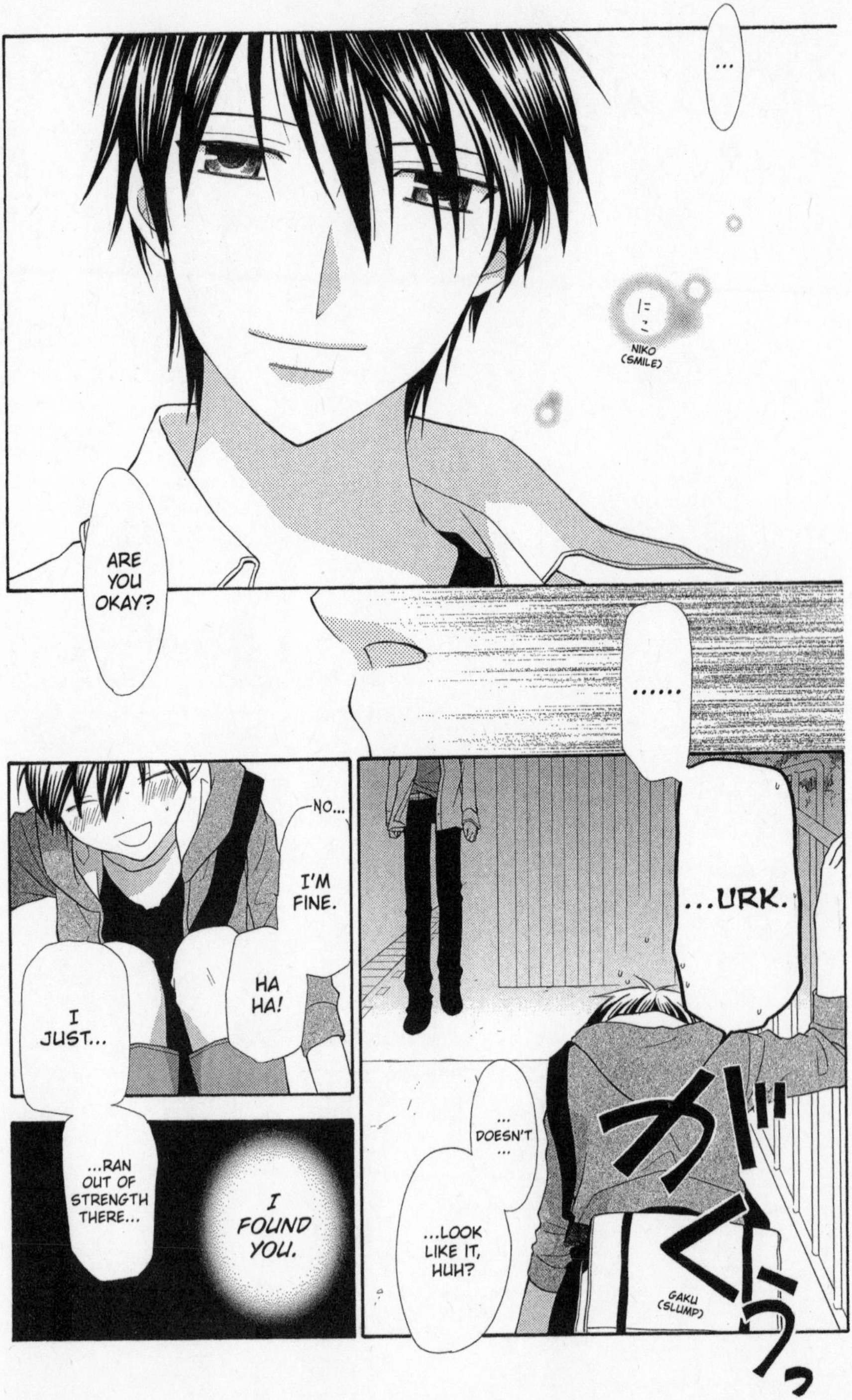
...
にこ
NIKO (SMILE)
ARE YOU OKAY?
......
...URK.
... DOESN'T ...
...LOOK LIKE IT, HUH?
がくっ
GAKU (SLUMP)
NO...
I'M FINE.
HA HA!
I JUST...
...RAN OUT OF STRENGTH THERE...
I FOUND YOU.

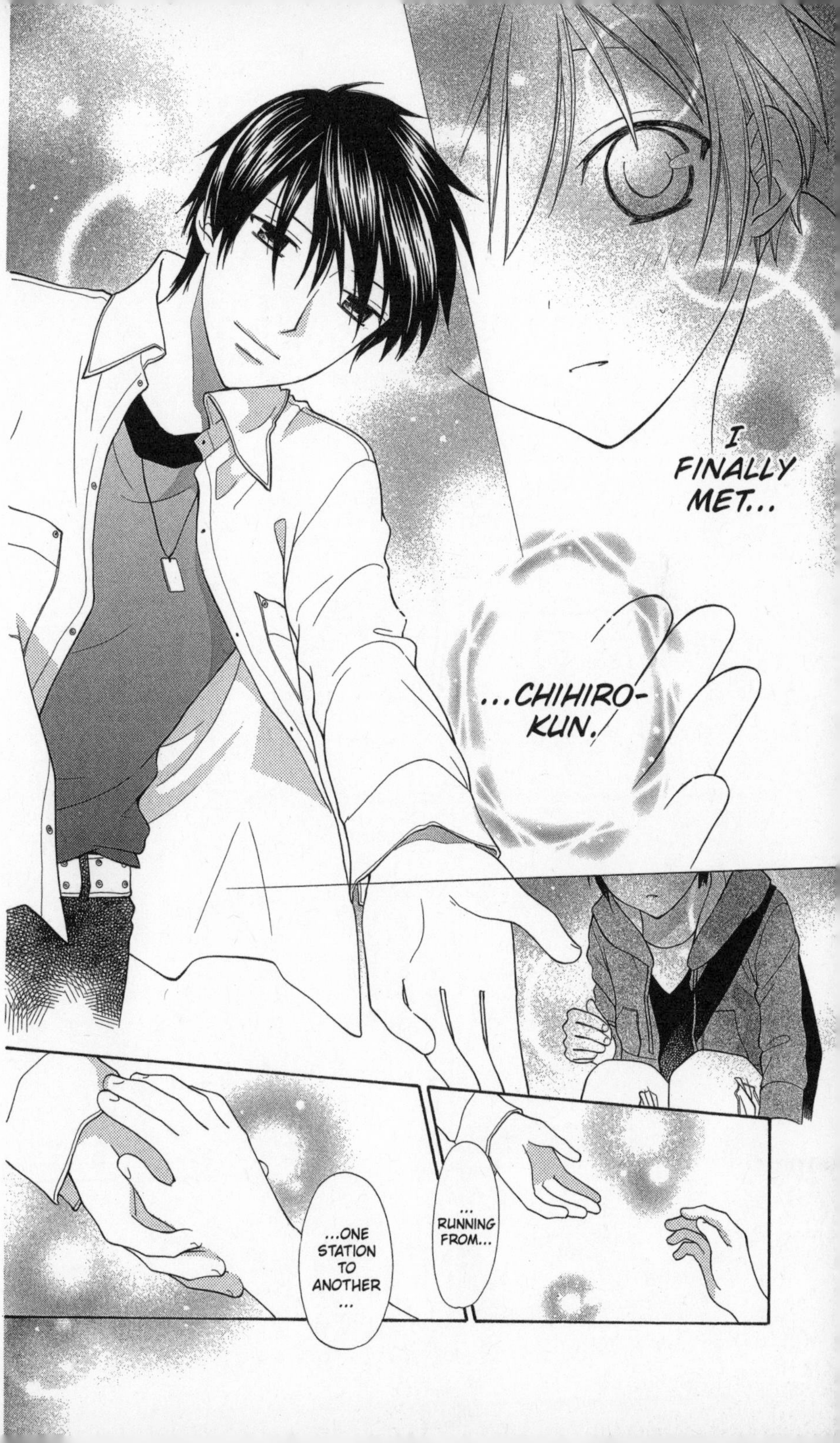
I FINALLY MET...
...CHIHIRO-KUN.
...RUNNING FROM...
...ONE STATION TO ANOTHER...

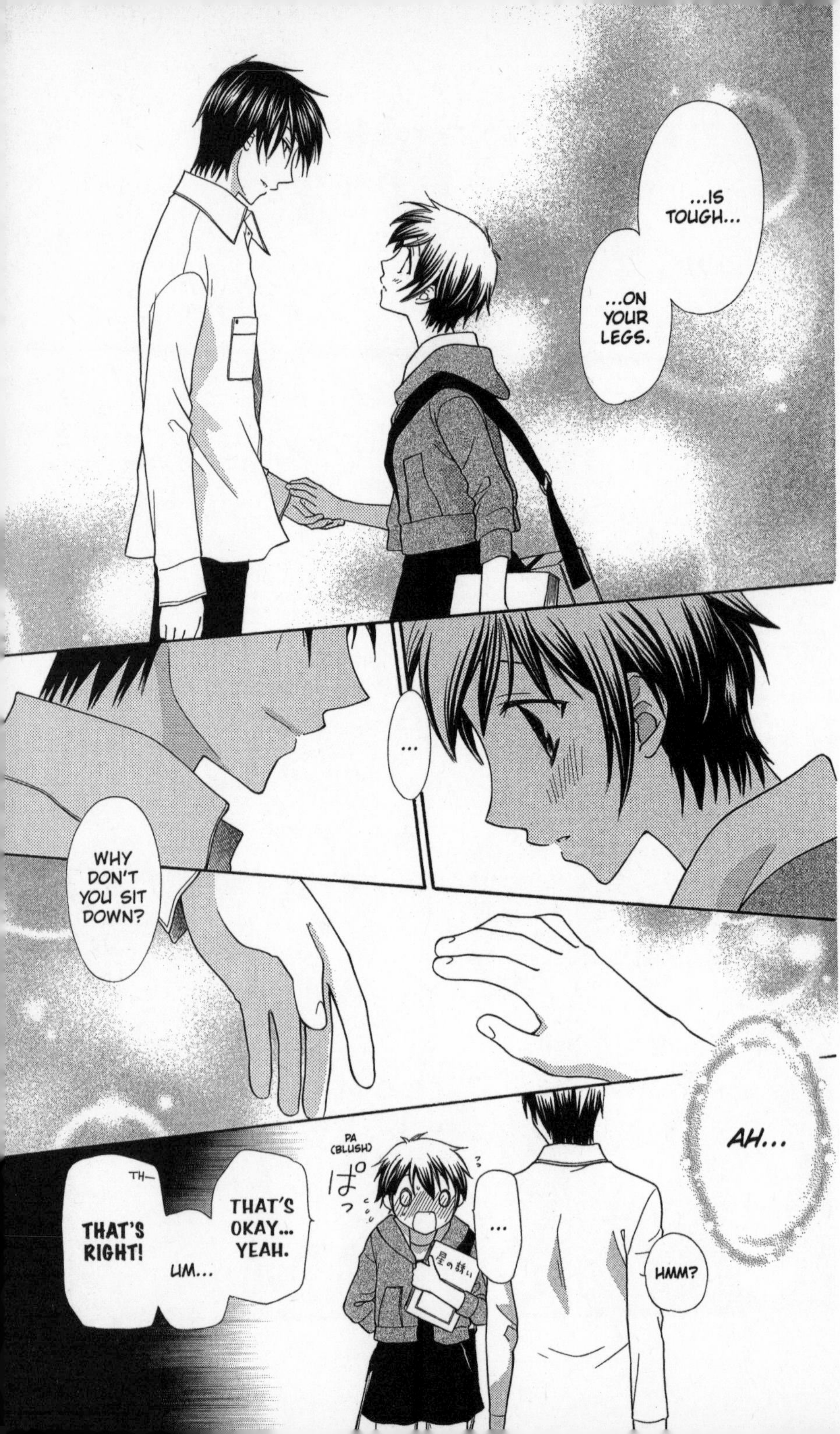
...IS TOUGH...
...ON YOUR LEGS.
...
WHY DON'T YOU SIT DOWN?
AH...
HMM?
...
PA (BLUSH)
ぱっ
星の誘い
THAT'S OKAY... YEAH.
UM...
TH— THAT'S RIGHT!

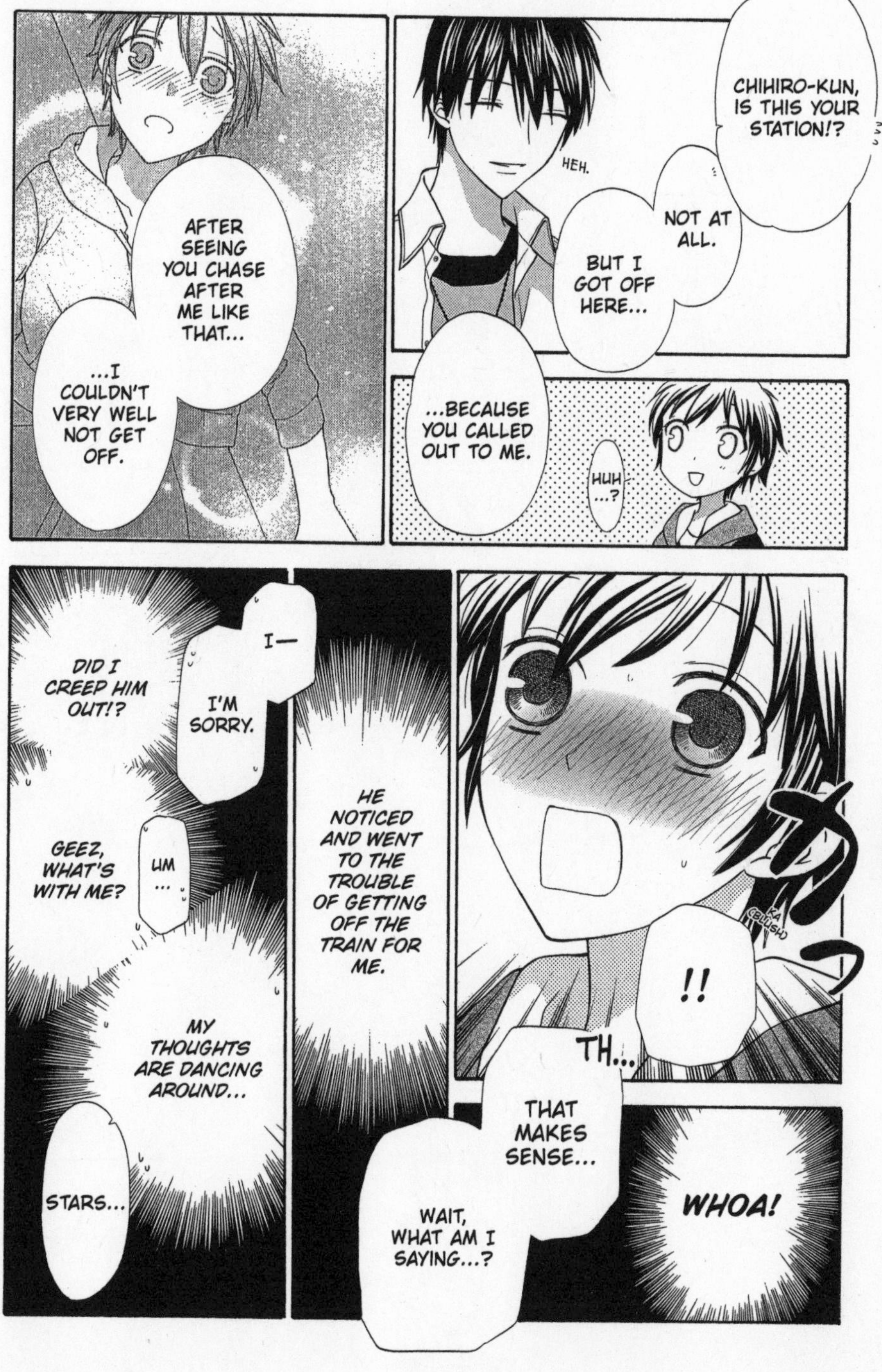
CHIHIRO-KUN, IS THIS YOUR STATION!?
HEH.
NOT AT ALL.
BUT I GOT OFF HERE...
...BECAUSE YOU CALLED OUT TO ME.
HUH ...?
AFTER SEEING YOU CHASE AFTER ME LIKE THAT...
...I COULDN'T VERY WELL NOT GET OFF.
KA (BLUSH)
!!
TH...
THAT MAKES SENSE...
WHOA!
WAIT, WHAT AM I SAYING...?
HE NOTICED AND WENT TO THE TROUBLE OF GETTING OFF THE TRAIN FOR ME.
I—
DID I CREEP HIM OUT!?
I'M SORRY.
UM ...
GEEZ, WHAT'S WITH ME?
MY THOUGHTS ARE DANCING AROUND...
STARS...

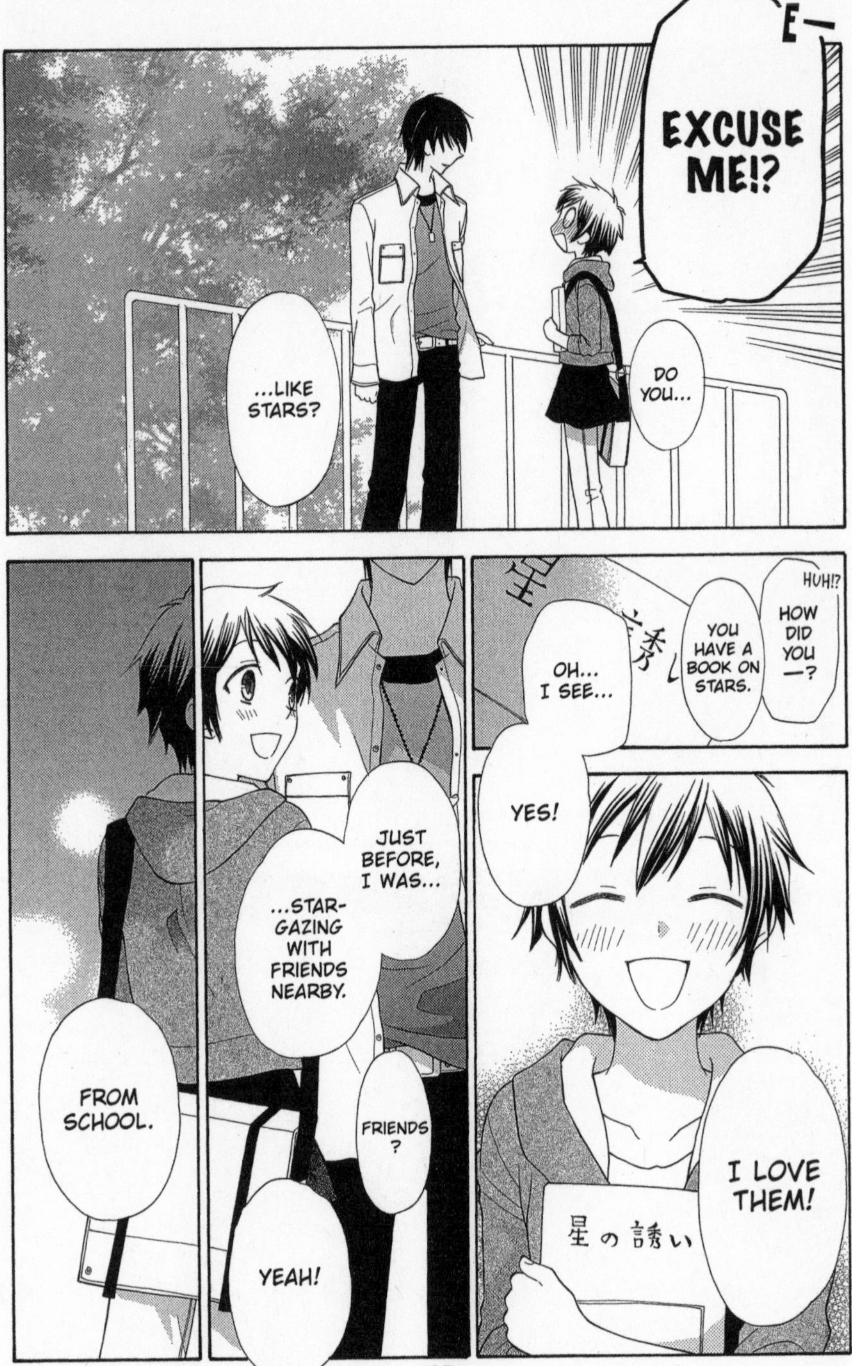
DO YOU...
...LIKE STARS?
E— EXCUSE ME!?
HUH!? HOW DID YOU—?
YOU HAVE A BOOK ON STARS.
OH... I SEE...
YES!
I LOVE THEM!
星の誘い
JUST BEFORE, I WAS...
...STAR-GAZING WITH FRIENDS NEARBY.
FRIENDS?
YEAH!
FROM SCHOOL.

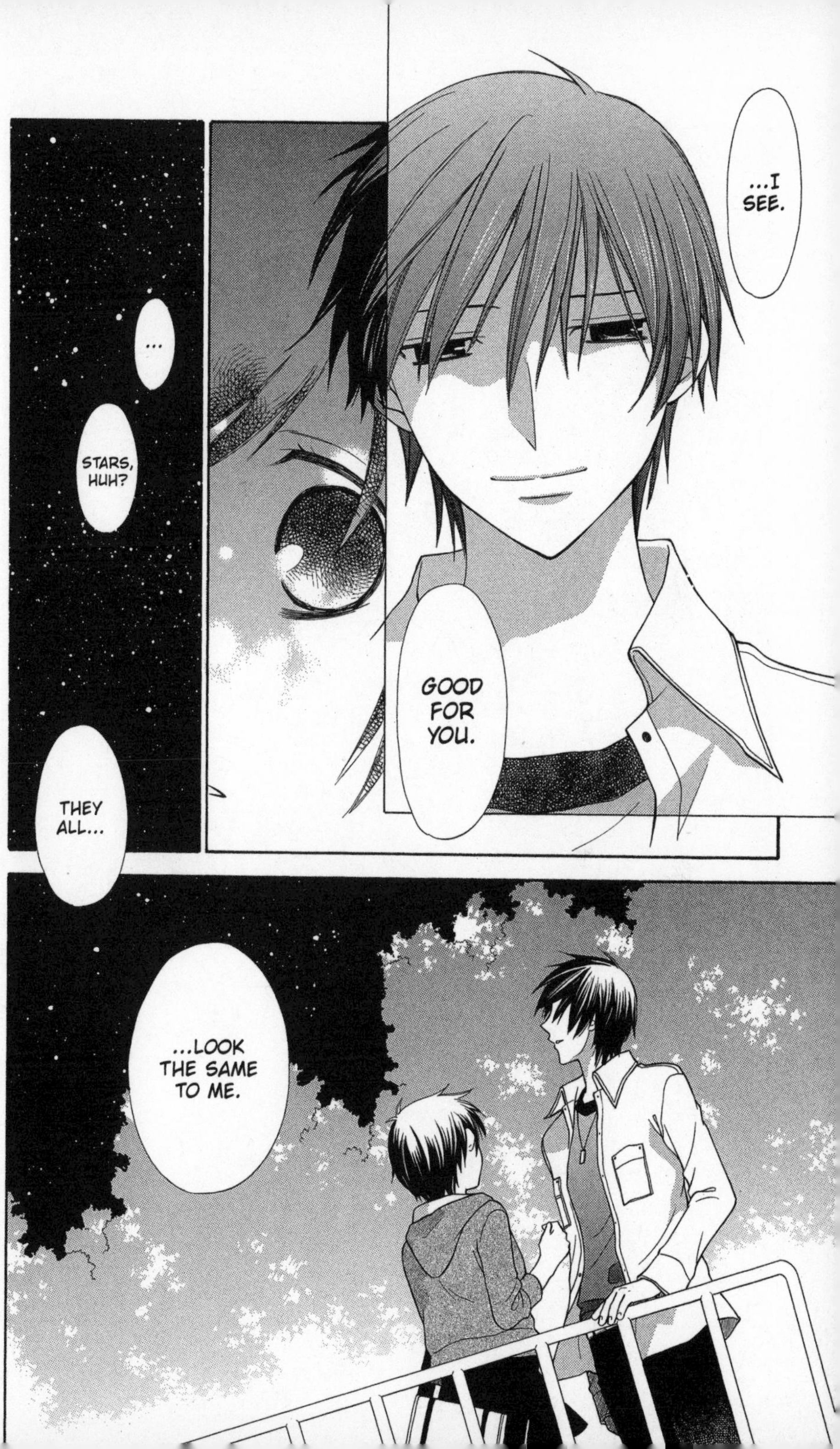
...I SEE.
GOOD FOR YOU.
...
STARS, HUH?
THEY ALL...
...LOOK THE SAME TO ME.

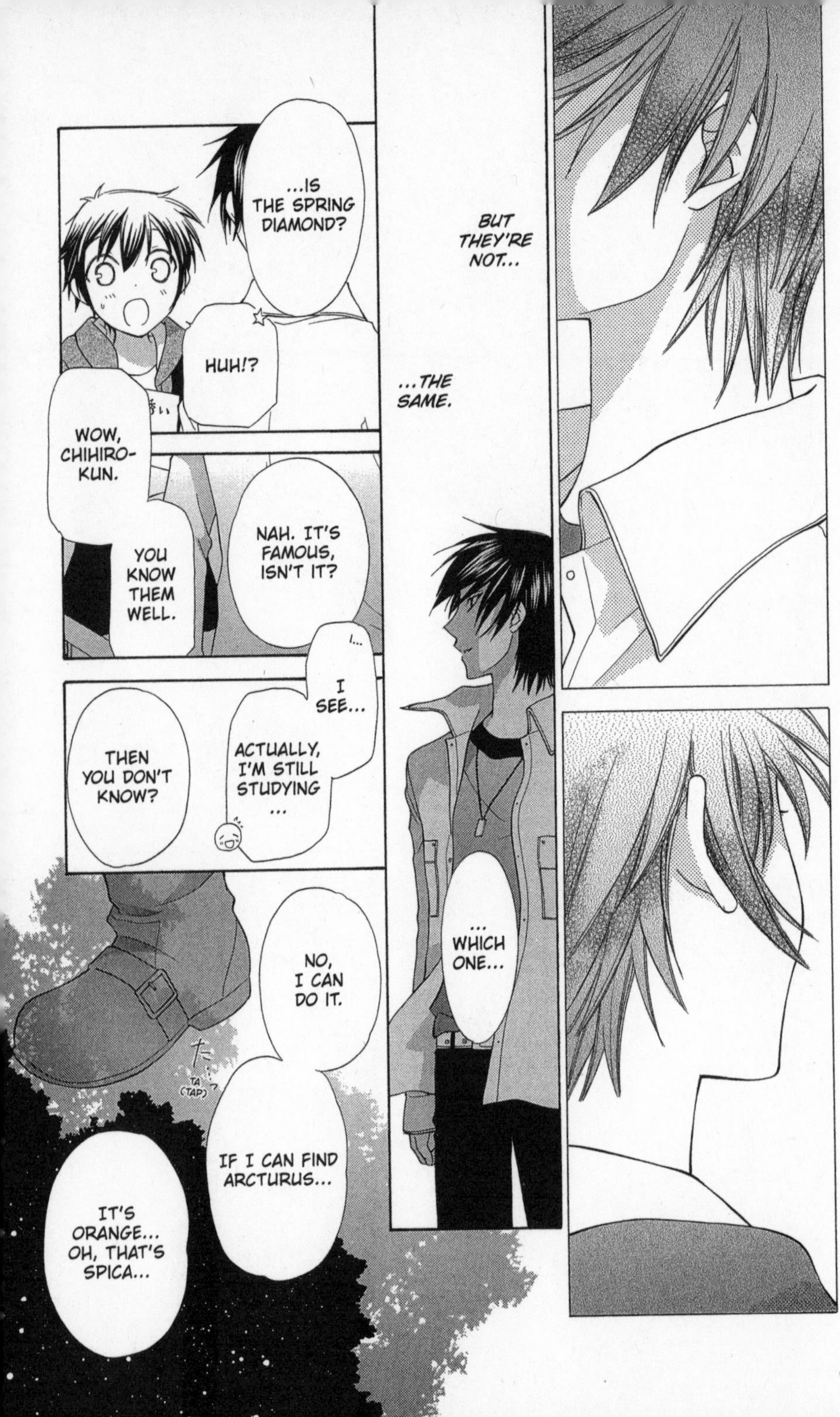
BUT THEY'RE NOT...
...THE SAME.
...WHICH ONE...
...IS THE SPRING DIAMOND?
HUH!?
WOW, CHIHIRO-KUN.
YOU KNOW THEM WELL.
NAH. IT'S FAMOUS, ISN'T IT?
I... I SEE...
ACTUALLY, I'M STILL STUDYING...
THEN YOU DON'T KNOW?
NO, I CAN DO IT.
IF I CAN FIND ARCTURUS...
TA (TAP)
IT'S ORANGE... OH, THAT'S SPICA...

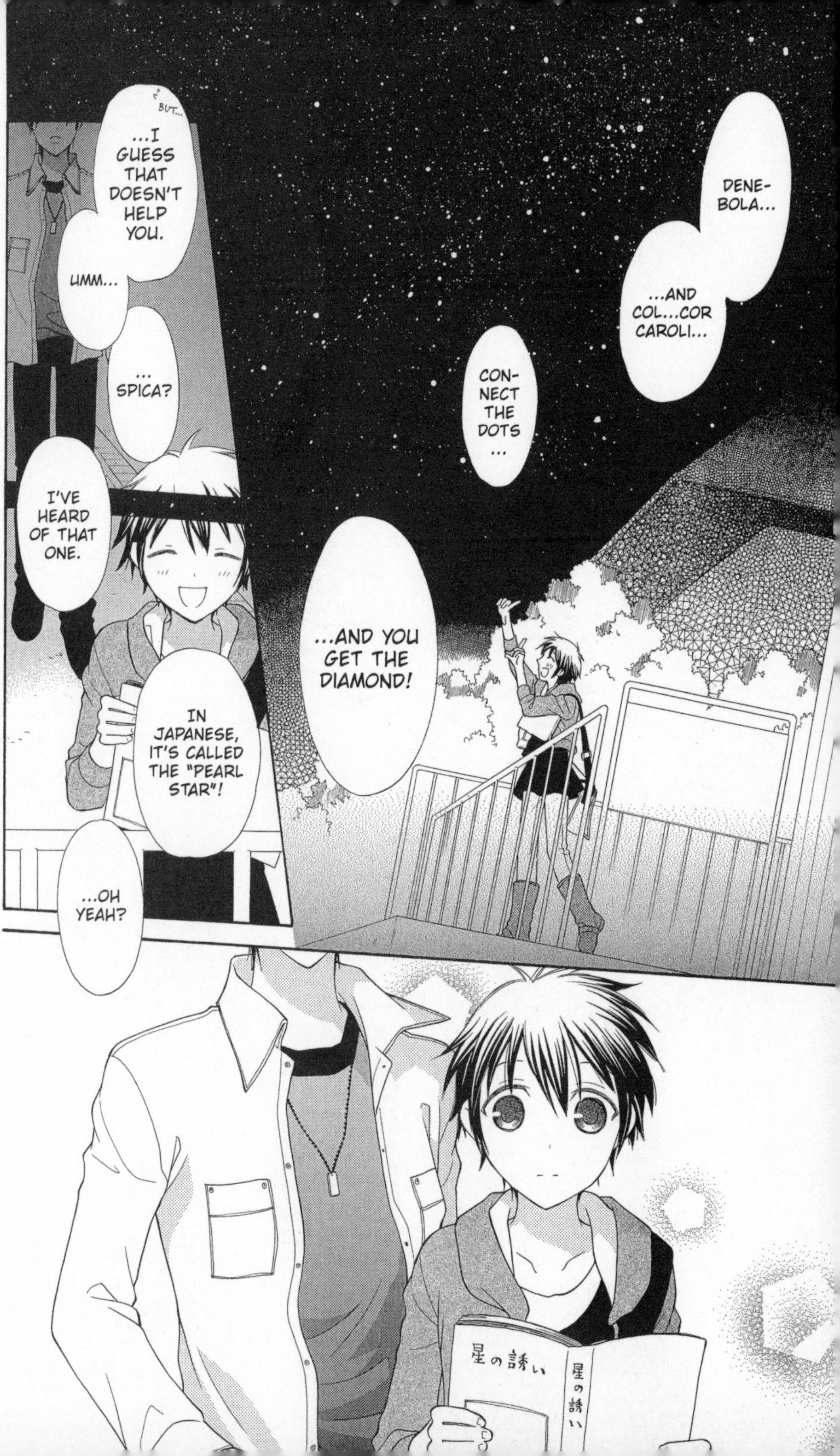
DENE-BOLA...
...AND COL...COR CAROLI...
CON-NECT THE DOTS...
...AND YOU GET THE DIAMOND!
BUT...
...I GUESS THAT DOESN'T HELP YOU.
UMM...
...SPICA?
I'VE HEARD OF THAT ONE.
IN JAPANESE, IT'S CALLED THE "PEARL STAR"!
...OH YEAH?
星の誘い
星の誘い

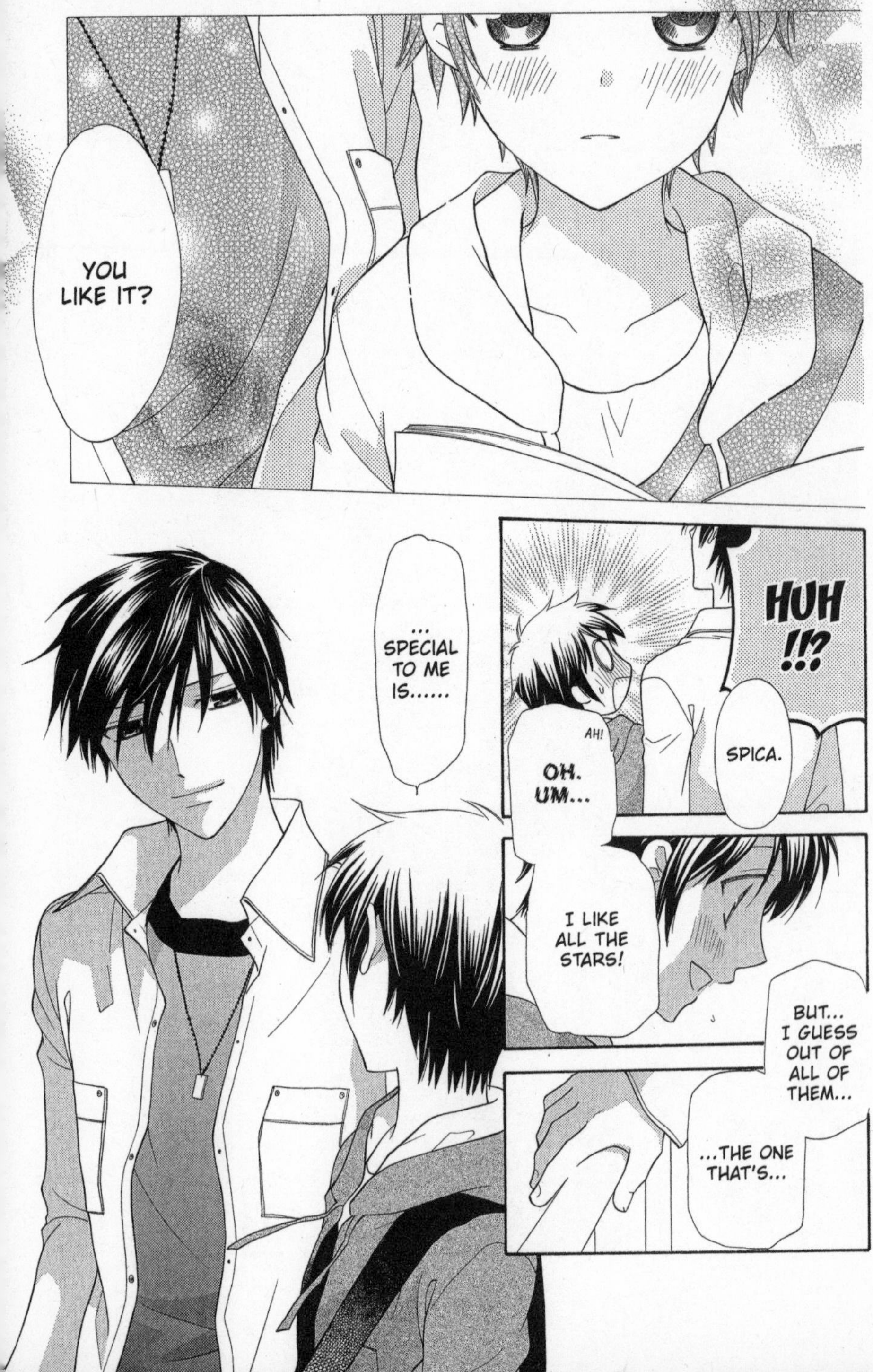
YOU LIKE IT?
HUH !!?
SPICA.
AH!
OH. UM...
I LIKE ALL THE STARS!
BUT... I GUESS OUT OF ALL OF THEM...
...THE ONE THAT'S...
... SPECIAL TO ME IS......

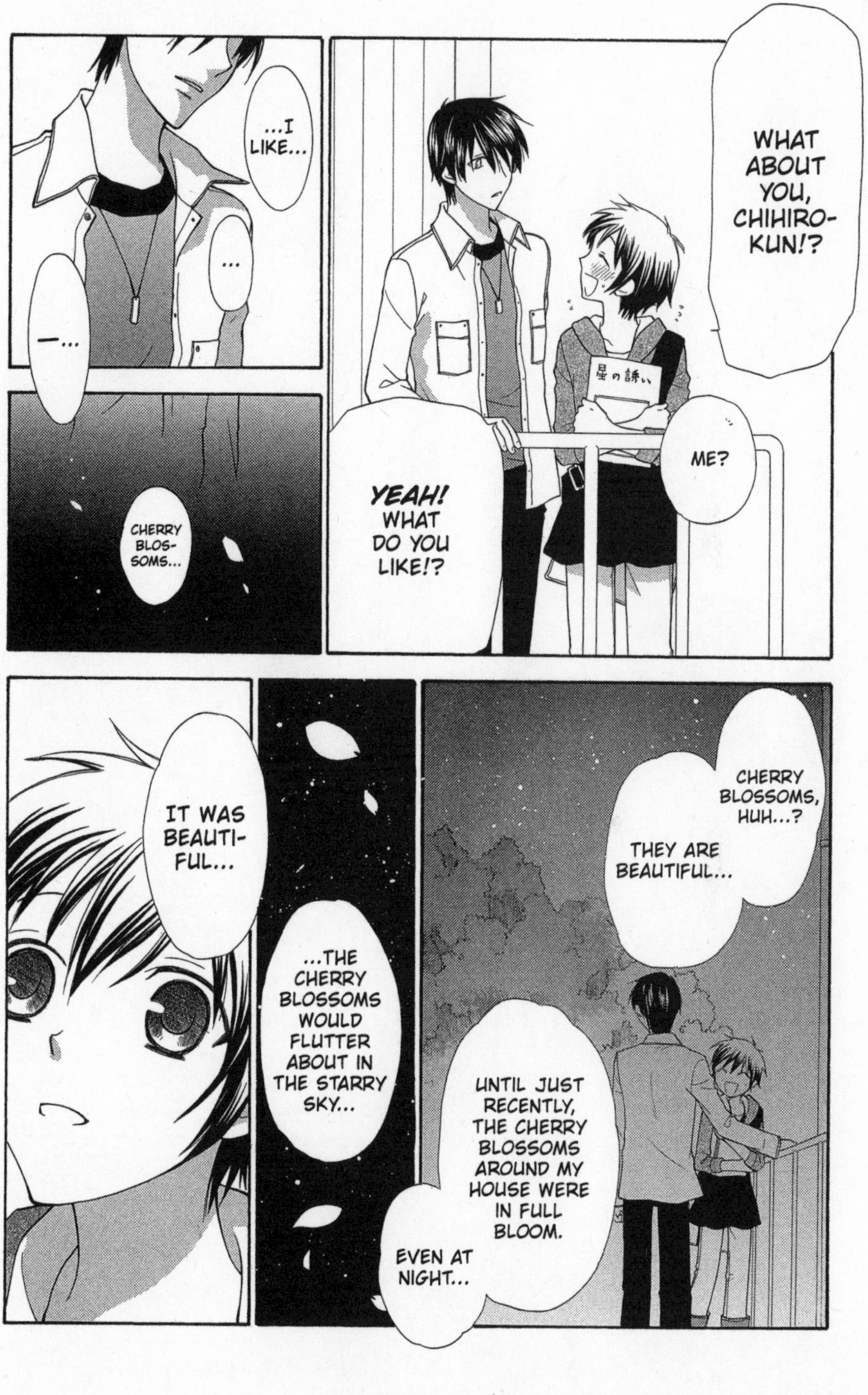
WHAT ABOUT YOU, CHIHIRO-KUN!?
星の誘い
ME?
YEAH! WHAT DO YOU LIKE!?
...I LIKE...
...
—...
CHERRY BLOSSOMS...
CHERRY BLOSSOMS, HUH...?
THEY ARE BEAUTIFUL...
UNTIL JUST RECENTLY, THE CHERRY BLOSSOMS AROUND MY HOUSE WERE IN FULL BLOOM.
EVEN AT NIGHT...
...THE CHERRY BLOSSOMS WOULD FLUTTER ABOUT IN THE STARRY SKY...
IT WAS BEAUTIFUL...

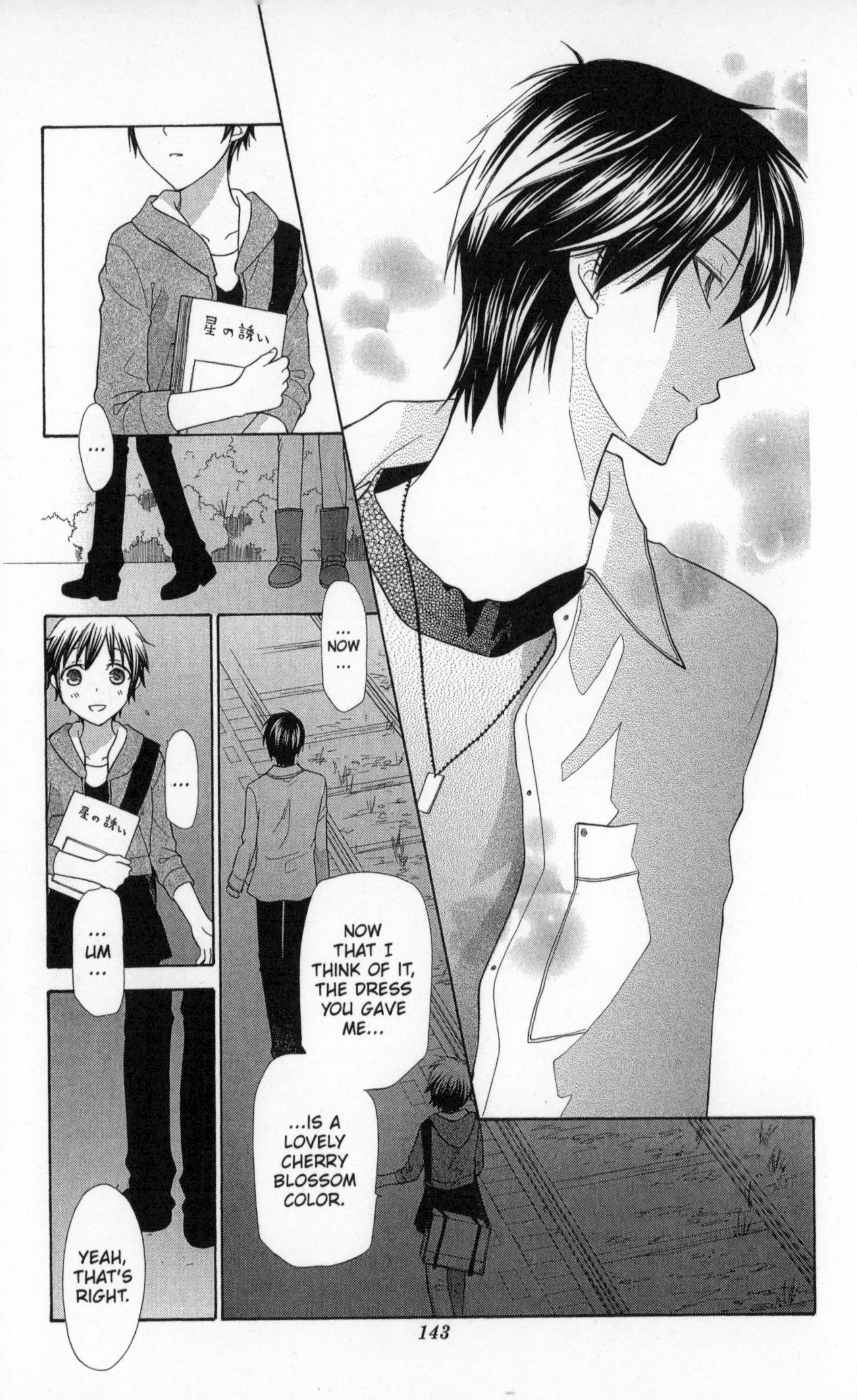
星の誘い
...
... NOW ...
...
星の誘い
... UM ...
NOW THAT I THINK OF IT, THE DRESS YOU GAVE ME...
...IS A LOVELY CHERRY BLOSSOM COLOR.
YEAH, THAT'S RIGHT.

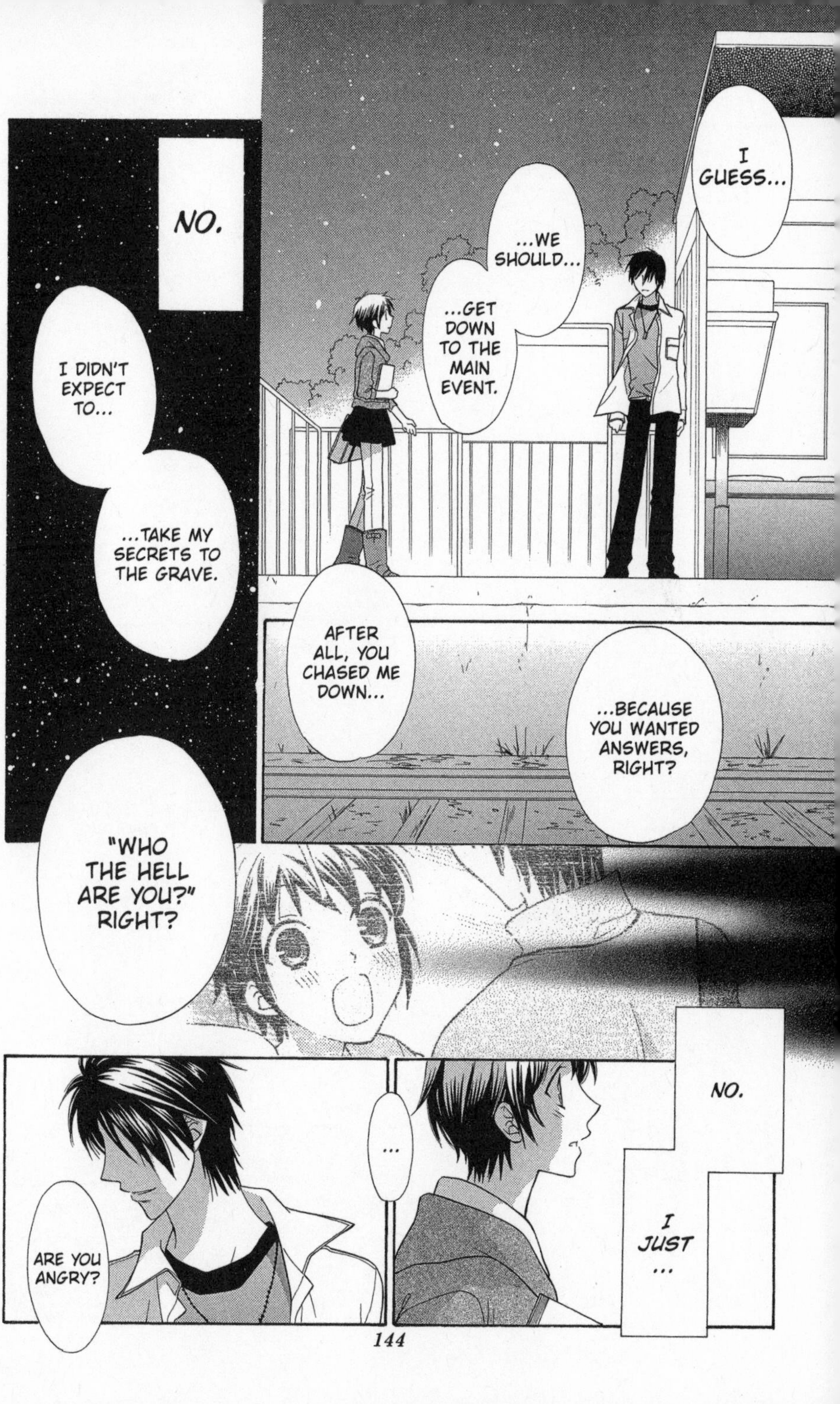
I GUESS...
...WE SHOULD...
...GET DOWN TO THE MAIN EVENT.
AFTER ALL, YOU CHASED ME DOWN...
...BECAUSE YOU WANTED ANSWERS, RIGHT?
"WHO THE HELL ARE YOU?" RIGHT?
NO.
I DIDN'T EXPECT TO...
...TAKE MY SECRETS TO THE GRAVE.
NO.
I JUST ...
...
ARE YOU ANGRY?

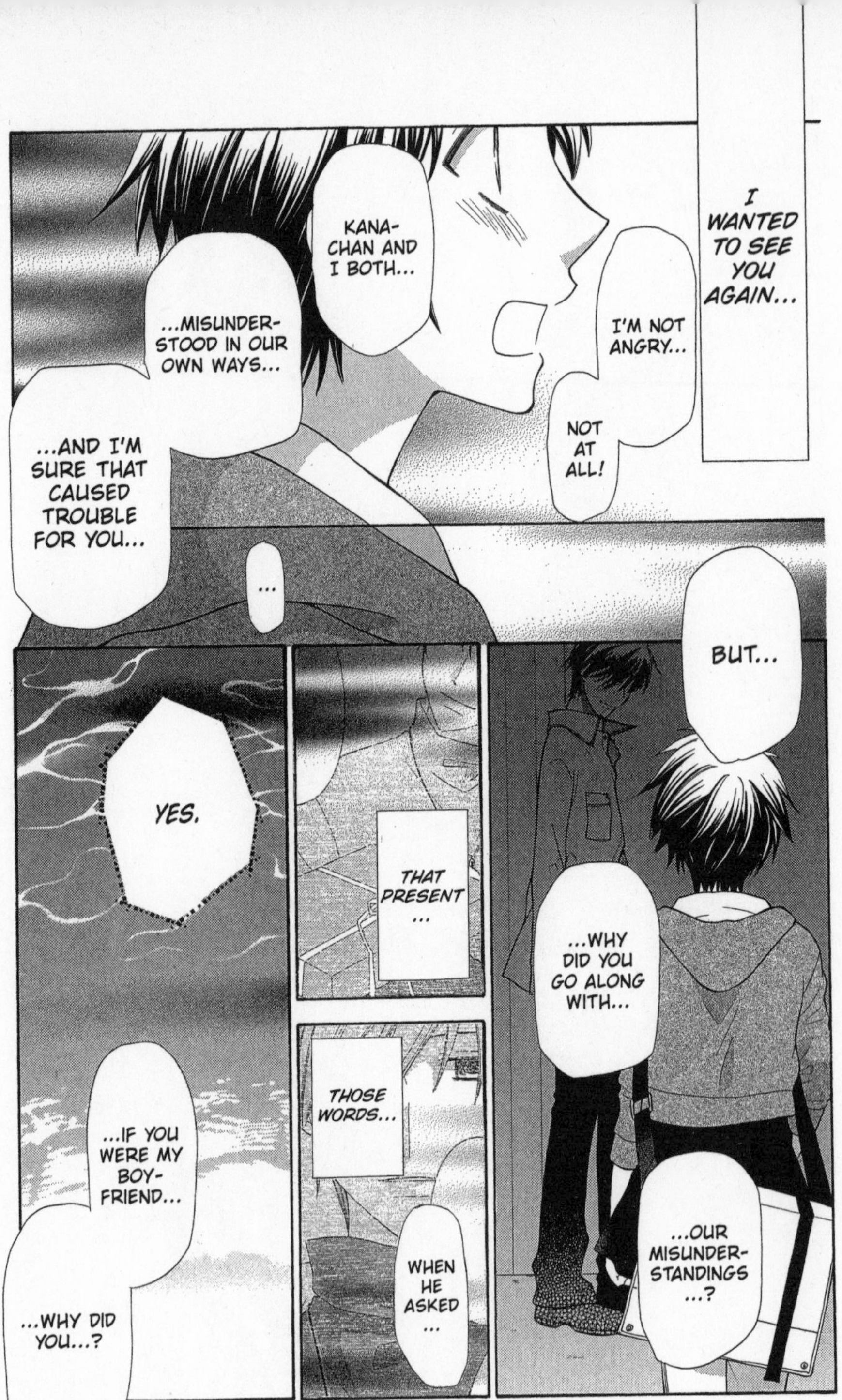
I WANTED TO SEE YOU AGAIN...
I'M NOT ANGRY...
NOT AT ALL!
KANA-CHAN AND I BOTH...
...MISUNDER-STOOD IN OUR OWN WAYS...
...AND I'M SURE THAT CAUSED TROUBLE FOR YOU...
...
BUT...
...WHY DID YOU GO ALONG WITH...
...OUR MISUNDER-STANDINGS...?
THAT PRESENT...
THOSE WORDS...
WHEN HE ASKED...
YES.
...IF YOU WERE MY BOY-FRIEND...
...WHY DID YOU...?

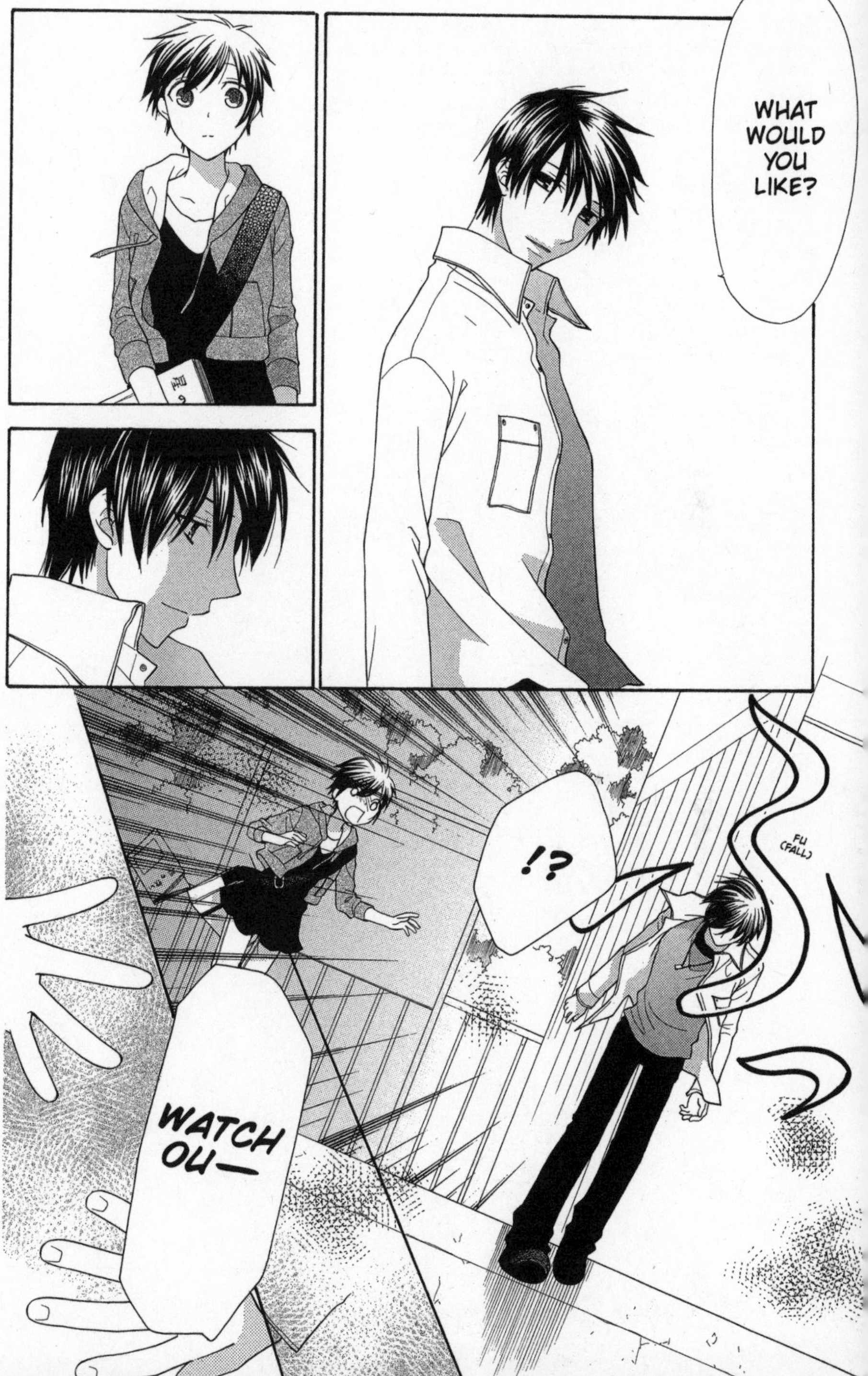
WHAT WOULD YOU LIKE?
FU (FALL)
!?
WATCH OU—

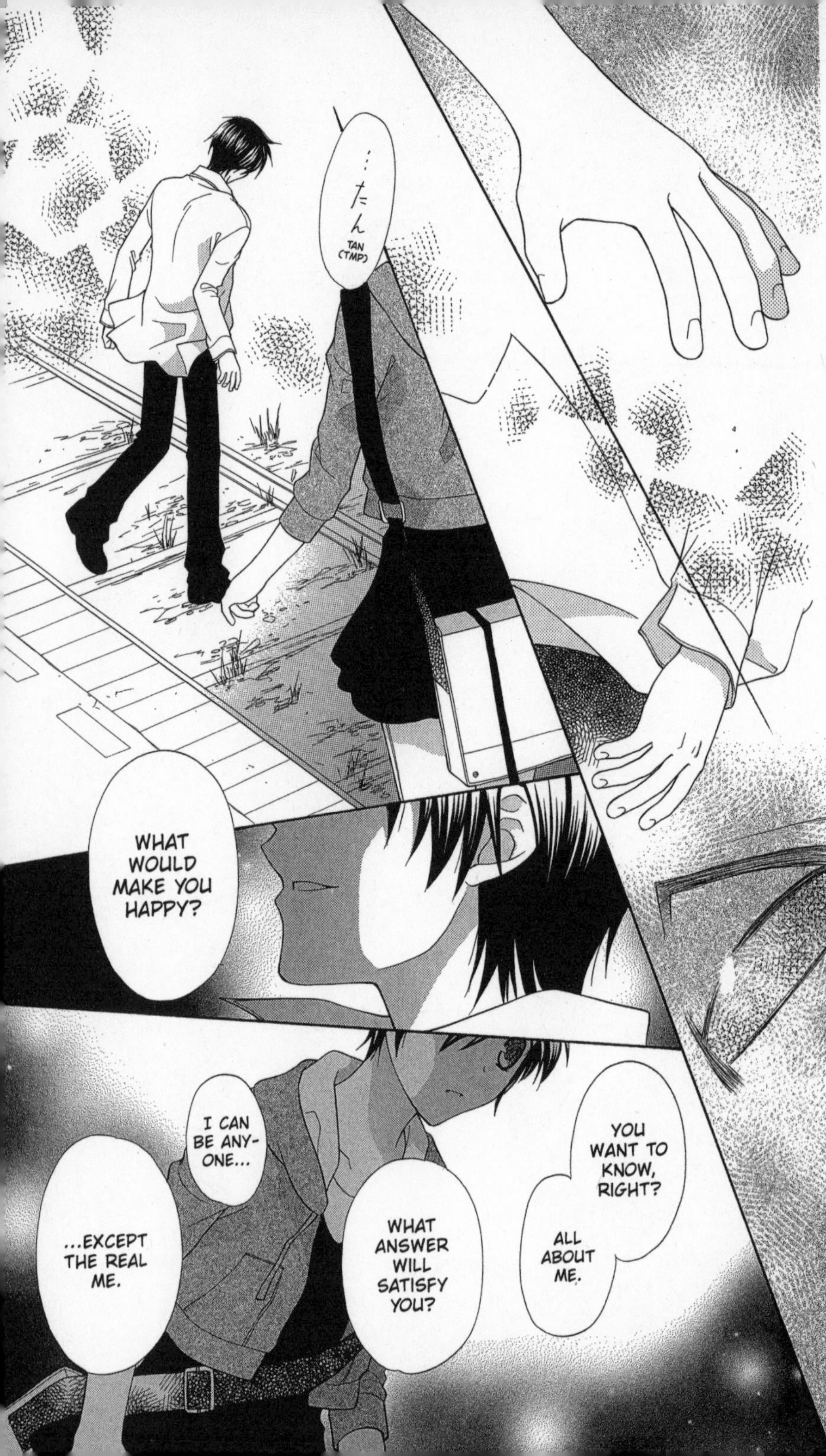
…たん
TAN (TMP)
WHAT WOULD MAKE YOU HAPPY?
YOU WANT TO KNOW, RIGHT?
ALL ABOUT ME.
WHAT ANSWER WILL SATISFY YOU?
I CAN BE ANY-ONE…
…EXCEPT THE REAL ME.

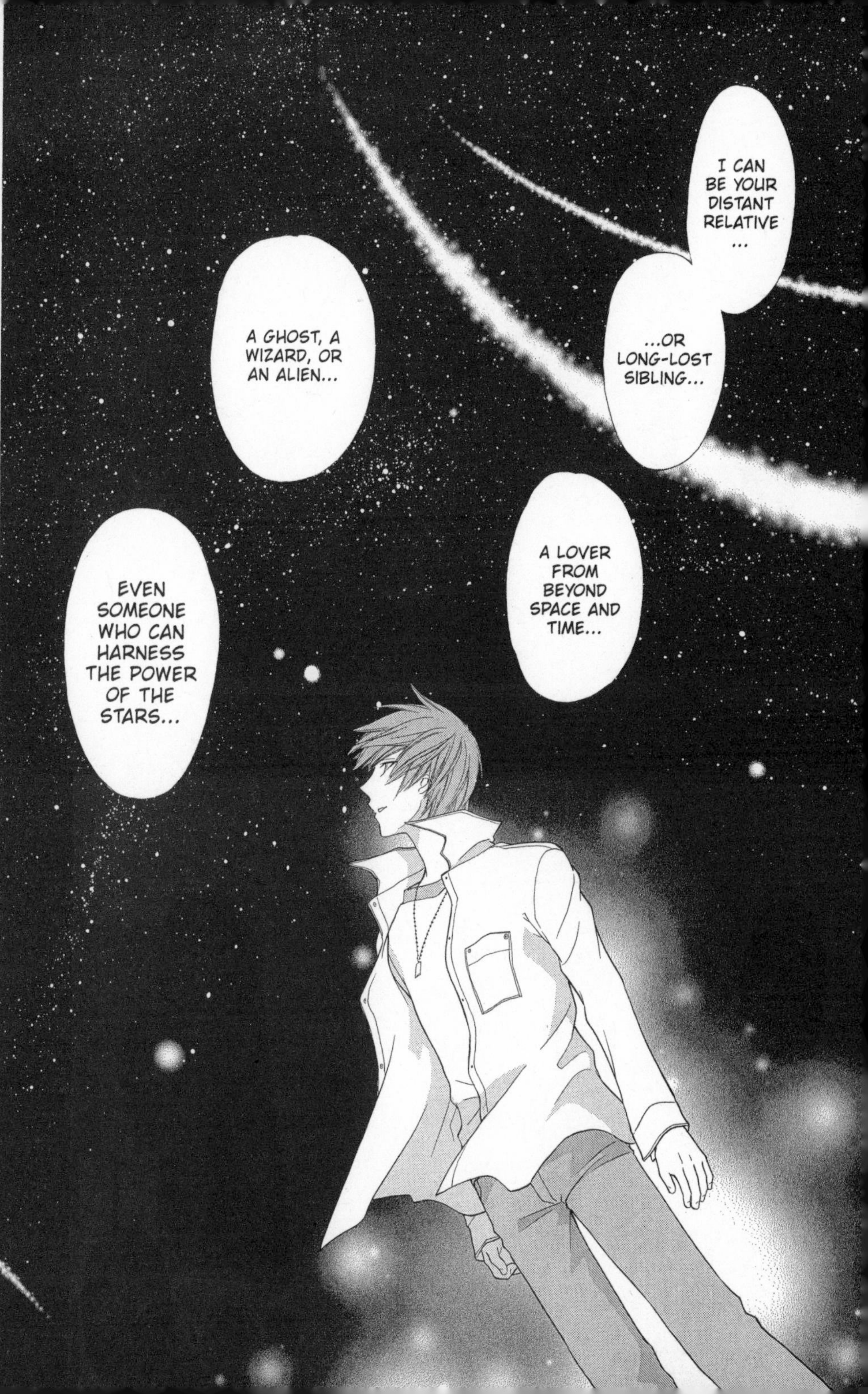
I CAN BE YOUR DISTANT RELATIVE ...
...OR LONG-LOST SIBLING...
A GHOST, A WIZARD, OR AN ALIEN...
A LOVER FROM BEYOND SPACE AND TIME...
EVEN SOMEONE WHO CAN HARNESS THE POWER OF THE STARS...

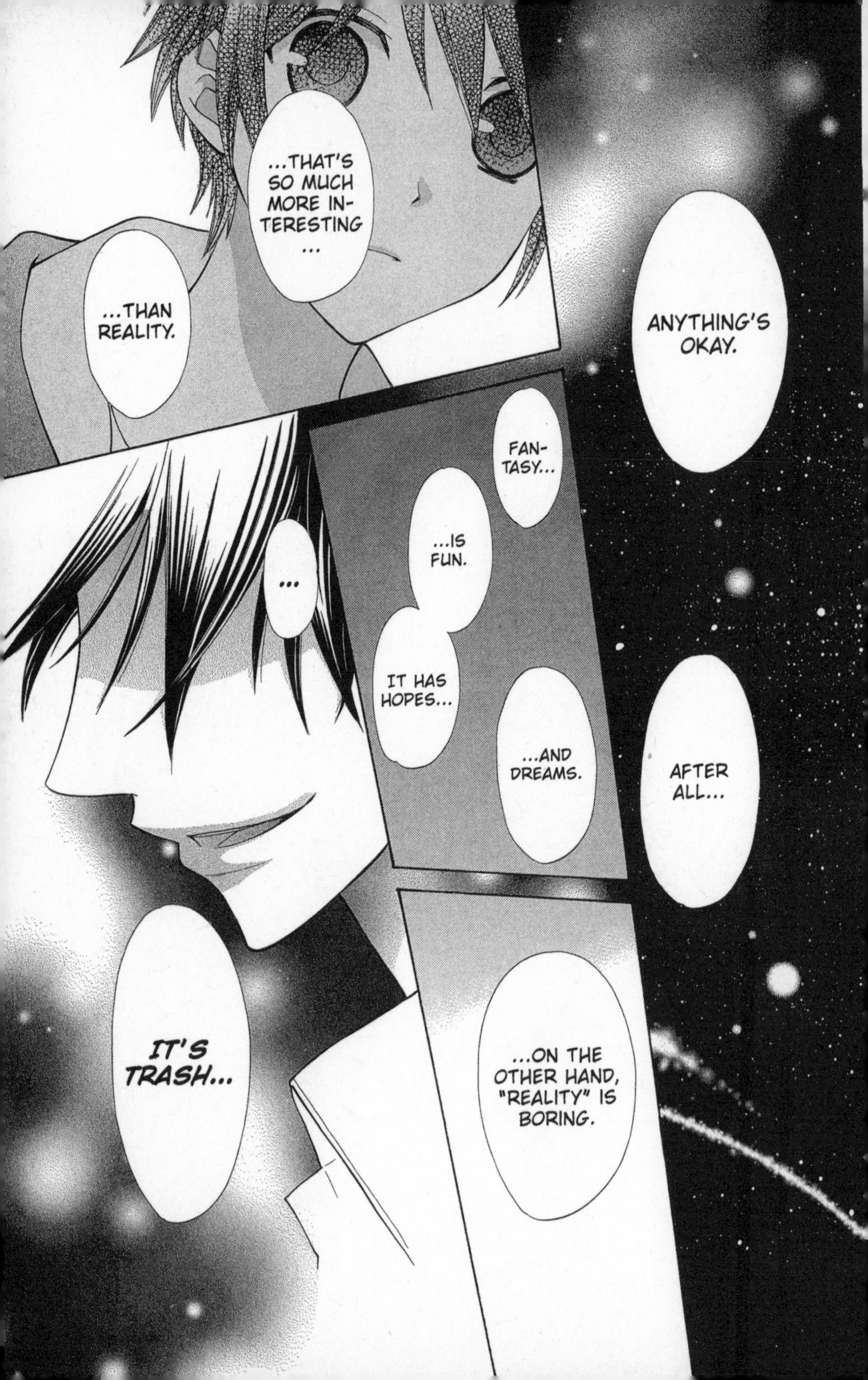
...THAT'S SO MUCH MORE IN-TERESTING ...
...THAN REALITY.
FAN-TASY...
...IS FUN.
...
IT HAS HOPES...
...AND DREAMS.
ANYTHING'S OKAY.
AFTER ALL...
...ON THE OTHER HAND, "REALITY" IS BORING.
IT'S TRASH...

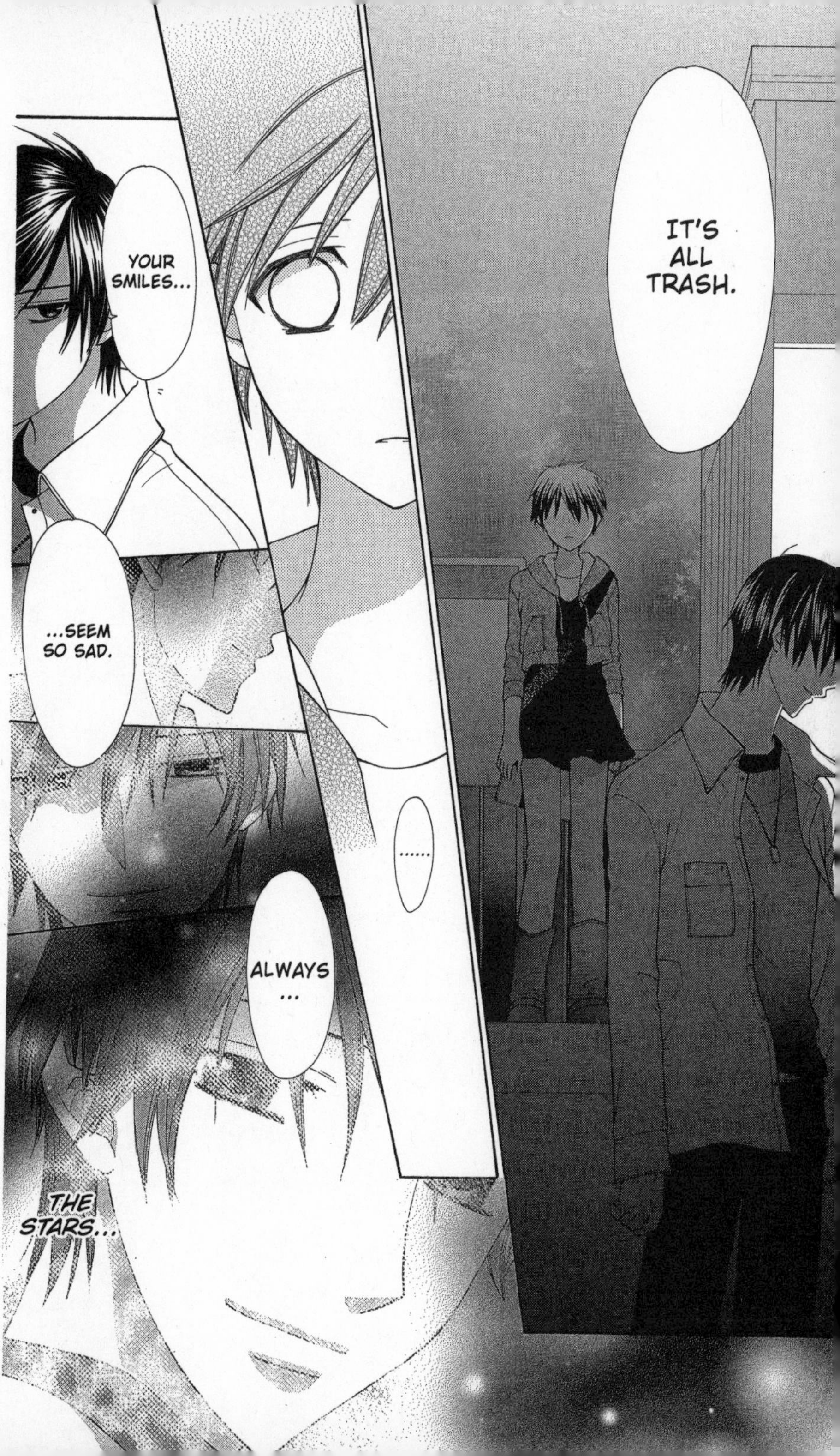
IT'S ALL TRASH.
......
YOUR SMILES...
...SEEM SO SAD.
ALWAYS ...
THE STARS...

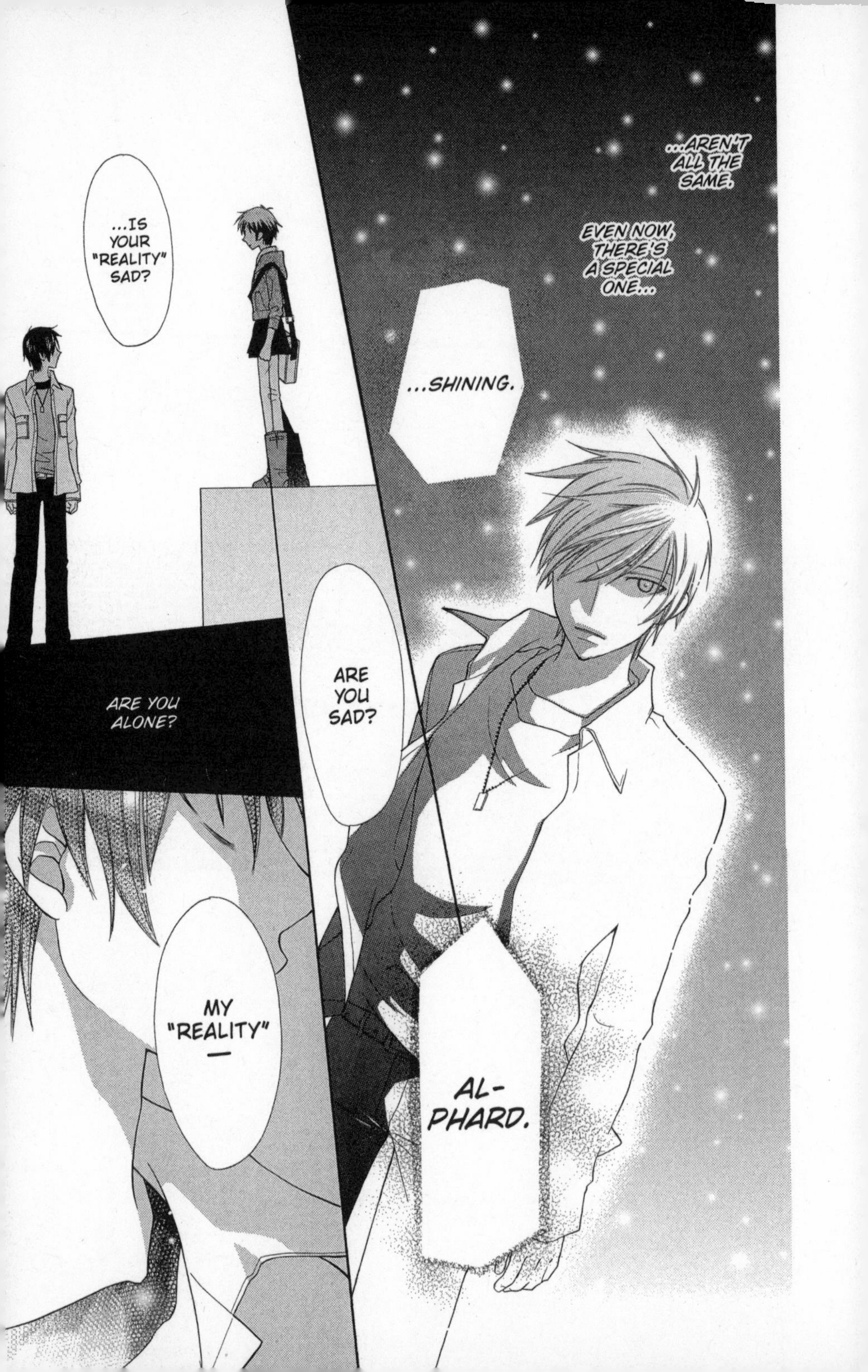
...AREN'T ALL THE SAME.
EVEN NOW, THERE'S A SPECIAL ONE...
...SHINING.
AL-PHARD.
...IS YOUR "REALITY" SAD?
ARE YOU ALONE?
ARE YOU SAD?
MY "REALITY" —

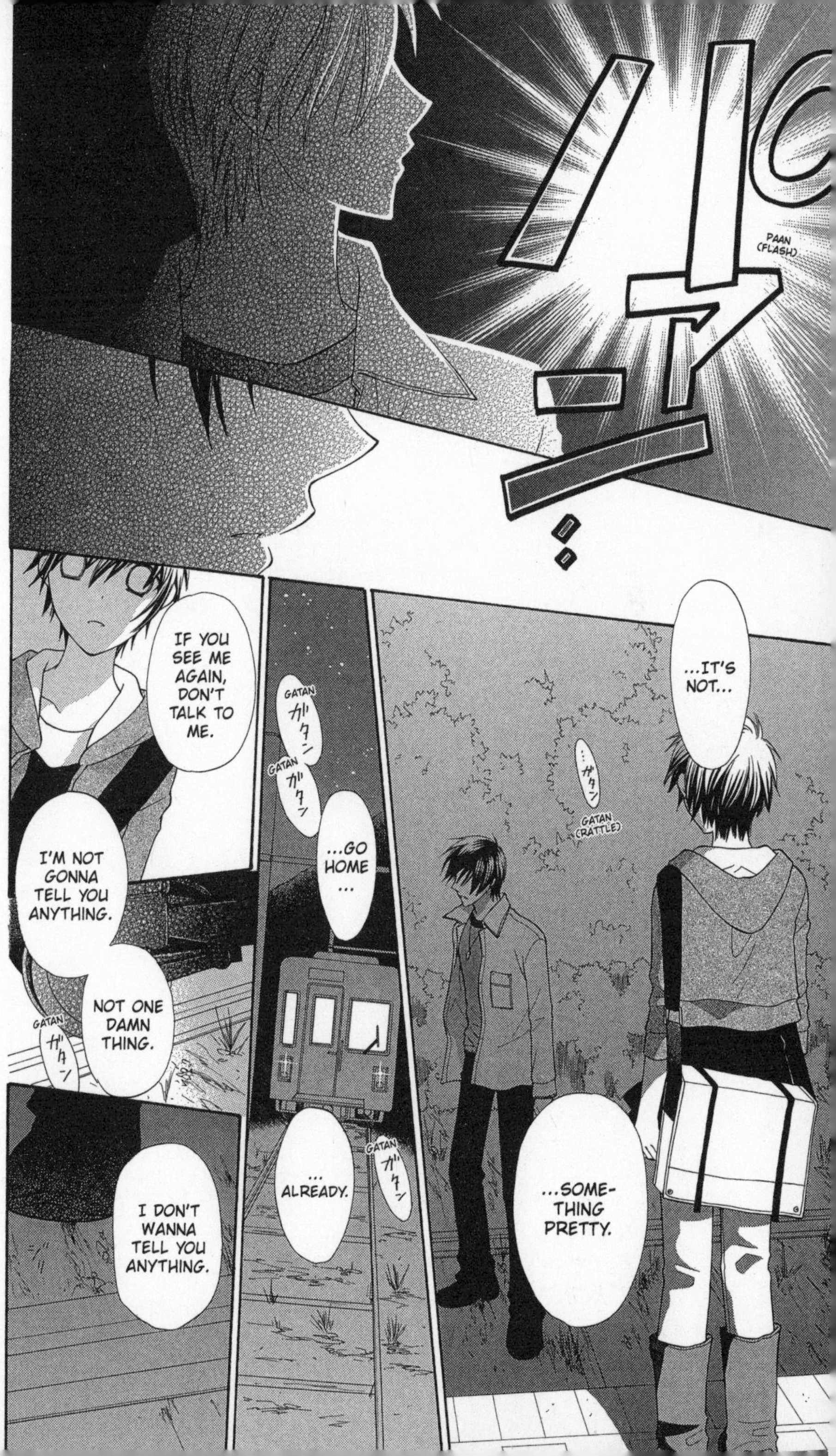
PAAN (FLASH)
...IT'S NOT...
...GATAN (RATTLE)
...SOME-THING PRETTY.
GATAN
GATAN
...GO HOME ...
GATAN
... ALREADY.
IF YOU SEE ME AGAIN, DON'T TALK TO ME.
I'M NOT GONNA TELL YOU ANYTHING.
NOT ONE DAMN THING.
GATAN
I DON'T WANNA TELL YOU ANYTHING.

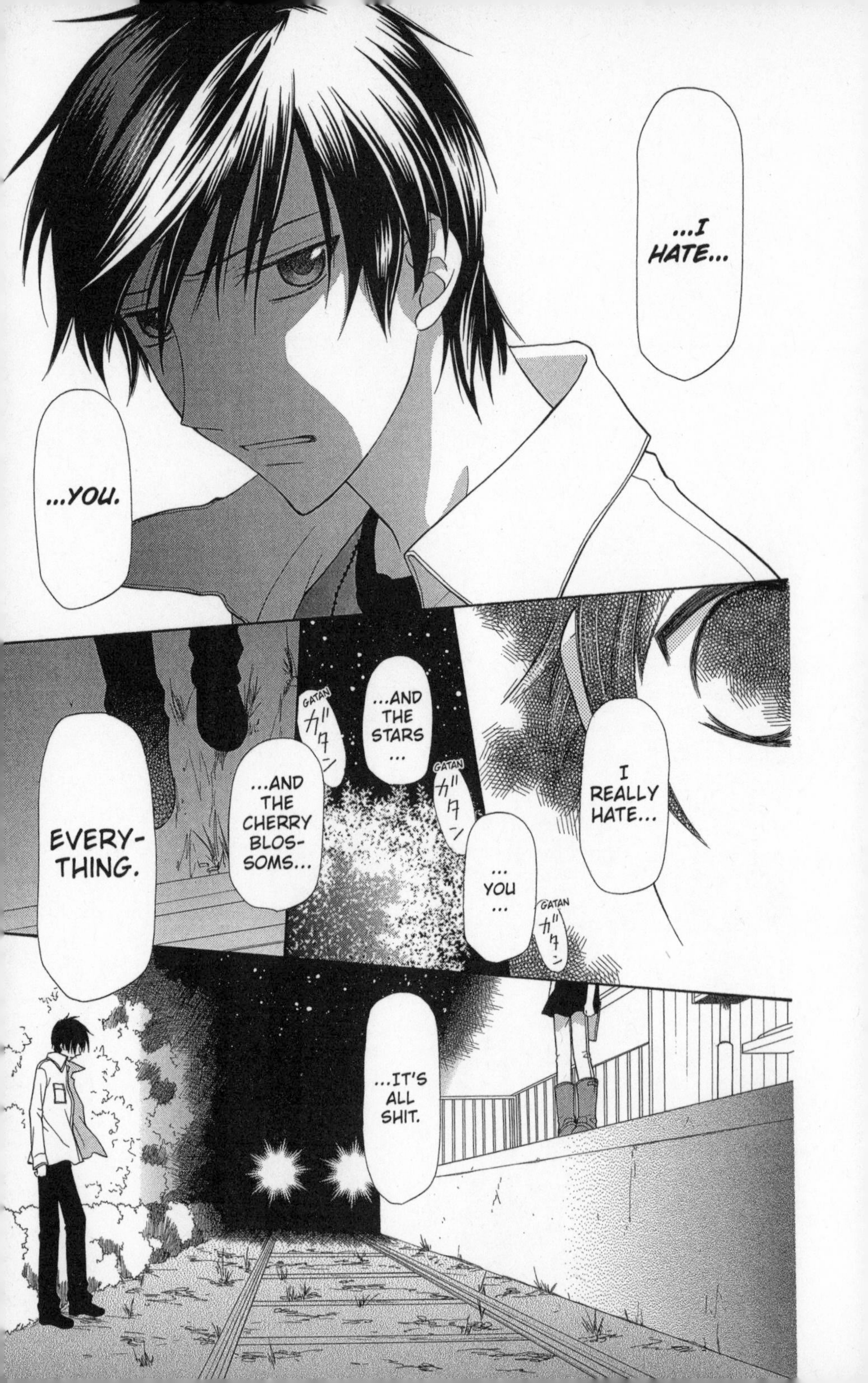
...I HATE...
...YOU.
I REALLY HATE...
GATAN ガタン
... YOU ...
GATAN ガタン
...AND THE STARS ...
GATAN ガタン
...AND THE CHERRY BLOS-SOMS...
EVERY-THING.
...IT'S ALL SHIT.

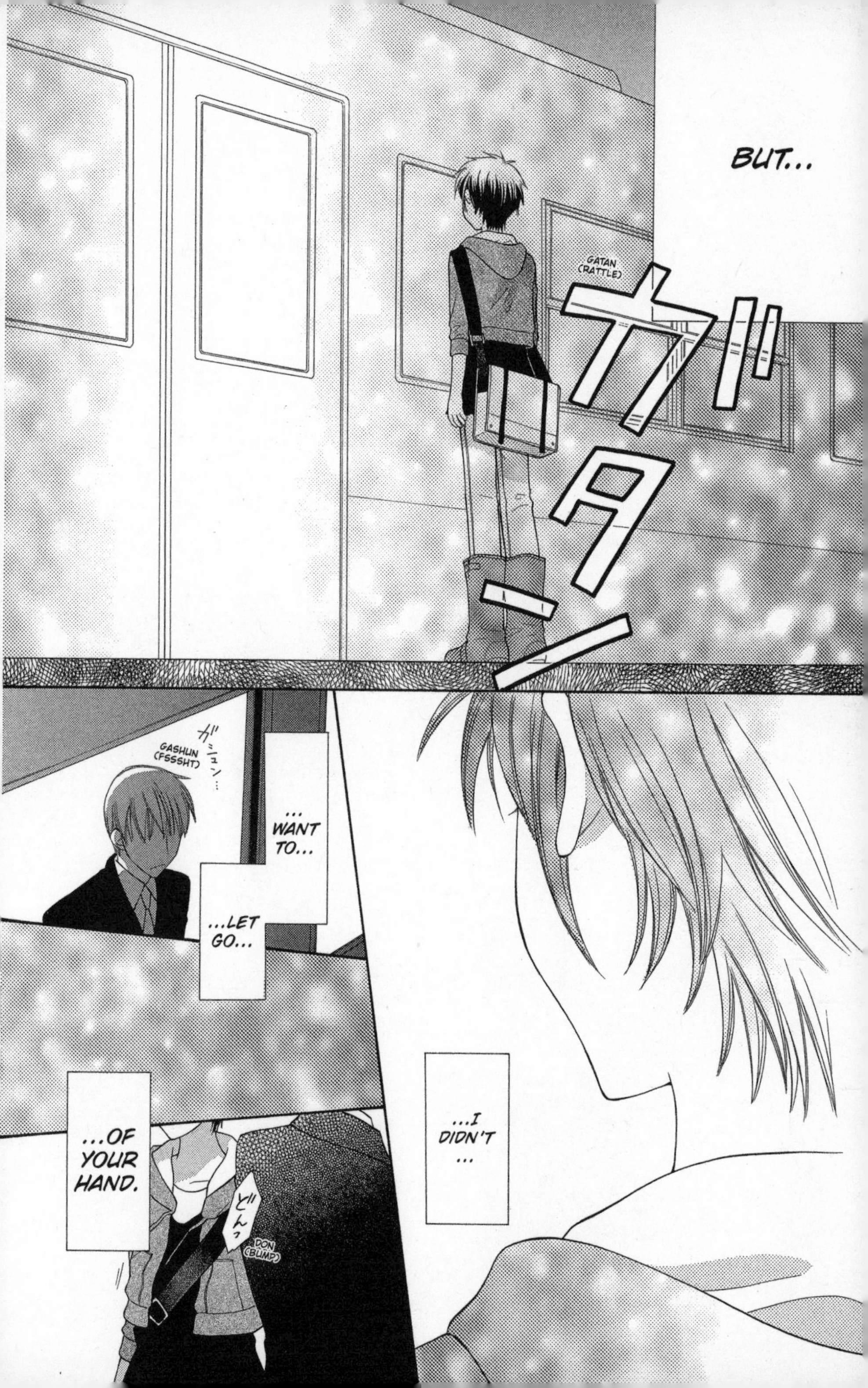

BUT...
GATAN (RATTLE)
ガターン
...I DIDN'T ...
... WANT TO...
GASHUN (FSSSHT)
ガシュン...
...LET GO...
...OF YOUR HAND.
DON (BUMP)
どんっ

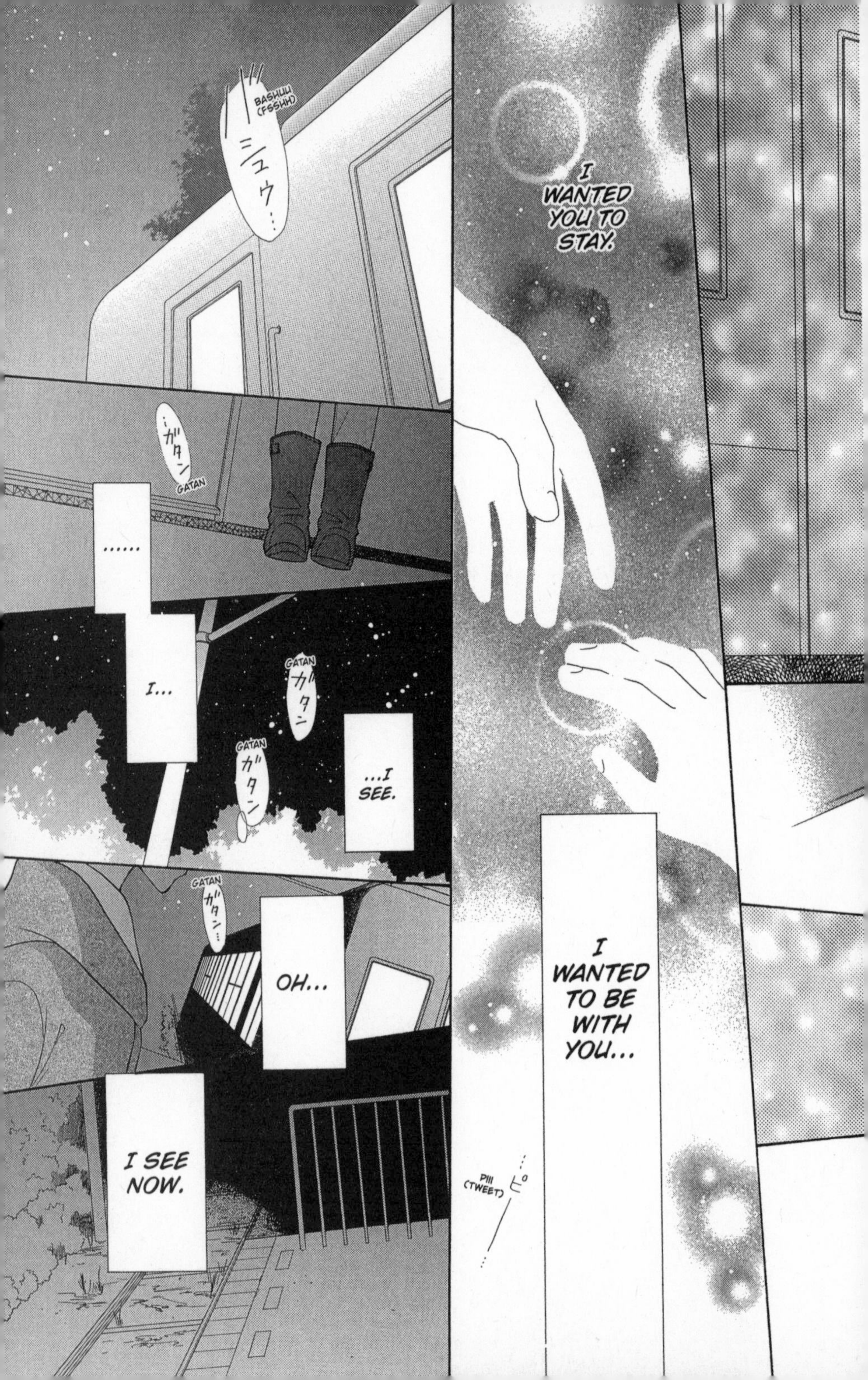
I WANTED YOU TO STAY.
I WANTED TO BE WITH YOU...
PIII (TWEET)
ピー…
BASHUU (FSSHH)
シュウ…
ガタン
GATAN
......
I...
GATAN
ガタン
GATAN
ガタン
...I SEE.
GATAN
ガタン…
OH...
I SEE NOW.

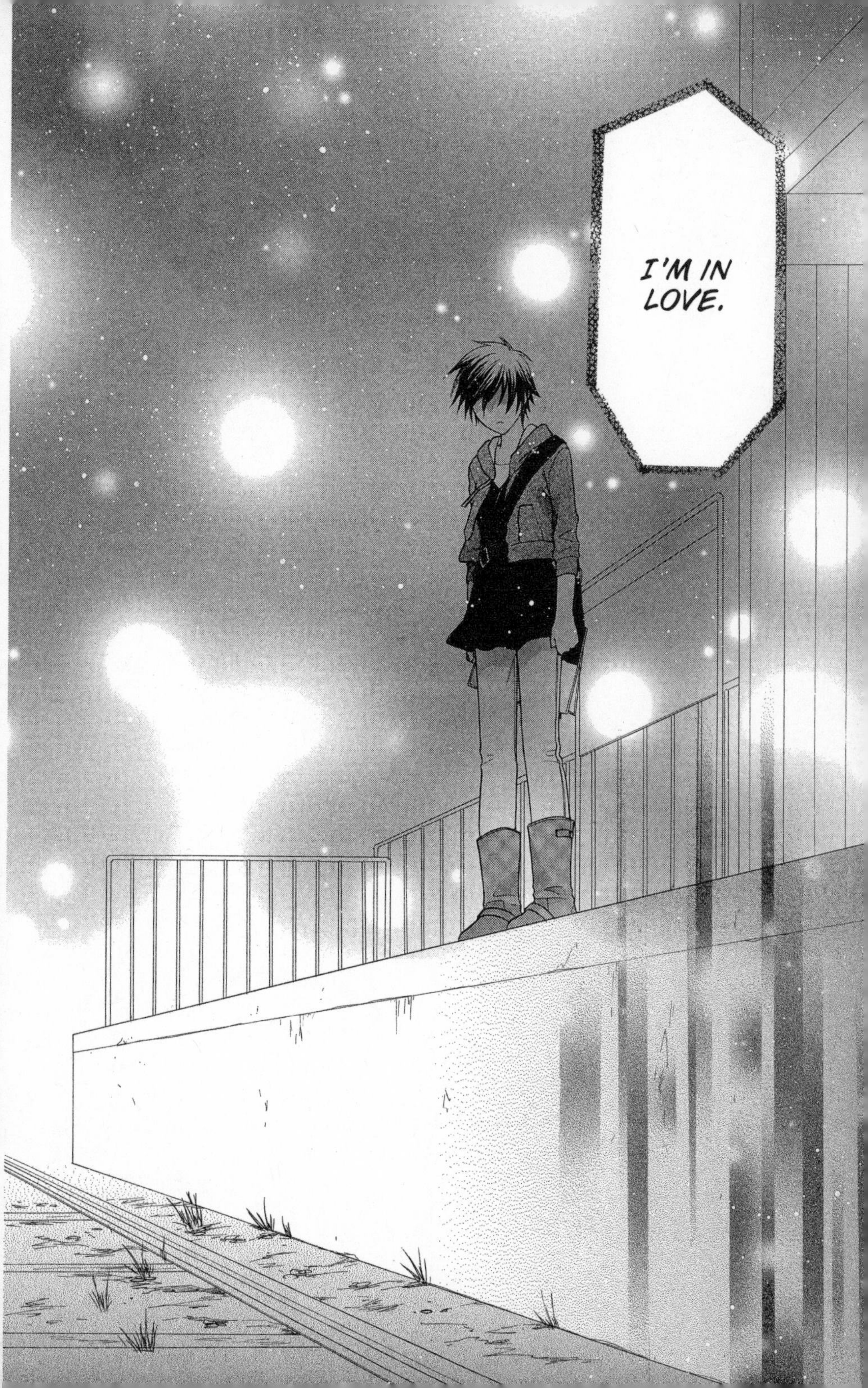
I'M IN LOVE.

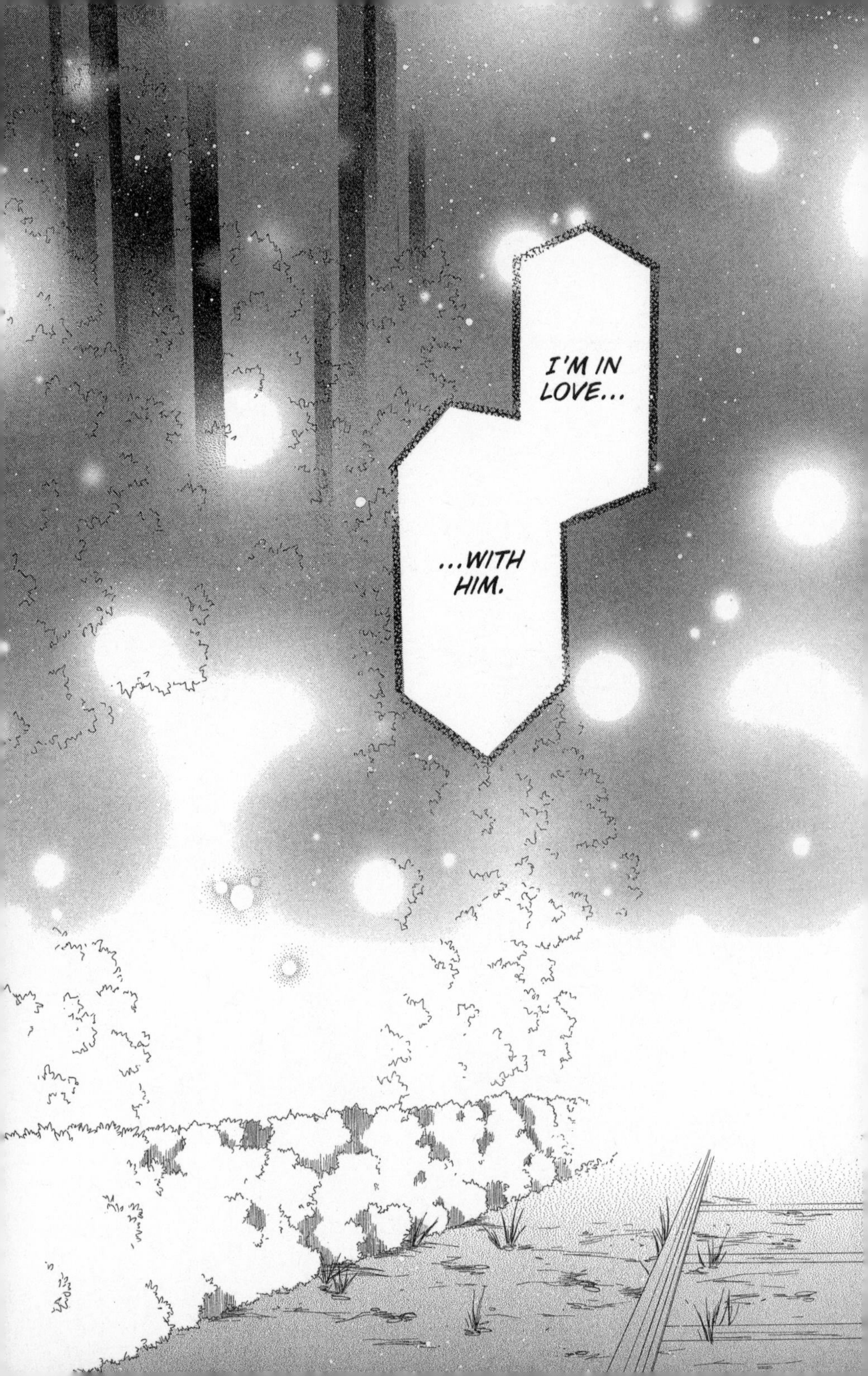
I'M IN LOVE...
...WITH HIM.

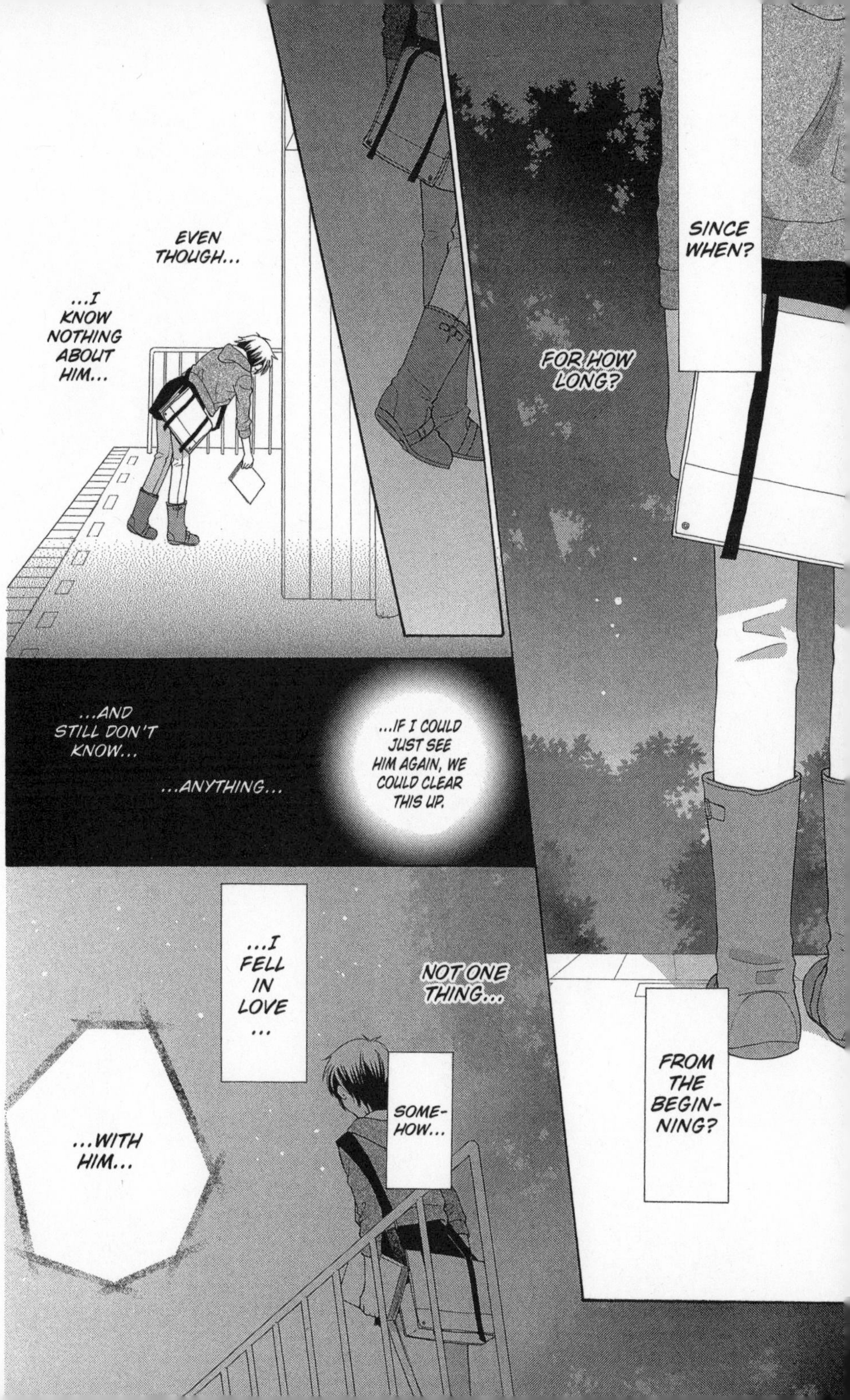
SINCE WHEN?
FOR HOW LONG?
FROM THE BEGINNING?
EVEN THOUGH...
...I KNOW NOTHING ABOUT HIM...
...AND STILL DON'T KNOW...
...ANYTHING...
...IF I COULD JUST SEE HIM AGAIN, WE COULD CLEAR THIS UP.
NOT ONE THING...
...I FELL IN LOVE...
SOME-HOW...
...WITH HIM...

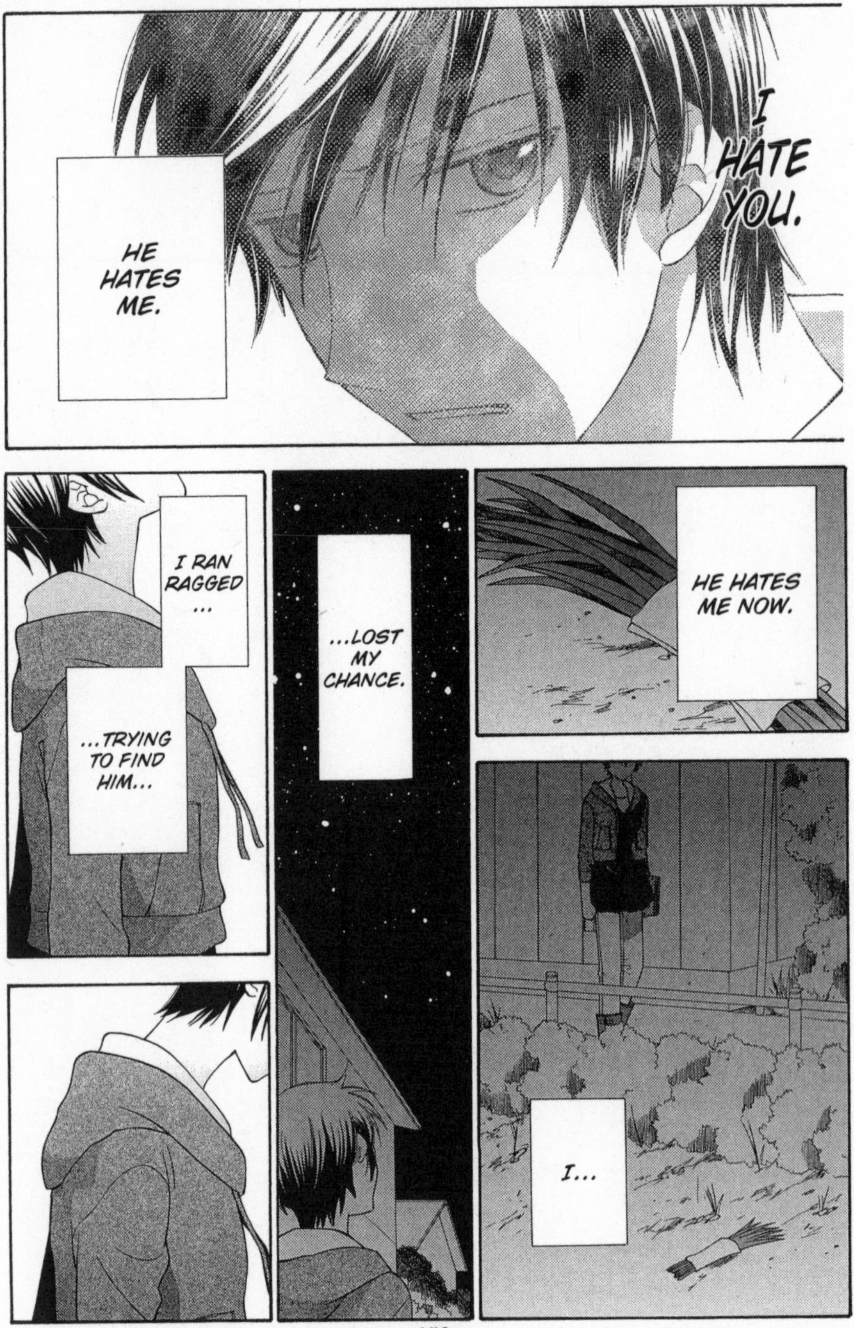
I HATE YOU.
HE HATES ME.
HE HATES ME NOW.
I...
...LOST MY CHANCE.
I RAN RAGGED ...
...TRYING TO FIND HIM...

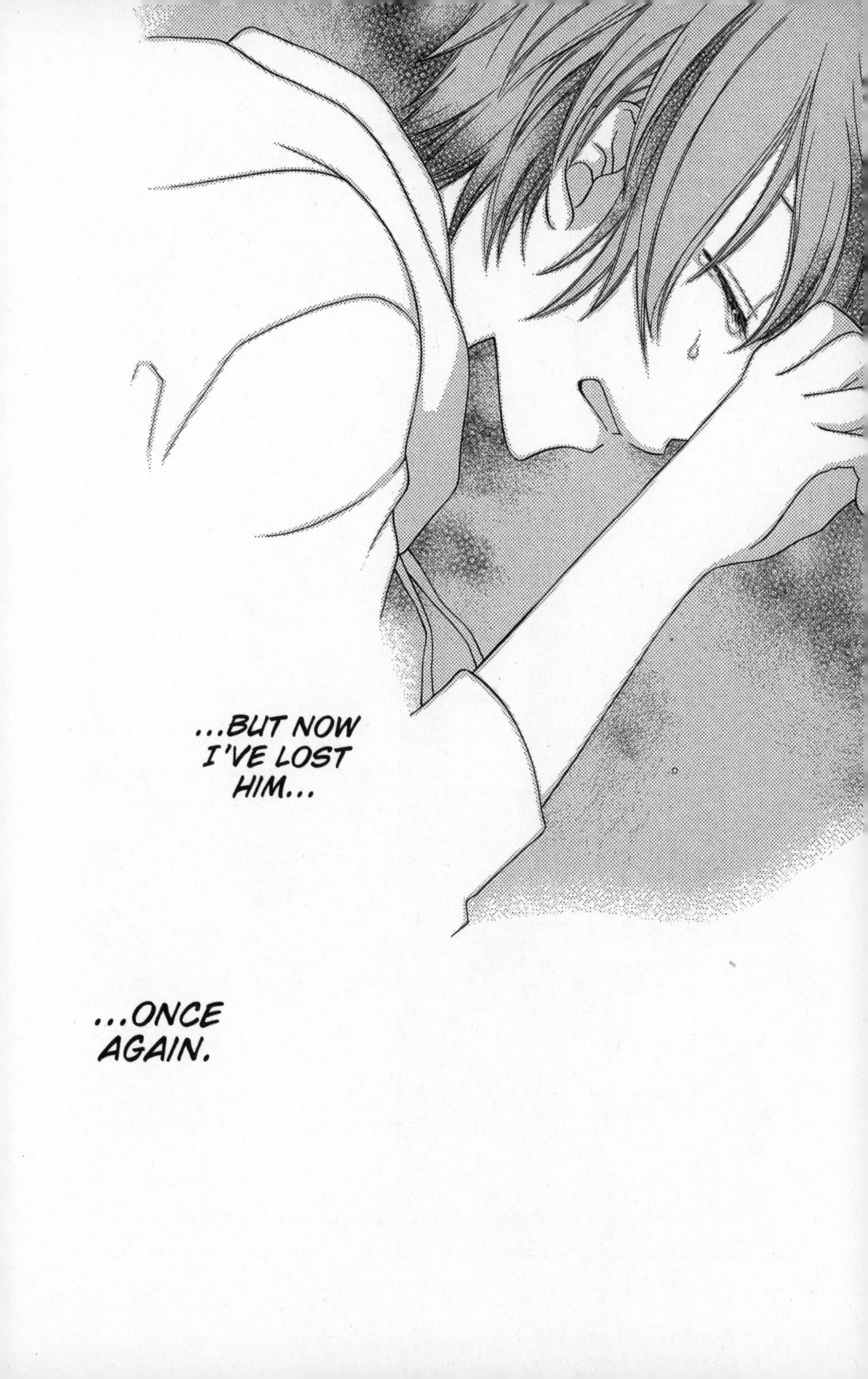
...BUT NOW I'VE LOST HIM...
...ONCE AGAIN.

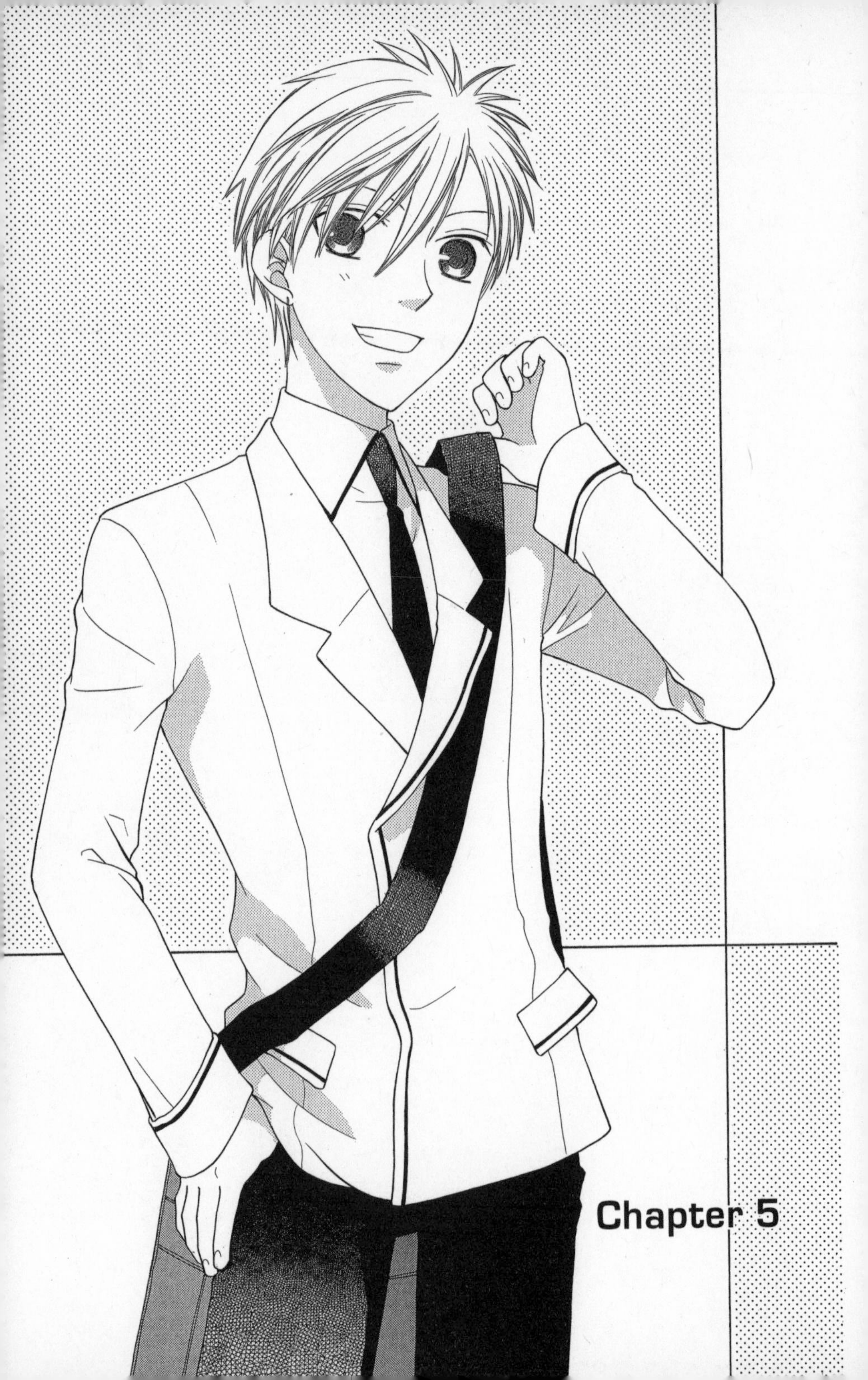

Chapter 5

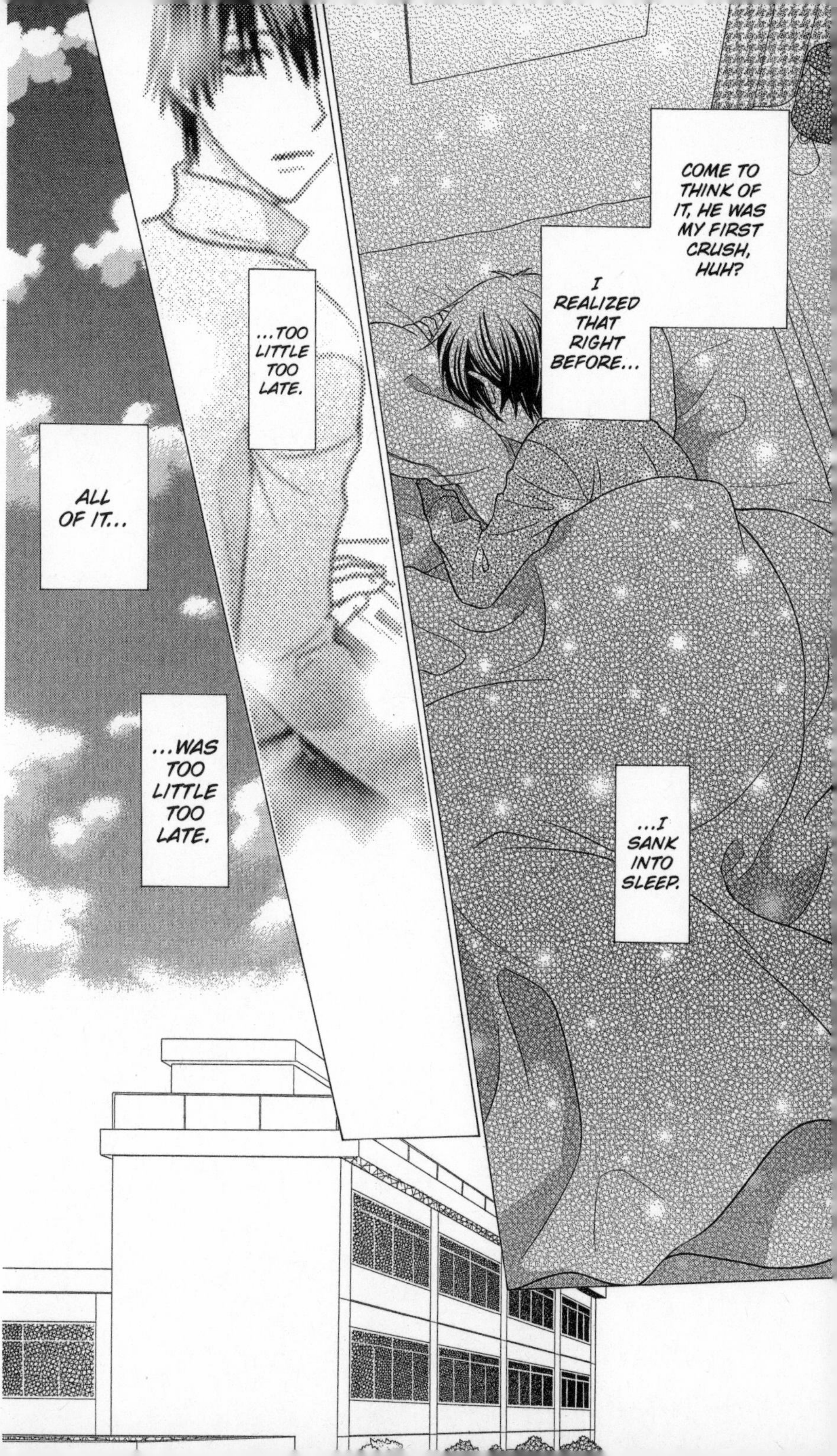
COME TO THINK OF IT, HE WAS MY FIRST CRUSH, HUH?
I REALIZED THAT RIGHT BEFORE...
...I SANK INTO SLEEP.
...TOO LITTLE TOO LATE.
ALL OF IT...
...WAS TOO LITTLE TOO LATE.

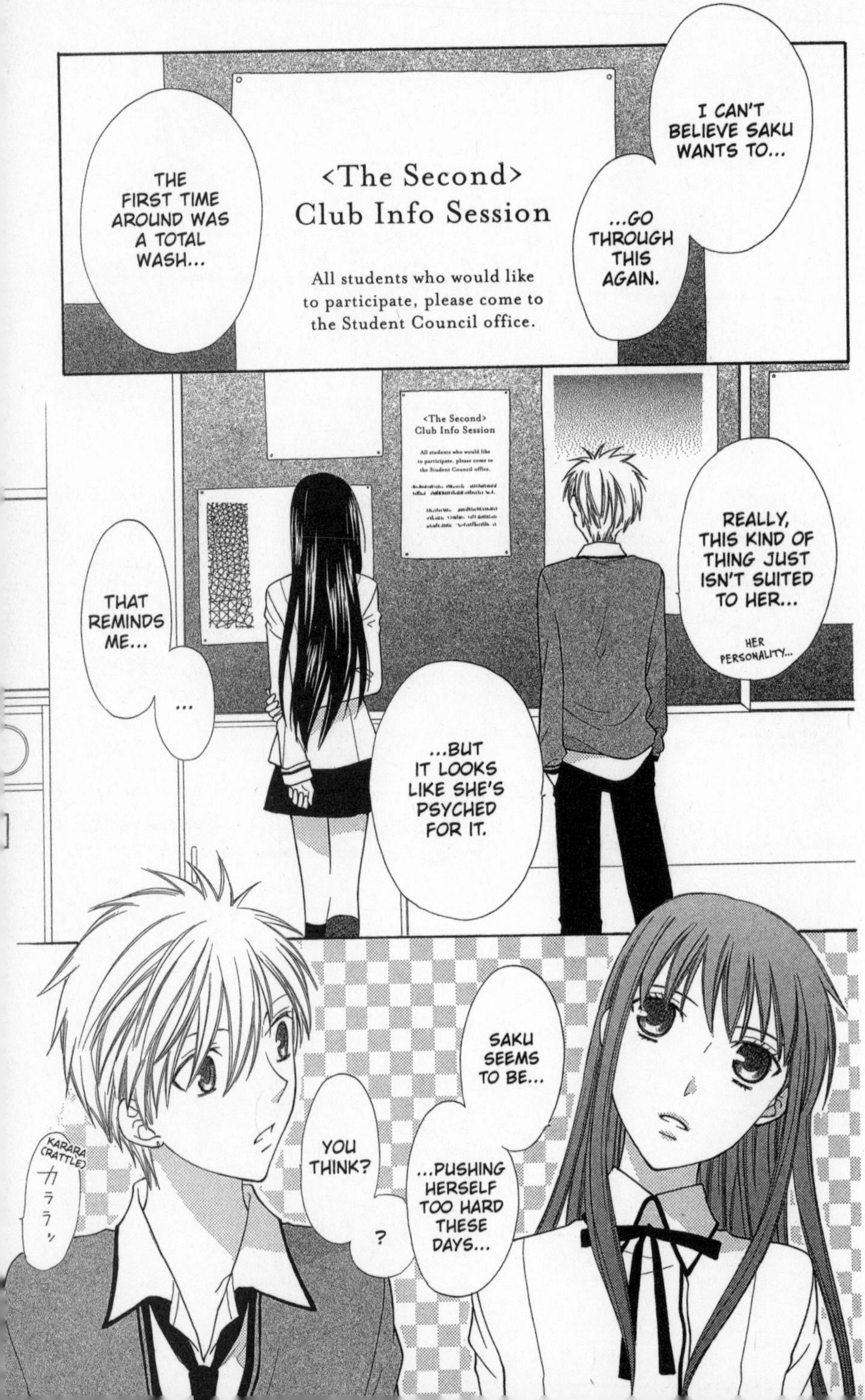
I CAN'T BELIEVE SAKU WANTS TO...
...GO THROUGH THIS AGAIN.
<The Second> Club Info Session
All students who would like to participate, please come to the Student Council office.
THE FIRST TIME AROUND WAS A TOTAL WASH...
REALLY, THIS KIND OF THING JUST ISN'T SUITED TO HER...
HER PERSONALITY...
<The Second> Club Info Session
All students who would like to participate, please come to the Student Council office.
...BUT IT LOOKS LIKE SHE'S PSYCHED FOR IT.
THAT REMINDS ME...
...
SAKU SEEMS TO BE...
...PUSHING HERSELF TOO HARD THESE DAYS...
YOU THINK?
?
KARARA (RATTLE)
カララッ

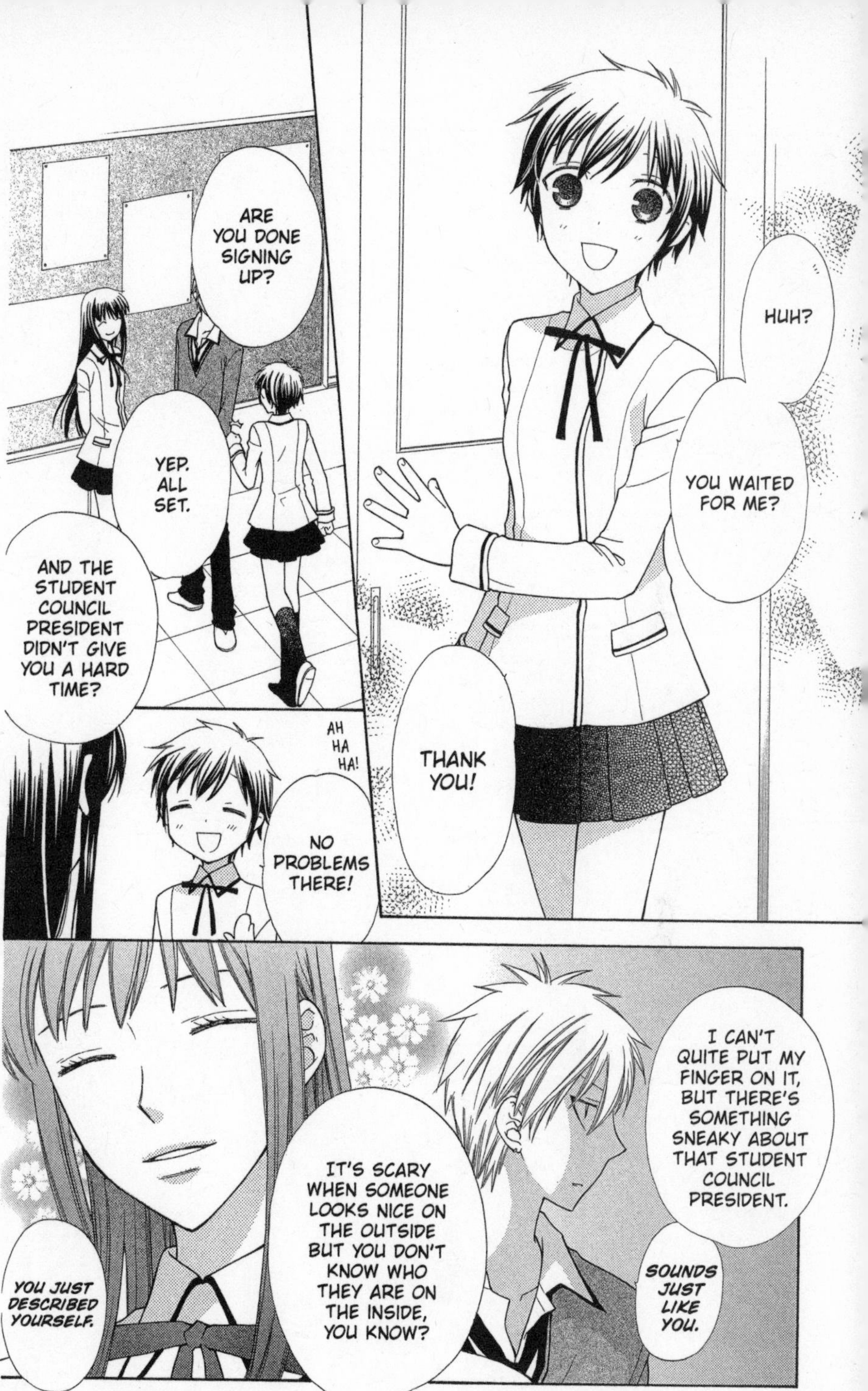
HUH?
YOU WAITED FOR ME?
THANK YOU!
ARE YOU DONE SIGNING UP?
YEP. ALL SET.
AND THE STUDENT COUNCIL PRESIDENT DIDN'T GIVE YOU A HARD TIME?
AH HA HA!
NO PROBLEMS THERE!
I CAN'T QUITE PUT MY FINGER ON IT, BUT THERE'S SOMETHING SNEAKY ABOUT THAT STUDENT COUNCIL PRESIDENT.
IT'S SCARY WHEN SOMEONE LOOKS NICE ON THE OUTSIDE BUT YOU DON'T KNOW WHO THEY ARE ON THE INSIDE, YOU KNOW?
SOUNDS JUST LIKE YOU.
YOU JUST DESCRIBED YOURSELF.

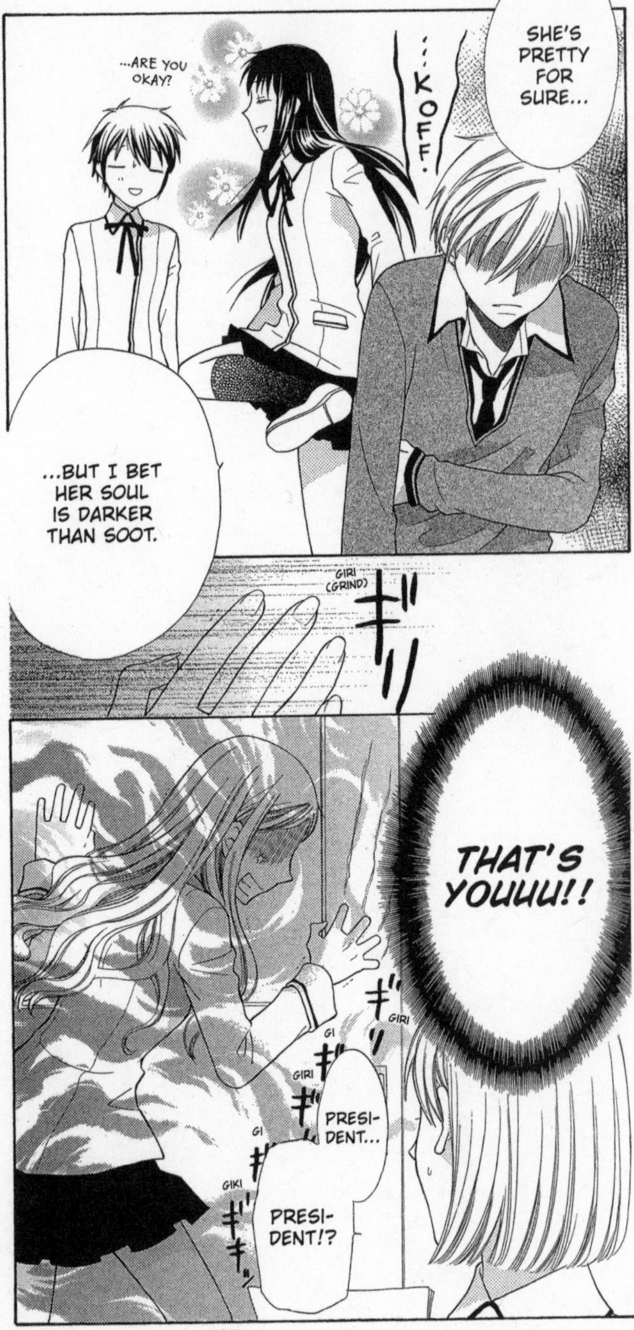
SHE'S PRETTY FOR SURE...
...KOFF...
...ARE YOU OKAY?
...BUT I BET HER SOUL IS DARKER THAN SOOT.
GIRI (GRIND)
THAT'S YOUUU!!
GIRI
GI
GIRI
GI
GIKI
PRESI-DENT...
PRESI-DENT!?

A short story, "Ponta Twinkles Too," is included at the end of this volume. He's in the first chapter as well. A cameo anyway. (LOL)

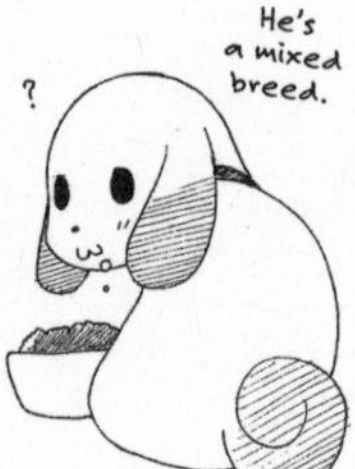
He's a mixed breed.
?

Saku and Yuuri are dog people. Sei and Kanade are cat people. That's the vibe I get.

I don't know about Chihiro.

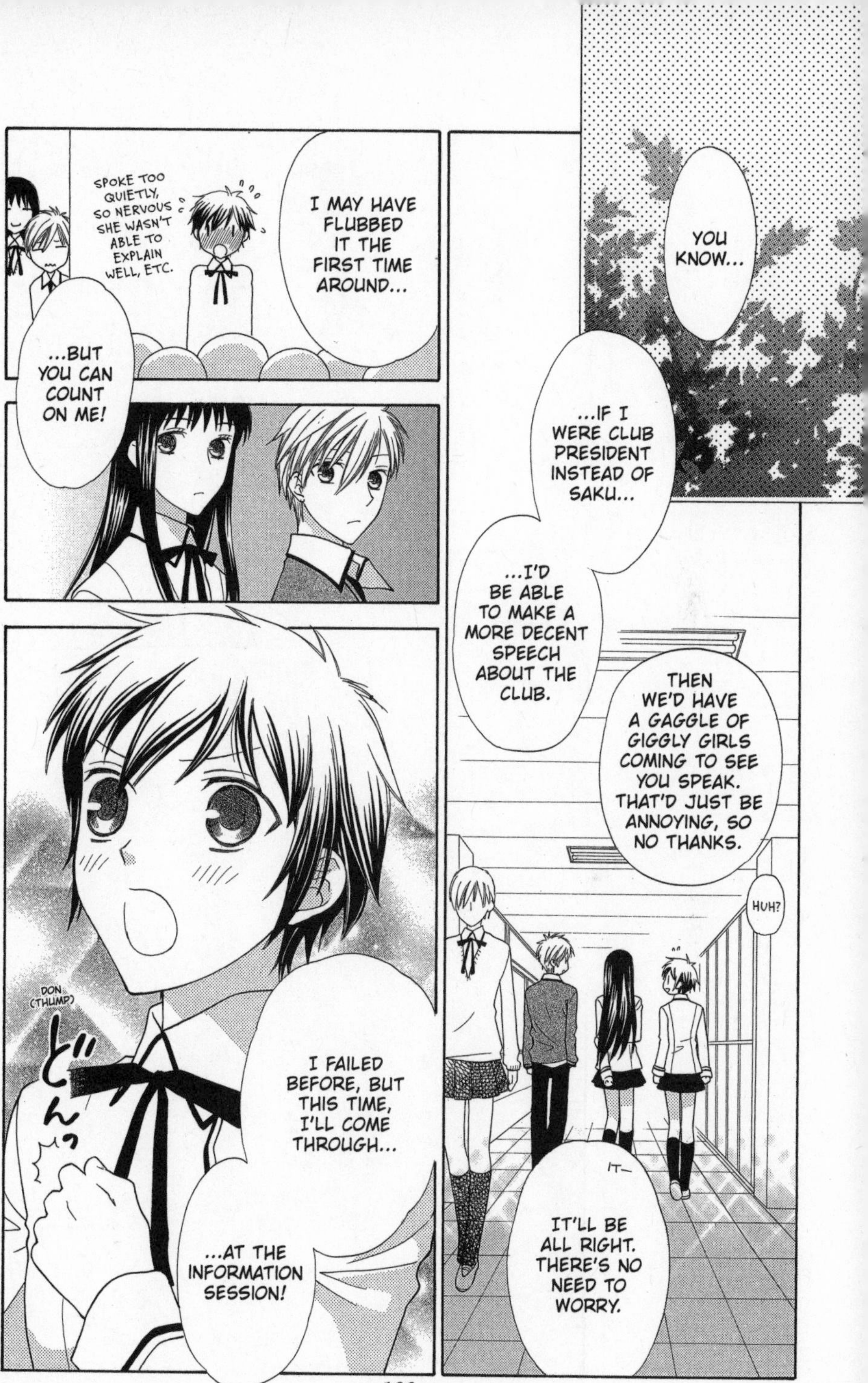
YOU KNOW...
...IF I WERE CLUB PRESIDENT INSTEAD OF SAKU...
...I'D BE ABLE TO MAKE A MORE DECENT SPEECH ABOUT THE CLUB.
THEN WE'D HAVE A GAGGLE OF GIGGLY GIRLS COMING TO SEE YOU SPEAK. THAT'D JUST BE ANNOYING, SO NO THANKS.
HUH?
IT—
IT'LL BE ALL RIGHT. THERE'S NO NEED TO WORRY.
I MAY HAVE FLUBBED IT THE FIRST TIME AROUND...
SPOKE TOO QUIETLY, SO NERVOUS SHE WASN'T ABLE TO EXPLAIN WELL, ETC.
...BUT YOU CAN COUNT ON ME!
DON (THUMP)
どんっ
I FAILED BEFORE, BUT THIS TIME, I'LL COME THROUGH...
...AT THE INFORMATION SESSION!

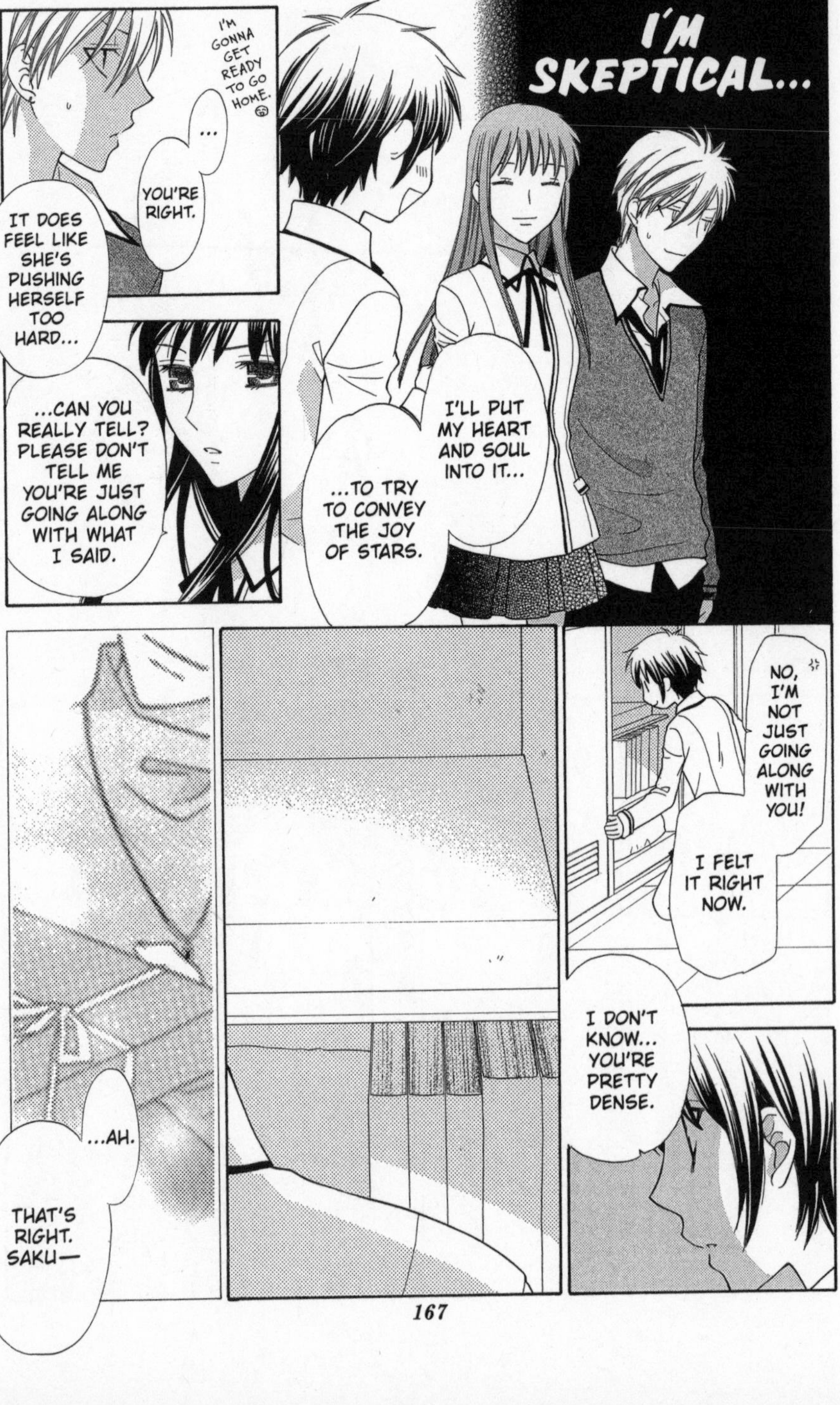
I'M SKEPTICAL...
I'LL PUT MY HEART AND SOUL INTO IT...
...TO TRY TO CONVEY THE JOY OF STARS.
I'M GONNA GET READY TO GO HOME.
...
YOU'RE RIGHT.
IT DOES FEEL LIKE SHE'S PUSHING HERSELF TOO HARD...
...CAN YOU REALLY TELL? PLEASE DON'T TELL ME YOU'RE JUST GOING ALONG WITH WHAT I SAID.
NO, I'M NOT JUST GOING ALONG WITH YOU!
I FELT IT RIGHT NOW.
I DON'T KNOW... YOU'RE PRETTY DENSE.
...AH.
THAT'S RIGHT. SAKU—

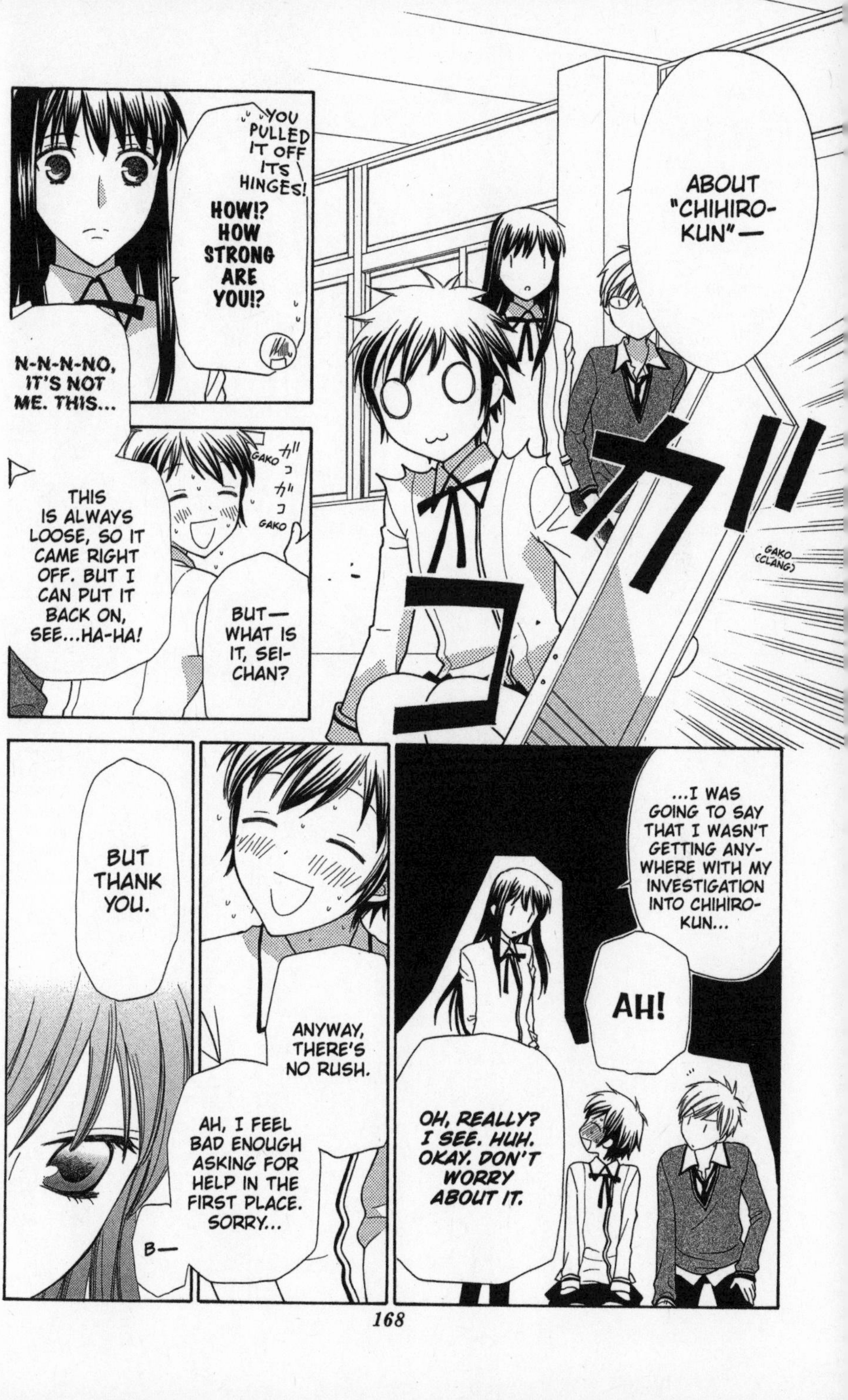
ABOUT "CHIHIRO-KUN"—
GAKO (CLANG)
...YOU PULLED IT OFF ITS HINGES!
HOW!? HOW STRONG ARE YOU!?
N-N-N-NO, IT'S NOT ME. THIS...
GAKO GAKO
THIS IS ALWAYS LOOSE, SO IT CAME RIGHT OFF. BUT I CAN PUT IT BACK ON, SEE...HA-HA!
BUT— WHAT IS IT, SEI-CHAN?
...I WAS GOING TO SAY THAT I WASN'T GETTING ANYWHERE WITH MY INVESTIGATION INTO CHIHIRO-KUN...
AH!
OH, REALLY? I SEE. HUH. OKAY. DON'T WORRY ABOUT IT.
ANYWAY, THERE'S NO RUSH.
AH, I FEEL BAD ENOUGH ASKING FOR HELP IN THE FIRST PLACE. SORRY...
BUT THANK YOU.
B—

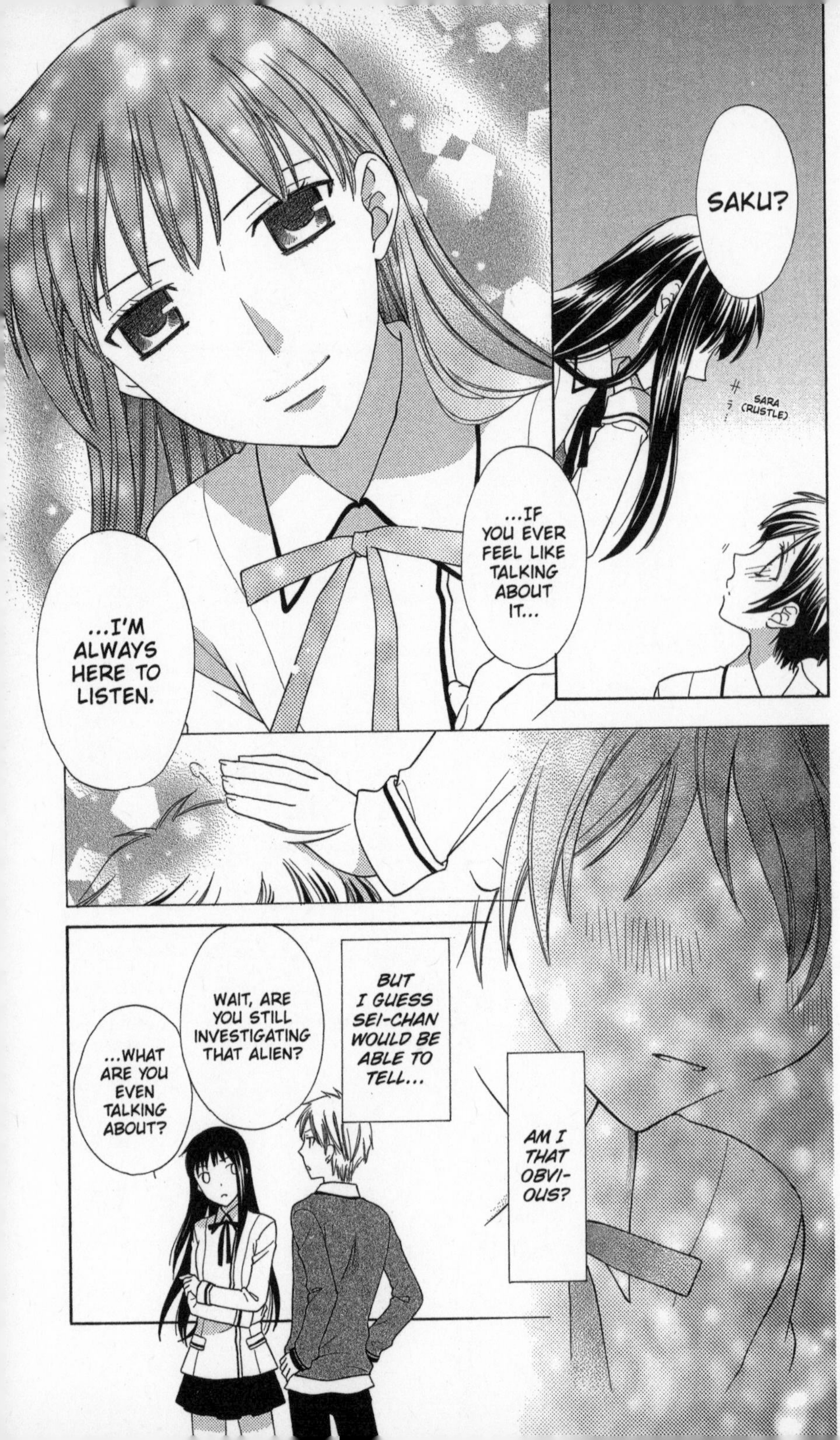
SAKU?
サラ
SARA (RUSTLE)
...IF YOU EVER FEEL LIKE TALKING ABOUT IT...
...I'M ALWAYS HERE TO LISTEN.
AM I THAT OBVI-OUS?
BUT I GUESS SEI-CHAN WOULD BE ABLE TO TELL...
WAIT, ARE YOU STILL INVESTIGATING THAT ALIEN?
...WHAT ARE YOU EVEN TALKING ABOUT?

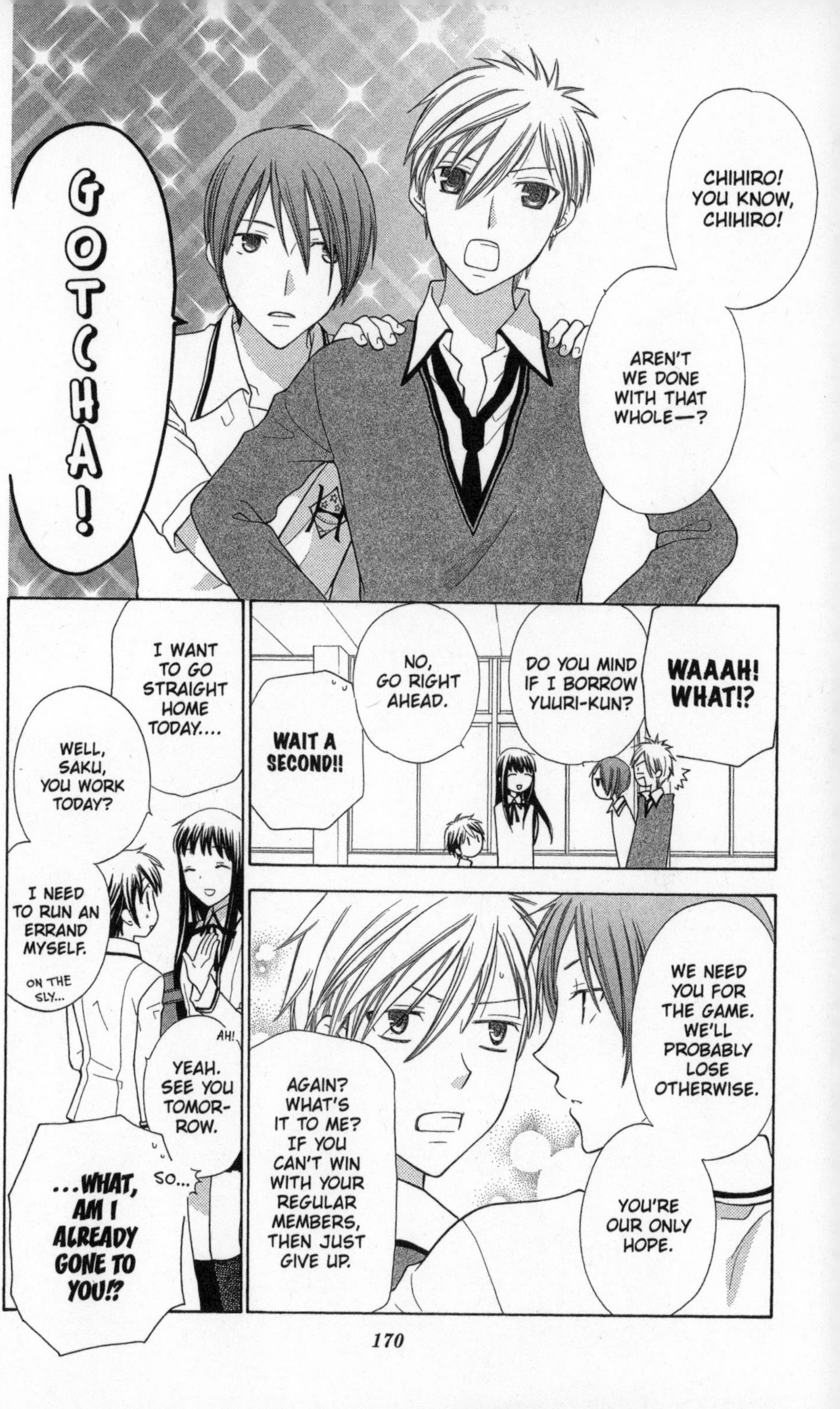
CHIHIRO! YOU KNOW, CHIHIRO!
AREN'T WE DONE WITH THAT WHOLE—?
GOTCHA!
WAAAH! WHAT!?
DO YOU MIND IF I BORROW YUURI-KUN?
NO, GO RIGHT AHEAD.
WAIT A SECOND!!
WE NEED YOU FOR THE GAME. WE'LL PROBABLY LOSE OTHERWISE.
YOU'RE OUR ONLY HOPE.
AGAIN? WHAT'S IT TO ME? IF YOU CAN'T WIN WITH YOUR REGULAR MEMBERS, THEN JUST GIVE UP.
I WANT TO GO STRAIGHT HOME TODAY....
WELL, SAKU, YOU WORK TODAY?
I NEED TO RUN AN ERRAND MYSELF.
ON THE SLY...
AH!
YEAH. SEE YOU TOMOR-ROW.
SO...
...WHAT, AM I ALREADY GONE TO YOU!?

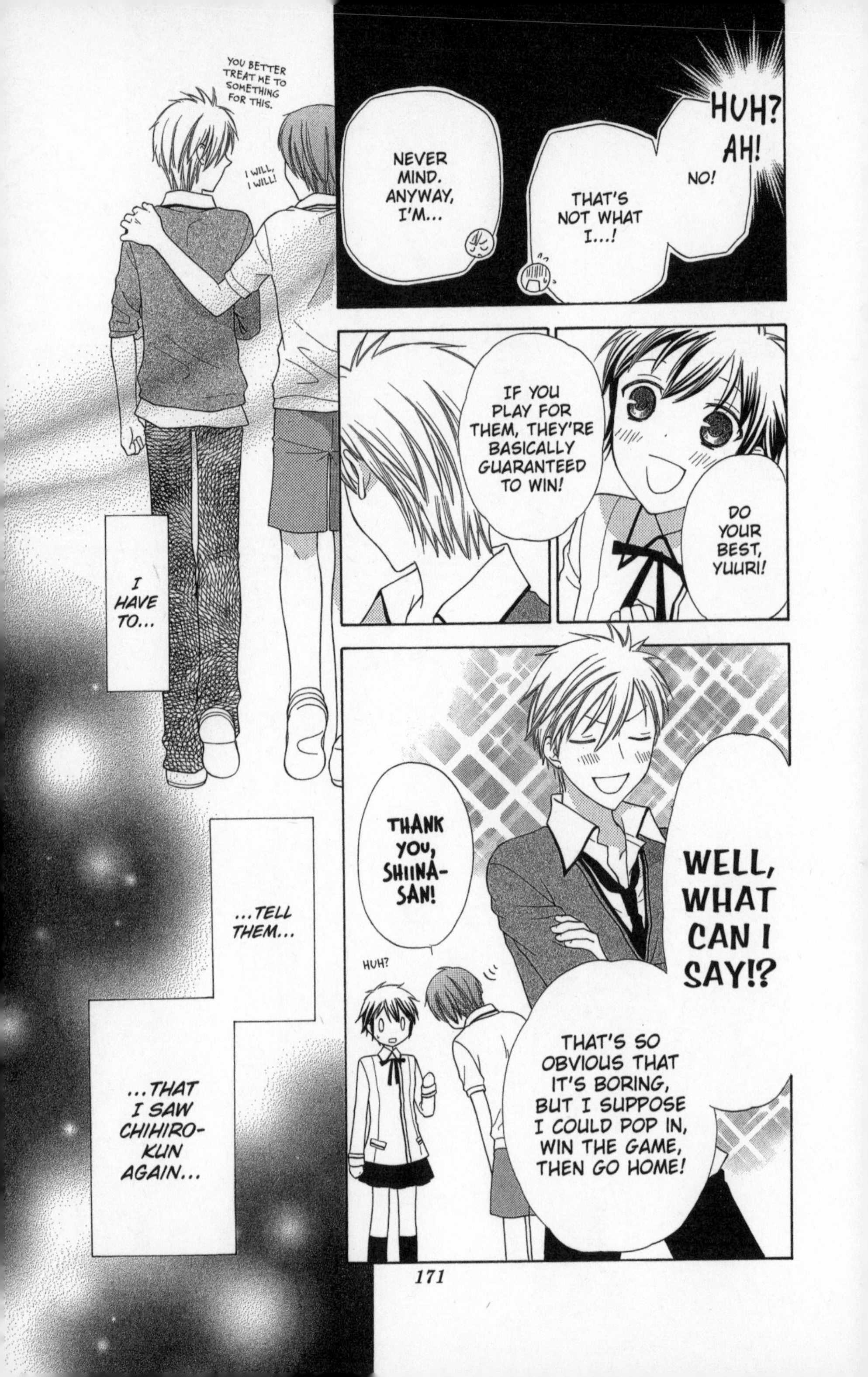
HUH? AH!
NO!
THAT'S NOT WHAT I...!
NEVER MIND. ANYWAY, I'M...
IF YOU PLAY FOR THEM, THEY'RE BASICALLY GUARANTEED TO WIN!
DO YOUR BEST, YUURI!
WELL, WHAT CAN I SAY!?
THAT'S SO OBVIOUS THAT IT'S BORING, BUT I SUPPOSE I COULD POP IN, WIN THE GAME, THEN GO HOME!
THANK YOU, SHIINA-SAN!
HUH?
YOU BETTER TREAT ME TO SOMETHING FOR THIS.
I WILL, I WILL!
I HAVE TO...
...TELL THEM...
...THAT I SAW CHIHIRO-KUN AGAIN...

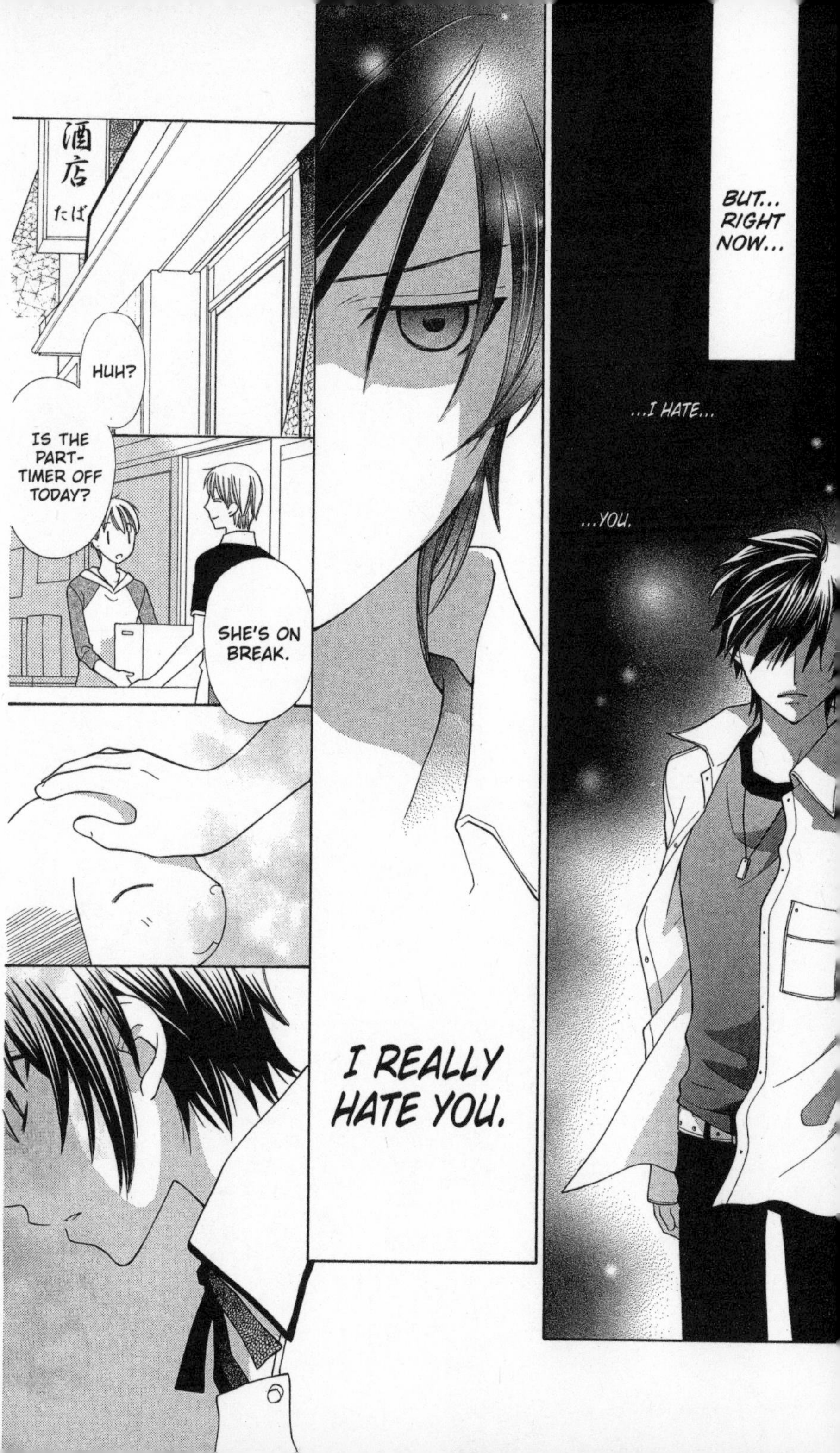
BUT... RIGHT NOW...
...I HATE...
...YOU.
I REALLY HATE YOU.
酒店
たば
HUH?
IS THE PART-TIMER OFF TODAY?
SHE'S ON BREAK.

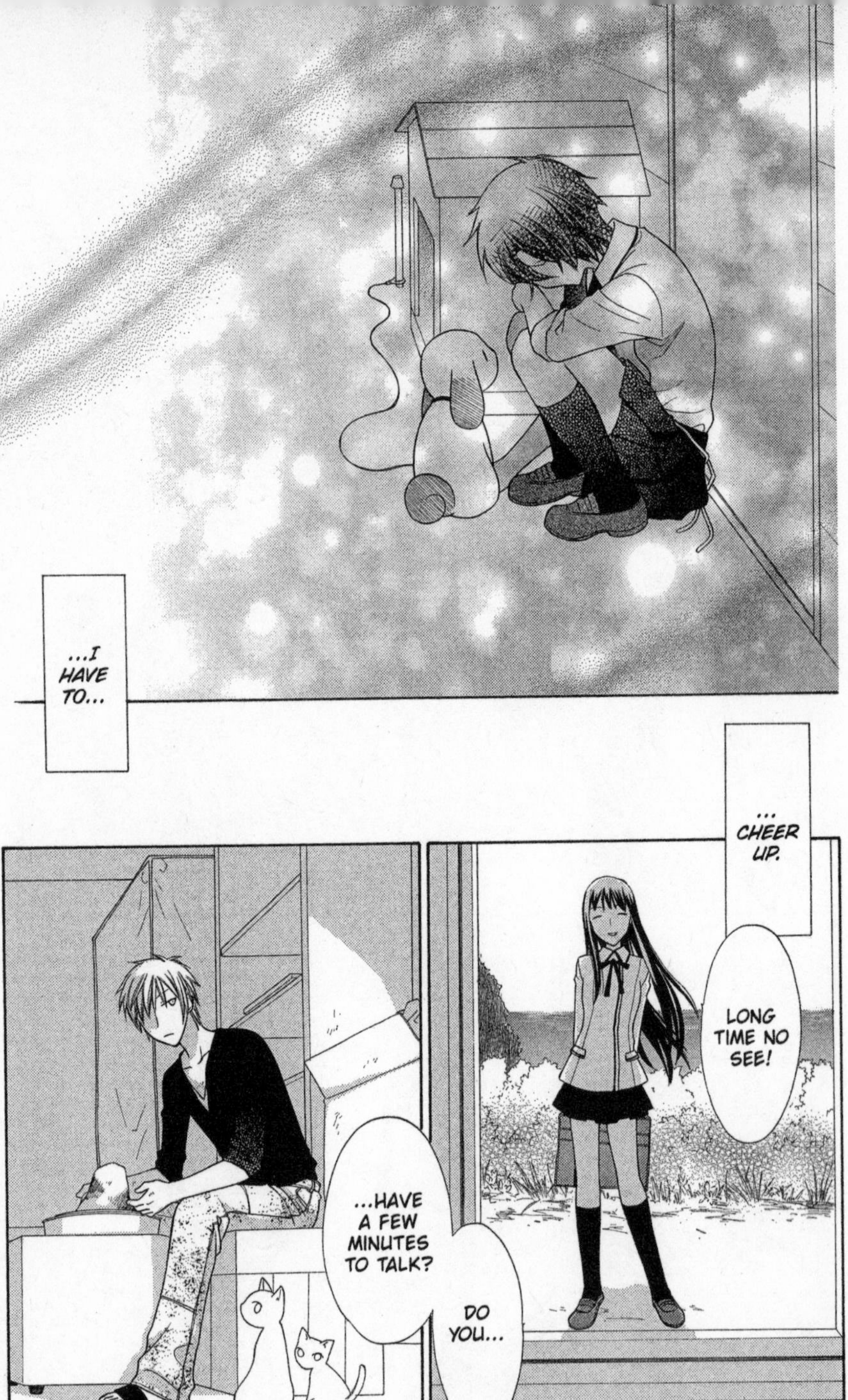
...I HAVE TO...
... CHEER UP.
LONG TIME NO SEE!
DO YOU...
...HAVE A FEW MINUTES TO TALK?

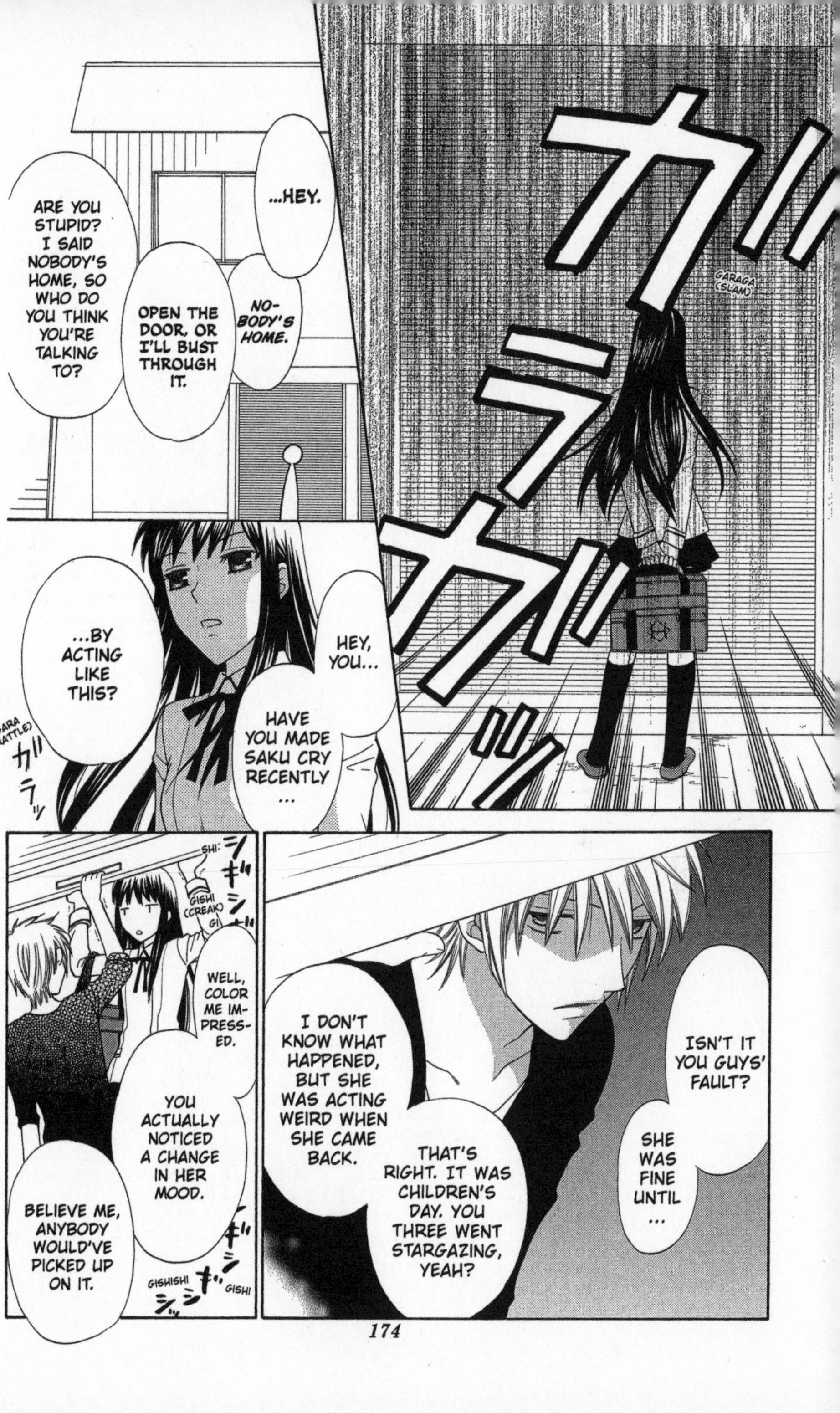
GARAGA (SLAM)
...HEY.
NO-BODY'S HOME.
OPEN THE DOOR, OR I'LL BUST THROUGH IT.
ARE YOU STUPID? I SAID NOBODY'S HOME, SO WHO DO YOU THINK YOU'RE TALKING TO?
HEY, YOU...
HAVE YOU MADE SAKU CRY RECENTLY ...
...BY ACTING LIKE THIS?
GARA (RATTLE)
ISN'T IT YOU GUYS' FAULT?
SHE WAS FINE UNTIL ...
THAT'S RIGHT. IT WAS CHILDREN'S DAY. YOU THREE WENT STARGAZING, YEAH?
I DON'T KNOW WHAT HAPPENED, BUT SHE WAS ACTING WEIRD WHEN SHE CAME BACK.
SHI-
GISHI (CREAK)
GI
WELL, COLOR ME IM-PRESS-ED.
YOU ACTUALLY NOTICED A CHANGE IN HER MOOD.
BELIEVE ME, ANYBODY WOULD'VE PICKED UP ON IT.
GISHISHI
GISHI

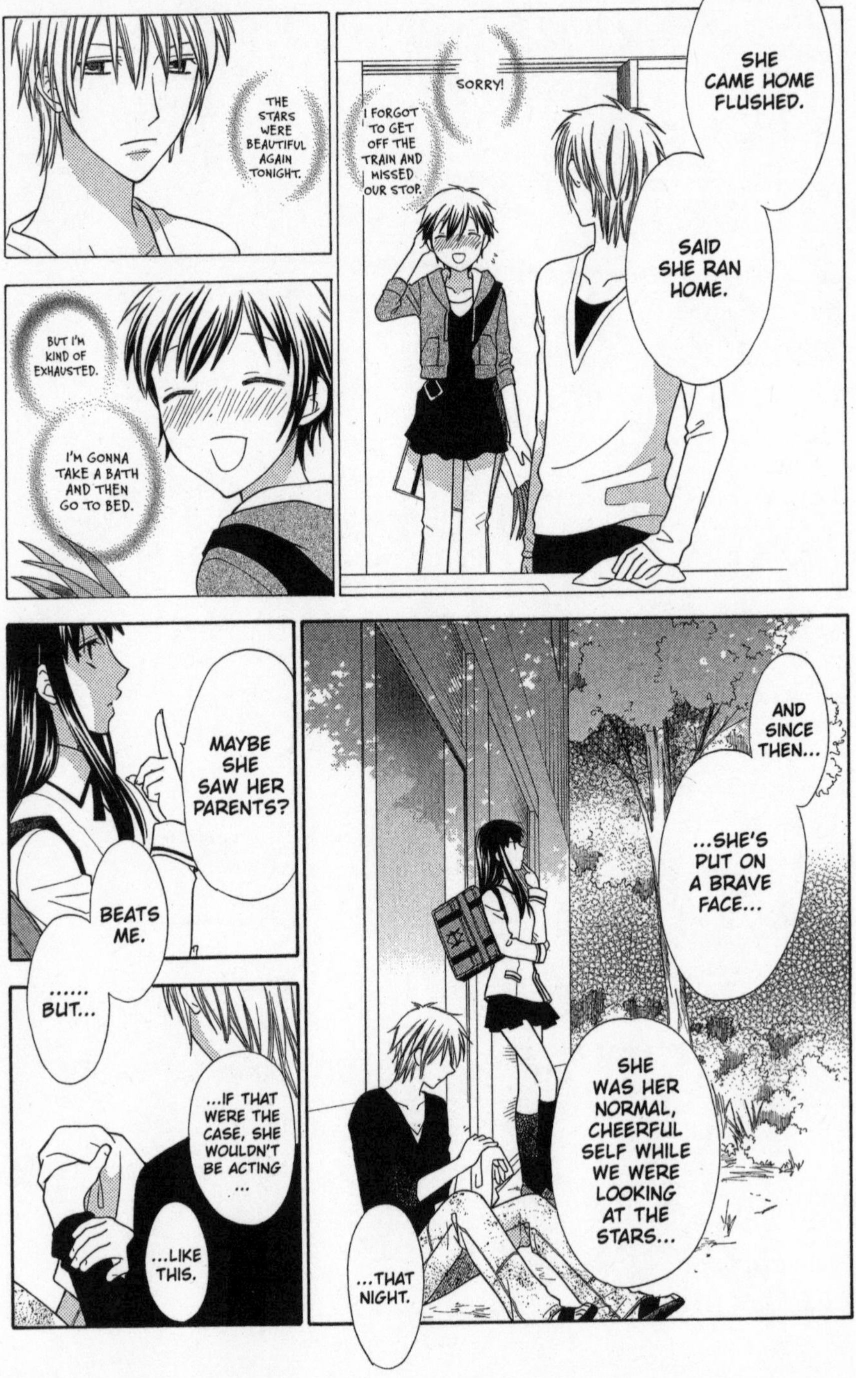
SHE CAME HOME FLUSHED.
SAID SHE RAN HOME.
SORRY!
I FORGOT TO GET OFF THE TRAIN AND MISSED OUR STOP.
THE STARS WERE BEAUTIFUL AGAIN TONIGHT.
BUT I'M KIND OF EXHAUSTED.
I'M GONNA TAKE A BATH AND THEN GO TO BED.
AND SINCE THEN...
...SHE'S PUT ON A BRAVE FACE...
SHE WAS HER NORMAL, CHEERFUL SELF WHILE WE WERE LOOKING AT THE STARS...
...THAT NIGHT.
MAYBE SHE SAW HER PARENTS?
BEATS ME.
...... BUT...
...IF THAT WERE THE CASE, SHE WOULDN'T BE ACTING ...
...LIKE THIS.

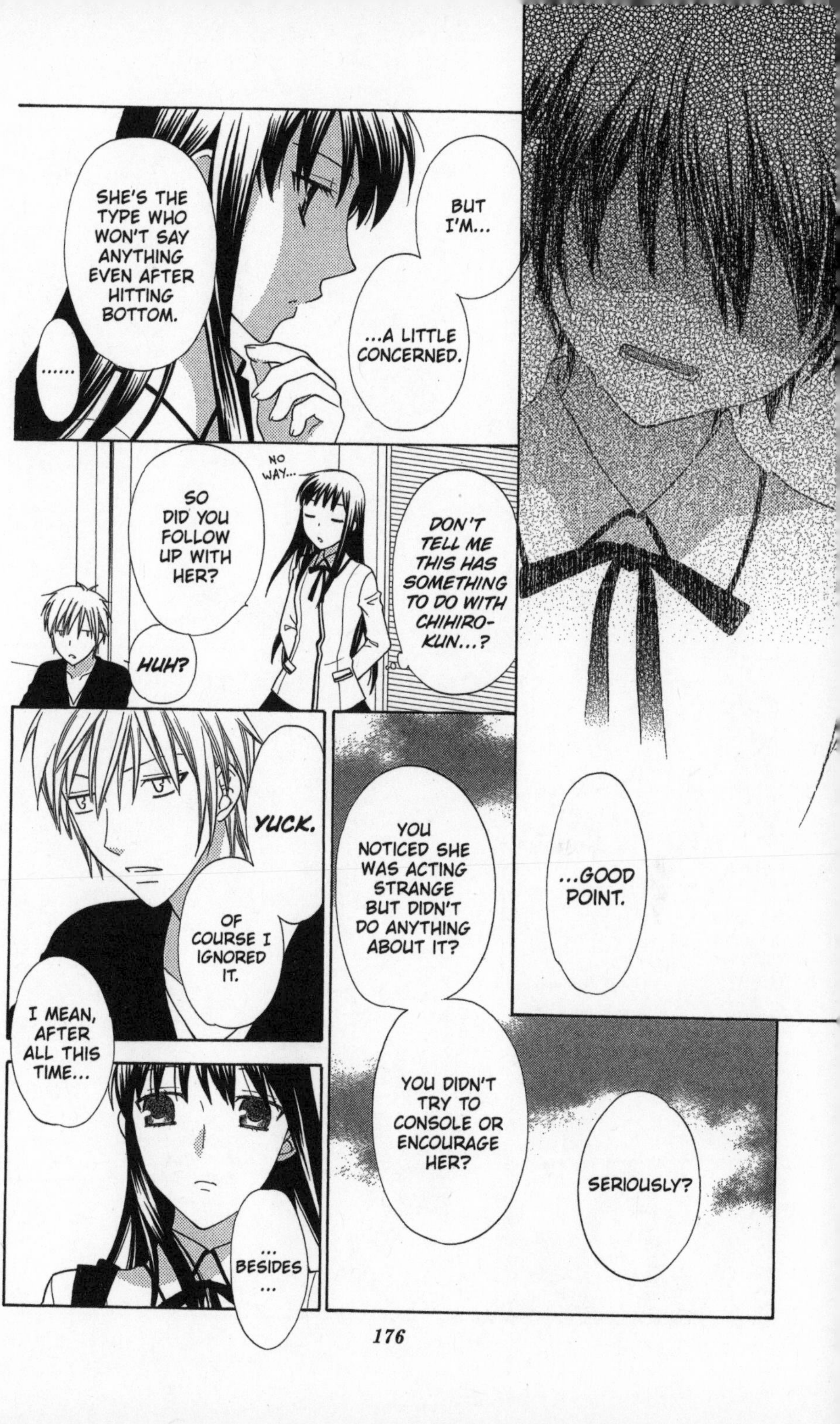
...GOOD POINT.
BUT I'M...
...A LITTLE CONCERNED.
SHE'S THE TYPE WHO WON'T SAY ANYTHING EVEN AFTER HITTING BOTTOM.
......
DON'T TELL ME THIS HAS SOMETHING TO DO WITH CHIHIRO-KUN...?
NO WAY...
SO DID YOU FOLLOW UP WITH HER?
HUH?
YOU NOTICED SHE WAS ACTING STRANGE BUT DIDN'T DO ANYTHING ABOUT IT?
YOU DIDN'T TRY TO CONSOLE OR ENCOURAGE HER?
SERIOUSLY?
YUCK.
OF COURSE I IGNORED IT.
I MEAN, AFTER ALL THIS TIME...
...BESIDES...

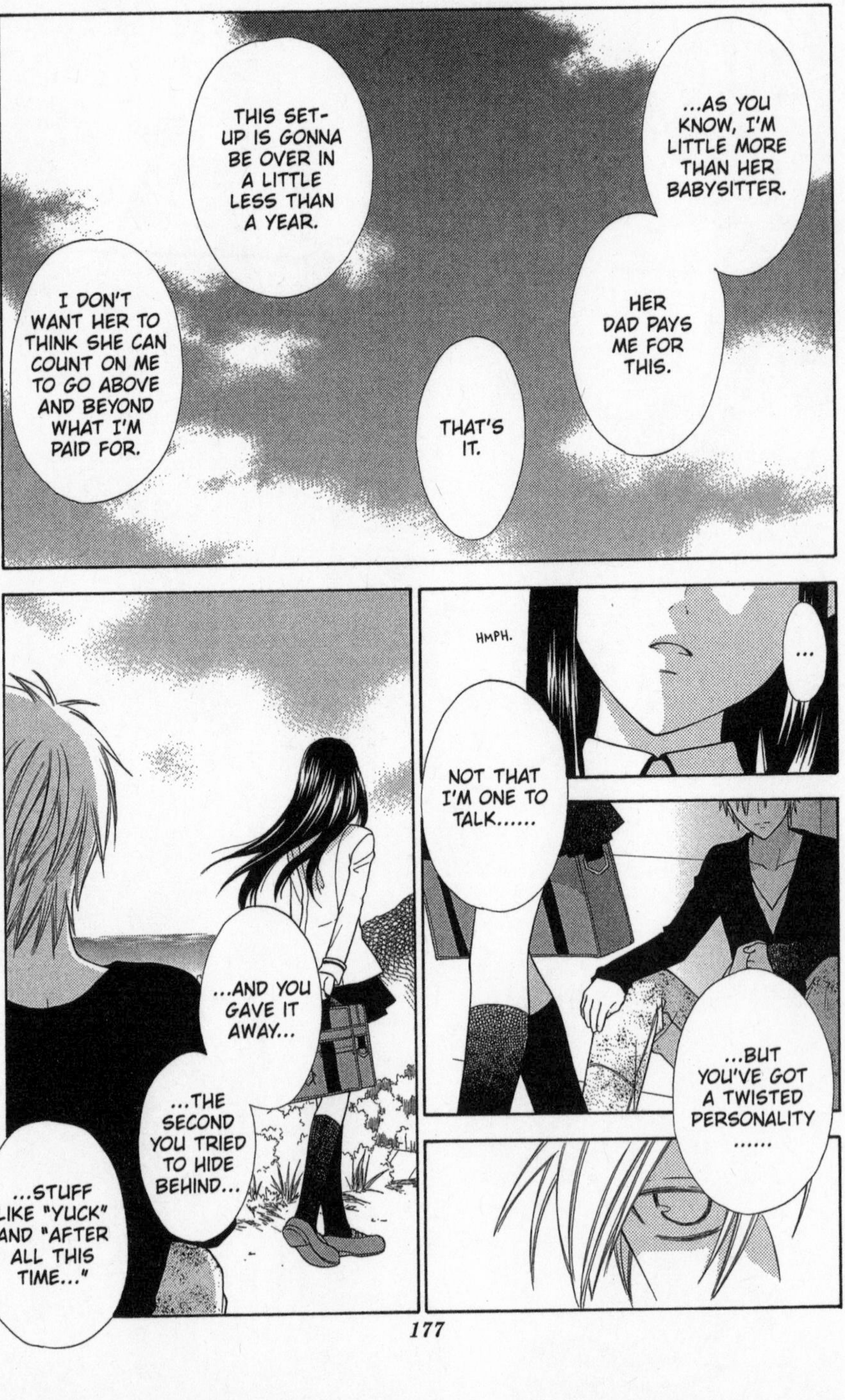

...AS YOU KNOW, I'M LITTLE MORE THAN HER BABYSITTER.
HER DAD PAYS ME FOR THIS.
THAT'S IT.
THIS SET-UP IS GONNA BE OVER IN A LITTLE LESS THAN A YEAR.
I DON'T WANT HER TO THINK SHE CAN COUNT ON ME TO GO ABOVE AND BEYOND WHAT I'M PAID FOR.
...
HMPH.
NOT THAT I'M ONE TO TALK......
...BUT YOU'VE GOT A TWISTED PERSONALITY ......
...AND YOU GAVE IT AWAY...
...THE SECOND YOU TRIED TO HIDE BEHIND...
...STUFF LIKE "YUCK" AND "AFTER ALL THIS TIME..."

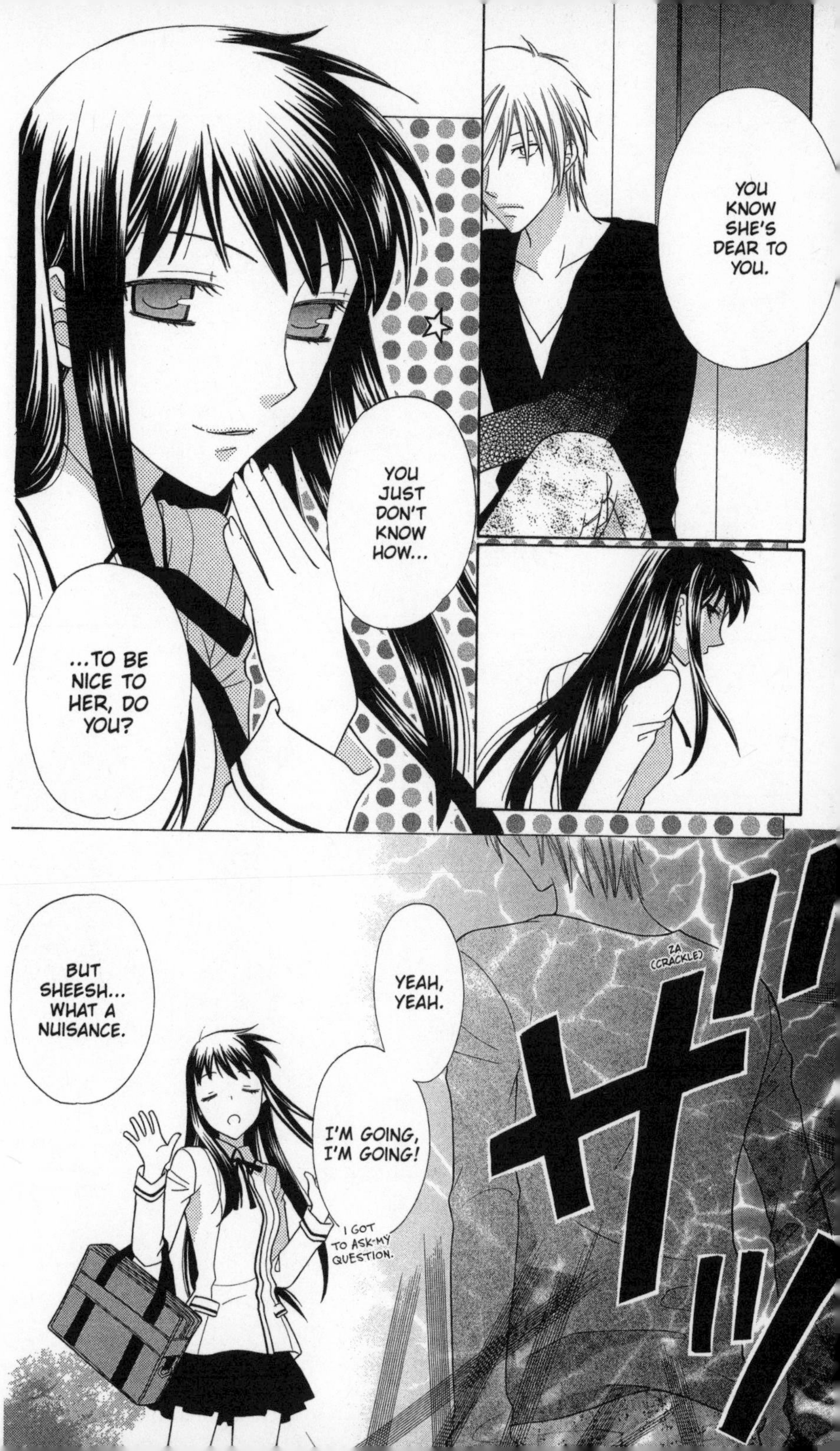
YOU KNOW SHE'S DEAR TO YOU.
YOU JUST DON'T KNOW HOW...
...TO BE NICE TO HER, DO YOU?
ZA (CRACKLE)
YEAH, YEAH.
BUT SHEESH... WHAT A NUISANCE.
I'M GOING, I'M GOING!
I GOT TO ASK MY QUESTION.

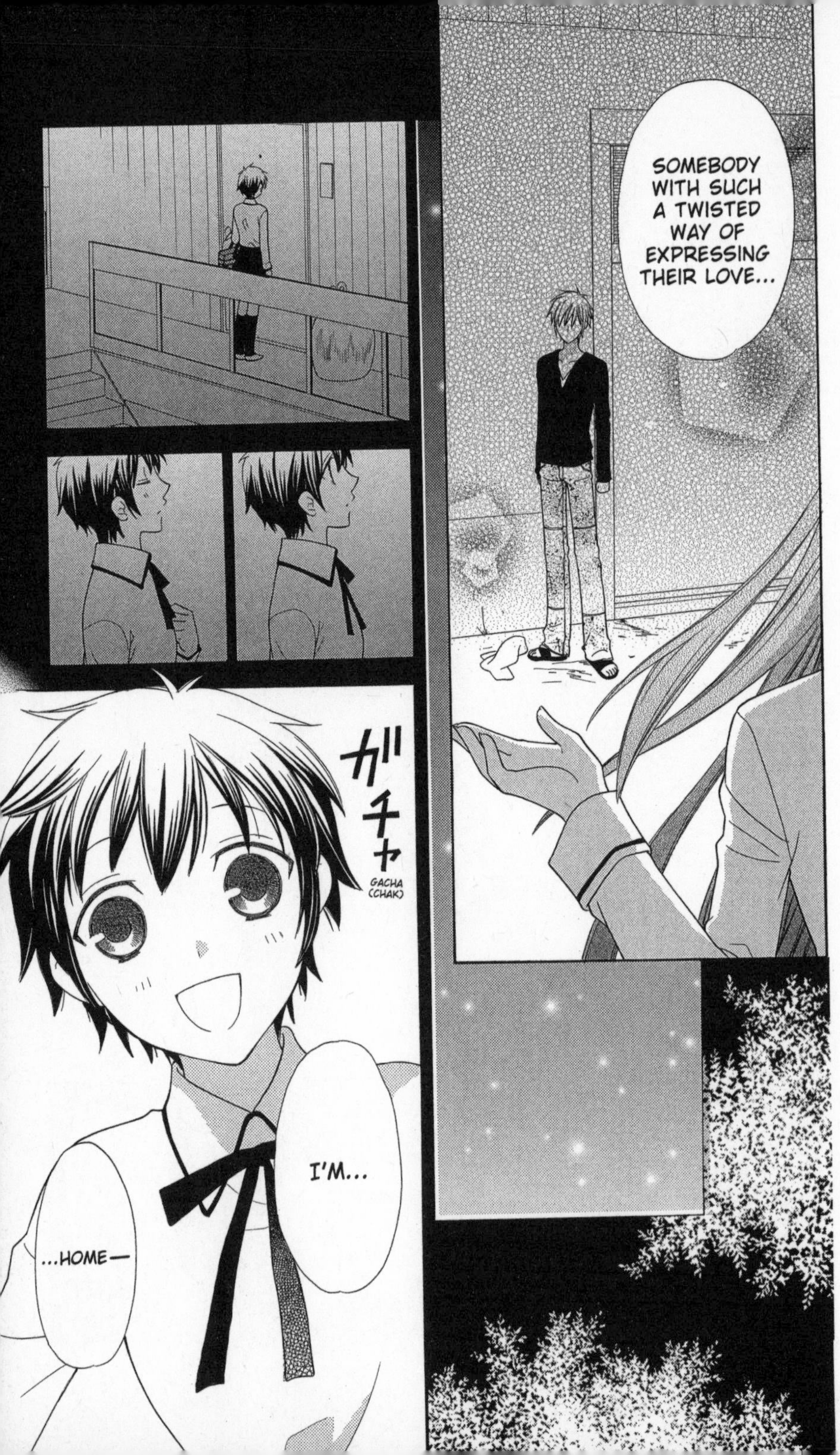
SOMEBODY WITH SUCH A TWISTED WAY OF EXPRESSING THEIR LOVE...
ガチャ
GACHA (CHAK)
I'M...
...HOME—

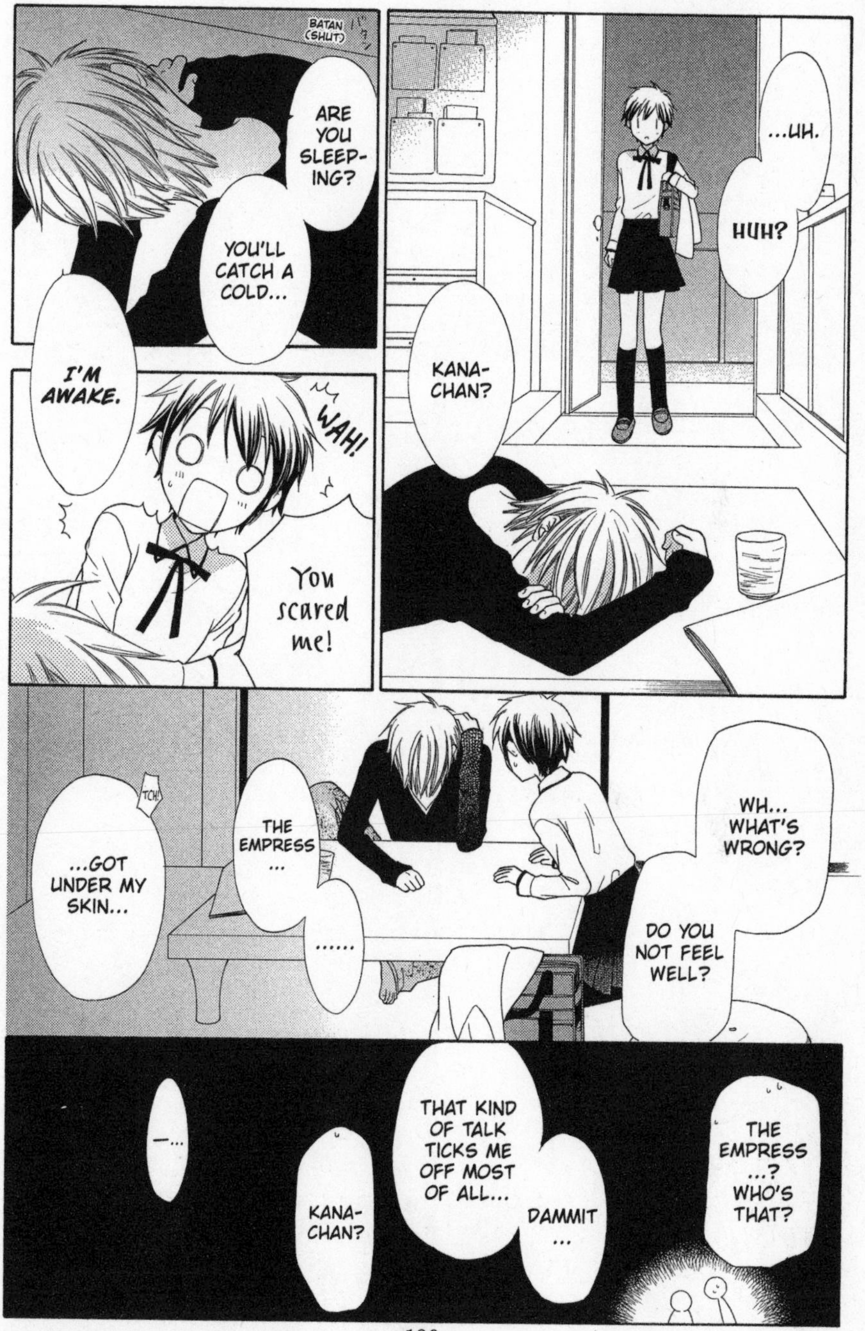
...UH.
HUH?
KANA-CHAN?
BATAN (SHUT)
ARE YOU SLEEPING?
YOU'LL CATCH A COLD...
I'M AWAKE.
WAH!
You scared me!
WH... WHAT'S WRONG?
DO YOU NOT FEEL WELL?
THE EMPRESS ...
......
TCH!
...GOT UNDER MY SKIN...
THE EMPRESS ...? WHO'S THAT?
DAMMIT ...
THAT KIND OF TALK TICKS ME OFF MOST OF ALL...
KANA-CHAN?
—...

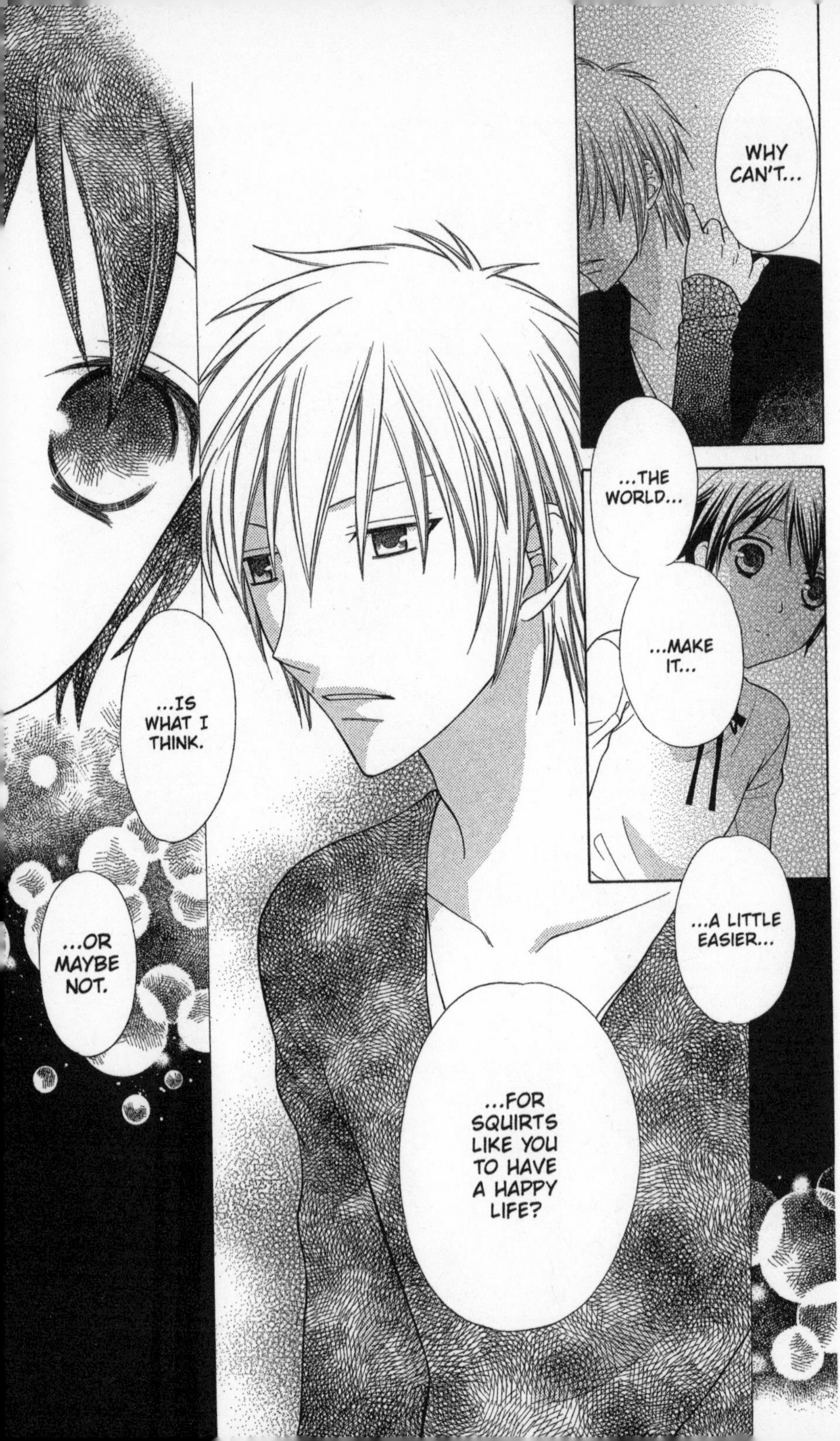
WHY CAN'T...
...THE WORLD...
...MAKE IT...
...A LITTLE EASIER...
...FOR SQUIRTS LIKE YOU TO HAVE A HAPPY LIFE?
...IS WHAT I THINK.
...OR MAYBE NOT.

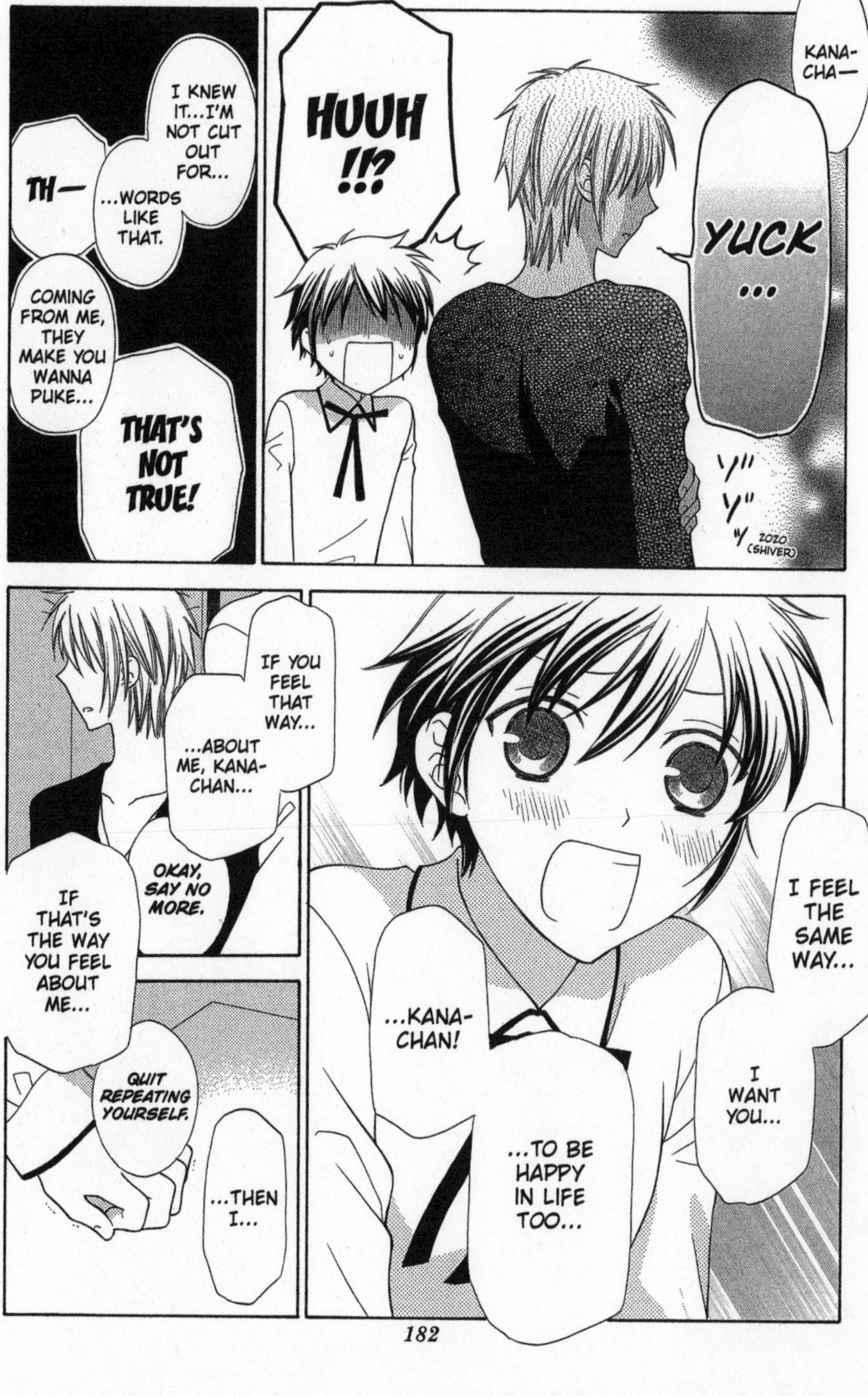
KANA-CHA—
YUCK...
HUUH!!?
ZOZO (SHIVER)
I KNEW IT...I'M NOT CUT OUT FOR...
...WORDS LIKE THAT.
TH—
COMING FROM ME, THEY MAKE YOU WANNA PUKE...
THAT'S NOT TRUE!
I FEEL THE SAME WAY...
I WANT YOU...
...TO BE HAPPY IN LIFE TOO...
...KANA-CHAN!
IF YOU FEEL THAT WAY...
...ABOUT ME, KANA-CHAN...
OKAY, SAY NO MORE.
IF THAT'S THE WAY YOU FEEL ABOUT ME...
QUIT REPEATING YOURSELF.
...THEN I...

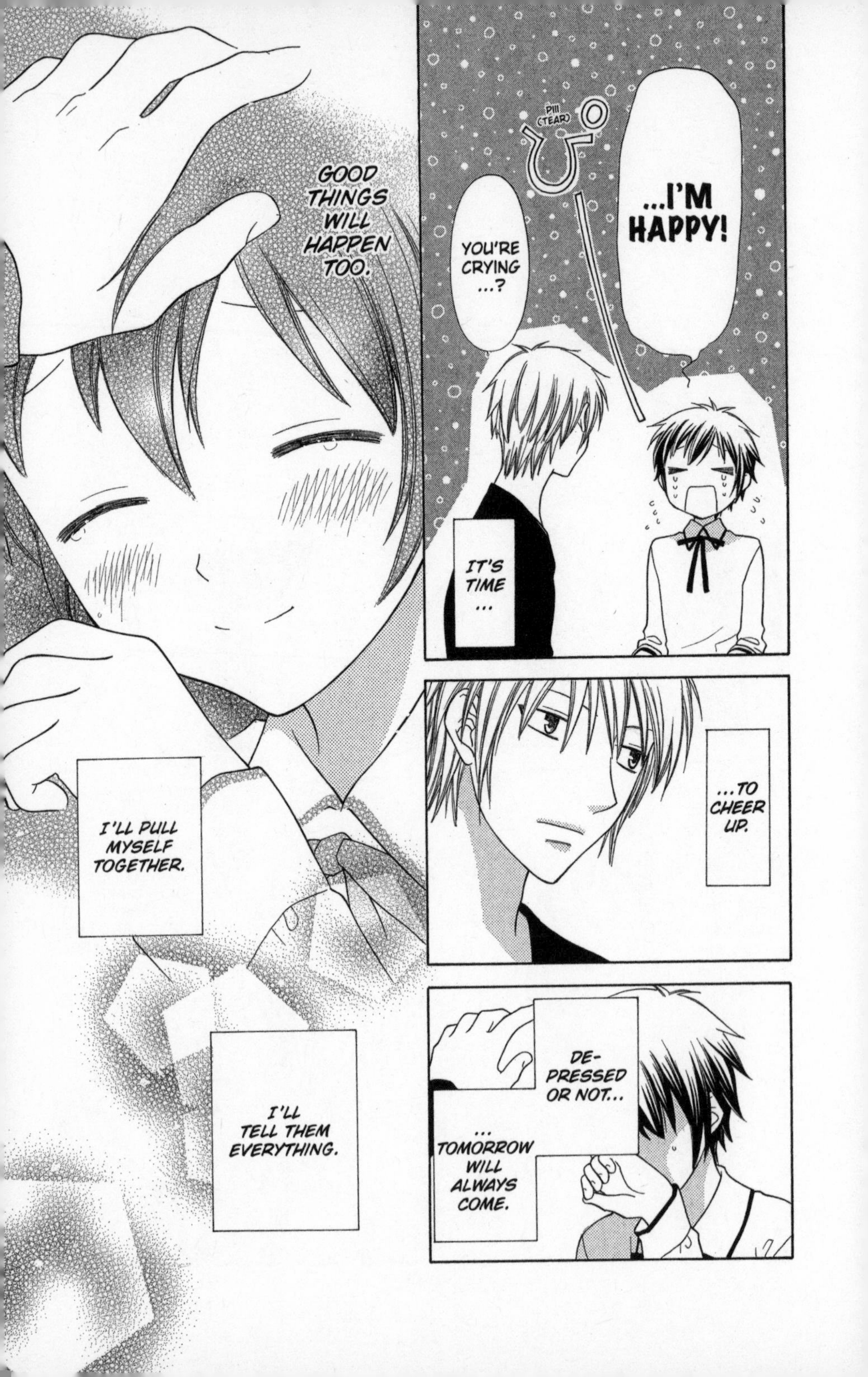
...I'M HAPPY!
PIII (TEAR)
YOU'RE CRYING ...?
IT'S TIME ...
...TO CHEER UP.
DE-PRESSED OR NOT...
... TOMORROW WILL ALWAYS COME.
GOOD THINGS WILL HAPPEN TOO.
I'LL PULL MYSELF TOGETHER.
I'LL TELL THEM EVERYTHING.

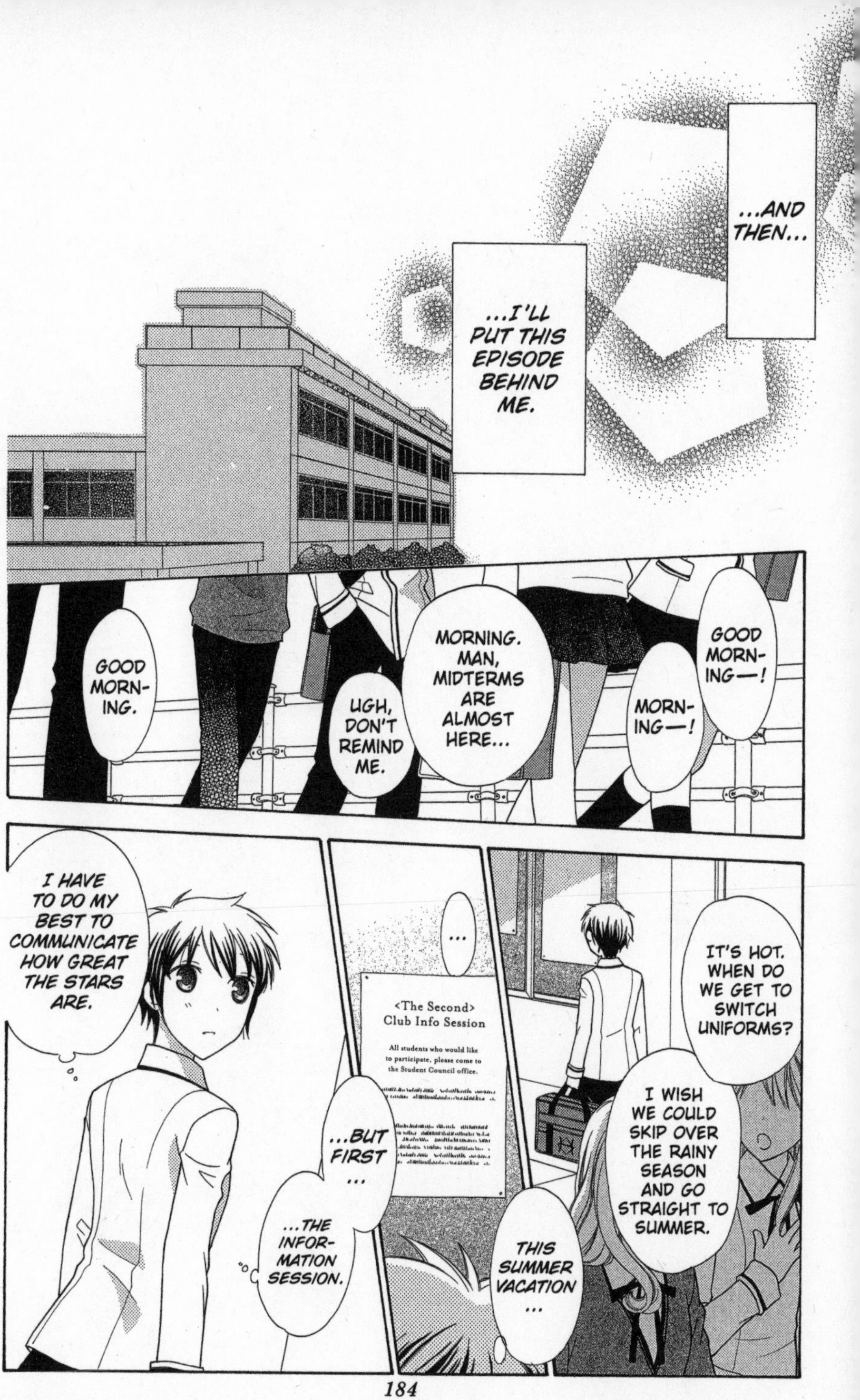
...AND THEN...
...I'LL PUT THIS EPISODE BEHIND ME.
GOOD MORNING—!
MORNING—!
MORNING. MAN, MIDTERMS ARE ALMOST HERE...
UGH, DON'T REMIND ME.
GOOD MORNING.
IT'S HOT. WHEN DO WE GET TO SWITCH UNIFORMS?
I WISH WE COULD SKIP OVER THE RAINY SEASON AND GO STRAIGHT TO SUMMER.
THIS SUMMER VACATION ...
...
<The Second> Club Info Session
All students who would like to participate, please come to the Student Council office.
...BUT FIRST ...
...THE INFORMATION SESSION.
I HAVE TO DO MY BEST TO COMMUNICATE HOW GREAT THE STARS ARE.

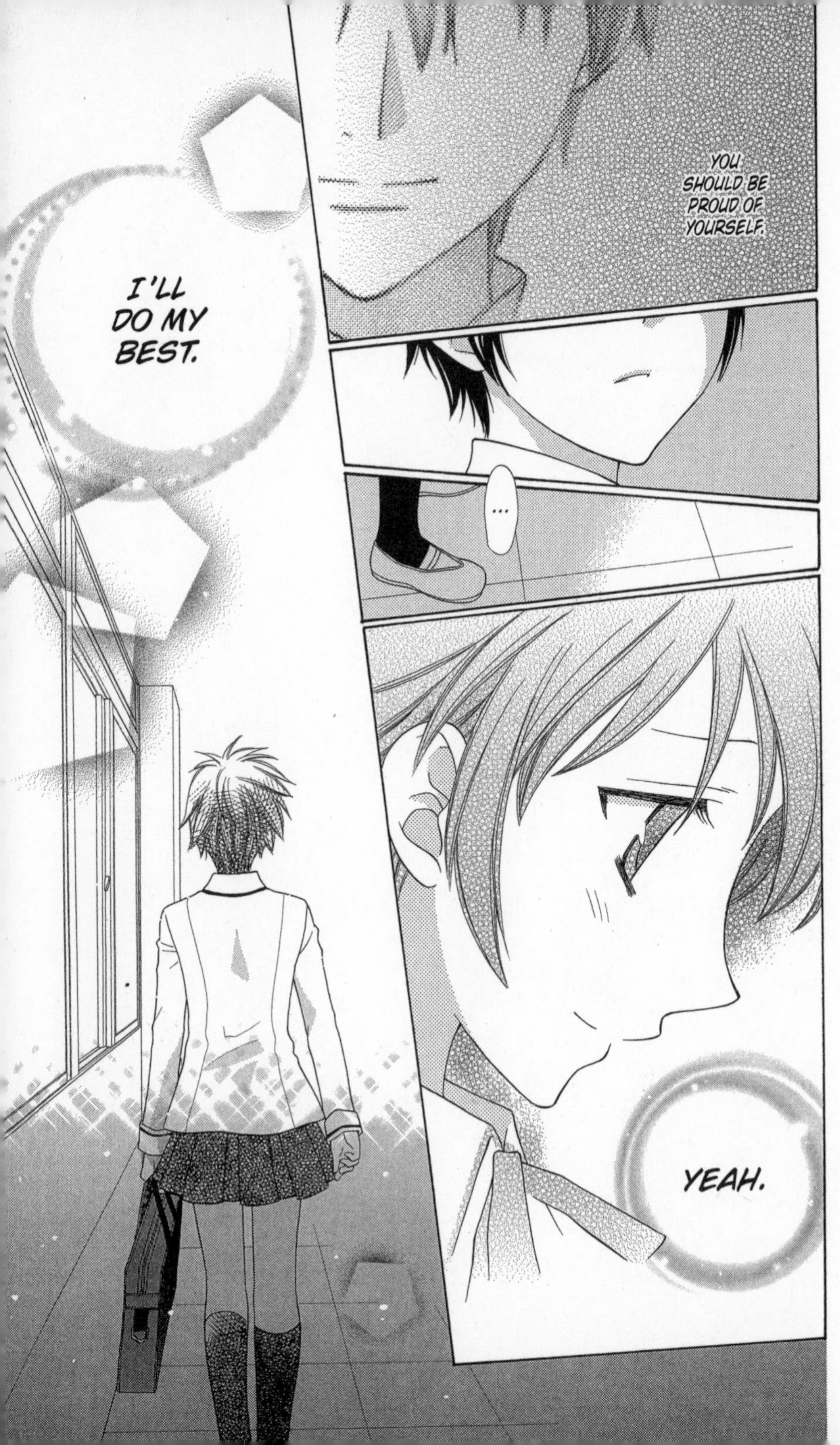
YOU SHOULD BE PROUD OF YOURSELF.
...
YEAH.
I'LL DO MY BEST.

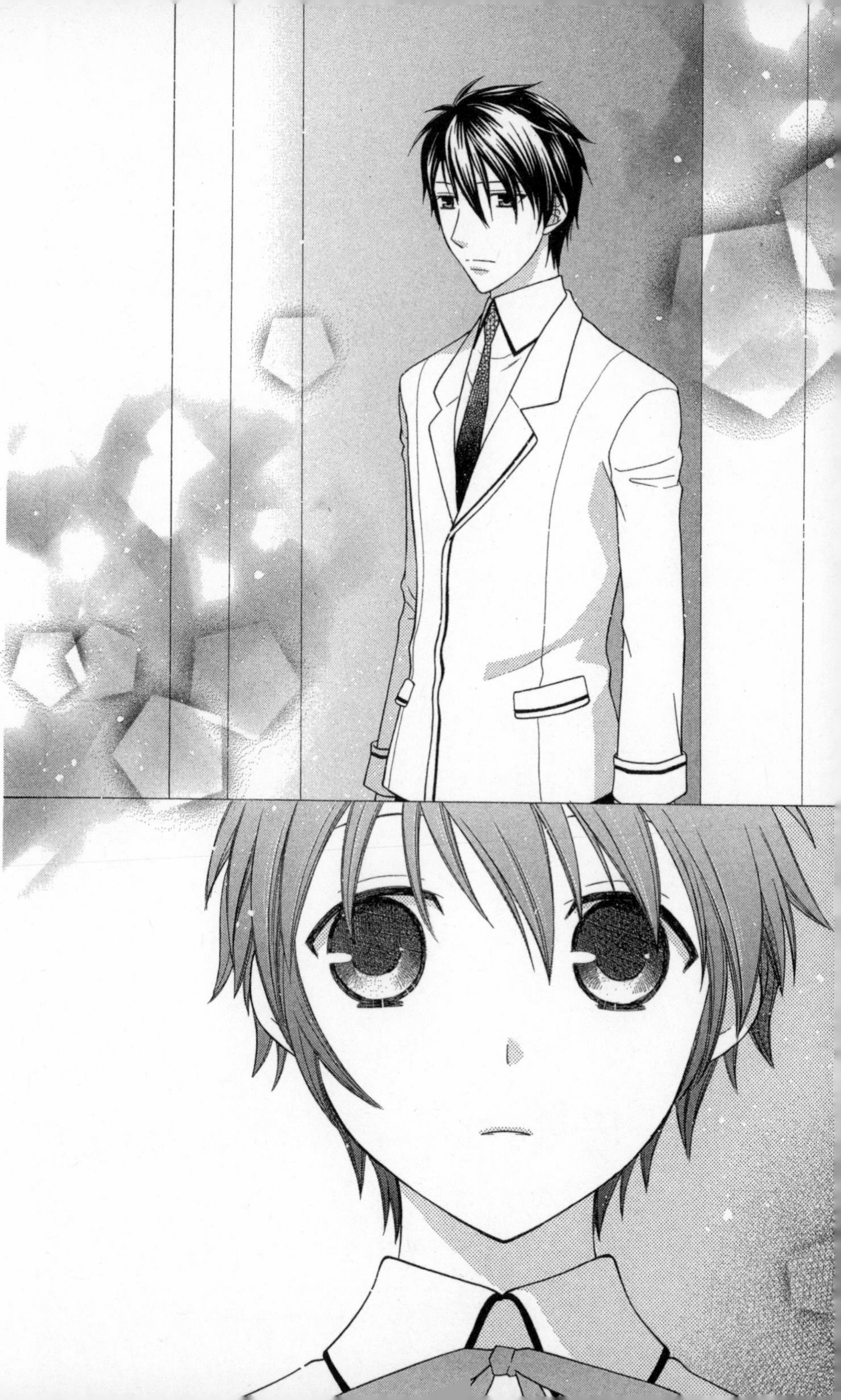

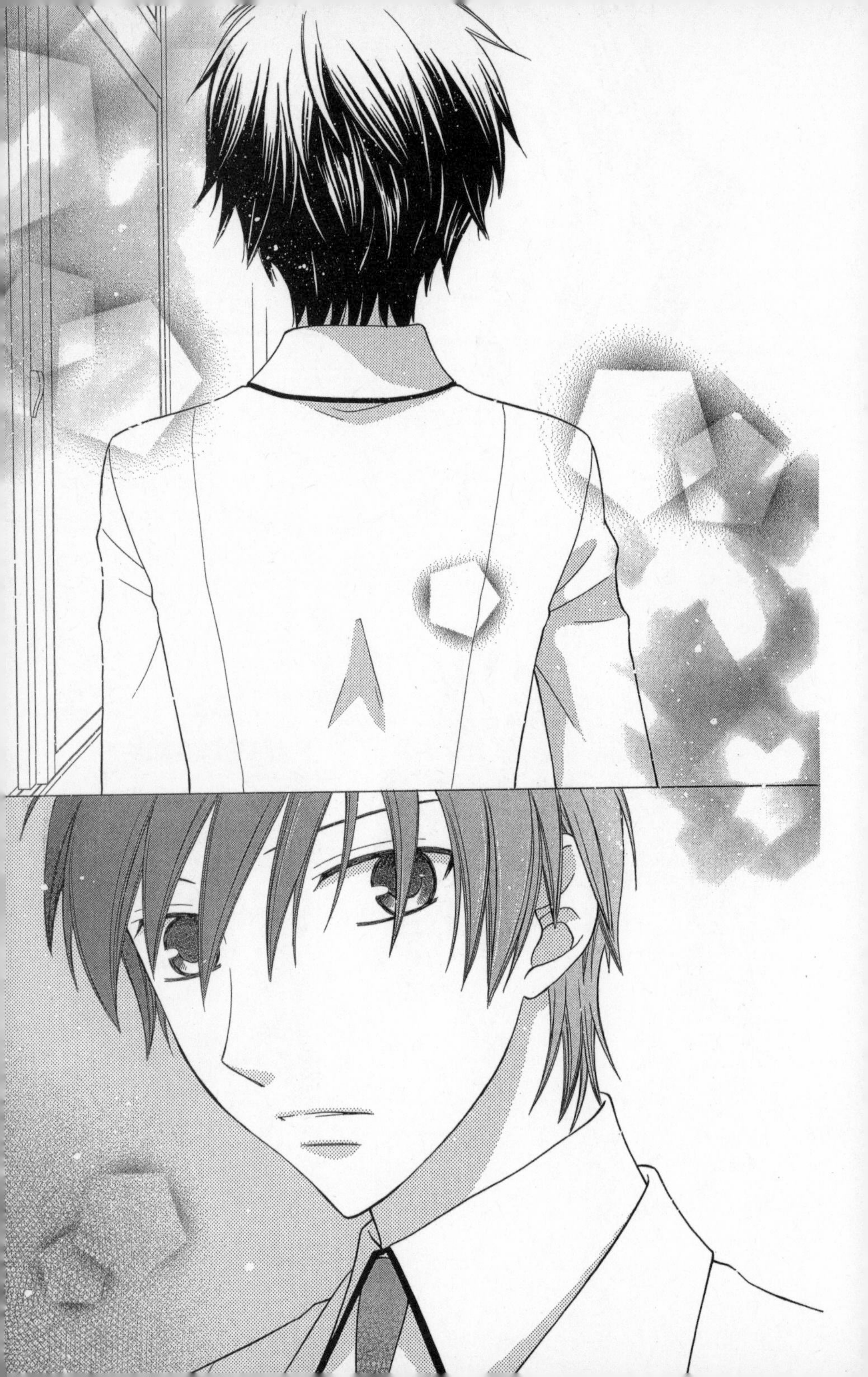

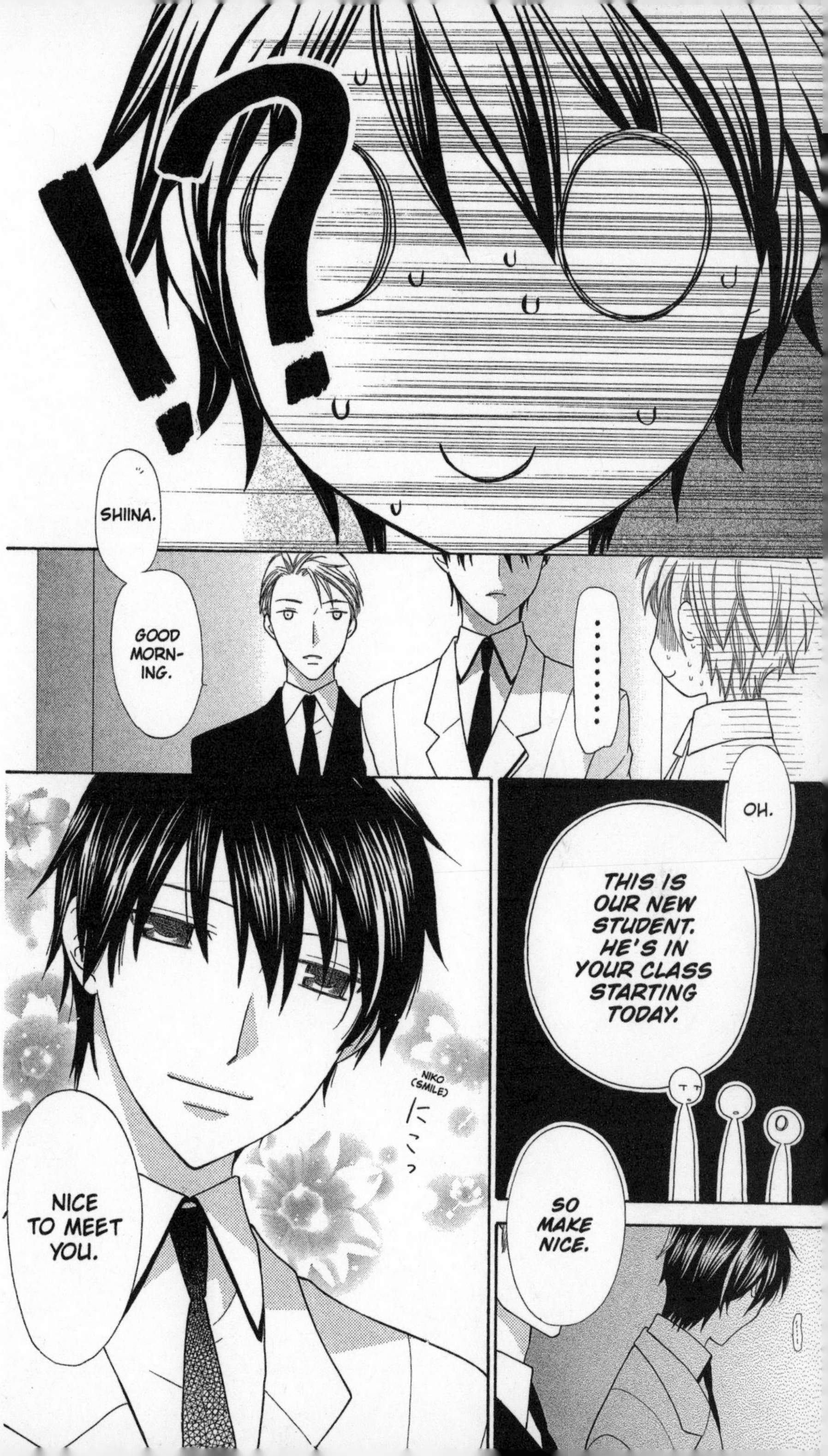
!?
SHIINA.
GOOD MORNING.
....
OH.
THIS IS OUR NEW STUDENT. HE'S IN YOUR CLASS STARTING TODAY.
SO MAKE NICE.
NICE TO MEET YOU.
NIKO (SMILE)
にこっ

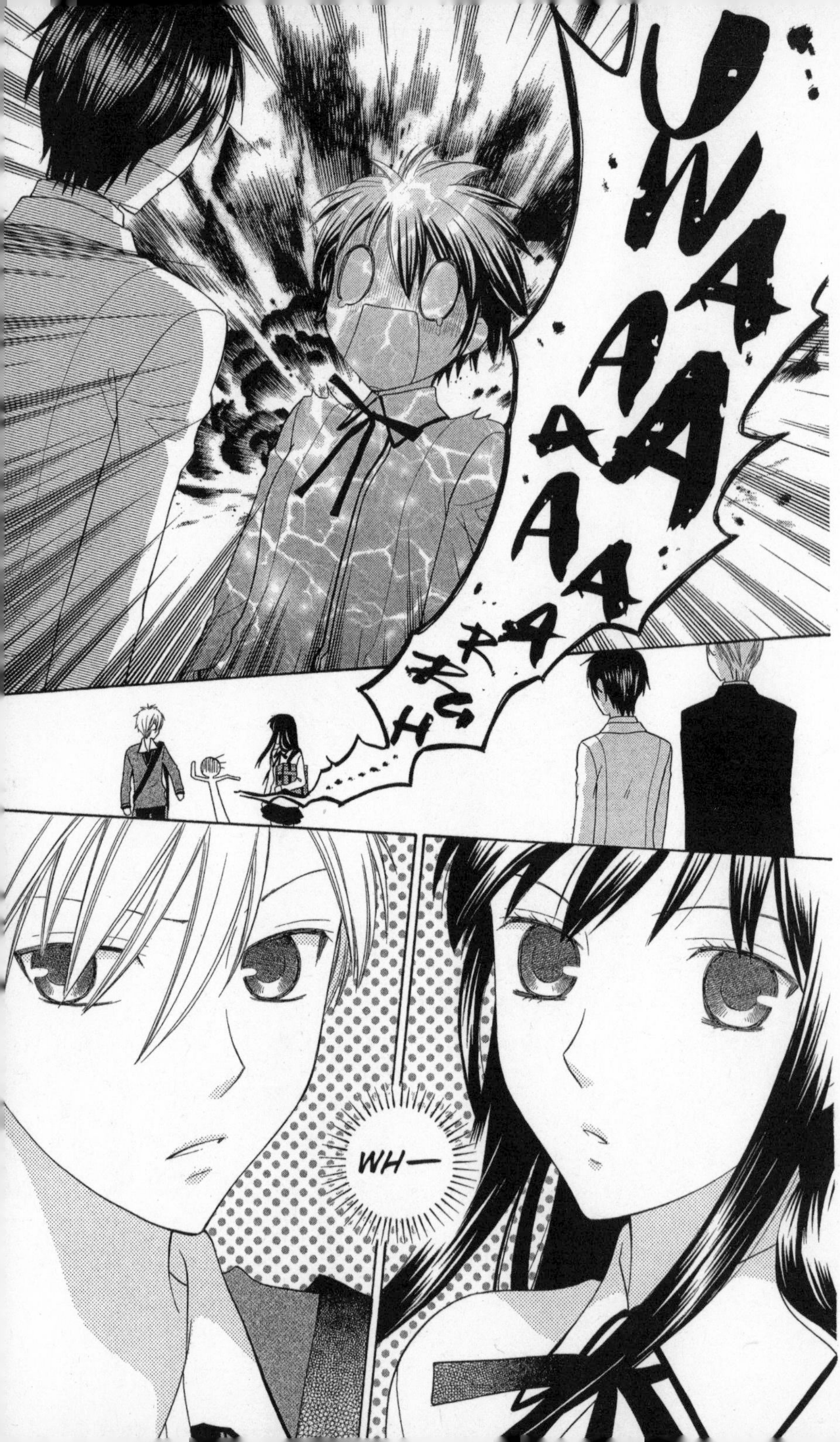
UWAAAAAAAAARRGH
WH—

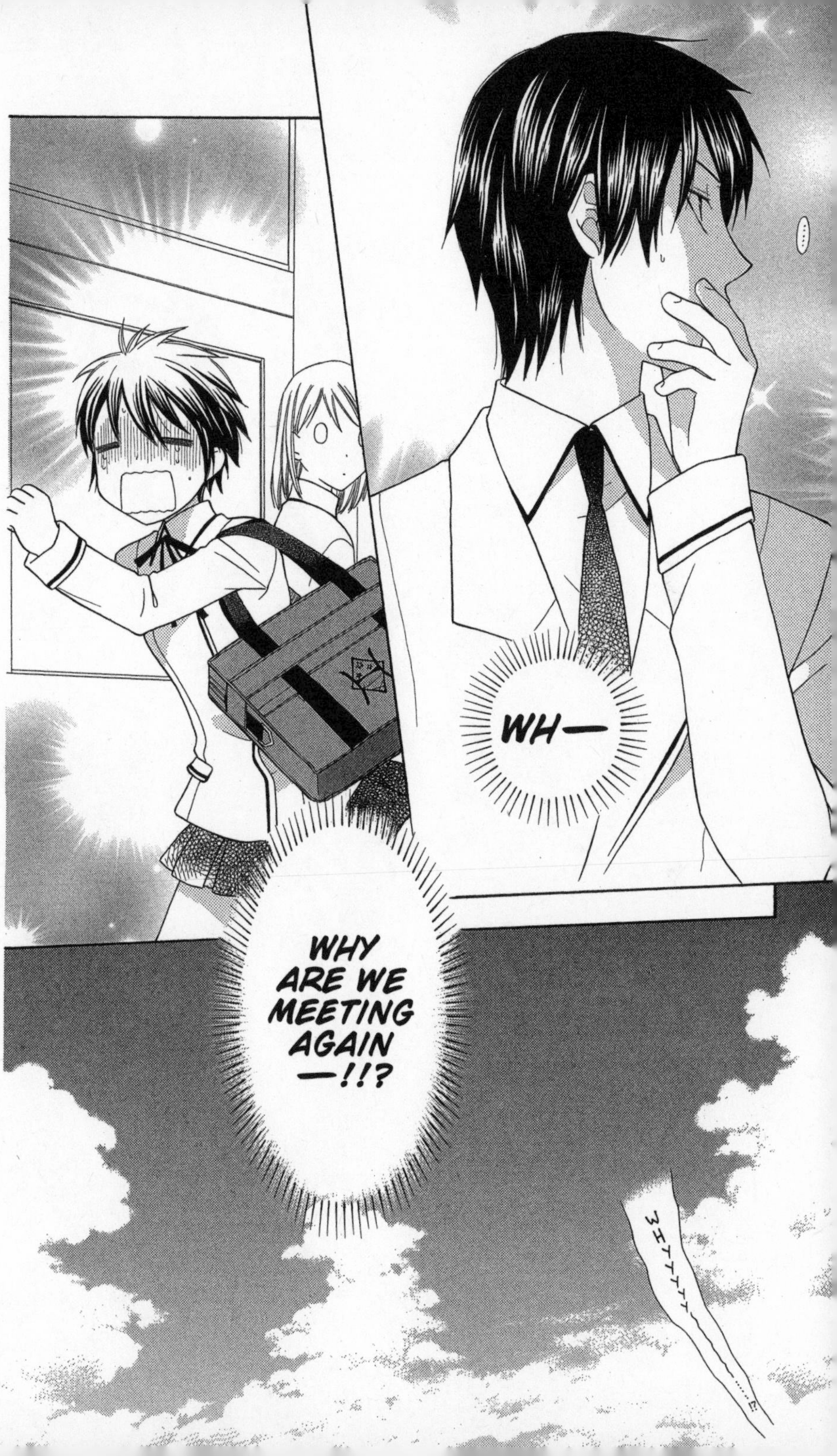
......
WH—
WHY ARE WE MEETING AGAIN—!!?
WHYYYYYY......!!

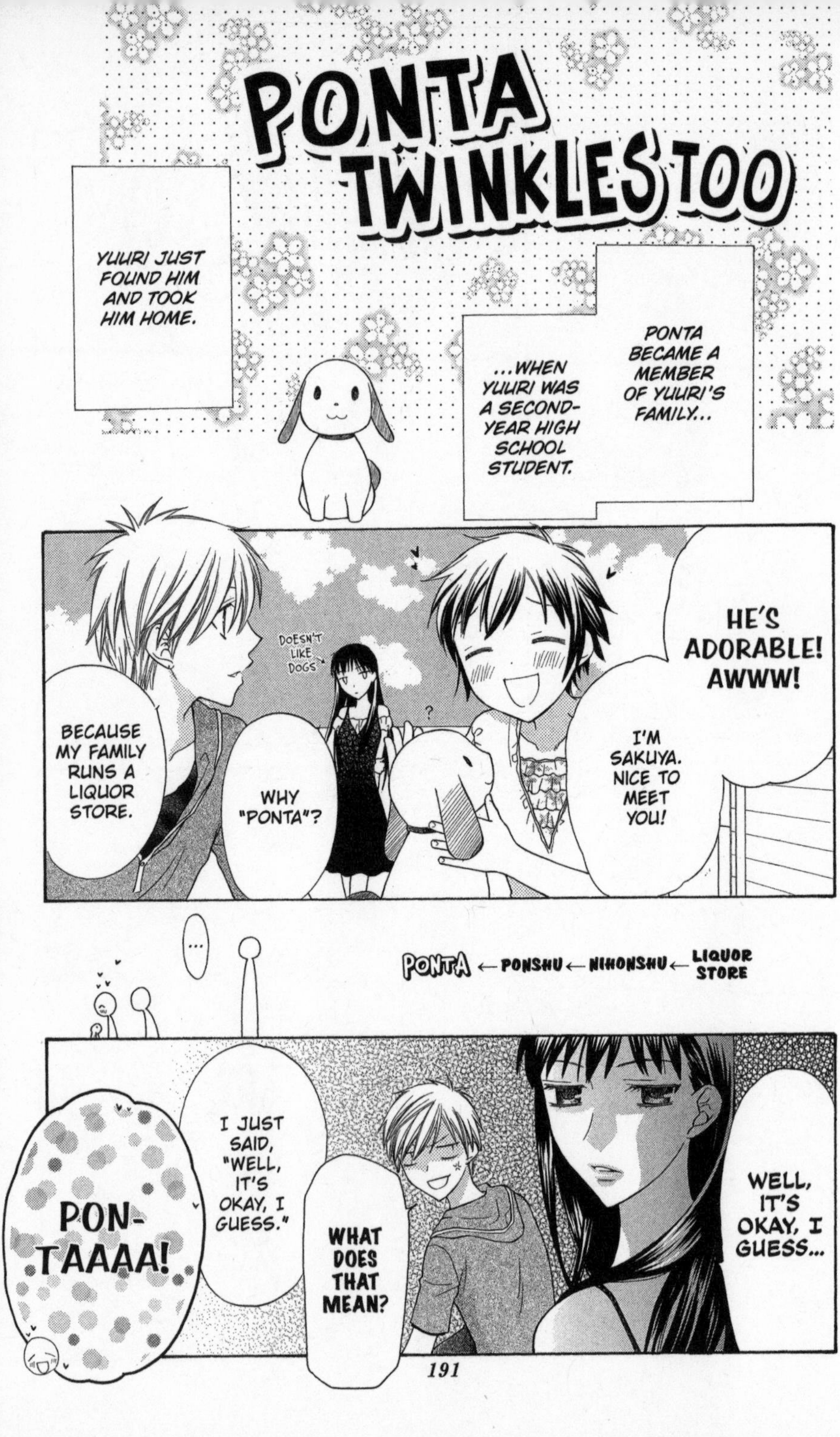
PONTA TWINKLES TOO
PONTA BECAME A MEMBER OF YUURI'S FAMILY...
...WHEN YUURI WAS A SECOND-YEAR HIGH SCHOOL STUDENT.
YUURI JUST FOUND HIM AND TOOK HIM HOME.
HE'S ADORABLE! AWWW!
I'M SAKUYA. NICE TO MEET YOU!
DOESN'T LIKE DOGS
?
WHY "PONTA"?
BECAUSE MY FAMILY RUNS A LIQUOR STORE.
PONTA ← PONSHU ← NIHONSHU ← LIQUOR STORE
...
WELL, IT'S OKAY, I GUESS...
WHAT DOES THAT MEAN?
I JUST SAID, "WELL, IT'S OKAY, I GUESS."
PON-TAAAA!

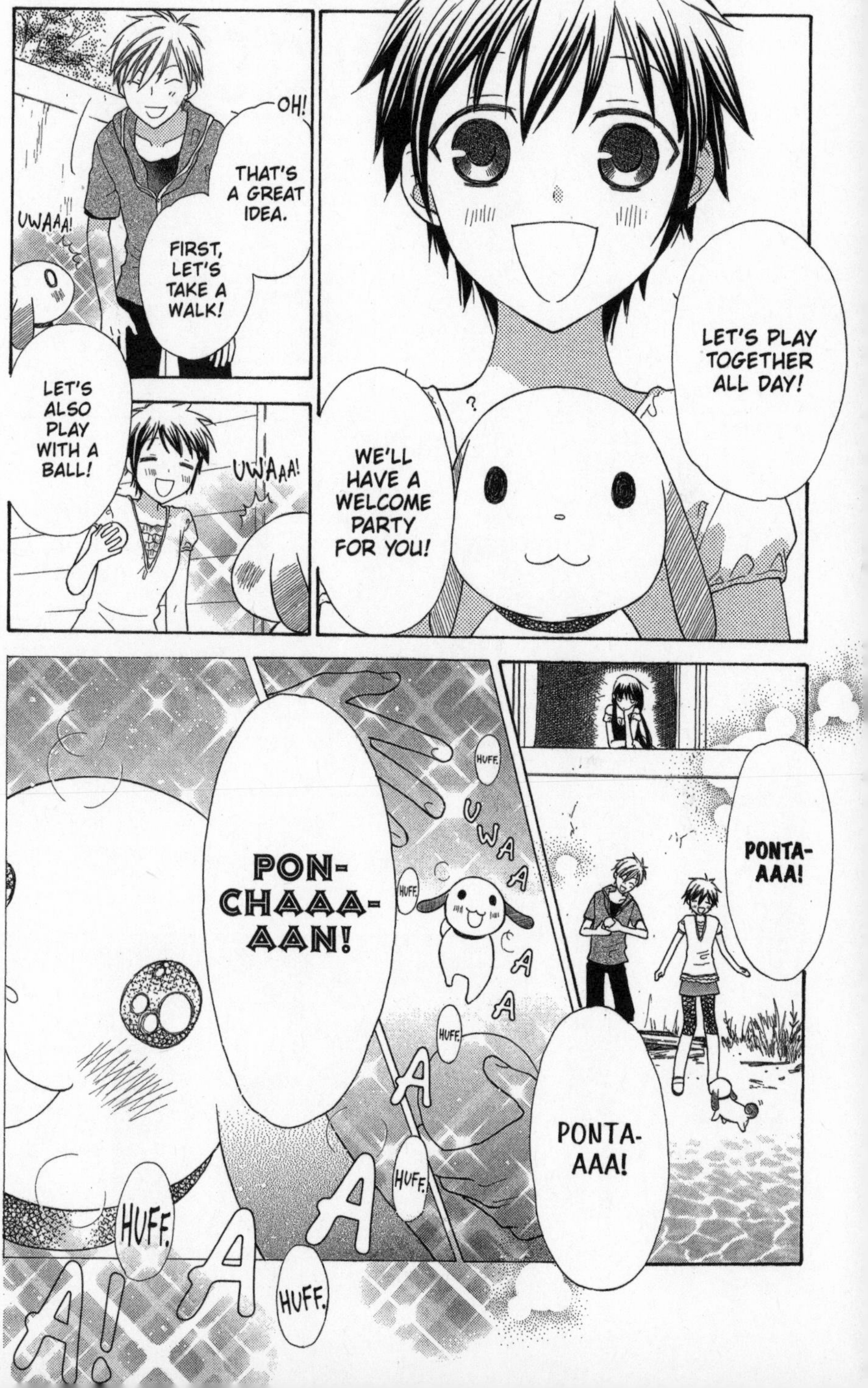
LET'S PLAY TOGETHER ALL DAY!
WE'LL HAVE A WELCOME PARTY FOR YOU!
OH!
THAT'S A GREAT IDEA.
FIRST, LET'S TAKE A WALK!
UWAAA!
LET'S ALSO PLAY WITH A BALL!
UWAAA!
PONTA-AAA!
PONTA-AAA!
HUFF.
UWAAAAAAA
HUFF.
HUFF.
HUFF.
PON-CHAAAA-AAN!
HUFF.
HUFF.
A! A A

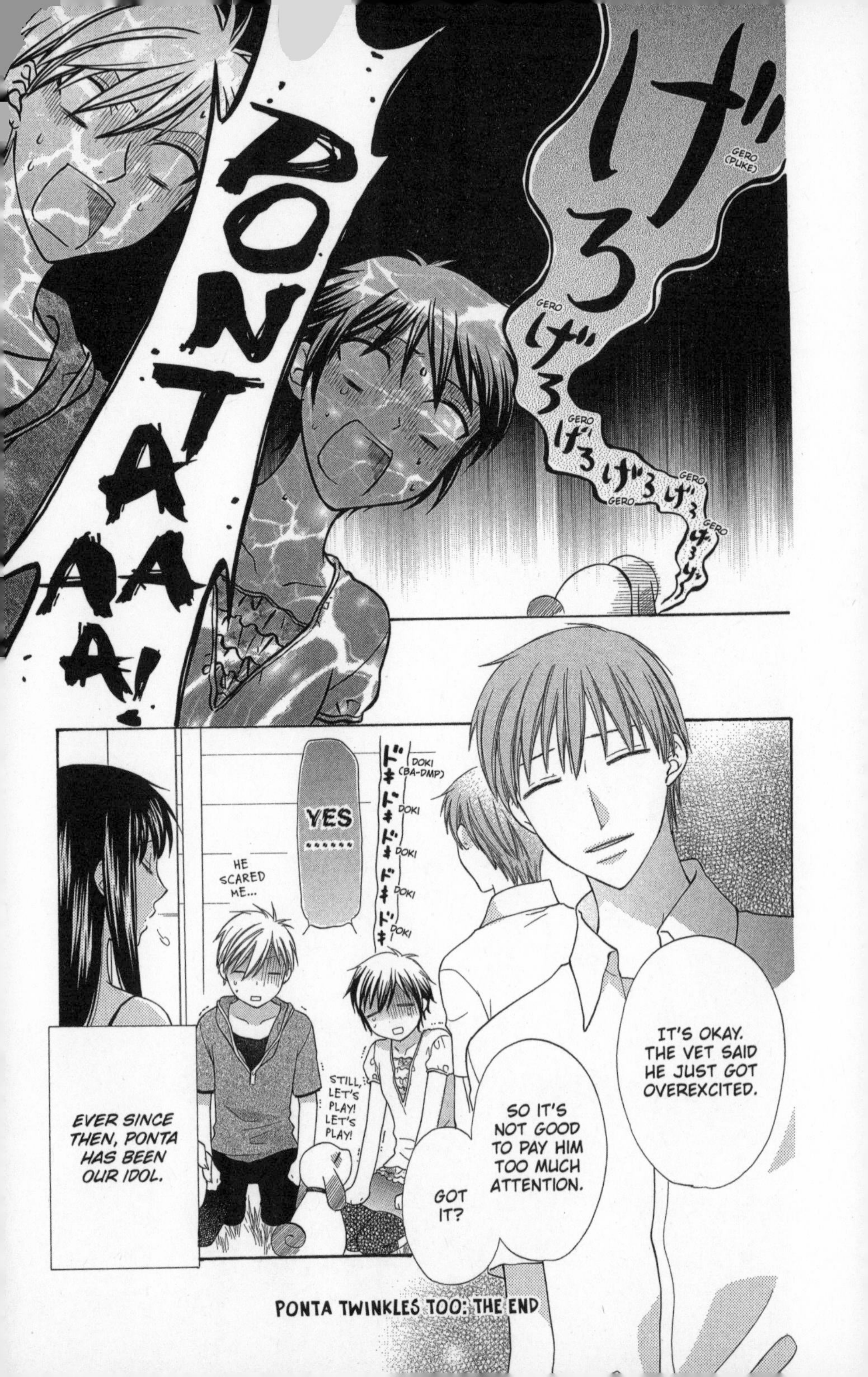

げろ GERO (PUKE)
げろ GERO
げろ GERO
げろ GERO
げろ GERO
げろ GERO
PONTAAAAAA!
IT'S OKAY. THE VET SAID HE JUST GOT OVEREXCITED.
SO IT'S NOT GOOD TO PAY HIM TOO MUCH ATTENTION.
GOT IT?
ドキ DOKI (BA-DMP)
ドキ DOKI
ドキ DOKI
ドキ DOKI
ドキ DOKI
YES ......
HE SCARED ME...
STILL, LET'S PLAY! LET'S PLAY!
EVER SINCE THEN, PONTA HAS BEEN OUR IDOL.
PONTA TWINKLES TOO: THE END

Feeling of Gratitude

Harada-sama   Araki-sama
Mother   My editor

Everyone who supports me
and reads this series

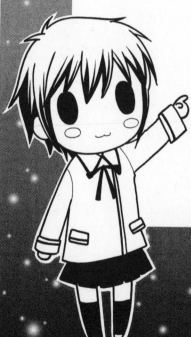

See you again ❀

高屋 奈月。
Natsuki Takaya

Twinkle Stars

NATSUKI TAKAYA

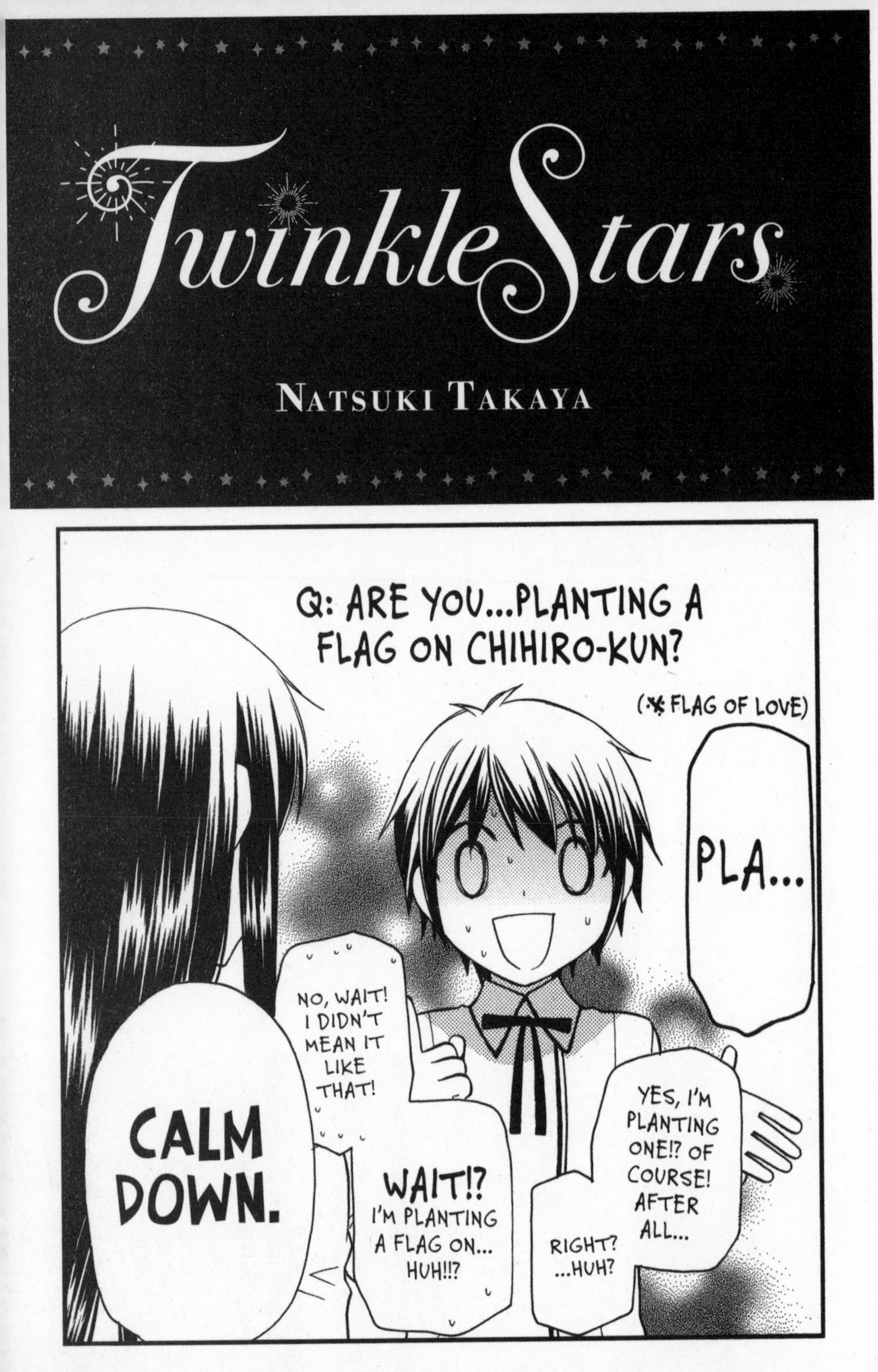
Q: ARE YOU...PLANTING A FLAG ON CHIHIRO-KUN?
(※ FLAG OF LOVE)
PLA...
YES, I'M PLANTING ONE!? OF COURSE! AFTER ALL...
RIGHT? ...HUH?
NO, WAIT! I DIDN'T MEAN IT LIKE THAT!
WAIT!? I'M PLANTING A FLAG ON... HUH!!?
CALM DOWN.

Twinkle Stars

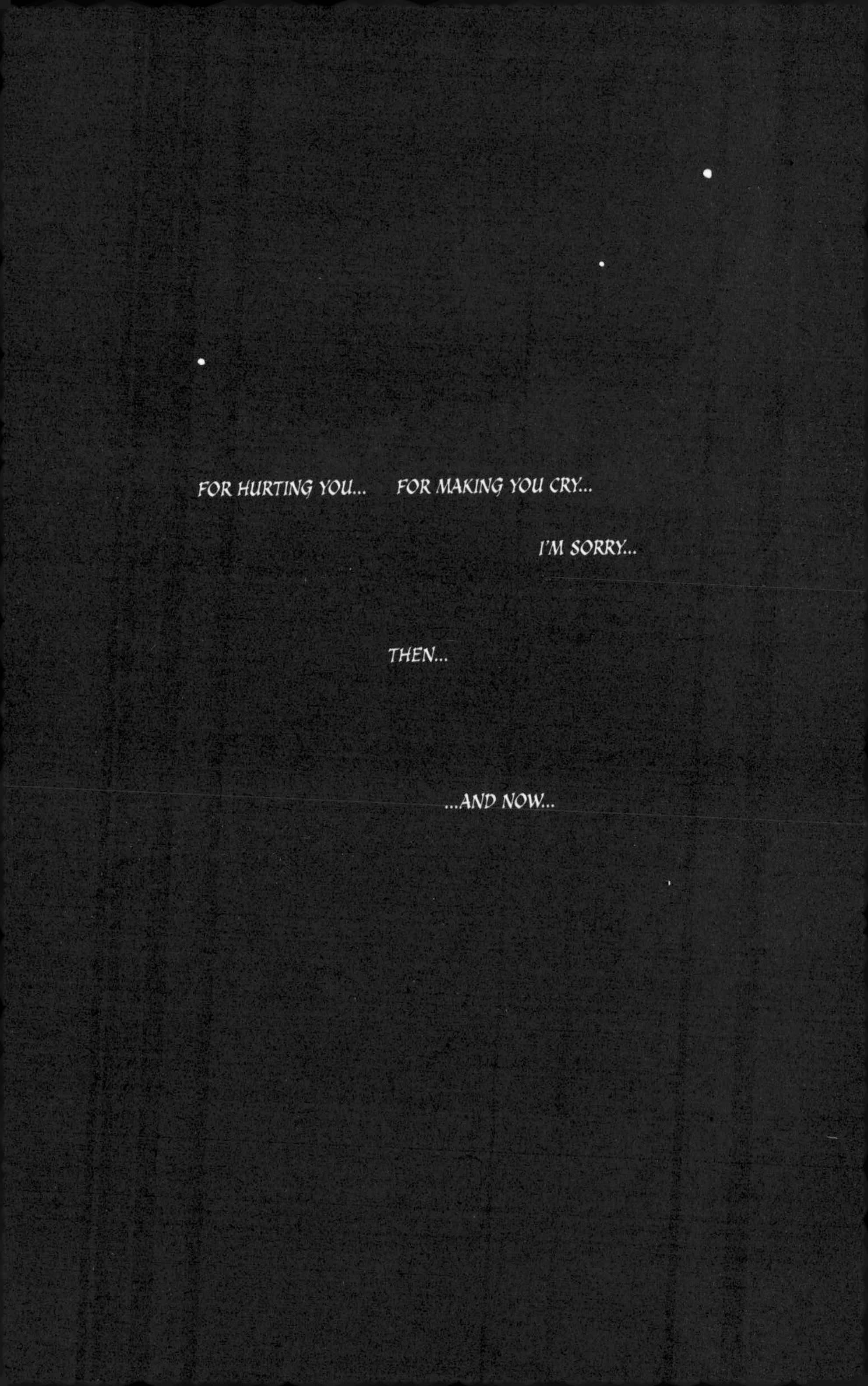
FOR HURTING YOU... FOR MAKING YOU CRY...
I'M SORRY...
THEN...
...AND NOW...

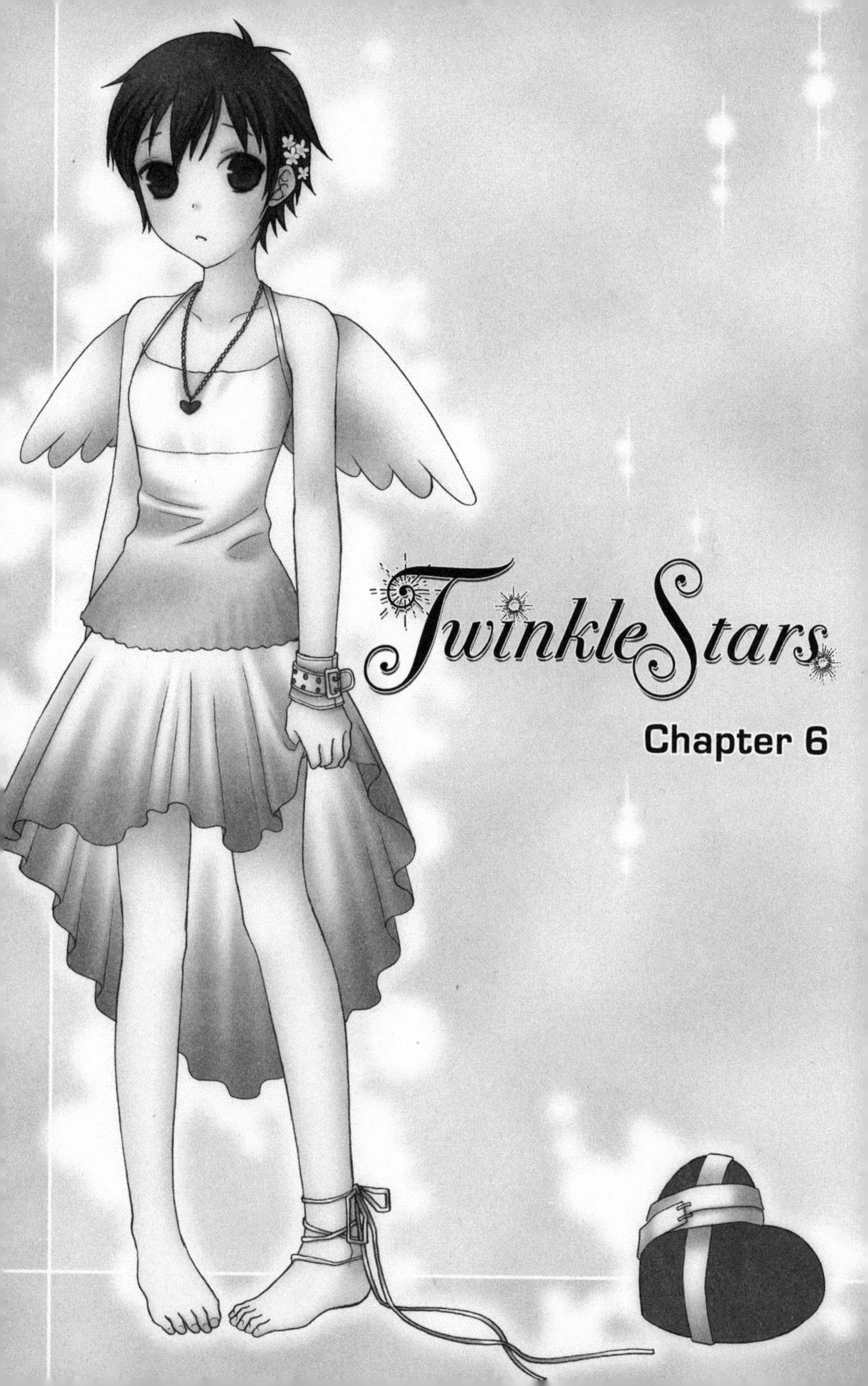
Twinkle Stars
Chapter 6

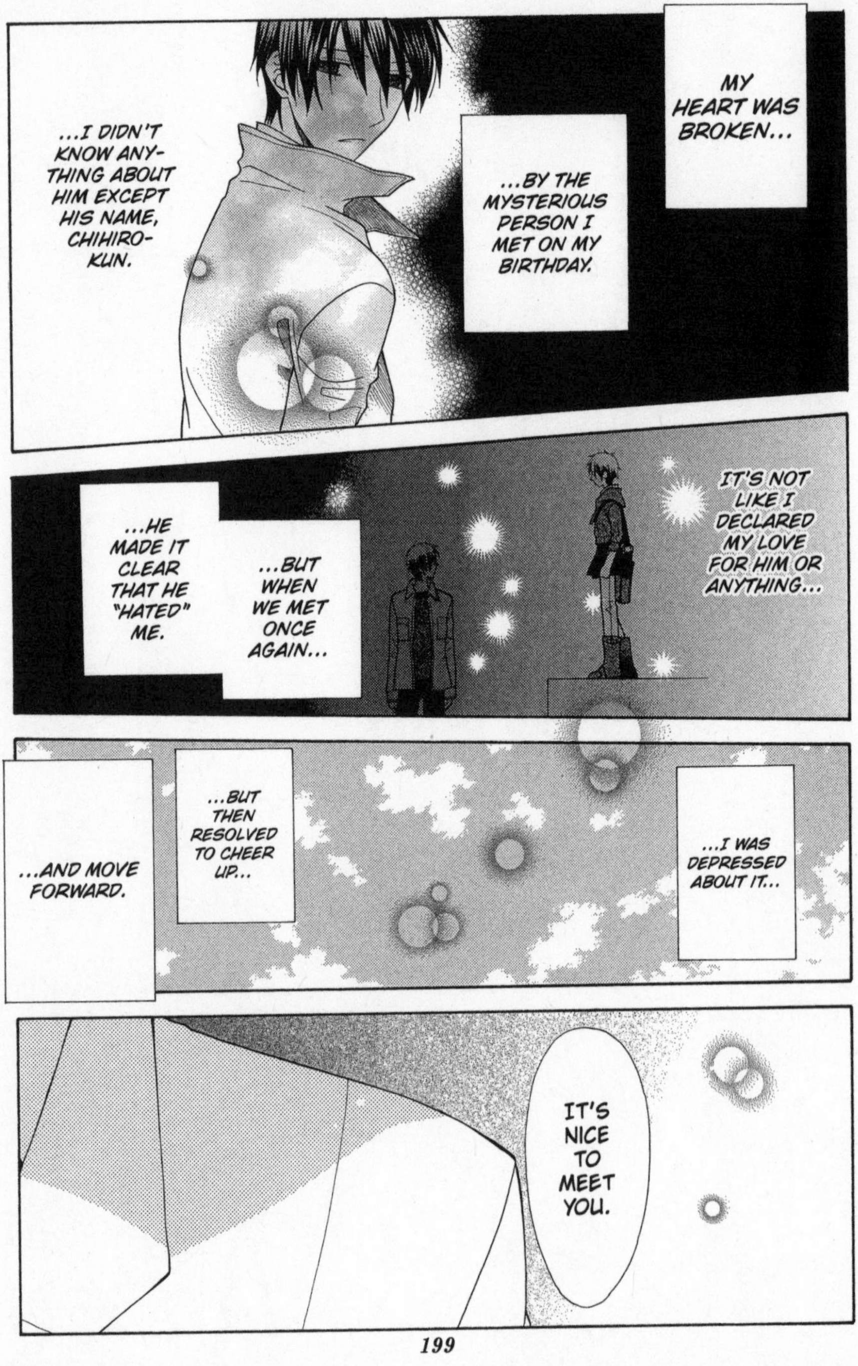
MY HEART WAS BROKEN...
...BY THE MYSTERIOUS PERSON I MET ON MY BIRTHDAY.
...I DIDN'T KNOW ANY-THING ABOUT HIM EXCEPT HIS NAME, CHIHIRO-KUN.
IT'S NOT LIKE I DECLARED MY LOVE FOR HIM OR ANYTHING...
...BUT WHEN WE MET ONCE AGAIN...
...HE MADE IT CLEAR THAT HE "HATED" ME.
...I WAS DEPRESSED ABOUT IT...
...BUT THEN RESOLVED TO CHEER UP...
...AND MOVE FORWARD.
IT'S NICE TO MEET YOU.

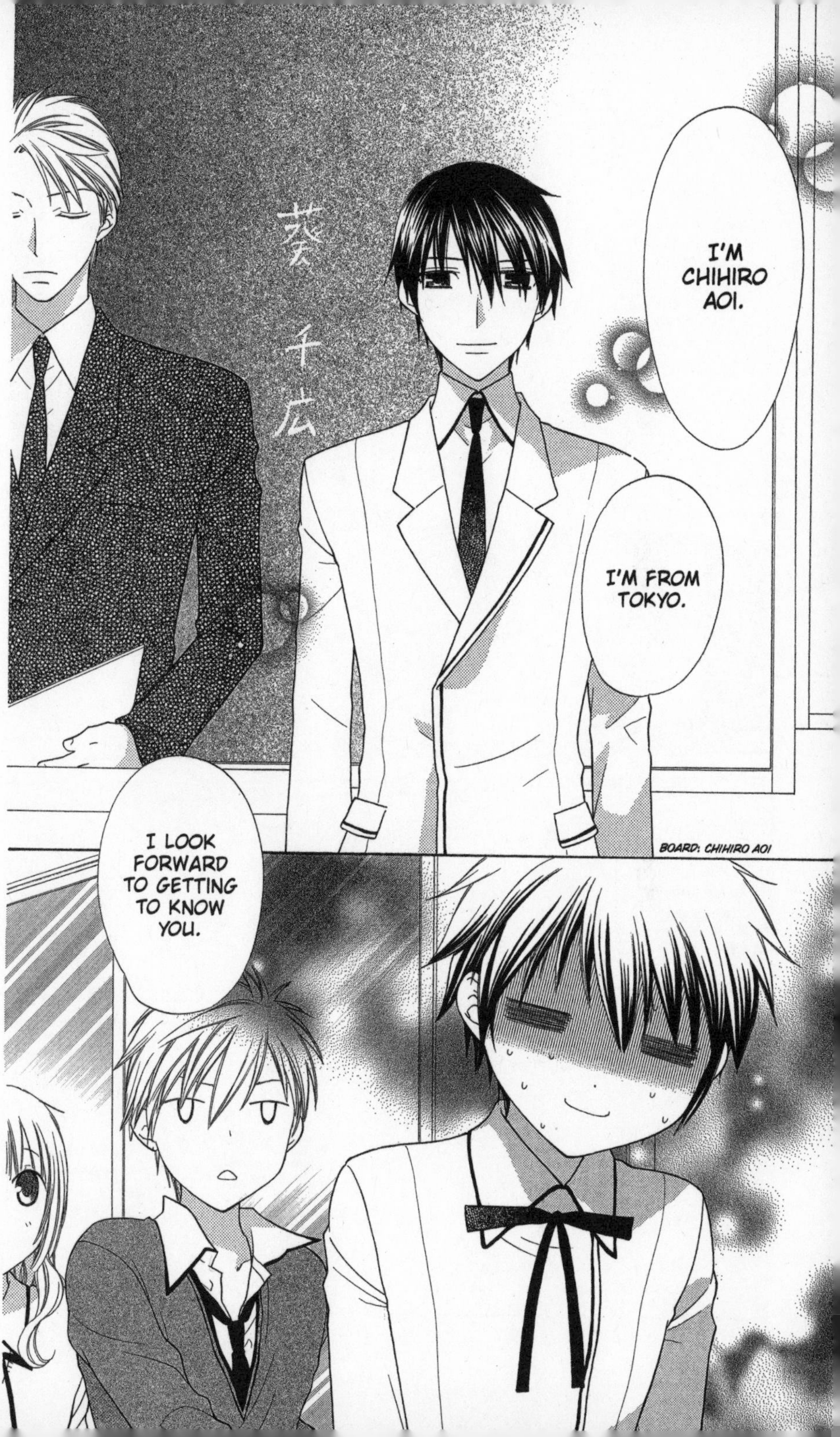
I'M CHIHIRO AOI.
I'M FROM TOKYO.
葵 千広
BOARD: CHIHIRO AOI
I LOOK FORWARD TO GETTING TO KNOW YOU.

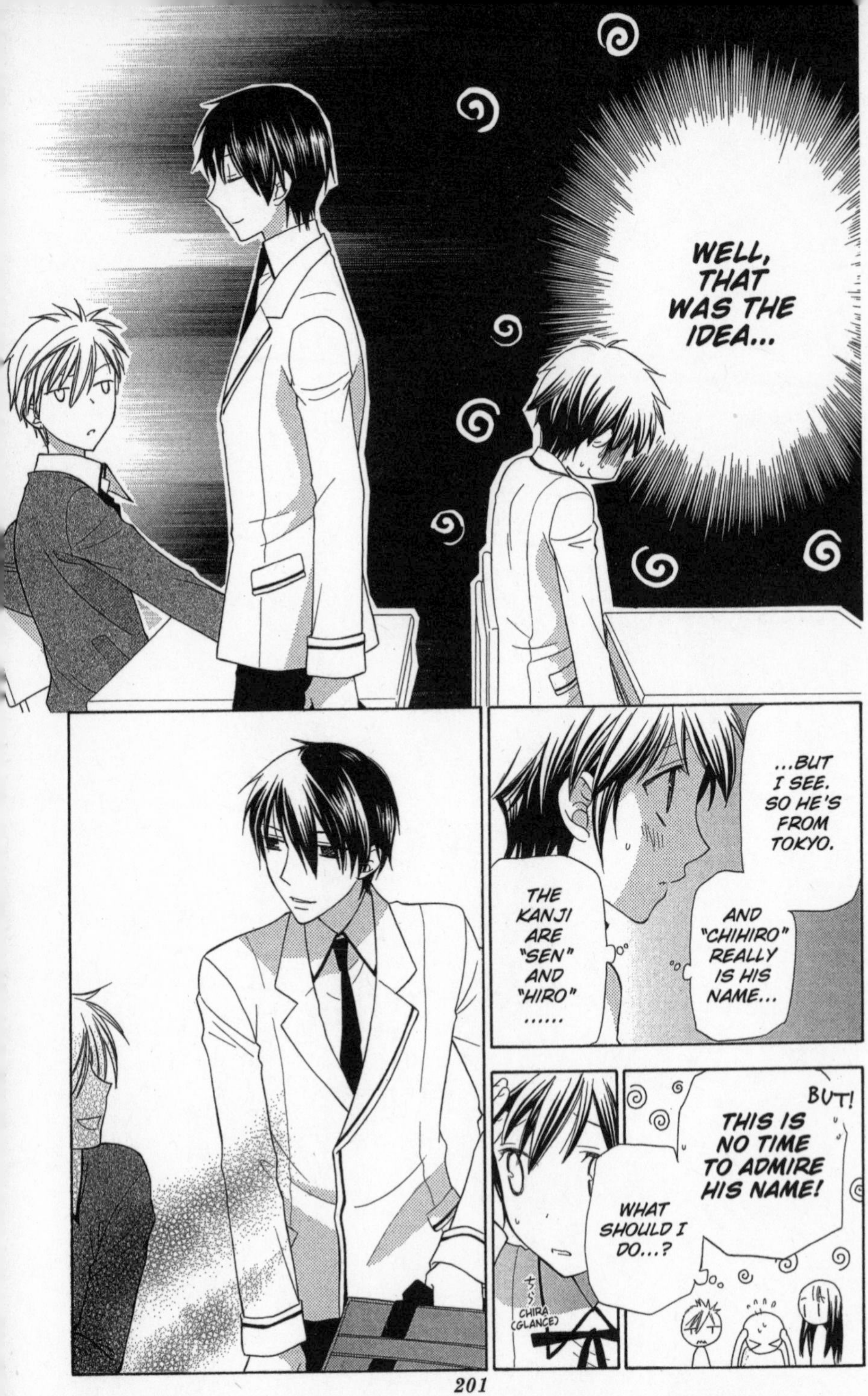
WELL, THAT WAS THE IDEA...
...BUT I SEE. SO HE'S FROM TOKYO.
AND "CHIHIRO" REALLY IS HIS NAME...
THE KANJI ARE "SEN" AND "HIRO" ......
BUT!
THIS IS NO TIME TO ADMIRE HIS NAME!
WHAT SHOULD I DO...?
ちら
CHIRA (GLANCE)

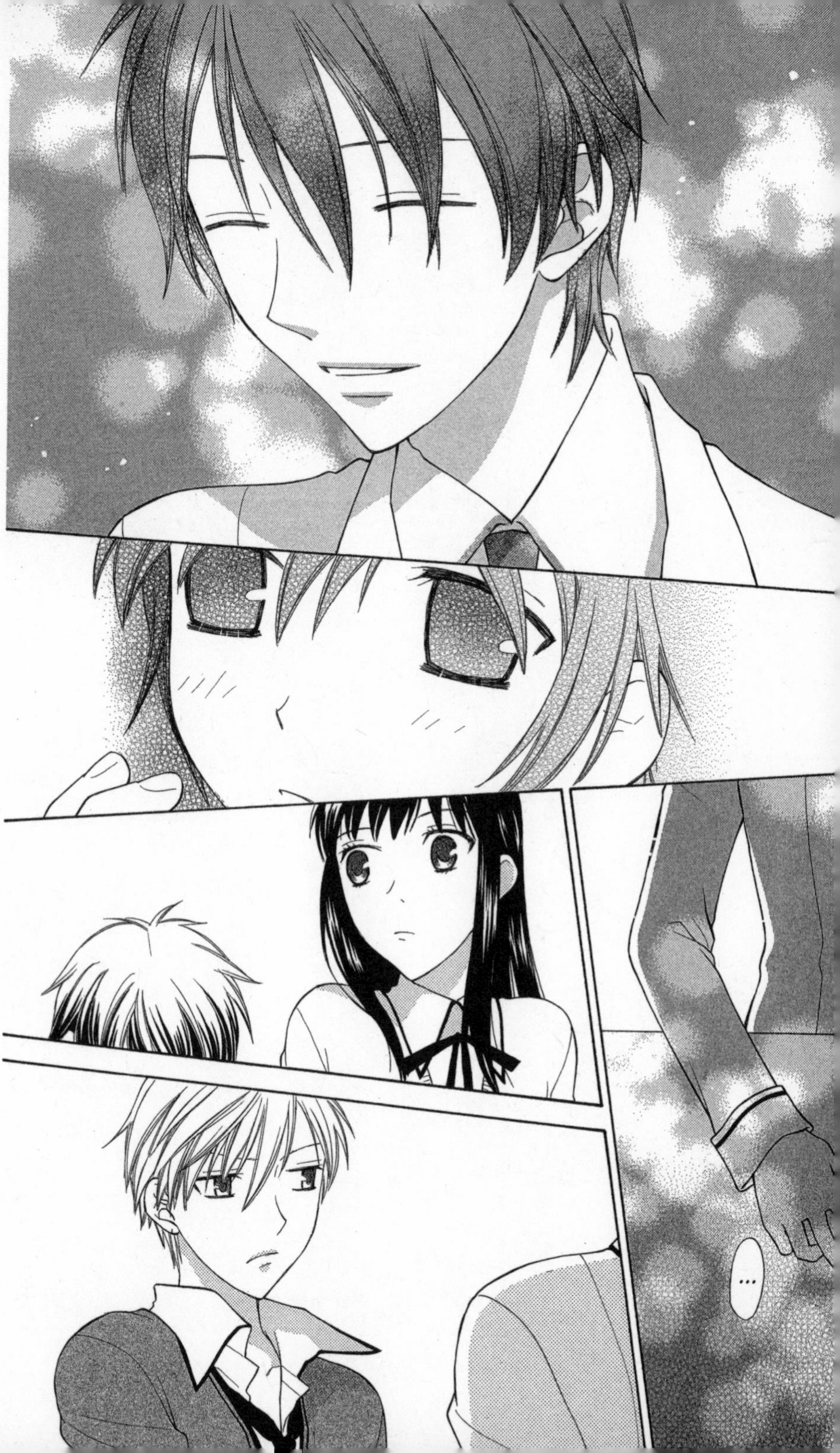
...

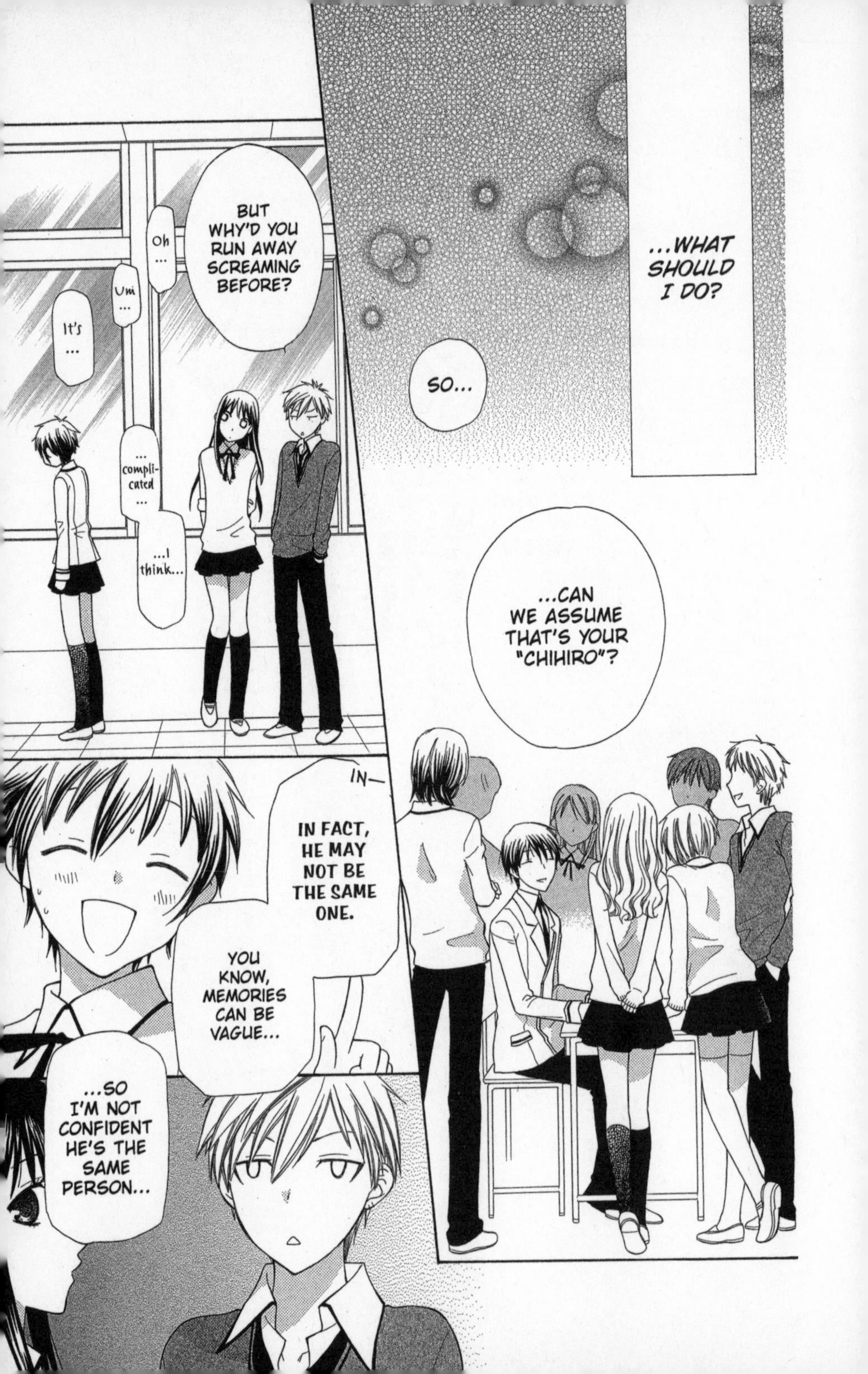
...WHAT SHOULD I DO?
SO...
...CAN WE ASSUME THAT'S YOUR "CHIHIRO"?
BUT WHY'D YOU RUN AWAY SCREAMING BEFORE?
Oh...
Um...
It's...
...complicated...
...I think...
IN—
IN FACT, HE MAY NOT BE THE SAME ONE.
YOU KNOW, MEMORIES CAN BE VAGUE...
...SO I'M NOT CONFIDENT HE'S THE SAME PERSON...

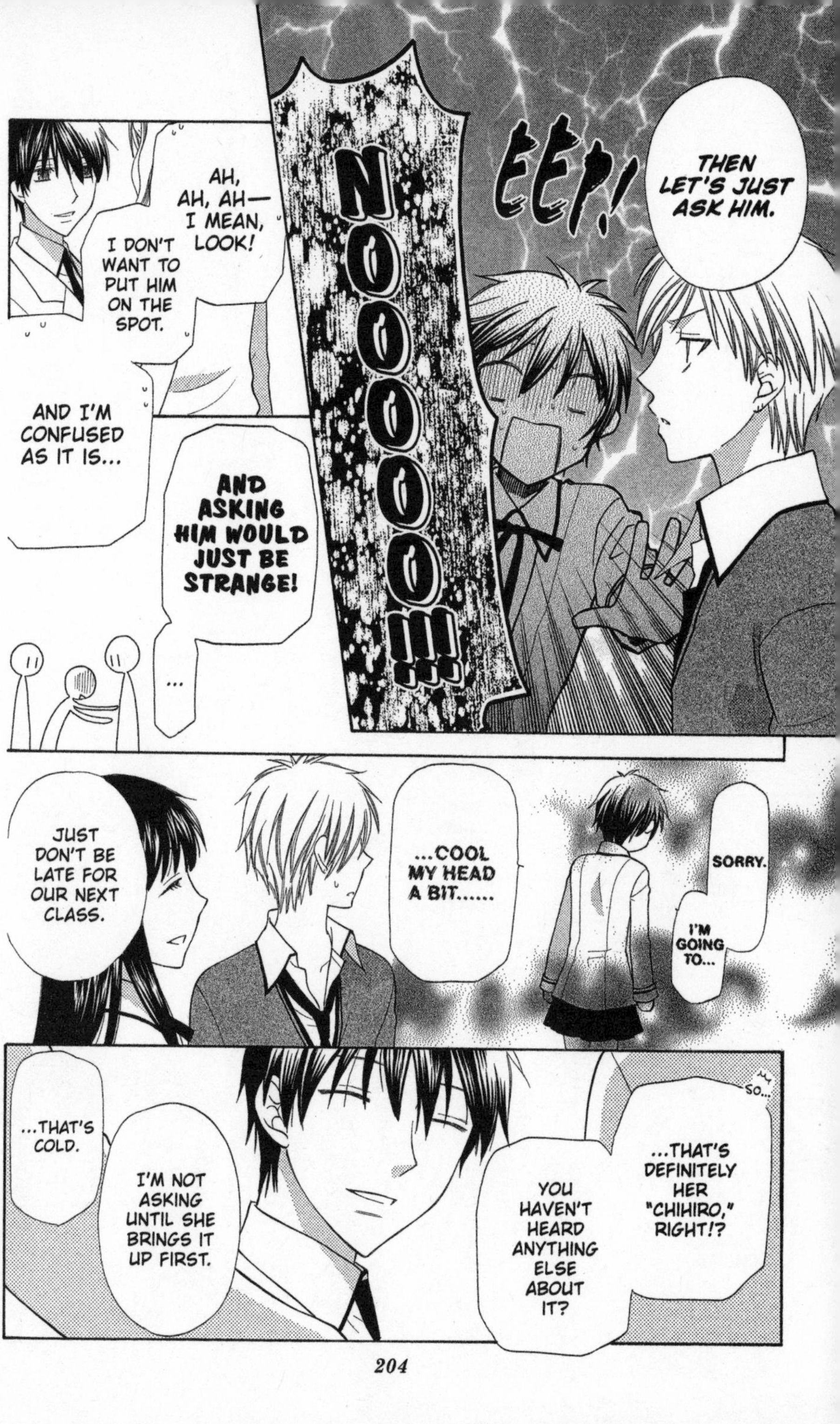
THEN LET'S JUST ASK HIM.
EEP!
NOOOOOOO!!!
AH, AH, AH— I MEAN, LOOK!
I DON'T WANT TO PUT HIM ON THE SPOT.
AND I'M CONFUSED AS IT IS...
AND ASKING HIM WOULD JUST BE STRANGE!
...
SORRY.
I'M GOING TO...
...COOL MY HEAD A BIT......
JUST DON'T BE LATE FOR OUR NEXT CLASS.
SO...
...THAT'S DEFINITELY HER "CHIHIRO," RIGHT!?
YOU HAVEN'T HEARD ANYTHING ELSE ABOUT IT?
I'M NOT ASKING UNTIL SHE BRINGS IT UP FIRST.
...THAT'S COLD.

Twinkle Stars

Nice to meet you and hello. I'm Takaya. This is Volume 2 of *Twinkle Stars*. Around this volume, Sakuya's hair starts to slowly but steadily grow longer. Have you heard the old chestnut about naturally becoming prettier when you're in love? It's like that. So her hair's gradually getting longer. I wonder how long it will be by the end. I don't think it'll be as long as Sei-chan's hair though...

And so Volume 2 begins...

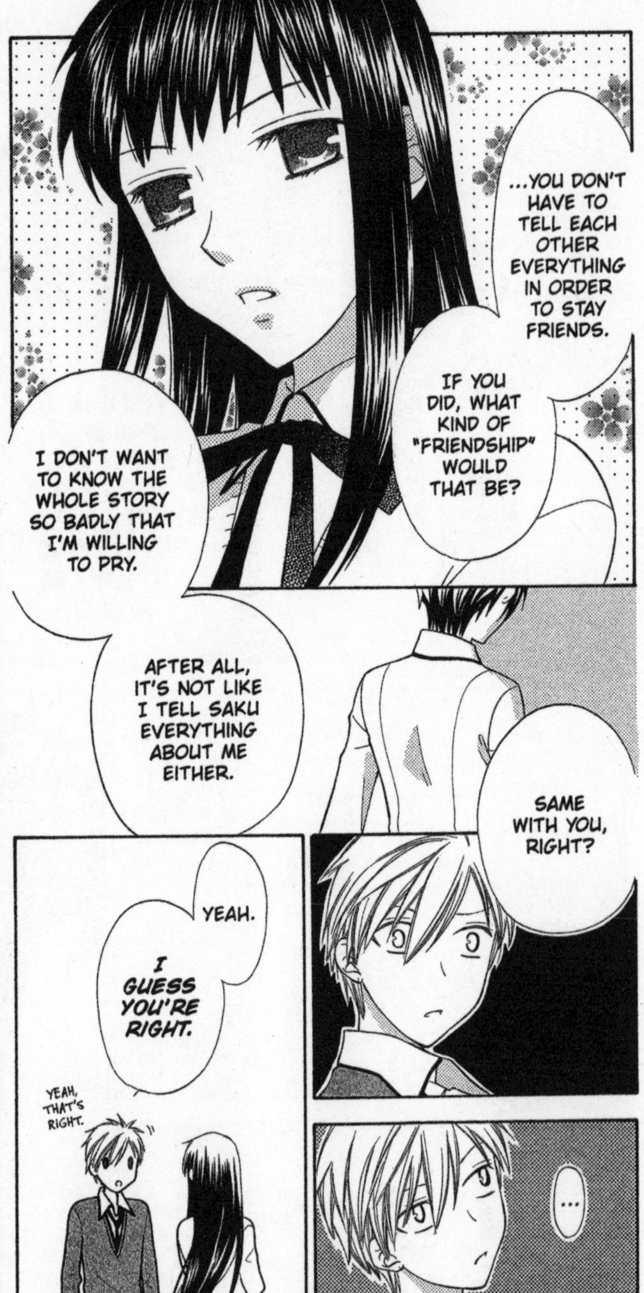
...YOU DON'T HAVE TO TELL EACH OTHER EVERYTHING IN ORDER TO STAY FRIENDS.
IF YOU DID, WHAT KIND OF "FRIENDSHIP" WOULD THAT BE?
I DON'T WANT TO KNOW THE WHOLE STORY SO BADLY THAT I'M WILLING TO PRY.
AFTER ALL, IT'S NOT LIKE I TELL SAKU EVERYTHING ABOUT ME EITHER.
SAME WITH YOU, RIGHT?
...
YEAH.
I GUESS YOU'RE RIGHT.
YEAH, THAT'S RIGHT.

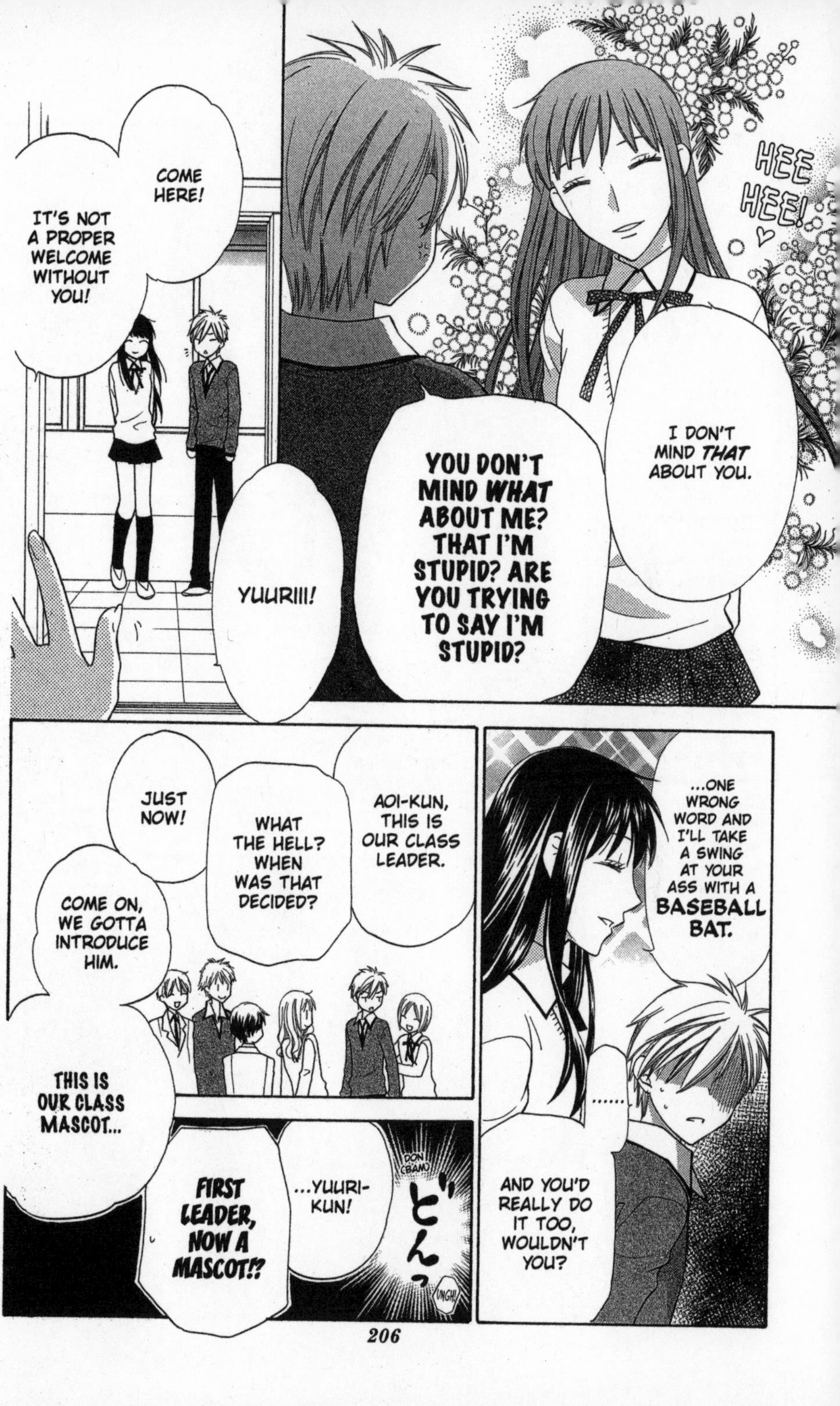
HEE HEE!
I DON'T MIND *THAT* ABOUT YOU.
YOU DON'T MIND *WHAT* ABOUT ME? THAT I'M STUPID? ARE YOU TRYING TO SAY I'M STUPID?
YUURIII!
COME HERE!
IT'S NOT A PROPER WELCOME WITHOUT YOU!
...ONE WRONG WORD AND I'LL TAKE A SWING AT YOUR ASS WITH A **BASEBALL BAT.**
......
AND YOU'D REALLY DO IT TOO, WOULDN'T YOU?
AOI-KUN, THIS IS OUR CLASS LEADER.
WHAT THE HELL? WHEN WAS THAT DECIDED?
JUST NOW!
COME ON, WE GOTTA INTRODUCE HIM.
THIS IS OUR CLASS MASCOT...
DON (BAM)
どんっ
UNGH!
...YUURI-KUN!
FIRST LEADER, NOW A MASCOT!?

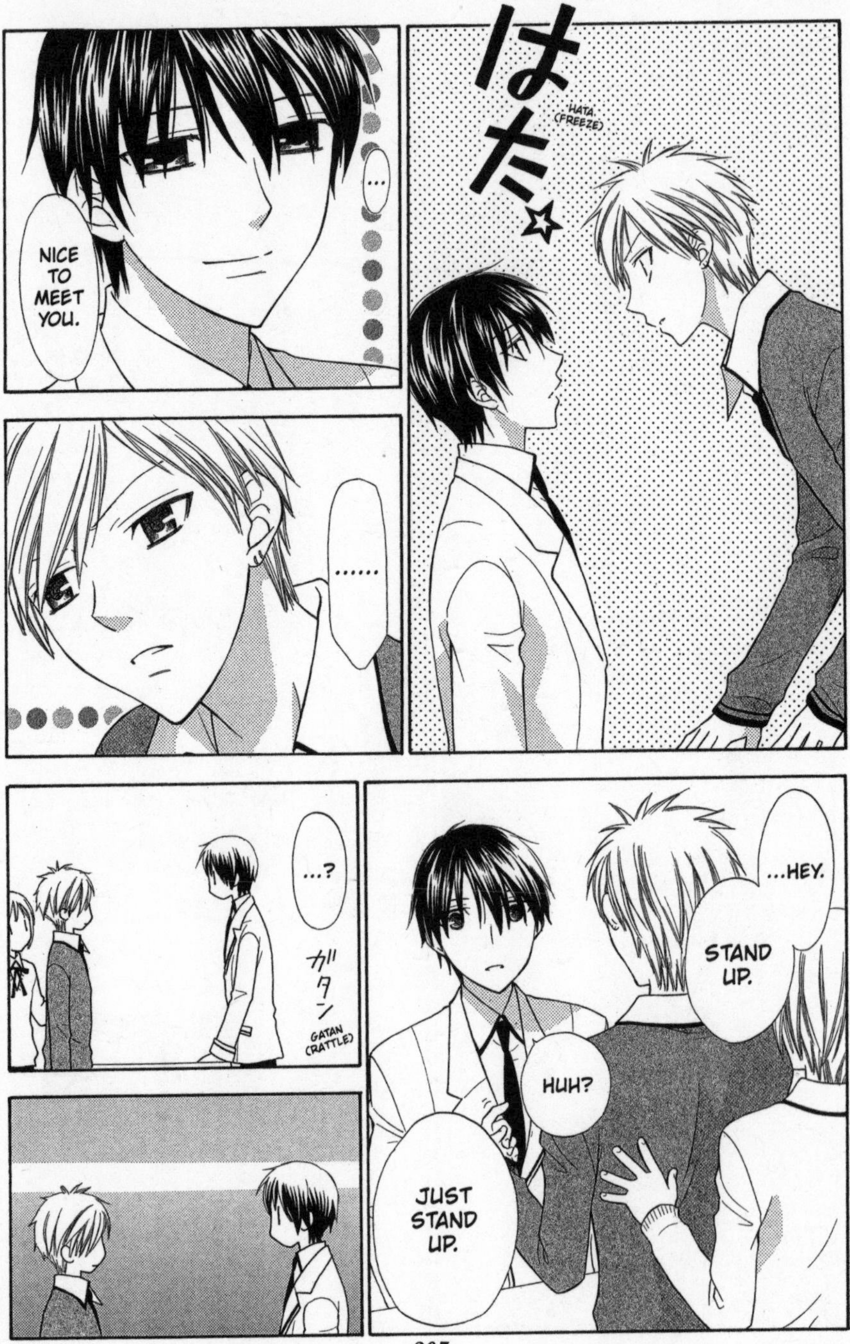
はた
HATA (FREEZE)
...
NICE TO MEET YOU.
......
...HEY.
STAND UP.
HUH?
JUST STAND UP.
...?
ガタン
GATAN (RATTLE)

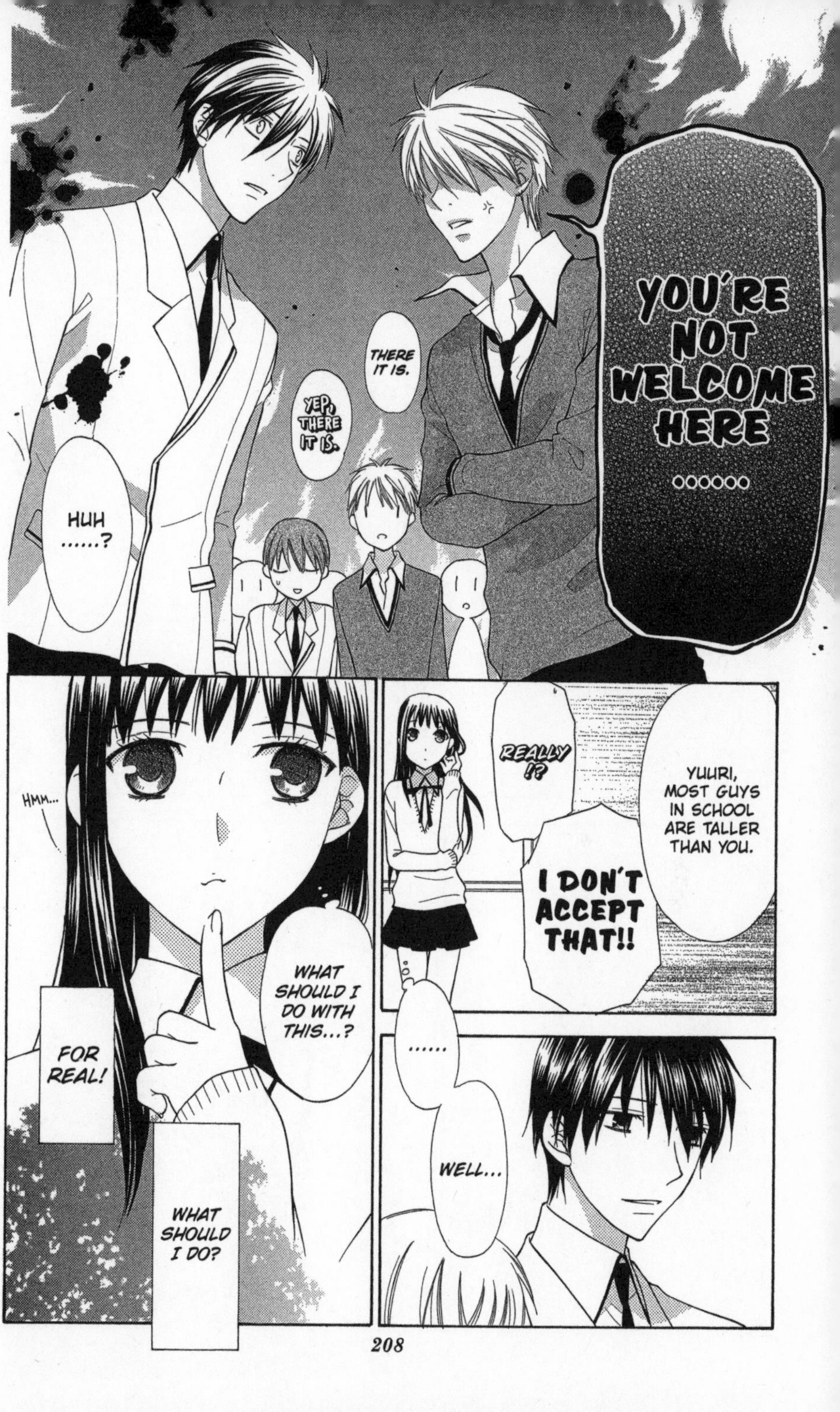
YOU'RE NOT WELCOME HERE ......
THERE IT IS.
YEP, THERE IT IS.
HUH ......?
YUURI, MOST GUYS IN SCHOOL ARE TALLER THAN YOU.
REALLY!?
I DON'T ACCEPT THAT!!
......
WELL...
HMM...
WHAT SHOULD I DO WITH THIS...?
FOR REAL!
WHAT SHOULD I DO?

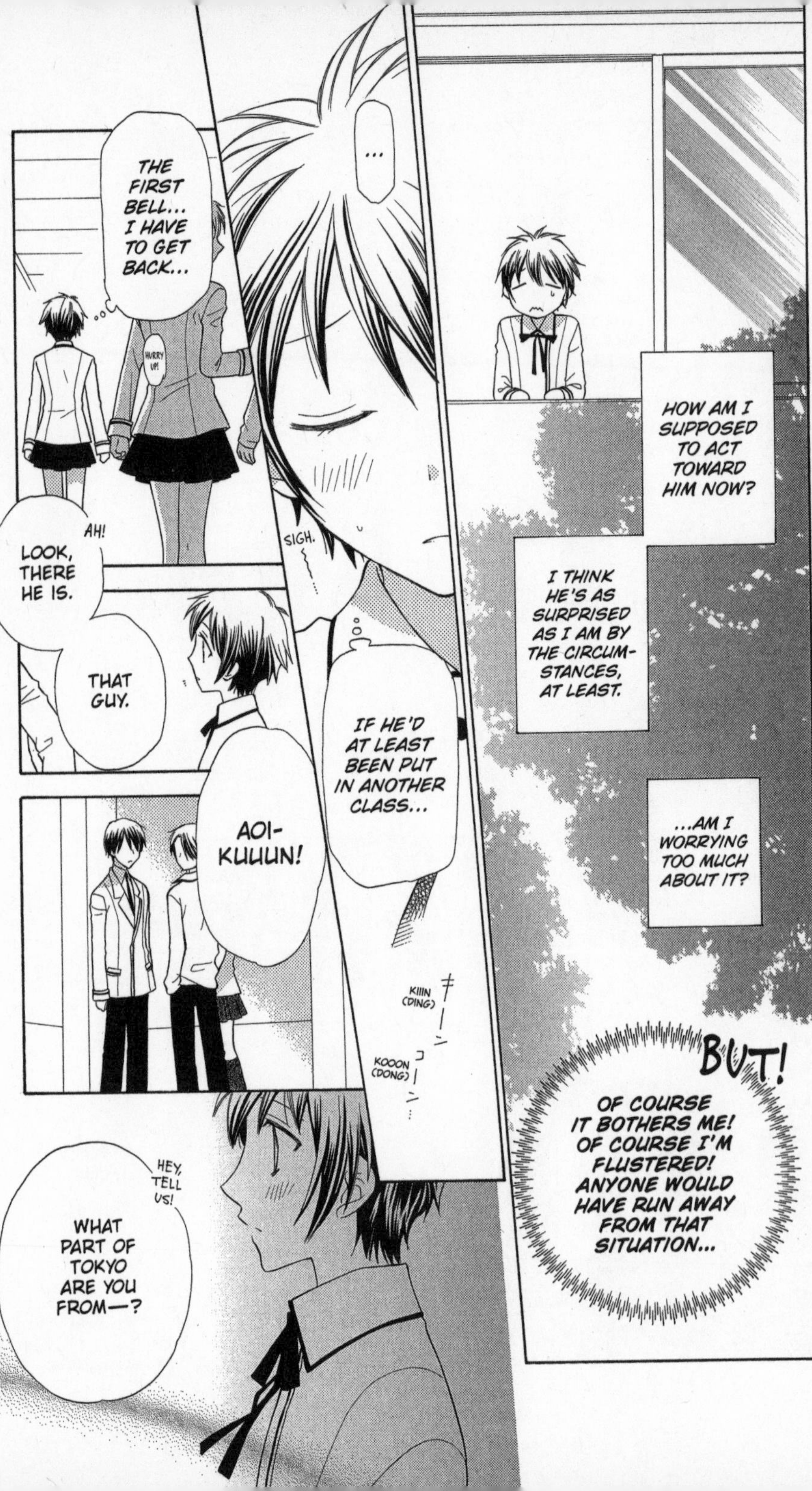
HOW AM I SUPPOSED TO ACT TOWARD HIM NOW?
I THINK HE'S AS SURPRISED AS I AM BY THE CIRCUM-STANCES, AT LEAST.
...AM I WORRYING TOO MUCH ABOUT IT?
BUT!
OF COURSE IT BOTHERS ME! OF COURSE I'M FLUSTERED! ANYONE WOULD HAVE RUN AWAY FROM THAT SITUATION...
...
SIGH.
IF HE'D AT LEAST BEEN PUT IN ANOTHER CLASS...
KIIN (DING)
KOOON (DONG)
THE FIRST BELL... I HAVE TO GET BACK...
HURRY UP!
AH!
LOOK, THERE HE IS.
THAT GUY.
AOI-KUUUN!
HEY, TELL US!
WHAT PART OF TOKYO ARE YOU FROM—?

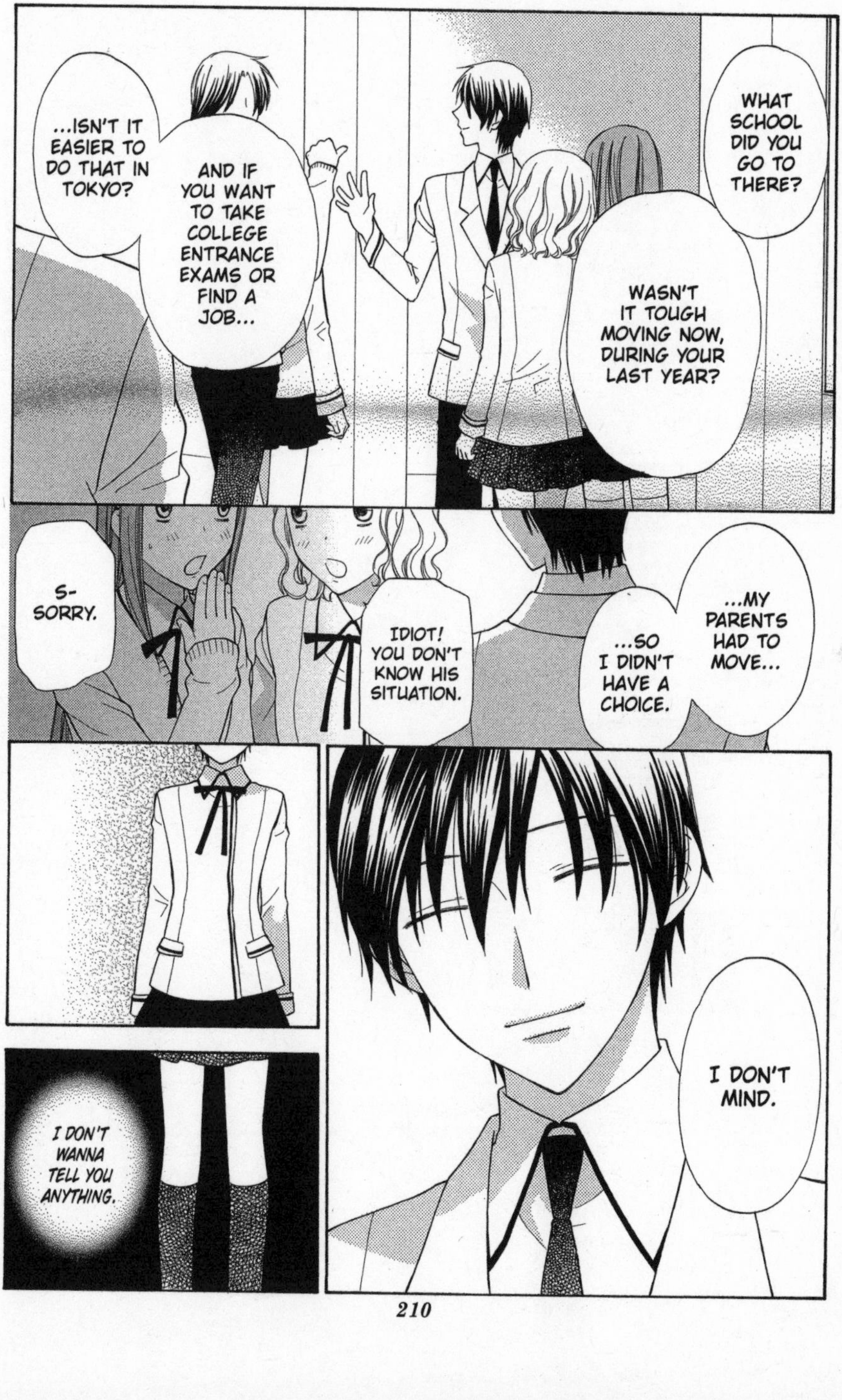
WHAT SCHOOL DID YOU GO TO THERE?
WASN'T IT TOUGH MOVING NOW, DURING YOUR LAST YEAR?
AND IF YOU WANT TO TAKE COLLEGE ENTRANCE EXAMS OR FIND A JOB...
...ISN'T IT EASIER TO DO THAT IN TOKYO?
...MY PARENTS HAD TO MOVE...
...SO I DIDN'T HAVE A CHOICE.
IDIOT! YOU DON'T KNOW HIS SITUATION.
S-SORRY.
I DON'T MIND.
I DON'T WANNA TELL YOU ANYTHING.

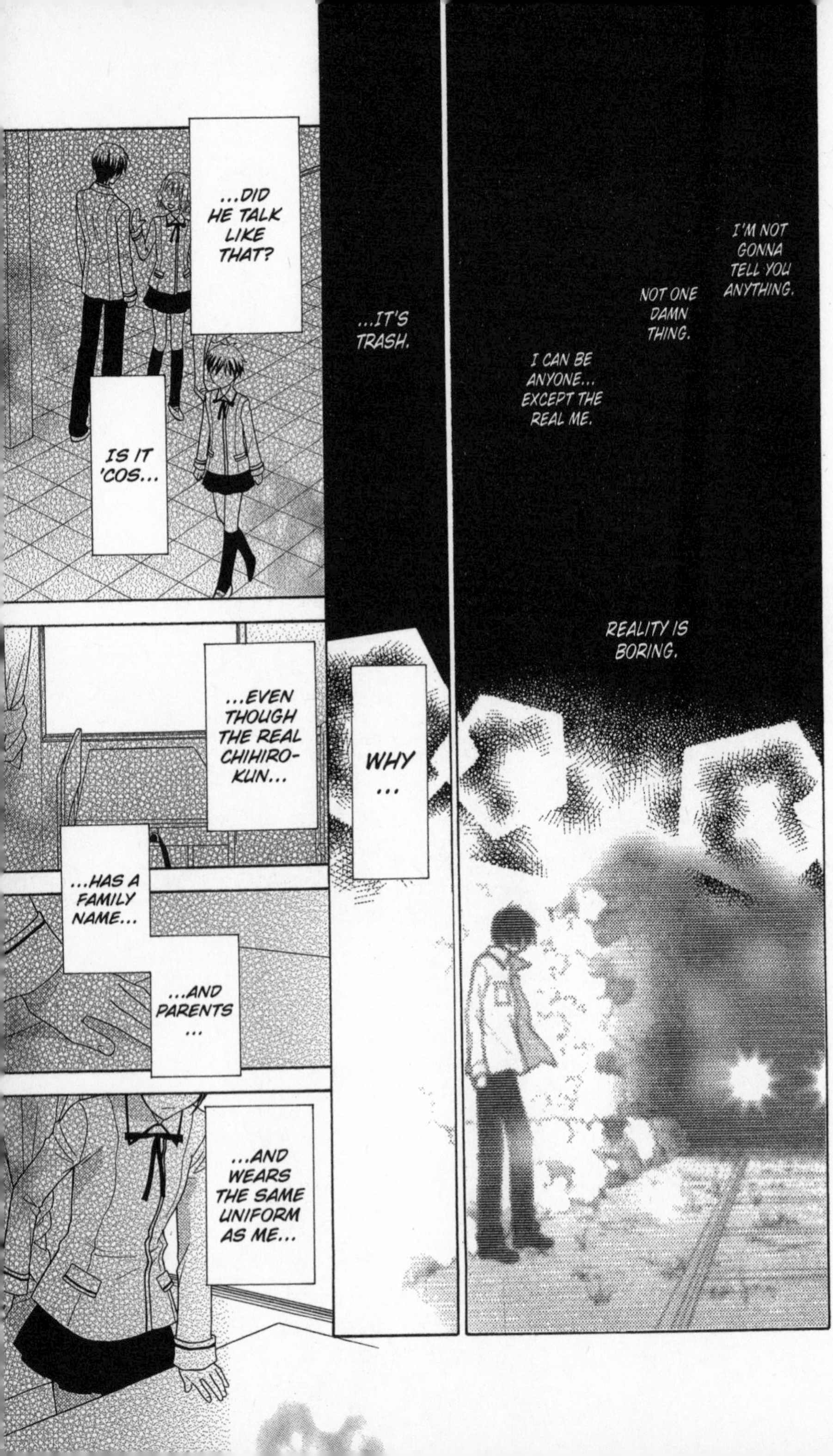
I'M NOT GONNA TELL YOU ANYTHING.
NOT ONE DAMN THING.
I CAN BE ANYONE... EXCEPT THE REAL ME.
REALITY IS BORING.
...IT'S TRASH.
WHY...
...DID HE TALK LIKE THAT?
IS IT 'COS...
...EVEN THOUGH THE REAL CHIHIRO-KUN...
...HAS A FAMILY NAME...
...AND PARENTS...
...AND WEARS THE SAME UNIFORM AS ME...

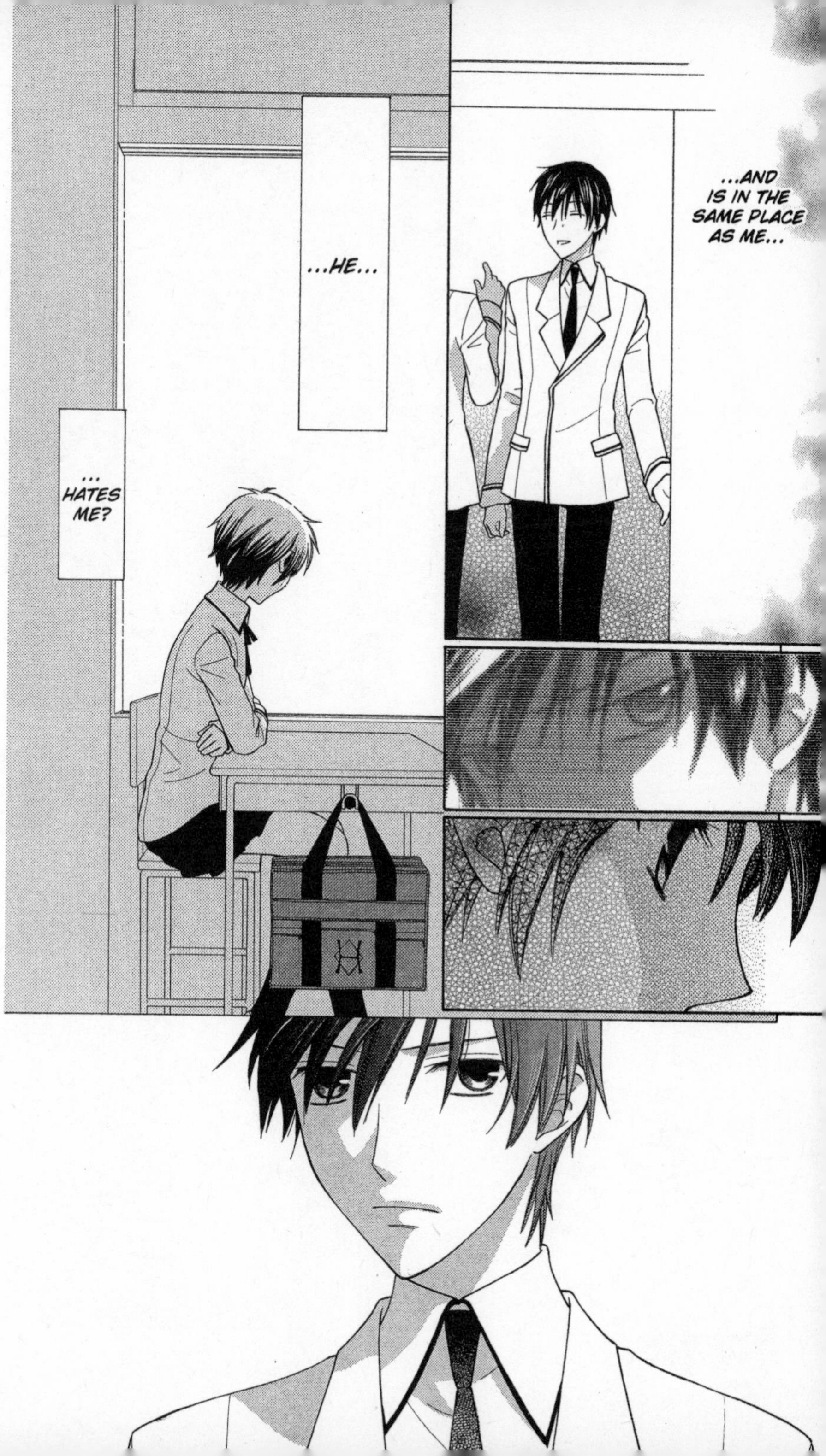
...AND IS IN THE SAME PLACE AS ME...
...HE...
... HATES ME?

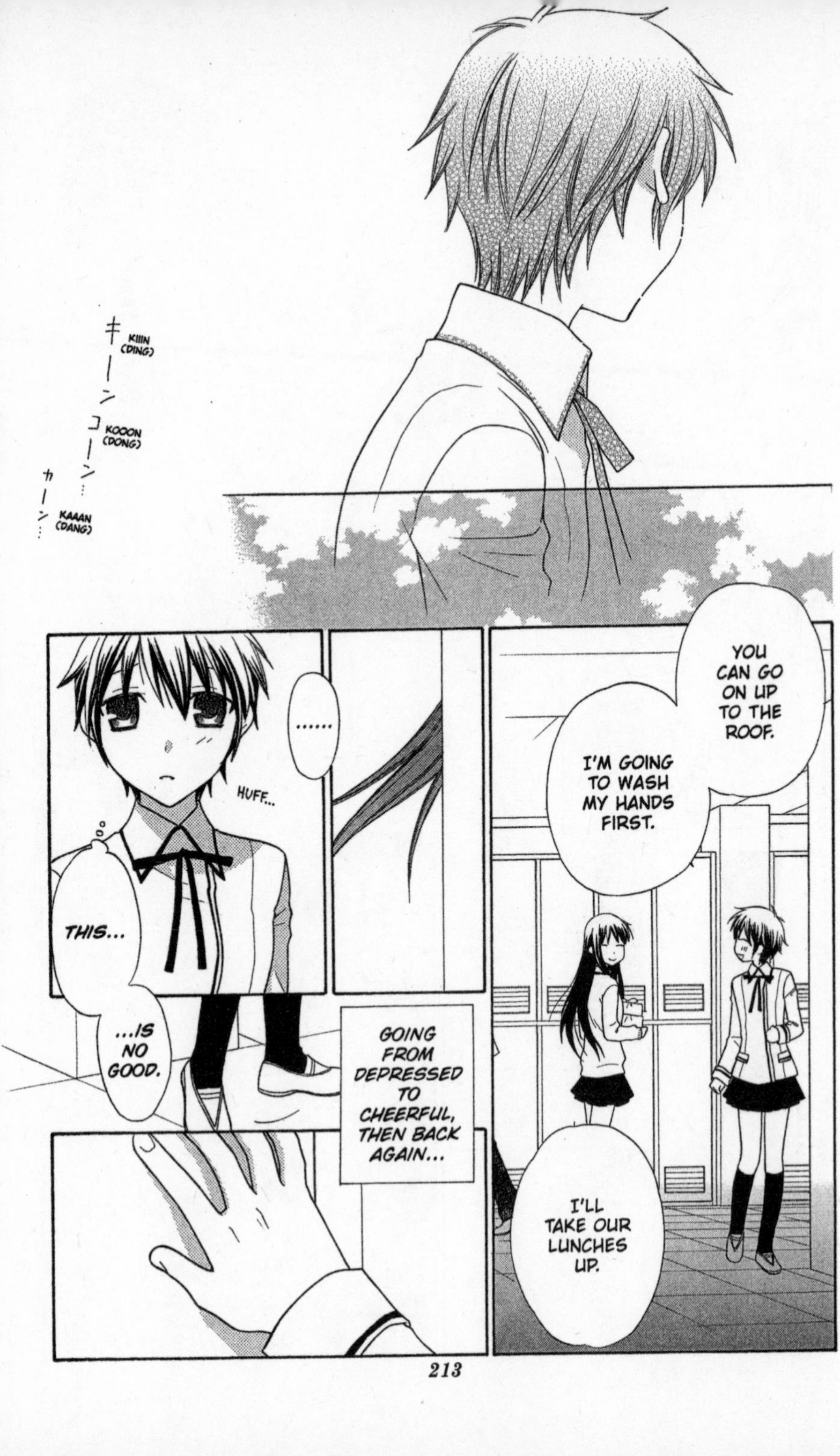
KIIIN (DING)
KOOON (DONG)
KAAAN (DANG)
YOU CAN GO ON UP TO THE ROOF.
I'M GOING TO WASH MY HANDS FIRST.
I'LL TAKE OUR LUNCHES UP.
......
HUFF...
THIS...
...IS NO GOOD.
GOING FROM DEPRESSED TO CHEERFUL, THEN BACK AGAIN...

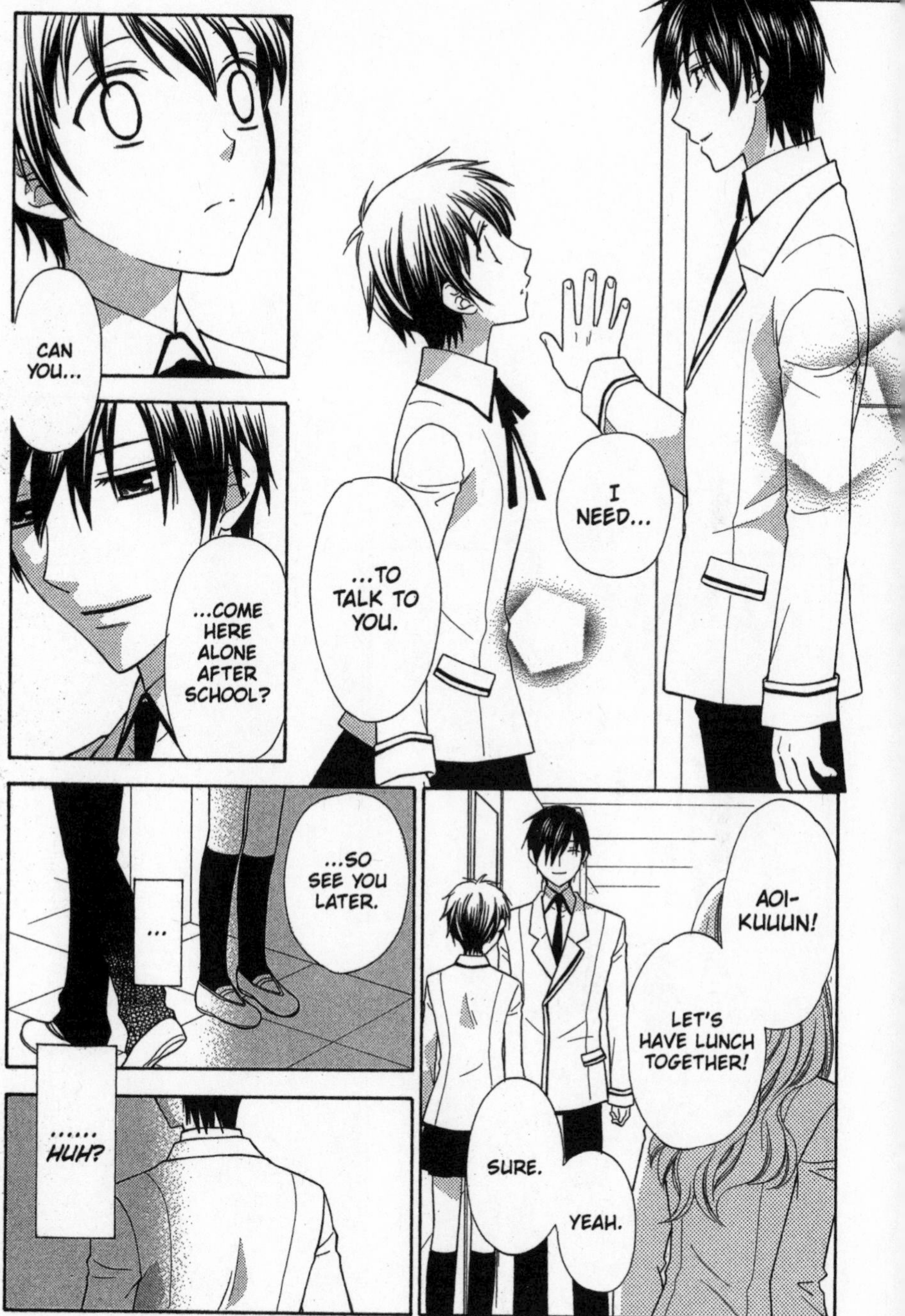
I NEED...
...TO TALK TO YOU.
CAN YOU...
...COME HERE ALONE AFTER SCHOOL?
AOI-KUUUN!
LET'S HAVE LUNCH TOGETHER!
SURE.
YEAH.
...SO SEE YOU LATER.
...
...... HUH?

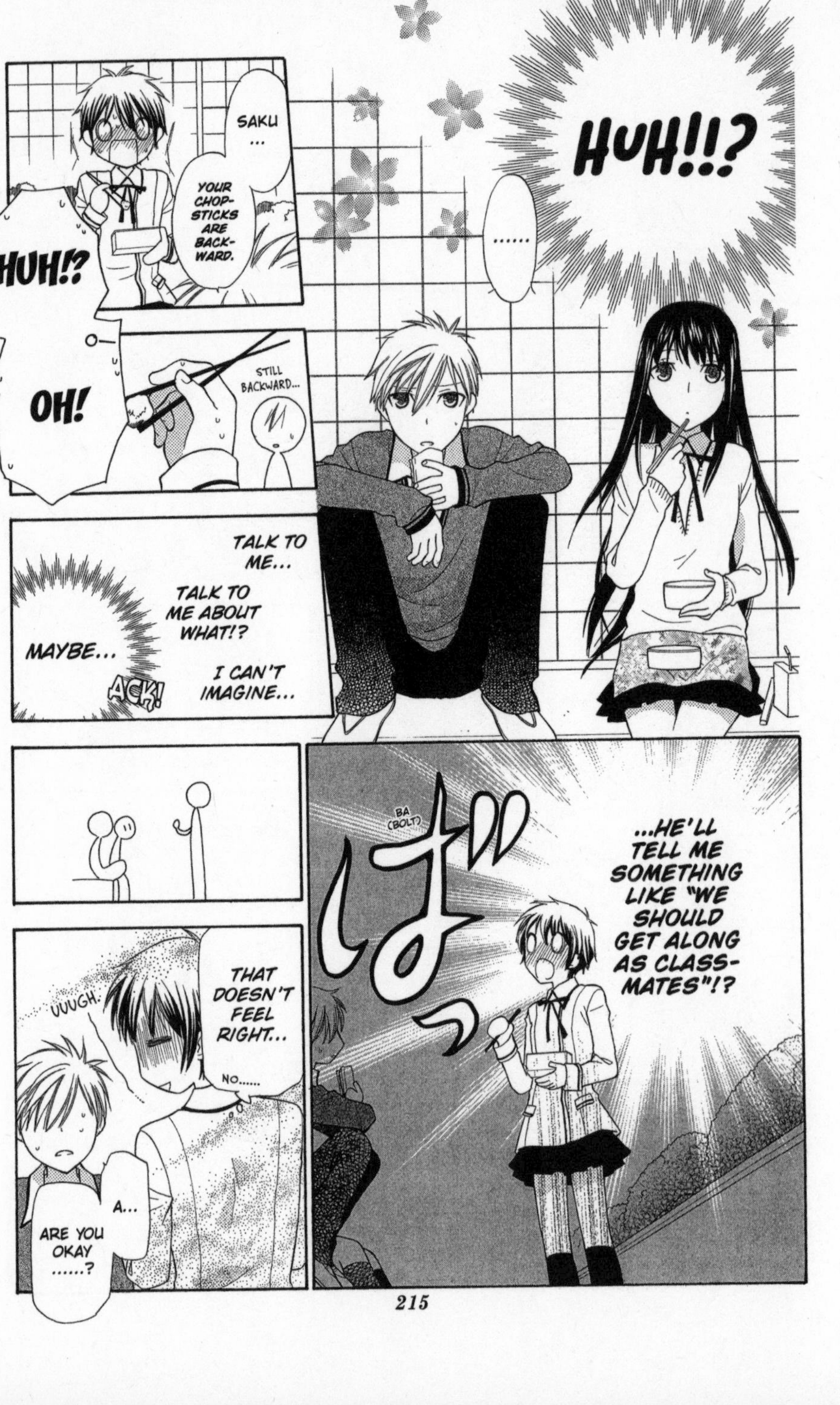

HUH!!?
......
SAKU ...
YOUR CHOP-STICKS ARE BACK-WARD.
HUH!?
STILL BACKWARD...
OH!
TALK TO ME...
TALK TO ME ABOUT WHAT!?
I CAN'T IMAGINE...
MAYBE...
ACK!
BA (BOLT)
...HE'LL TELL ME SOMETHING LIKE "WE SHOULD GET ALONG AS CLASS-MATES"!?
THAT DOESN'T FEEL RIGHT...
UUUGH.
NO......
A...
ARE YOU OKAY ......?

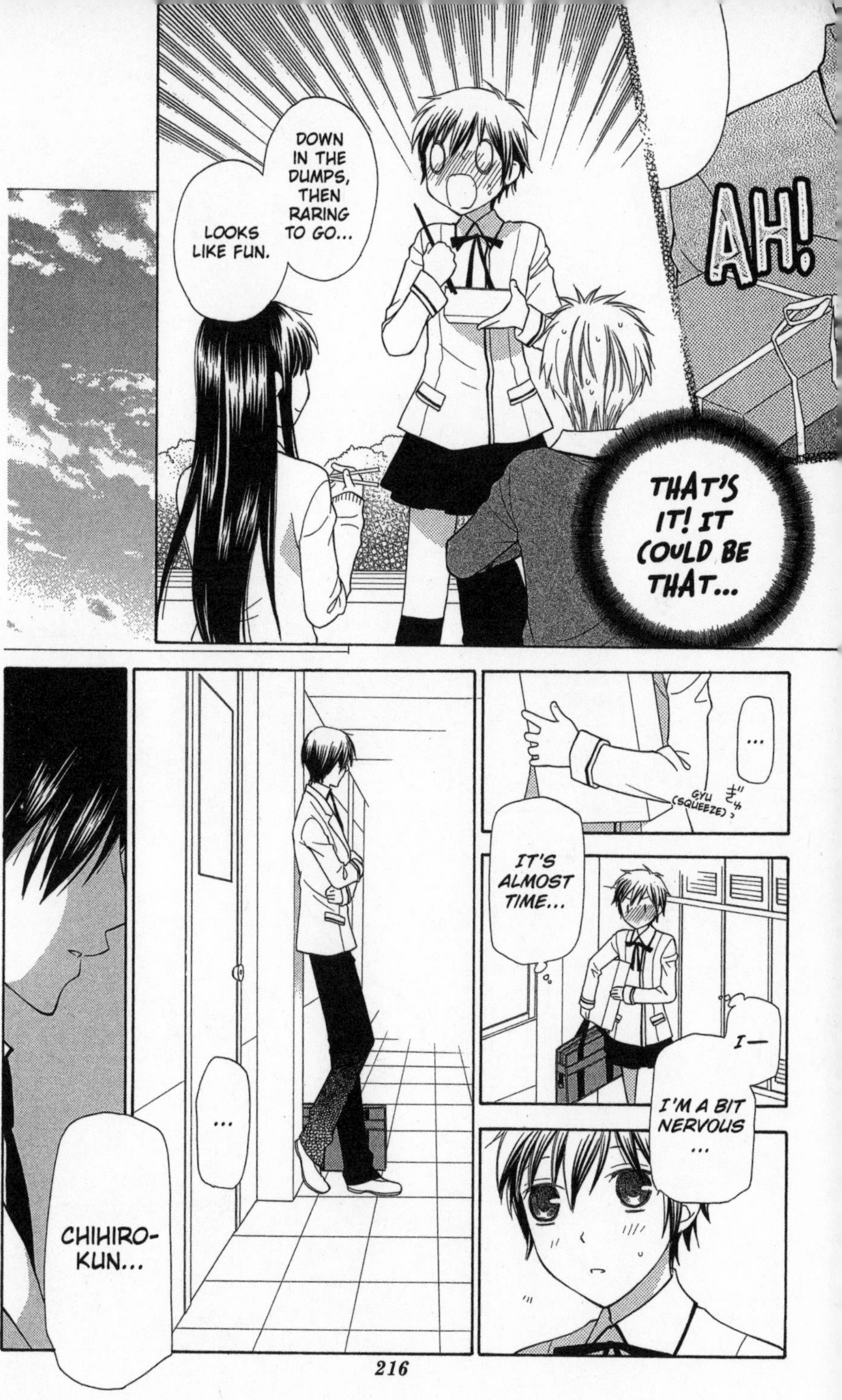
AH!
DOWN IN THE DUMPS, THEN RARING TO GO...
LOOKS LIKE FUN.
THAT'S IT! IT COULD BE THAT...
...
GYU (SQUEEZE)
IT'S ALMOST TIME...
I—
I'M A BIT NERVOUS...
...
CHIHIRO-KUN...

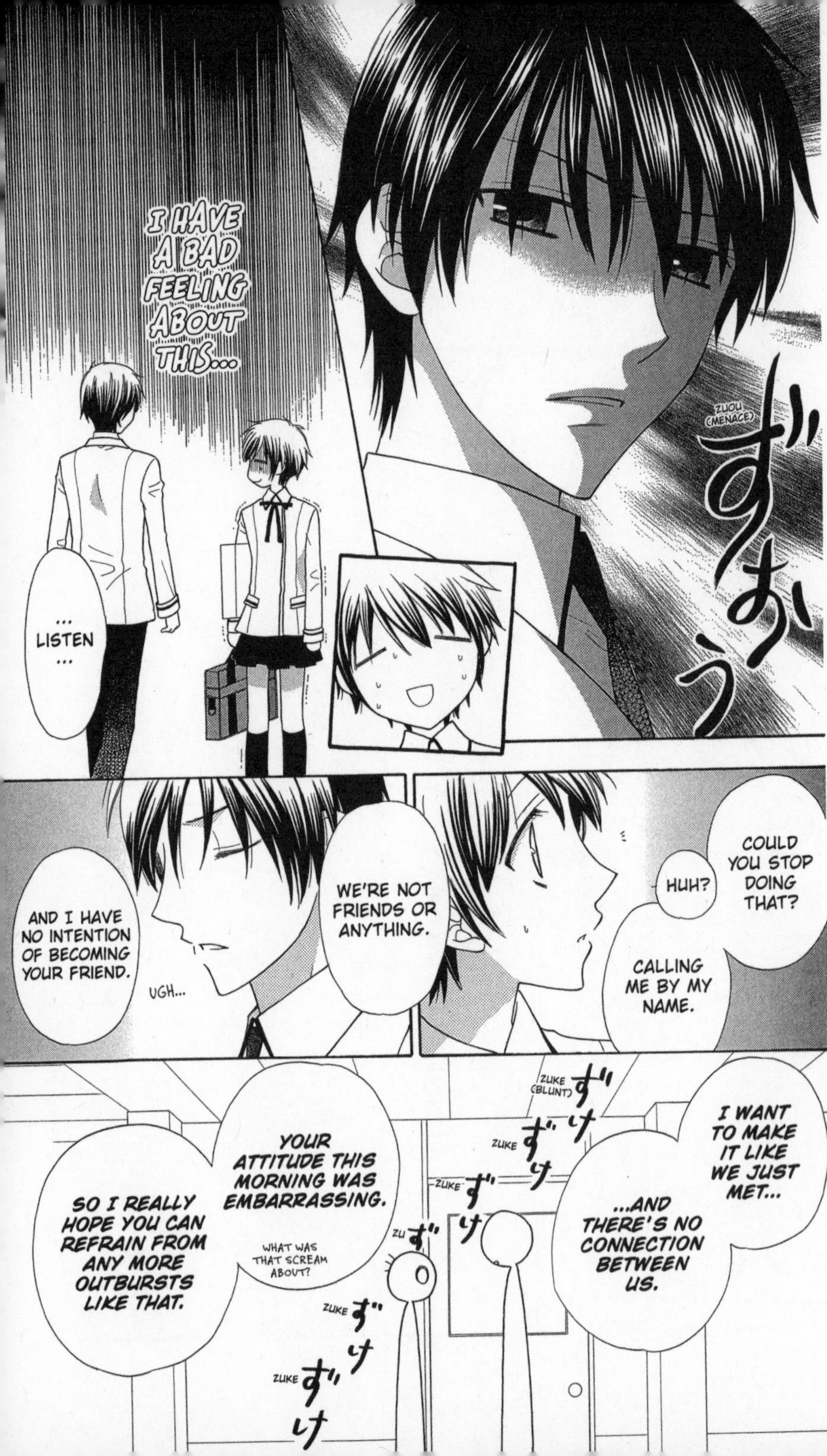
ZUOU (MENACE)
ずおう
I HAVE A BAD FEELING ABOUT THIS...
... LISTEN ...
COULD YOU STOP DOING THAT?
HUH?
CALLING ME BY MY NAME.
WE'RE NOT FRIENDS OR ANYTHING.
AND I HAVE NO INTENTION OF BECOMING YOUR FRIEND.
UGH...
ZUKE (BLUNT) ずけ
ZUKE ずけ
ZUKE ずけ
I WANT TO MAKE IT LIKE WE JUST MET...
...AND THERE'S NO CONNECTION BETWEEN US.
ZU ず
YOUR ATTITUDE THIS MORNING WAS EMBARRASSING.
WHAT WAS THAT SCREAM ABOUT?
SO I REALLY HOPE YOU CAN REFRAIN FROM ANY MORE OUTBURSTS LIKE THAT.
ZUKE ずけ
ZUKE ずけ

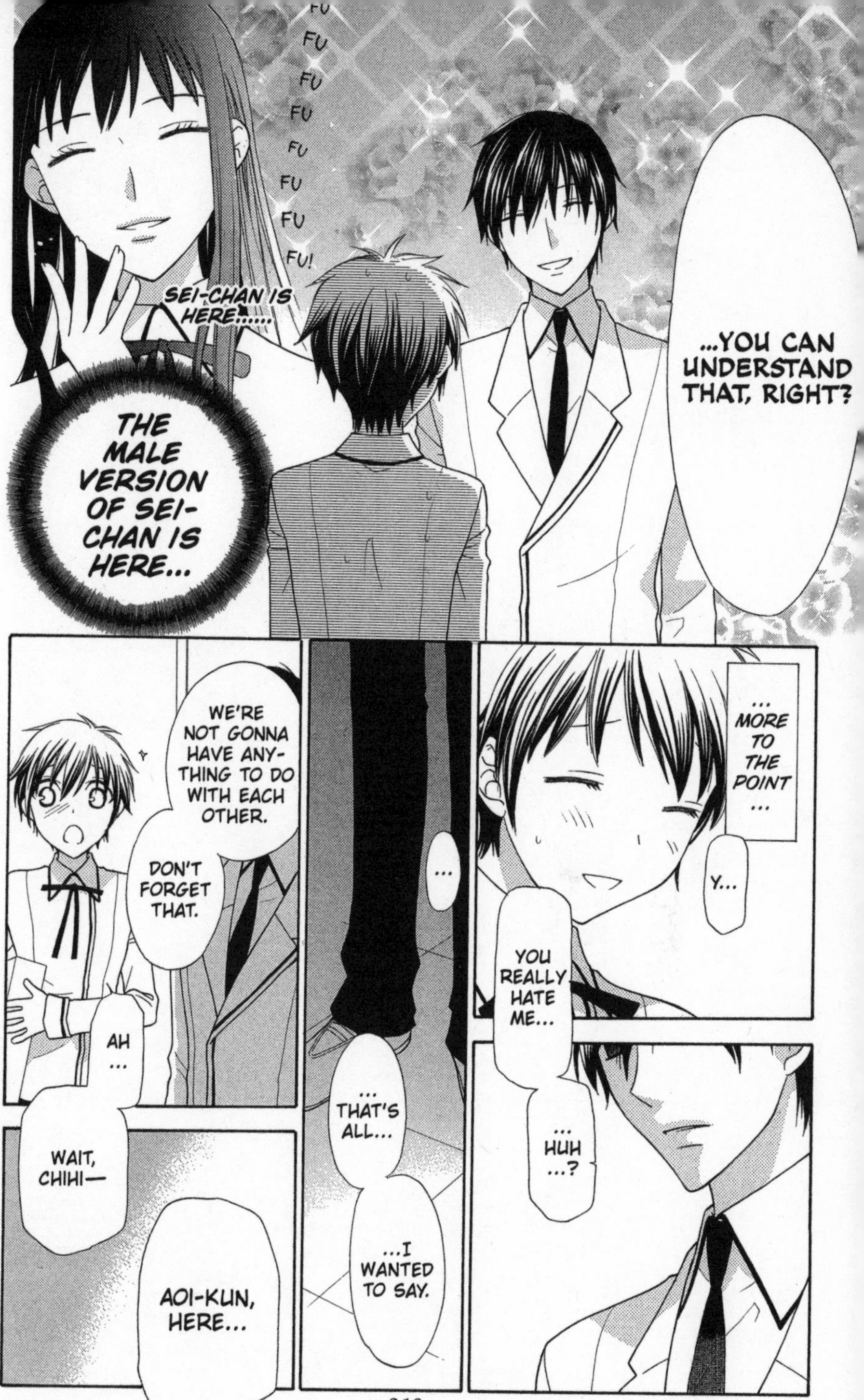

...YOU CAN UNDERSTAND THAT, RIGHT?
FU FU FU FU FU FU FU FU!
SEI-CHAN IS HERE......
THE MALE VERSION OF SEI-CHAN IS HERE...
...MORE TO THE POINT...
Y...
YOU REALLY HATE ME...
...HUH...?
...
...THAT'S ALL...
...I WANTED TO SAY.
WE'RE NOT GONNA HAVE ANYTHING TO DO WITH EACH OTHER.
DON'T FORGET THAT.
AH...
WAIT, CHIHI—
AOI-KUN, HERE...

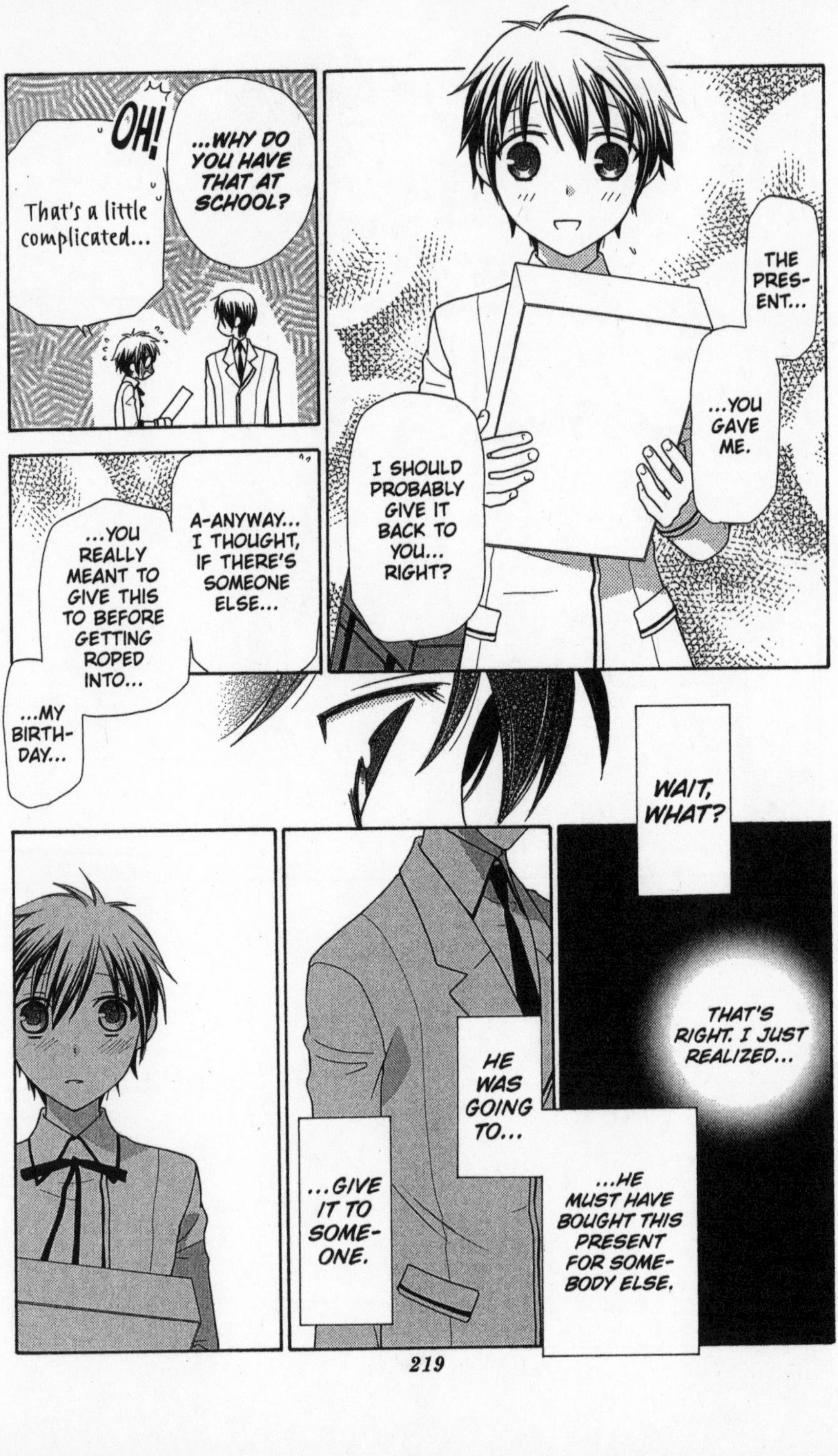
THE PRESENT...
...YOU GAVE ME.
I SHOULD PROBABLY GIVE IT BACK TO YOU... RIGHT?
OH!
...WHY DO YOU HAVE THAT AT SCHOOL?
That's a little complicated...
A-ANYWAY... I THOUGHT, IF THERE'S SOMEONE ELSE...
...YOU REALLY MEANT TO GIVE THIS TO BEFORE GETTING ROPED INTO...
...MY BIRTHDAY...
WAIT, WHAT?
THAT'S RIGHT. I JUST REALIZED...
...HE MUST HAVE BOUGHT THIS PRESENT FOR SOMEBODY ELSE.
HE WAS GOING TO...
...GIVE IT TO SOMEONE.

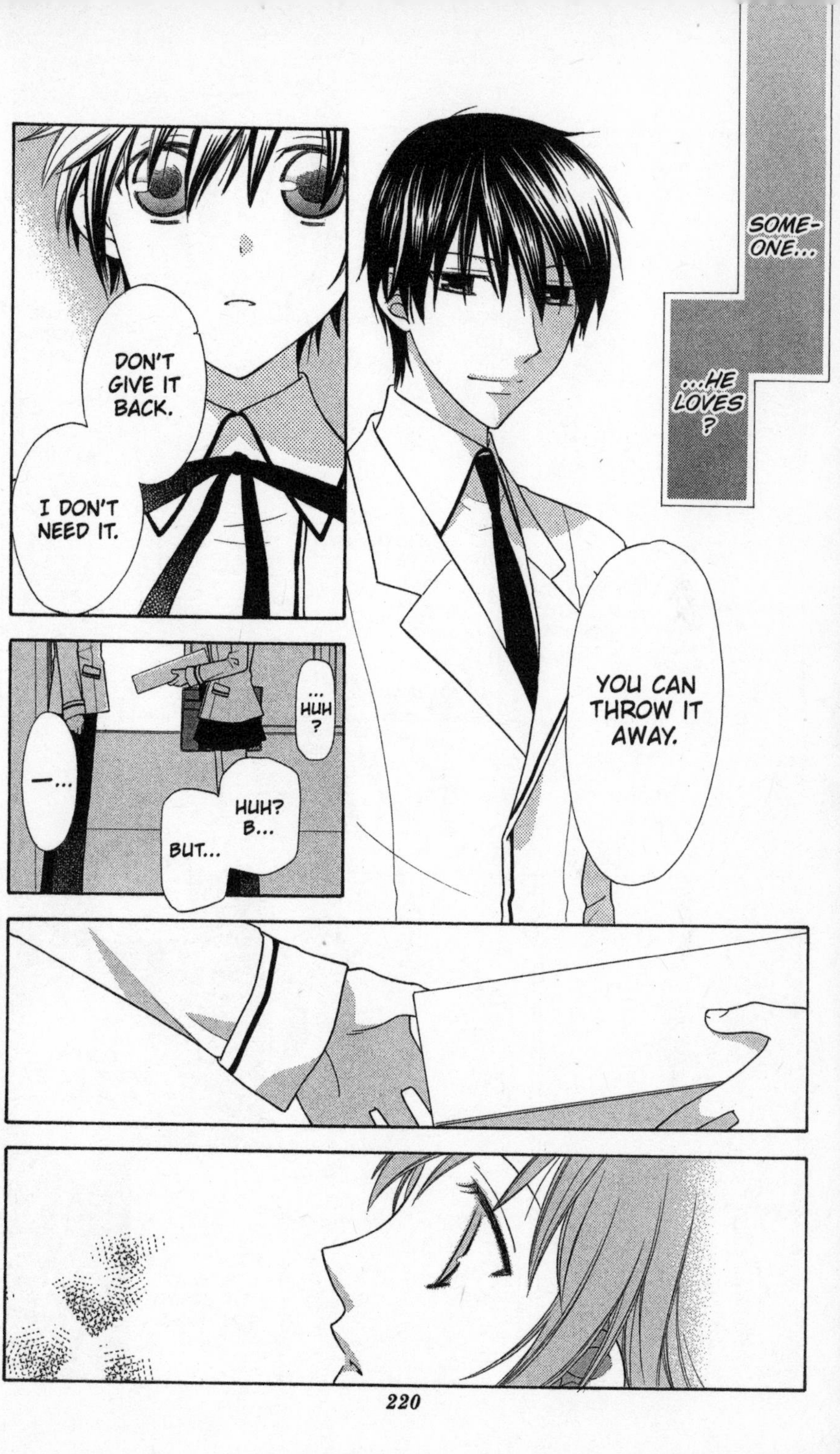
SOME-ONE...
...HE LOVES ?
YOU CAN THROW IT AWAY.
DON'T GIVE IT BACK.
I DON'T NEED IT.
... HUH ?
HUH? B... BUT...
—...

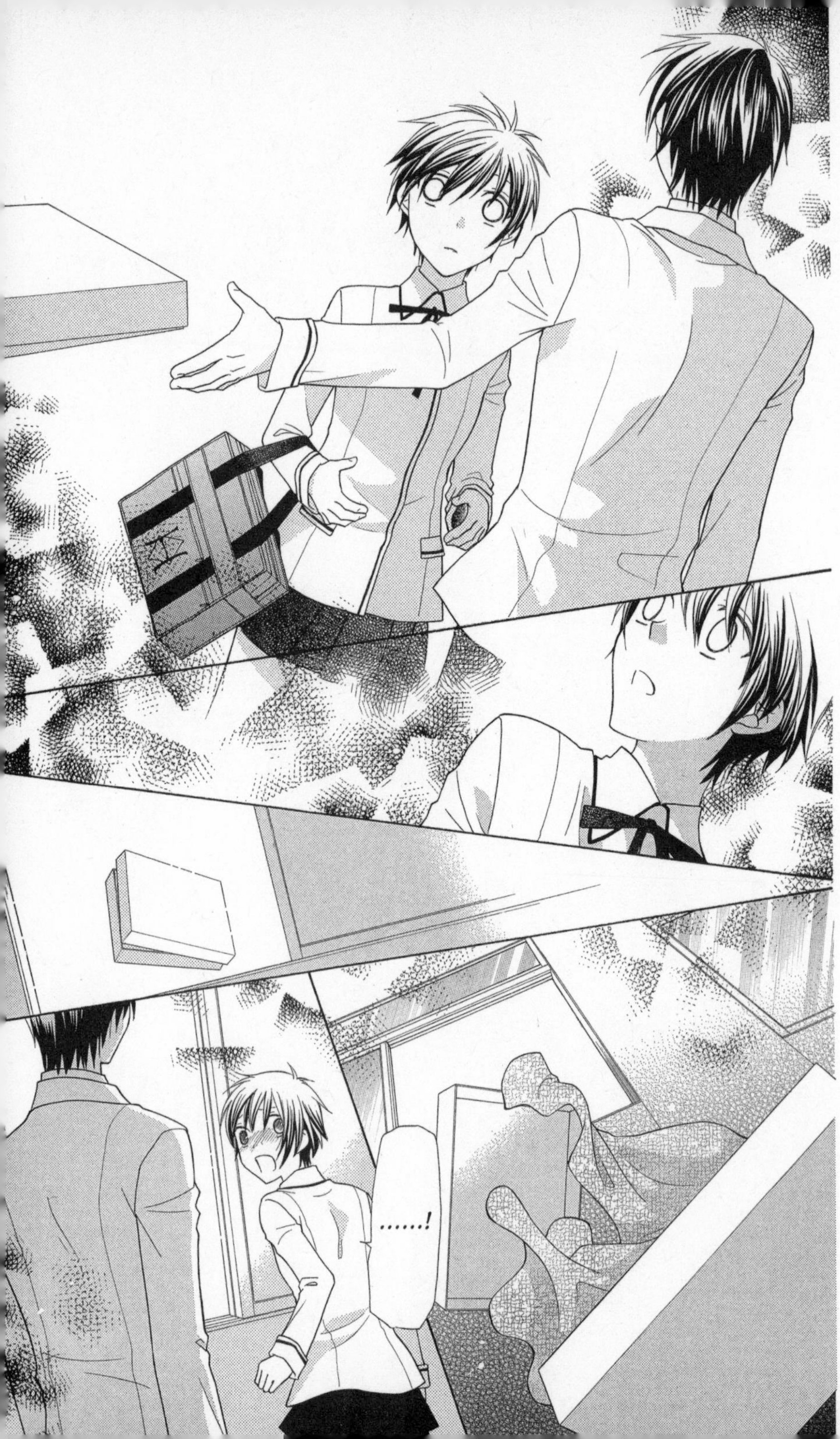
......!

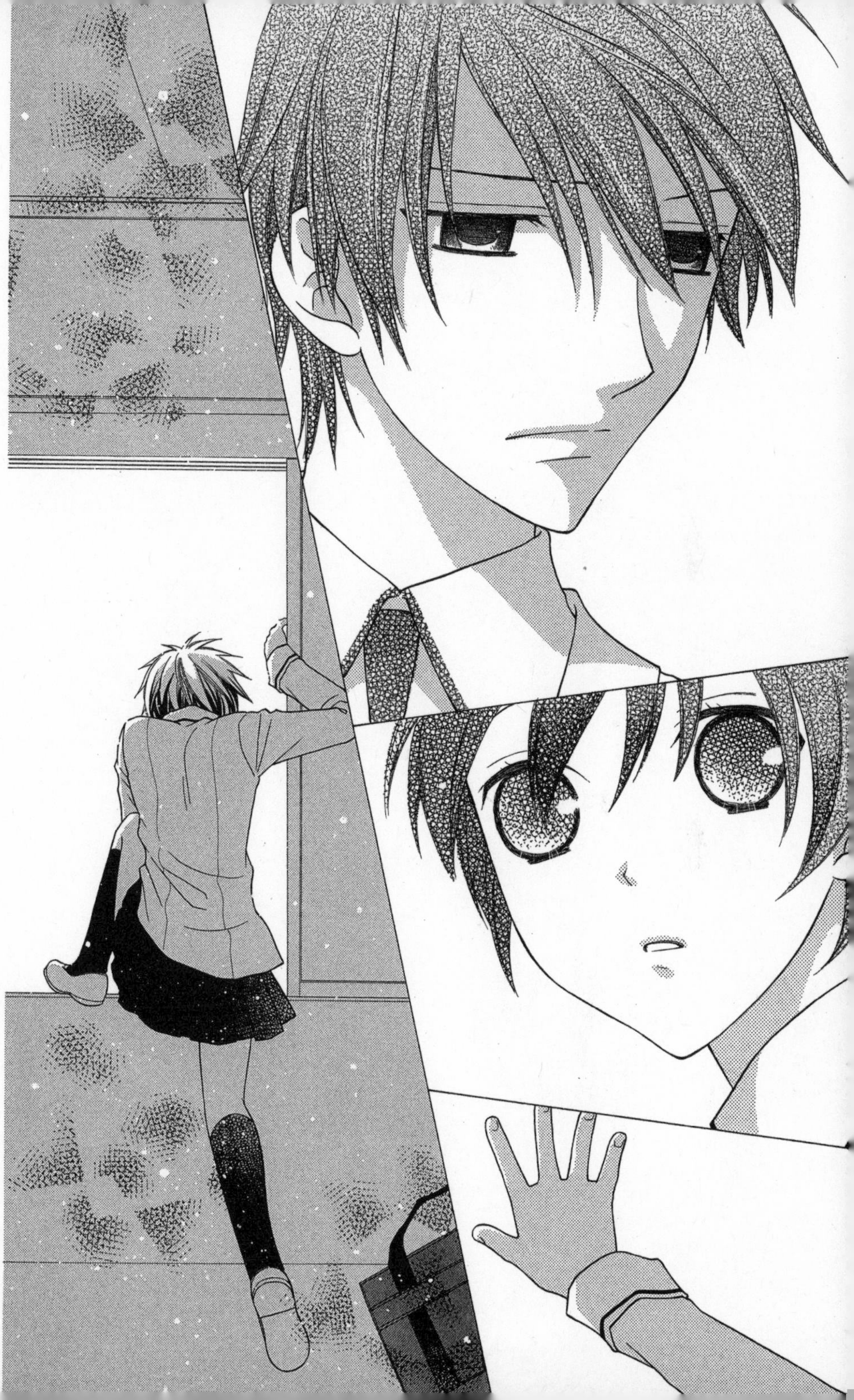

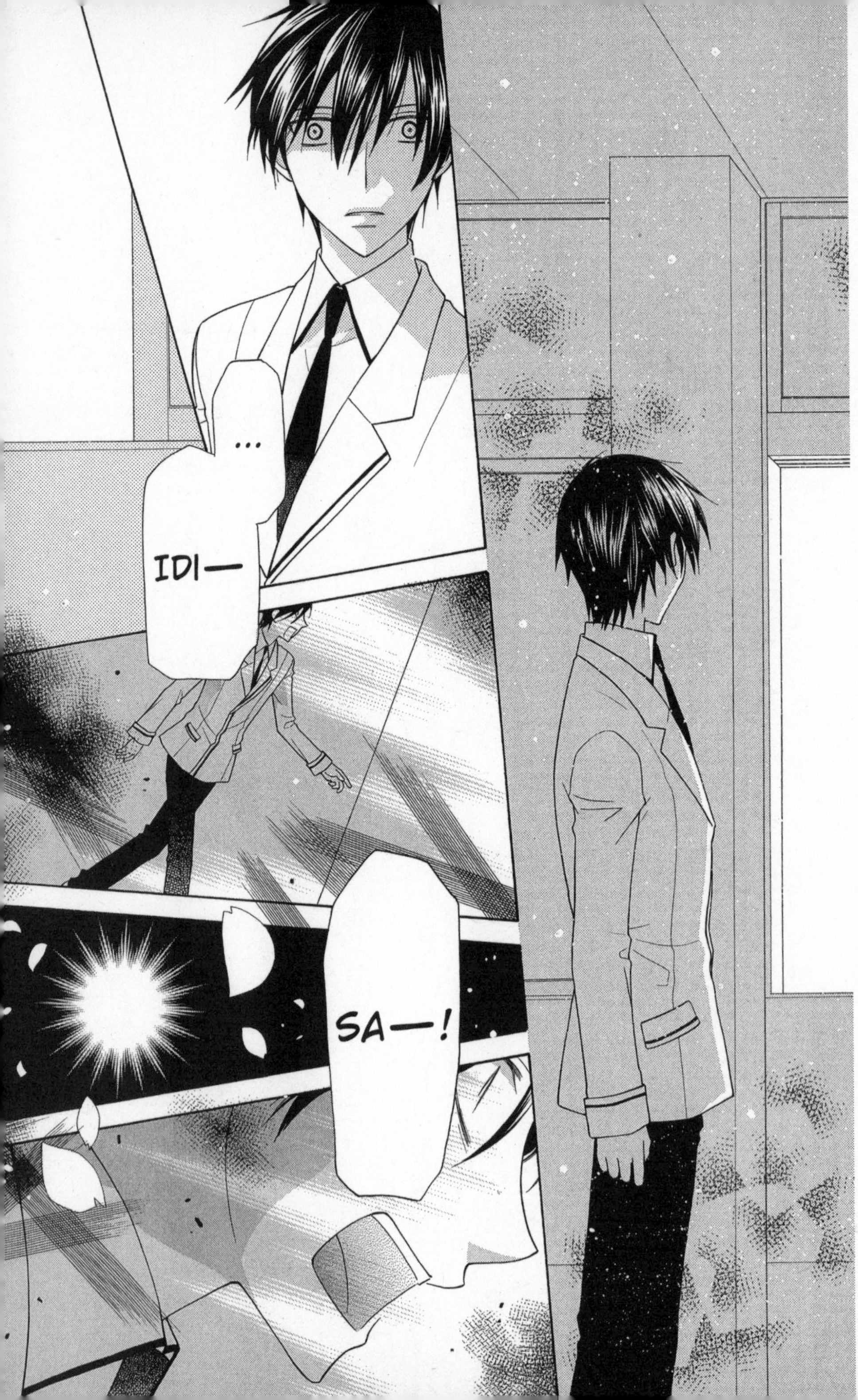
...
IDI—
SA—!

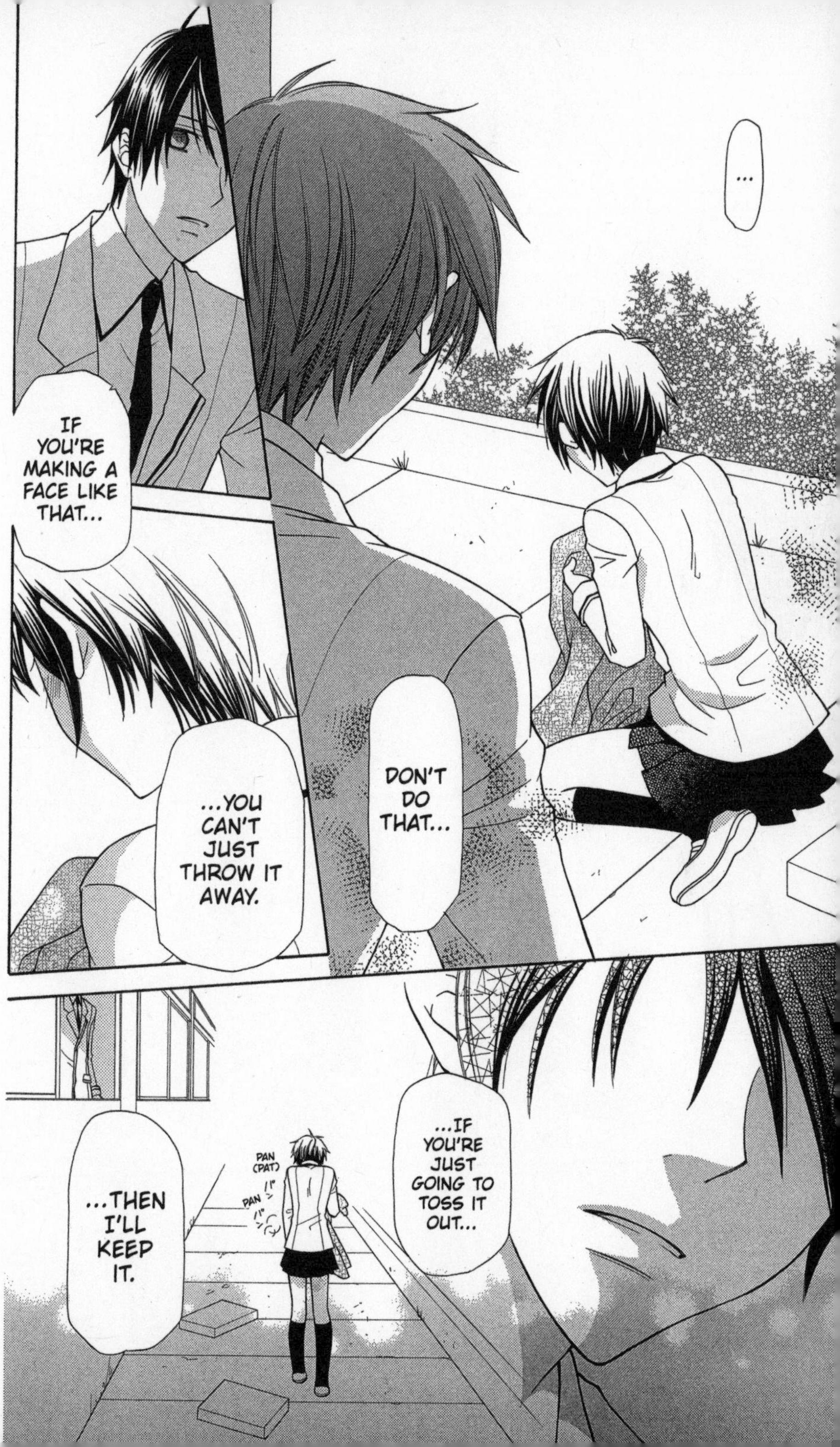
...
DON'T DO THAT...
IF YOU'RE MAKING A FACE LIKE THAT...
...YOU CAN'T JUST THROW IT AWAY.
...IF YOU'RE JUST GOING TO TOSS IT OUT...
PAN (PAT)
PAN
...THEN I'LL KEEP IT.

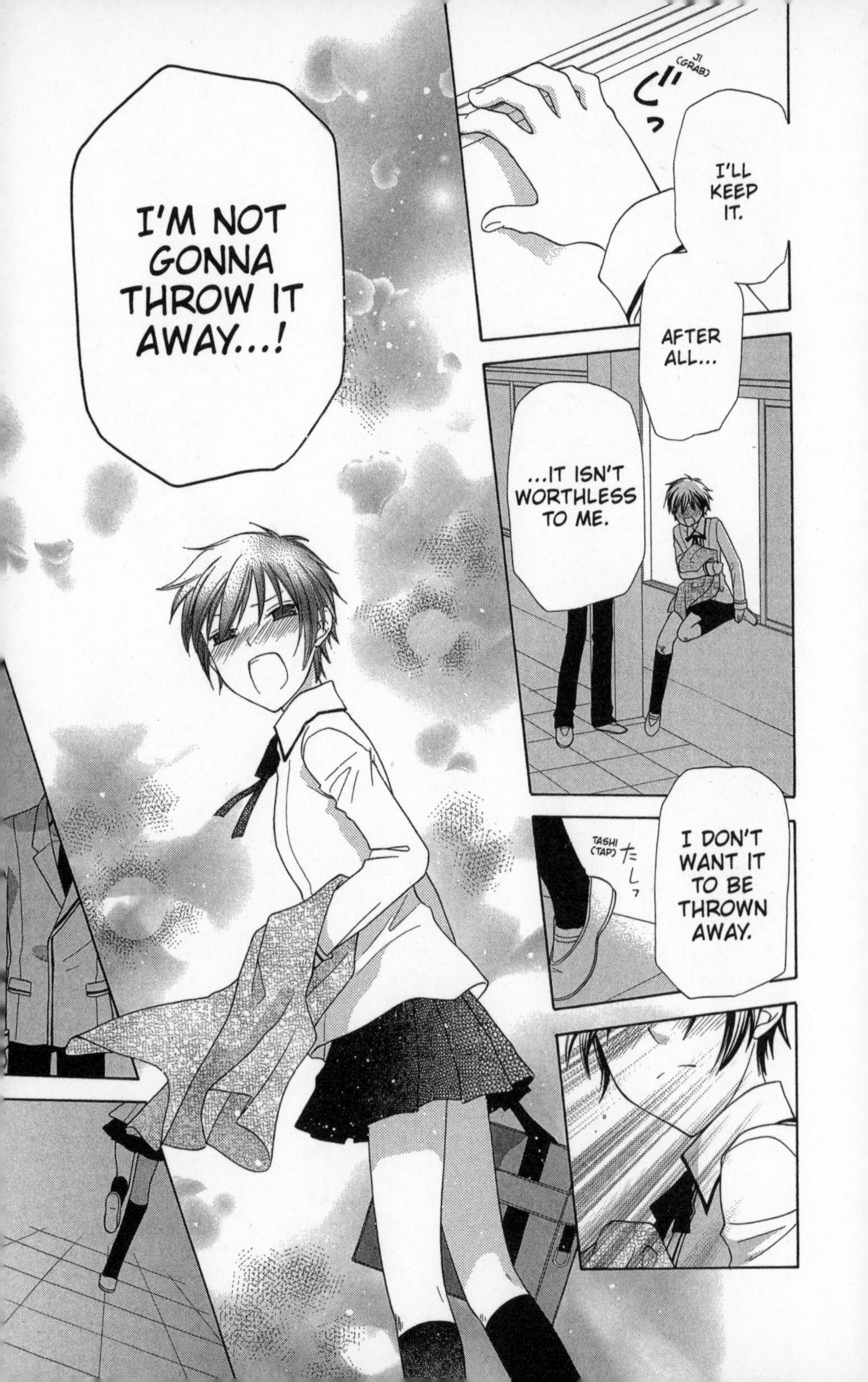
JI (GRAB)
ぐっ
I'LL KEEP IT.
AFTER ALL...
...IT ISN'T WORTHLESS TO ME.
TASHI (TAP)
たしっ
I DON'T WANT IT TO BE THROWN AWAY.
I'M NOT GONNA THROW IT AWAY...!

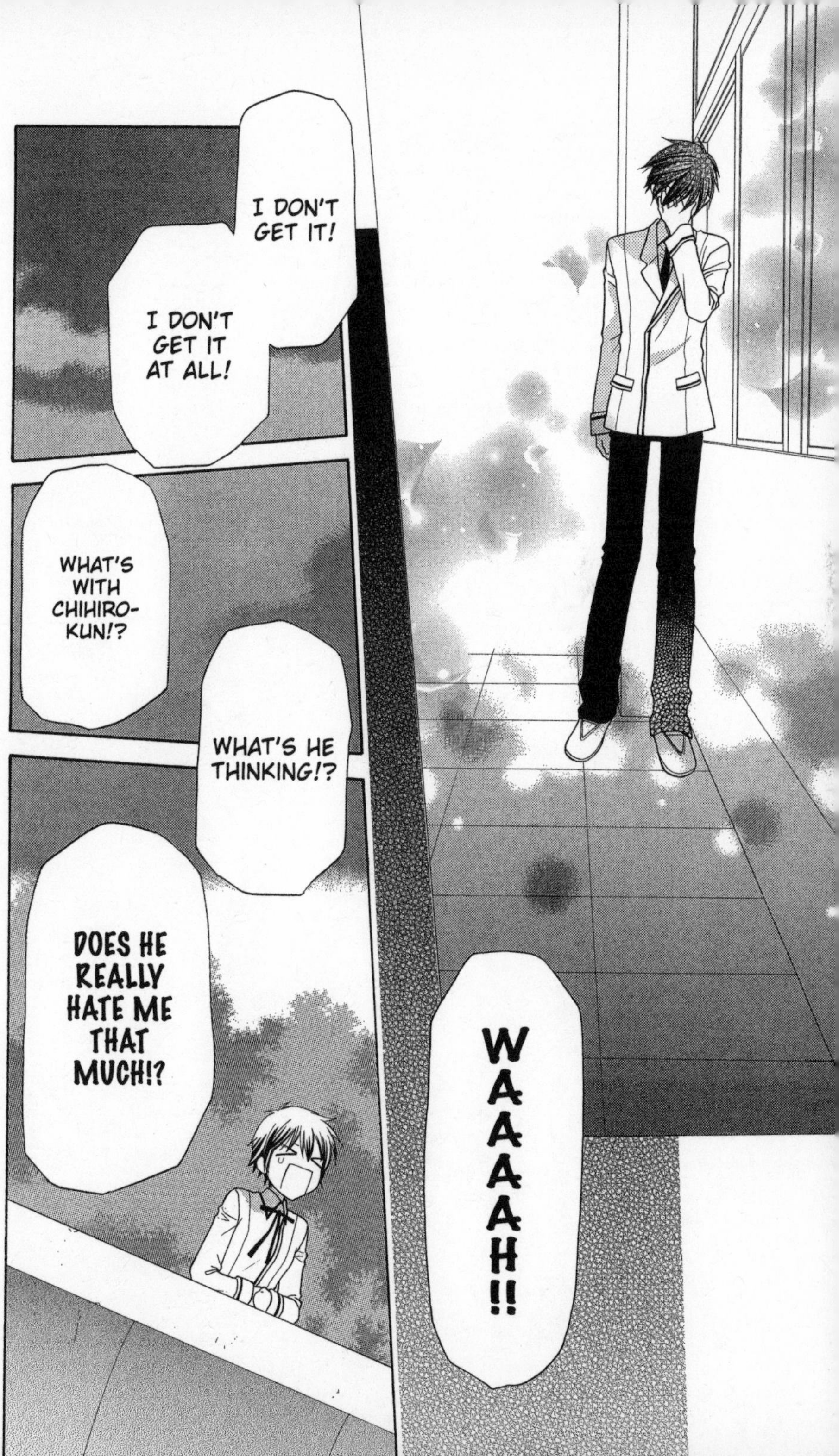
WAAAAAH!!
I DON'T GET IT!
I DON'T GET IT AT ALL!
WHAT'S WITH CHIHIRO-KUN!?
WHAT'S HE THINKING!?
DOES HE REALLY HATE ME THAT MUCH!?

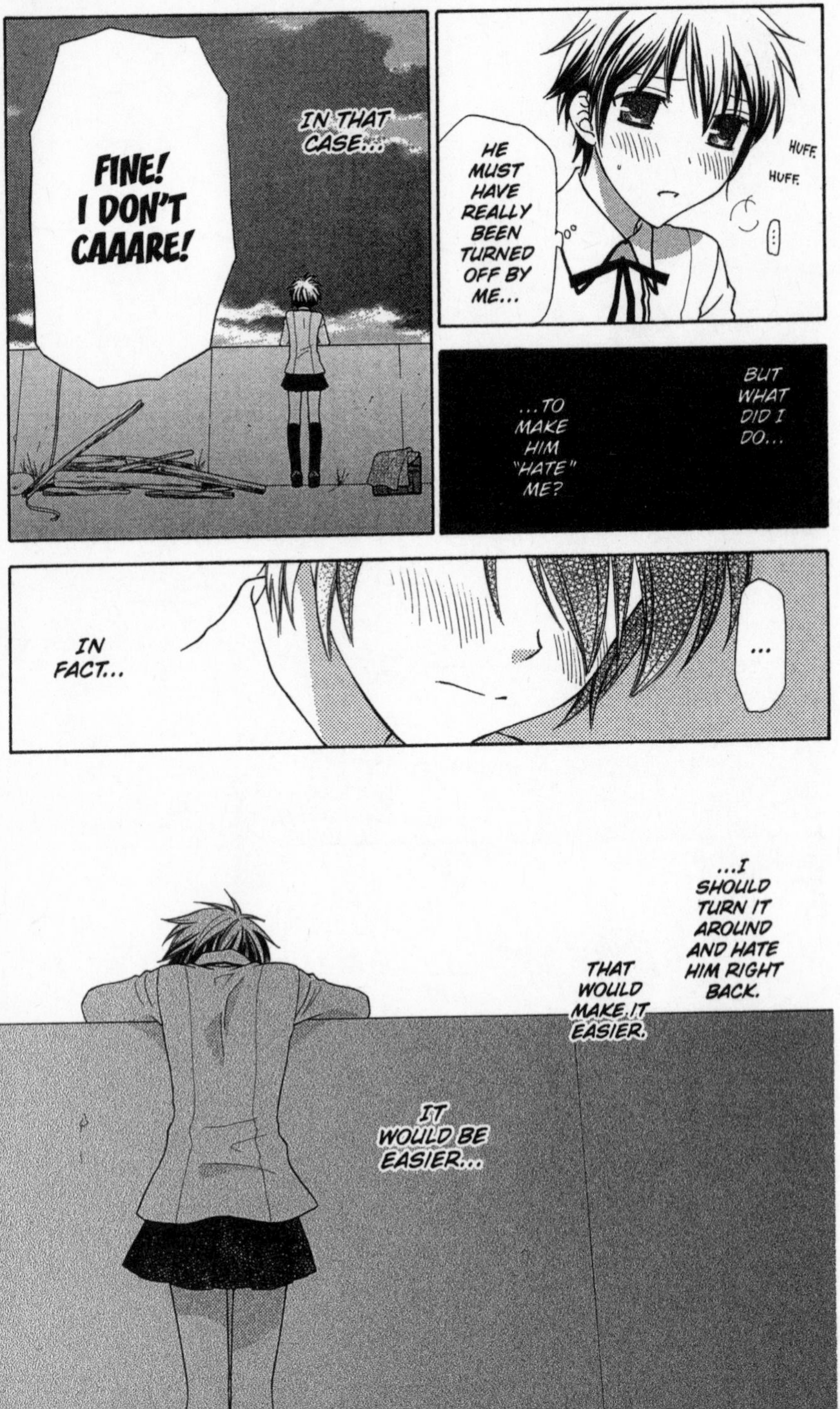

HE MUST HAVE REALLY BEEN TURNED OFF BY ME...
HUFF
HUFF
...
BUT WHAT DID I DO...
...TO MAKE HIM "HATE" ME?
FINE! I DON'T CAAARE!
IN THAT CASE...
...
IN FACT...
...I SHOULD TURN IT AROUND AND HATE HIM RIGHT BACK.
THAT WOULD MAKE IT EASIER.
IT WOULD BE EASIER...

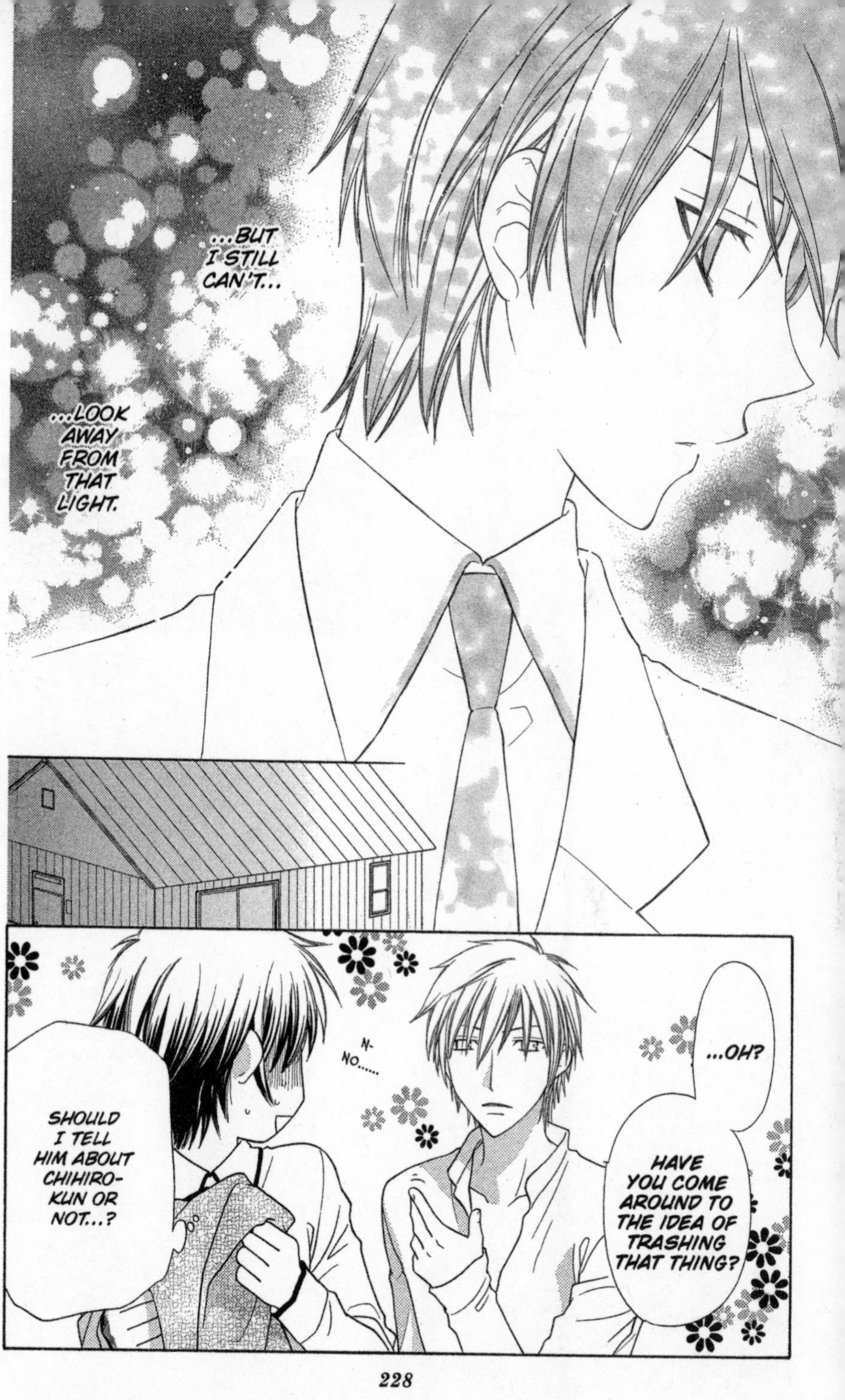
...BUT I STILL CAN'T...
...LOOK AWAY FROM THAT LIGHT.
...OH?
HAVE YOU COME AROUND TO THE IDEA OF TRASHING THAT THING?
N- NO......
SHOULD I TELL HIM ABOUT CHIHIRO-KUN OR NOT...?

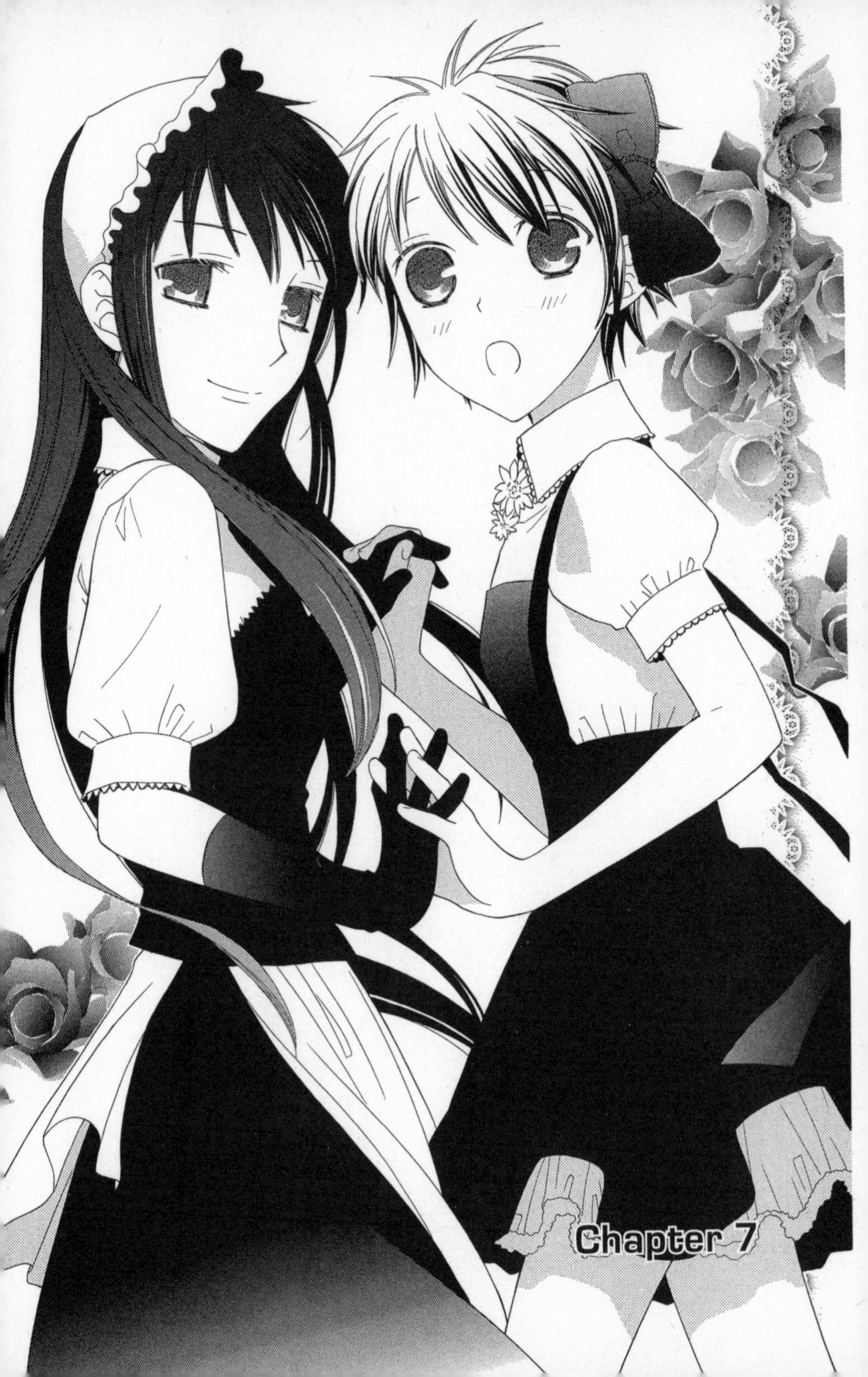
Chapter 7

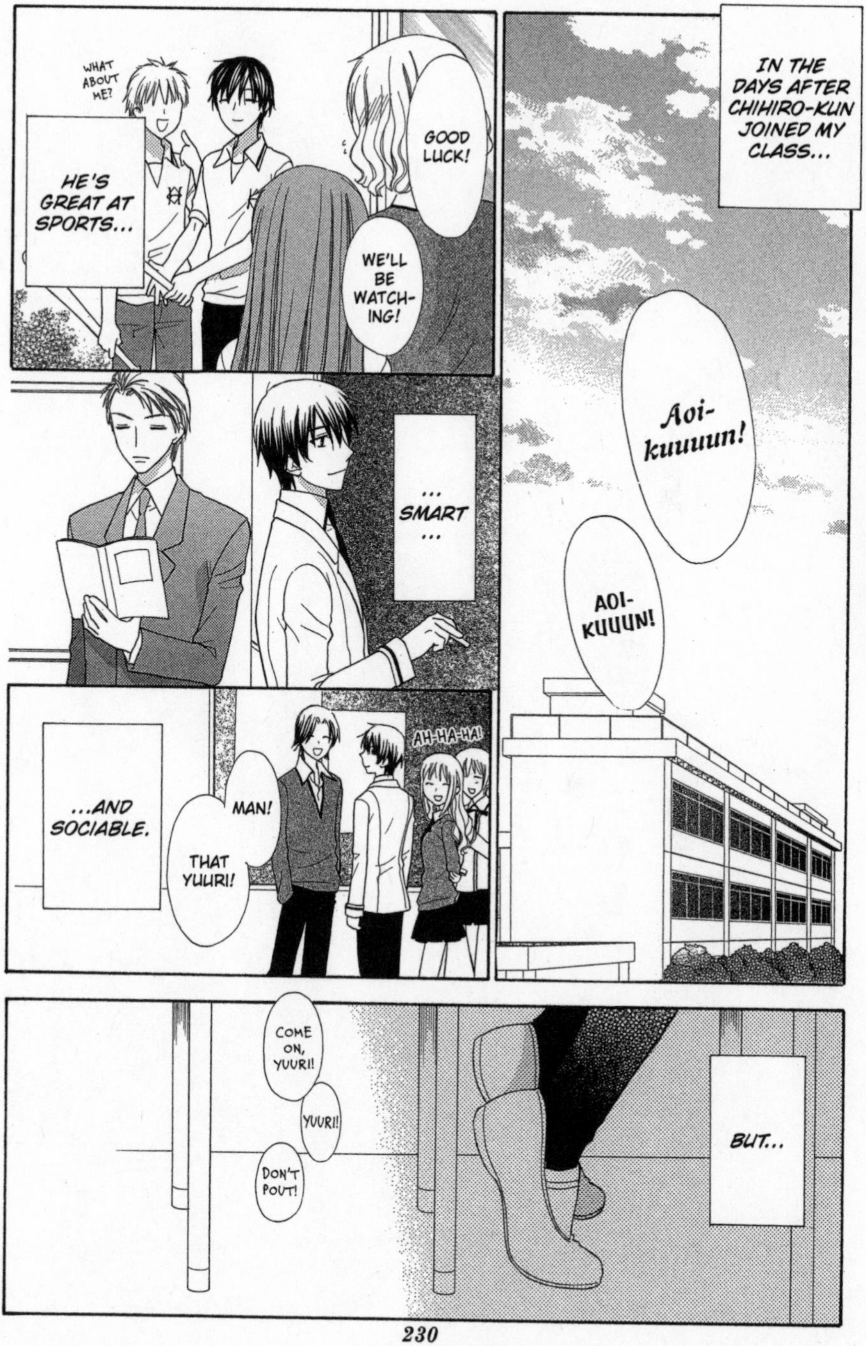
IN THE DAYS AFTER CHIHIRO-KUN JOINED MY CLASS...
Aoi-kuuuun!
AOI-KUUUN!
GOOD LUCK!
WE'LL BE WATCHING!
WHAT ABOUT ME?
HE'S GREAT AT SPORTS...
... SMART ...
AH-HA-HA!
MAN!
THAT YUURI!
...AND SOCIABLE.
BUT...
COME ON, YUURI!
YUURI!
DON'T POUT!

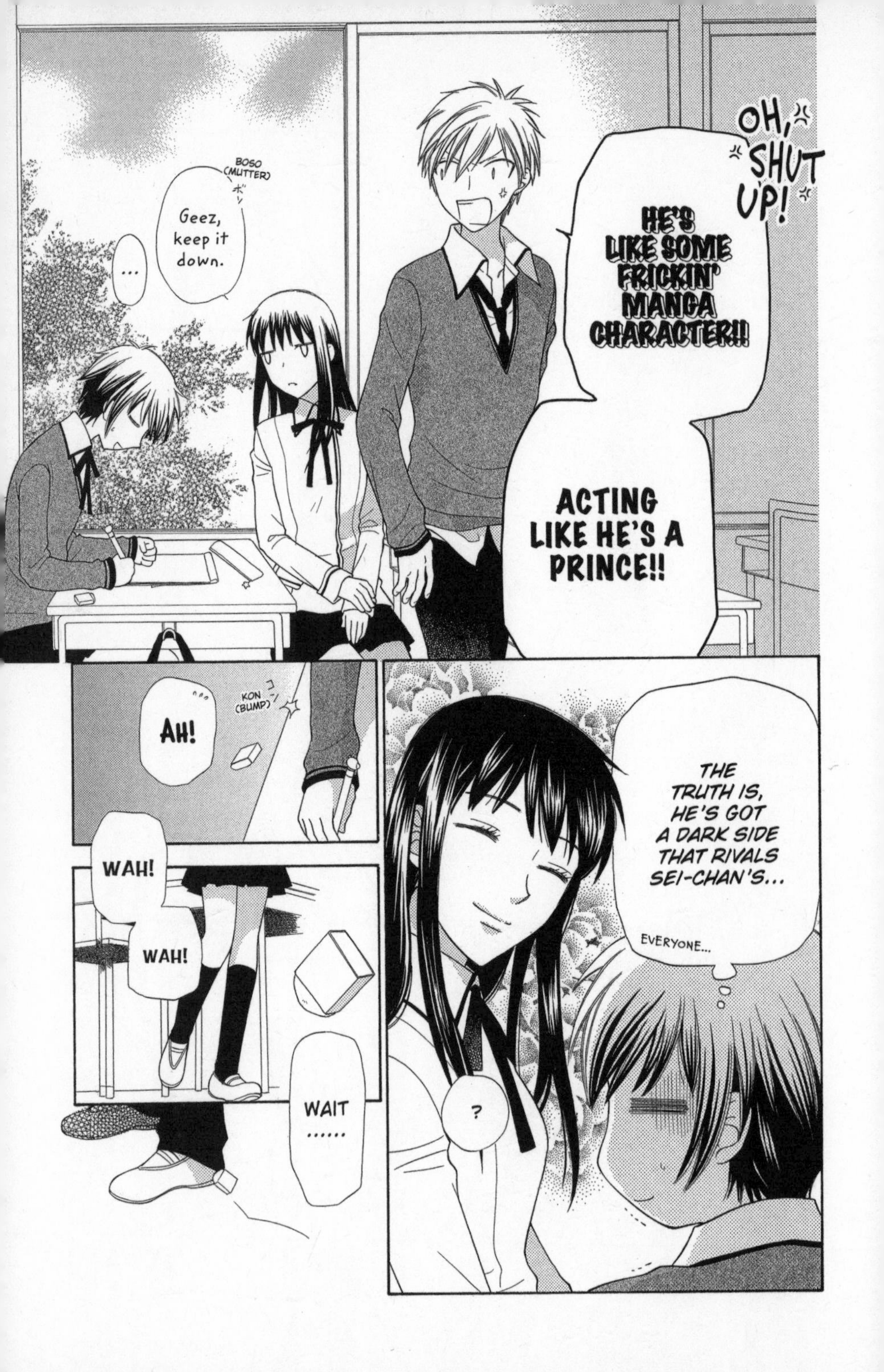
OH, SHUT UP!
HE'S LIKE SOME FRICKIN' MANGA CHARACTER!!
ACTING LIKE HE'S A PRINCE!!
BOSO (MUTTER)
Geez, keep it down.
...
THE TRUTH IS, HE'S GOT A DARK SIDE THAT RIVALS SEI-CHAN'S...
EVERYONE...
?
KON (BUMP)
AH!
WAH!
WAH!
WAIT ......

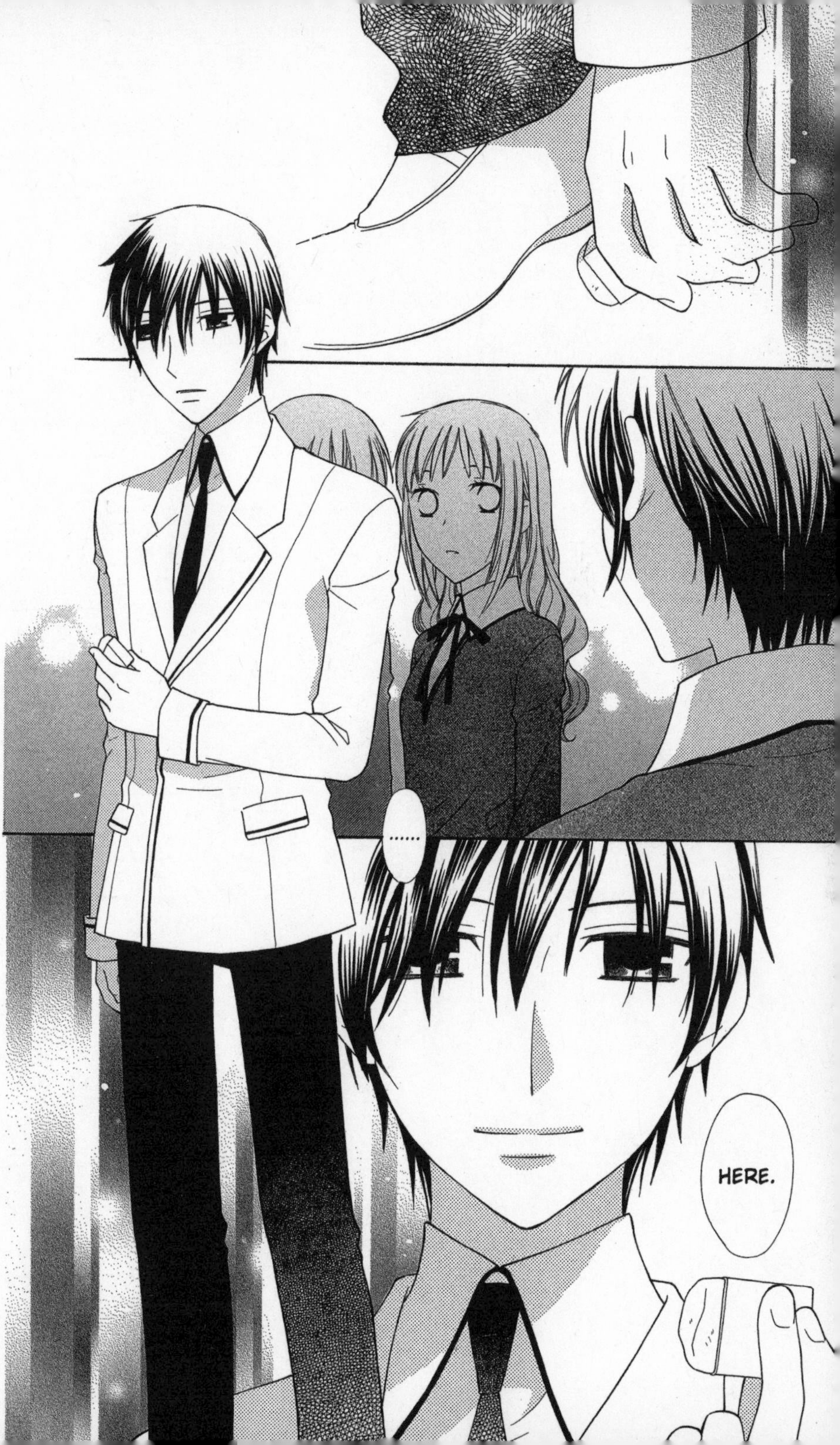
......
HERE.

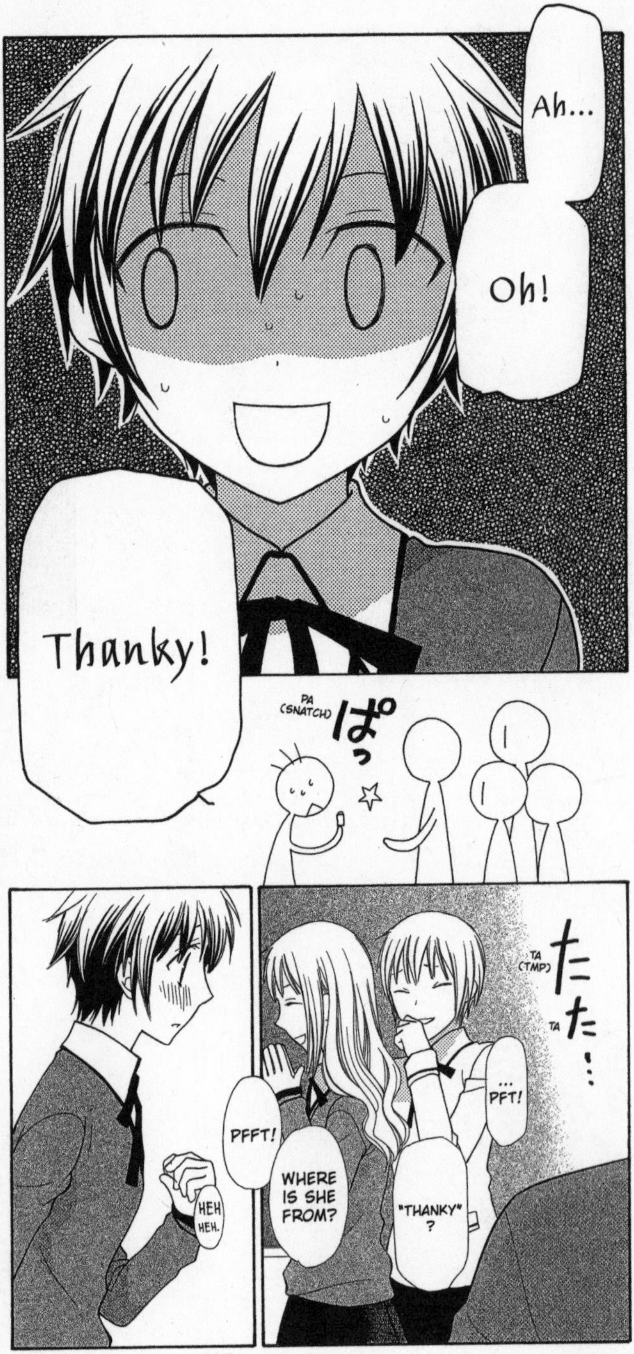
Ah...
Oh!
Thanky!
PA (SNATCH) ぱっ
TA (TMP) たた
TA
...PFT!
"THANKY"?
PFFT!
WHERE IS SHE FROM?
HEH HEH.

I made the collars on Saku's and the others' uniforms higher than average (kind of), so even as I draw it, I wonder if it's hard for them to breathe.

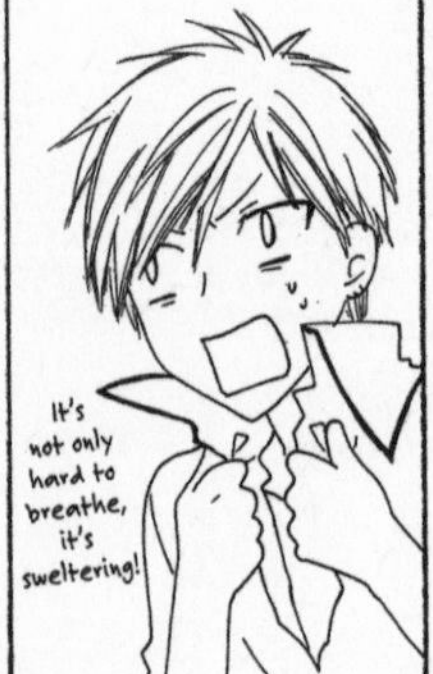
It's not only hard to breathe, it's sweltering!

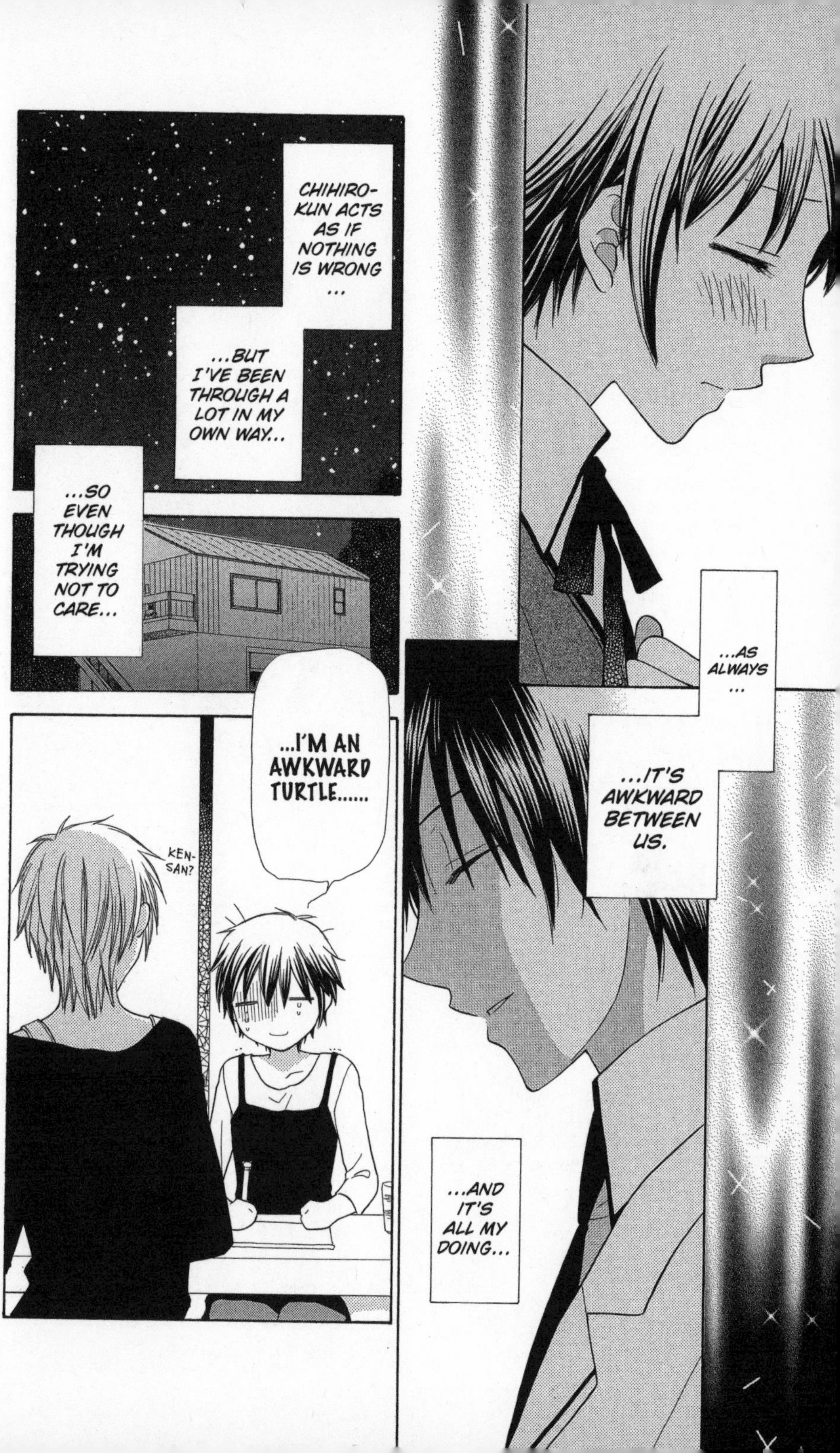
...AS ALWAYS...
...IT'S AWKWARD BETWEEN US.
...AND IT'S ALL MY DOING...
CHIHIRO-KUN ACTS AS IF NOTHING IS WRONG...
...BUT I'VE BEEN THROUGH A LOT IN MY OWN WAY...
...SO EVEN THOUGH I'M TRYING NOT TO CARE...
...I'M AN AWKWARD TURTLE......
KEN-SAN?

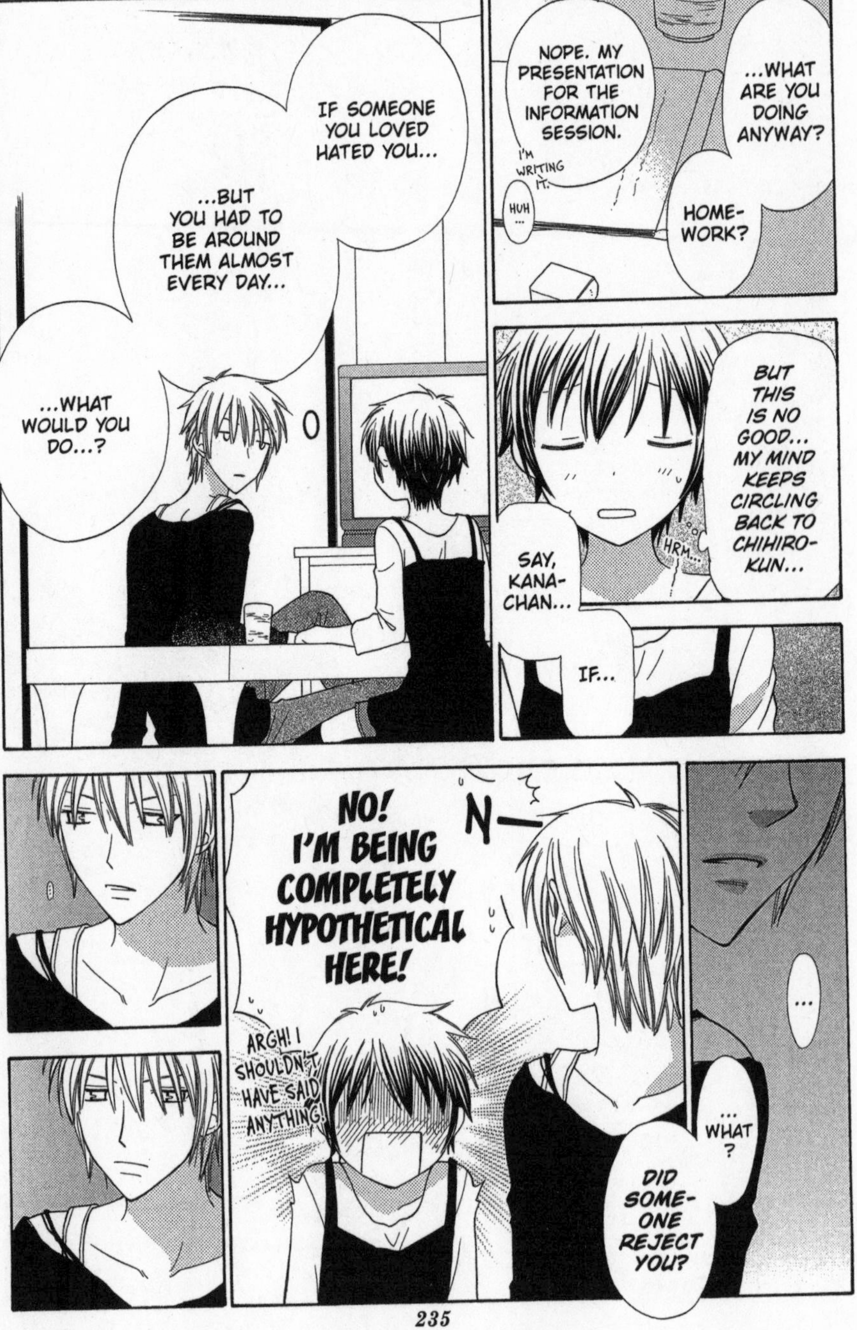
...WHAT ARE YOU DOING ANYWAY?
HOME-WORK?
NOPE. MY PRESENTATION FOR THE INFORMATION SESSION.
I'M WRITING IT.
HUH...
BUT THIS IS NO GOOD... MY MIND KEEPS CIRCLING BACK TO CHIHIRO-KUN...
HRM...
SAY, KANA-CHAN...
IF...
IF SOMEONE YOU LOVED HATED YOU...
...BUT YOU HAD TO BE AROUND THEM ALMOST EVERY DAY...
...WHAT WOULD YOU DO...?
...
...WHAT?
DID SOME-ONE REJECT YOU?
N—
NO! I'M BEING COMPLETELY HYPOTHETICAL HERE!
ARGH! I SHOULDN'T HAVE SAID ANYTHING!
...

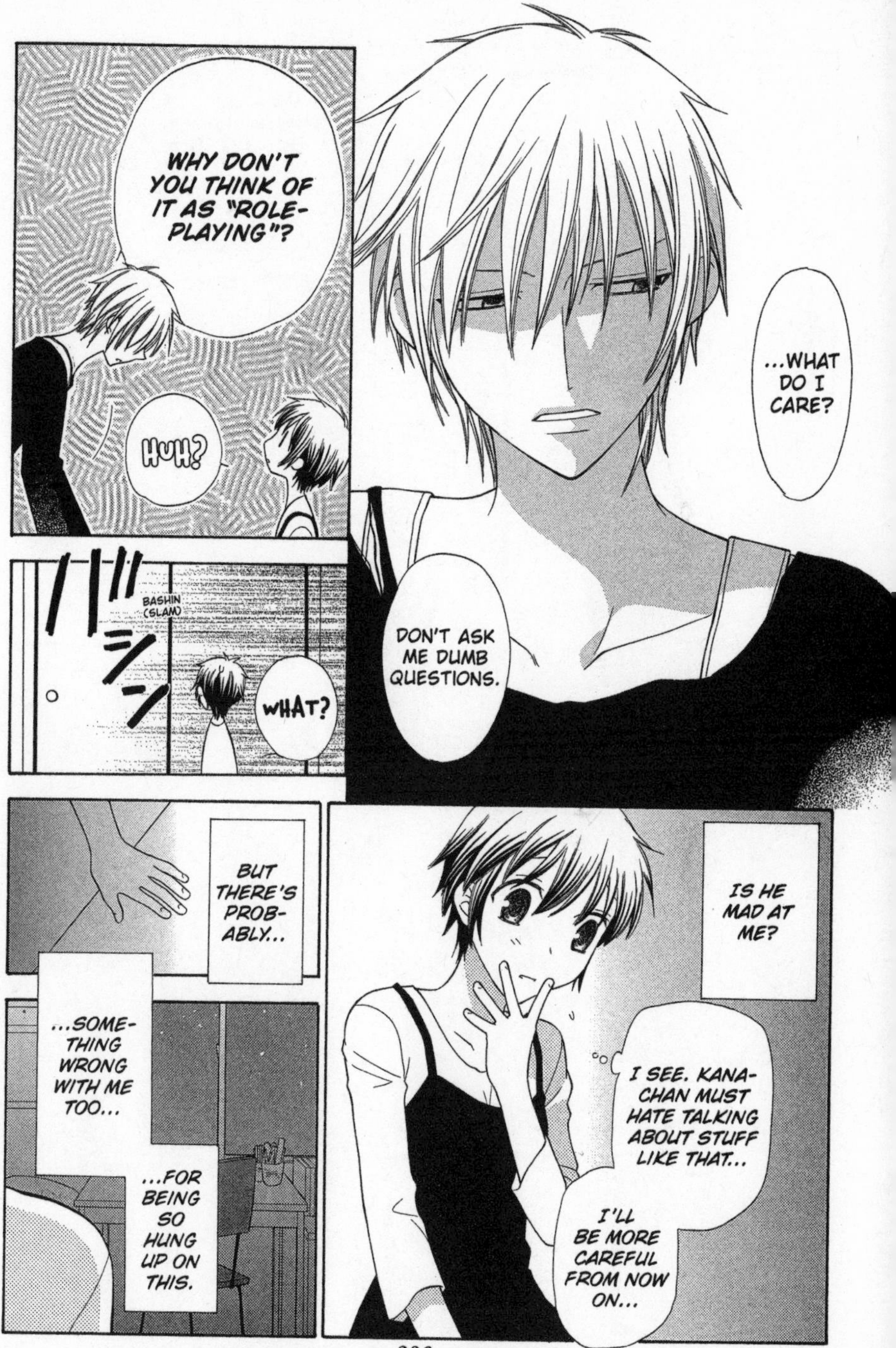
...WHAT DO I CARE?
DON'T ASK ME DUMB QUESTIONS.
WHY DON'T YOU THINK OF IT AS "ROLE-PLAYING"?
HUH?
BASHIN (SLAM)
WHAT?
IS HE MAD AT ME?
I SEE. KANA-CHAN MUST HATE TALKING ABOUT STUFF LIKE THAT...
I'LL BE MORE CAREFUL FROM NOW ON...
BUT THERE'S PROBABLY...
...SOMETHING WRONG WITH ME TOO...
...FOR BEING SO HUNG UP ON THIS.

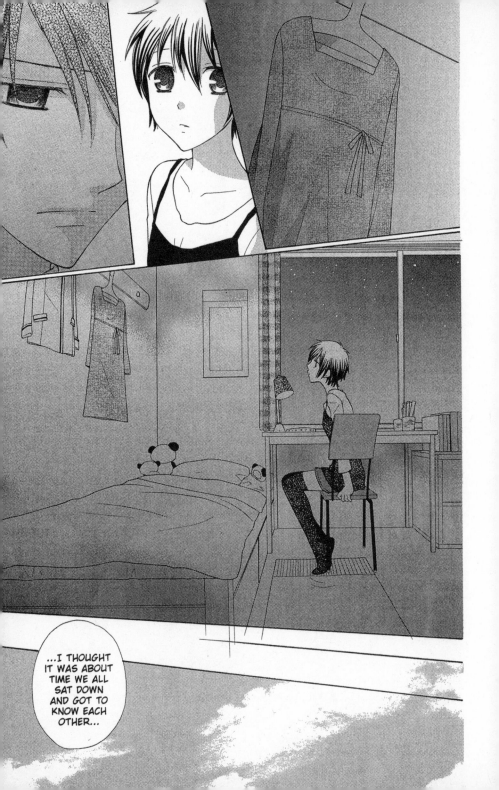

...I THOUGHT IT WAS ABOUT TIME WE ALL SAT DOWN AND GOT TO KNOW EACH OTHER...

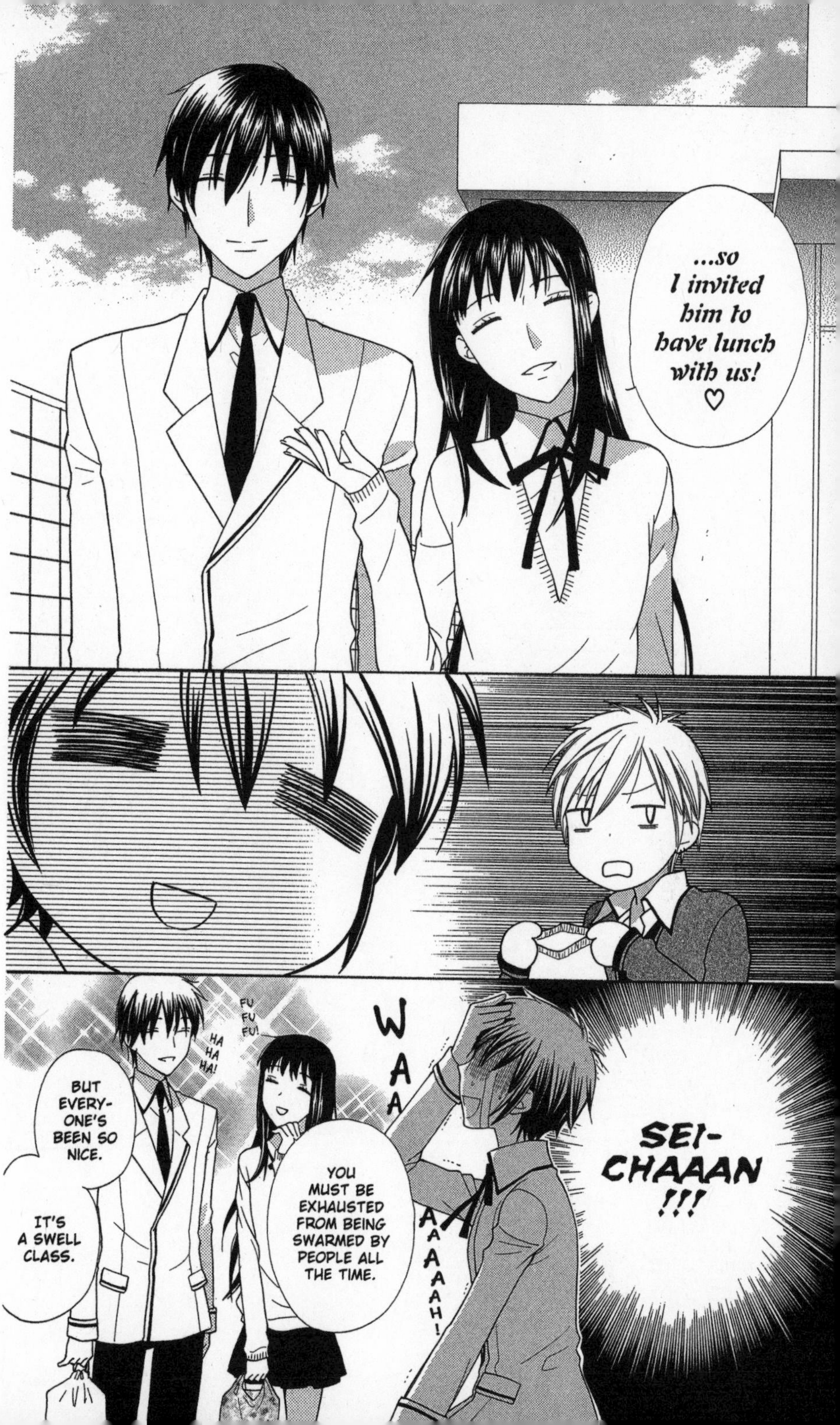

...so I invited him to have lunch with us! ♡
SEI-CHAAAN!!!
WAAAAAAAAAH!
FU FU FU!
HA HA HA!
YOU MUST BE EXHAUSTED FROM BEING SWARMED BY PEOPLE ALL THE TIME.
BUT EVERYONE'S BEEN SO NICE.
IT'S A SWELL CLASS.

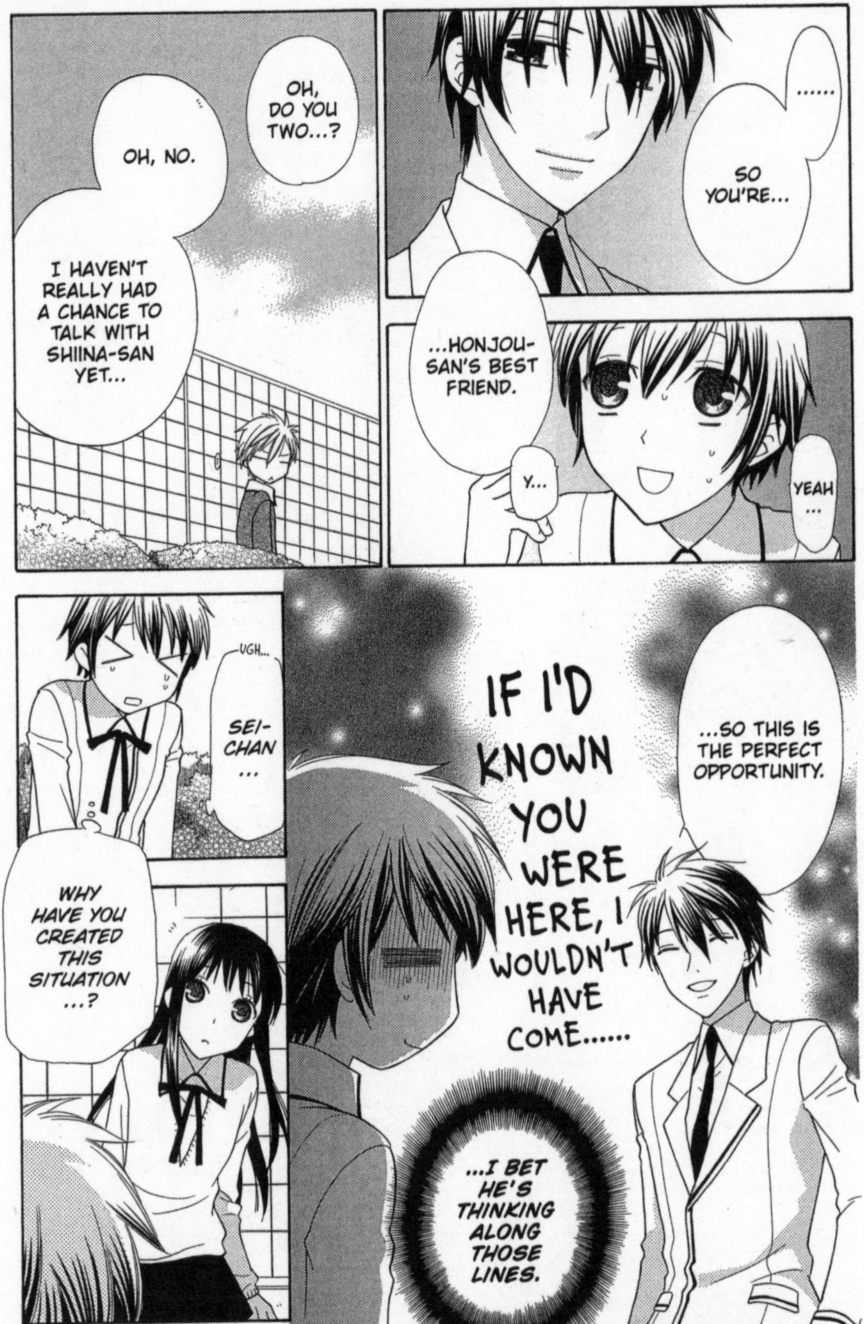
......
SO YOU'RE...
...HONJOU-SAN'S BEST FRIEND.
YEAH ...
Y...
OH, DO YOU TWO...?
OH, NO.
I HAVEN'T REALLY HAD A CHANCE TO TALK WITH SHIINA-SAN YET...
...SO THIS IS THE PERFECT OPPORTUNITY.
IF I'D KNOWN YOU WERE HERE, I WOULDN'T HAVE COME......
...I BET HE'S THINKING ALONG THOSE LINES.
UGH...
SEI-CHAN ...
WHY HAVE YOU CREATED THIS SITUATION ...?

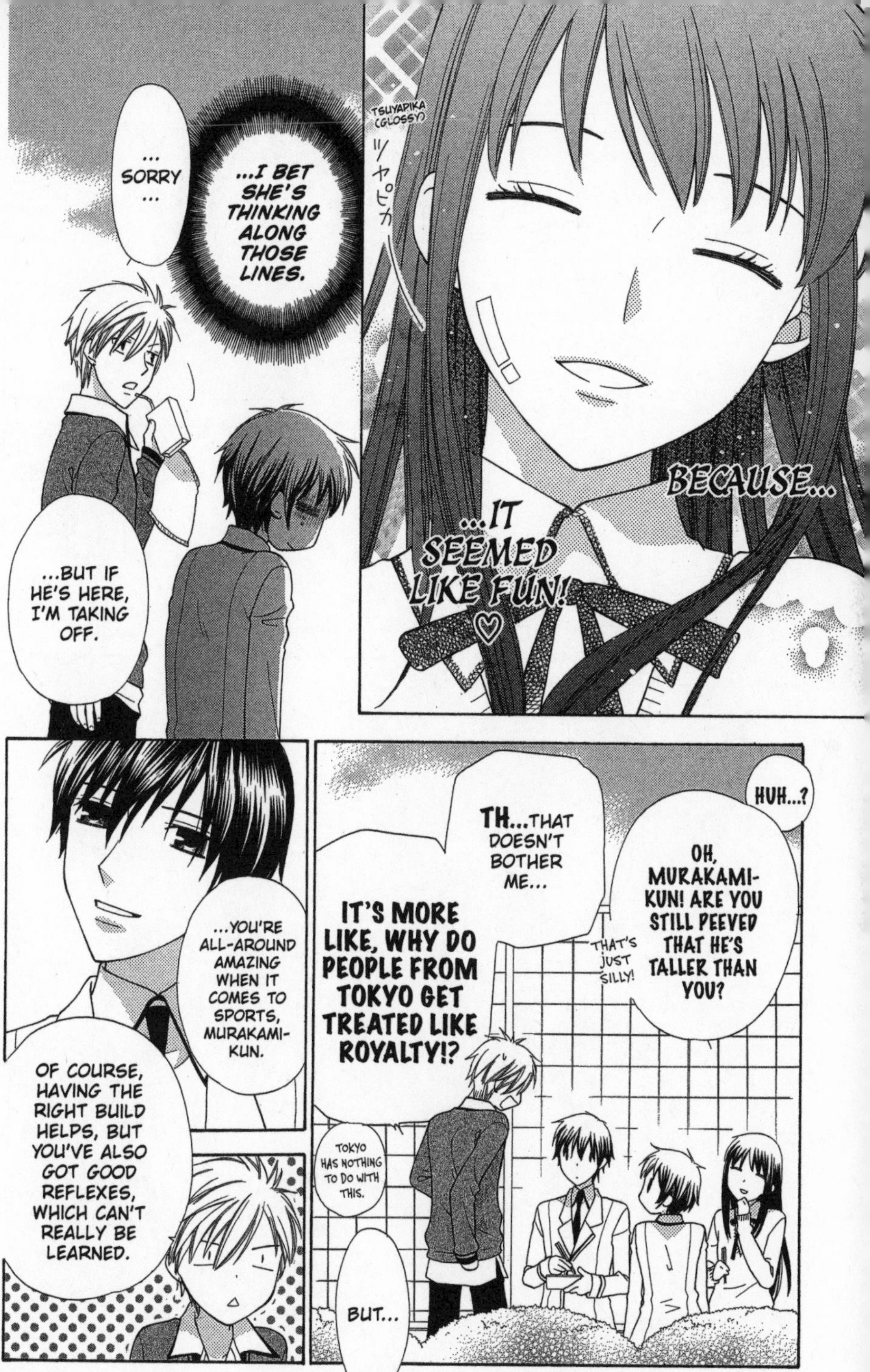
TSUYAPIKA (GLOSSY)
ツヤピカ
BECAUSE...
...IT SEEMED LIKE FUN! ♡
...I BET SHE'S THINKING ALONG THOSE LINES.
... SORRY ...
...BUT IF HE'S HERE, I'M TAKING OFF.
HUH...?
OH, MURAKAMI-KUN! ARE YOU STILL PEEVED THAT HE'S TALLER THAN YOU?
THAT'S JUST SILLY!
TH...THAT DOESN'T BOTHER ME...
IT'S MORE LIKE, WHY DO PEOPLE FROM TOKYO GET TREATED LIKE ROYALTY!?
TOKYO HAS NOTHING TO DO WITH THIS.
...YOU'RE ALL-AROUND AMAZING WHEN IT COMES TO SPORTS, MURAKAMI-KUN.
OF COURSE, HAVING THE RIGHT BUILD HELPS, BUT YOU'VE ALSO GOT GOOD REFLEXES, WHICH CAN'T REALLY BE LEARNED.
BUT...

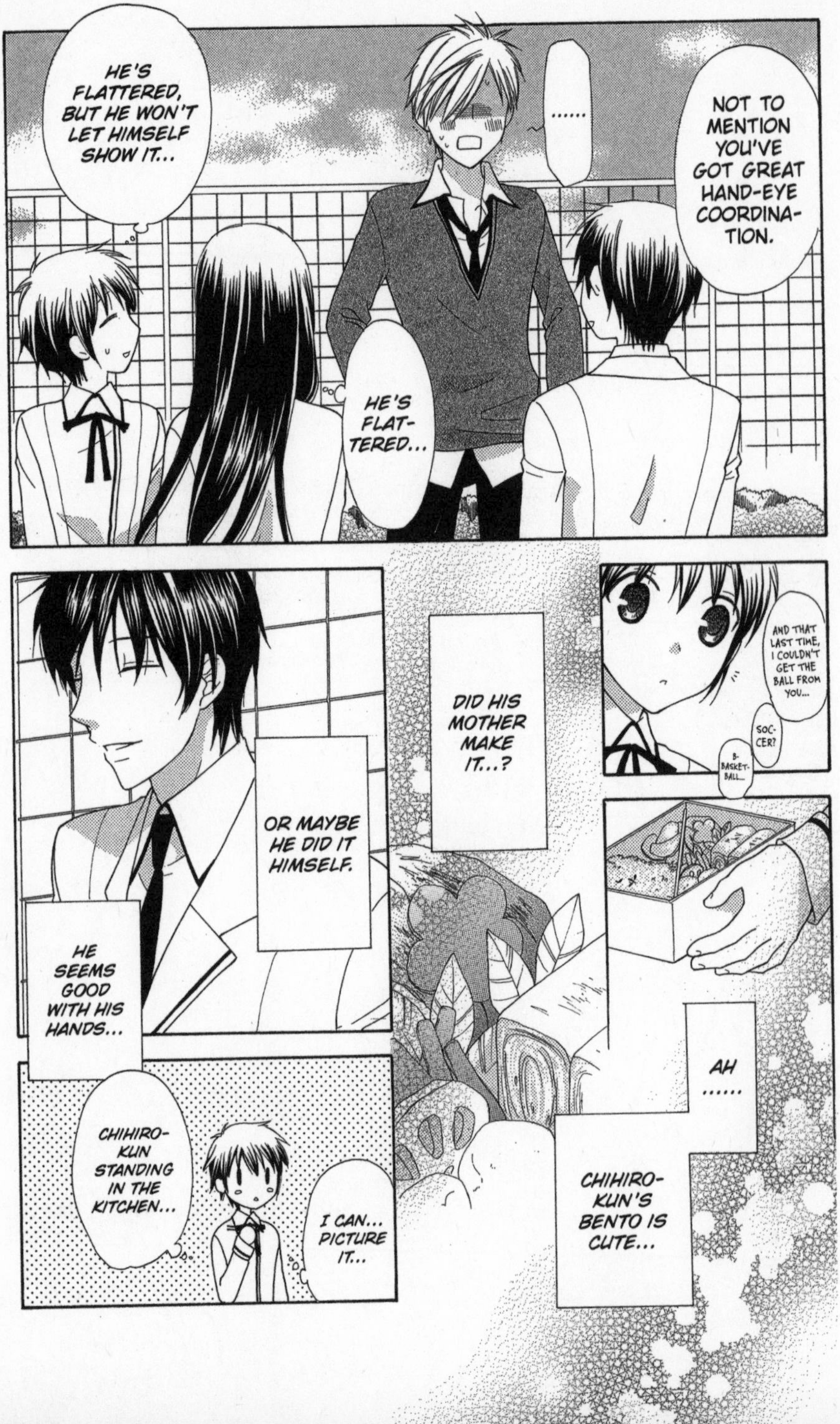

NOT TO MENTION YOU'VE GOT GREAT HAND-EYE COORDINA-TION.
......
HE'S FLAT-TERED...
HE'S FLATTERED, BUT HE WON'T LET HIMSELF SHOW IT...
AND THAT LAST TIME, I COULDN'T GET THE BALL FROM YOU...
SOC-CER?
B-BASKET-BALL...
AH ......
CHIHIRO-KUN'S BENTO IS CUTE...
DID HIS MOTHER MAKE IT...?
OR MAYBE HE DID IT HIMSELF.
HE SEEMS GOOD WITH HIS HANDS...
CHIHIRO-KUN STANDING IN THE KITCHEN...
I CAN... PICTURE IT...

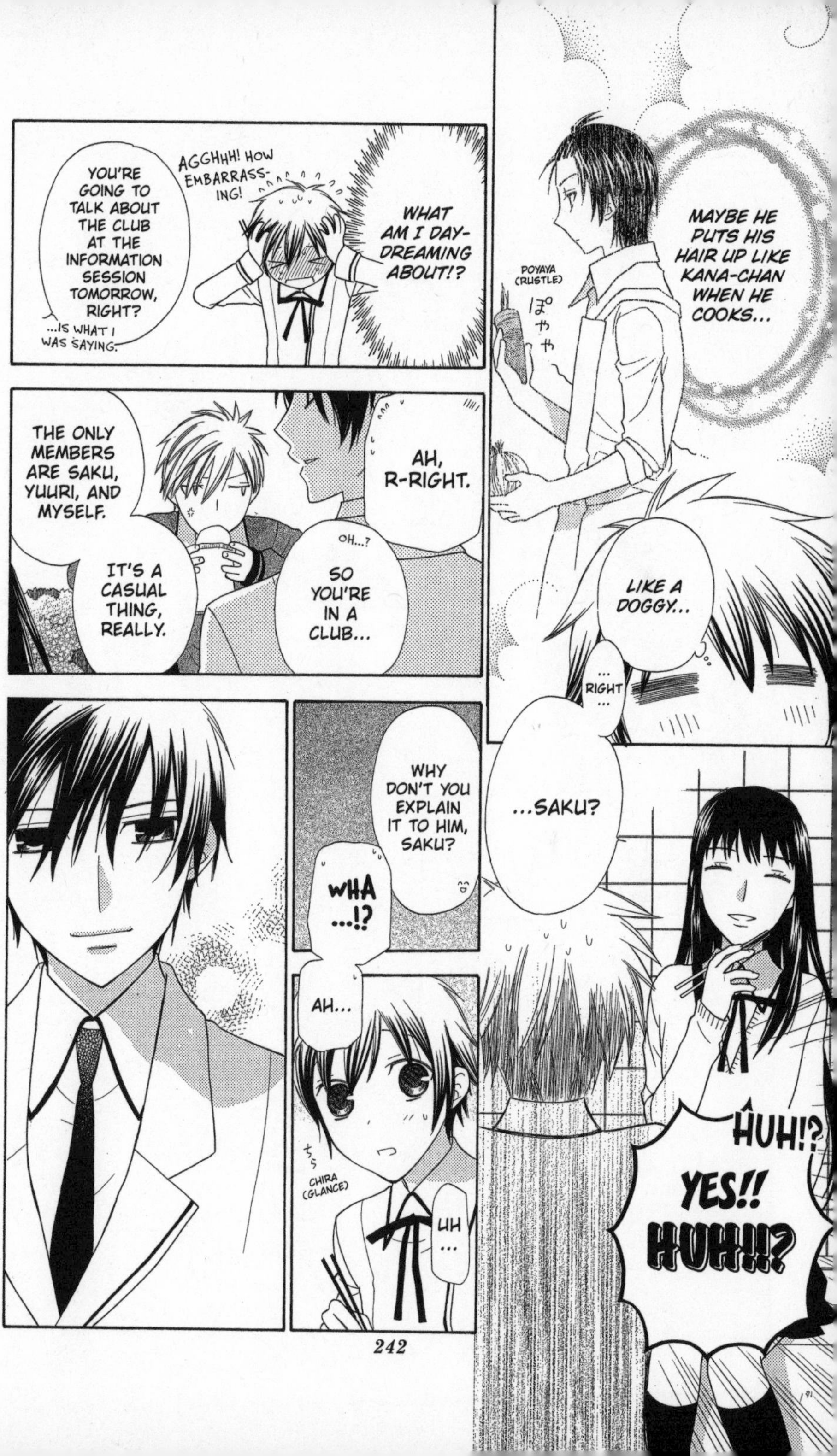
MAYBE HE PUTS HIS HAIR UP LIKE KANA-CHAN WHEN HE COOKS...
POYAYA (RUSTLE)
ぽやや
LIKE A DOGGY...
...RIGHT...
...SAKU?
HUH!?
YES!!
HUH!!?
YOU'RE GOING TO TALK ABOUT THE CLUB AT THE INFORMATION SESSION TOMORROW, RIGHT?
...IS WHAT I WAS SAYING.
AGGHHH! HOW EMBARRASS-ING!
WHAT AM I DAY-DREAMING ABOUT!?
AH, R-RIGHT.
OH...?
SO YOU'RE IN A CLUB...
THE ONLY MEMBERS ARE SAKU, YUURI, AND MYSELF.
IT'S A CASUAL THING, REALLY.
WHY DON'T YOU EXPLAIN IT TO HIM, SAKU?
WHA ...!?
AH...
ちら
CHIRA (GLANCE)
UH ...

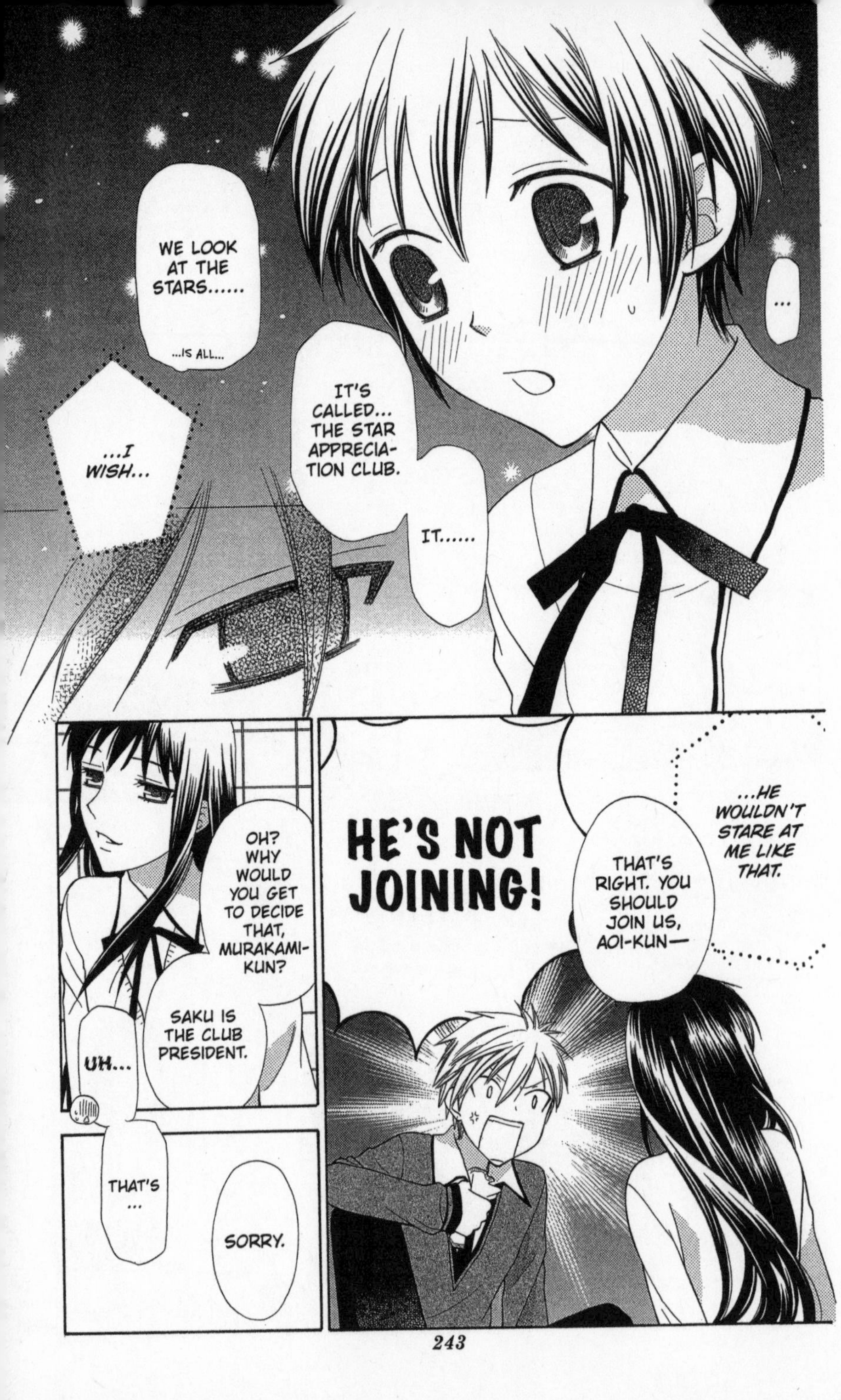
...
IT......
IT'S CALLED... THE STAR APPRECIATION CLUB.
WE LOOK AT THE STARS......
...IS ALL...
...I WISH...
...HE WOULDN'T STARE AT ME LIKE THAT.
THAT'S RIGHT. YOU SHOULD JOIN US, AOI-KUN—
HE'S NOT JOINING!
OH? WHY WOULD YOU GET TO DECIDE THAT, MURAKAMI-KUN?
SAKU IS THE CLUB PRESIDENT.
UH...
THAT'S ...
SORRY.

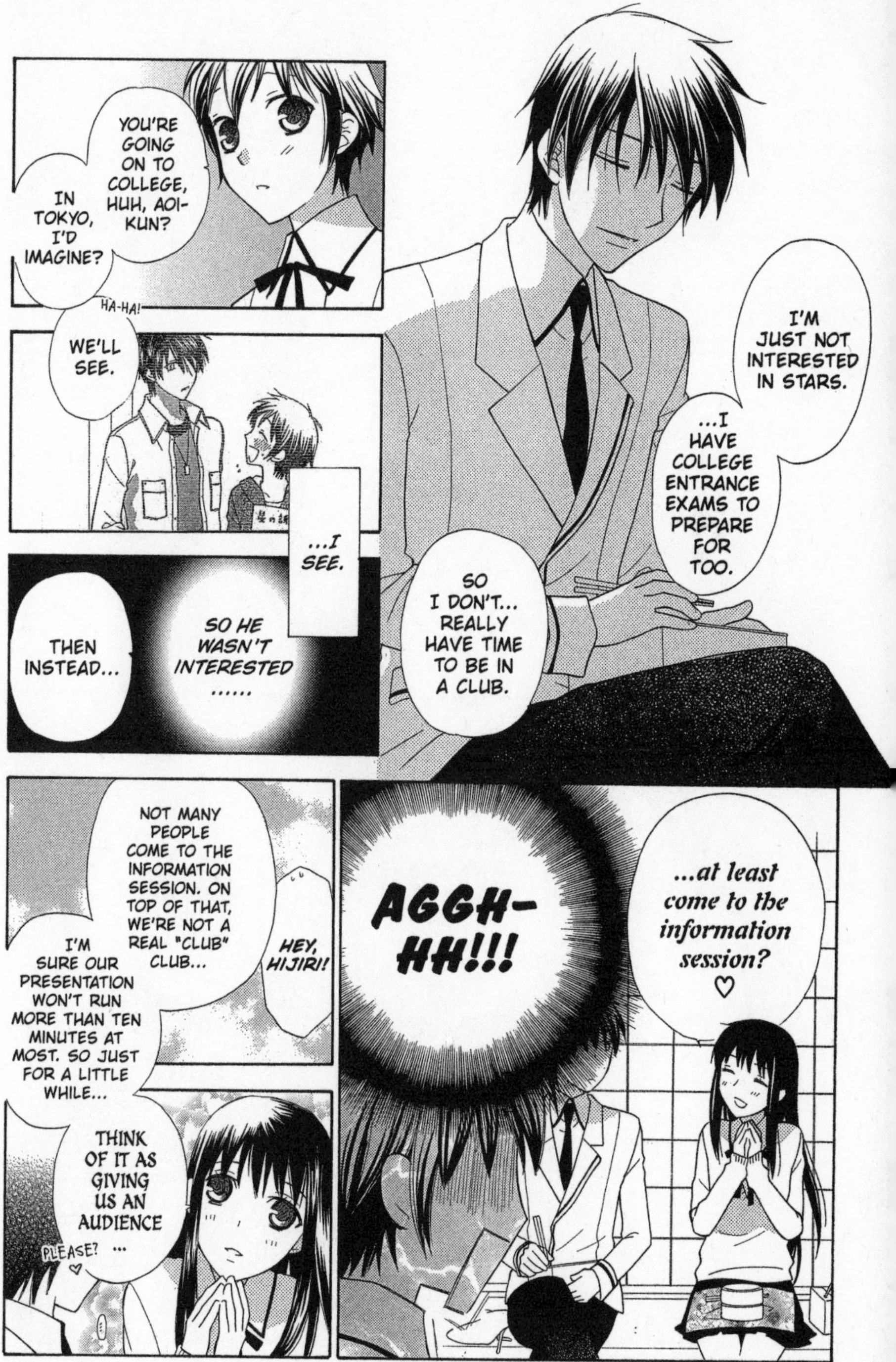
I'M JUST NOT INTERESTED IN STARS.
...I HAVE COLLEGE ENTRANCE EXAMS TO PREPARE FOR TOO.
SO I DON'T... REALLY HAVE TIME TO BE IN A CLUB.
YOU'RE GOING ON TO COLLEGE, HUH, AOI-KUN?
IN TOKYO, I'D IMAGINE?
HA-HA!
WE'LL SEE.
...I SEE.
SO HE WASN'T INTERESTED ......
THEN INSTEAD...
...at least come to the information session? ♡
AGGH-HH!!!
NOT MANY PEOPLE COME TO THE INFORMATION SESSION. ON TOP OF THAT, WE'RE NOT A REAL "CLUB" CLUB...
HEY, HIJIRI!
I'M SURE OUR PRESENTATION WON'T RUN MORE THAN TEN MINUTES AT MOST. SO JUST FOR A LITTLE WHILE...
THINK OF IT AS GIVING US AN AUDIENCE ...
PLEASE? ♡

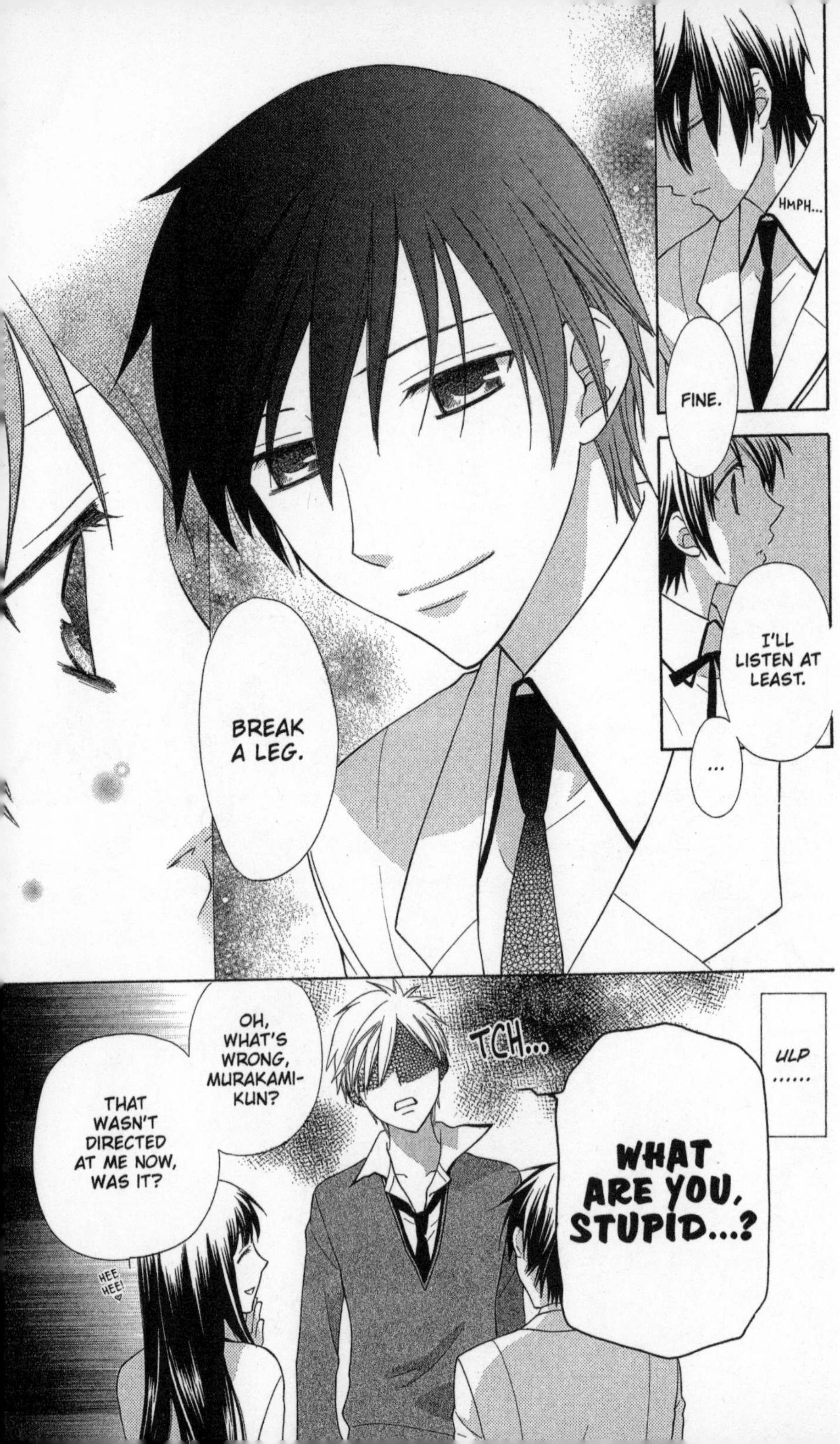
HMPH...
FINE.
I'LL LISTEN AT LEAST.
...
BREAK A LEG.
ULP ......
WHAT ARE YOU, STUPID...?
TCH...
OH, WHAT'S WRONG, MURAKAMI-KUN?
THAT WASN'T DIRECTED AT ME NOW, WAS IT?
HEE HEE!

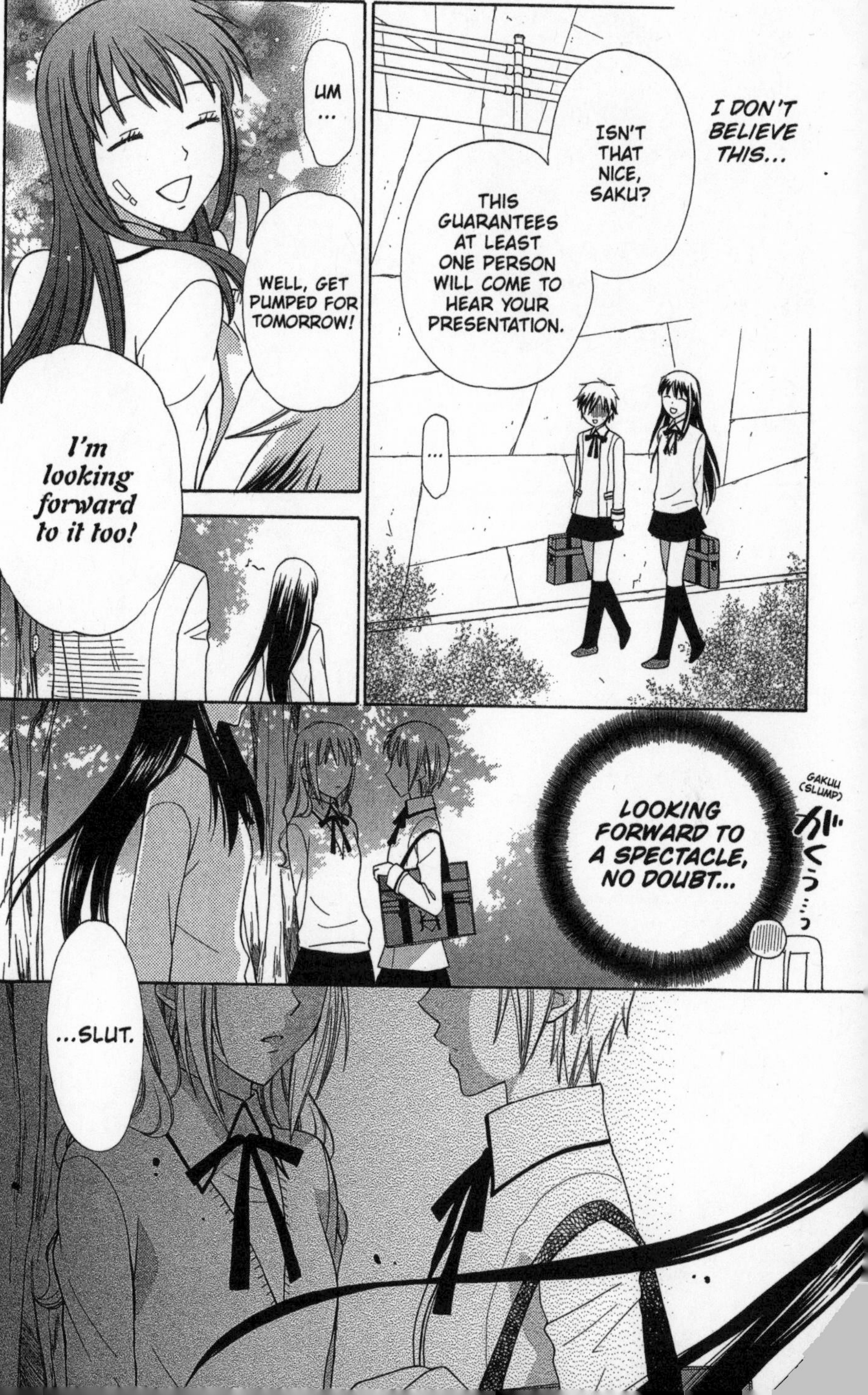
I DON'T BELIEVE THIS...
ISN'T THAT NICE, SAKU?
THIS GUARANTEES AT LEAST ONE PERSON WILL COME TO HEAR YOUR PRESENTATION.
...
UM ...
WELL, GET PUMPED FOR TOMORROW!
I'm looking forward to it too!
GAKUU (SLUMP)
がくぅ…っ
LOOKING FORWARD TO A SPECTACLE, NO DOUBT...
...SLUT.

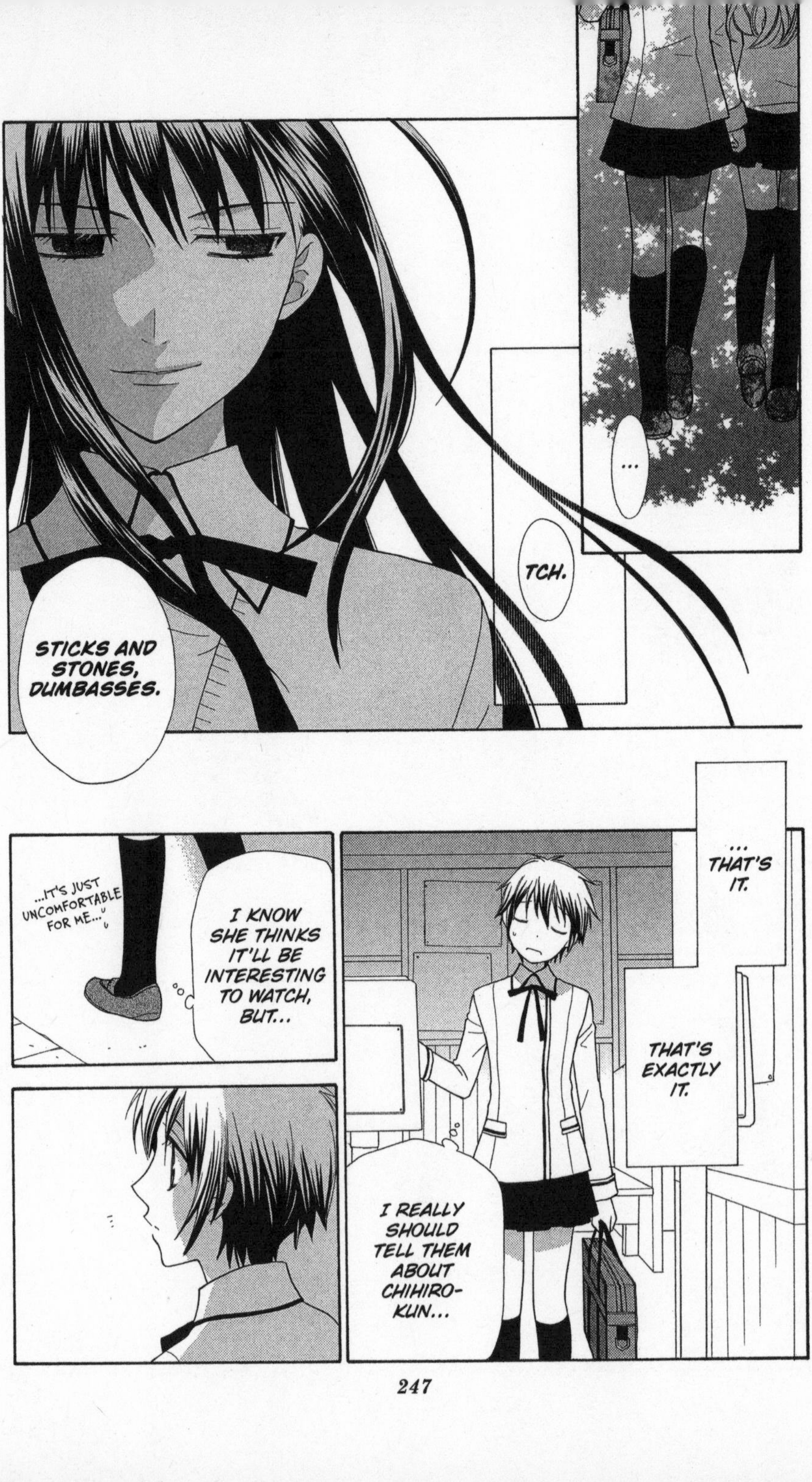
...
TCH.
STICKS AND STONES, DUMBASSES.
... THAT'S IT.
THAT'S EXACTLY IT.
I REALLY SHOULD TELL THEM ABOUT CHIHIRO-KUN...
I KNOW SHE THINKS IT'LL BE INTERESTING TO WATCH, BUT...
...IT'S JUST UNCOMFORTABLE FOR ME...

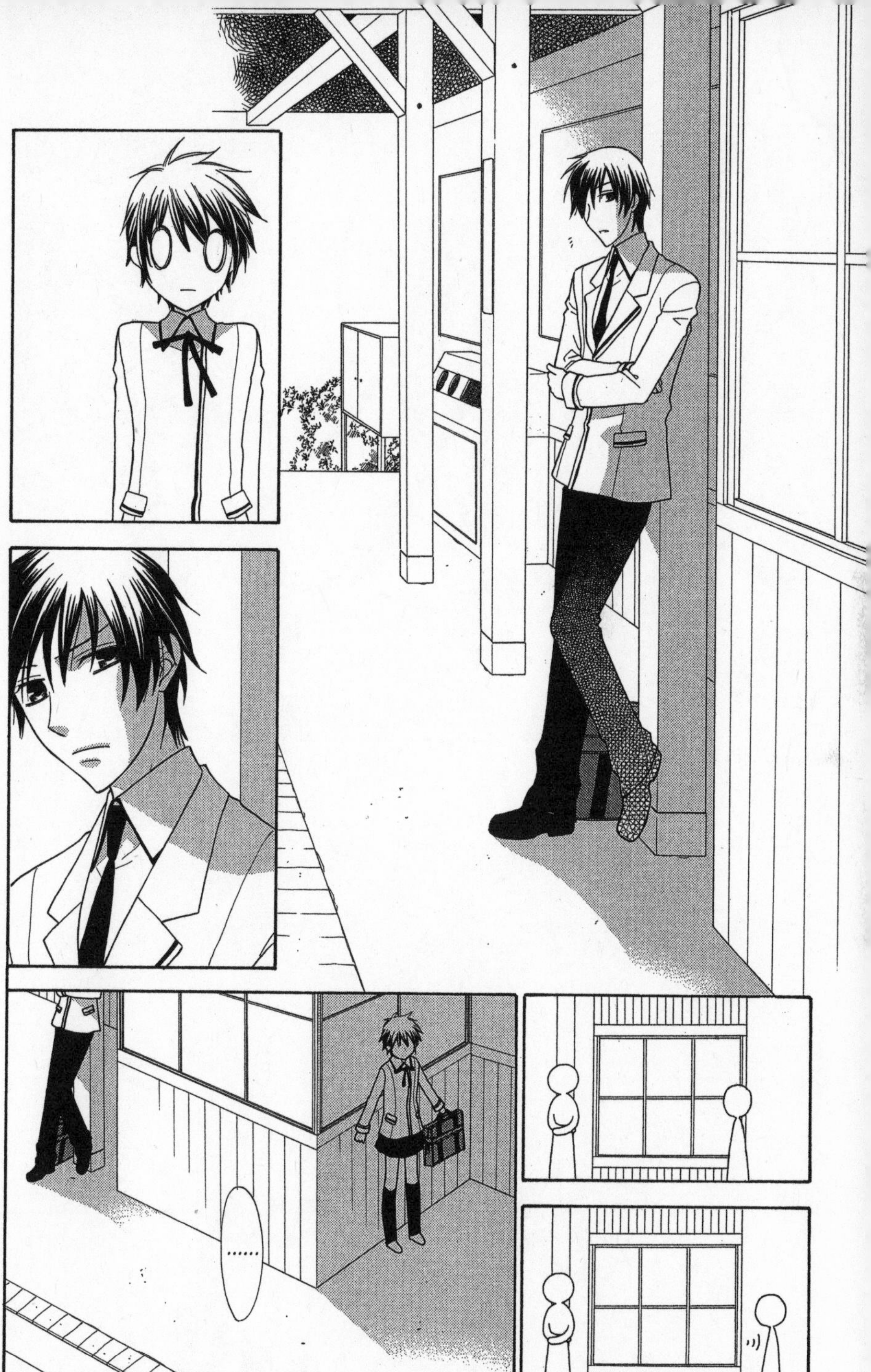
……

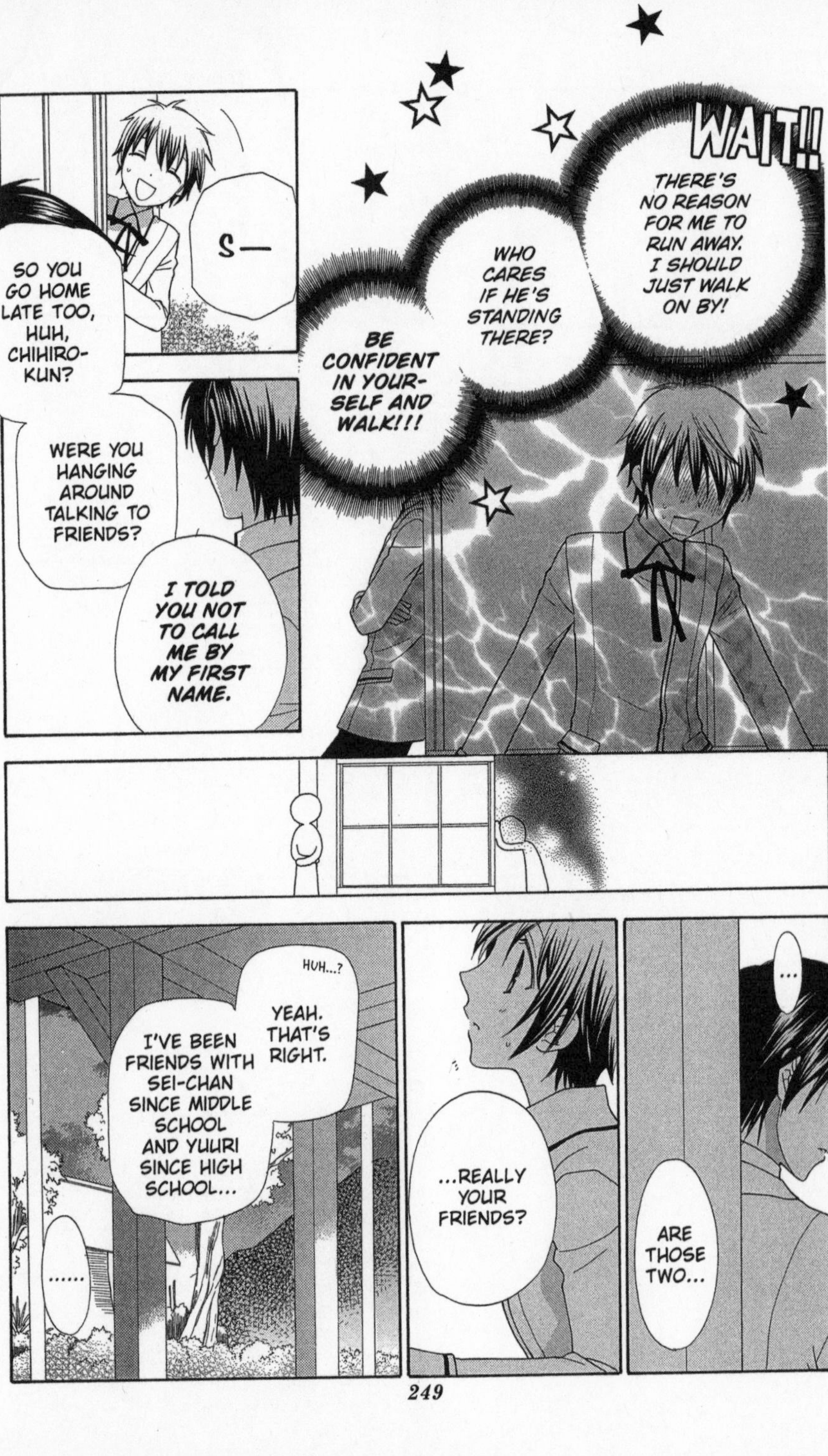
WAIT!!
THERE'S NO REASON FOR ME TO RUN AWAY. I SHOULD JUST WALK ON BY!
WHO CARES IF HE'S STANDING THERE?
BE CONFIDENT IN YOURSELF AND WALK!!!
S—
SO YOU GO HOME LATE TOO, HUH, CHIHIRO-KUN?
WERE YOU HANGING AROUND TALKING TO FRIENDS?
I TOLD YOU NOT TO CALL ME BY MY FIRST NAME.
...
ARE THOSE TWO...
...REALLY YOUR FRIENDS?
HUH...?
YEAH. THAT'S RIGHT.
I'VE BEEN FRIENDS WITH SEI-CHAN SINCE MIDDLE SCHOOL AND YUURI SINCE HIGH SCHOOL...
......

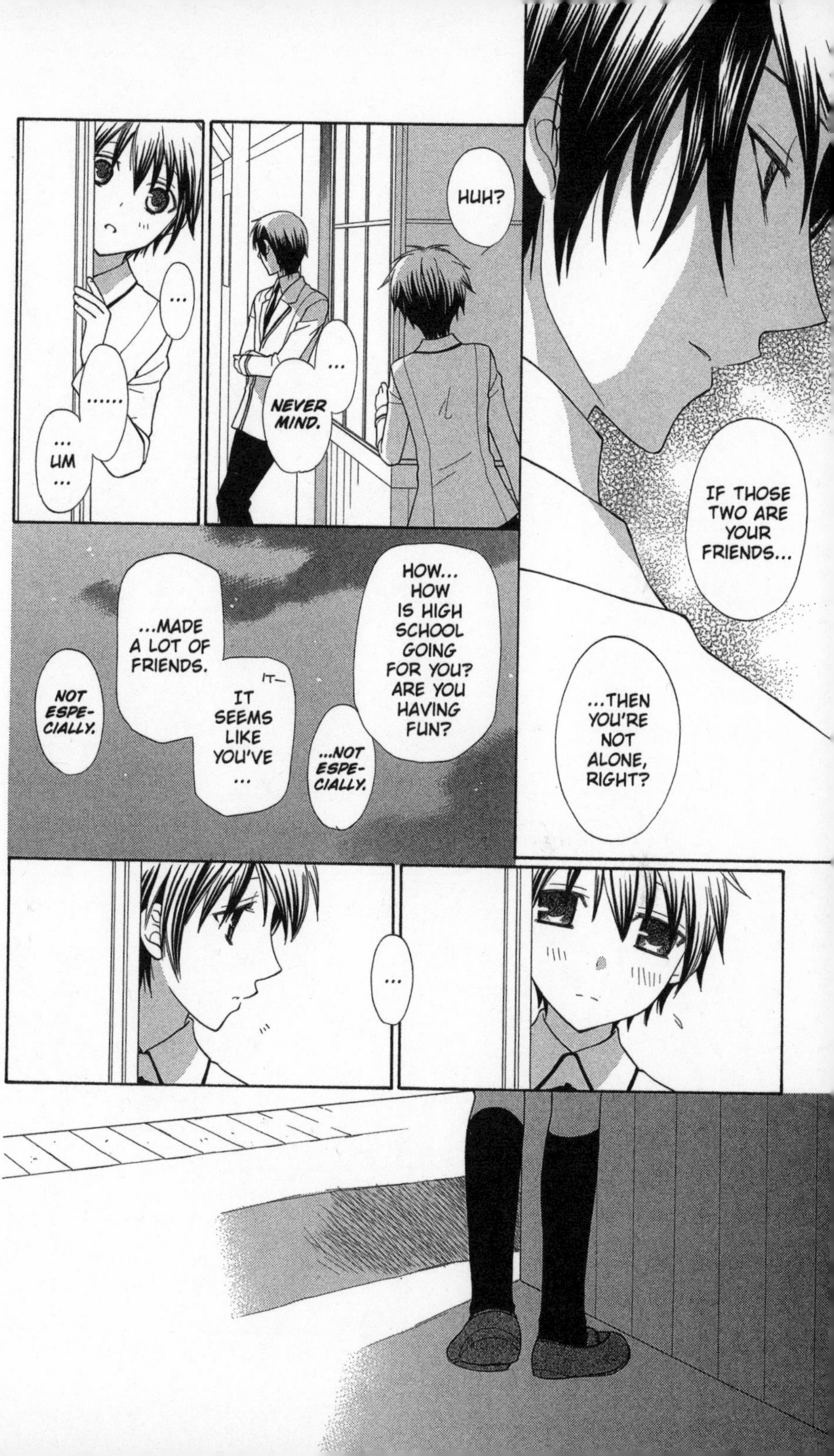
IF THOSE TWO ARE YOUR FRIENDS...
...THEN YOU'RE NOT ALONE, RIGHT?
HUH?
...
NEVER MIND.
...
......
...UM...
HOW... HOW IS HIGH SCHOOL GOING FOR YOU? ARE YOU HAVING FUN?
...NOT ESPECIALLY.
IT—
IT SEEMS LIKE YOU'VE...
...MADE A LOT OF FRIENDS.
NOT ESPECIALLY.
...

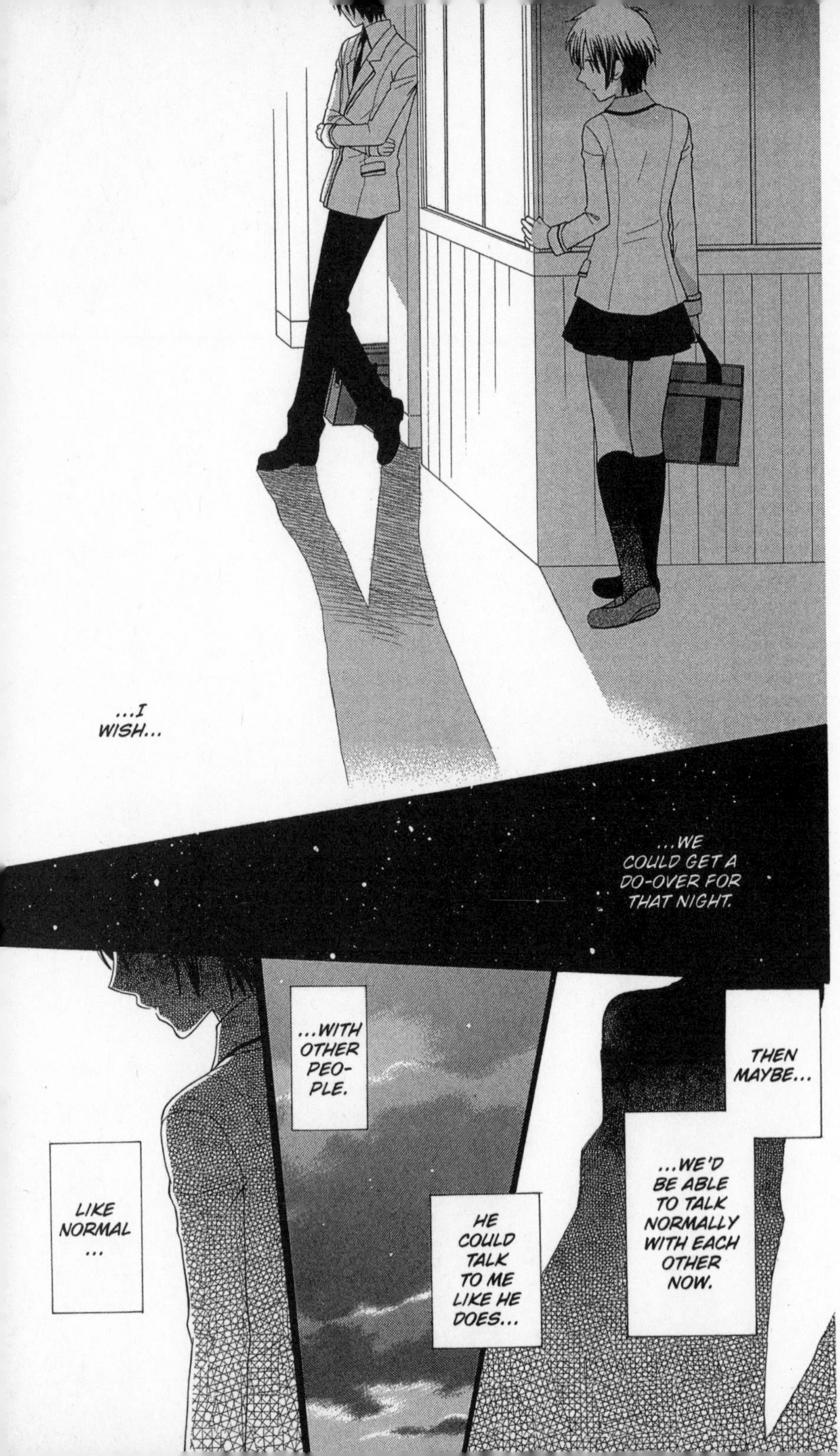
...I WISH...
...WE COULD GET A DO-OVER FOR THAT NIGHT.
THEN MAYBE...
...WE'D BE ABLE TO TALK NORMALLY WITH EACH OTHER NOW.
HE COULD TALK TO ME LIKE HE DOES...
...WITH OTHER PEO-PLE.
LIKE NORMAL ...

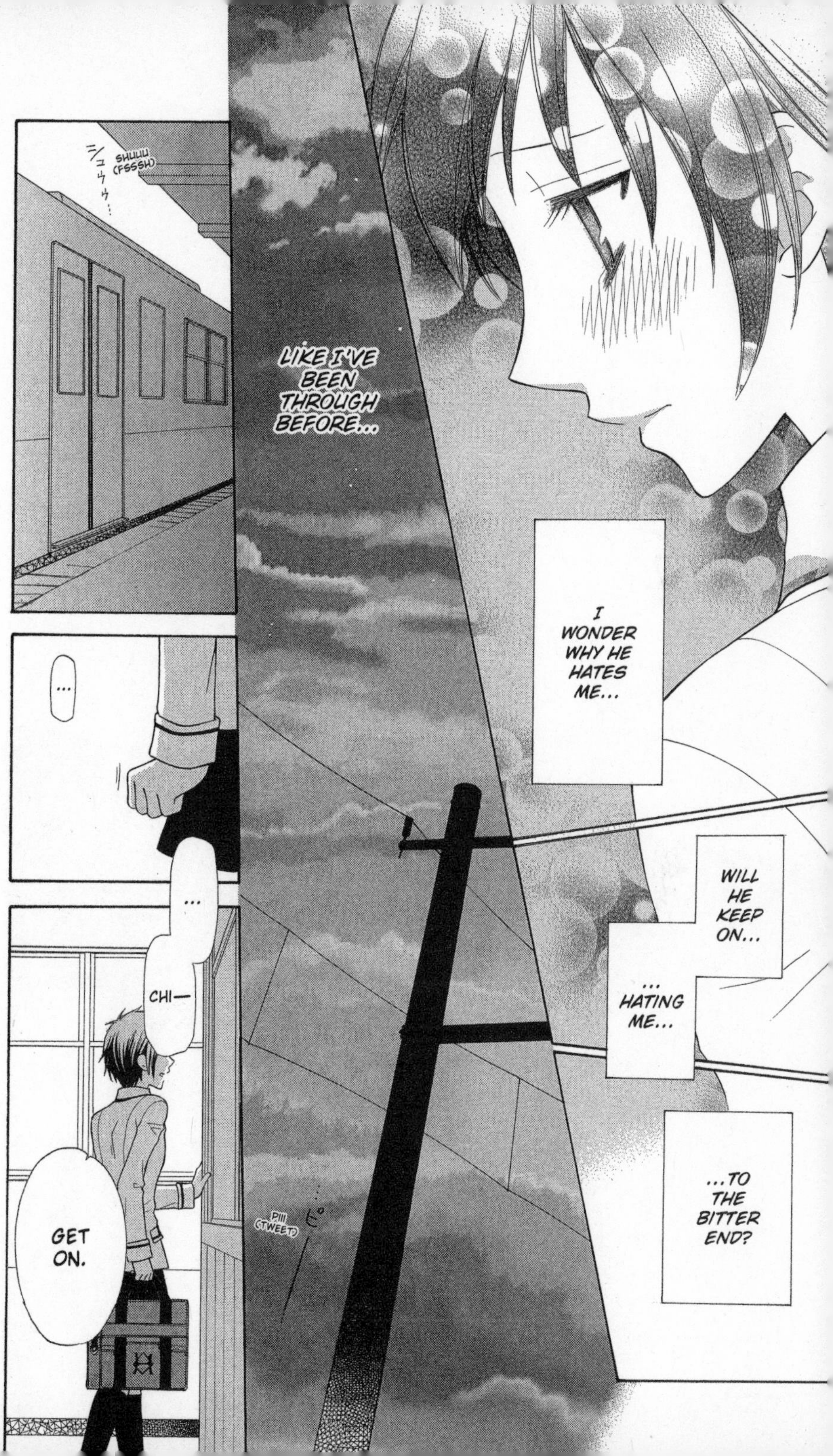
I WONDER WHY HE HATES ME...
WILL HE KEEP ON...
... HATING ME...
...TO THE BITTER END?
LIKE I'VE BEEN THROUGH BEFORE...
PIII (TWEET)
シュウゥ…
SHUUU (FSSSH)
...
...
CHI—
GET ON.

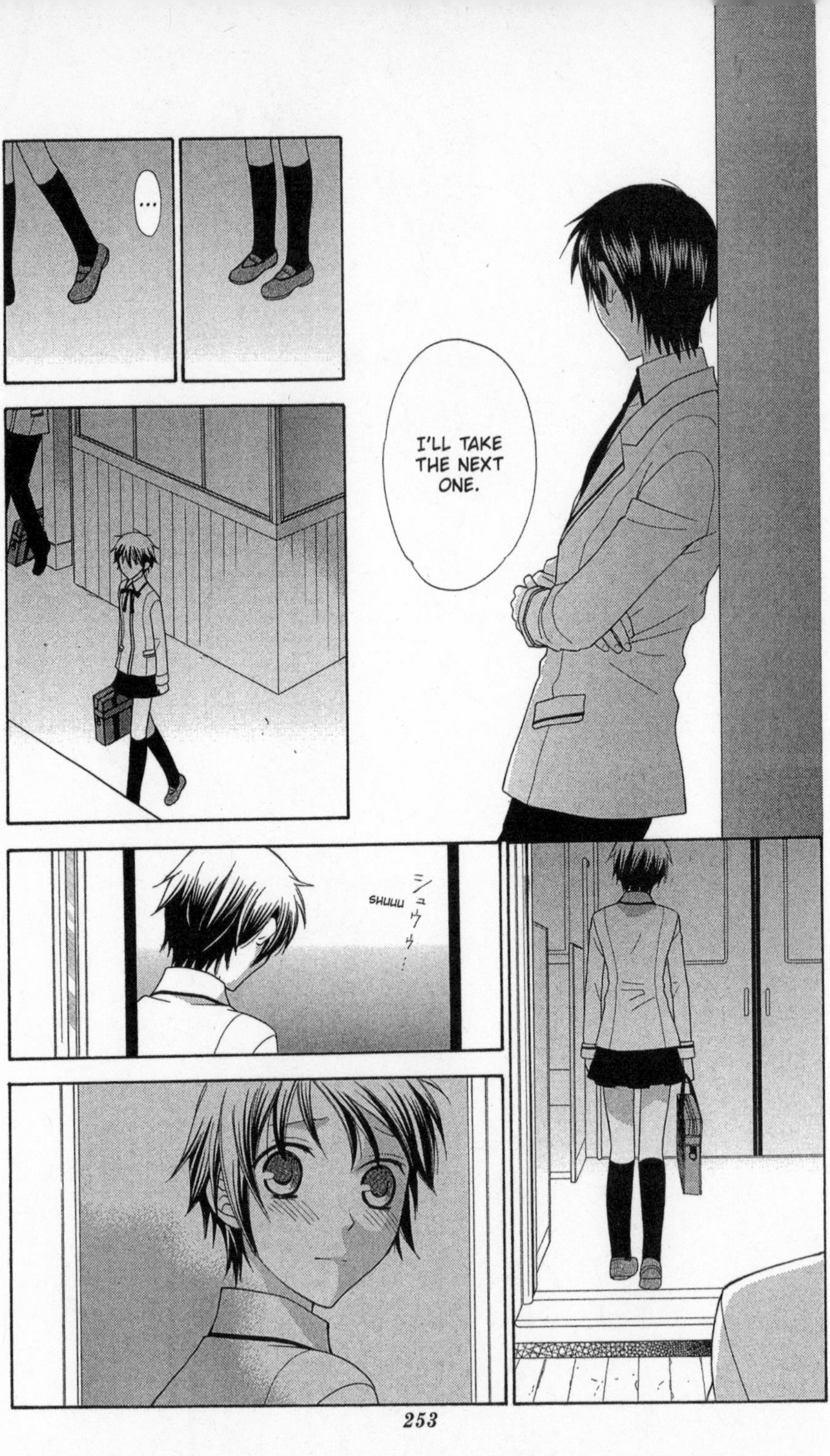
I'LL TAKE THE NEXT ONE.
...
シュウゥ…
SHUUU

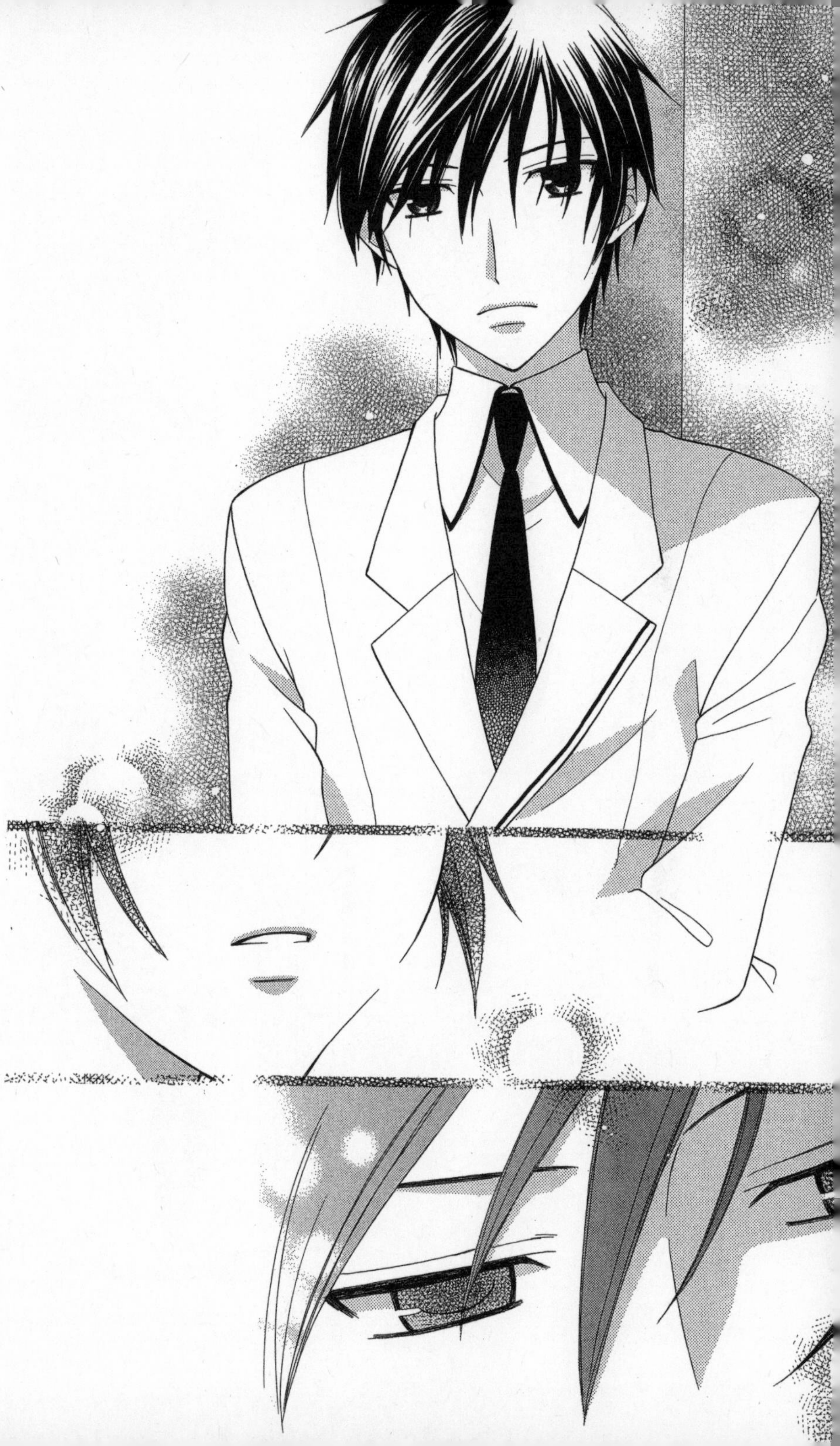

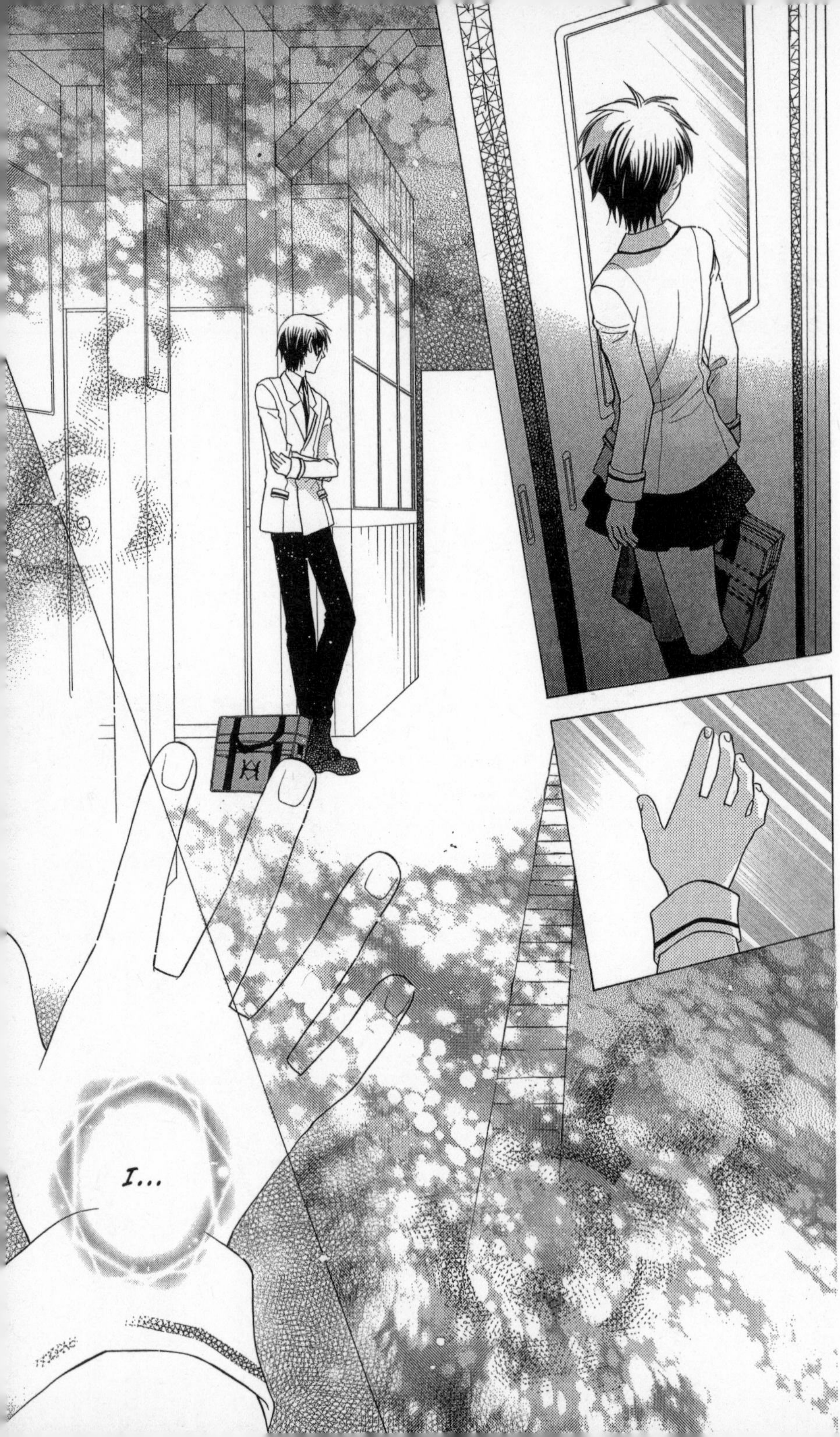
I...

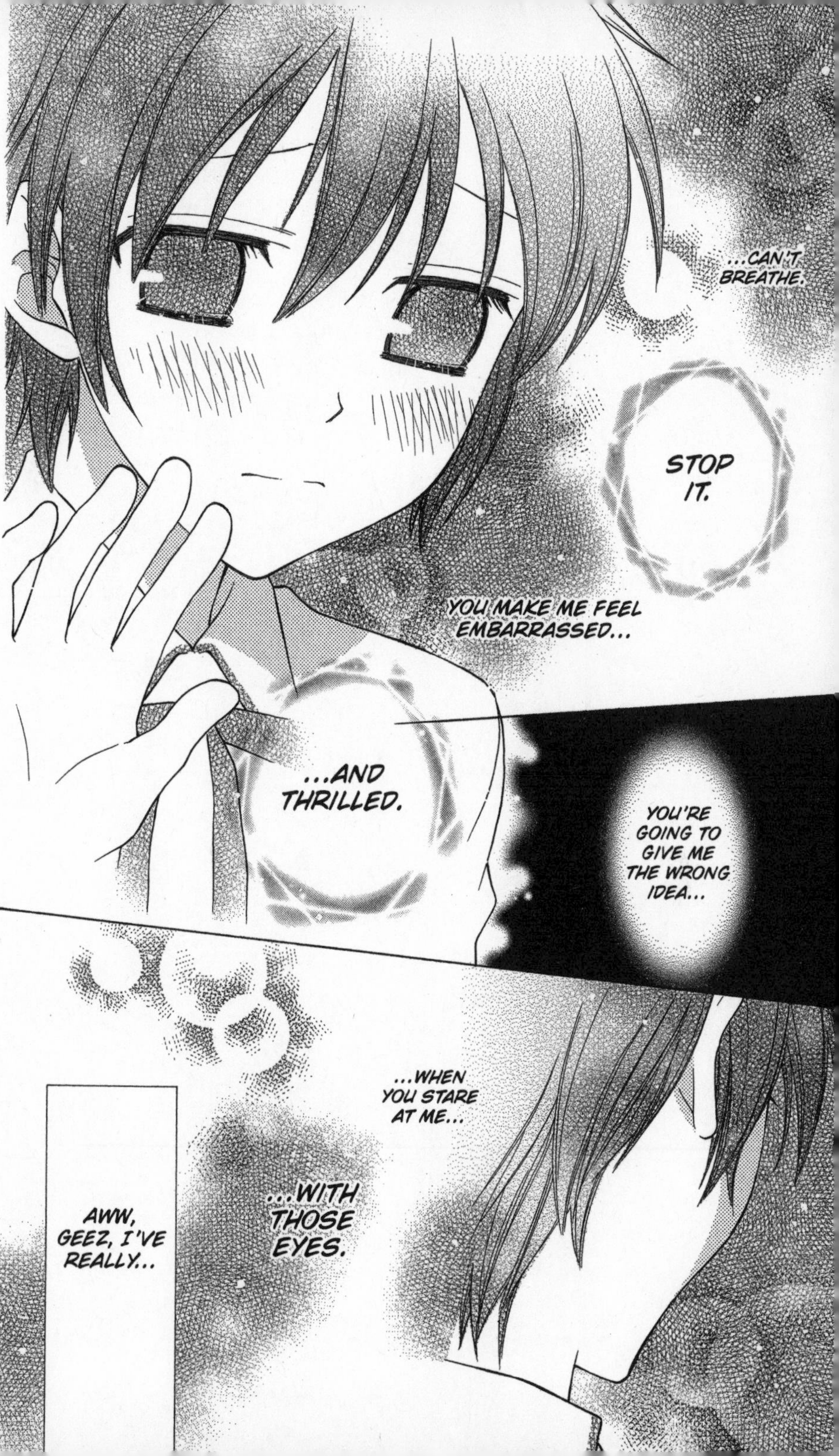
...CAN'T BREATHE.
STOP IT.
YOU MAKE ME FEEL EMBARRASSED...
...AND THRILLED.
YOU'RE GOING TO GIVE ME THE WRONG IDEA...
...WHEN YOU STARE AT ME...
...WITH THOSE EYES.
AWW, GEEZ, I'VE REALLY...

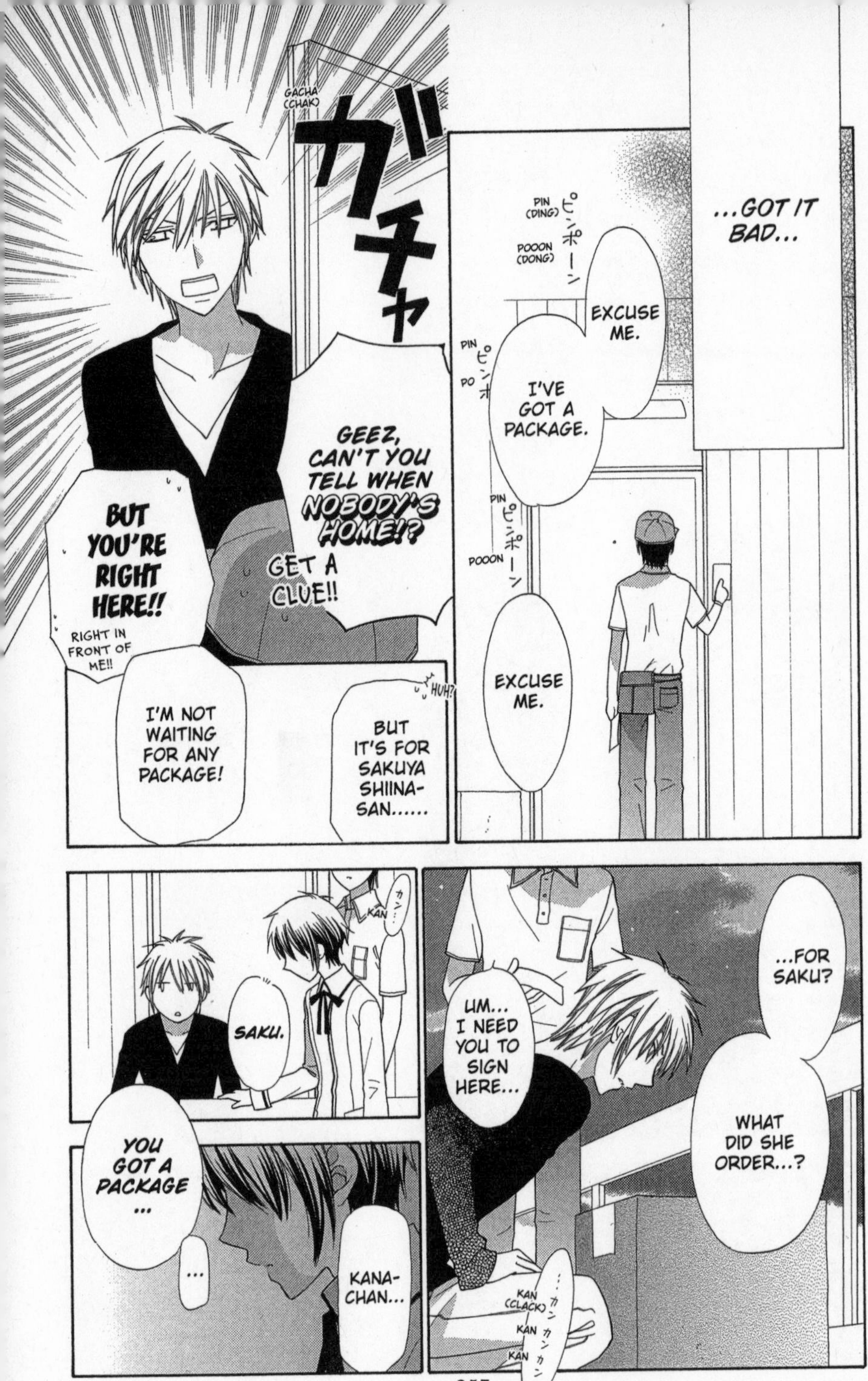
...GOT IT BAD...
PIN (DING)
POOON (DONG)
EXCUSE ME.
PIN
PO
I'VE GOT A PACKAGE.
PIN
POOON
EXCUSE ME.
GACHA (CHAK)
GEEZ, CAN'T YOU TELL WHEN NOBODY'S HOME!?
GET A CLUE!!
BUT YOU'RE RIGHT HERE!!
RIGHT IN FRONT OF ME!!
HUH?
BUT IT'S FOR SAKUYA SHIINA-SAN......
I'M NOT WAITING FOR ANY PACKAGE!
...FOR SAKU?
WHAT DID SHE ORDER...?
UM... I NEED YOU TO SIGN HERE...
KAN
SAKU.
...
KAN (CLACK)
KAN
KAN
KANA-CHAN...
YOU GOT A PACKAGE...
...

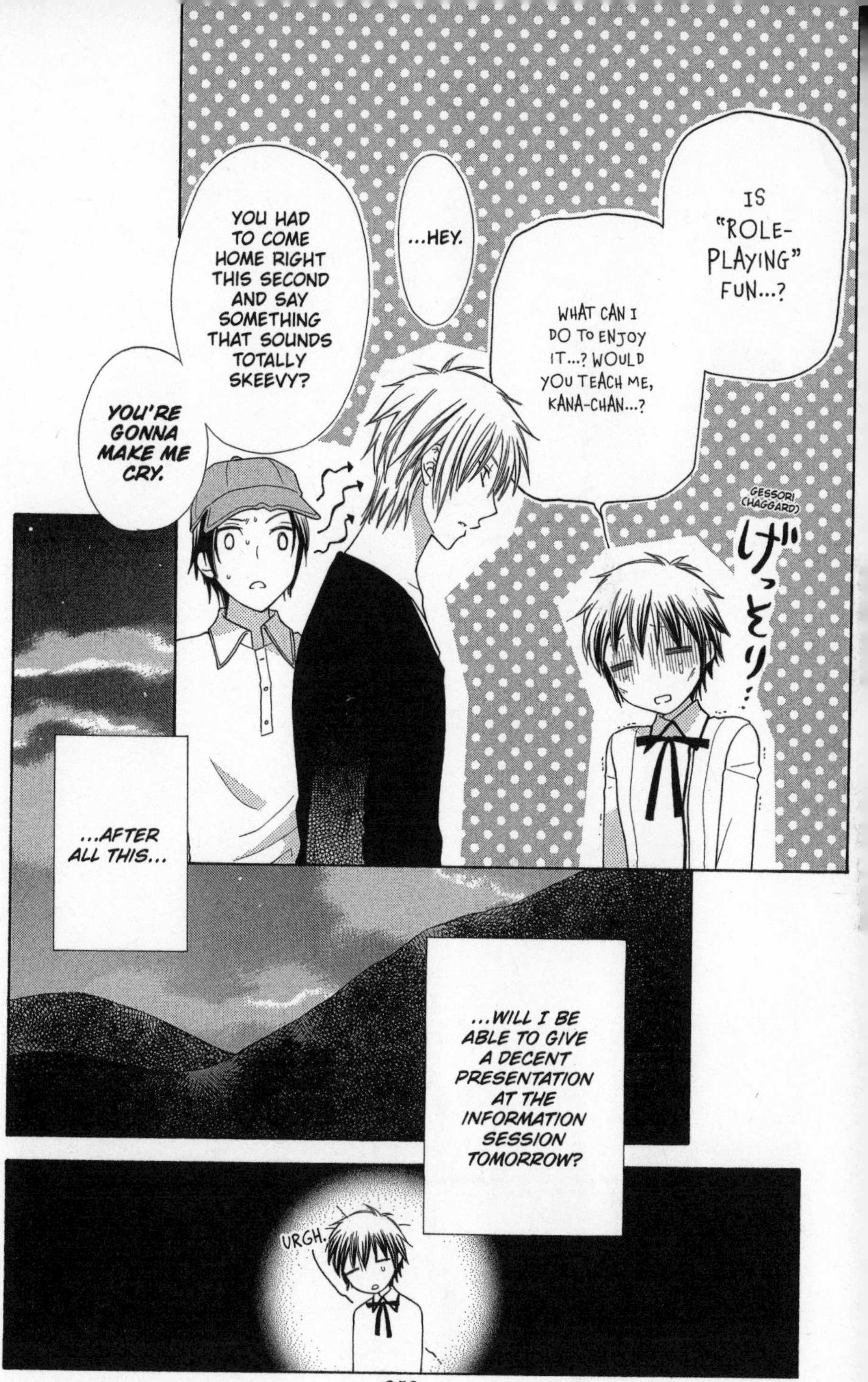
IS "ROLE-PLAYING" FUN...?
WHAT CAN I DO TO ENJOY IT...? WOULD YOU TEACH ME, KANA-CHAN...?
GESSORI (CHAGGARD)
げっそり
...HEY.
YOU HAD TO COME HOME RIGHT THIS SECOND AND SAY SOMETHING THAT SOUNDS TOTALLY SKEEVY?
YOU'RE GONNA MAKE ME CRY.
...AFTER ALL THIS...
...WILL I BE ABLE TO GIVE A DECENT PRESENTATION AT THE INFORMATION SESSION TOMORROW?
URGH.

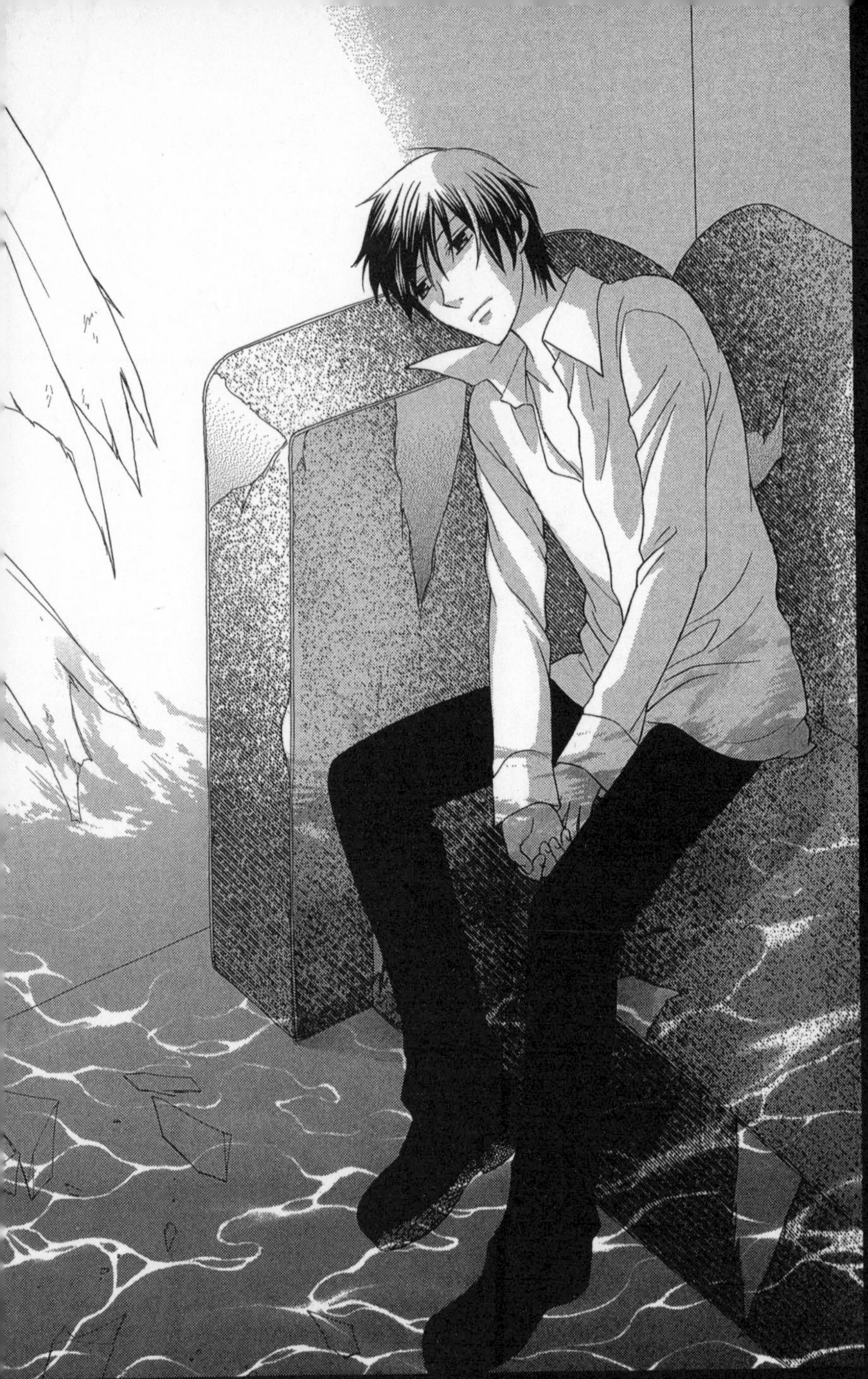

Chapter 8

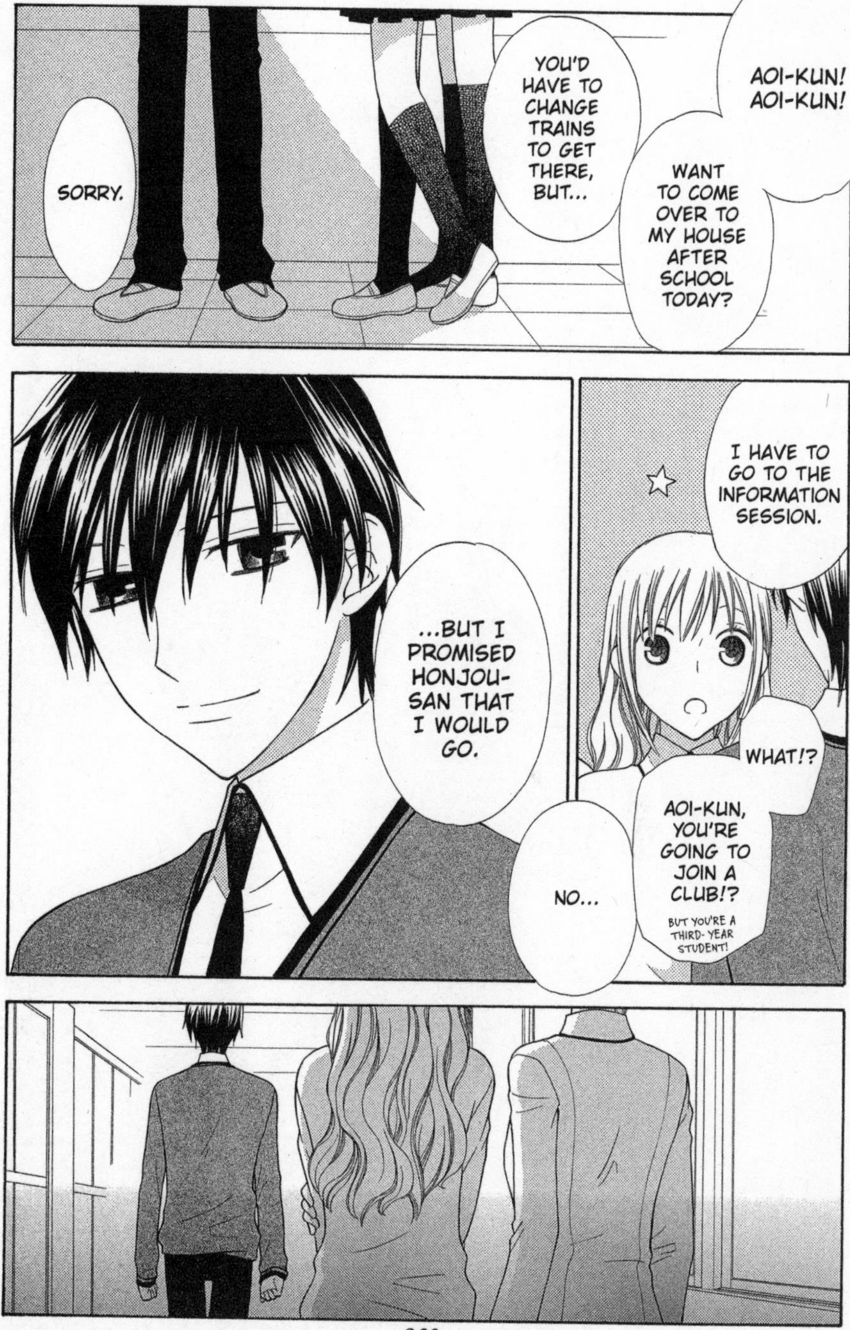
AOI-KUN! AOI-KUN!
WANT TO COME OVER TO MY HOUSE AFTER SCHOOL TODAY?
YOU'D HAVE TO CHANGE TRAINS TO GET THERE, BUT...
SORRY.
I HAVE TO GO TO THE INFORMATION SESSION.
WHAT!?
AOI-KUN, YOU'RE GOING TO JOIN A CLUB!?
BUT YOU'RE A THIRD-YEAR STUDENT!
NO...
...BUT I PROMISED HONJOU-SAN THAT I WOULD GO.

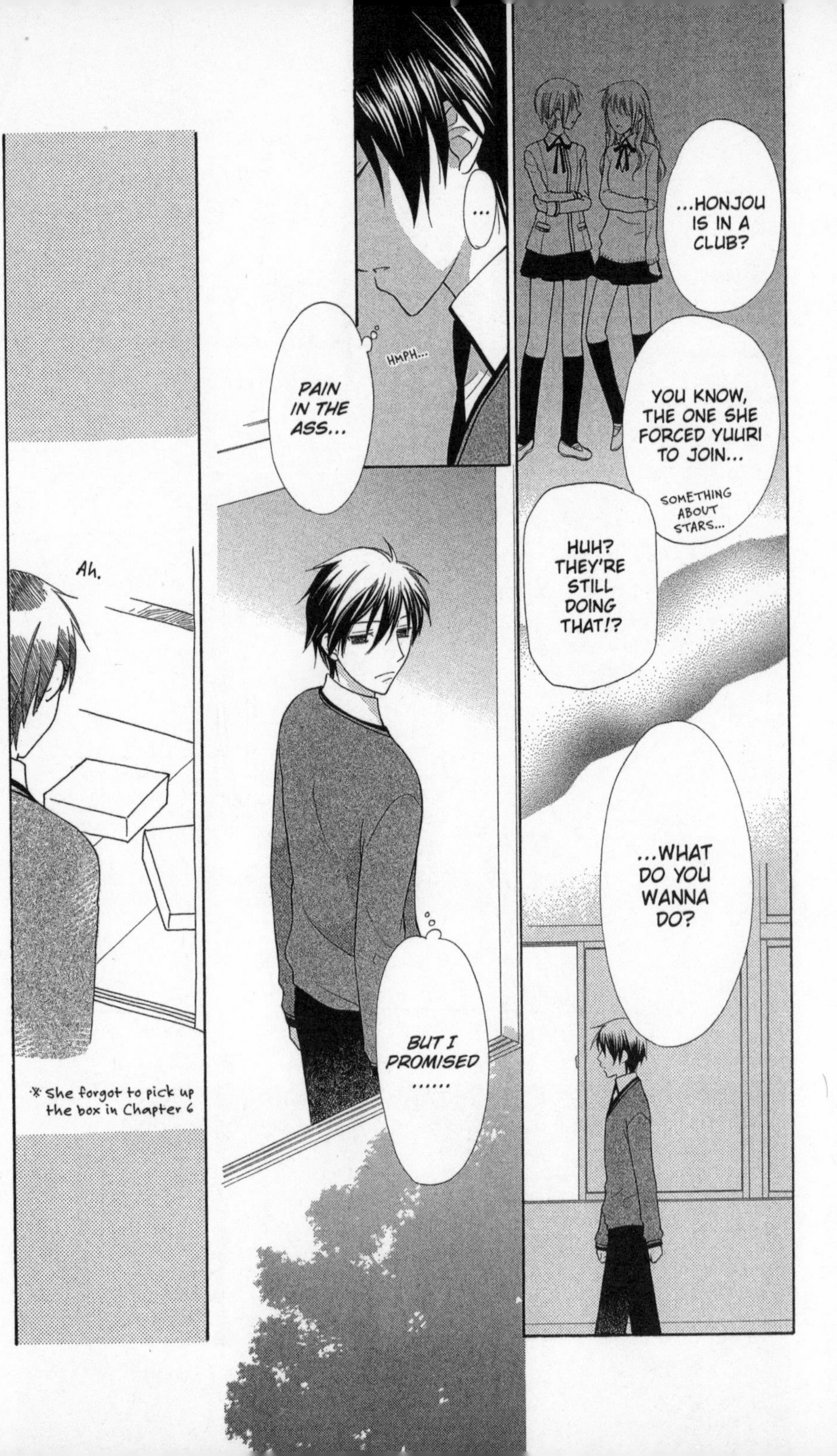
...HONJOU IS IN A CLUB?
YOU KNOW, THE ONE SHE FORCED YUURI TO JOIN...
SOMETHING ABOUT STARS...
HUH? THEY'RE STILL DOING THAT!?
...WHAT DO YOU WANNA DO?
...
HMPH...
PAIN IN THE ASS...
BUT I PROMISED ......
Ah.
※She forgot to pick up the box in Chapter 6

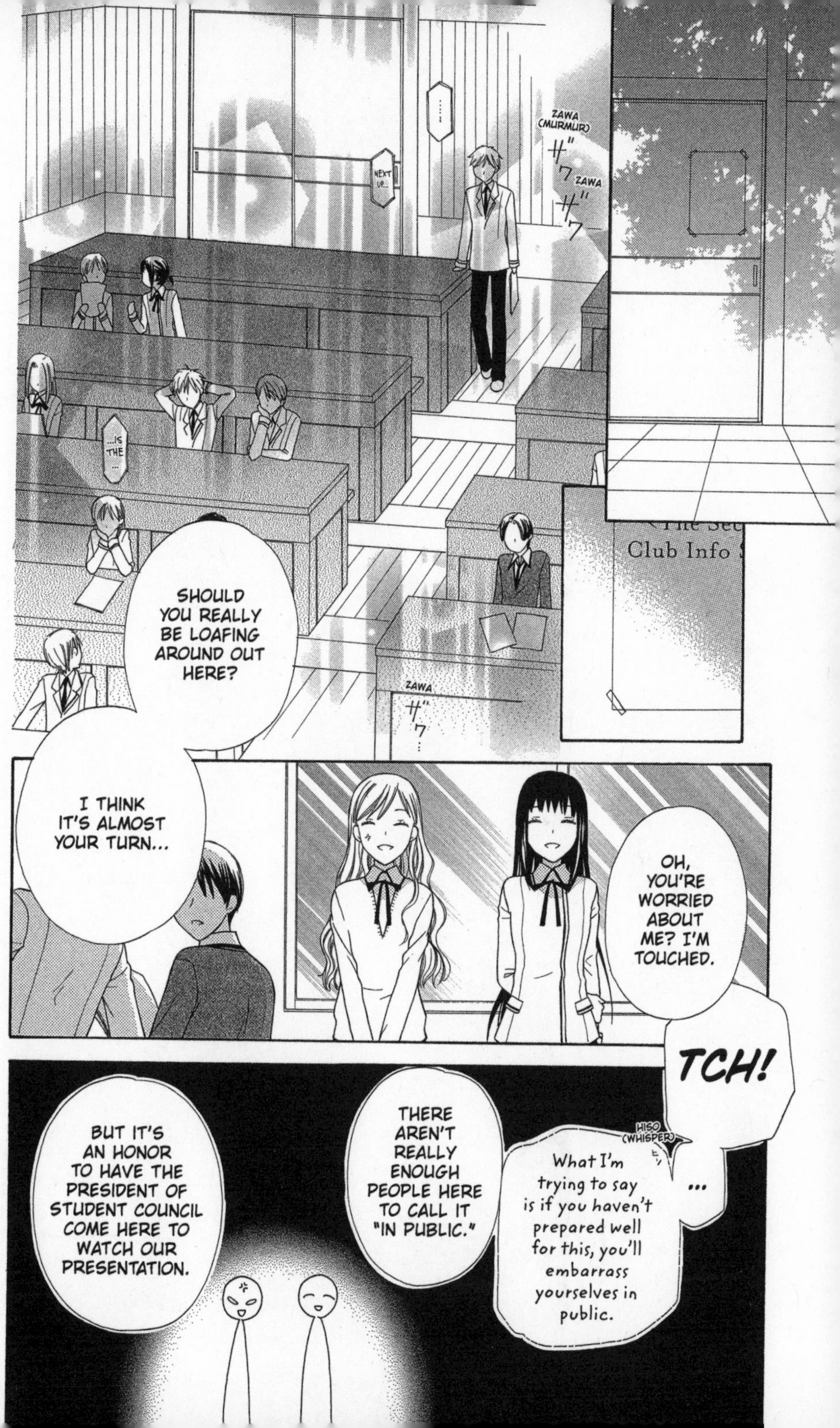
Club Info
...?
NEXT UP...
ZAWA (MURMUR)
ZAWA
...IS THE ...
SHOULD YOU REALLY BE LOAFING AROUND OUT HERE?
ZAWA
I THINK IT'S ALMOST YOUR TURN...
OH, YOU'RE WORRIED ABOUT ME? I'M TOUCHED.
TCH!
...
HISO (WHISPER)
What I'm trying to say is if you haven't prepared well for this, you'll embarrass yourselves in public.
THERE AREN'T REALLY ENOUGH PEOPLE HERE TO CALL IT "IN PUBLIC."
BUT IT'S AN HONOR TO HAVE THE PRESIDENT OF STUDENT COUNCIL COME HERE TO WATCH OUR PRESENTATION.

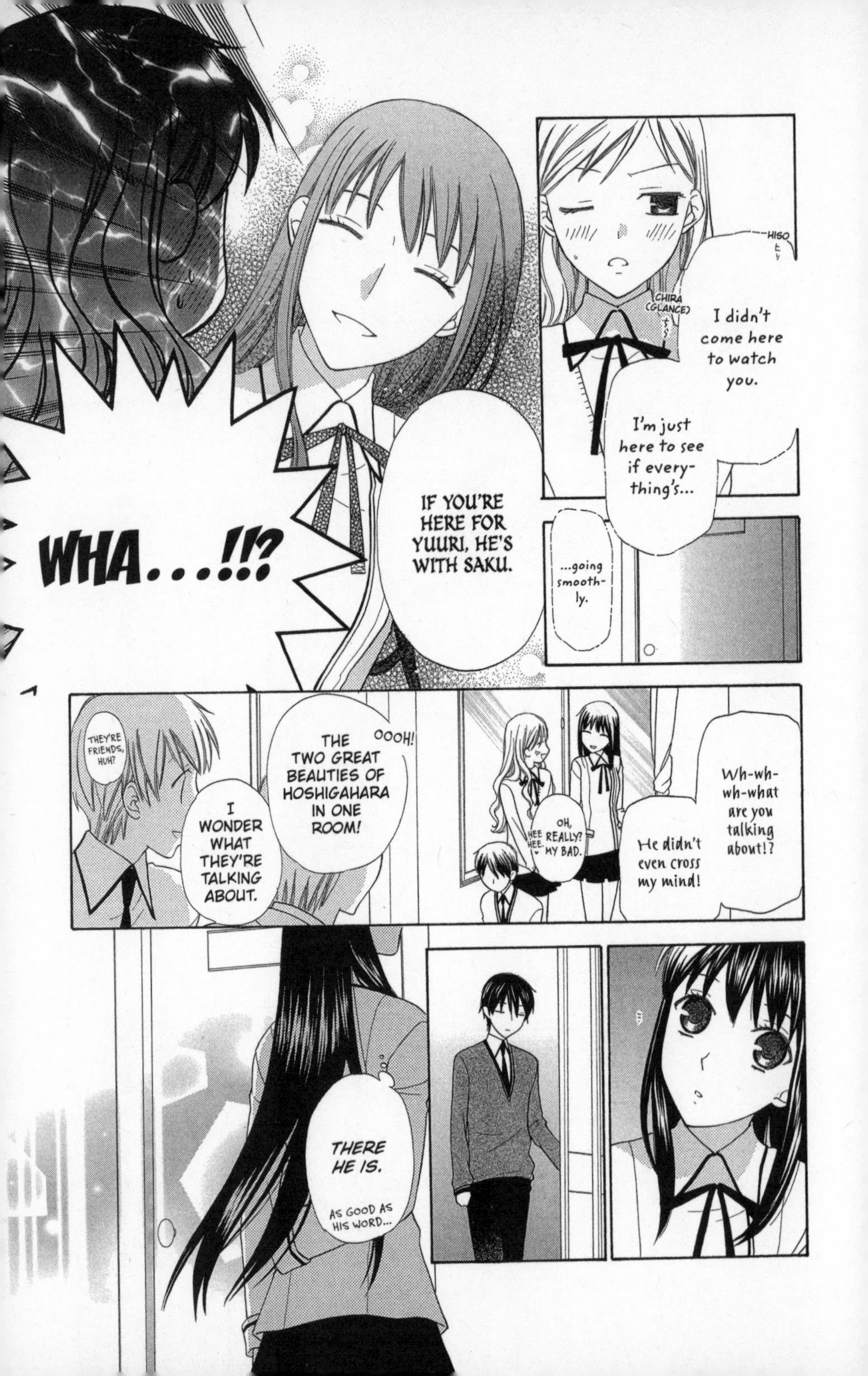
HISO
CHIRA (GLANCE)
I didn't come here to watch you.
I'm just here to see if every-thing's...
...going smooth-ly.
IF YOU'RE HERE FOR YUURI, HE'S WITH SAKU.
WHA...!!?
Wh-wh-wh-what are you talking about!?
He didn't even cross my mind!
OH, REALLY? MY BAD.
HEE HEE.
OOOH!
THE TWO GREAT BEAUTIES OF HOSHIGAHARA IN ONE ROOM!
THEY'RE FRIENDS, HUH?
I WONDER WHAT THEY'RE TALKING ABOUT.
THERE HE IS.
AS GOOD AS HIS WORD...

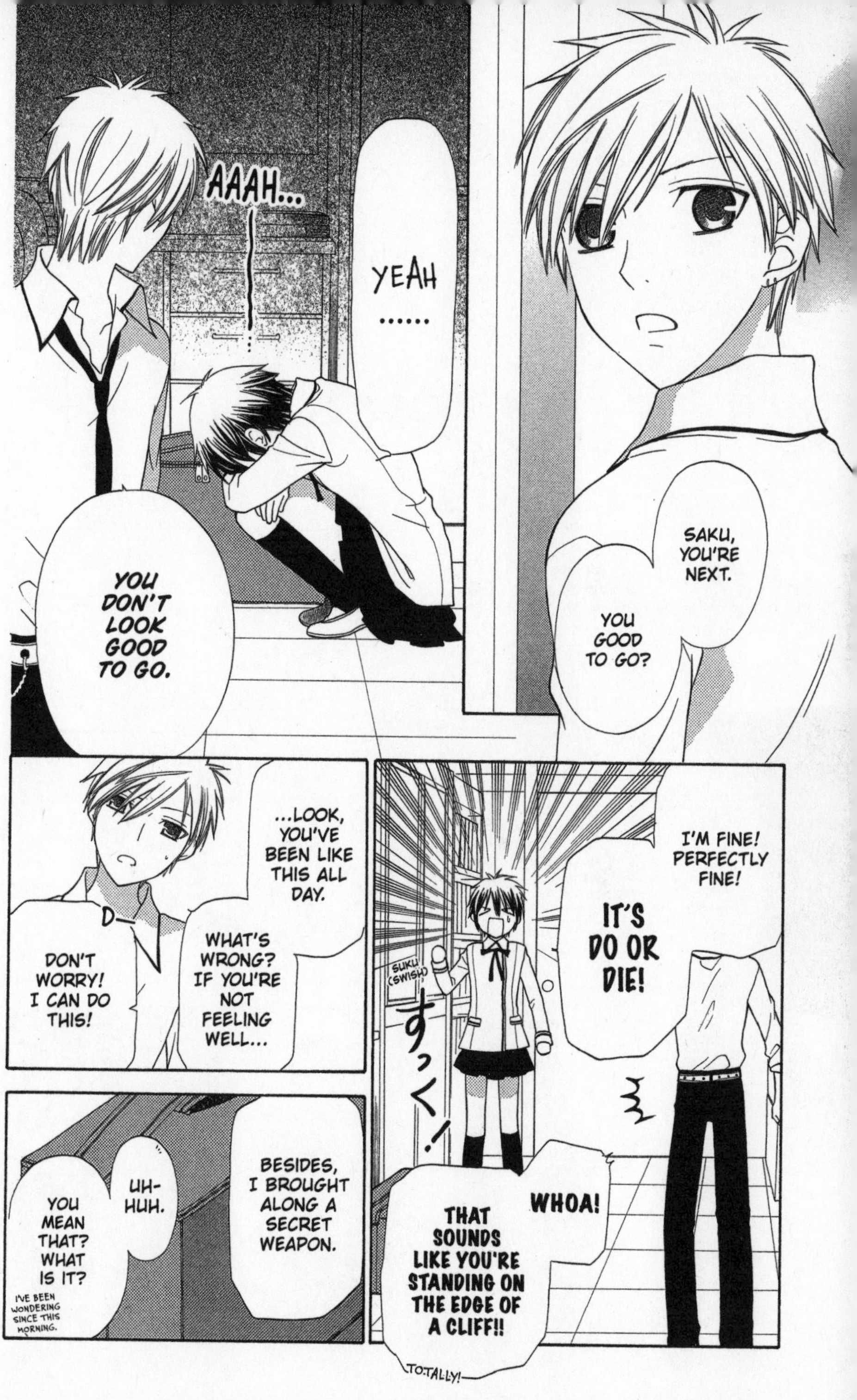
SAKU, YOU'RE NEXT.
YOU GOOD TO GO?
YEAH ......
AAAH...
YOU DON'T LOOK GOOD TO GO.
I'M FINE! PERFECTLY FINE!
IT'S DO OR DIE!
SUKU (SWISH)
すっく!
WHOA!
THAT SOUNDS LIKE YOU'RE STANDING ON THE EDGE OF A CLIFF!!
TO-TALLY!
...LOOK, YOU'VE BEEN LIKE THIS ALL DAY.
WHAT'S WRONG? IF YOU'RE NOT FEELING WELL...
D—
DON'T WORRY! I CAN DO THIS!
BESIDES, I BROUGHT ALONG A SECRET WEAPON.
UH-HUH.
YOU MEAN THAT? WHAT IS IT?
I'VE BEEN WONDERING SINCE THIS MORNING.

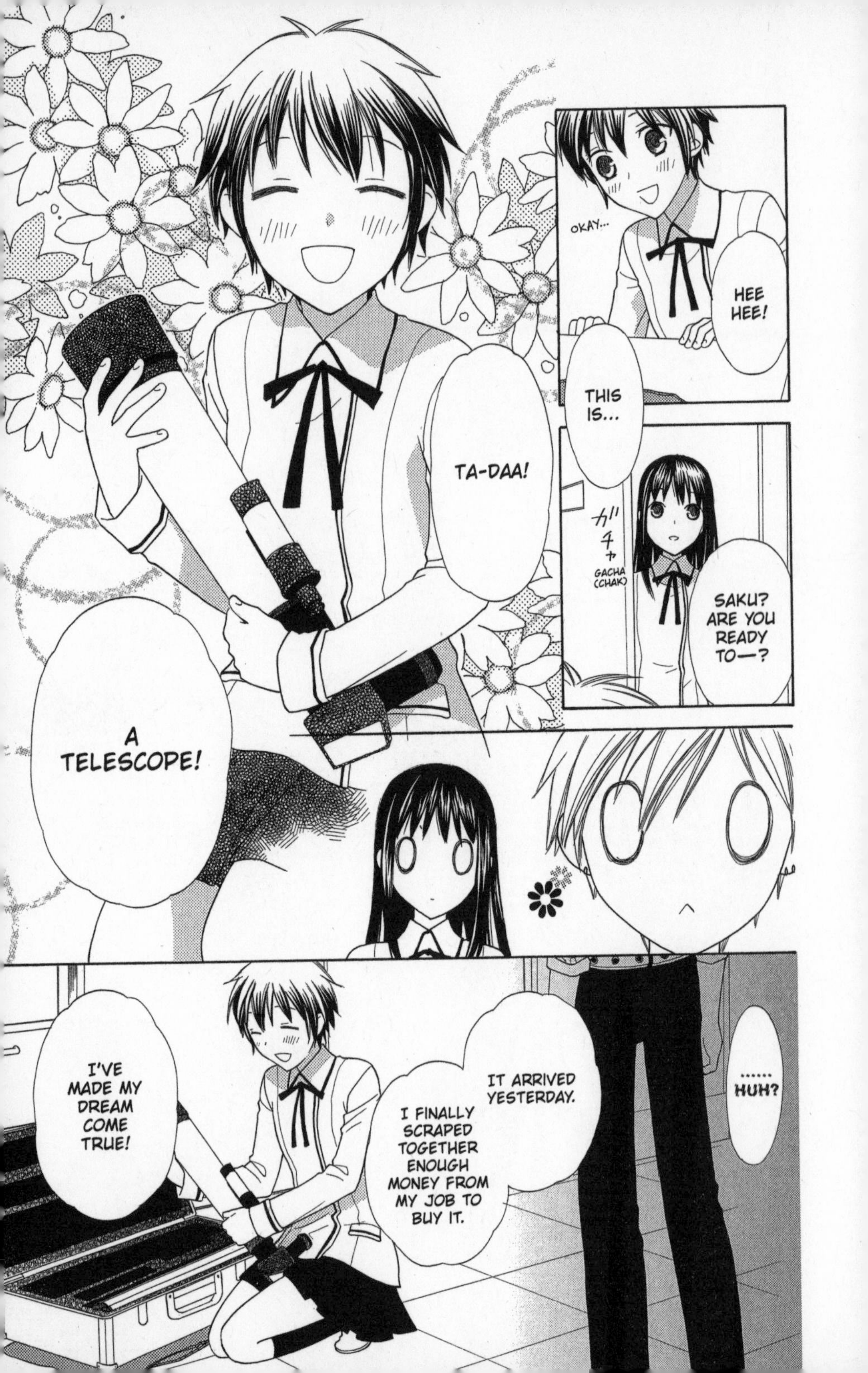

HEE HEE!
OKAY...
THIS IS...
SAKU? ARE YOU READY TO—?
ガチャ
GACHA (CHAK)
TA-DAA!
A TELESCOPE!
......HUH?
IT ARRIVED YESTERDAY.
I FINALLY SCRAPED TOGETHER ENOUGH MONEY FROM MY JOB TO BUY IT.
I'VE MADE MY DREAM COME TRUE!

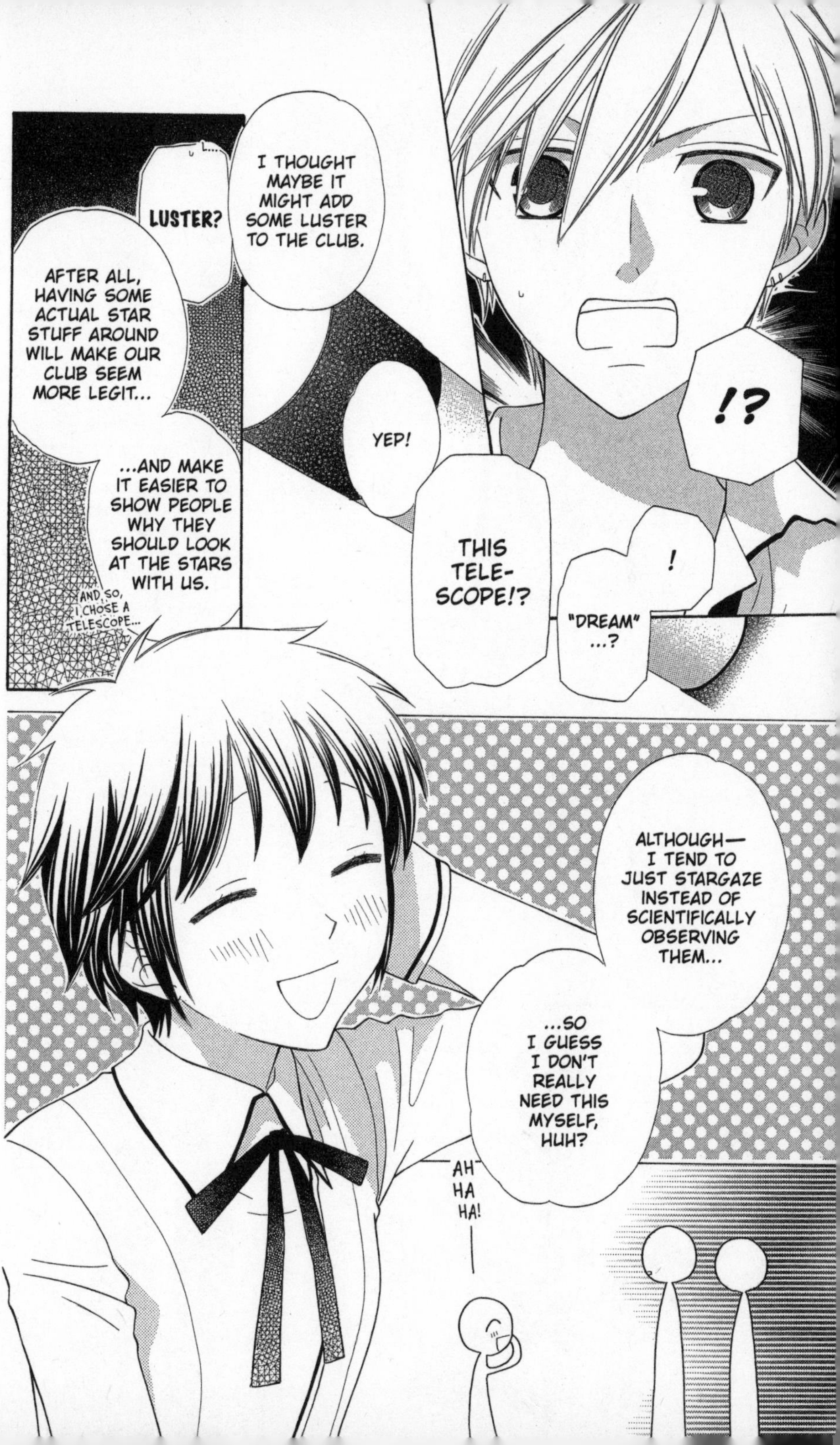
!?
YEP!
THIS TELE-SCOPE!?
!
"DREAM" ...?
I THOUGHT MAYBE IT MIGHT ADD SOME LUSTER TO THE CLUB.
I...
LUSTER?
AFTER ALL, HAVING SOME ACTUAL STAR STUFF AROUND WILL MAKE OUR CLUB SEEM MORE LEGIT...
...AND MAKE IT EASIER TO SHOW PEOPLE WHY THEY SHOULD LOOK AT THE STARS WITH US.
AND SO, I CHOSE A TELESCOPE...
ALTHOUGH— I TEND TO JUST STARGAZE INSTEAD OF SCIENTIFICALLY OBSERVING THEM...
...SO I GUESS I DON'T REALLY NEED THIS MYSELF, HUH?
AH HA HA!

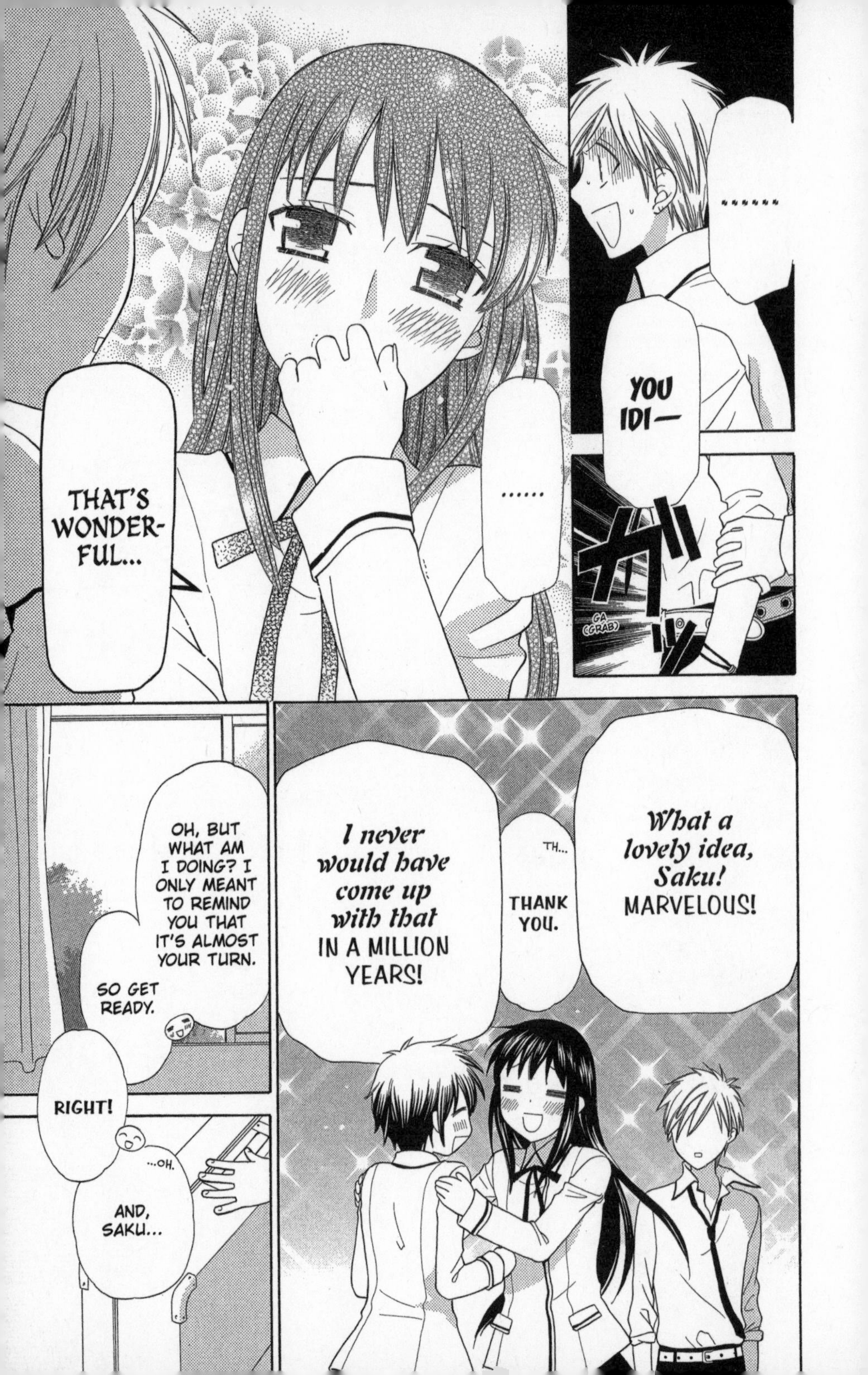
......
YOU IDI—
GA (GRAB)
......
THAT'S WONDER-FUL...
What a lovely idea, Saku! MARVELOUS!
TH...
THANK YOU.
I never would have come up with that IN A MILLION YEARS!
OH, BUT WHAT AM I DOING? I ONLY MEANT TO REMIND YOU THAT IT'S ALMOST YOUR TURN.
SO GET READY.
RIGHT!
...OH.
AND, SAKU...

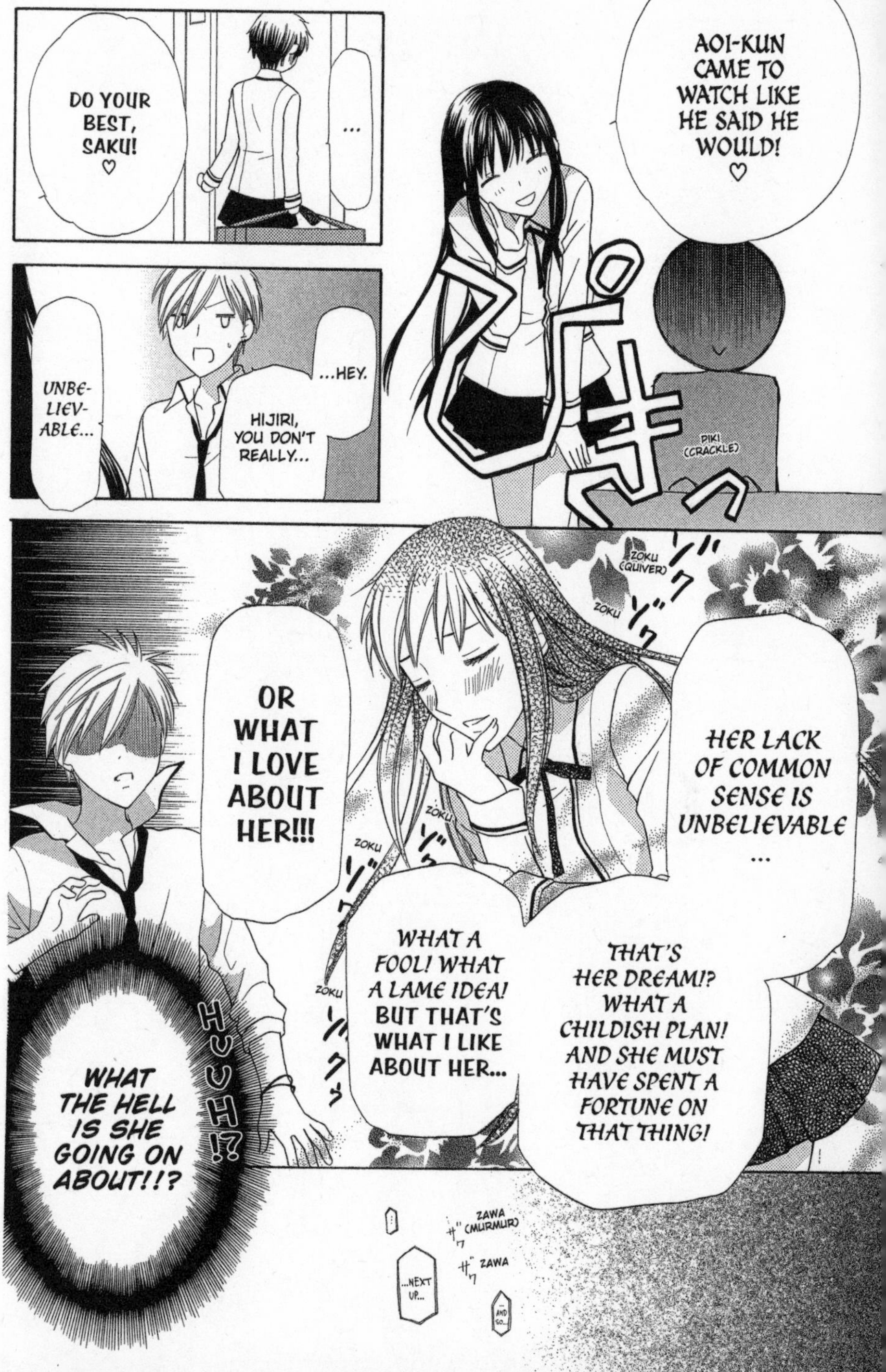
AOI-KUN CAME TO WATCH LIKE HE SAID HE WOULD! ♡
PIKI (CRACKLE)
...
DO YOUR BEST, SAKU! ♡
...HEY.
HIJIRI, YOU DON'T REALLY...
UNBE-LIEV-ABLE...
ZOKU (QUIVER)
ZOKU
HER LACK OF COMMON SENSE IS UNBELIEVABLE ...
OR WHAT I LOVE ABOUT HER!!!
ZOKU
ZOKU
THAT'S HER DREAM!? WHAT A CHILDISH PLAN! AND SHE MUST HAVE SPENT A FORTUNE ON THAT THING!
WHAT A FOOL! WHAT A LAME IDEA! BUT THAT'S WHAT I LIKE ABOUT HER...
ZOKU
HUUUH!?
WHAT THE HELL IS SHE GOING ON ABOUT!!?
ZAWA (MURMUR)
ZAWA
...AND SO...
...NEXT UP...
...

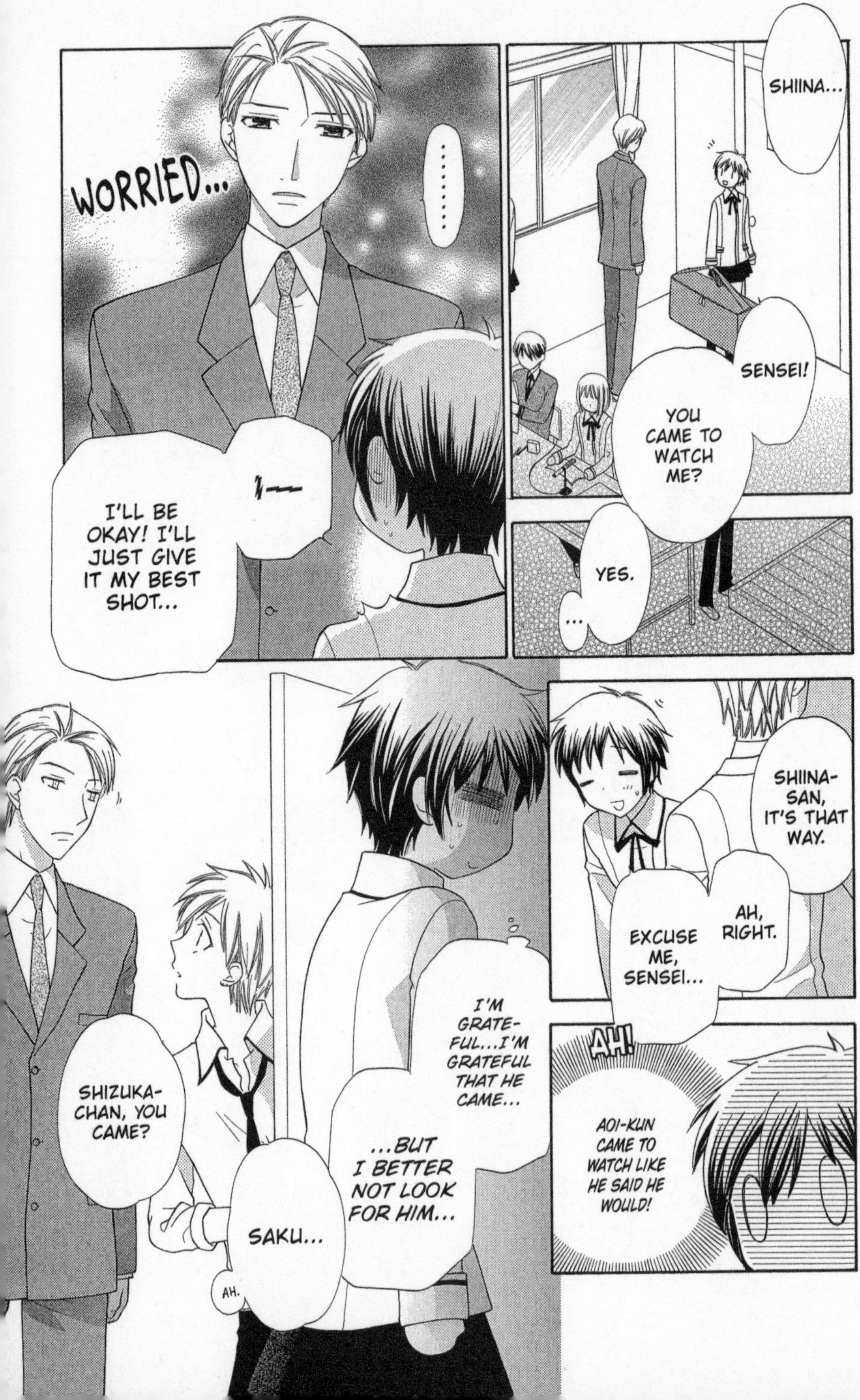
SHIINA...
SENSEI!
YOU CAME TO WATCH ME?
YES.
...
......
WORRIED...
I'LL BE OKAY! I'LL JUST GIVE IT MY BEST SHOT...
SHIINA-SAN, IT'S THAT WAY.
AH, RIGHT.
EXCUSE ME, SENSEI...
AH!
AOI-KUN CAME TO WATCH LIKE HE SAID HE WOULD!
I'M GRATEFUL...I'M GRATEFUL THAT HE CAME...
...BUT I BETTER NOT LOOK FOR HIM...
SHIZUKA-CHAN, YOU CAME?
SAKU...
AH.

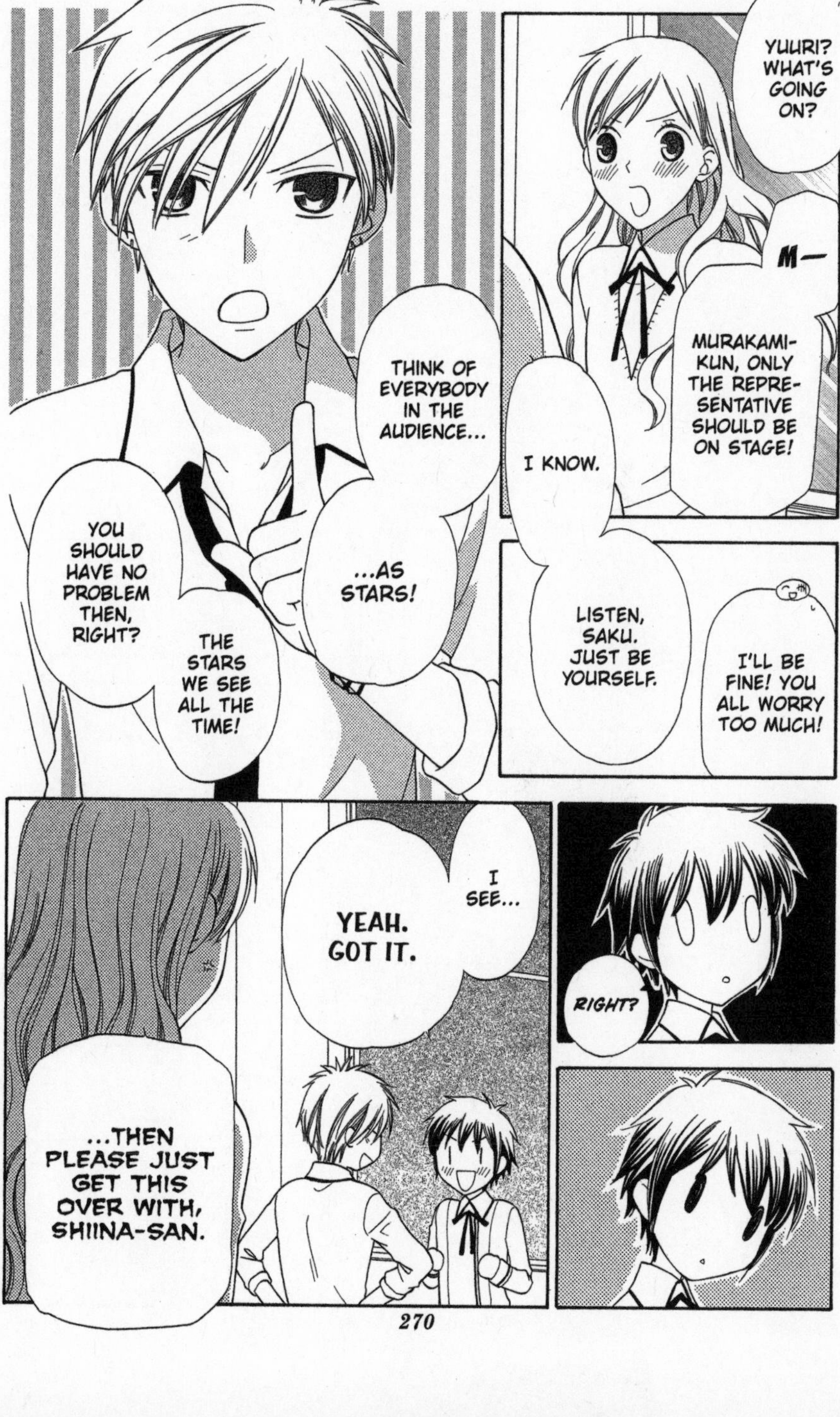
YUURI? WHAT'S GOING ON?
M—
MURAKAMI-KUN, ONLY THE REPRESENTATIVE SHOULD BE ON STAGE!
I KNOW.
LISTEN, SAKU. JUST BE YOURSELF.
I'LL BE FINE! YOU ALL WORRY TOO MUCH!
THINK OF EVERYBODY IN THE AUDIENCE...
...AS STARS!
THE STARS WE SEE ALL THE TIME!
YOU SHOULD HAVE NO PROBLEM THEN, RIGHT?
RIGHT?
I SEE...
YEAH. GOT IT.
...THEN PLEASE JUST GET THIS OVER WITH, SHIINA-SAN.

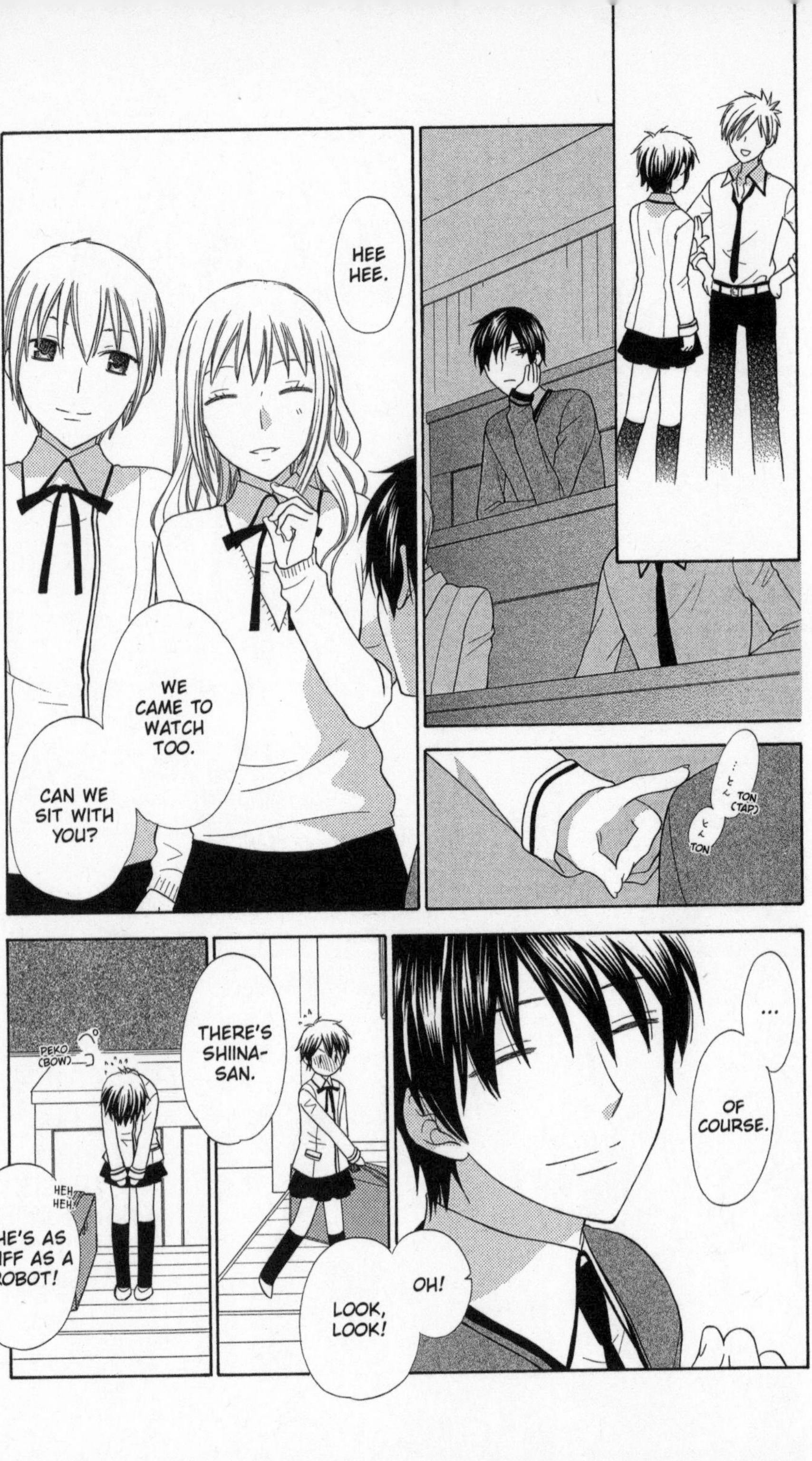
…とん
TON (TAP)
とん
TON
HEE HEE.
WE CAME TO WATCH TOO.
CAN WE SIT WITH YOU?
… OF COURSE.
OH!
LOOK, LOOK!
THERE'S SHIINA-SAN.
PEKO (BOW)
HEH HEH
SHE'S AS STIFF AS A ROBOT!

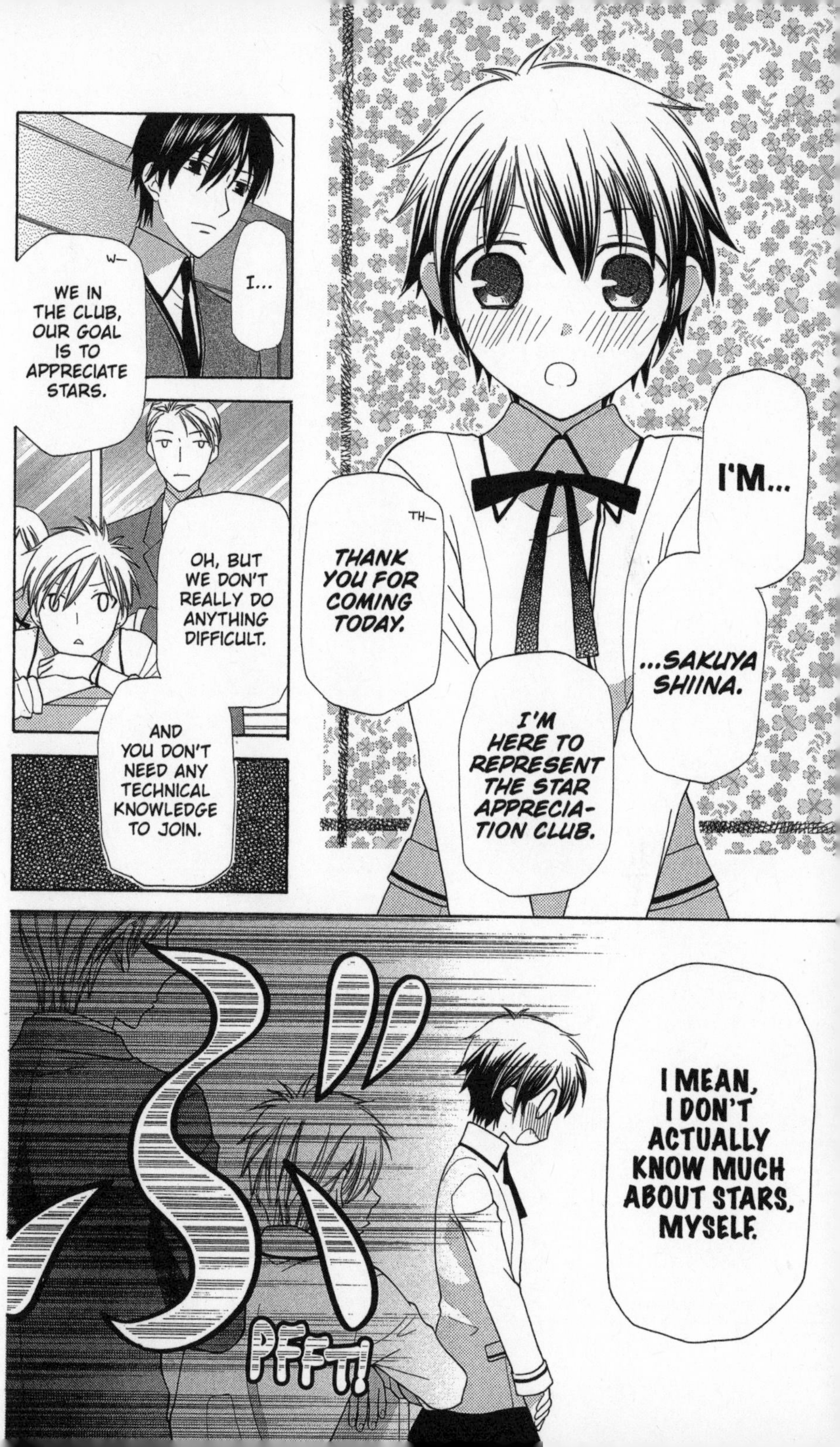
I'M...
...SAKUYA SHIINA.
TH— THANK YOU FOR COMING TODAY.
I'M HERE TO REPRESENT THE STAR APPRECIA-TION CLUB.
I...
W— WE IN THE CLUB, OUR GOAL IS TO APPRECIATE STARS.
OH, BUT WE DON'T REALLY DO ANYTHING DIFFICULT.
AND YOU DON'T NEED ANY TECHNICAL KNOWLEDGE TO JOIN.
I MEAN, I DON'T ACTUALLY KNOW MUCH ABOUT STARS, MYSELF.
PFFT!

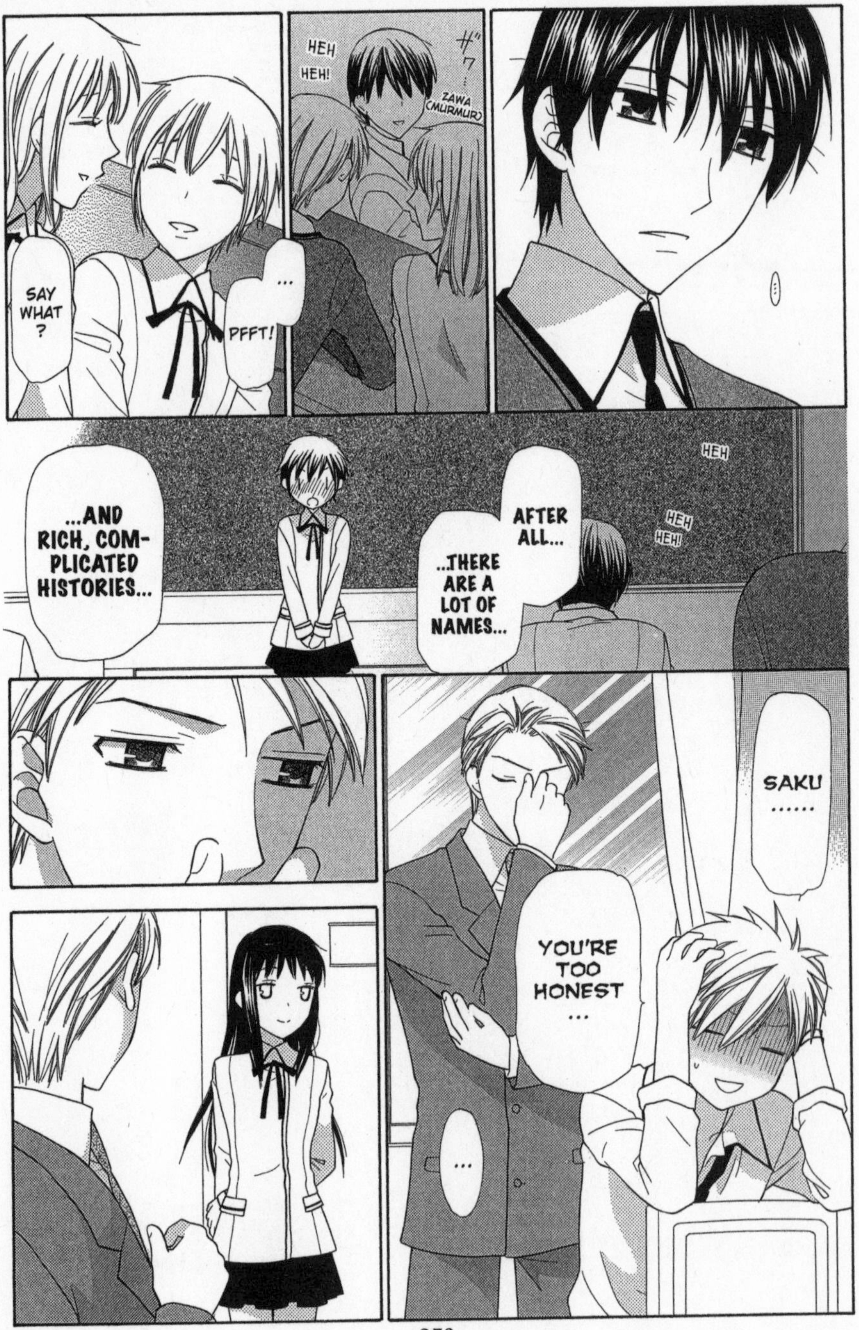

⋮
HEH
HEH!
ザワ…
ZAWA (MURMUR)
...
PFFT!
SAY WHAT ?
HEH
HEH
HEH!
AFTER ALL...
...THERE ARE A LOT OF NAMES...
...AND RICH, COM-PLICATED HISTORIES...
SAKU ......
YOU'RE TOO HONEST ...
...

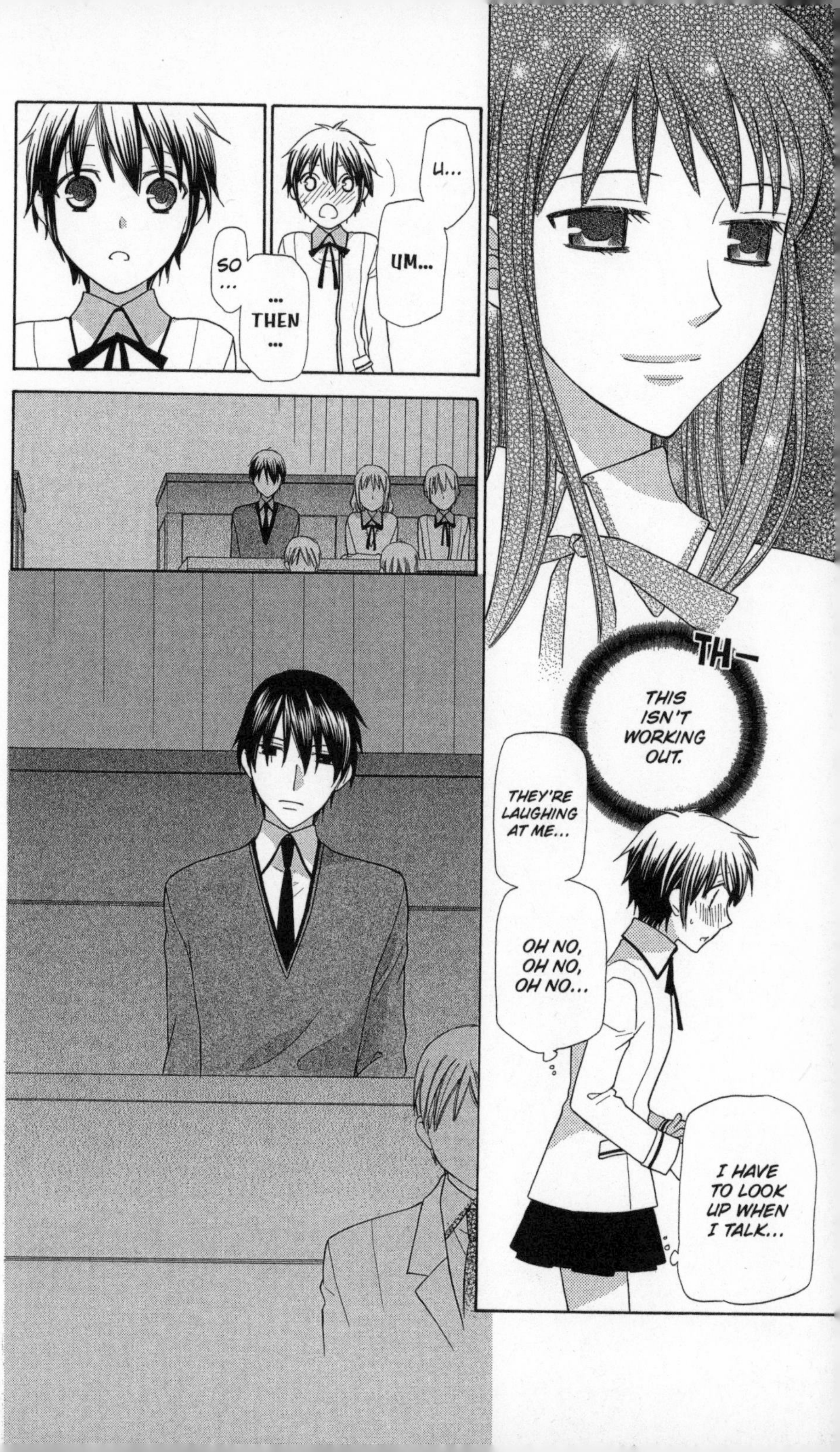
TH—
THIS ISN'T WORKING OUT.
THEY'RE LAUGHING AT ME...
OH NO, OH NO, OH NO...
I HAVE TO LOOK UP WHEN I TALK...
U...
UM...
SO ...
... THEN ...

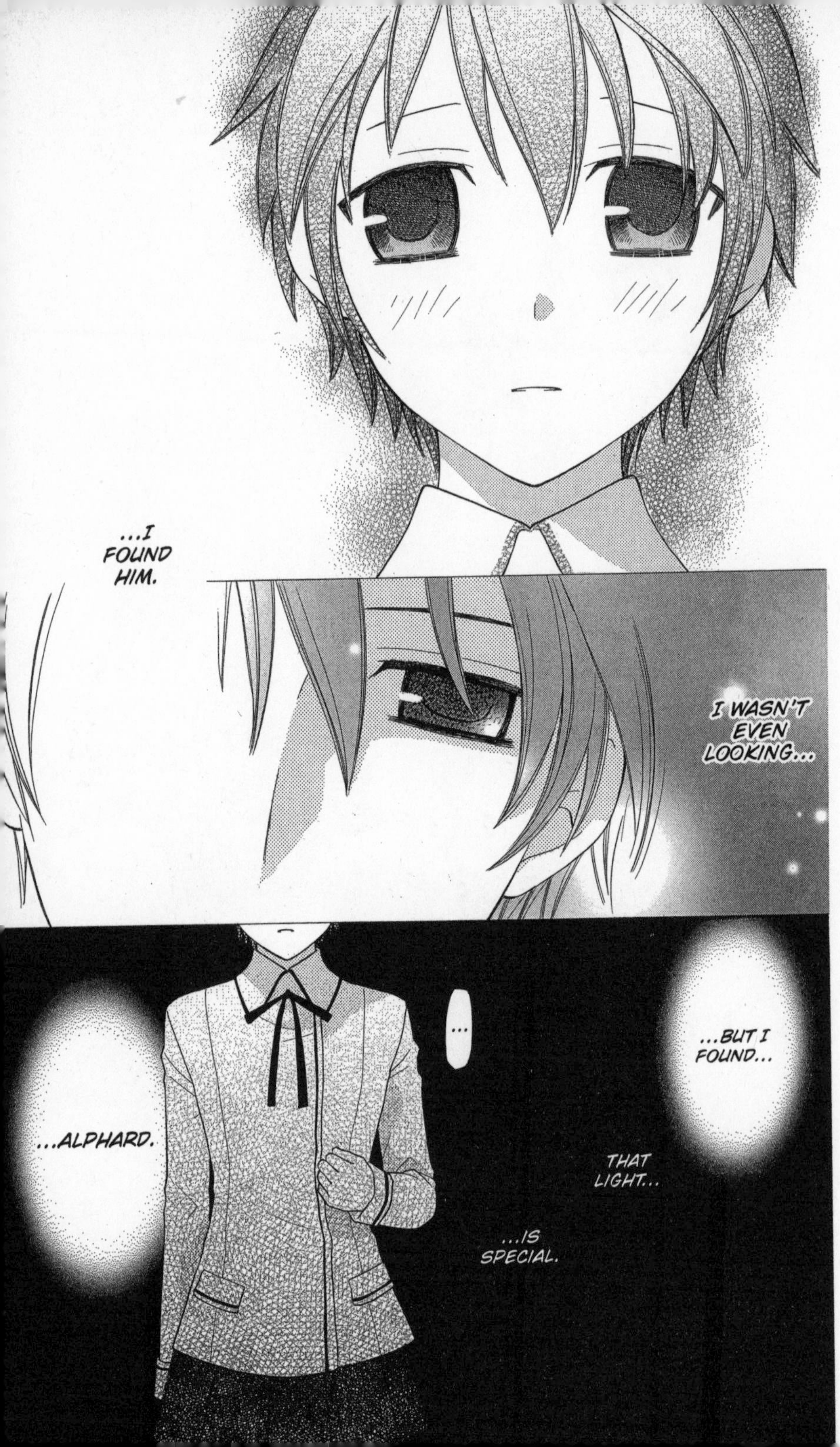
...I FOUND HIM.
I WASN'T EVEN LOOKING...
...BUT I FOUND...
...
...ALPHARD.
THAT LIGHT...
...IS SPECIAL.

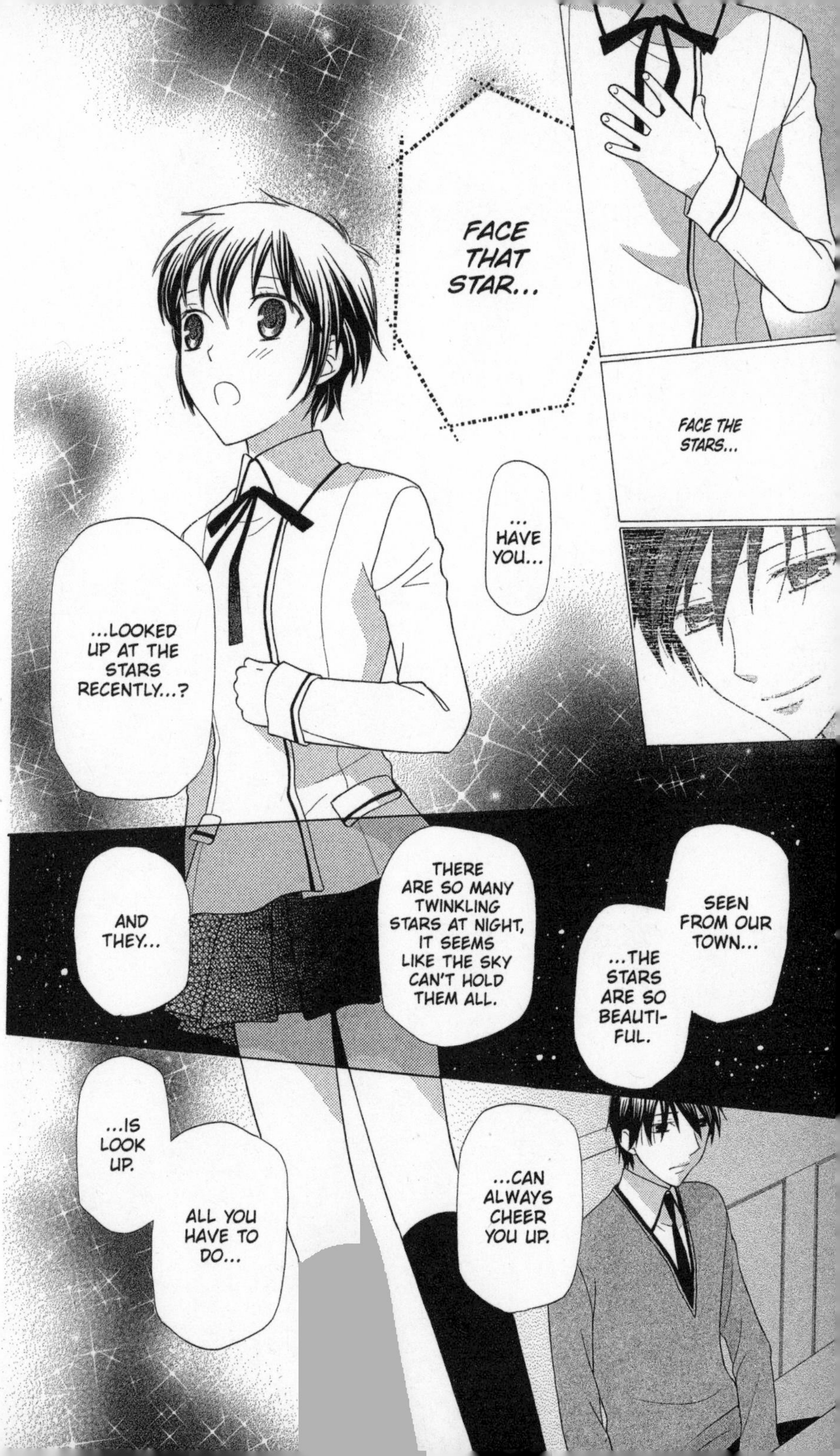
FACE THE STARS...
FACE THAT STAR...
...HAVE YOU...
...LOOKED UP AT THE STARS RECENTLY...?
SEEN FROM OUR TOWN...
...THE STARS ARE SO BEAUTIFUL.
THERE ARE SO MANY TWINKLING STARS AT NIGHT, IT SEEMS LIKE THE SKY CAN'T HOLD THEM ALL.
AND THEY...
...CAN ALWAYS CHEER YOU UP.
ALL YOU HAVE TO DO...
...IS LOOK UP.

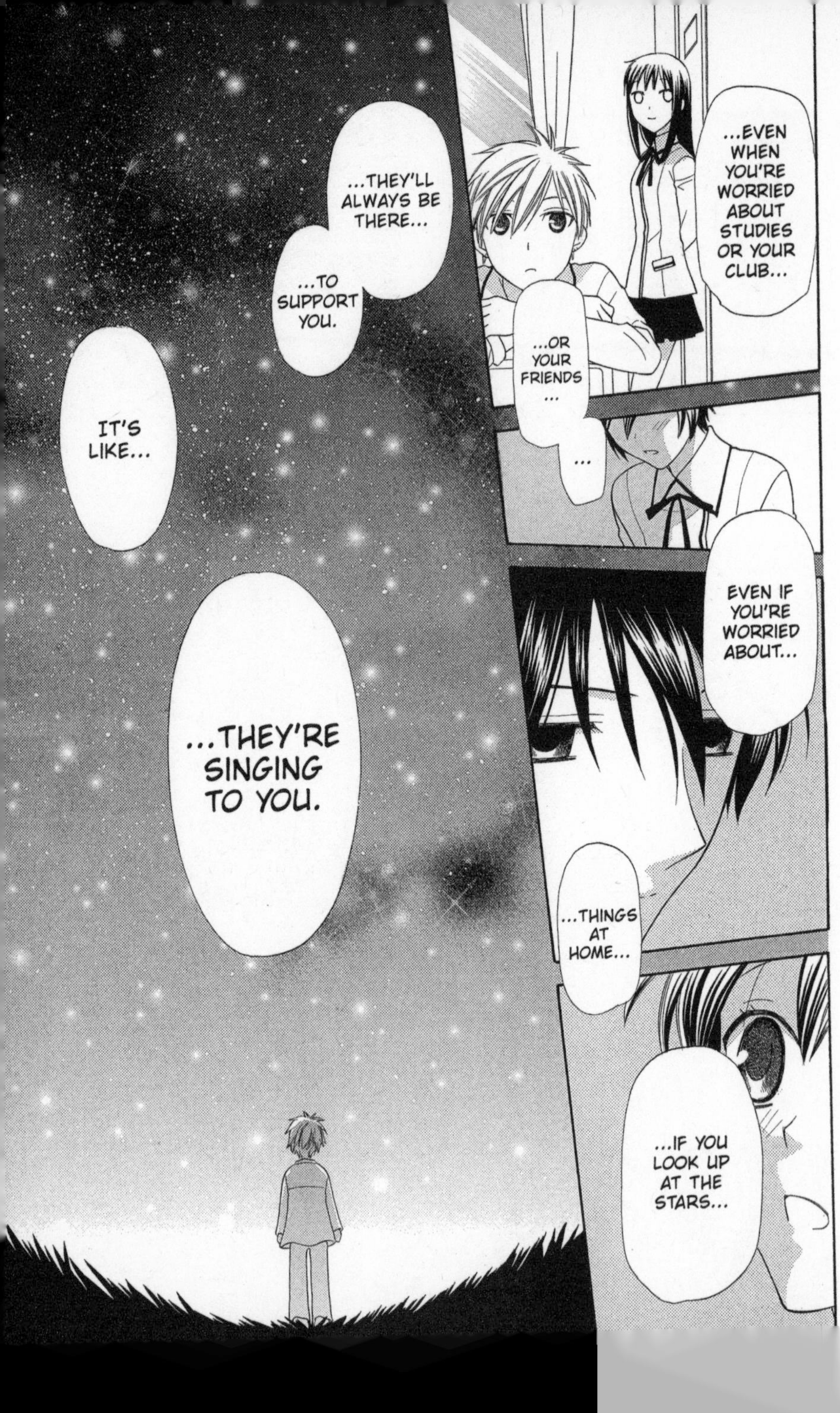
...EVEN WHEN YOU'RE WORRIED ABOUT STUDIES OR YOUR CLUB...
...OR YOUR FRIENDS...
...
EVEN IF YOU'RE WORRIED ABOUT...
...THINGS AT HOME...
...IF YOU LOOK UP AT THE STARS...
...THEY'LL ALWAYS BE THERE...
...TO SUPPORT YOU.
IT'S LIKE...
...THEY'RE SINGING TO YOU.

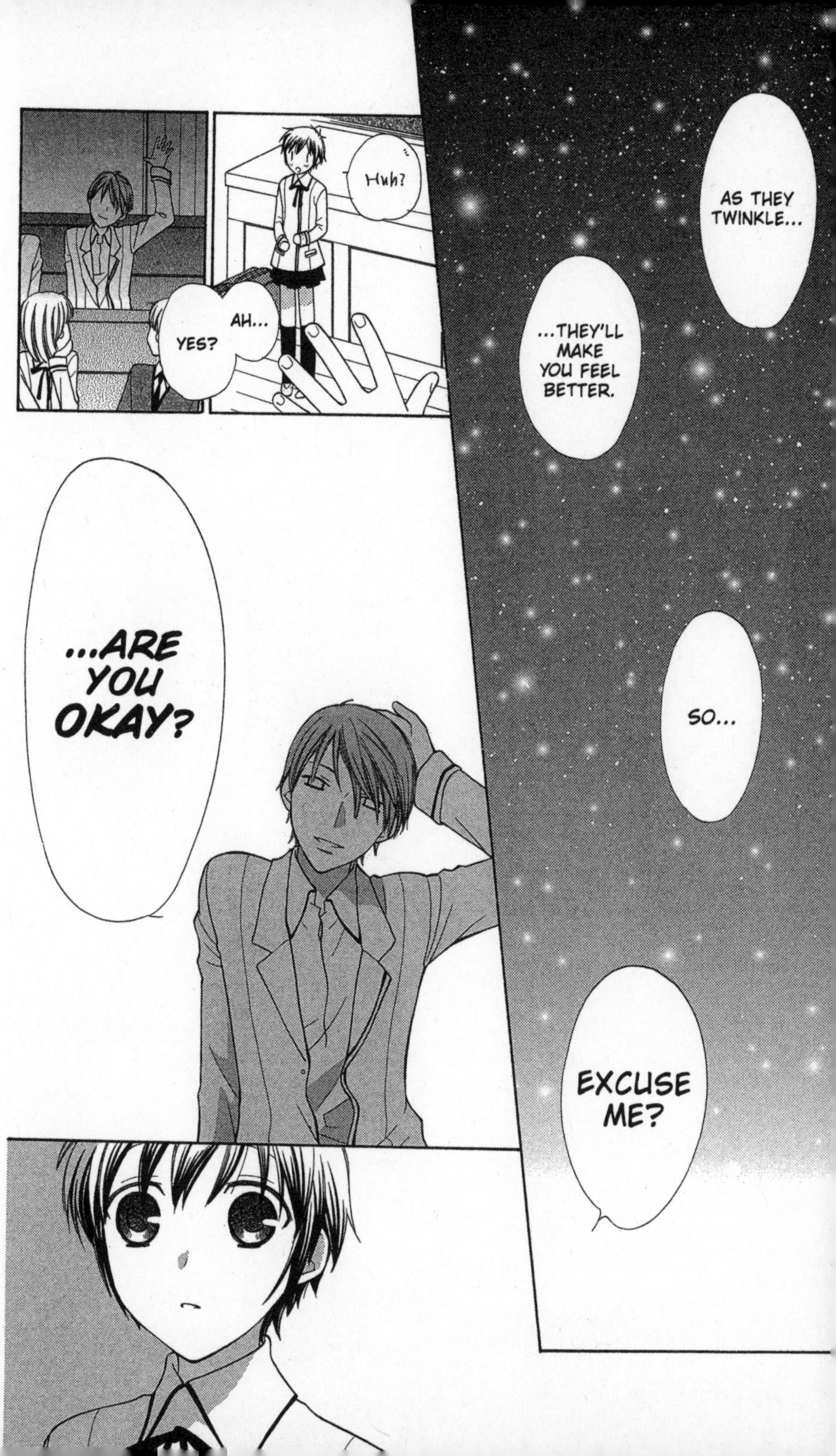
AS THEY TWINKLE...
...THEY'LL MAKE YOU FEEL BETTER.
SO...
EXCUSE ME?
Huh?
AH...
YES?
...ARE YOU OKAY?

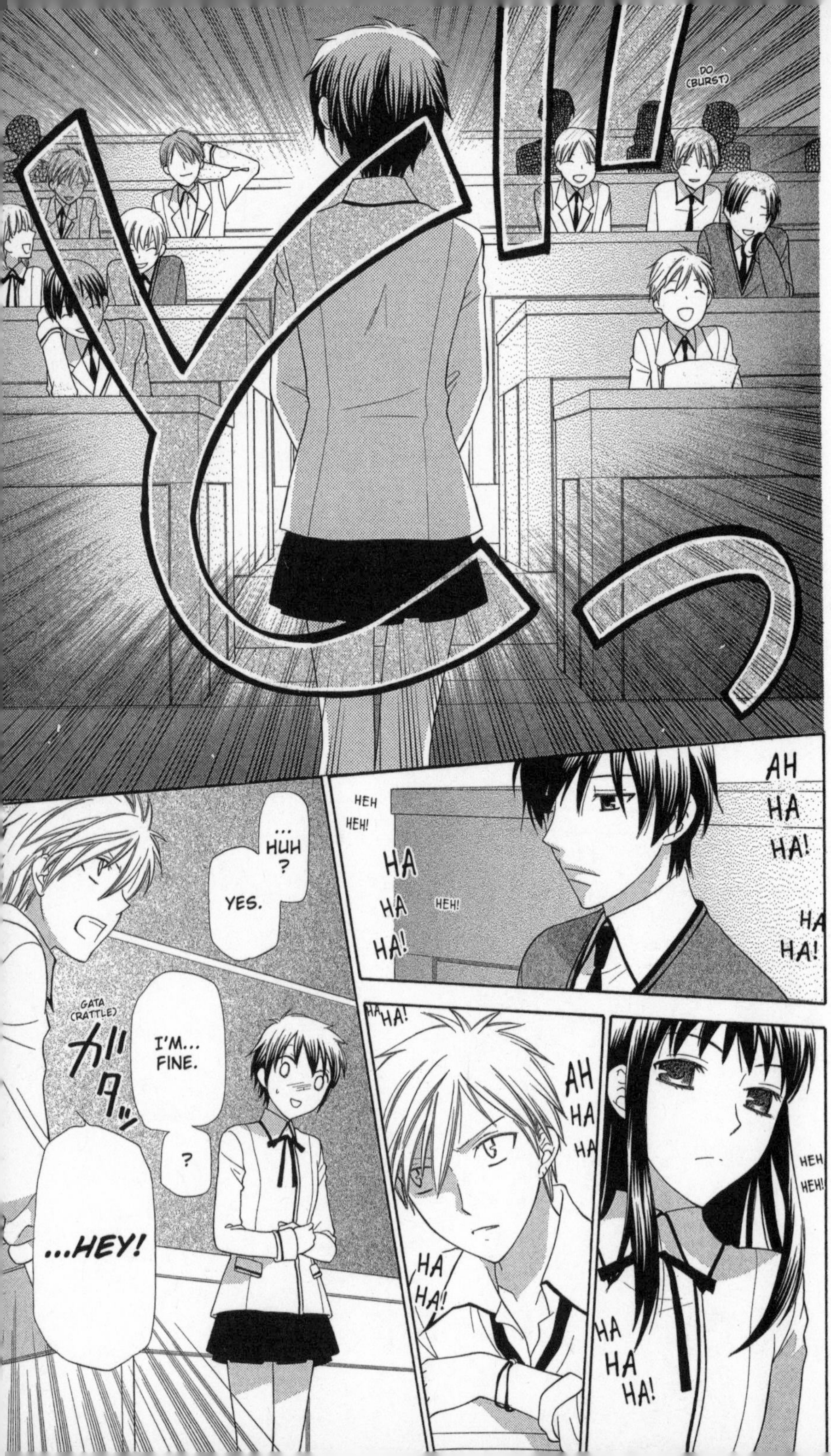
DO (BURST)
AH HA HA!
HEH HEH!
HA HA HA!
HEH!
HA HA!
HA HA!
HEH HEH!
HA HA HA!
AH HA HA HA
HA HA!
...HUH?
YES.
GATA (RATTLE)
I'M... FINE.
?
...HEY!

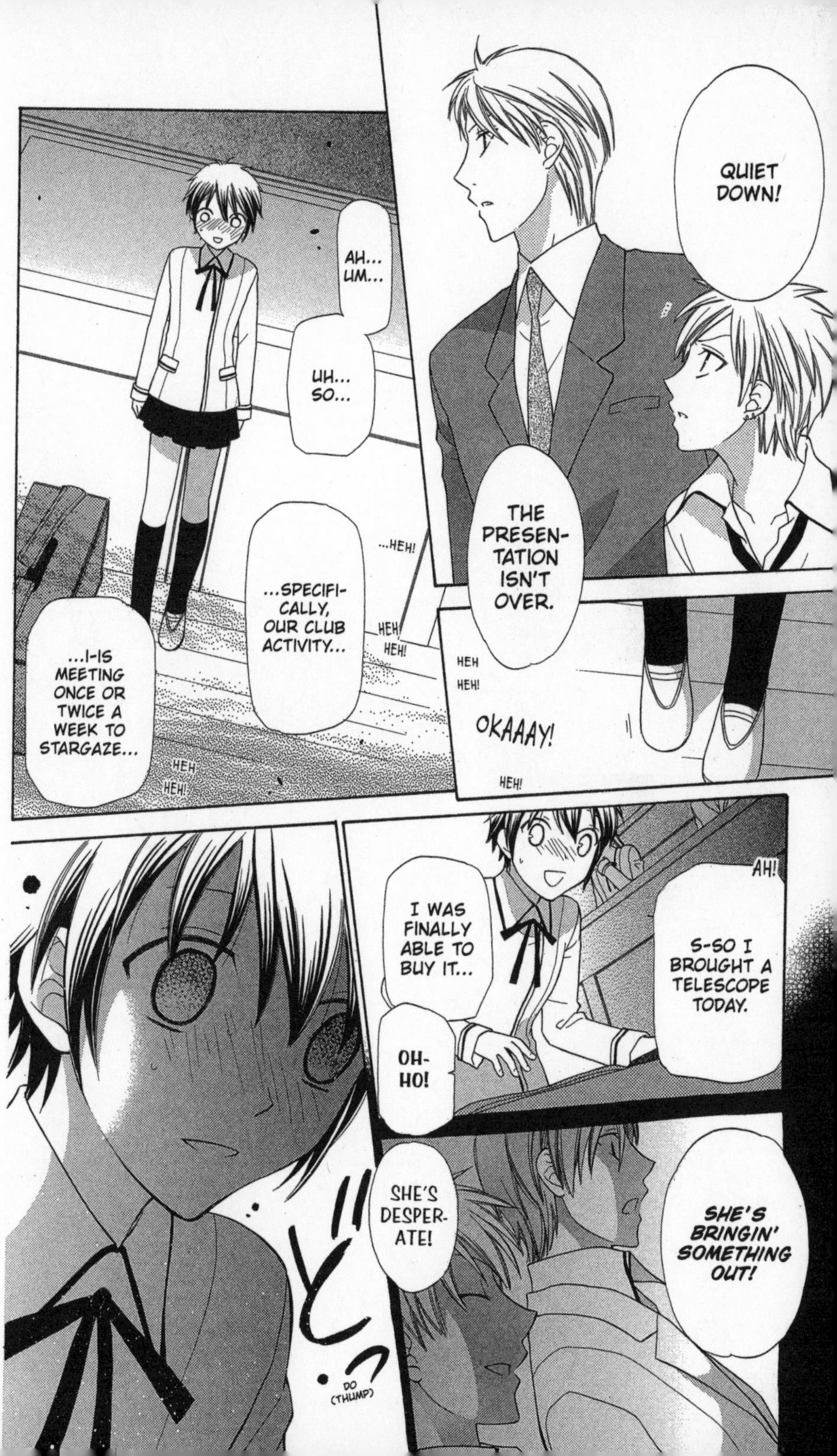
QUIET DOWN!
THE PRESEN-TATION ISN'T OVER.
HEH HEH!
OKAAAY!
HEH!
AH... UM...
UH... SO...
...SPECIFI-CALLY, OUR CLUB ACTIVITY...
...HEH!
HEH HEH!
...I-IS MEETING ONCE OR TWICE A WEEK TO STARGAZE...
HEH HEH!
AH!
S-SO I BROUGHT A TELESCOPE TODAY.
I WAS FINALLY ABLE TO BUY IT...
OH-HO!
SHE'S BRINGIN' SOMETHING OUT!
SHE'S DESPERATE!
DO (THUMP)

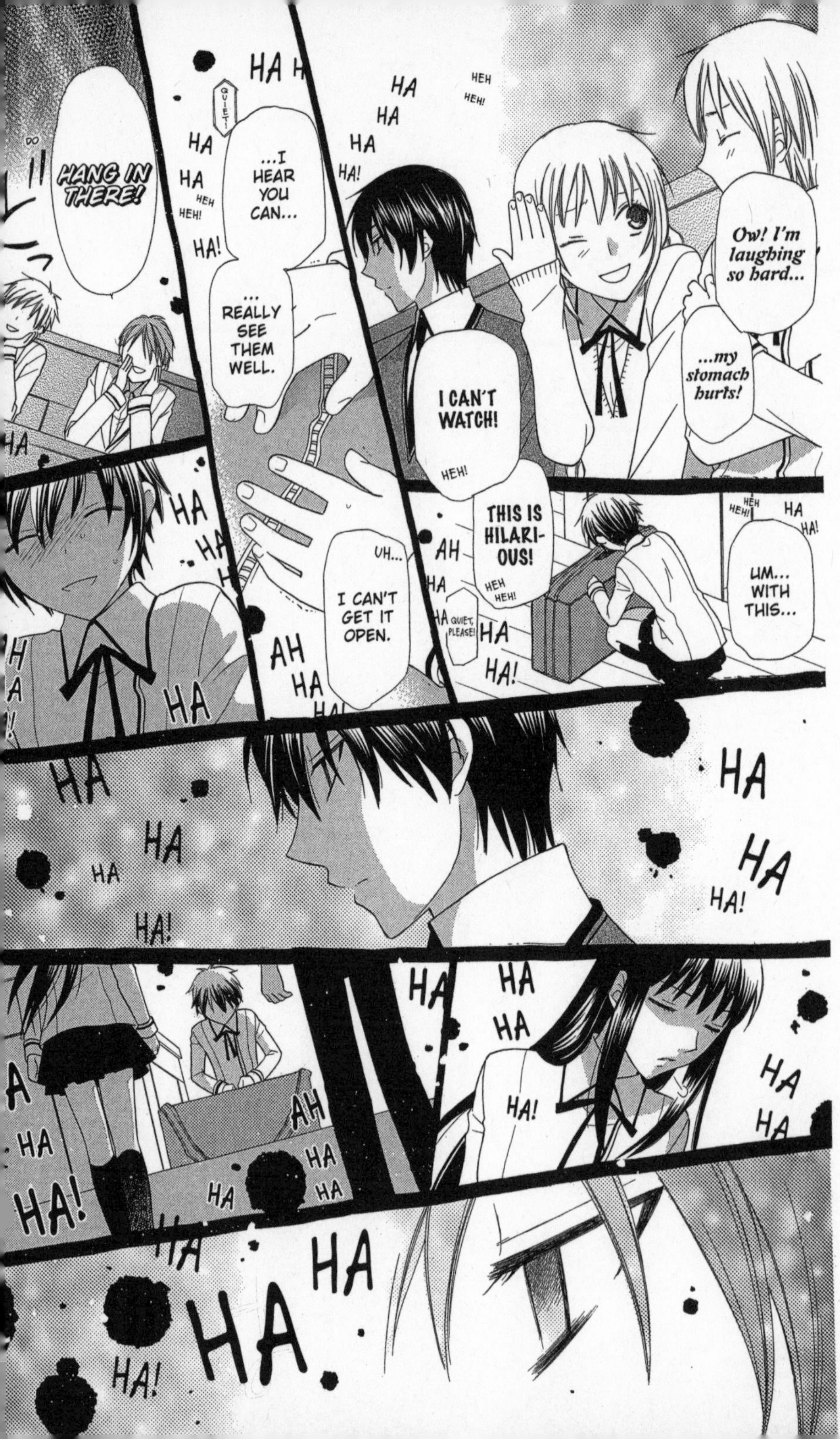

HEH HEH!
Ow! I'm laughing so hard...
...my stomach hurts!
HA HA HA HA!
I CAN'T WATCH!
HEH!
HA H
QUIET!
...I HEAR YOU CAN...
...REALLY SEE THEM WELL.
HA HA HEH HEH! HA!
DO
HANG IN THERE!
HA
HEH HEH!
HA HA!
UM... WITH THIS...
THIS IS HILARIOUS!
HEH HEH!
QUIET, PLEASE!
AH HA HA HA HA!
UH...
I CAN'T GET IT OPEN.
AH HA HA
HA HA
HA HA!
HA HA HA HA!
HA HA
HA HA HA HA
HA!
AH HA HA HA HA
A HA HA!
HA HA HA HA!

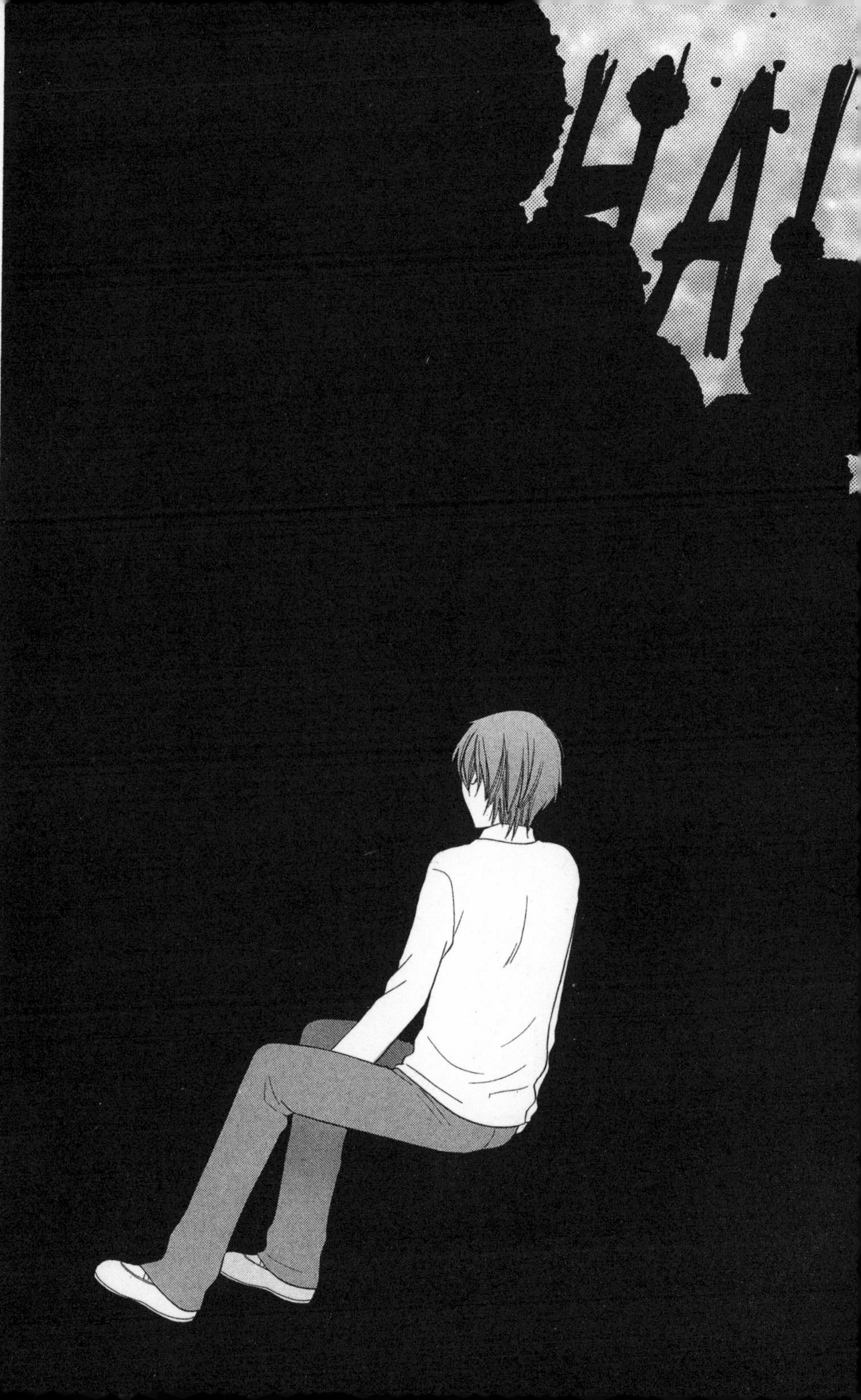
HA!

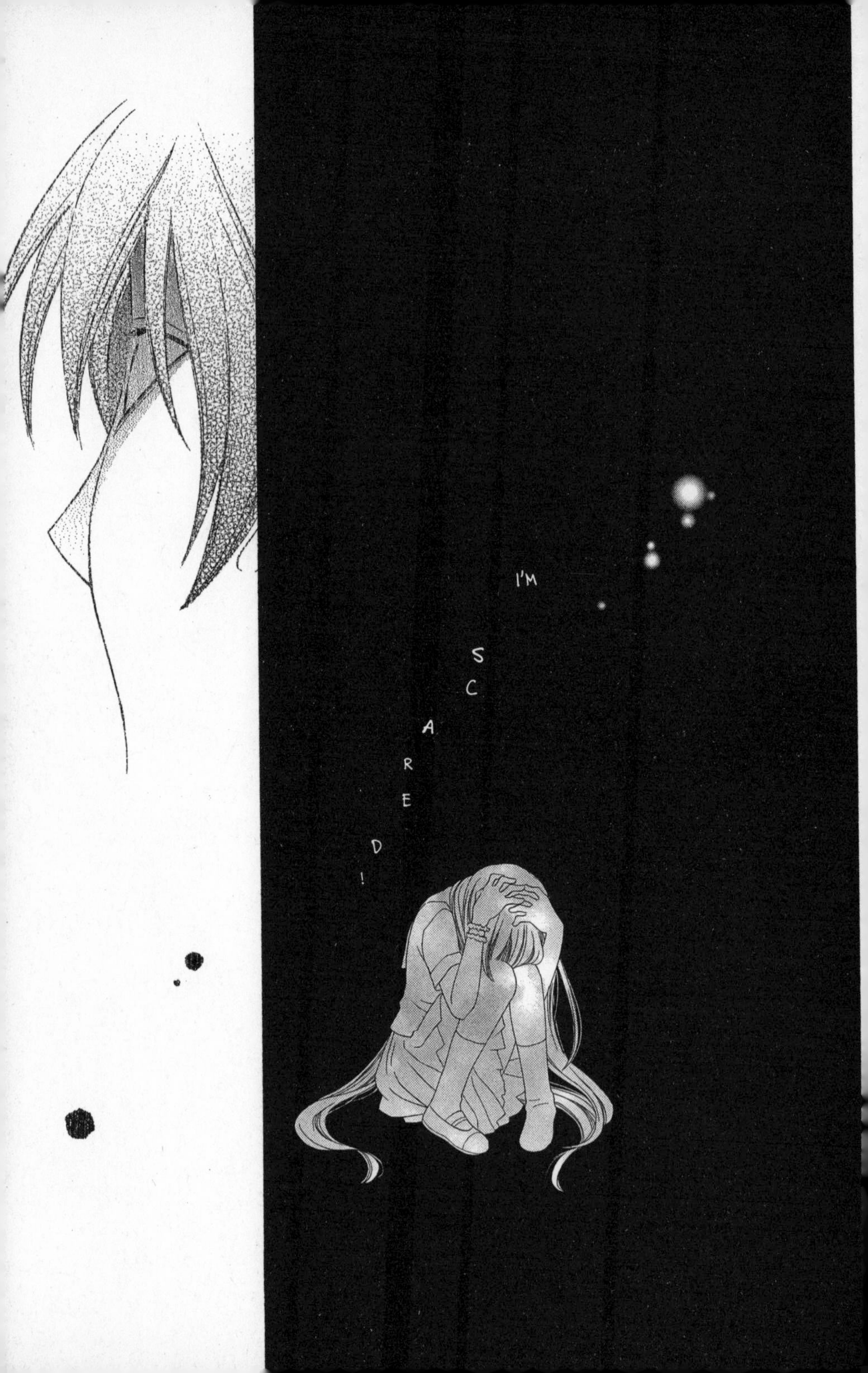
I'M SCARED!

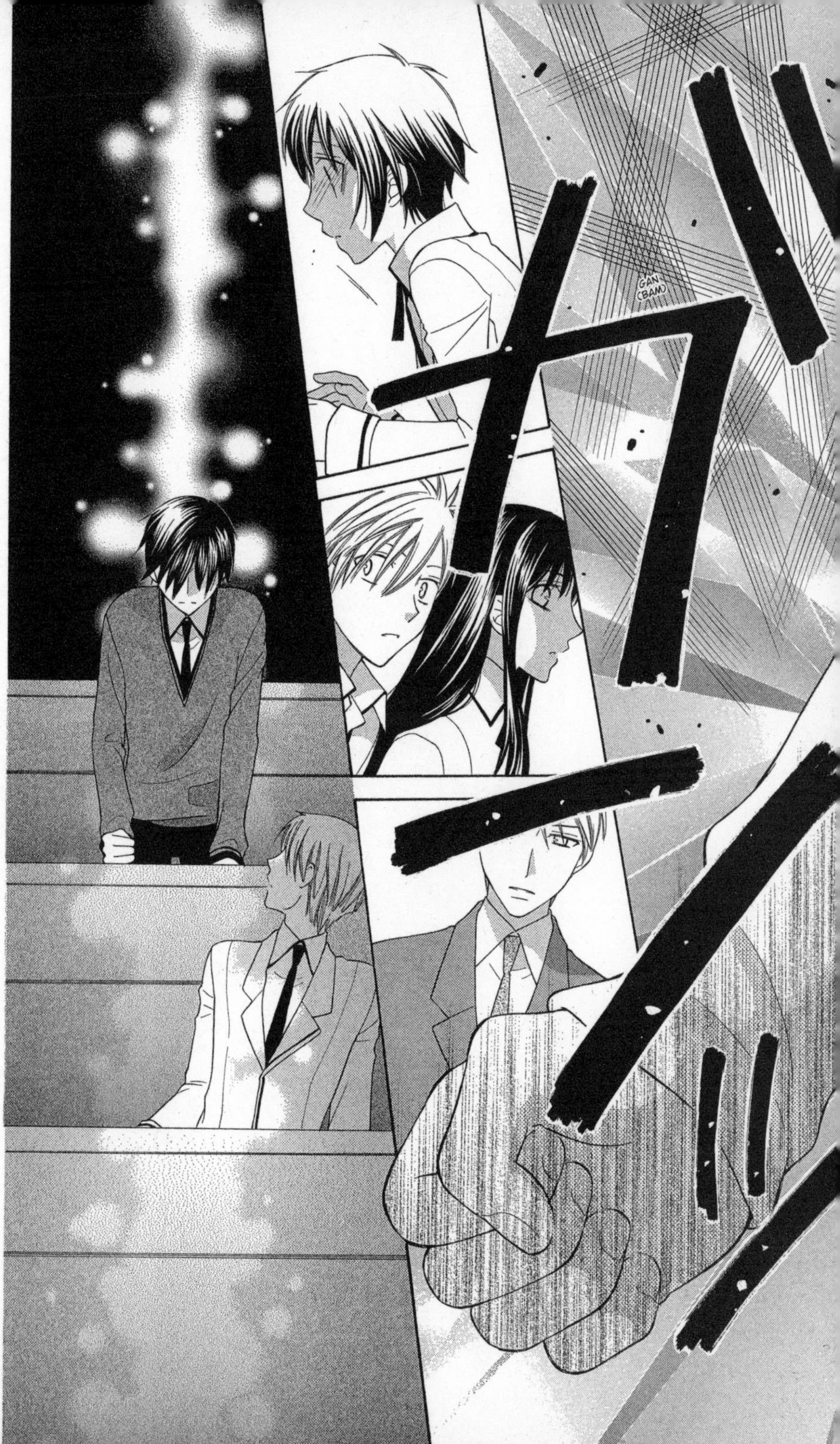
GAN
(BAM)

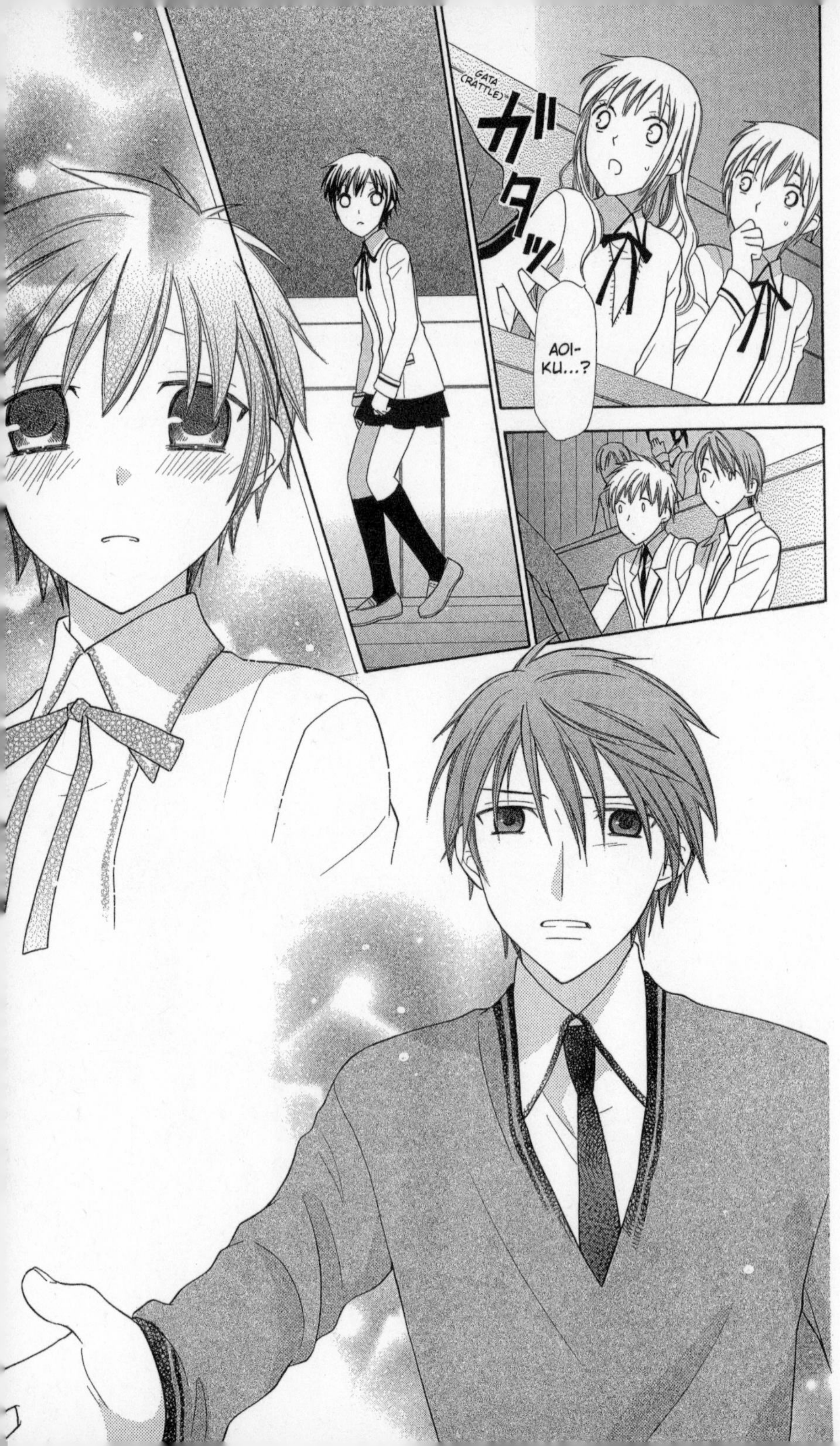
GATA (RATTLE)
ガタッ
AOI-KU...?

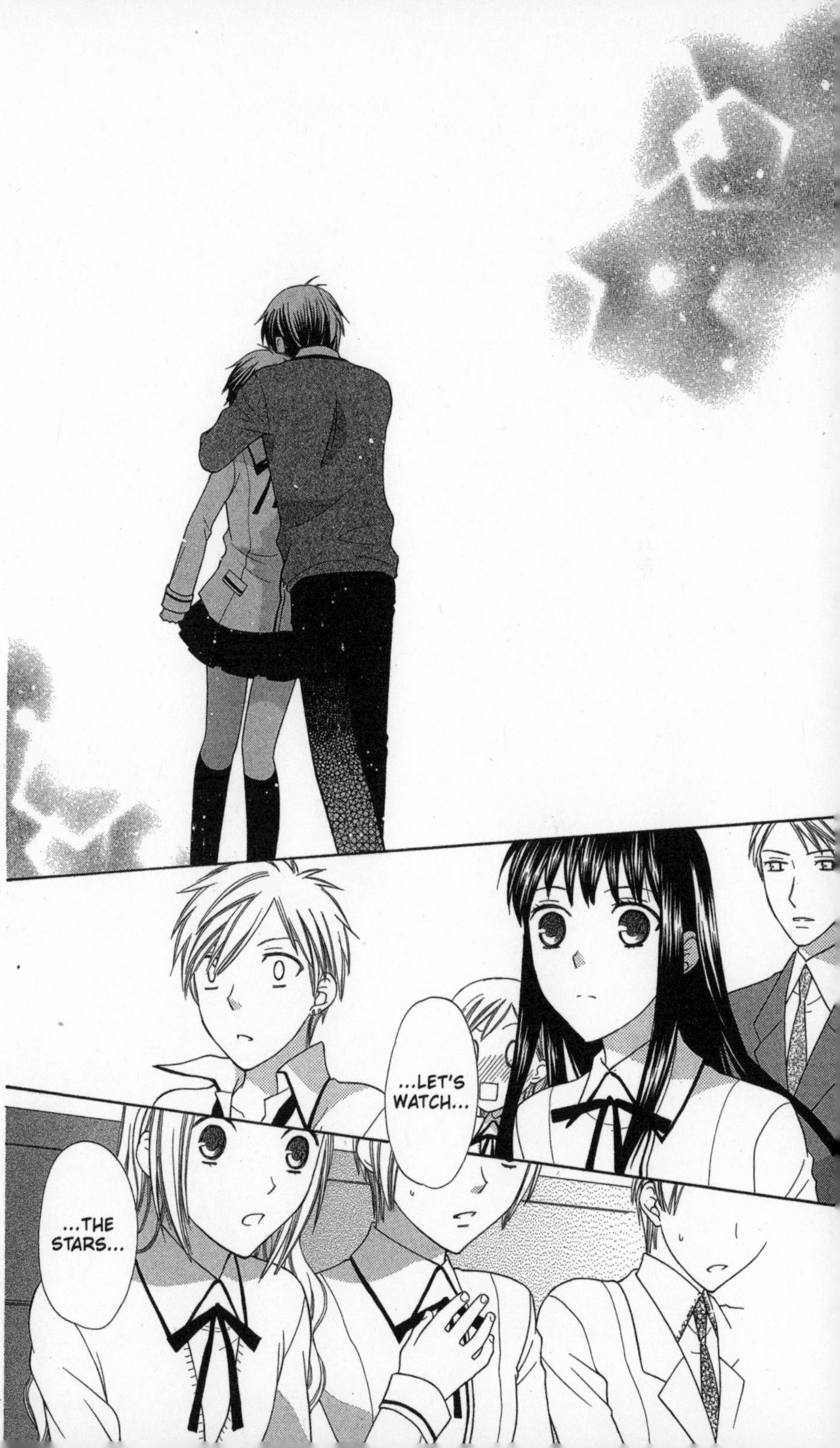
...LET'S WATCH...
...THE STARS...

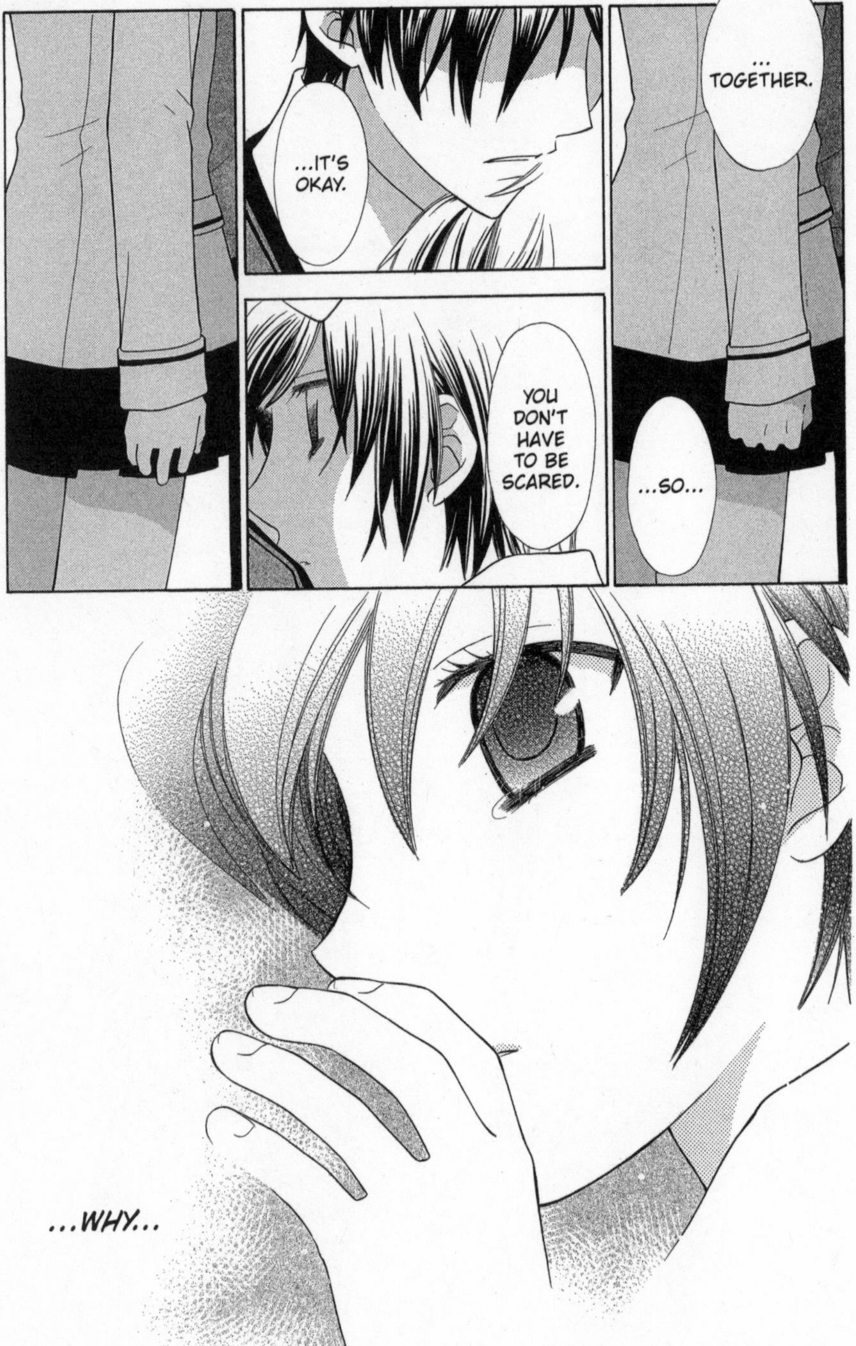
...TOGETHER.
...SO...
...IT'S OKAY.
YOU DON'T HAVE TO BE SCARED.
...WHY...

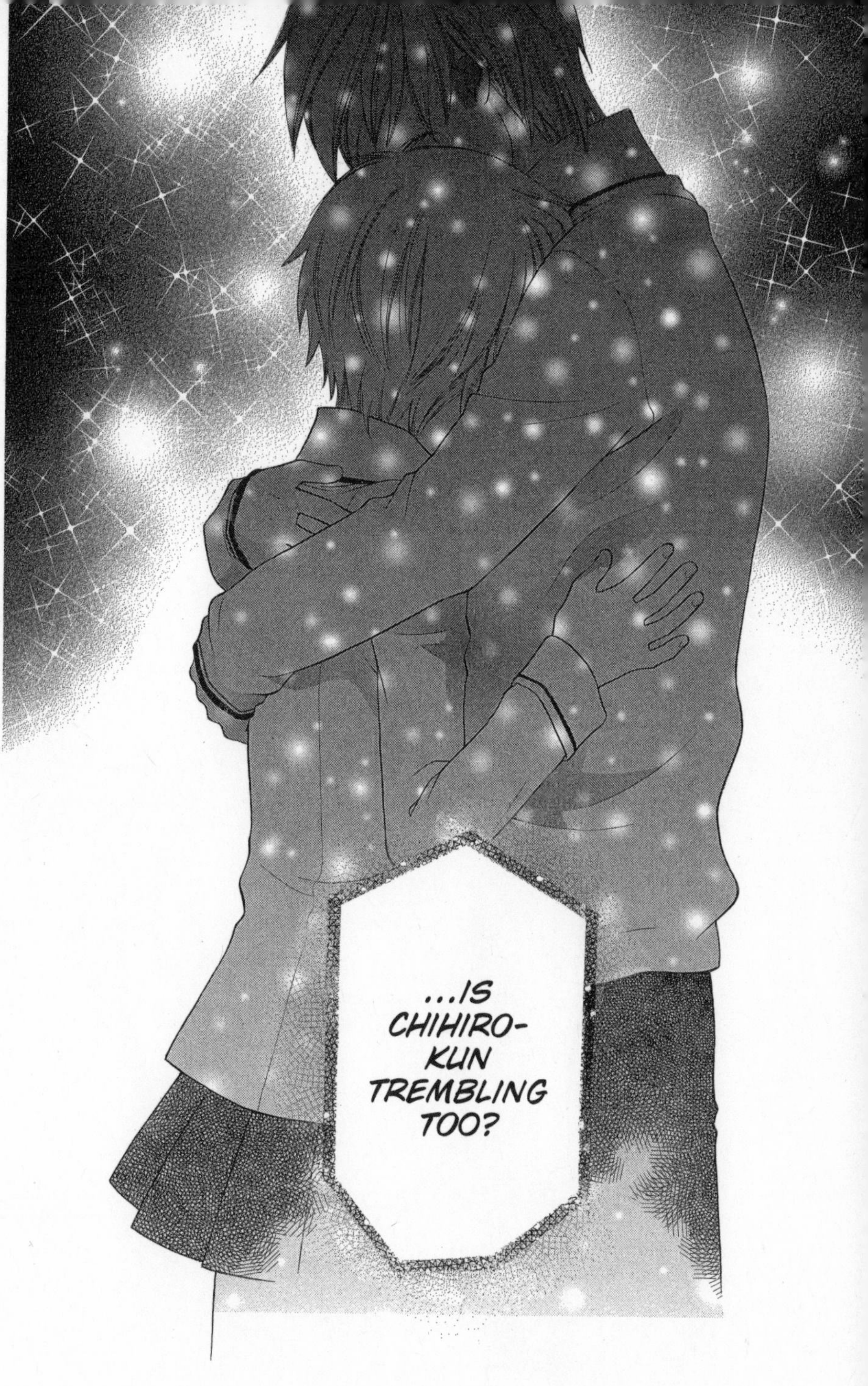
...IS CHIHIRO-KUN TREMBLING TOO?

※ONE EXAMPLE OF EXTENDED EYELASHES

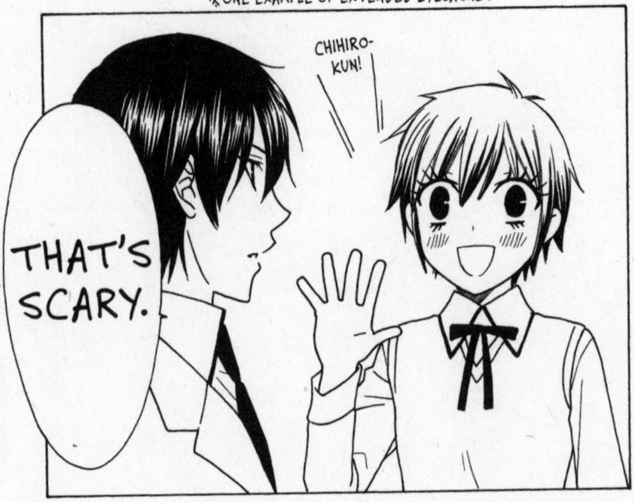
CHIHIRO-KUN!
THAT'S SCARY.

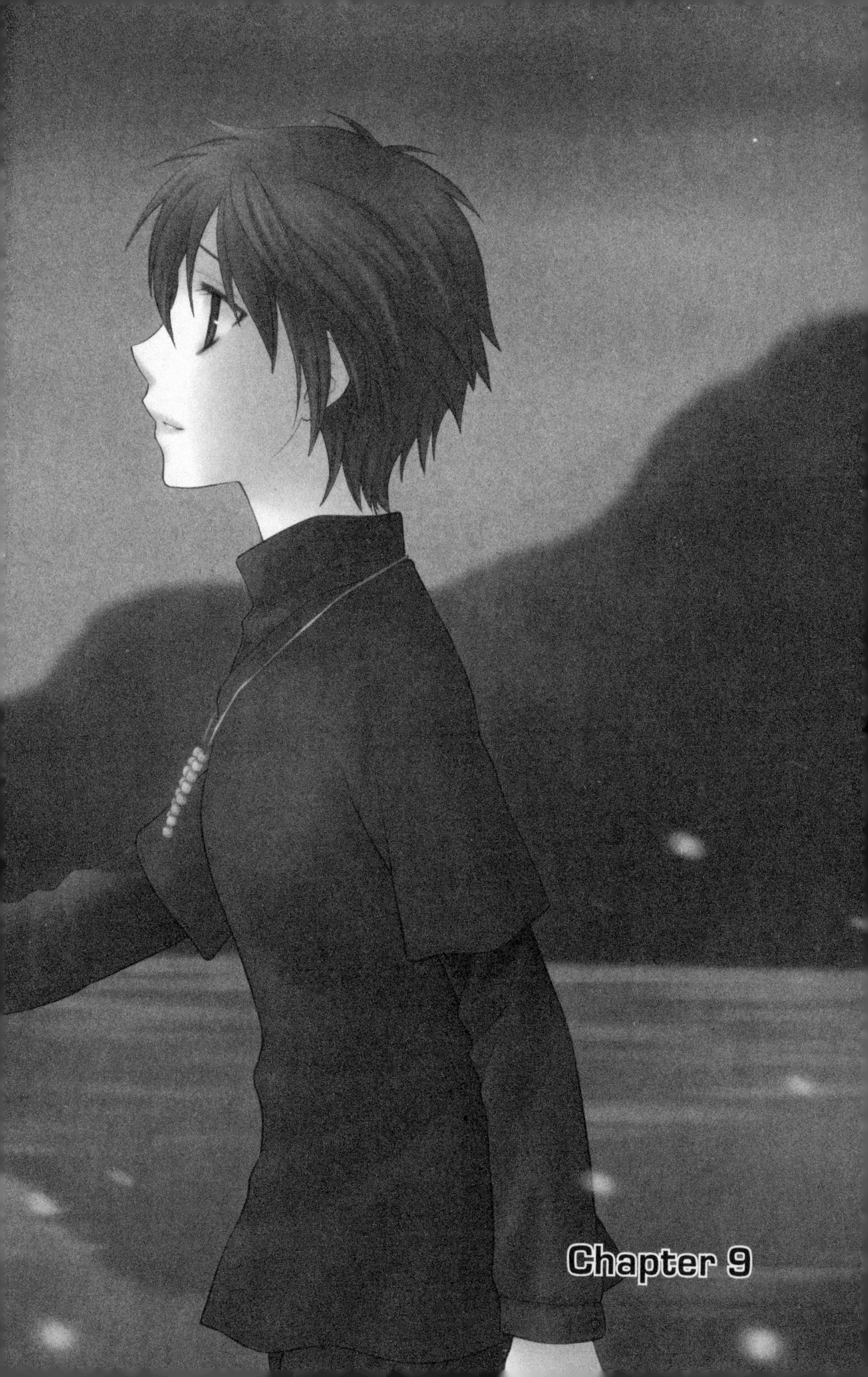
Chapter 9

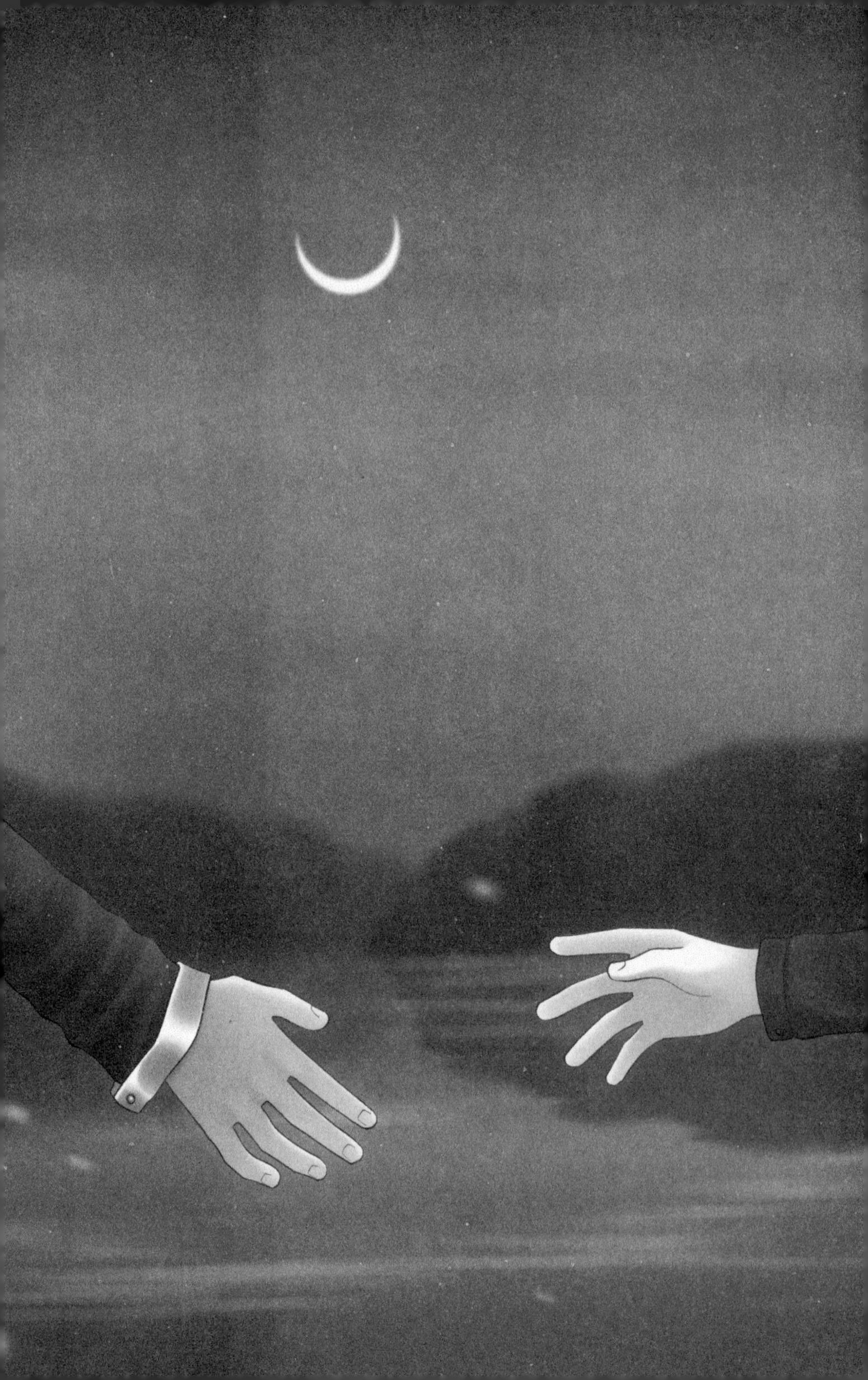

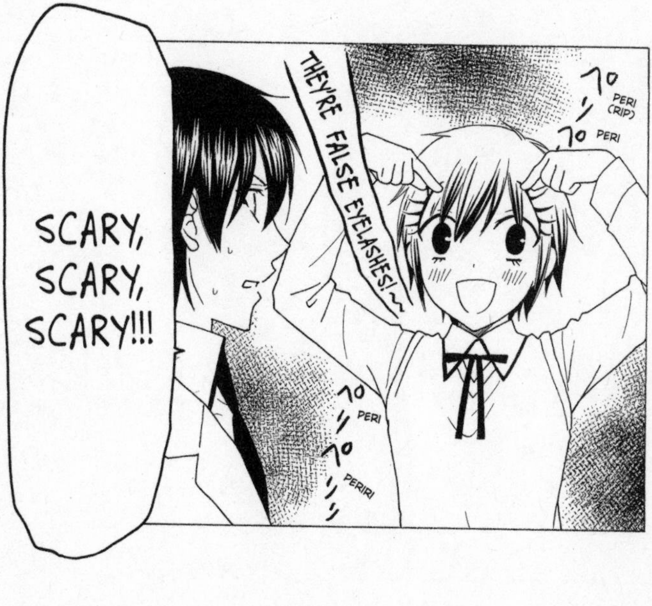
PERI (RIP)
PERI
THEY'RE FALSE EYELASHES!~
PERI
PERIRI
SCARY, SCARY, SCARY!!!

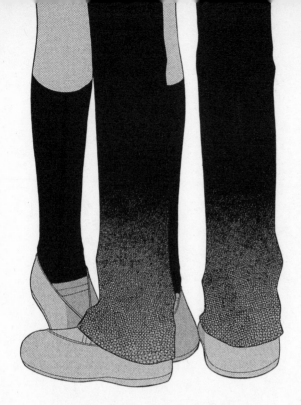

LET'S
WATCH...

...THE
STARS...

...TOGETHER.

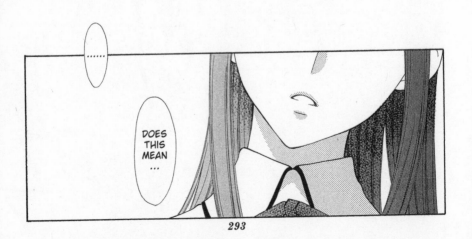

......

DOES
THIS
MEAN
...

293

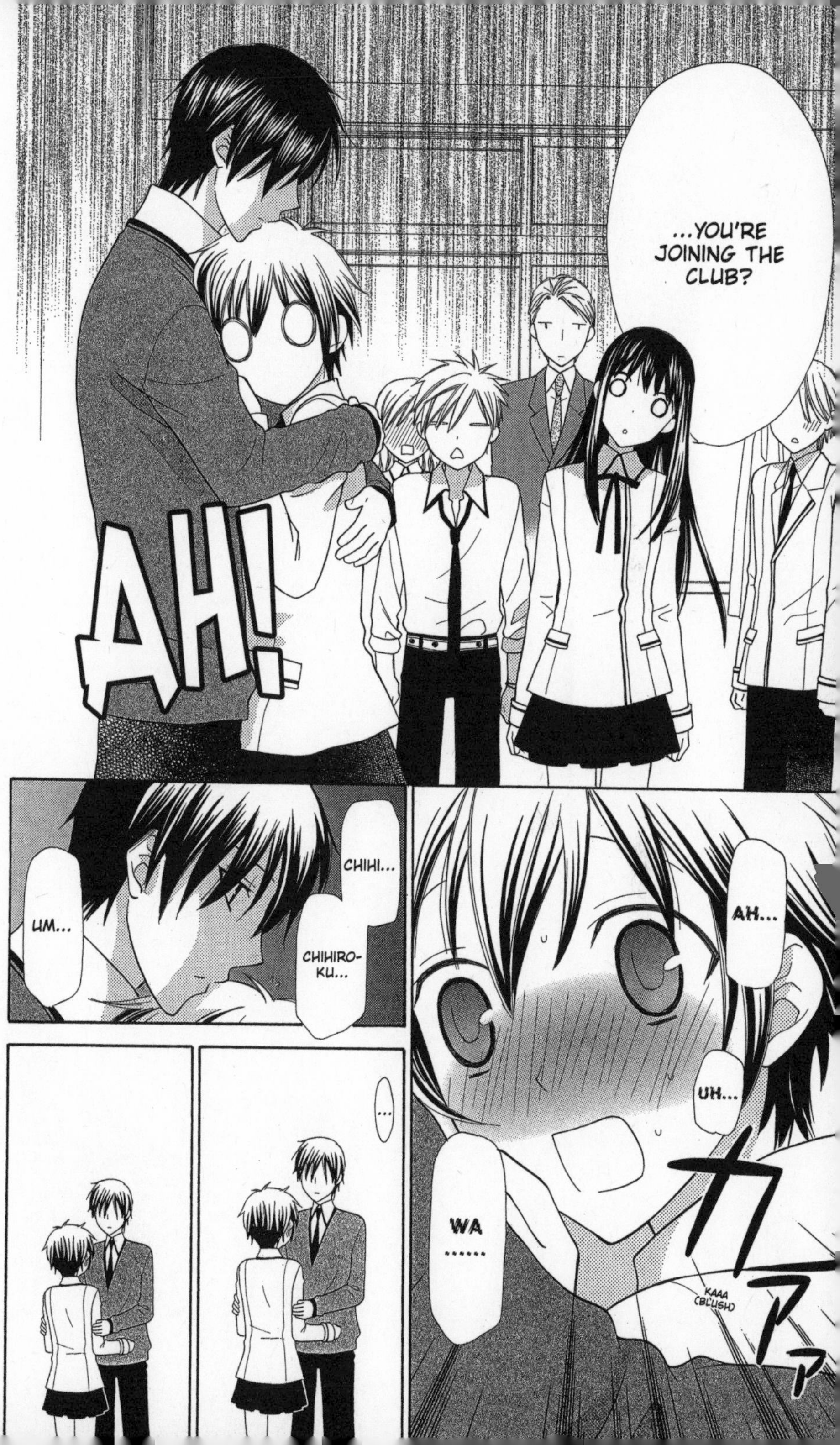
...YOU'RE JOINING THE CLUB?
AH!
AH...
UH...
WA ......
カァァ
KAAA (BLUSH)
CHIHI...
CHIHIRO-KU...
UM...
...

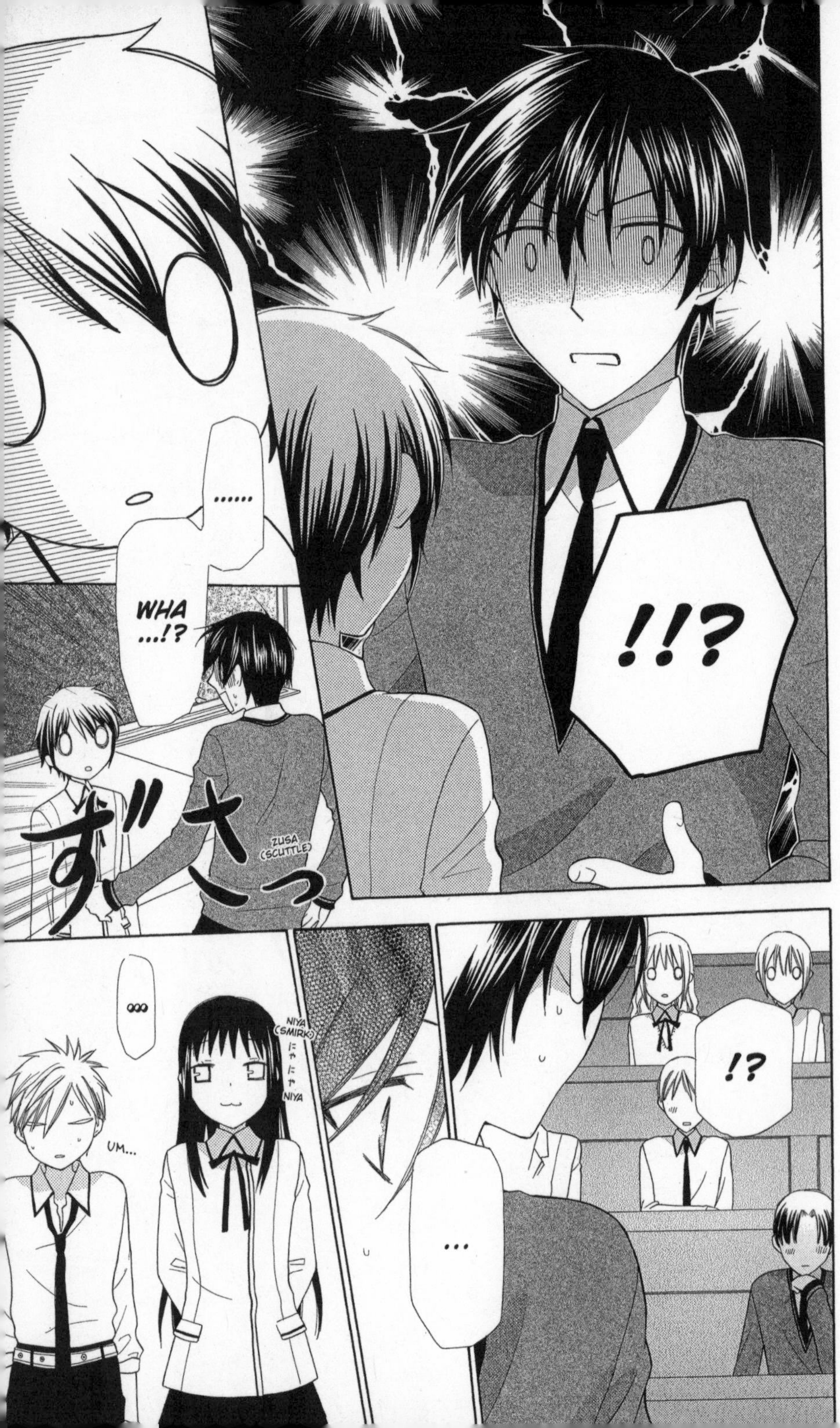
!!?
......
WHA ...!?
ずさっ
ZUSA (SCUTTLE)
!?
...
...
NIYA (SMIRK)
にやにや
NIYA
UM...

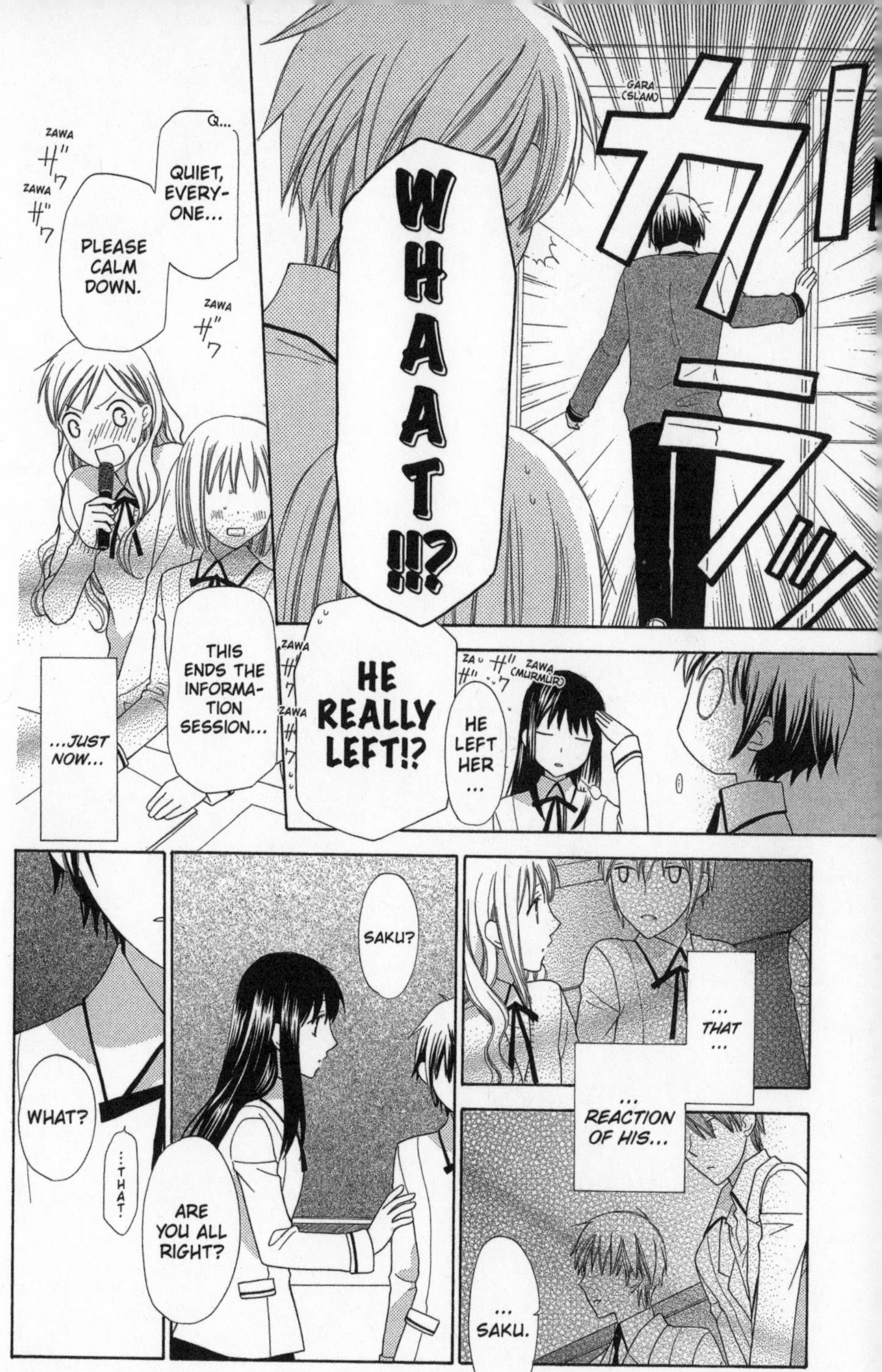
GARA (SLAM)
WHAAT!!?
ZAWA
ZAWA
Q...
QUIET, EVERYONE...
PLEASE CALM DOWN.
ZAWA
THIS ENDS THE INFORMATION SESSION...
ZAWA (MURMUR)
HE LEFT HER...
HE REALLY LEFT!!?
ZAWA
ZAWA
...JUST NOW...
...THAT...
...REACTION OF HIS...
...SAKU.
SAKU?
ARE YOU ALL RIGHT?
WHAT?
...THAT...

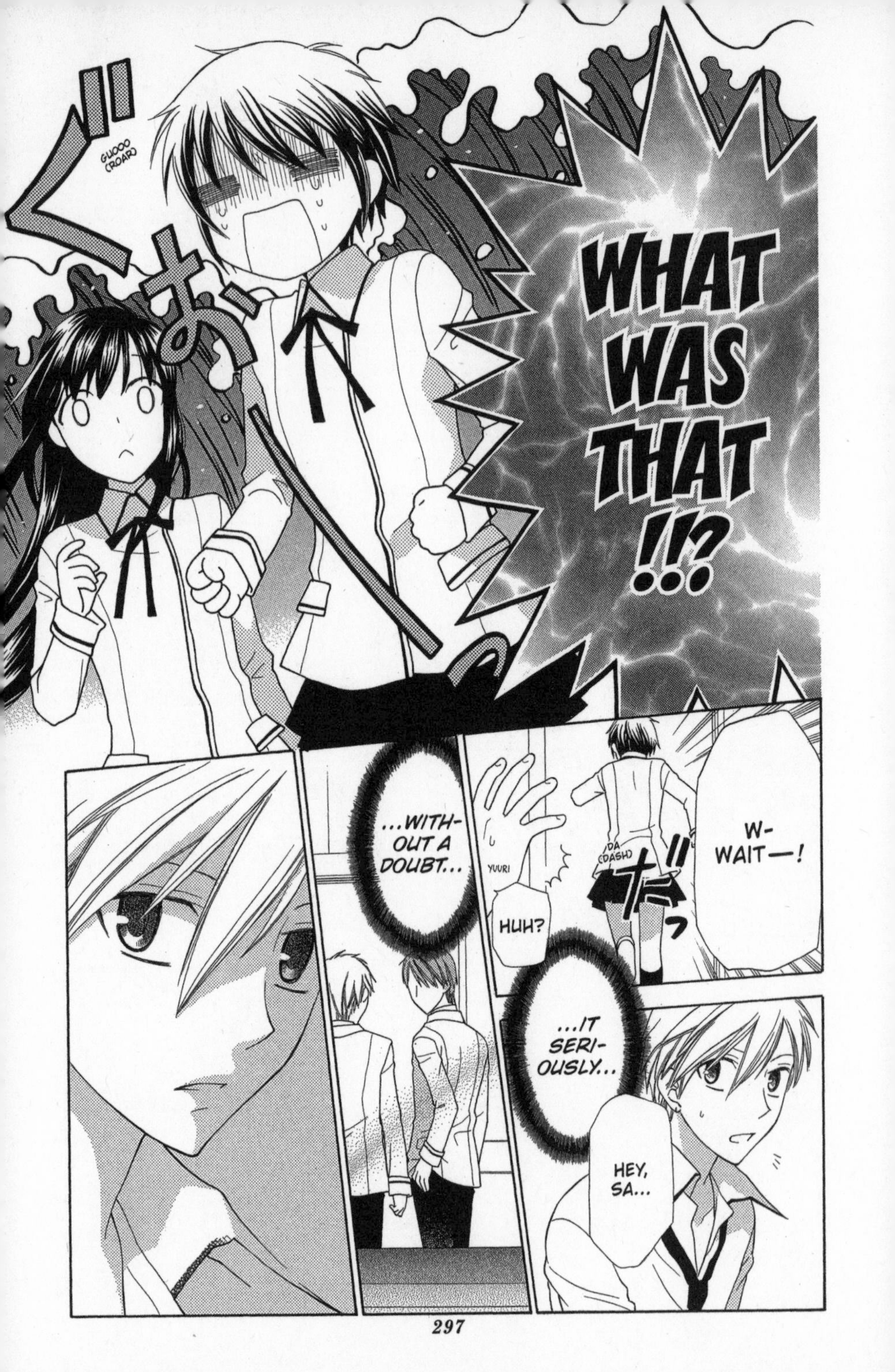
WHAT WAS THAT !!?
GUOOO (ROAR)
W-WAIT—!
DA (DASH)
YUURI
HUH?
...IT SERI-OUSLY...
HEY, SA...
...WITH-OUT A DOUBT...

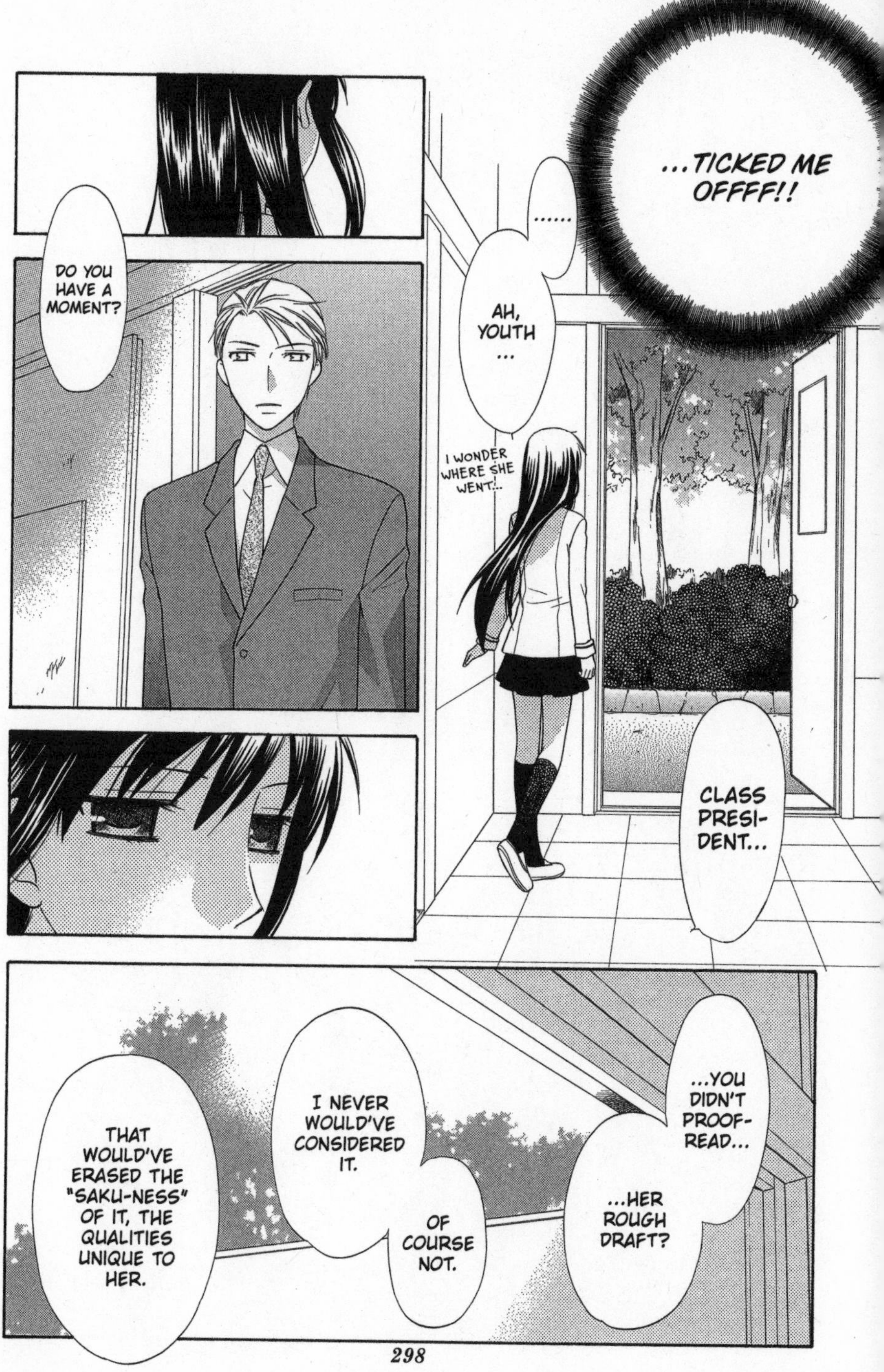
...TICKED ME OFFFF!!
......
AH, YOUTH ...
I WONDER WHERE SHE WENT!..
CLASS PRESI-DENT...
DO YOU HAVE A MOMENT?
...YOU DIDN'T PROOF-READ...
...HER ROUGH DRAFT?
OF COURSE NOT.
I NEVER WOULD'VE CONSIDERED IT.
THAT WOULD'VE ERASED THE "SAKU-NESS" OF IT, THE QUALITIES UNIQUE TO HER.

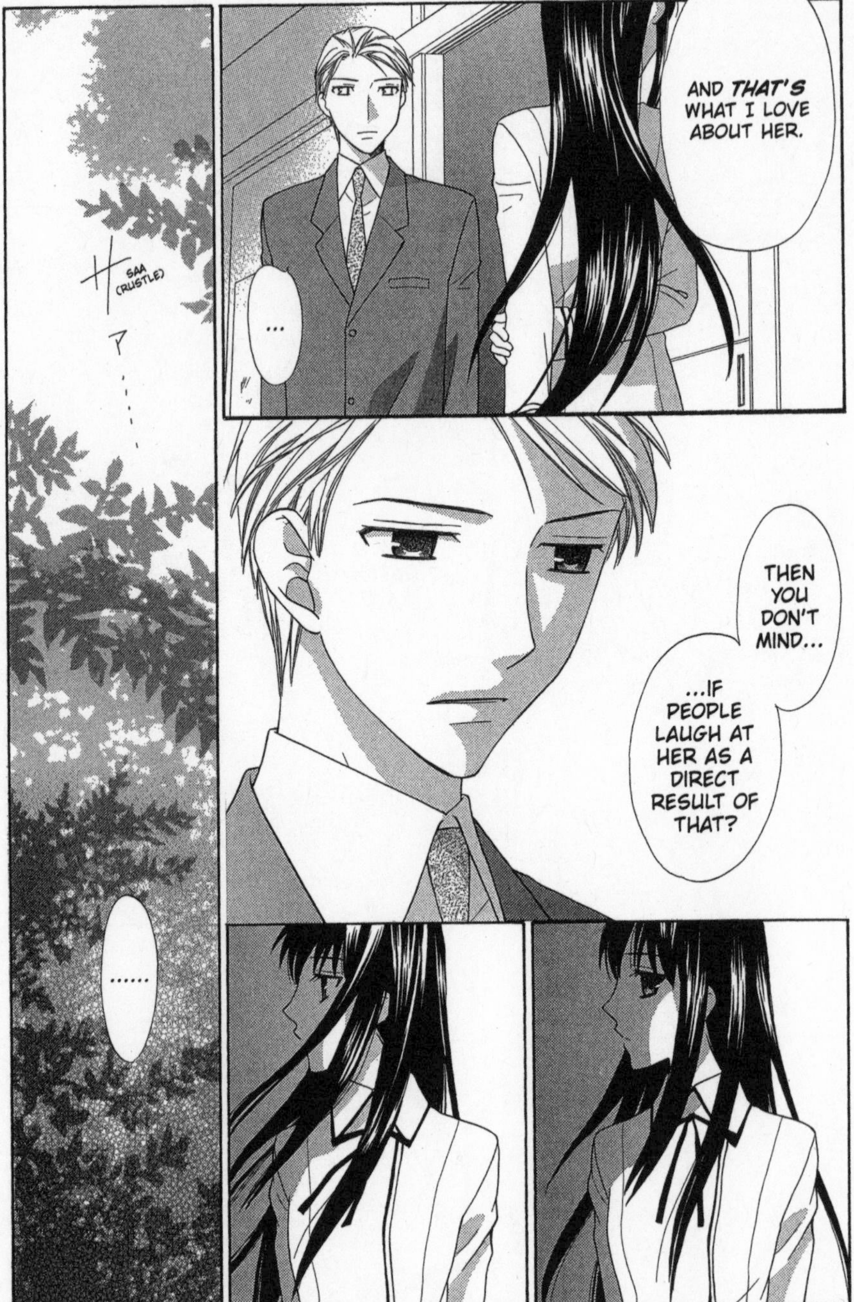
AND *THAT'S* WHAT I LOVE ABOUT HER.
...
THEN YOU DON'T MIND...
...IF PEOPLE LAUGH AT HER AS A DIRECT RESULT OF THAT?
SAA (RUSTLE)
....

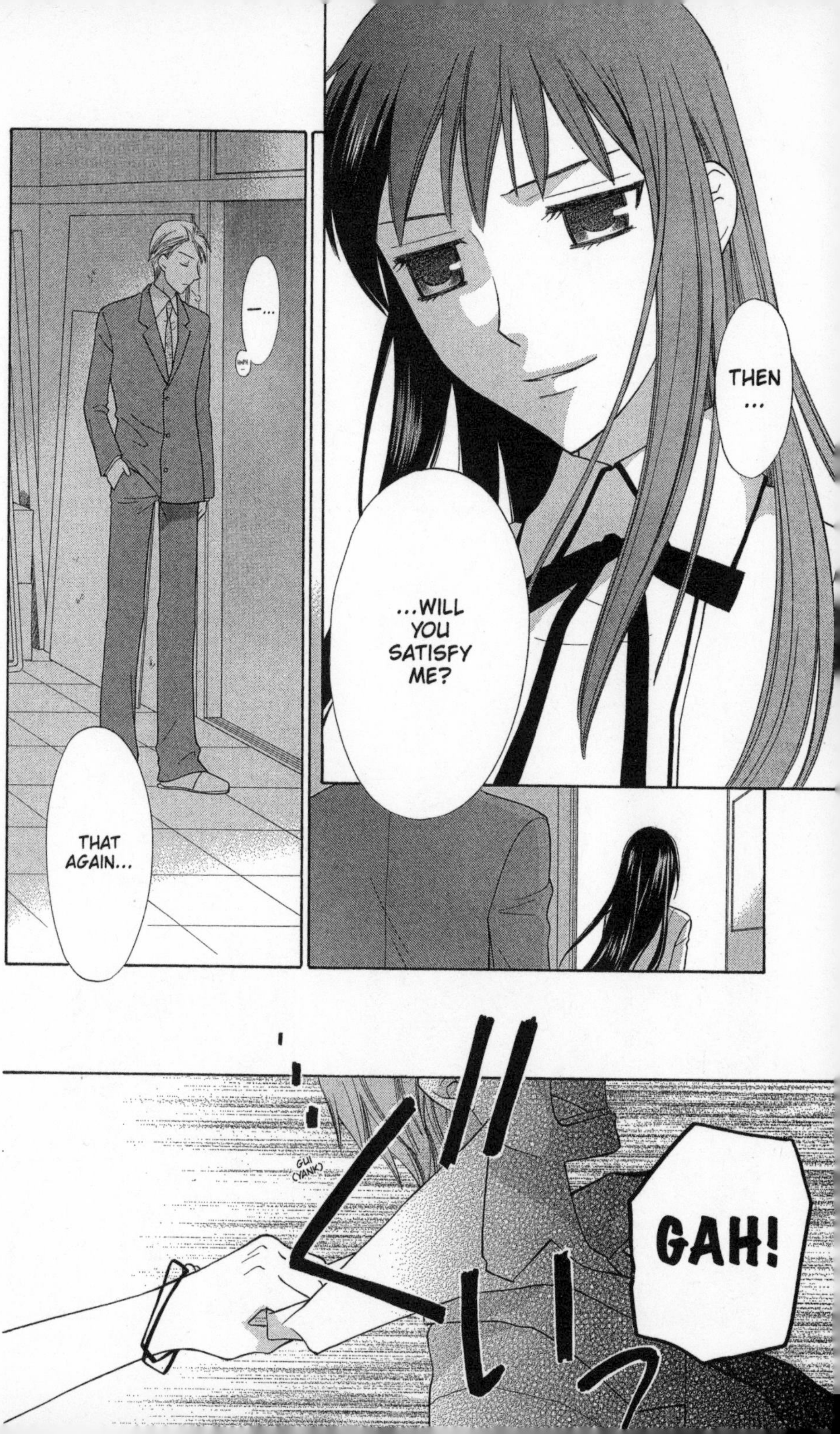
THEN...
...WILL YOU SATISFY ME?
—...
HMPH...
THAT AGAIN...
GUI (YANK)
GAH!

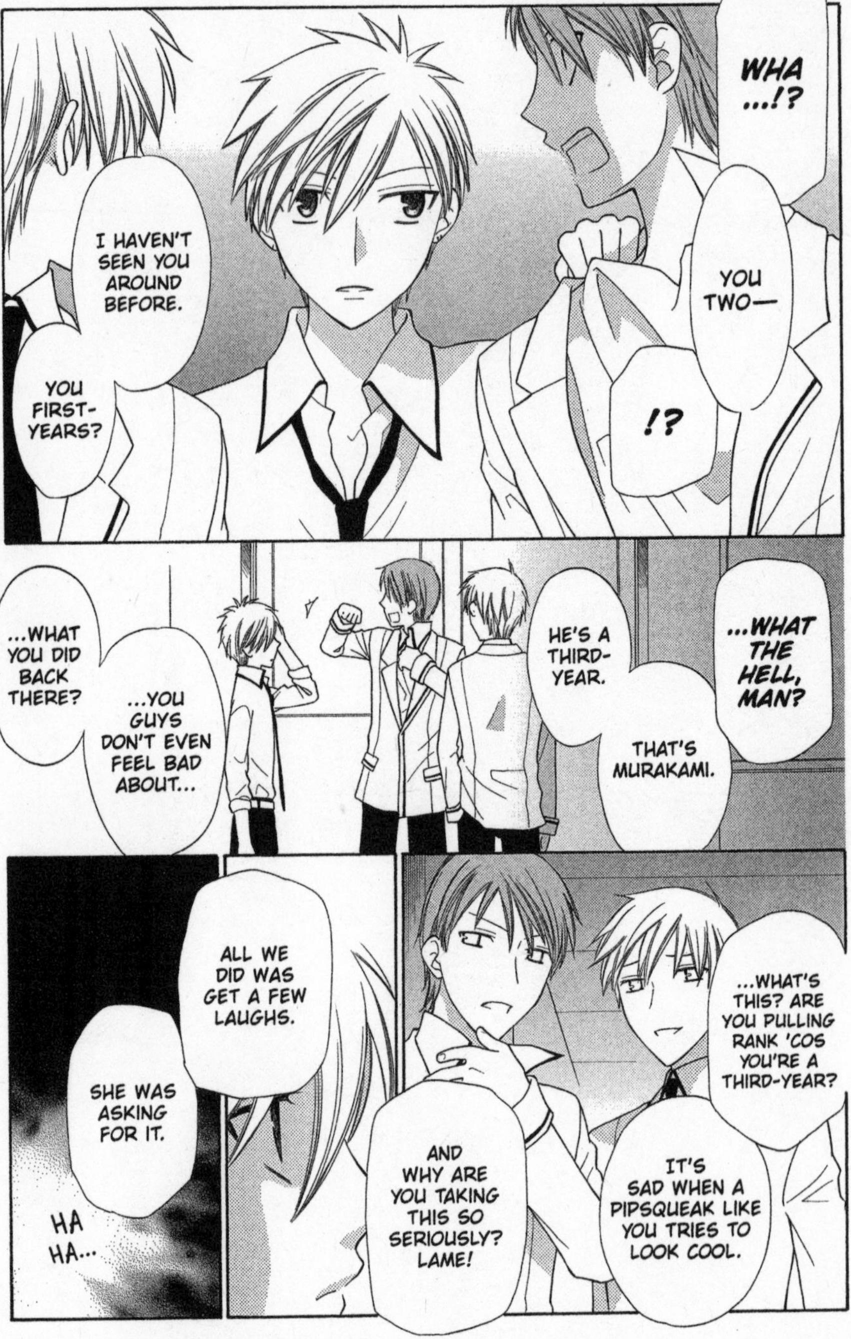
WHA ...!?
YOU TWO—
!?
I HAVEN'T SEEN YOU AROUND BEFORE.
YOU FIRST-YEARS?
...WHAT THE HELL, MAN?
HE'S A THIRD-YEAR.
THAT'S MURAKAMI.
...YOU GUYS DON'T EVEN FEEL BAD ABOUT...
...WHAT YOU DID BACK THERE?
...WHAT'S THIS? ARE YOU PULLING RANK 'COS YOU'RE A THIRD-YEAR?
IT'S SAD WHEN A PIPSQUEAK LIKE YOU TRIES TO LOOK COOL.
AND WHY ARE YOU TAKING THIS SO SERIOUSLY? LAME!
ALL WE DID WAS GET A FEW LAUGHS.
SHE WAS ASKING FOR IT.
HA HA...

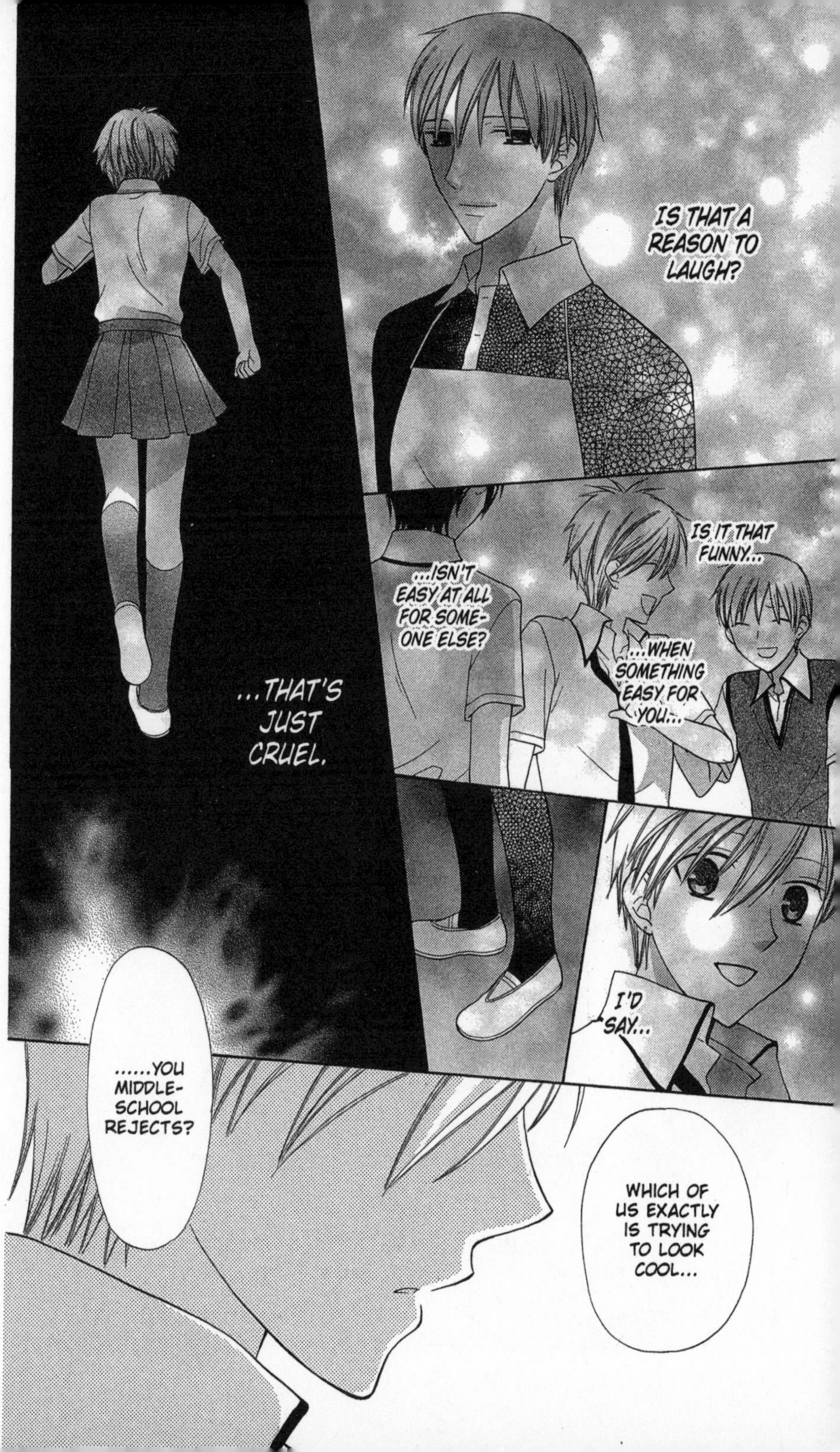
IS THAT A REASON TO LAUGH?
IS IT THAT FUNNY...
...WHEN SOMETHING EASY FOR YOU...
...ISN'T EASY AT ALL FOR SOME-ONE ELSE?
I'D SAY...
...THAT'S JUST CRUEL.
WHICH OF US EXACTLY IS TRYING TO LOOK COOL...
......YOU MIDDLE-SCHOOL REJECTS?

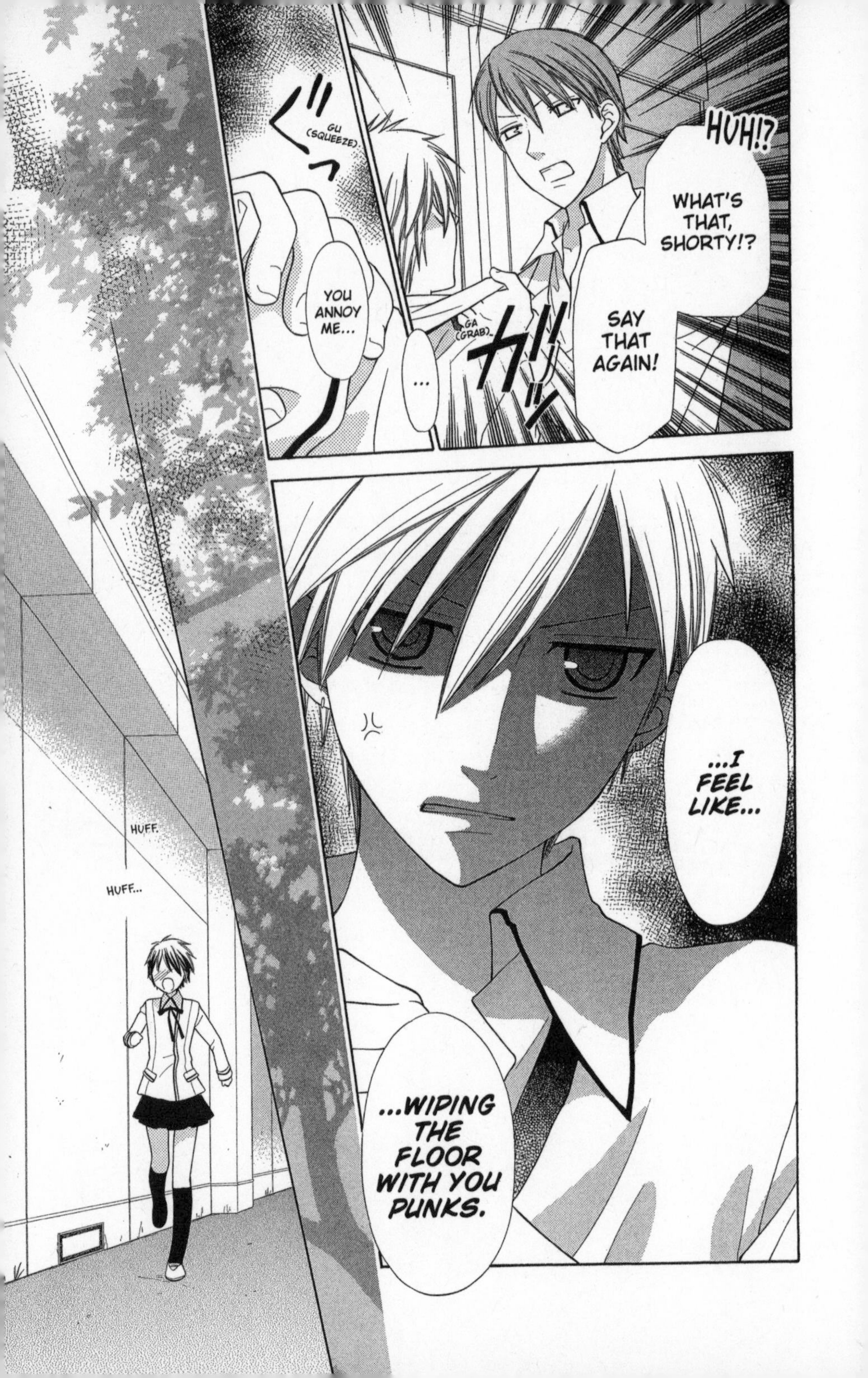
HUH!?
WHAT'S THAT, SHORTY!?
SAY THAT AGAIN!
GA (GRAB)
...
YOU ANNOY ME...
GU (SQUEEZE)
...I FEEL LIKE...
...WIPING THE FLOOR WITH YOU PUNKS.
HUFF.
HUFF...

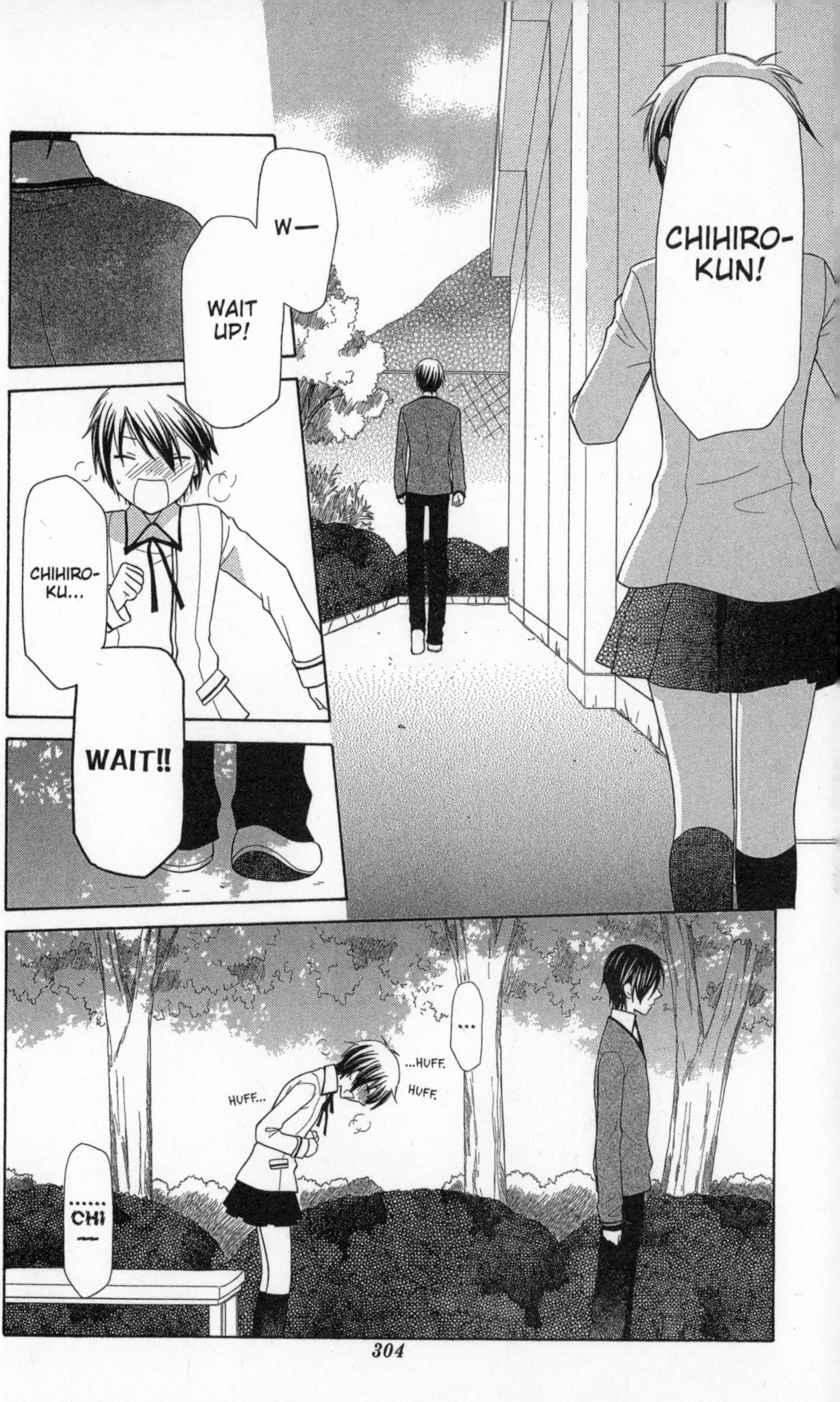
CHIHIRO-KUN!
W— WAIT UP!
CHIHIRO-KU...
WAIT!!
...
...HUFF.
HUFF.
HUFF...
......CHI—

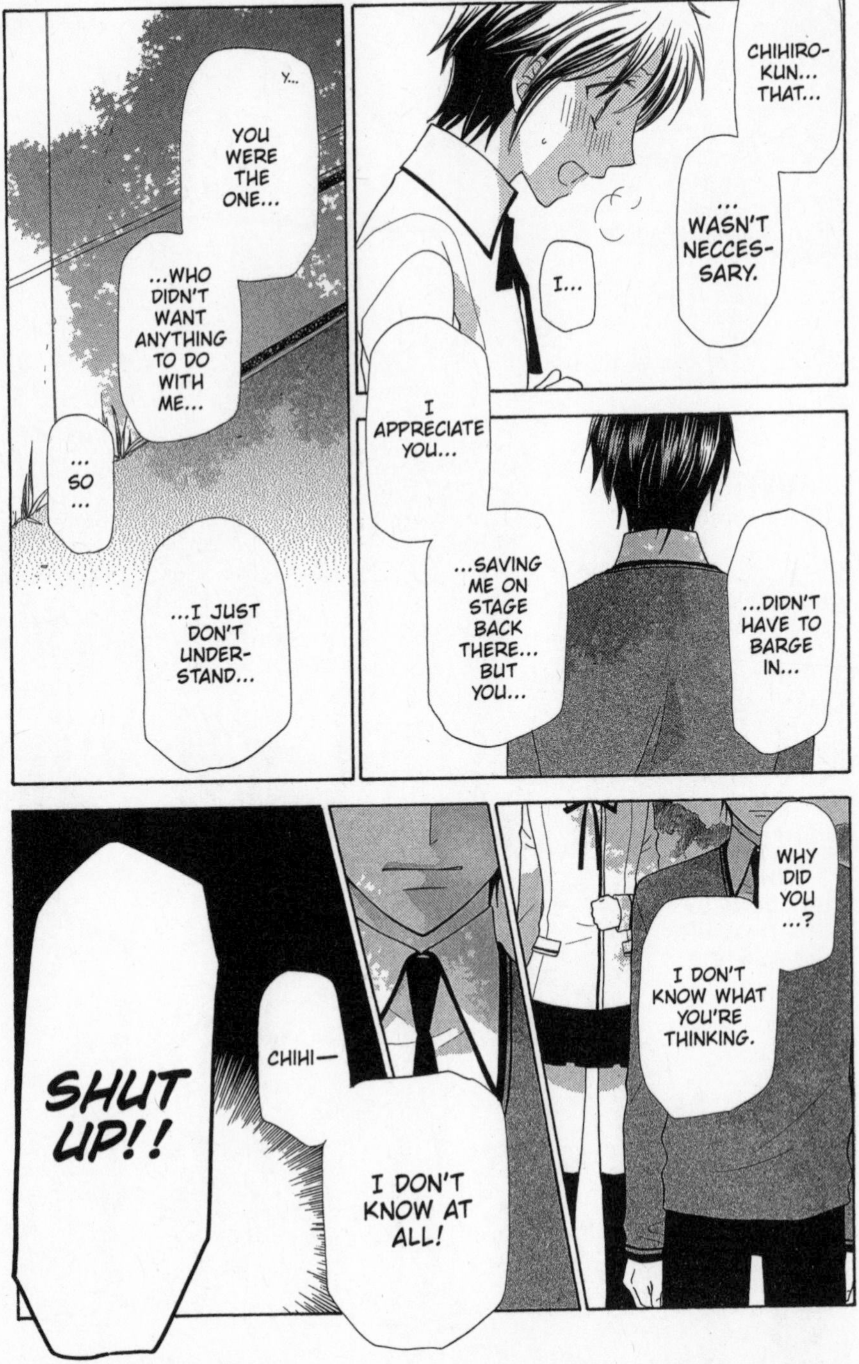
CHIHIRO-KUN... THAT...
...WASN'T NECCES-SARY.
I...
I APPRECIATE YOU...
...SAVING ME ON STAGE BACK THERE... BUT YOU...
...DIDN'T HAVE TO BARGE IN...
Y...
YOU WERE THE ONE...
...WHO DIDN'T WANT ANYTHING TO DO WITH ME...
...SO...
...I JUST DON'T UNDER-STAND...
WHY DID YOU...?
I DON'T KNOW WHAT YOU'RE THINKING.
CHIHI—
I DON'T KNOW AT ALL!
SHUT UP!!

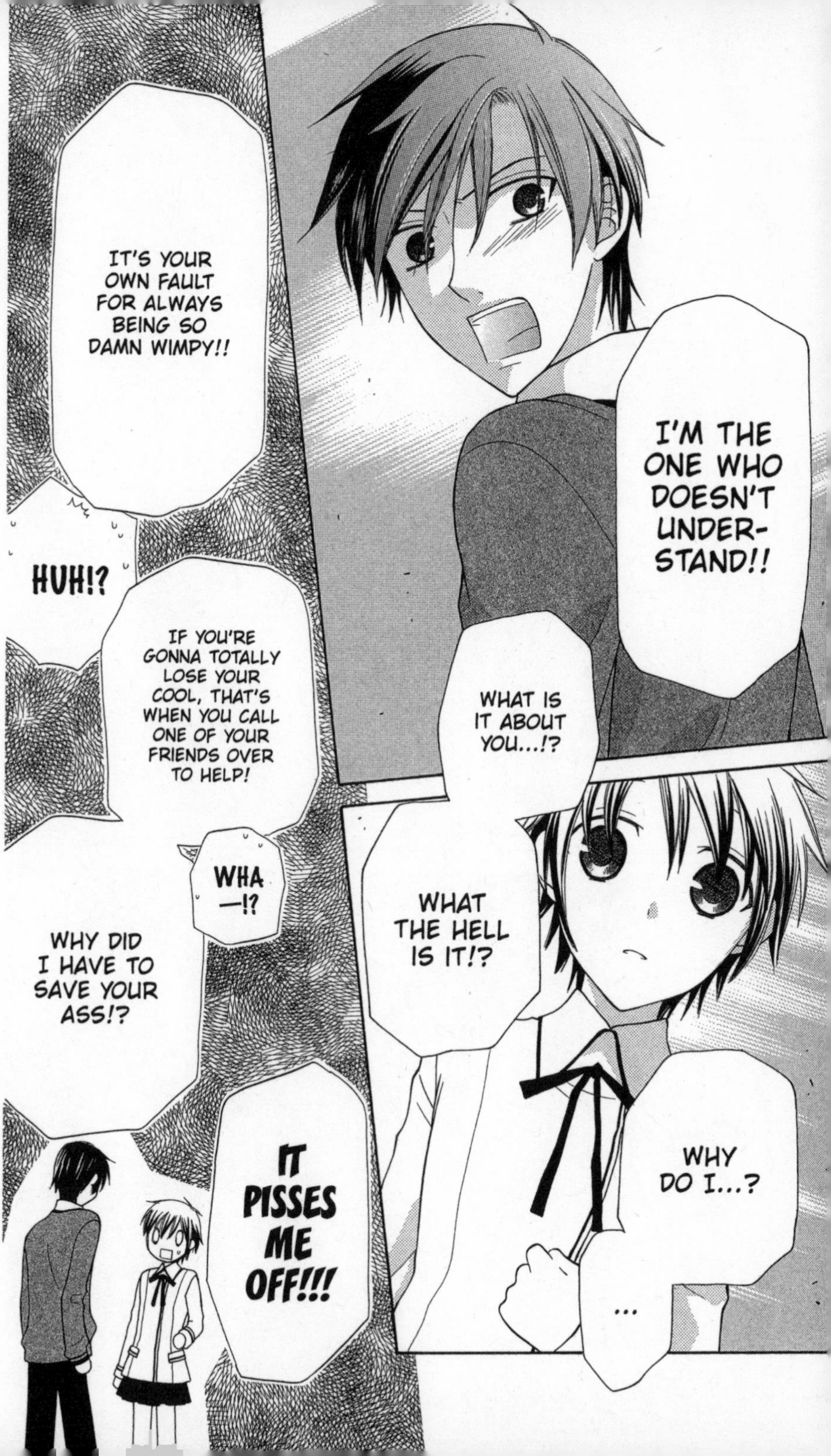

I'M THE ONE WHO DOESN'T UNDERSTAND!!
WHAT IS IT ABOUT YOU...!?
WHAT THE HELL IS IT!?
WHY DO I...?
...
IT'S YOUR OWN FAULT FOR ALWAYS BEING SO DAMN WIMPY!!
HUH!?
IF YOU'RE GONNA TOTALLY LOSE YOUR COOL, THAT'S WHEN YOU CALL ONE OF YOUR FRIENDS OVER TO HELP!
WHA—!?
WHY DID I HAVE TO SAVE YOUR ASS!?
IT PISSES ME OFF!!!

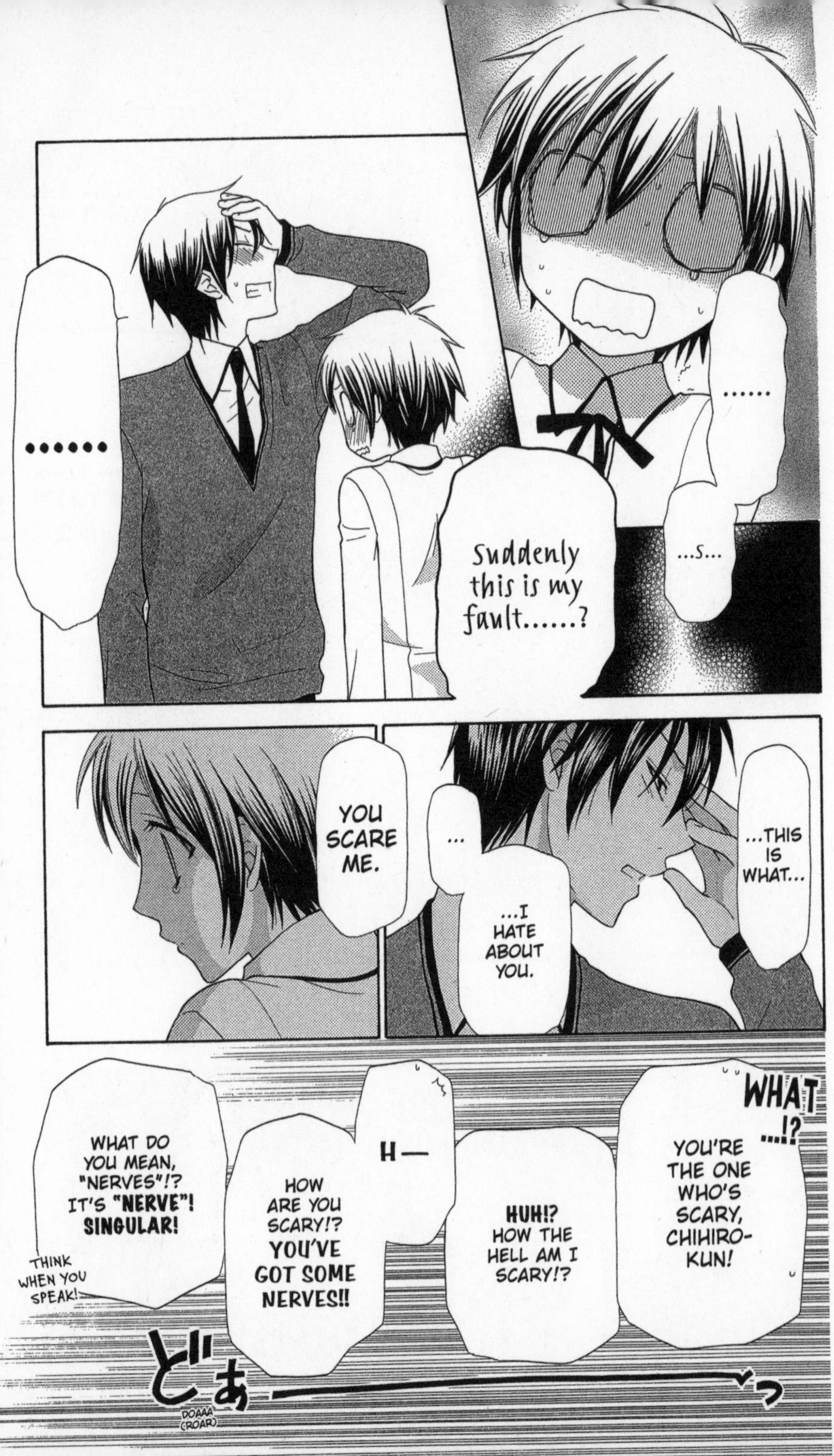
......
...S...
Suddenly this is my fault......?
......
...THIS IS WHAT...
...
...I HATE ABOUT YOU.
YOU SCARE ME.
WHAT ...!?
YOU'RE THE ONE WHO'S SCARY, CHIHIRO-KUN!
HUH!? HOW THE HELL AM I SCARY!?
H—
HOW ARE YOU SCARY!? YOU'VE GOT SOME NERVES!!
WHAT DO YOU MEAN, "NERVES"!? IT'S "NERVE"! SINGULAR!
THINK WHEN YOU SPEAK!
どあ
DOAAA (ROAR)

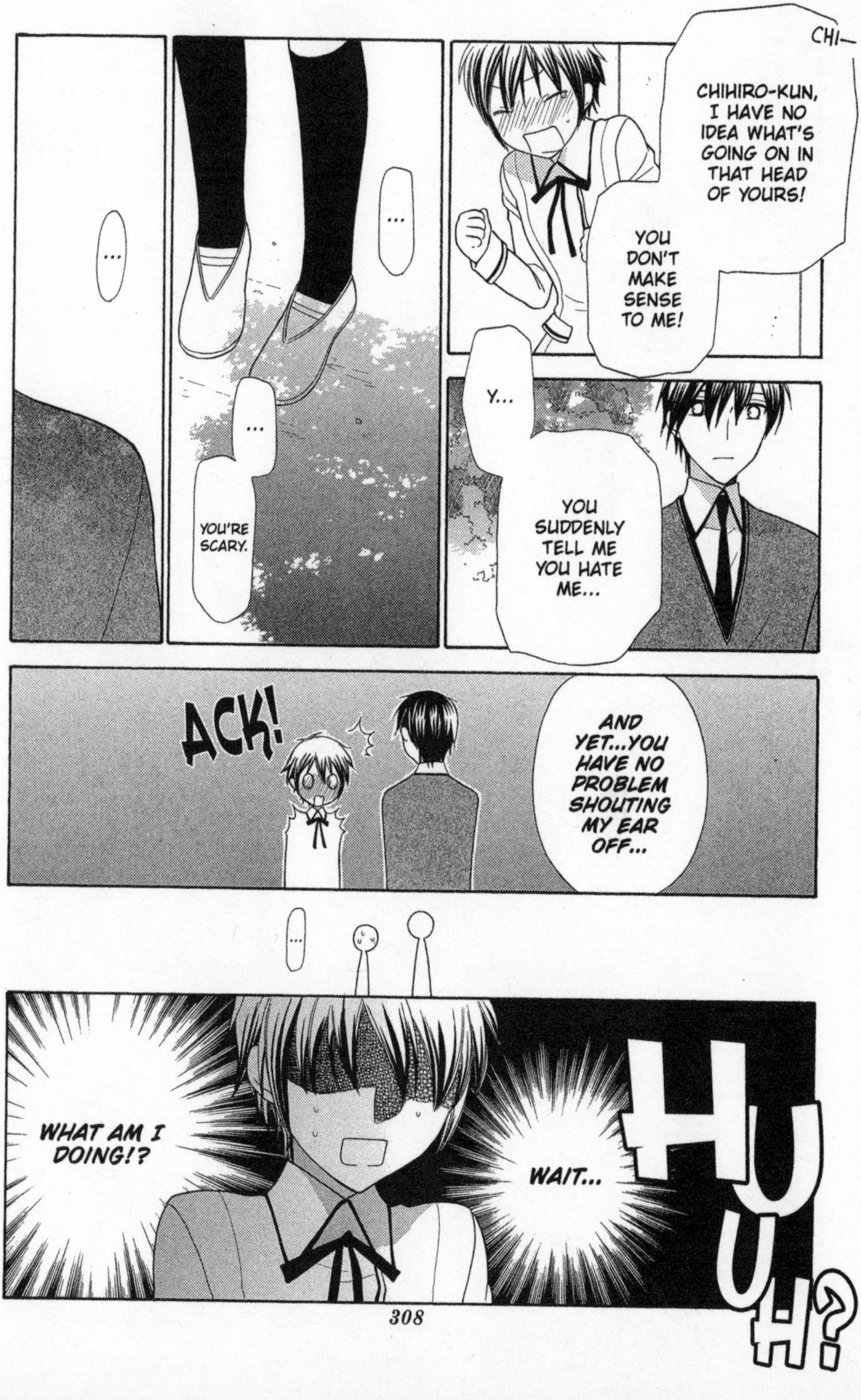

CHI—
CHIHIRO-KUN, I HAVE NO IDEA WHAT'S GOING ON IN THAT HEAD OF YOURS!
YOU DON'T MAKE SENSE TO ME!
Y...
YOU SUDDENLY TELL ME YOU HATE ME...
...
...
YOU'RE SCARY.
...
AND YET...YOU HAVE NO PROBLEM SHOUTING MY EAR OFF...
ACK!
...
HUH?
WAIT...
WHAT AM I DOING!?

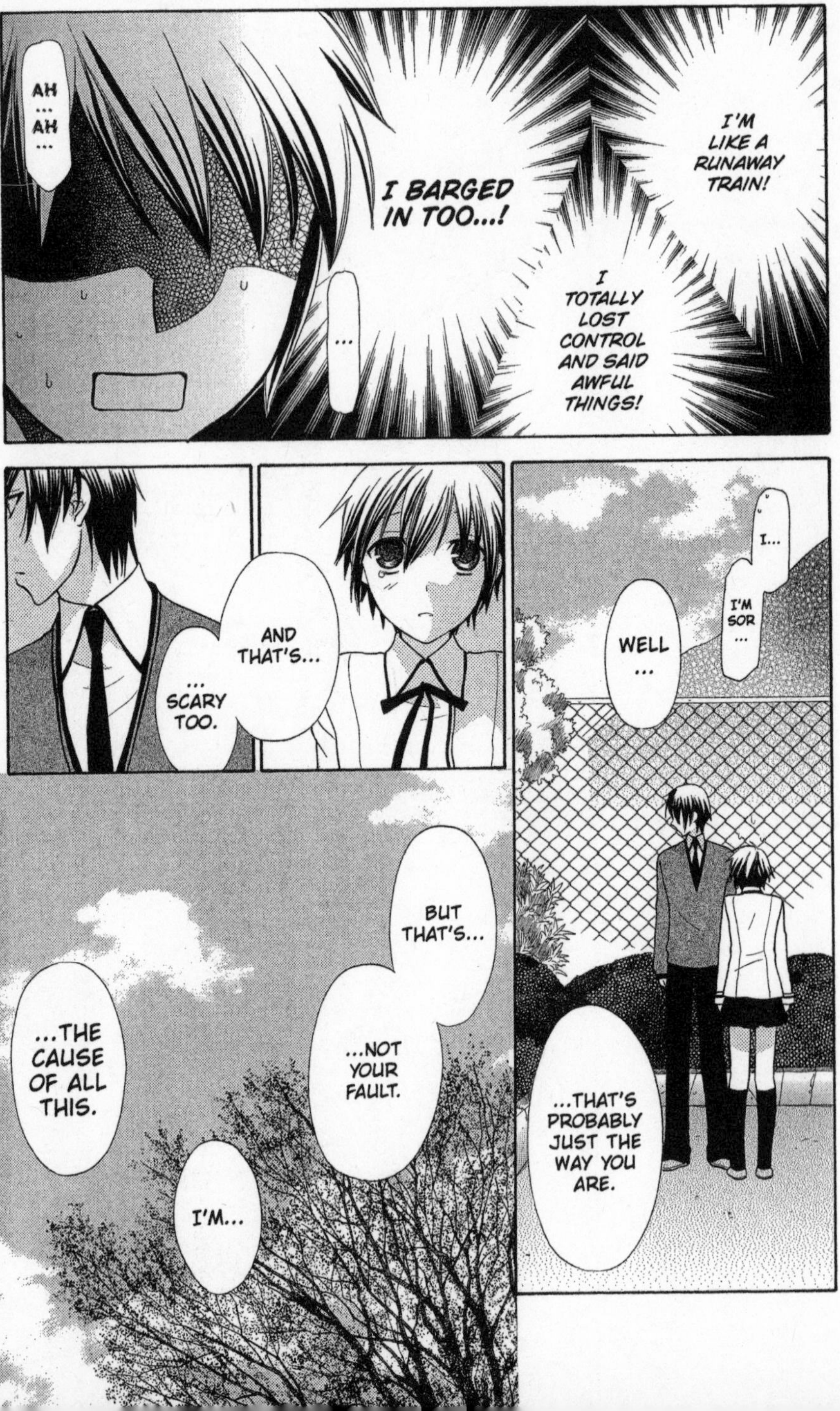
I'M LIKE A RUNAWAY TRAIN!
I TOTALLY LOST CONTROL AND SAID AWFUL THINGS!
I BARGED IN TOO...!
...
AH... AH...
I... I'M SOR...
WELL...
...THAT'S PROBABLY JUST THE WAY YOU ARE.
AND THAT'S...
...SCARY TOO.
BUT THAT'S...
...NOT YOUR FAULT.
I'M...
...THE CAUSE OF ALL THIS.

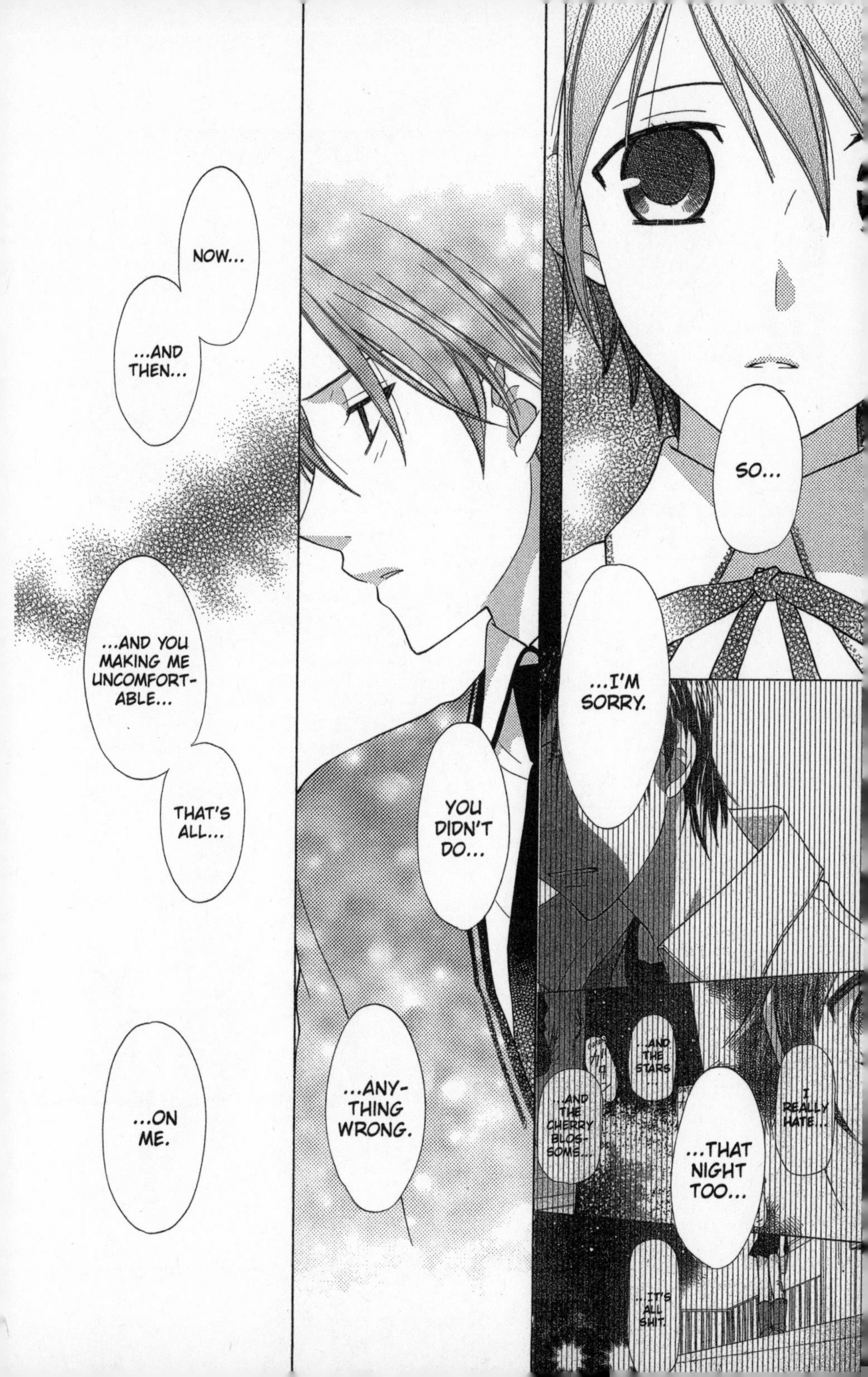
SO...
...I'M SORRY.
I REALLY HATE...
...THAT NIGHT TOO...
...AND THE STARS...
...AND THE CHERRY BLOSSOMS...
...IT'S ALL SHIT.
YOU DIDN'T DO...
...ANYTHING WRONG.
NOW...
...AND THEN...
...AND YOU MAKING ME UNCOMFORTABLE...
THAT'S ALL...
...ON ME.

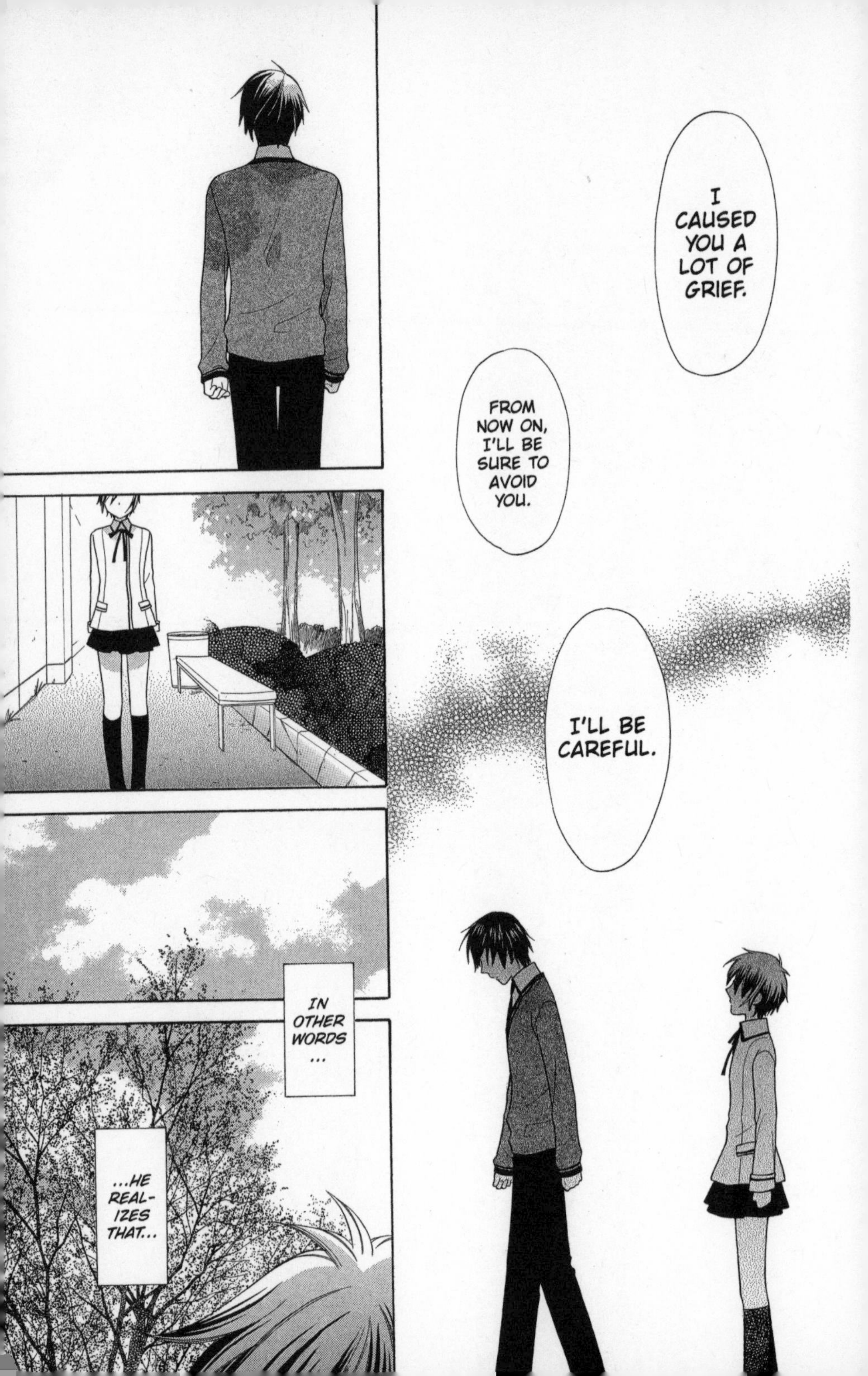
I CAUSED YOU A LOT OF GRIEF.
FROM NOW ON, I'LL BE SURE TO AVOID YOU.
I'LL BE CAREFUL.
IN OTHER WORDS...
...HE REALIZES THAT...

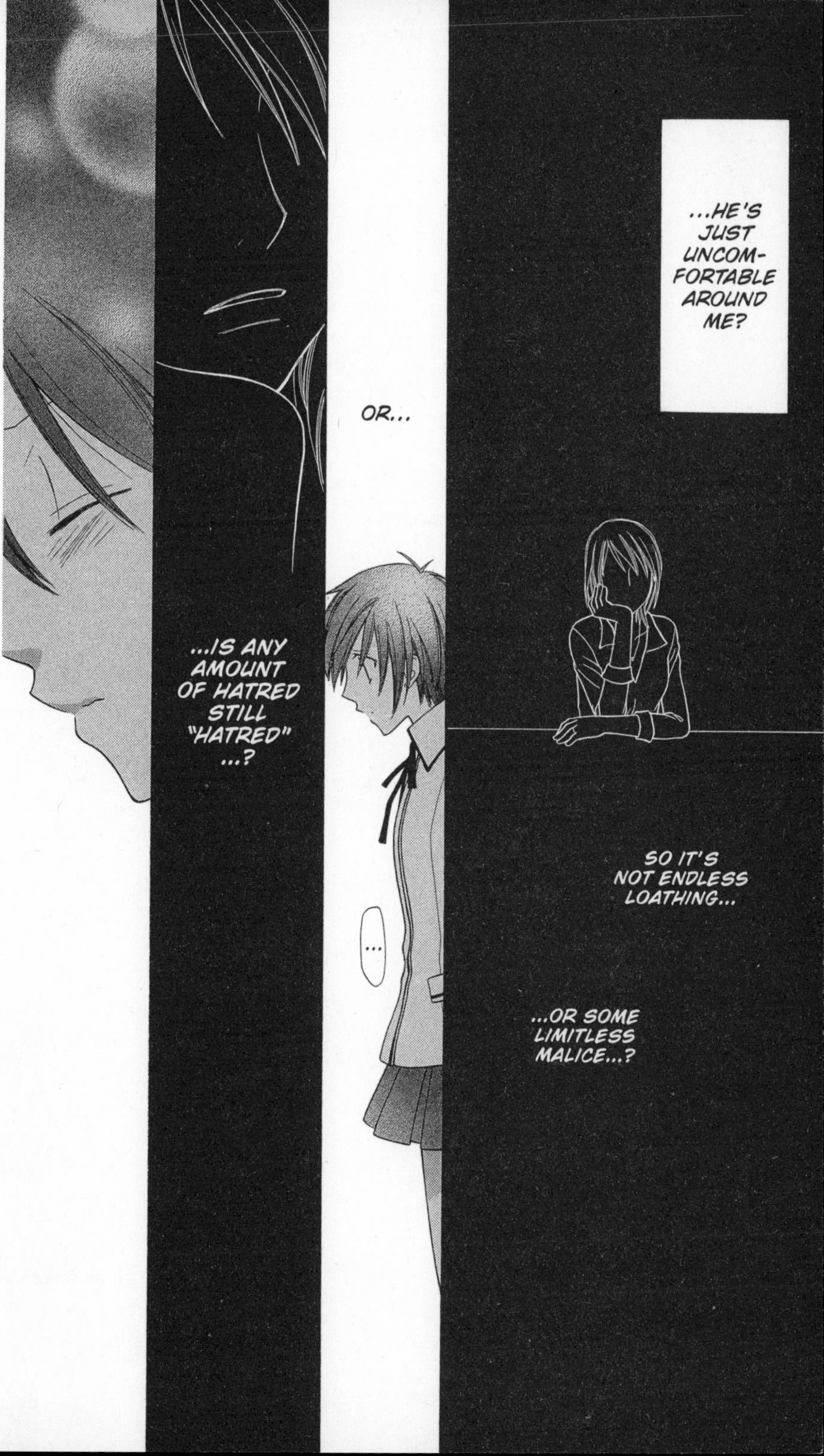
...HE'S JUST UNCOM-FORTABLE AROUND ME?
SO IT'S NOT ENDLESS LOATHING...
...OR SOME LIMITLESS MALICE...?
OR...
...
...IS ANY AMOUNT OF HATRED STILL "HATRED" ...?

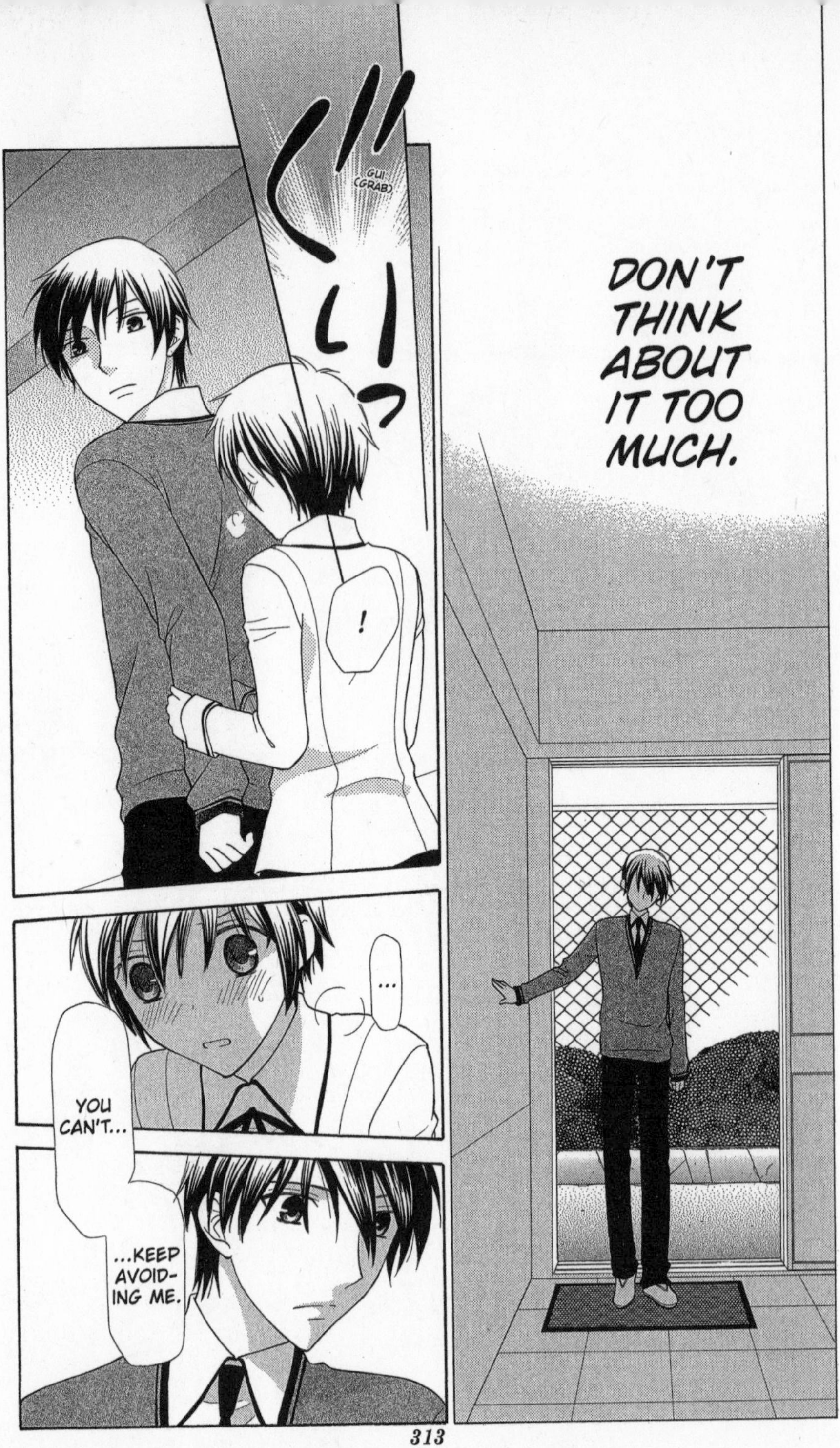
DON'T THINK ABOUT IT TOO MUCH.
GUI (GRAB)
!
...
YOU CAN'T...
...KEEP AVOID-ING ME.

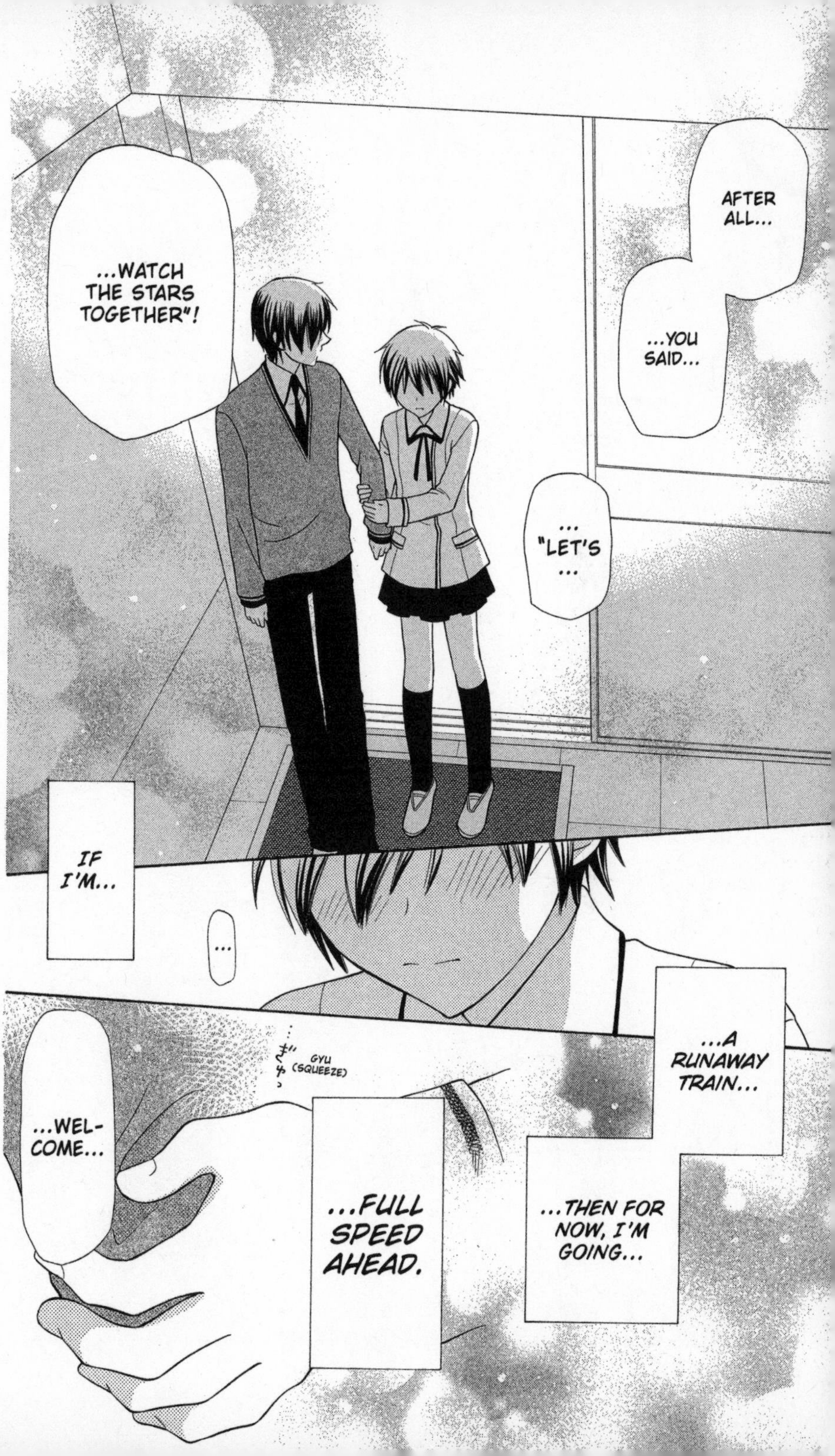
AFTER ALL...
...YOU SAID...
... "LET'S ...
...WATCH THE STARS TOGETHER"!
IF I'M...
...
...A RUNAWAY TRAIN...
GYU (SQUEEZE)
...THEN FOR NOW, I'M GOING...
...FULL SPEED AHEAD.
...WEL-COME...

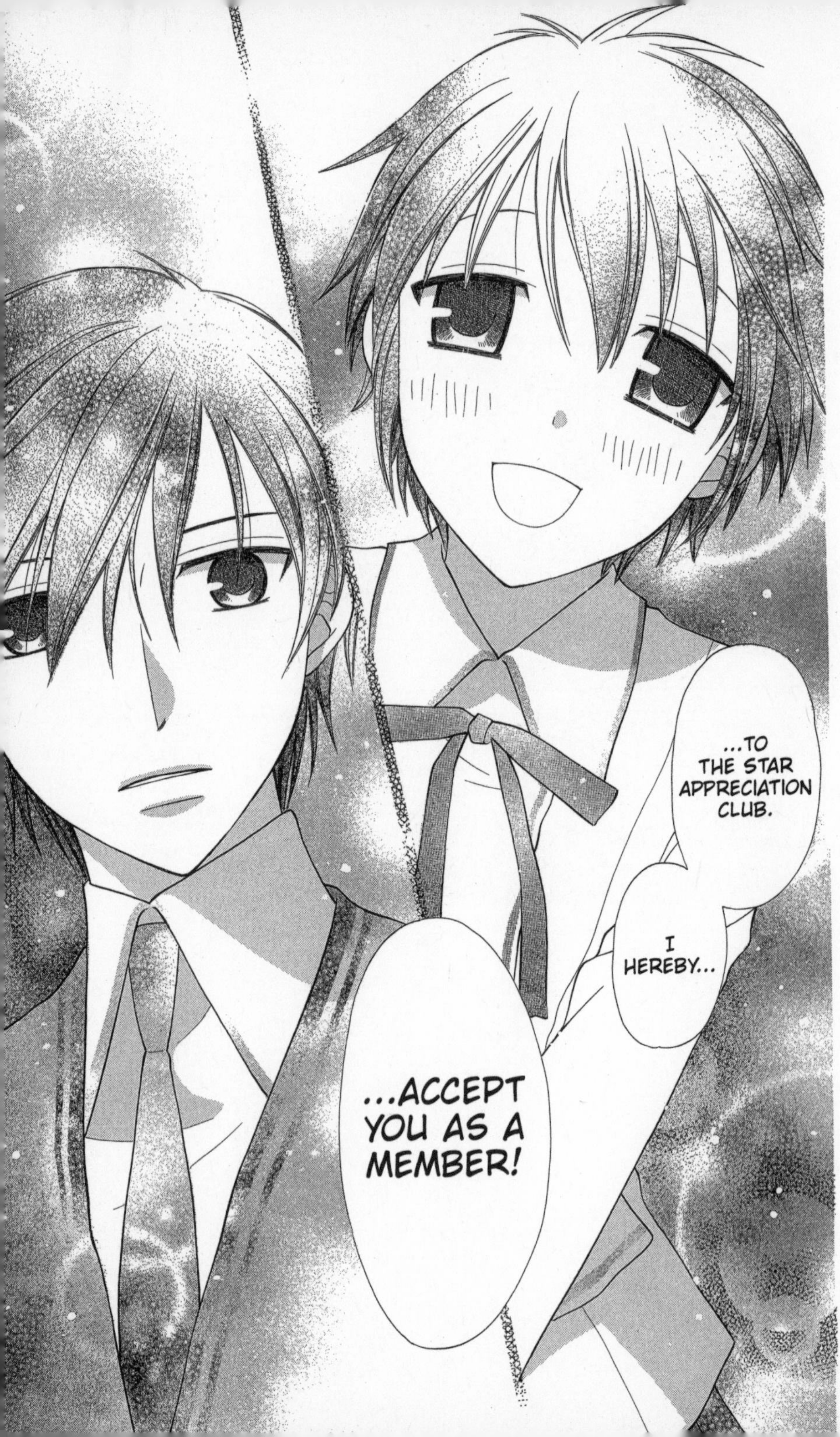
...TO THE STAR APPRECIATION CLUB.
I HEREBY...
...ACCEPT YOU AS A MEMBER!

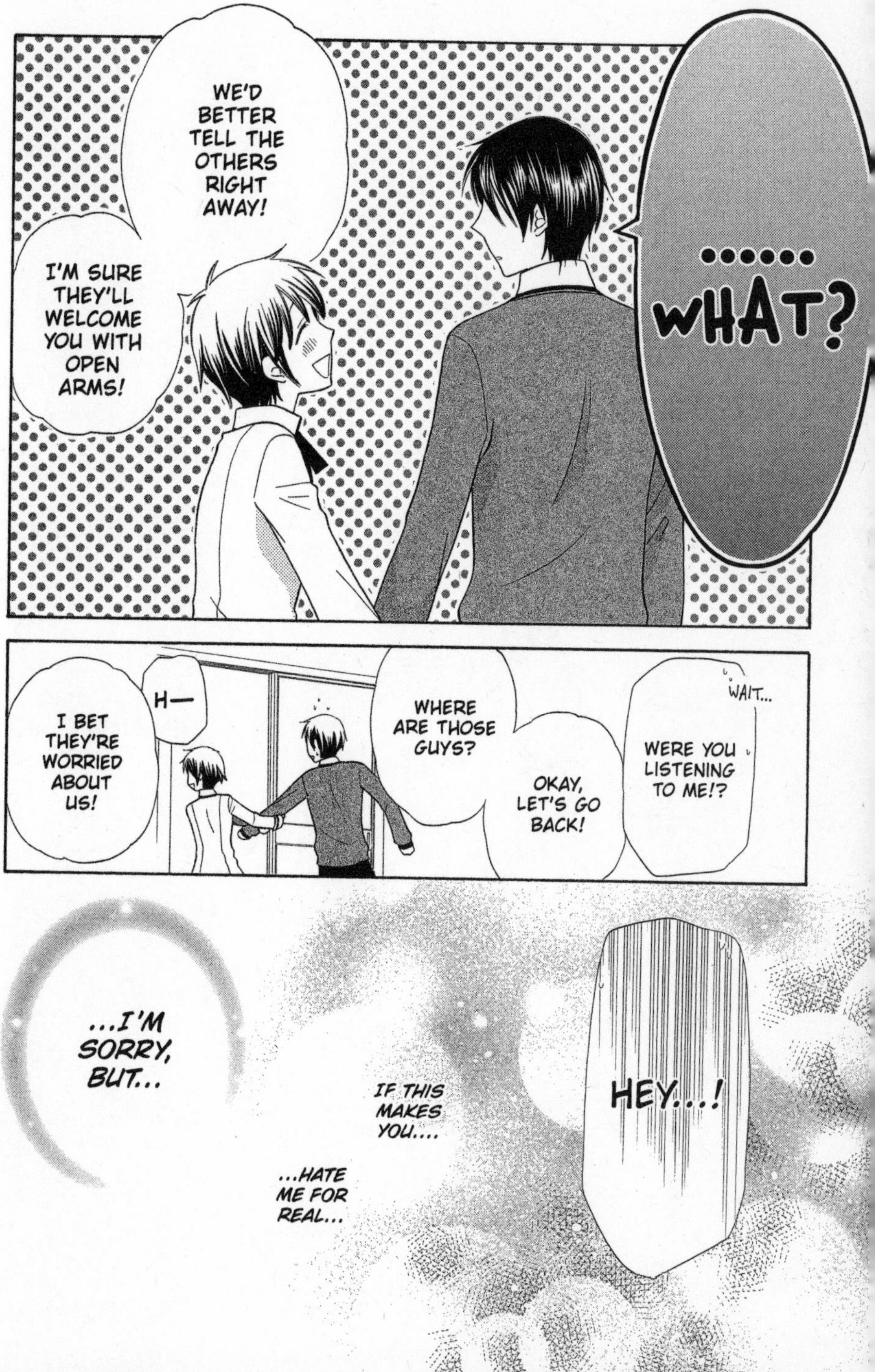
......WHAT?
WE'D BETTER TELL THE OTHERS RIGHT AWAY!
I'M SURE THEY'LL WELCOME YOU WITH OPEN ARMS!
WAIT...
WERE YOU LISTENING TO ME!?
WHERE ARE THOSE GUYS?
OKAY, LET'S GO BACK!
H—
I BET THEY'RE WORRIED ABOUT US!
HEY...!
IF THIS MAKES YOU....
...HATE ME FOR REAL...
...I'M SORRY, BUT...

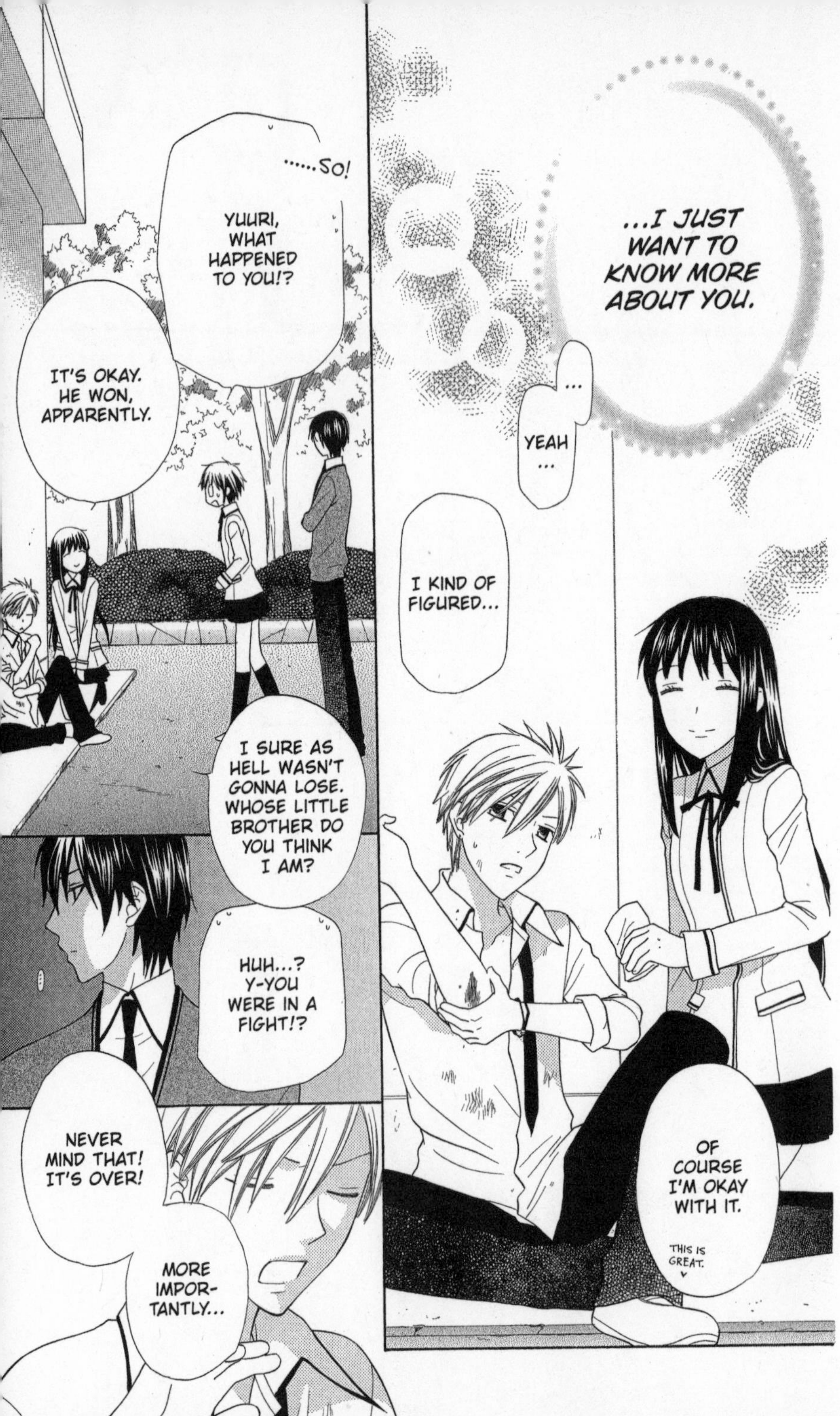
...I JUST WANT TO KNOW MORE ABOUT YOU.
... YEAH ...
I KIND OF FIGURED...
OF COURSE I'M OKAY WITH IT.
THIS IS GREAT.
......SO!
YUURI, WHAT HAPPENED TO YOU!?
IT'S OKAY. HE WON, APPARENTLY.
I SURE AS HELL WASN'T GONNA LOSE. WHOSE LITTLE BROTHER DO YOU THINK I AM?
HUH...? Y-YOU WERE IN A FIGHT!?
NEVER MIND THAT! IT'S OVER!
MORE IMPORTANTLY...

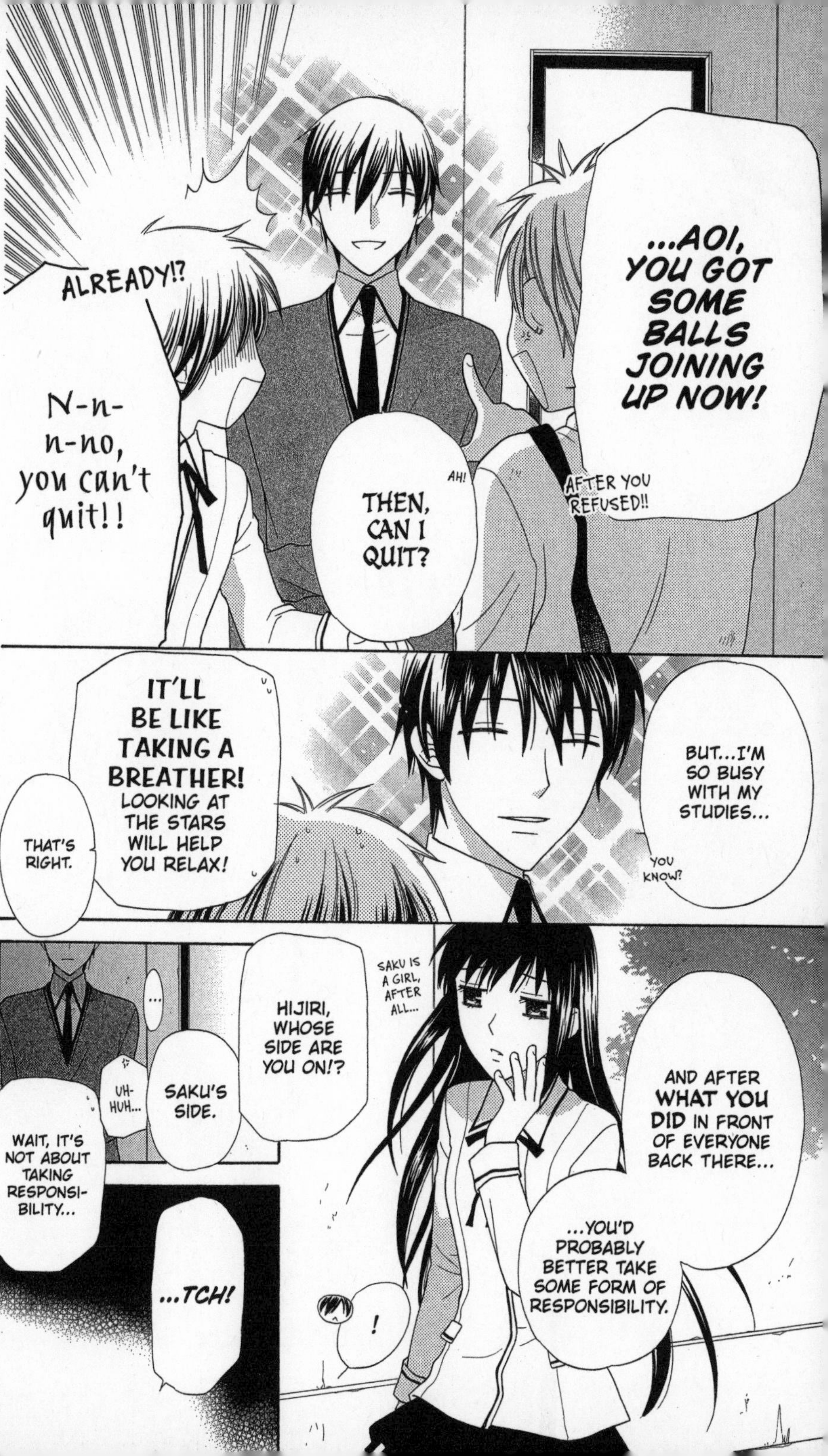
...AOI, YOU GOT SOME BALLS JOINING UP NOW!
AFTER YOU REFUSED!!
ALREADY!?
AH!
THEN, CAN I QUIT?
N-n-n-no, you can't quit!!
BUT...I'M SO BUSY WITH MY STUDIES...
YOU KNOW?
IT'LL BE LIKE TAKING A BREATHER! LOOKING AT THE STARS WILL HELP YOU RELAX!
THAT'S RIGHT.
AND AFTER WHAT YOU DID IN FRONT OF EVERYONE BACK THERE...
...YOU'D PROBABLY BETTER TAKE SOME FORM OF RESPONSIBILITY.
SAKU IS A GIRL, AFTER ALL...
!
HIJIRI, WHOSE SIDE ARE YOU ON!?
...
SAKU'S SIDE.
UH-HUH...
WAIT, IT'S NOT ABOUT TAKING RESPONSI-BILITY...
...TCH!

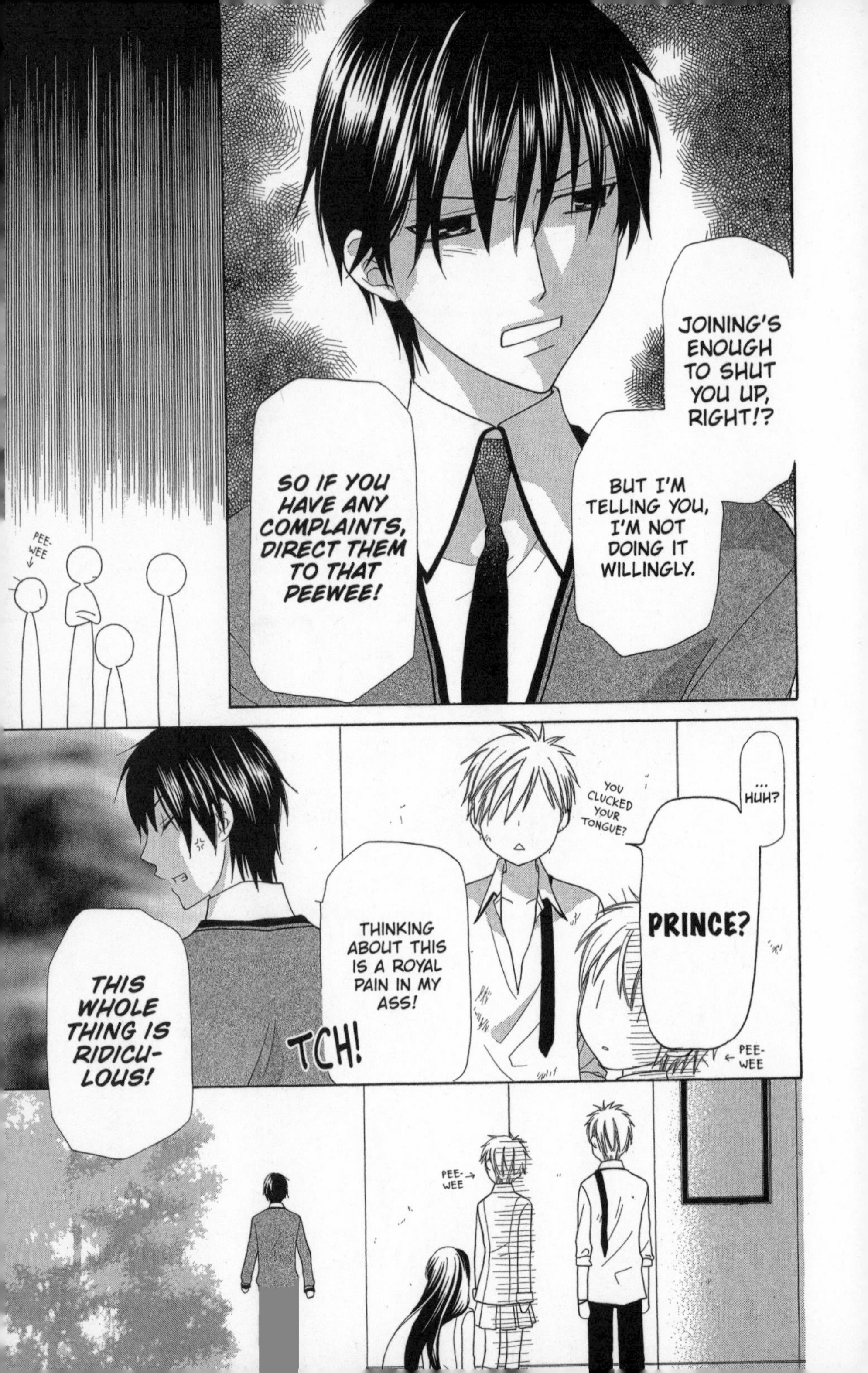
JOINING'S ENOUGH TO SHUT YOU UP, RIGHT!?
BUT I'M TELLING YOU, I'M NOT DOING IT WILLINGLY.
SO IF YOU HAVE ANY COMPLAINTS, DIRECT THEM TO THAT PEEWEE!
PEE-WEE
...HUH?
YOU CLUCKED YOUR TONGUE?
PRINCE?
PEE-WEE
THINKING ABOUT THIS IS A ROYAL PAIN IN MY ASS!
TCH!
THIS WHOLE THING IS RIDICU-LOUS!
PEE-WEE

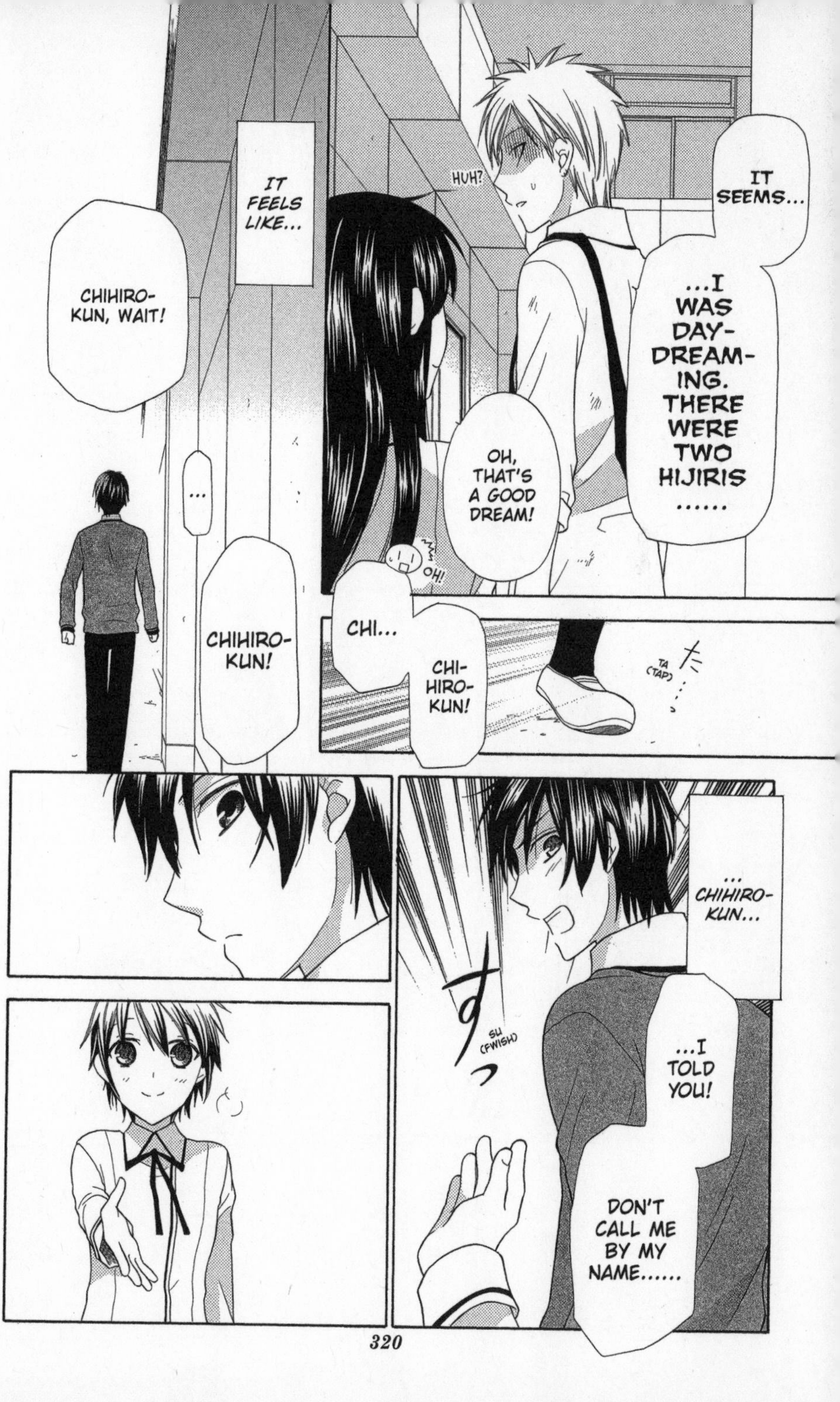
IT SEEMS...
...I WAS DAY-DREAM-ING. THERE WERE TWO HIJIRIS ......
HUH?
IT FEELS LIKE...
OH, THAT'S A GOOD DREAM!
OH!
CHI...
CHI-HIRO-KUN!
TA (TAP)
CHIHIRO-KUN, WAIT!
...
CHIHIRO-KUN!
... CHIHIRO-KUN...
SU (FWISH)
...I TOLD YOU!
DON'T CALL ME BY MY NAME......

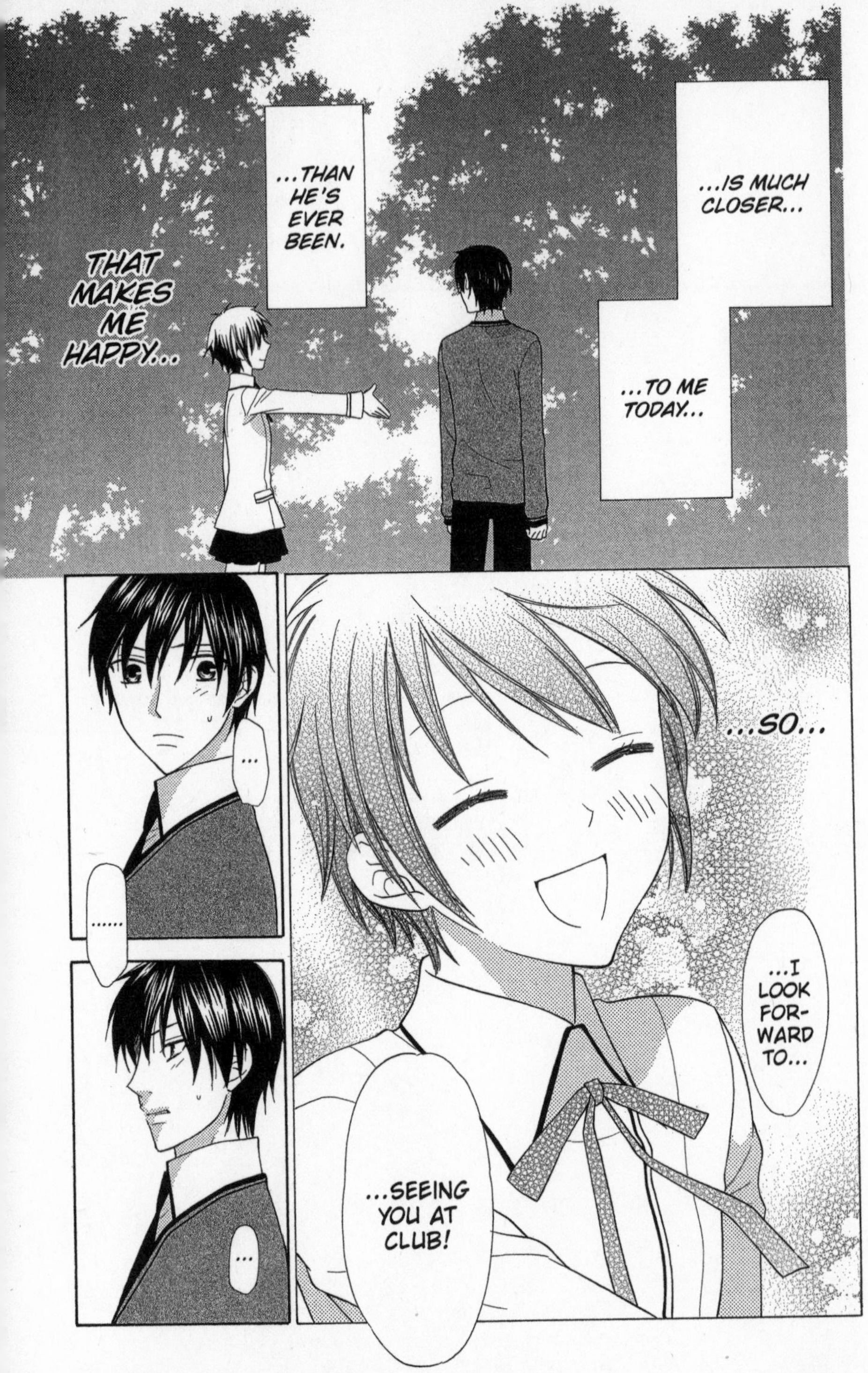
...IS MUCH CLOSER...
...TO ME TODAY...
...THAN HE'S EVER BEEN.
THAT MAKES ME HAPPY...
...SO...
...I LOOK FOR-WARD TO...
...SEEING YOU AT CLUB!
...
......
...

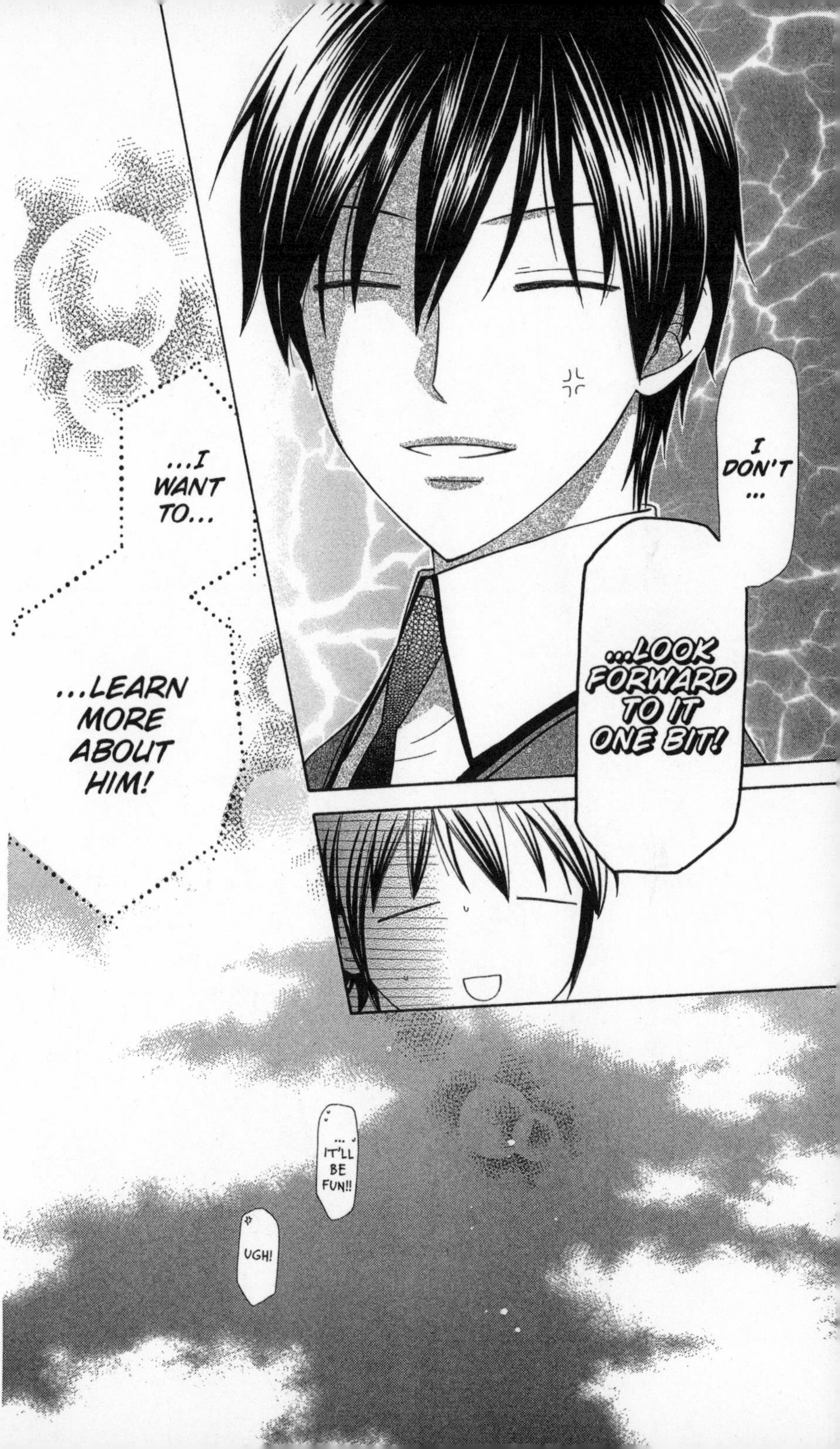
I DON'T ...
...LOOK FORWARD TO IT ONE BIT!
...I WANT TO...
...LEARN MORE ABOUT HIM!
...IT'LL BE FUN!!
UGH!

Chapter 10

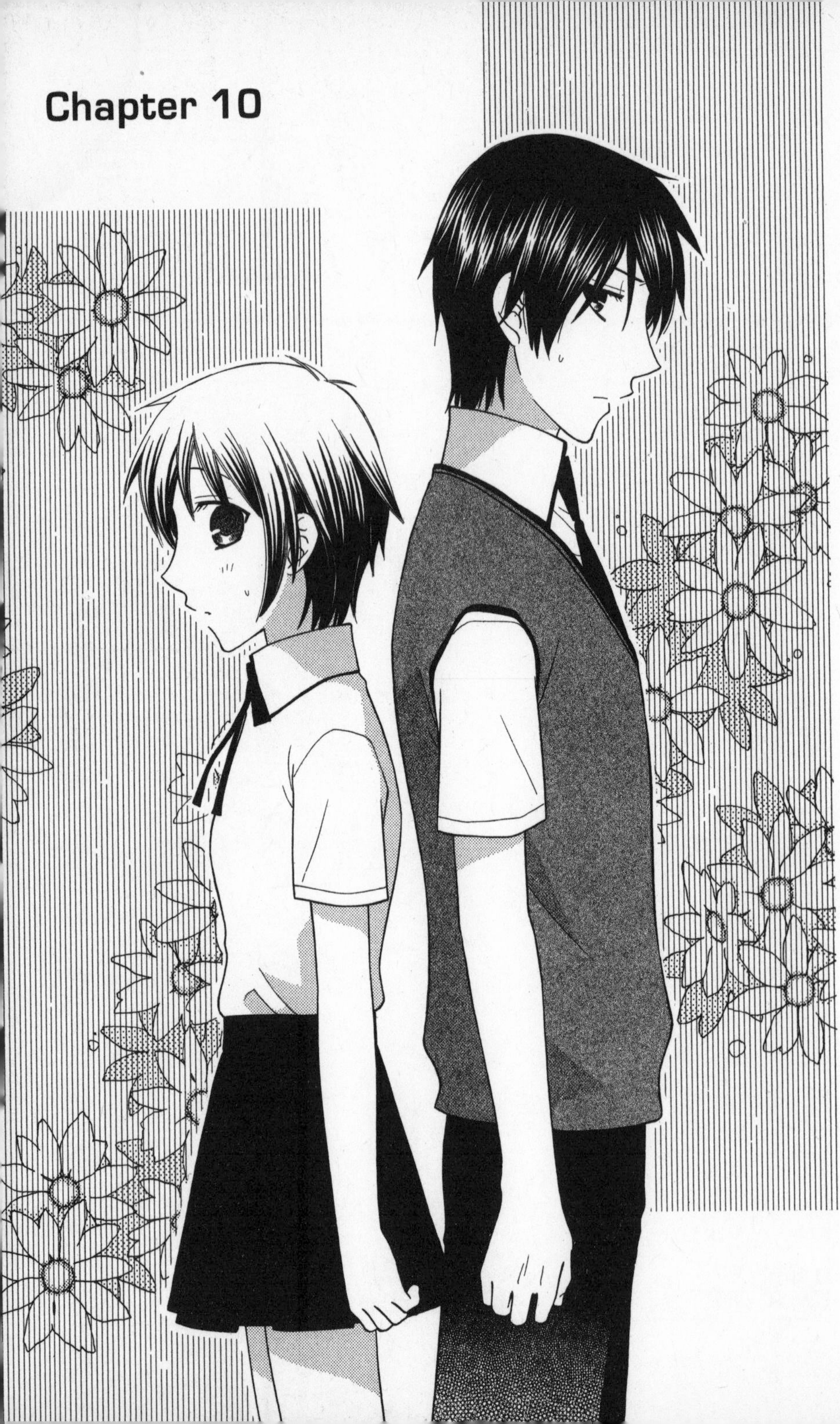

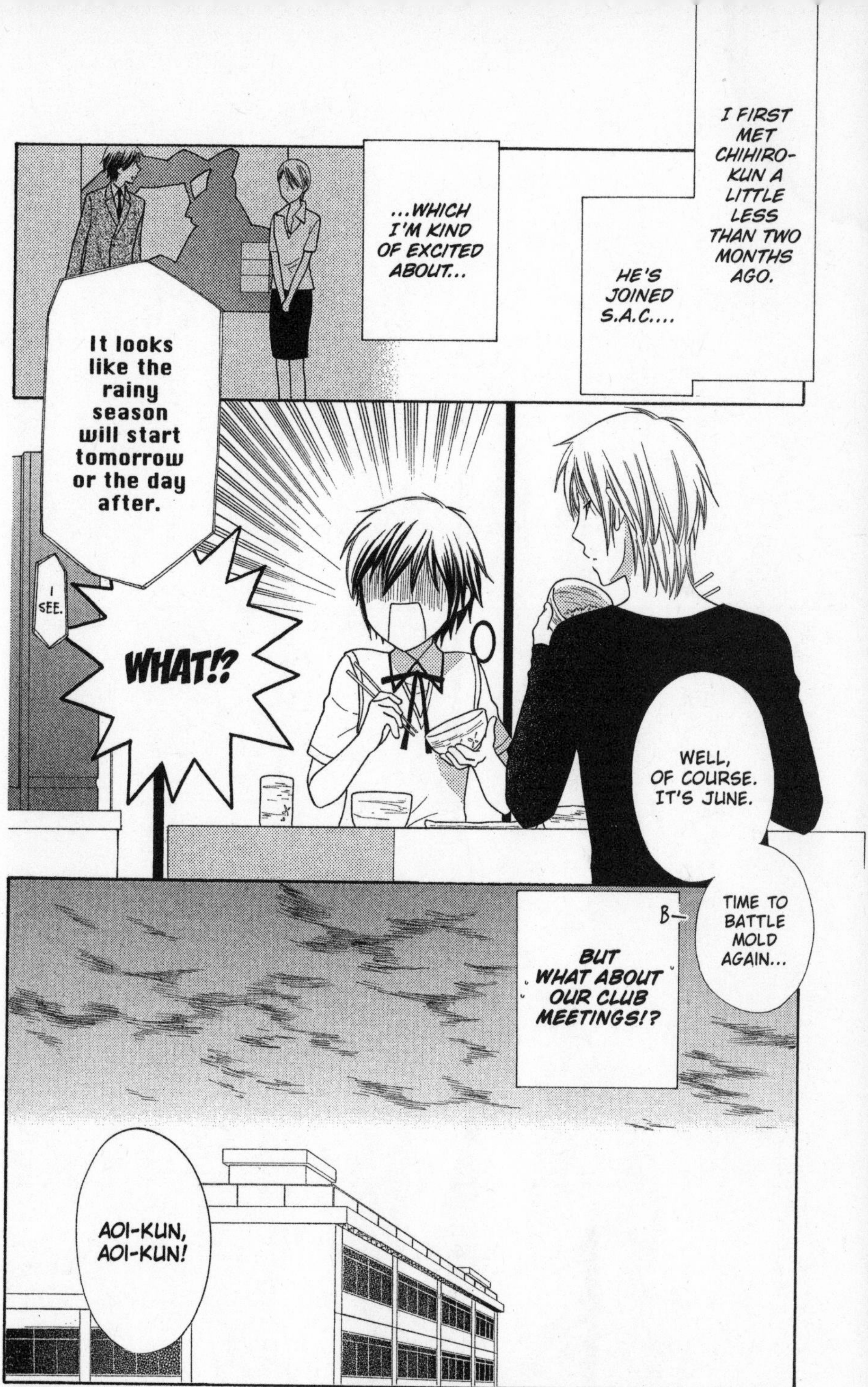
I FIRST MET CHIHIRO-KUN A LITTLE LESS THAN TWO MONTHS AGO.
HE'S JOINED S.A.C....
...WHICH I'M KIND OF EXCITED ABOUT...
It looks like the rainy season will start tomorrow or the day after.
I SEE.
WELL, OF COURSE. IT'S JUNE.
TIME TO BATTLE MOLD AGAIN...
WHAT!?
B—
BUT WHAT ABOUT OUR CLUB MEETINGS!?
AOI-KUN, AOI-KUN!

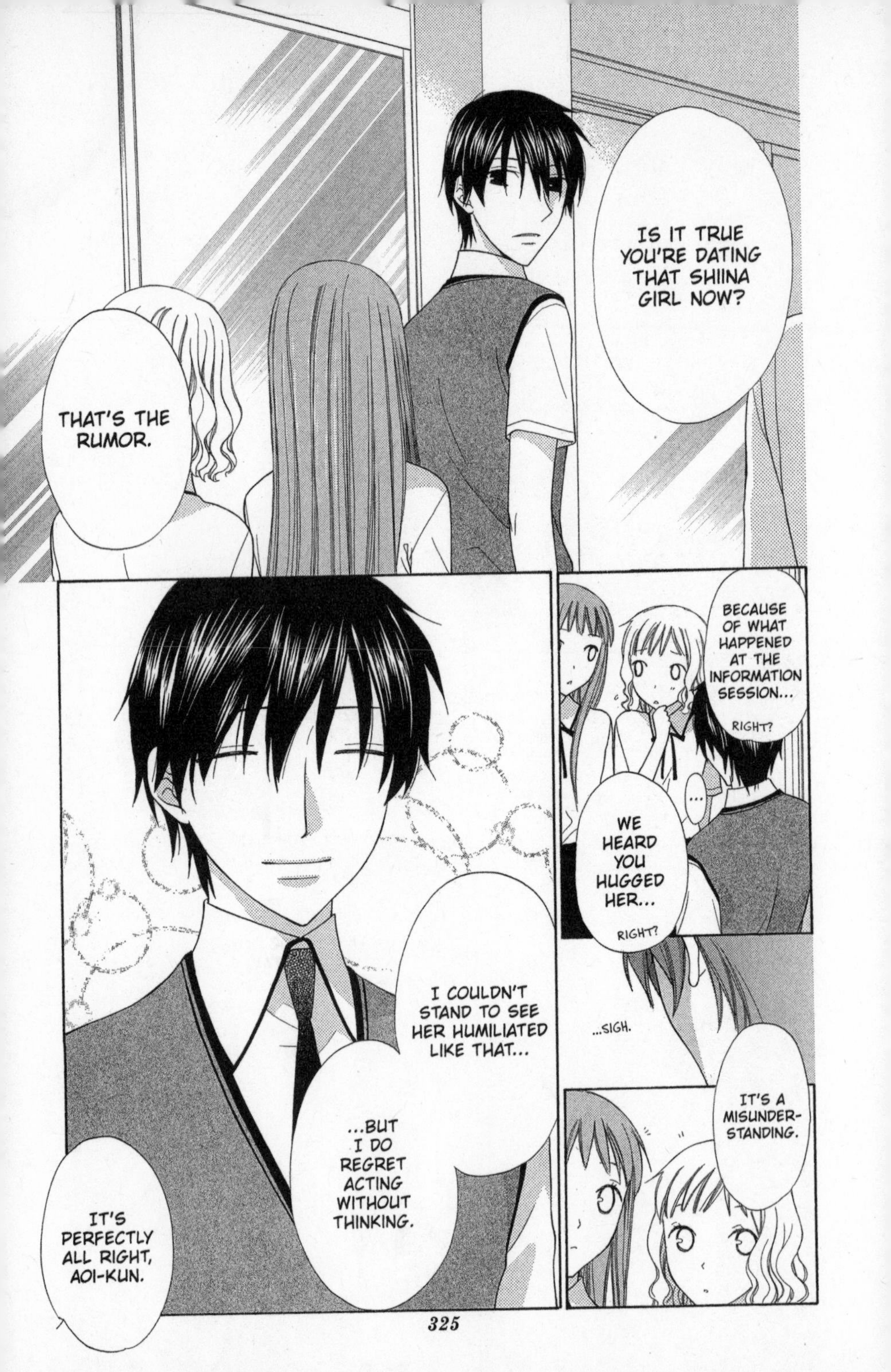
IS IT TRUE YOU'RE DATING THAT SHIINA GIRL NOW?
THAT'S THE RUMOR.
BECAUSE OF WHAT HAPPENED AT THE INFORMATION SESSION...
RIGHT?
...
WE HEARD YOU HUGGED HER...
RIGHT?
...SIGH.
IT'S A MISUNDER-STANDING.
I COULDN'T STAND TO SEE HER HUMILIATED LIKE THAT...
...BUT I DO REGRET ACTING WITHOUT THINKING.
IT'S PERFECTLY ALL RIGHT, AOI-KUN.

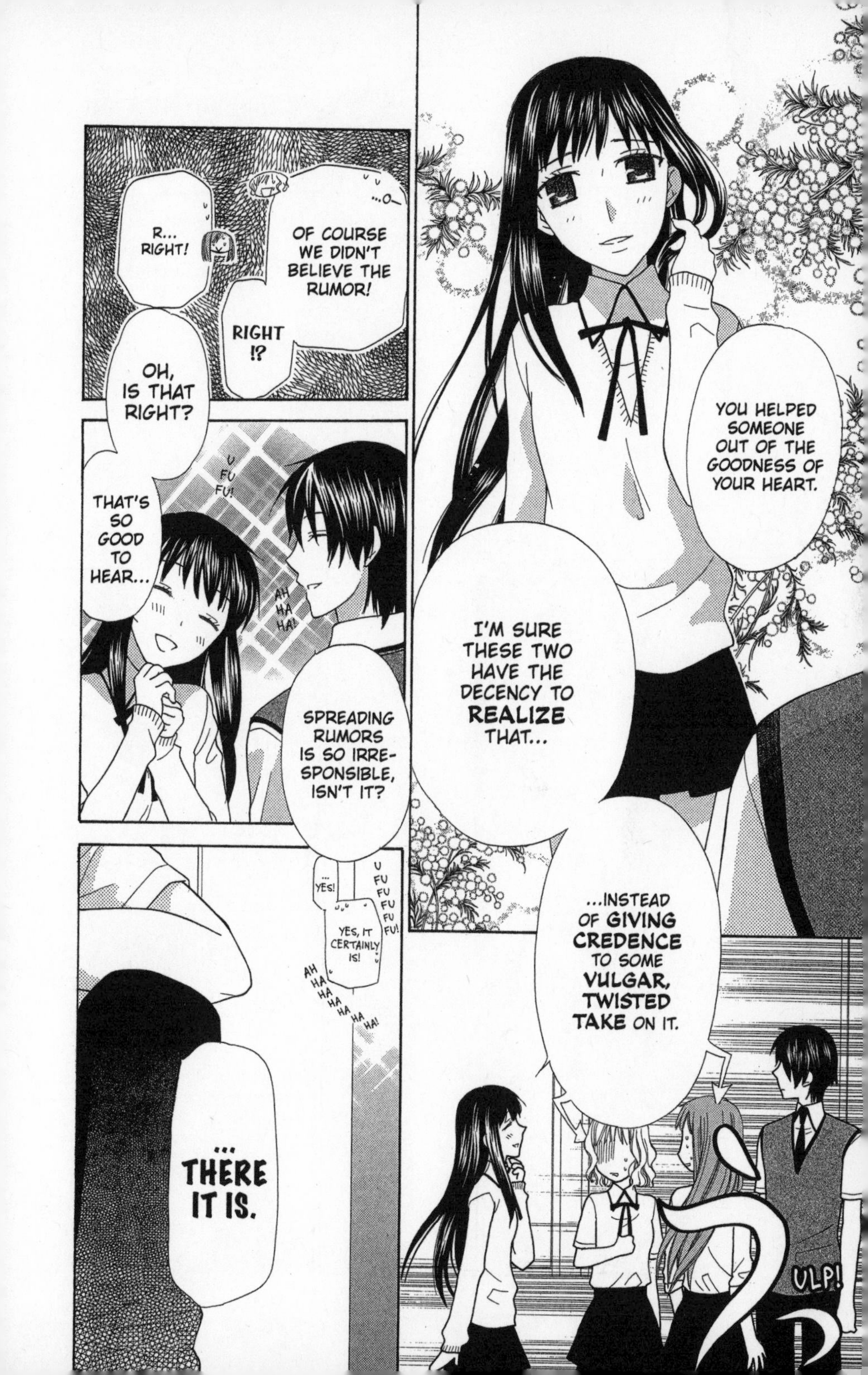
YOU HELPED SOMEONE OUT OF THE GOODNESS OF YOUR HEART.
I'M SURE THESE TWO HAVE THE DECENCY TO REALIZE THAT...
...INSTEAD OF GIVING CREDENCE TO SOME VULGAR, TWISTED TAKE ON IT.
ULP!
...O—
OF COURSE WE DIDN'T BELIEVE THE RUMOR!
RIGHT !?
R... RIGHT!
OH, IS THAT RIGHT?
THAT'S SO GOOD TO HEAR...
U FU FU!
AH HA HA!
SPREADING RUMORS IS SO IRRE-SPONSIBLE, ISN'T IT?
U FU FU FU FU FU!
...YES!
YES, IT CERTAINLY IS!
AH HA HA HA HA HA HA!
... THERE IT IS.

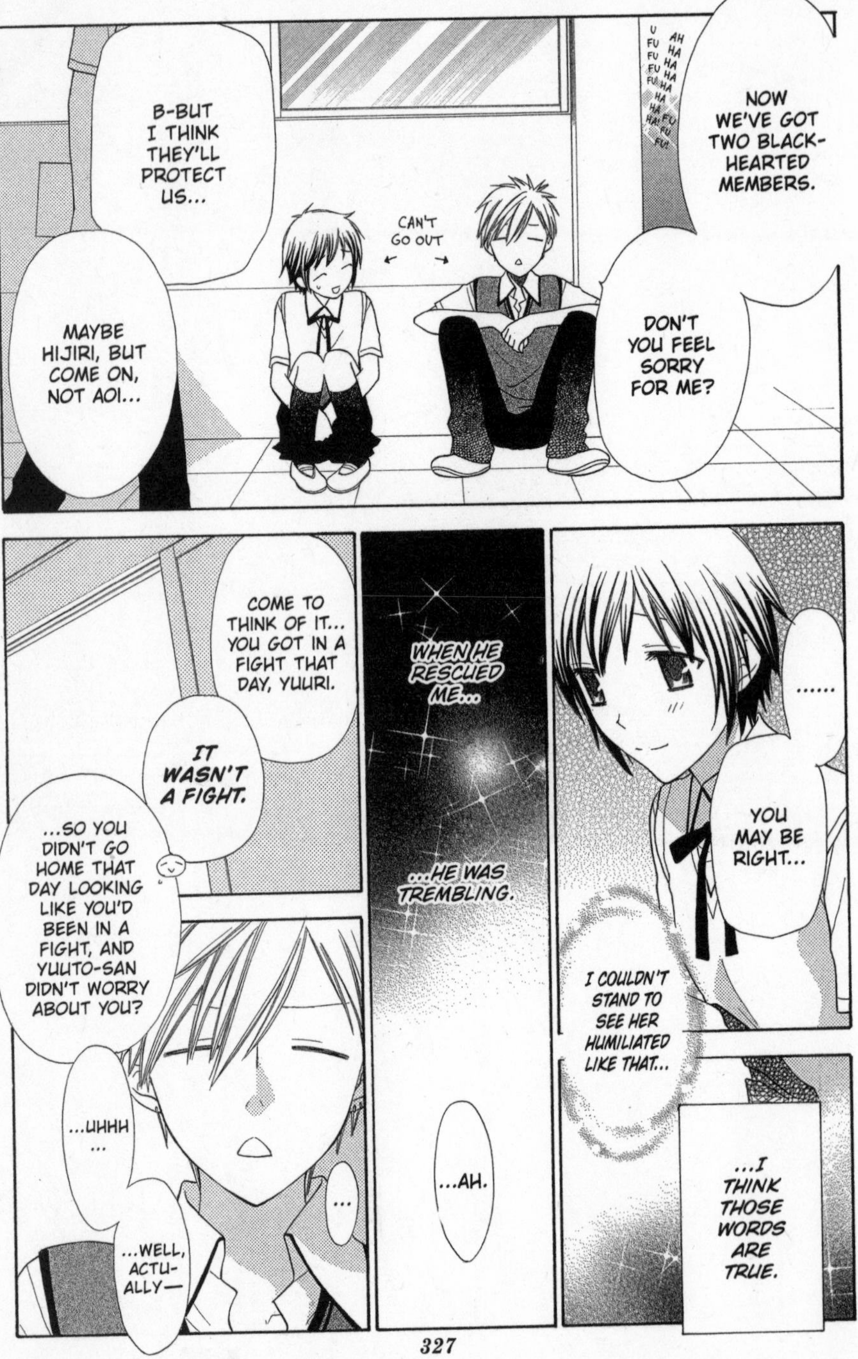
NOW WE'VE GOT TWO BLACK-HEARTED MEMBERS.
AH HA HA HA HA FU FU FU!
U FU FU FU FU! HA HA HA!
DON'T YOU FEEL SORRY FOR ME?
CAN'T GO OUT
B-BUT I THINK THEY'LL PROTECT US...
MAYBE HIJIRI, BUT COME ON, NOT AOI...
......
YOU MAY BE RIGHT...
I COULDN'T STAND TO SEE HER HUMILIATED LIKE THAT...
...I THINK THOSE WORDS ARE TRUE.
WHEN HE RESCUED ME...
...HE WAS TREMBLING.
...AH.
COME TO THINK OF IT... YOU GOT IN A FIGHT THAT DAY, YUURI.
IT WASN'T A FIGHT.
...SO YOU DIDN'T GO HOME THAT DAY LOOKING LIKE YOU'D BEEN IN A FIGHT, AND YUUTO-SAN DIDN'T WORRY ABOUT YOU?
...UHHH...
...
...WELL, ACTUALLY—

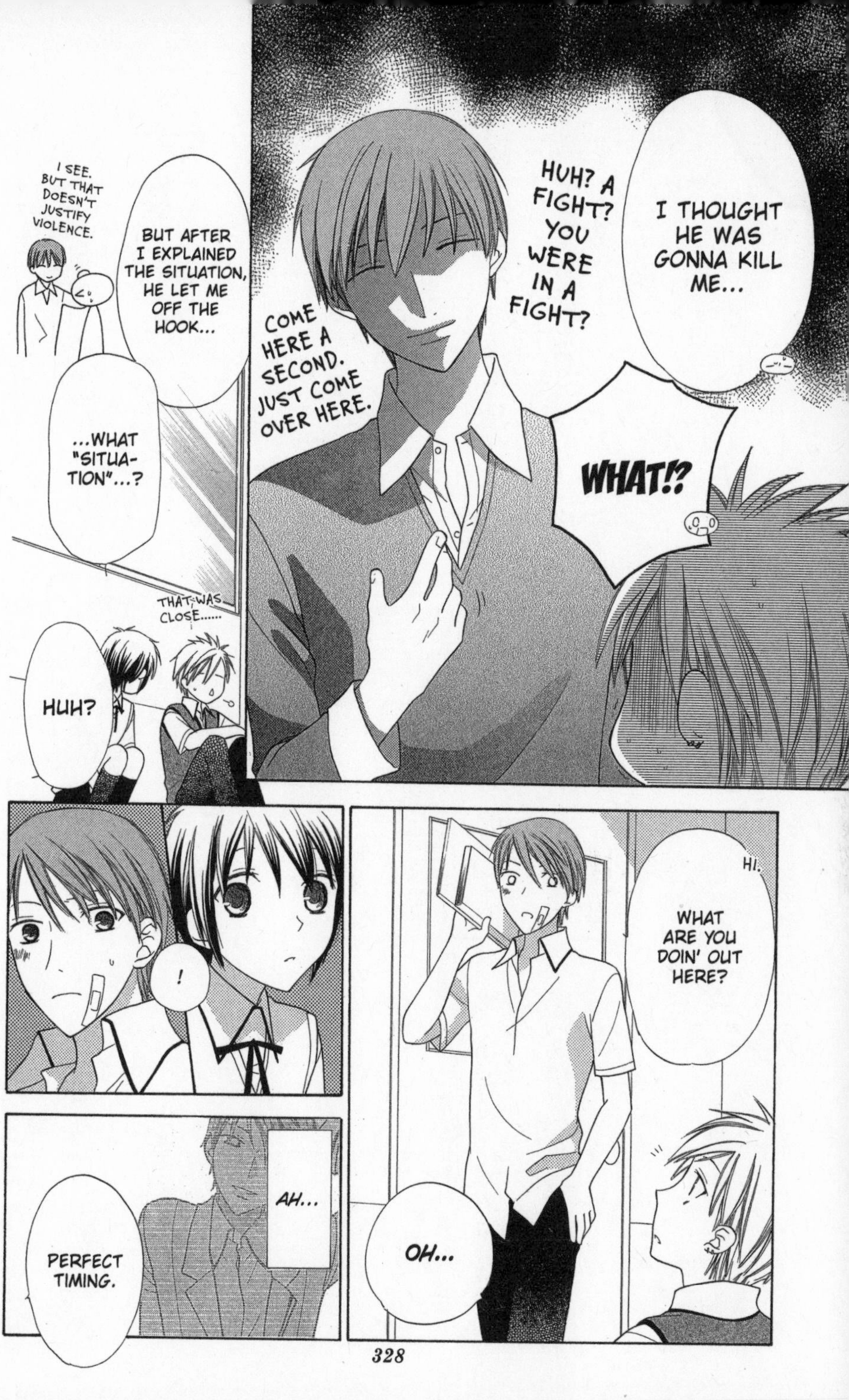
I THOUGHT HE WAS GONNA KILL ME...
HUH? A FIGHT? YOU WERE IN A FIGHT?
WHAT!?
COME HERE A SECOND. JUST COME OVER HERE.
BUT AFTER I EXPLAINED THE SITUATION, HE LET ME OFF THE HOOK...
I SEE. BUT THAT DOESN'T JUSTIFY VIOLENCE.
...WHAT "SITUATION"...?
THAT WAS CLOSE......
HUH?
HI.
WHAT ARE YOU DOIN' OUT HERE?
OH...
!
AH...
PERFECT TIMING.

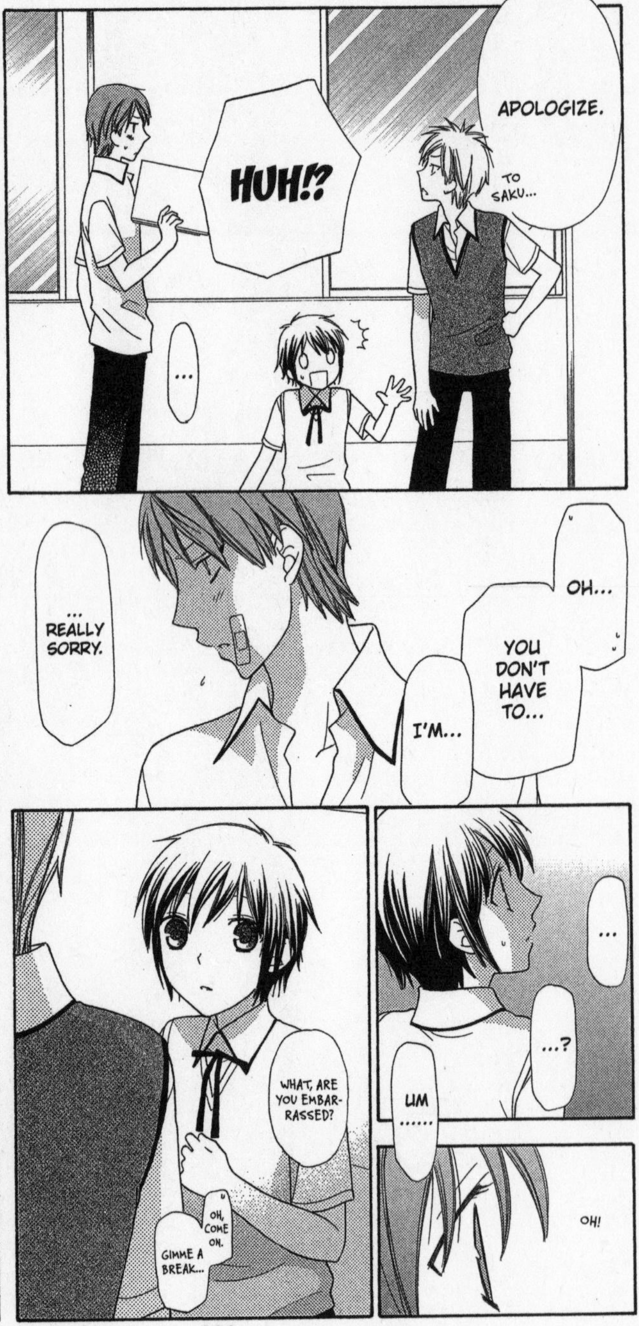
APOLOGIZE.
TO SAKU...
HUH!?
...
OH...
YOU DON'T HAVE TO...
I'M...
... REALLY SORRY.
...
...?
UM ......
OH!
WHAT, ARE YOU EMBARRASSED?
OH, COME ON.
GIMME A BREAK...

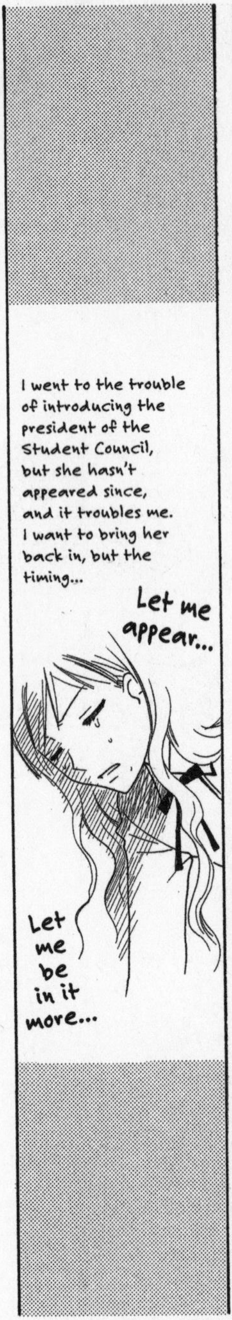
I went to the trouble of introducing the president of the Student Council, but she hasn't appeared since, and it troubles me. I want to bring her back in, but the timing...
Let me appear...
Let me be in it more...

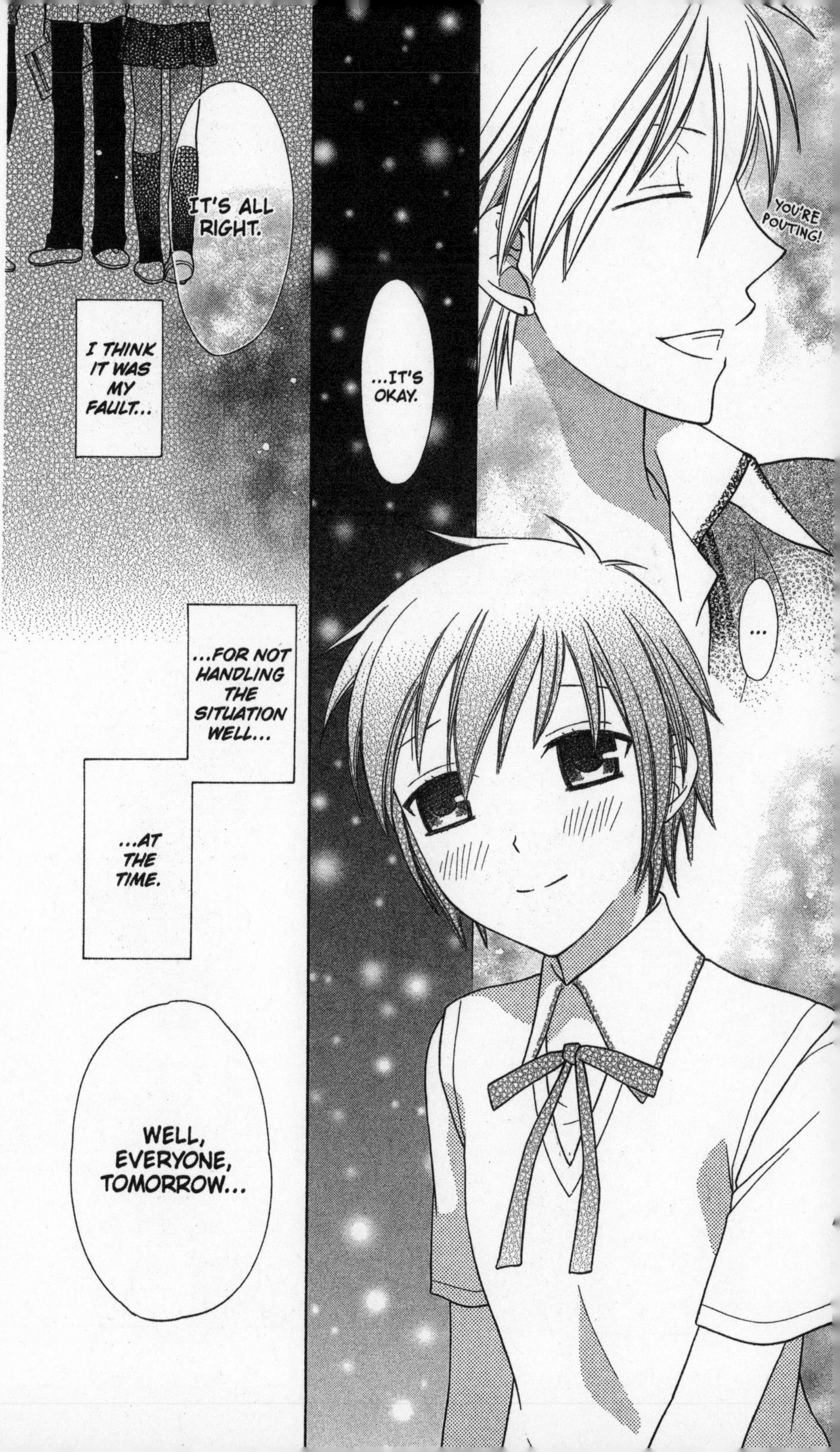
YOU'RE POUTING!
...
...IT'S OKAY.
IT'S ALL RIGHT.
I THINK IT WAS MY FAULT...
...FOR NOT HANDLING THE SITUATION WELL...
...AT THE TIME.
WELL, EVERYONE, TOMORROW...

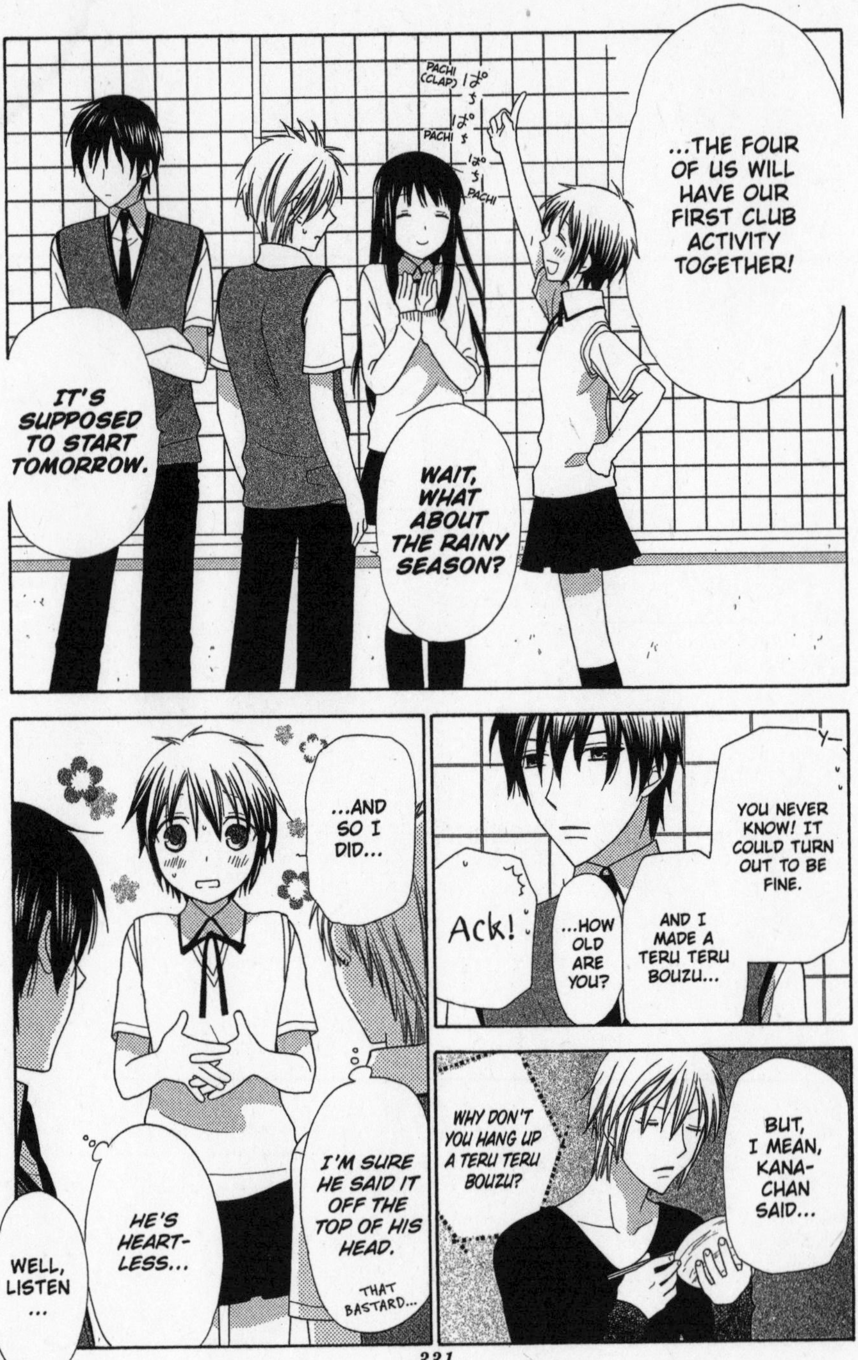
...THE FOUR OF US WILL HAVE OUR FIRST CLUB ACTIVITY TOGETHER!
PACHI (CLAP) ぱち
ぱち PACHI
ぱち PACHI
WAIT, WHAT ABOUT THE RAINY SEASON?
IT'S SUPPOSED TO START TOMORROW.
Y—
YOU NEVER KNOW! IT COULD TURN OUT TO BE FINE.
AND I MADE A TERU TERU BOUZU...
...HOW OLD ARE YOU?
Ack!
BUT, I MEAN, KANA-CHAN SAID...
WHY DON'T YOU HANG UP A TERU TERU BOUZU?
...AND SO I DID...
I'M SURE HE SAID IT OFF THE TOP OF HIS HEAD.
THAT BASTARD...
HE'S HEART-LESS...
WELL, LISTEN ...

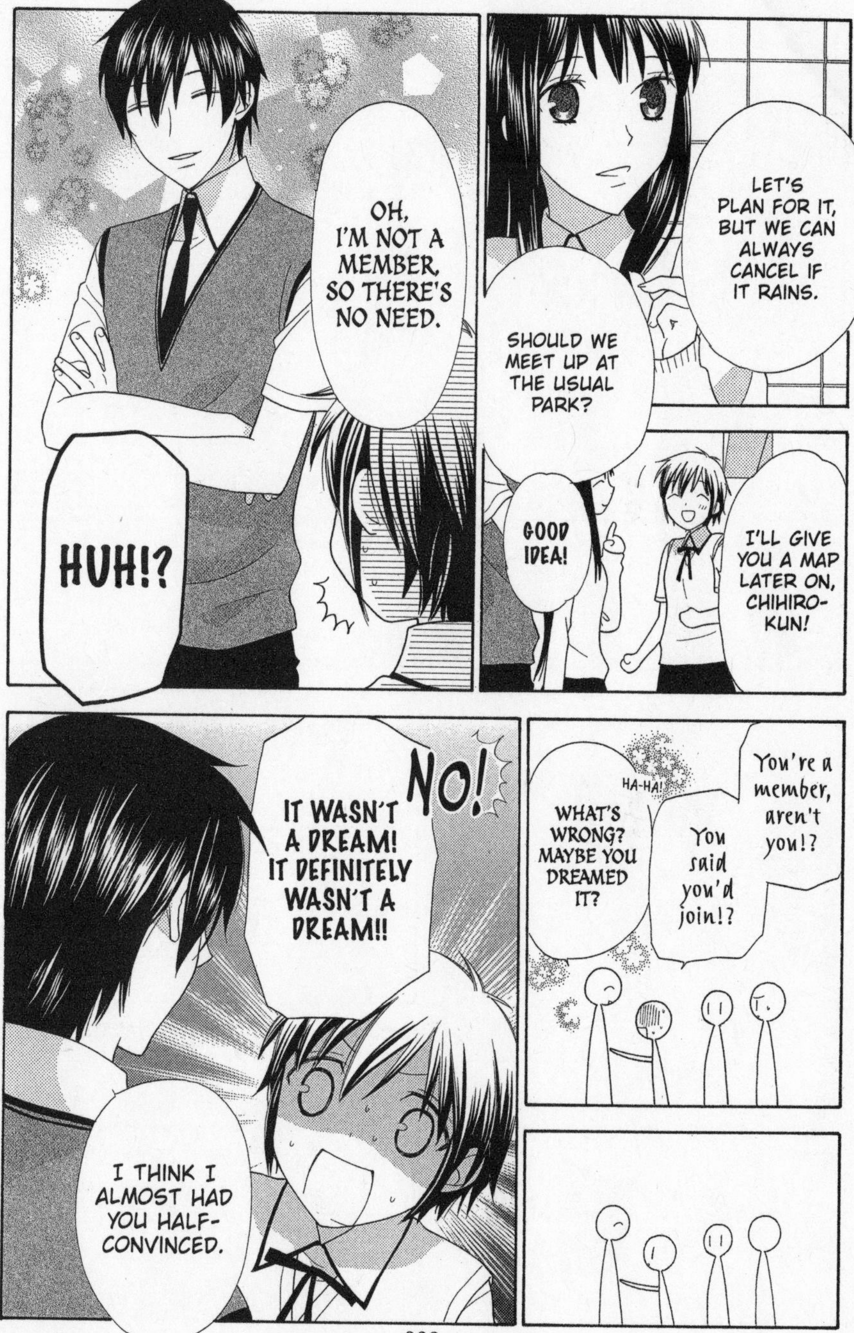
LET'S PLAN FOR IT, BUT WE CAN ALWAYS CANCEL IF IT RAINS.
SHOULD WE MEET UP AT THE USUAL PARK?
I'LL GIVE YOU A MAP LATER ON, CHIHIRO-KUN!
GOOD IDEA!
OH, I'M NOT A MEMBER, SO THERE'S NO NEED.
HUH!?
You're a member, aren't you!?
You said you'd join!?
HA-HA!
WHAT'S WRONG? MAYBE YOU DREAMED IT?
NO!
IT WASN'T A DREAM! IT DEFINITELY WASN'T A DREAM!!
I THINK I ALMOST HAD YOU HALF-CONVINCED.

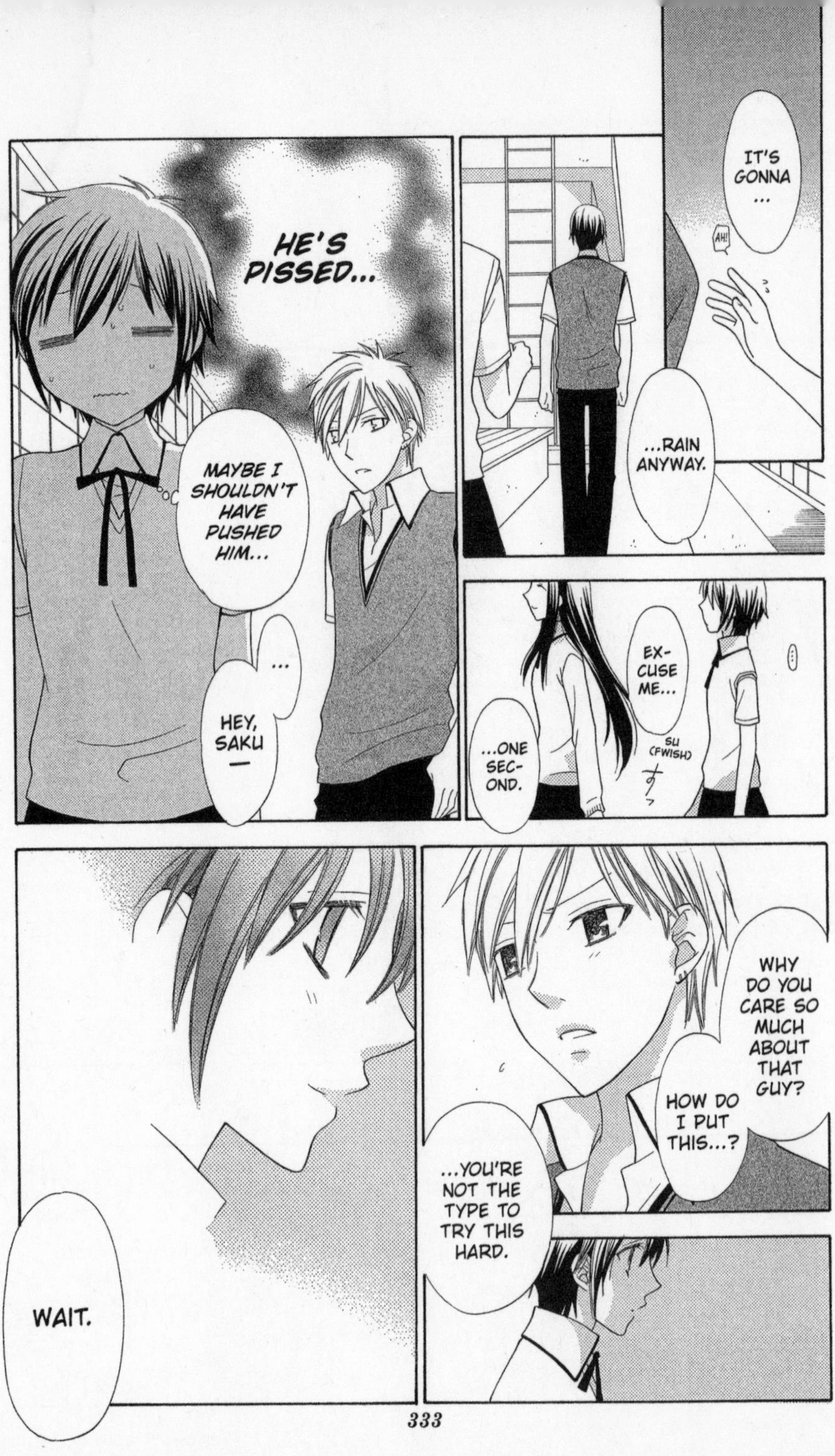

IT'S GONNA ...
AH!
...
...RAIN ANYWAY.
EX-CUSE ME...
!
SU (FWISH)
...ONE SEC-OND.
HE'S PISSED...
MAYBE I SHOULDN'T HAVE PUSHED HIM...
...
HEY, SAKU—
WHY DO YOU CARE SO MUCH ABOUT THAT GUY?
HOW DO I PUT THIS...?
...YOU'RE NOT THE TYPE TO TRY THIS HARD.
WAIT.

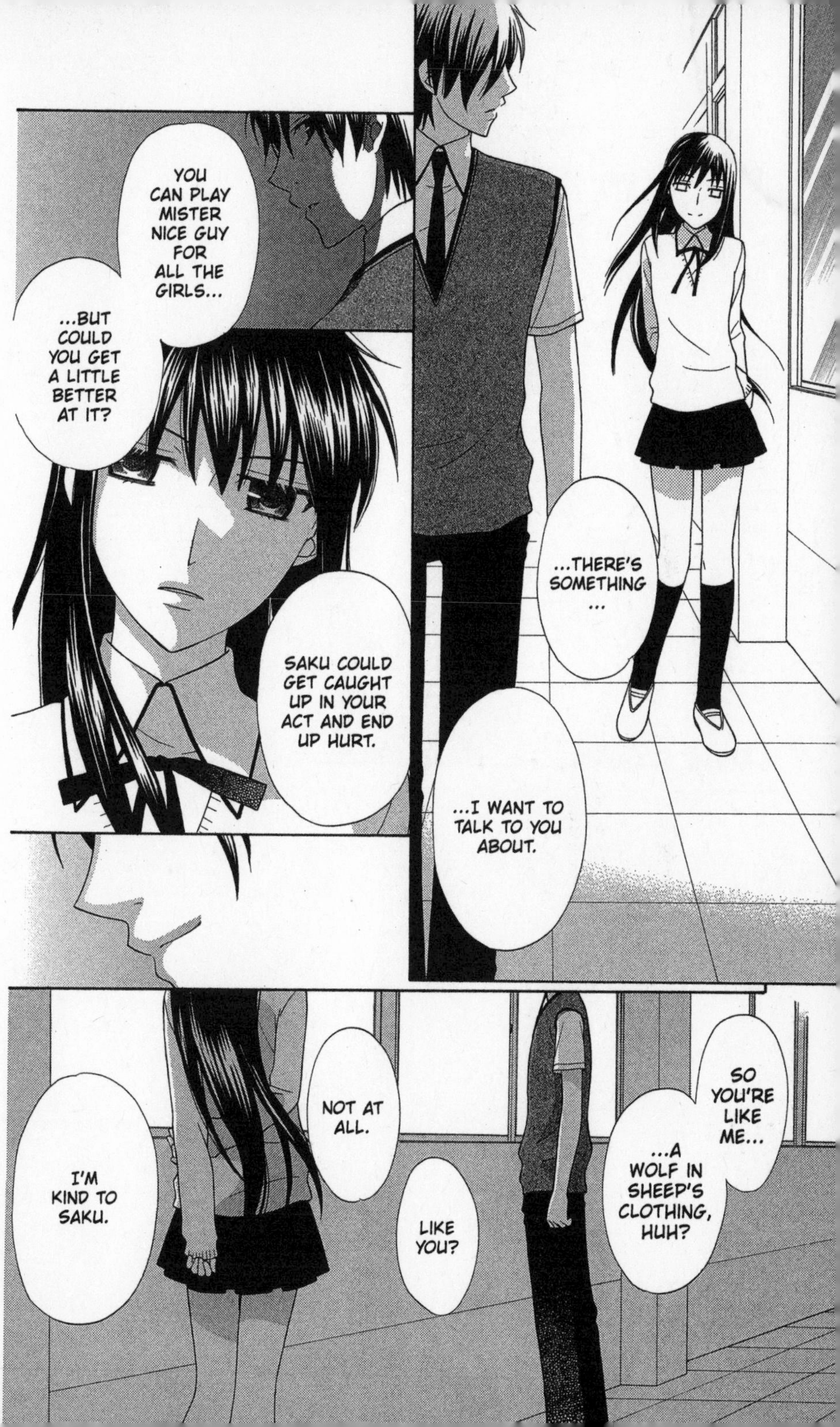
...THERE'S SOMETHING...
...I WANT TO TALK TO YOU ABOUT.
YOU CAN PLAY MISTER NICE GUY FOR ALL THE GIRLS...
...BUT COULD YOU GET A LITTLE BETTER AT IT?
SAKU COULD GET CAUGHT UP IN YOUR ACT AND END UP HURT.
SO YOU'RE LIKE ME...
...A WOLF IN SHEEP'S CLOTHING, HUH?
NOT AT ALL.
LIKE YOU?
I'M KIND TO SAKU.

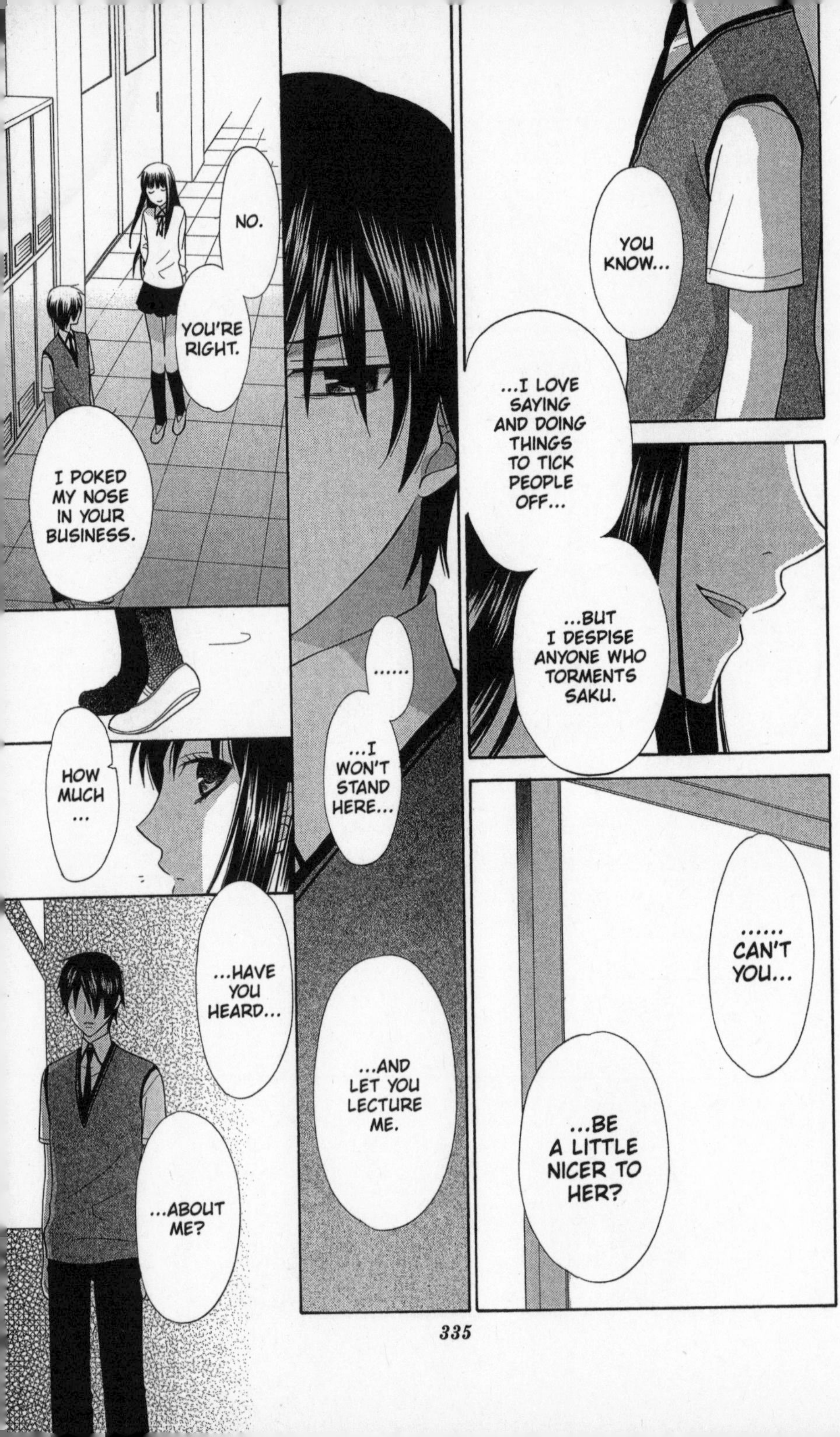
YOU KNOW...
...I LOVE SAYING AND DOING THINGS TO TICK PEOPLE OFF...
...BUT I DESPISE ANYONE WHO TORMENTS SAKU.
......CAN'T YOU...
...BE A LITTLE NICER TO HER?
......
...I WON'T STAND HERE...
...AND LET YOU LECTURE ME.
NO.
YOU'RE RIGHT.
I POKED MY NOSE IN YOUR BUSINESS.
HOW MUCH ...
...HAVE YOU HEARD...
...ABOUT ME?

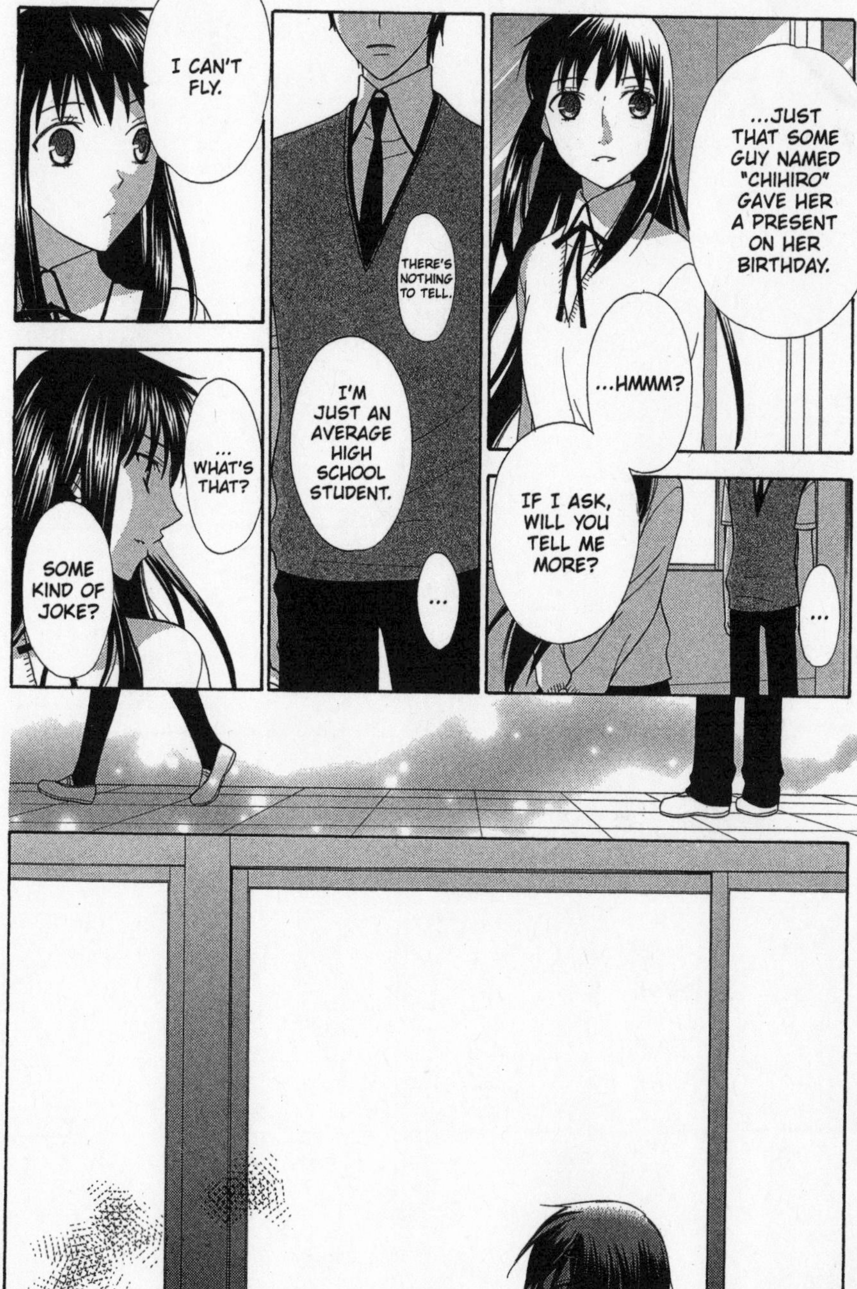
...JUST THAT SOME GUY NAMED "CHIHIRO" GAVE HER A PRESENT ON HER BIRTHDAY.
...HMMM?
IF I ASK, WILL YOU TELL ME MORE?
...
THERE'S NOTHING TO TELL.
I'M JUST AN AVERAGE HIGH SCHOOL STUDENT.
...
I CAN'T FLY.
...WHAT'S THAT?
SOME KIND OF JOKE?

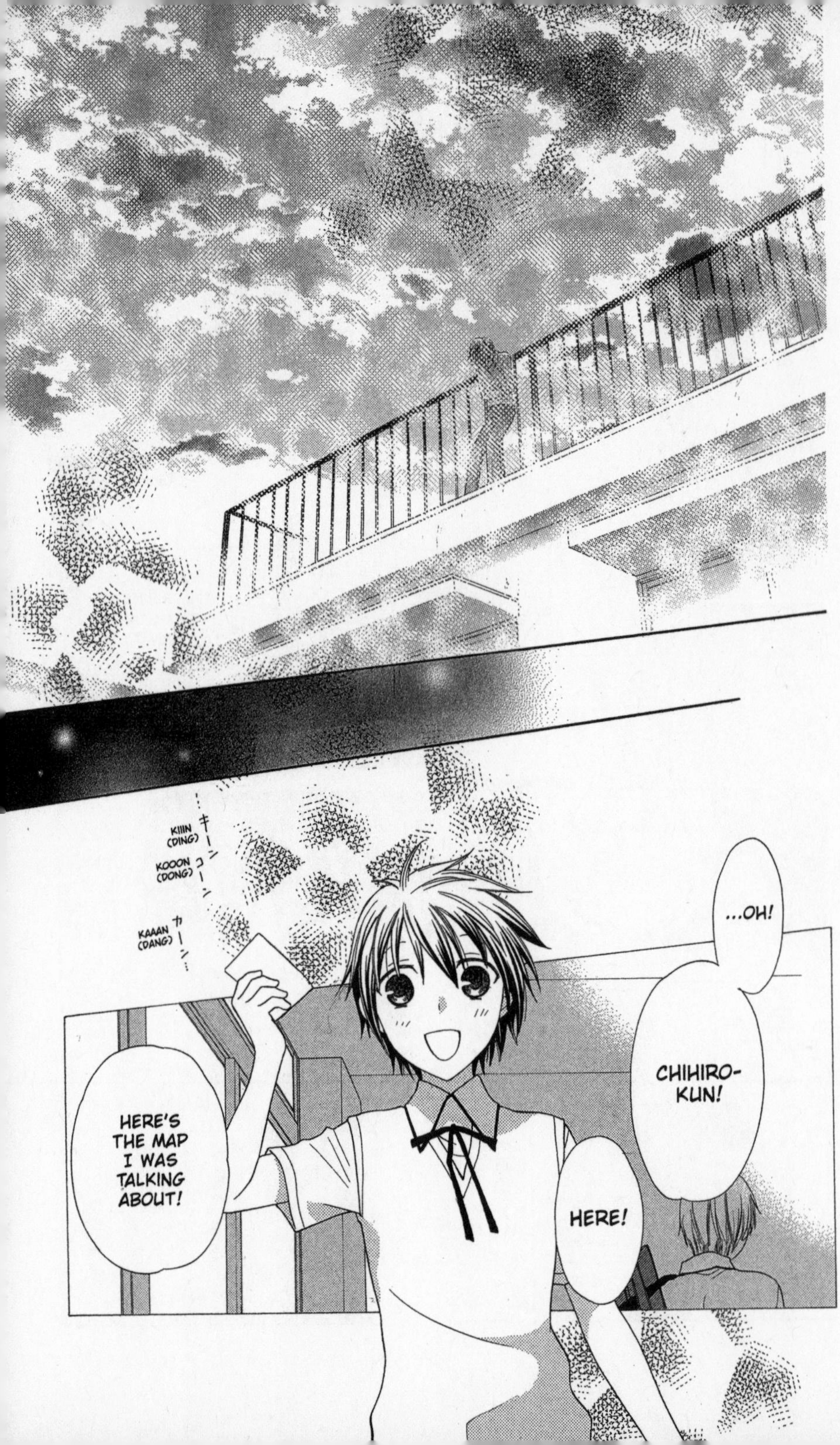
KIIIN (DING) キーン
KOOON (DONG) コーン
KAAAN (DANG) カーン
...OH!
CHIHIRO-KUN!
HERE!
HERE'S THE MAP I WAS TALKING ABOUT!

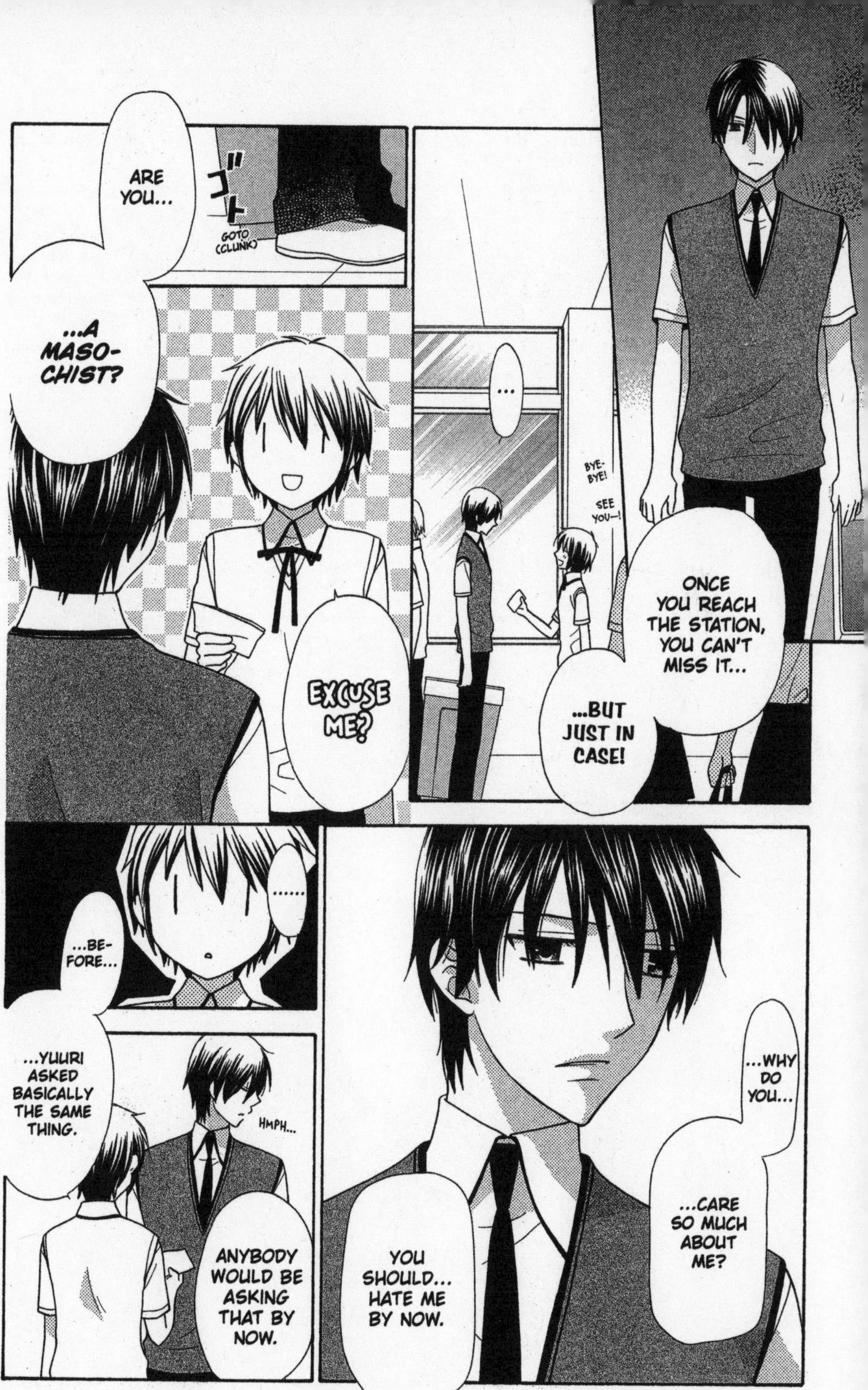
ONCE YOU REACH THE STATION, YOU CAN'T MISS IT...
...BUT JUST IN CASE!
...
BYE-BYE!
SEE YOU—!
ARE YOU...
GOTO (CLUNK)
...A MASO-CHIST?
EXCUSE ME?
...WHY DO YOU...
...CARE SO MUCH ABOUT ME?
YOU SHOULD... HATE ME BY NOW.
......
...BE-FORE...
...YUURI ASKED BASICALLY THE SAME THING.
HMPH...
ANYBODY WOULD BE ASKING THAT BY NOW.

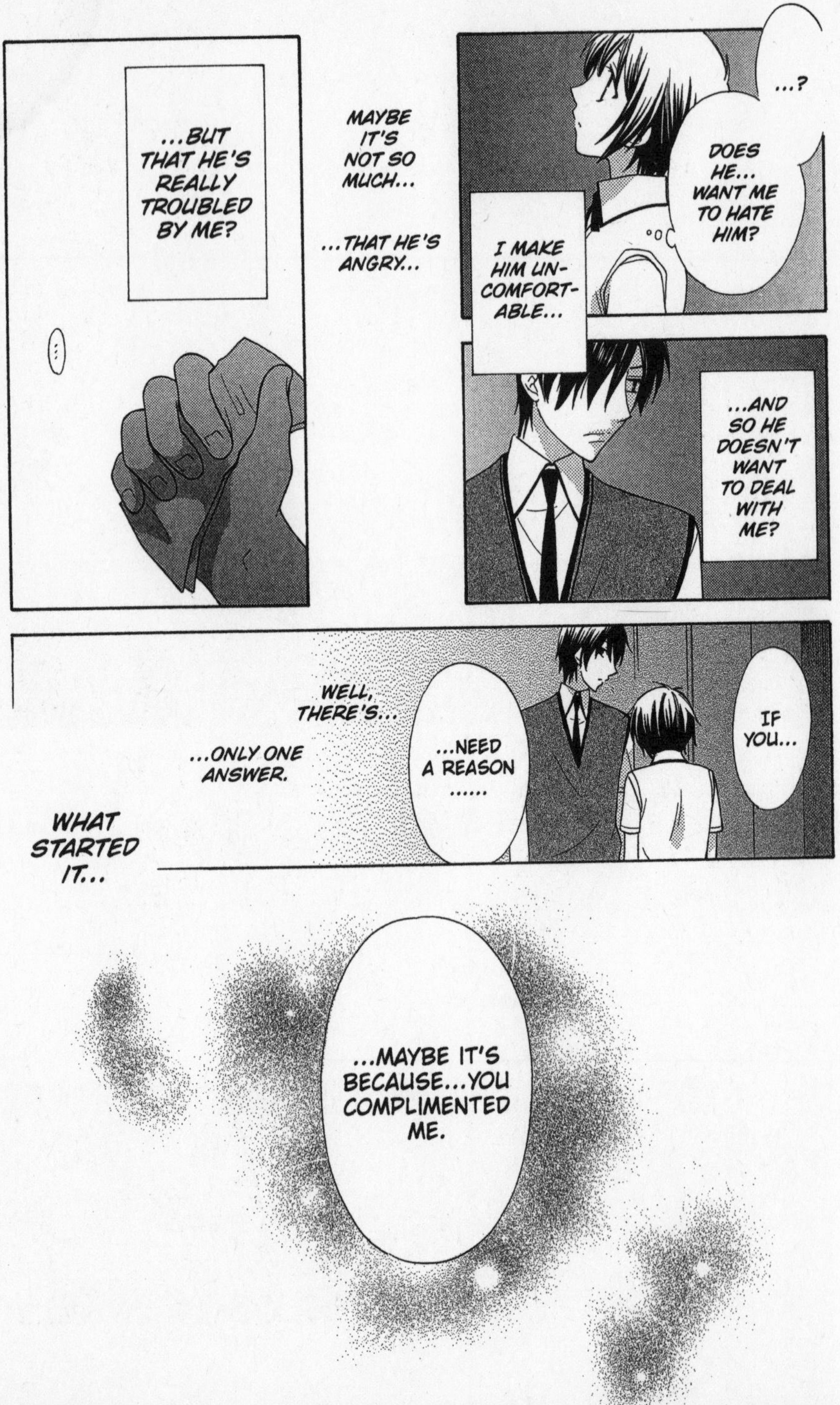
...?
DOES HE... WANT ME TO HATE HIM?
I MAKE HIM UN-COMFORT-ABLE...
...AND SO HE DOESN'T WANT TO DEAL WITH ME?
MAYBE IT'S NOT SO MUCH...
...THAT HE'S ANGRY...
...BUT THAT HE'S REALLY TROUBLED BY ME?
...
IF YOU...
...NEED A REASON ......
WELL, THERE'S...
...ONLY ONE ANSWER.
WHAT STARTED IT...
...MAYBE IT'S BECAUSE...YOU COMPLIMENTED ME.

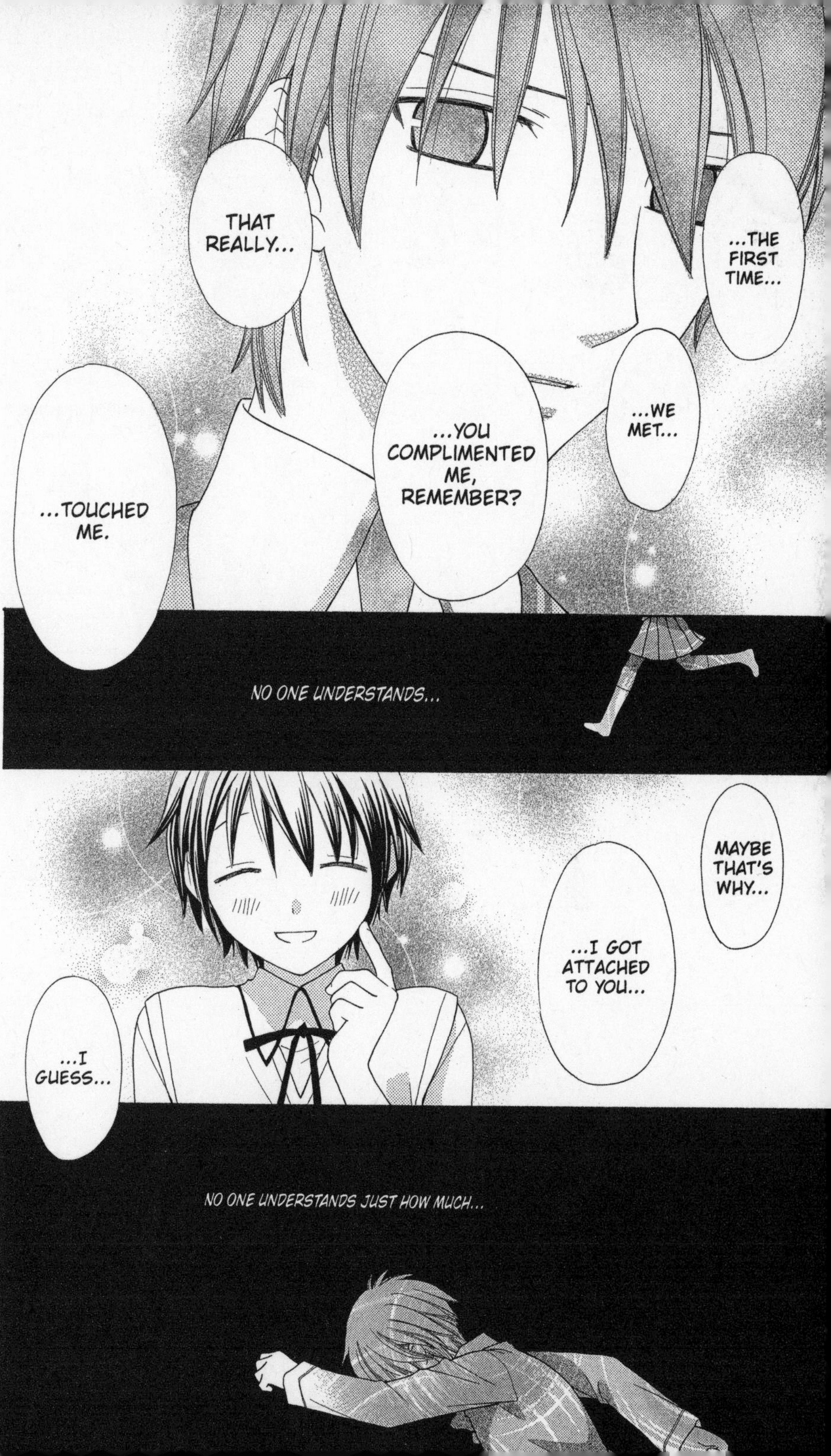
...THE FIRST TIME...
...WE MET...
...YOU COMPLIMENTED ME, REMEMBER?
THAT REALLY...
...TOUCHED ME.
NO ONE UNDERSTANDS...
MAYBE THAT'S WHY...
...I GOT ATTACHED TO YOU...
...I GUESS...
NO ONE UNDERSTANDS JUST HOW MUCH...

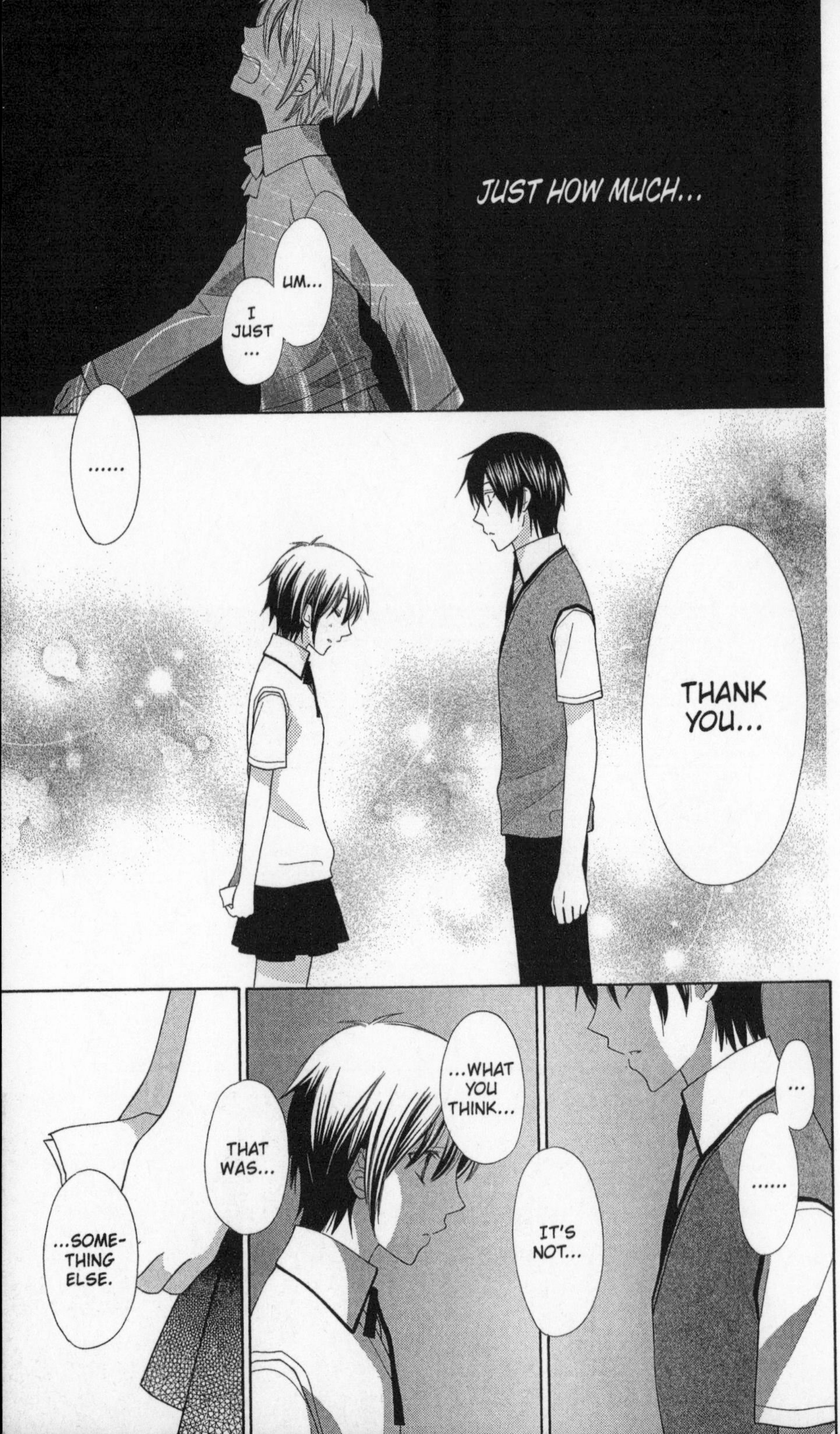

JUST HOW MUCH...
UM...
I JUST ...
THANK YOU...
......
...
......
IT'S NOT...
...WHAT YOU THINK...
THAT WAS...
...SOME-THING ELSE.

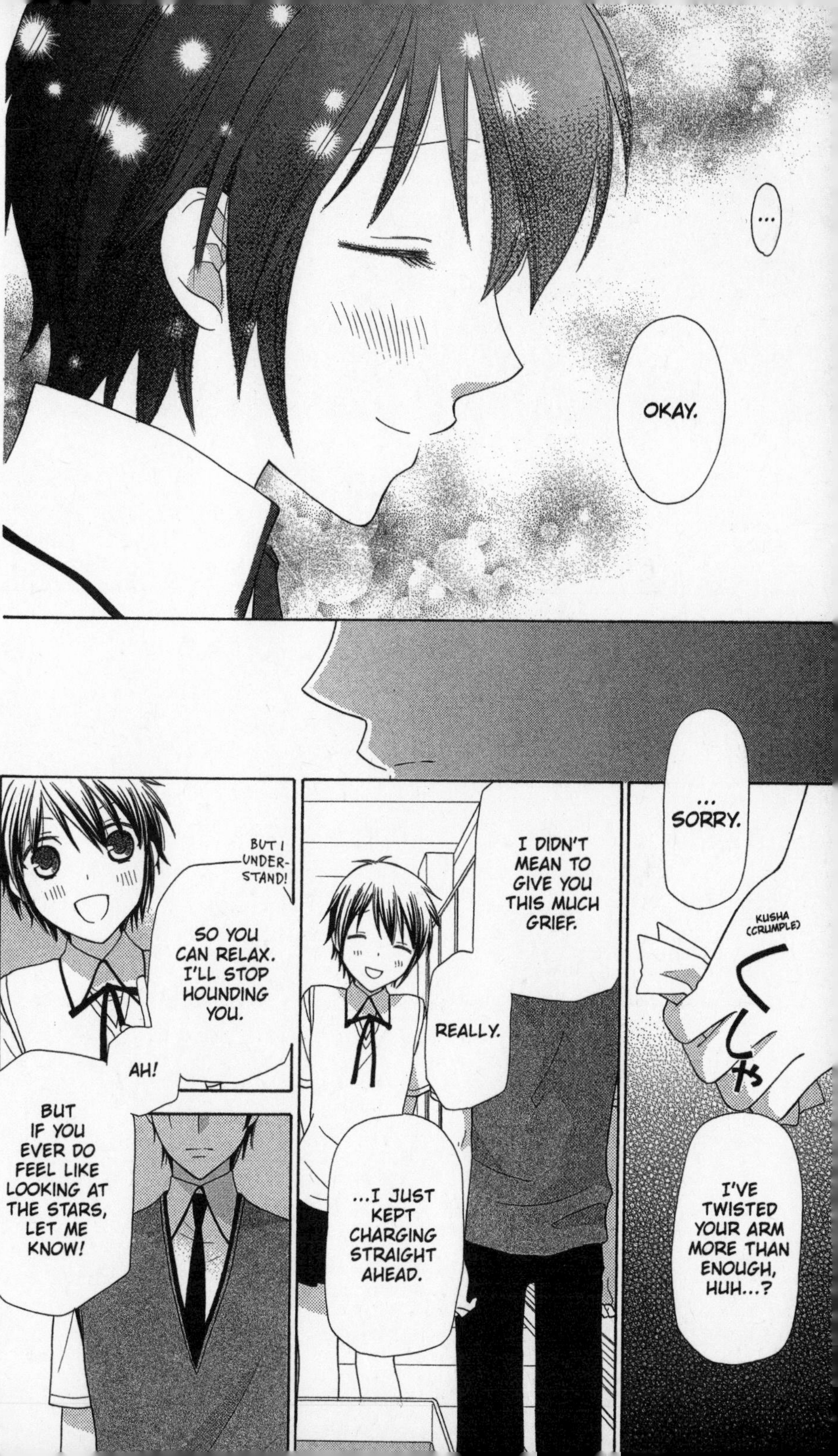
...
OKAY.
... SORRY.
KUSHA (CRUMPLE)
くしゃ
I'VE TWISTED YOUR ARM MORE THAN ENOUGH, HUH...?
I DIDN'T MEAN TO GIVE YOU THIS MUCH GRIEF.
REALLY.
...I JUST KEPT CHARGING STRAIGHT AHEAD.
BUT I UNDERSTAND!
SO YOU CAN RELAX. I'LL STOP HOUNDING YOU.
AH!
BUT IF YOU EVER DO FEEL LIKE LOOKING AT THE STARS, LET ME KNOW!

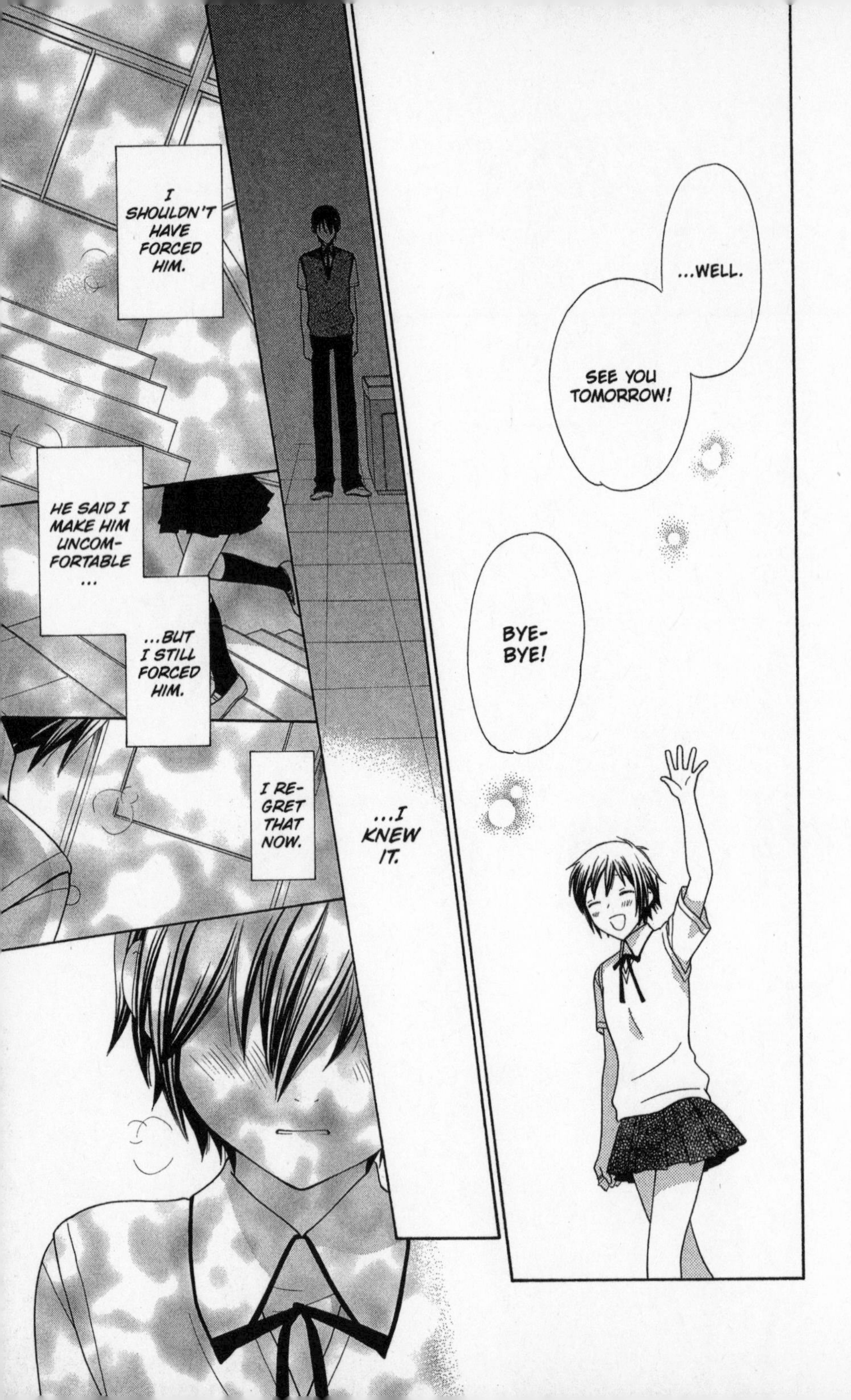
...WELL.
SEE YOU TOMORROW!
BYE-BYE!
...I KNEW IT.
I SHOULDN'T HAVE FORCED HIM.
HE SAID I MAKE HIM UNCOMFORTABLE ...
...BUT I STILL FORCED HIM.
I REGRET THAT NOW.

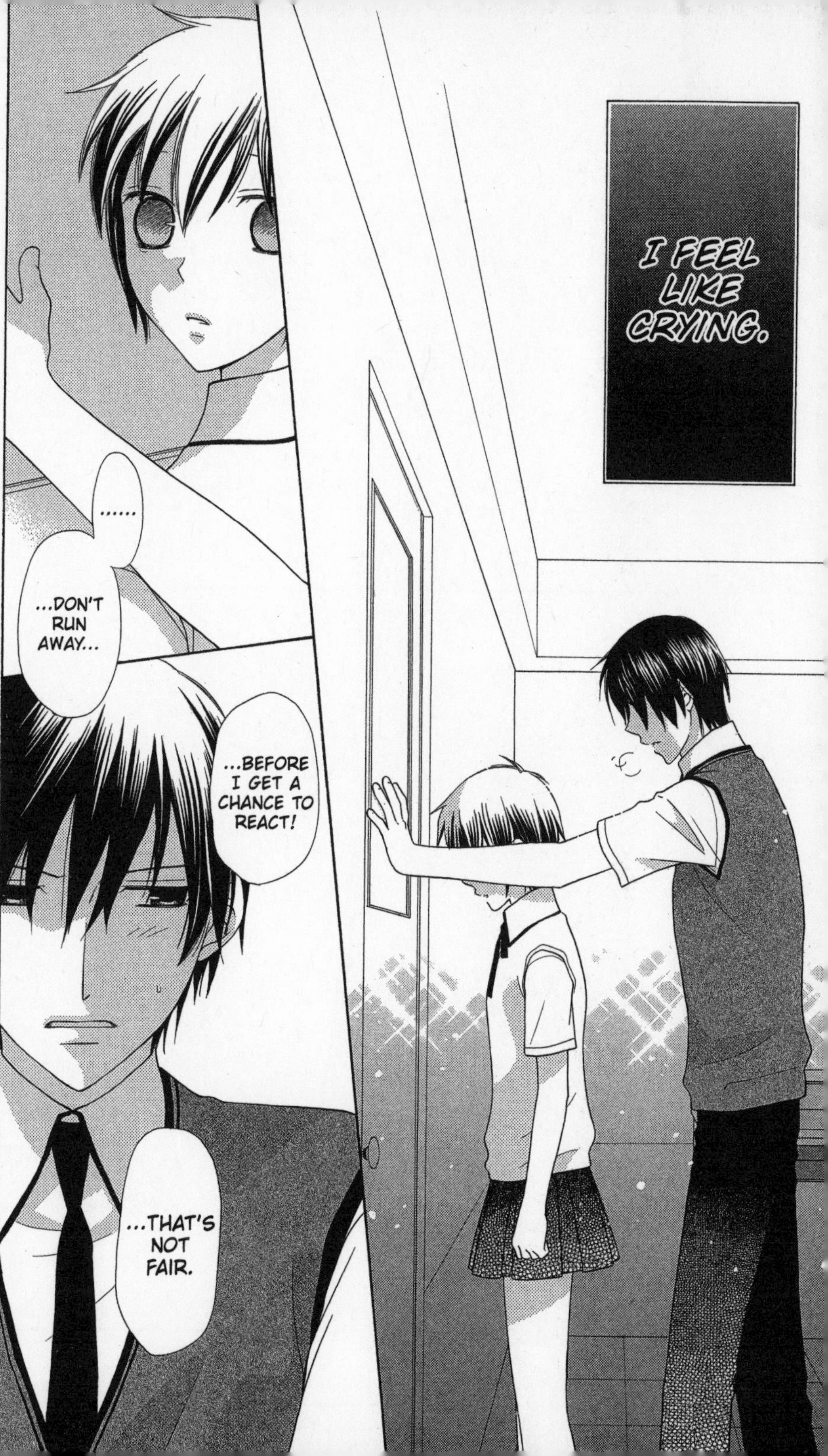
I FEEL LIKE CRYING.
......
...DON'T RUN AWAY...
...BEFORE I GET A CHANCE TO REACT!
...THAT'S NOT FAIR.

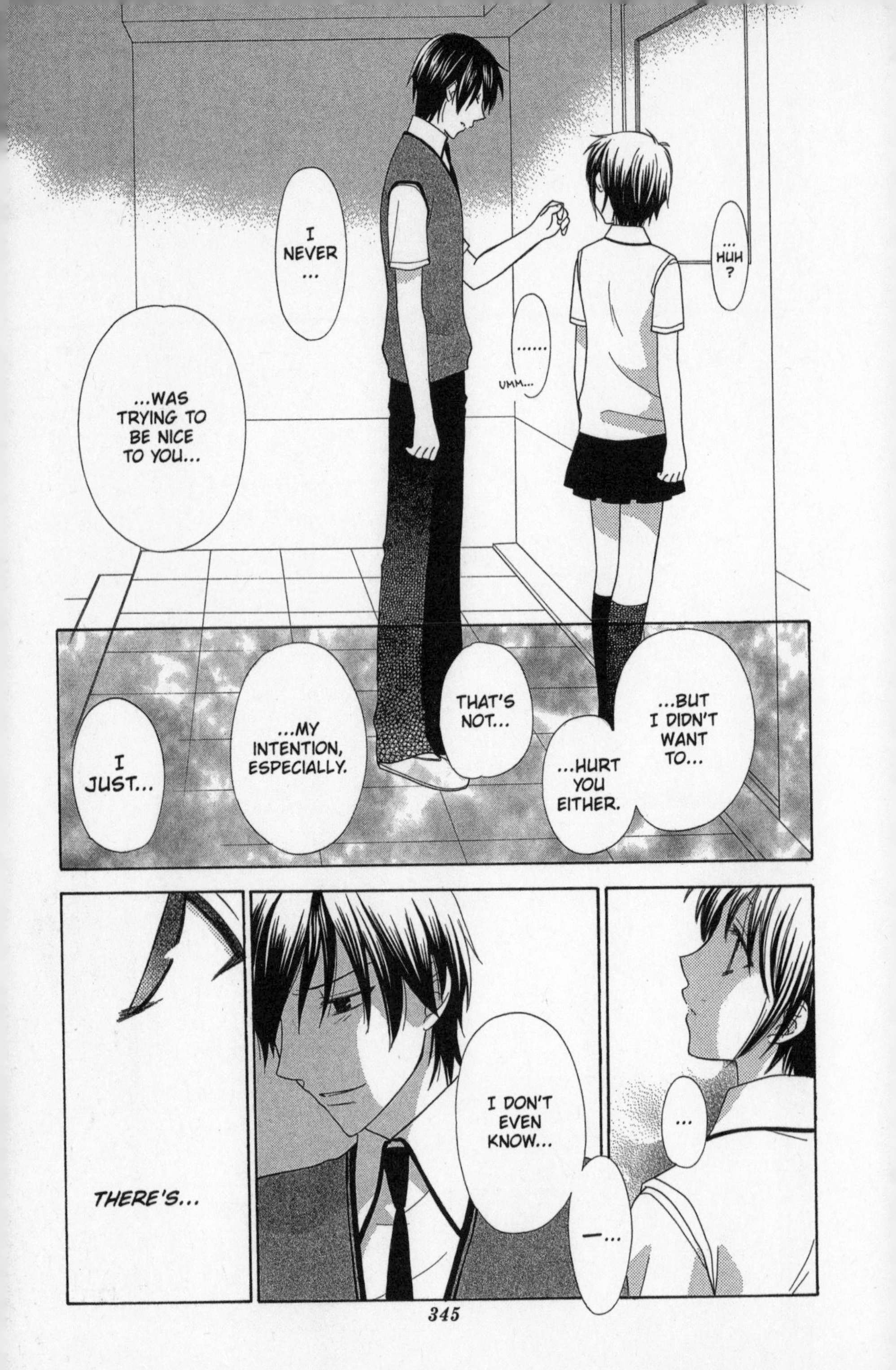
...HUH?
......
UMM...
I NEVER...
...WAS TRYING TO BE NICE TO YOU...
...BUT I DIDN'T WANT TO...
...HURT YOU EITHER.
THAT'S NOT...
...MY INTENTION, ESPECIALLY.
I JUST...
...
—...
I DON'T EVEN KNOW...
THERE'S...

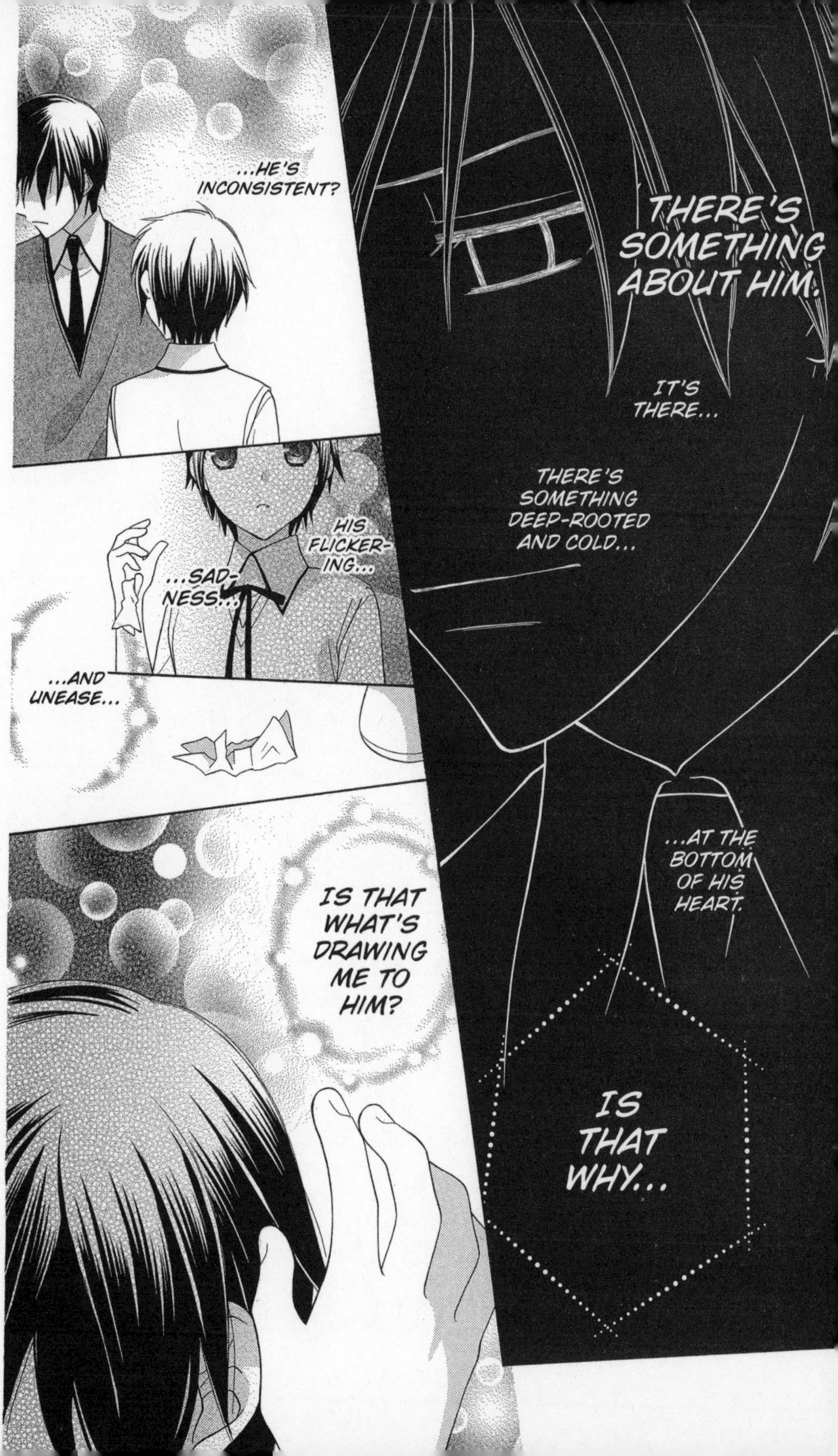
THERE'S SOMETHING ABOUT HIM.
IT'S THERE...
THERE'S SOMETHING DEEP-ROOTED AND COLD...
...AT THE BOTTOM OF HIS HEART.
IS THAT WHY...
...HE'S INCONSISTENT?
HIS FLICKERING...
...SADNESS...
...AND UNEASE...
IS THAT WHAT'S DRAWING ME TO HIM?

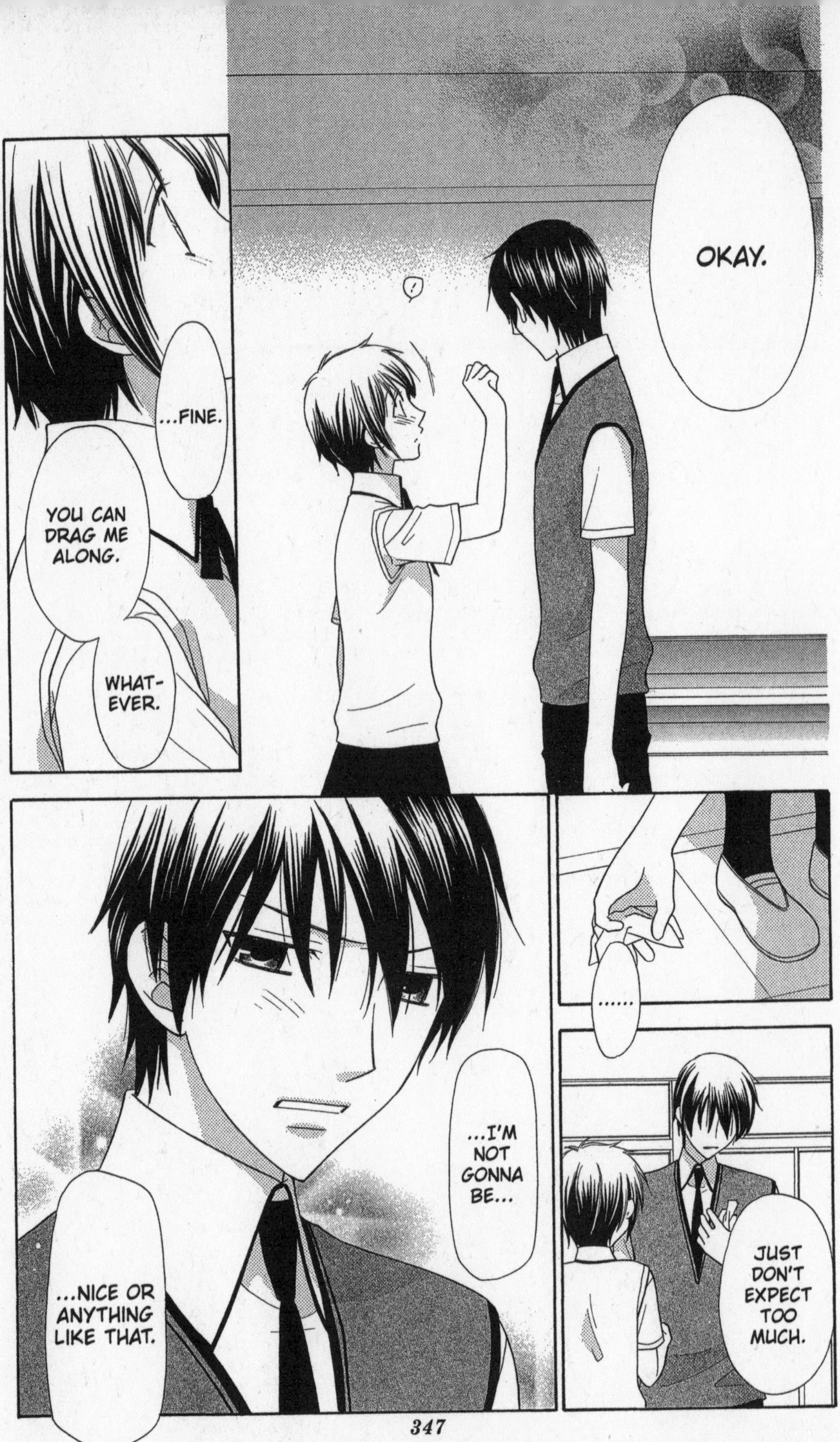
OKAY.
!
...FINE.
YOU CAN DRAG ME ALONG.
WHAT-EVER.
......
JUST DON'T EXPECT TOO MUCH.
...I'M NOT GONNA BE...
...NICE OR ANYTHING LIKE THAT.

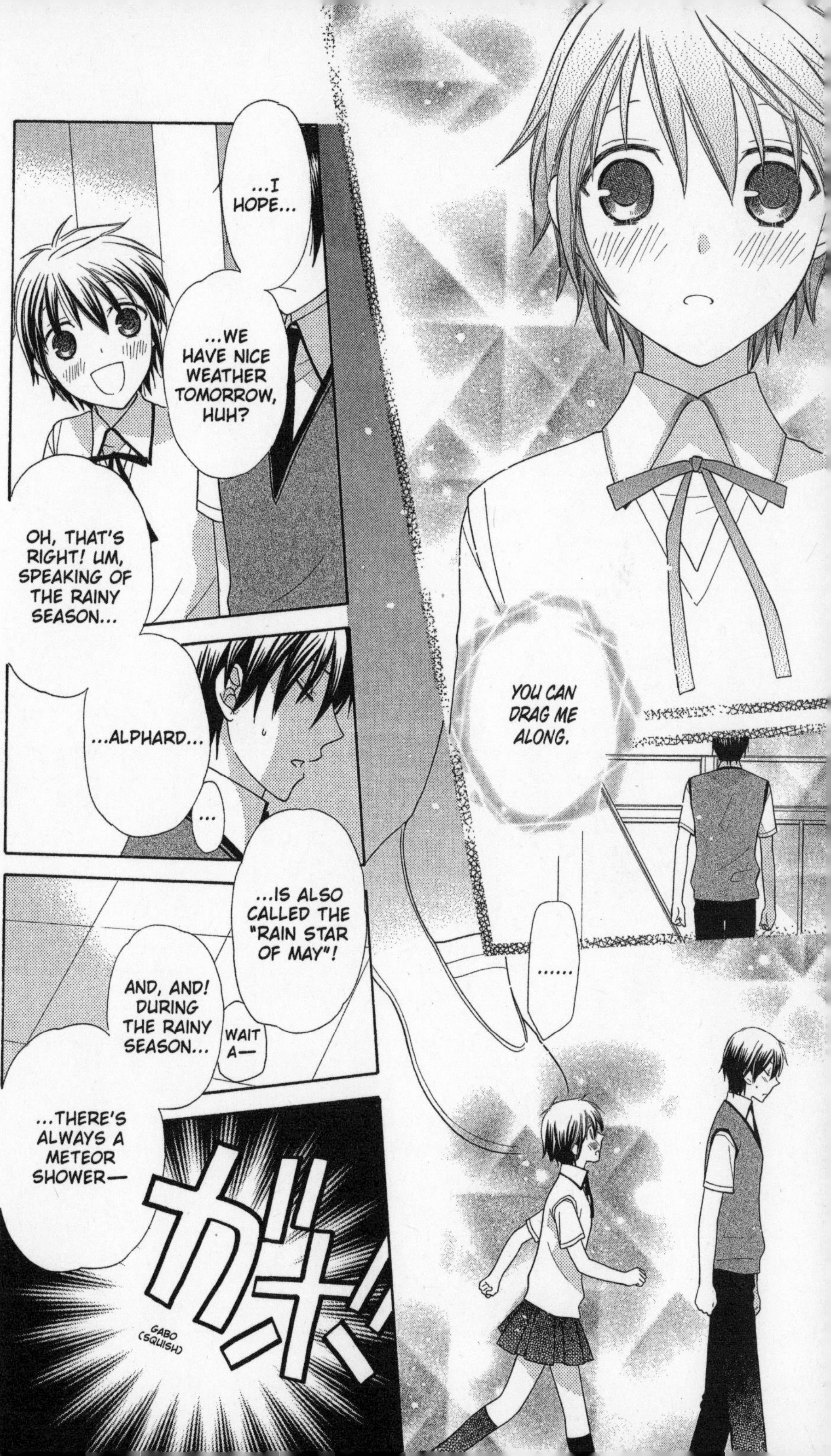
YOU CAN DRAG ME ALONG.
......
...I HOPE...
...WE HAVE NICE WEATHER TOMORROW, HUH?
OH, THAT'S RIGHT! UM, SPEAKING OF THE RAINY SEASON...
...ALPHARD...
...
...IS ALSO CALLED THE "RAIN STAR OF MAY"!
WAIT A—
AND, AND! DURING THE RAINY SEASON...
...THERE'S ALWAYS A METEOR SHOWER—
GABO (SQUISH)

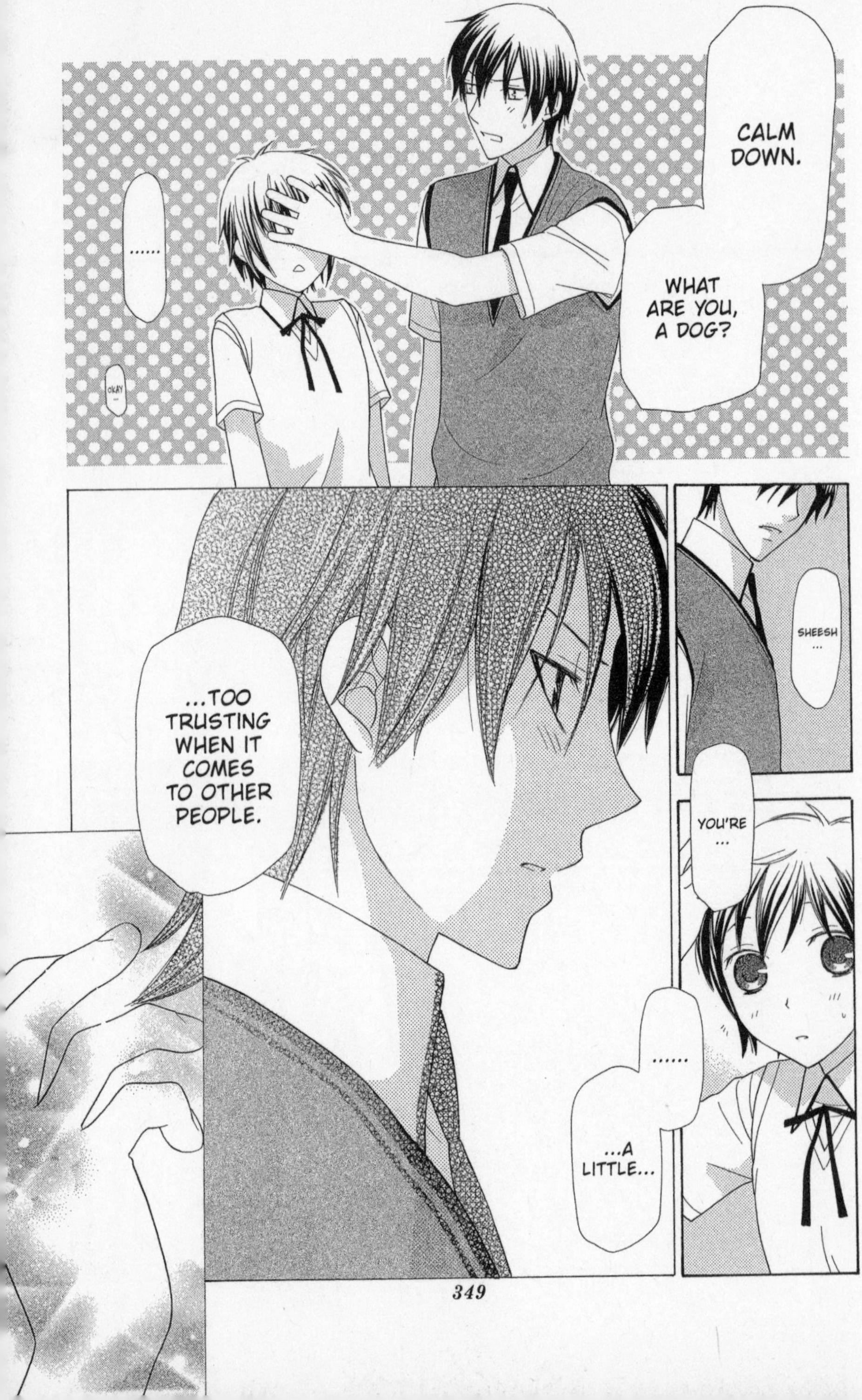
CALM DOWN.
WHAT ARE YOU, A DOG?
......
OKAY...
SHEESH...
YOU'RE...
......
...A LITTLE...
...TOO TRUSTING WHEN IT COMES TO OTHER PEOPLE.

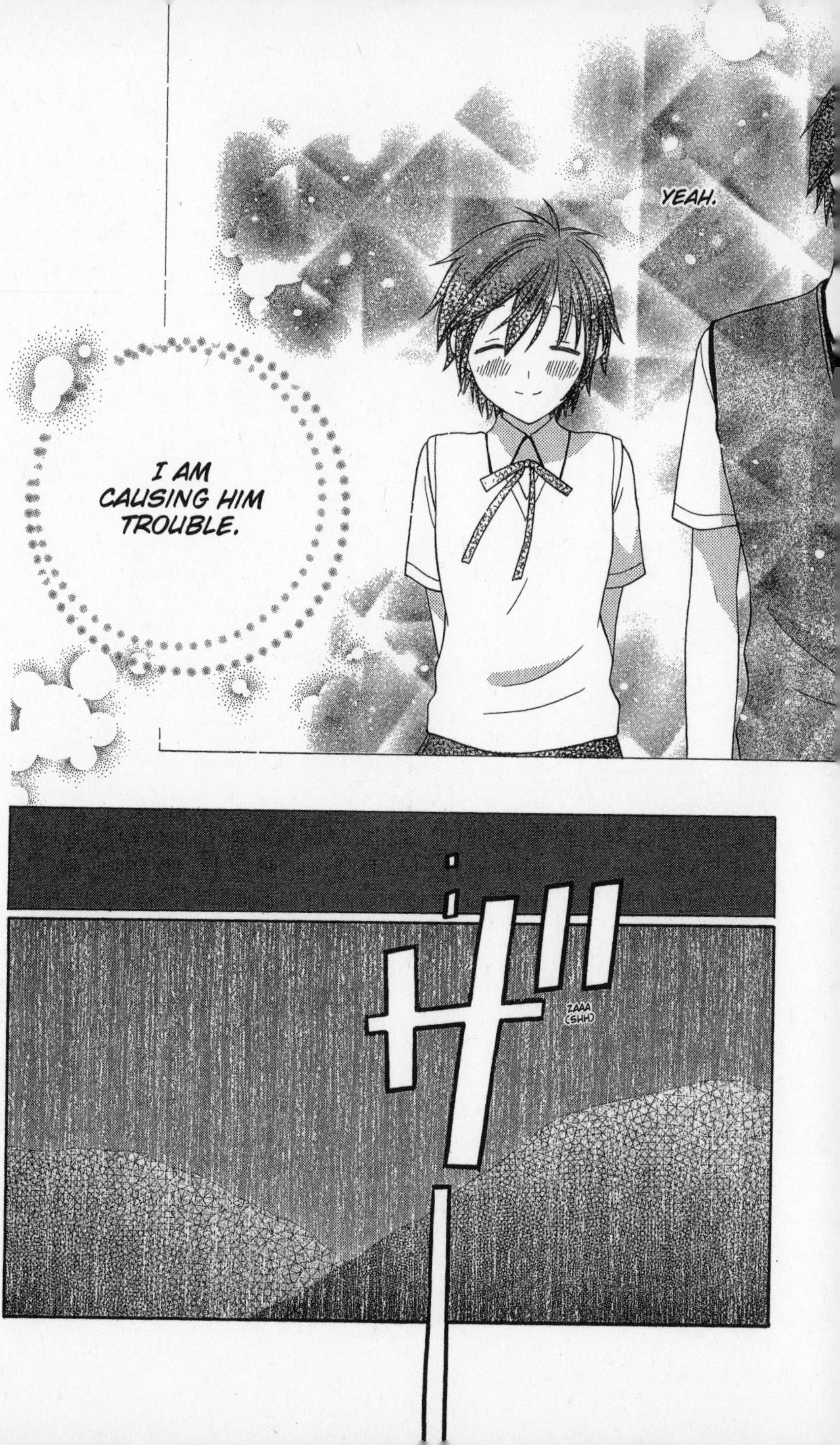
YEAH.
I AM CAUSING HIM TROUBLE.
ZAAA (SHH)

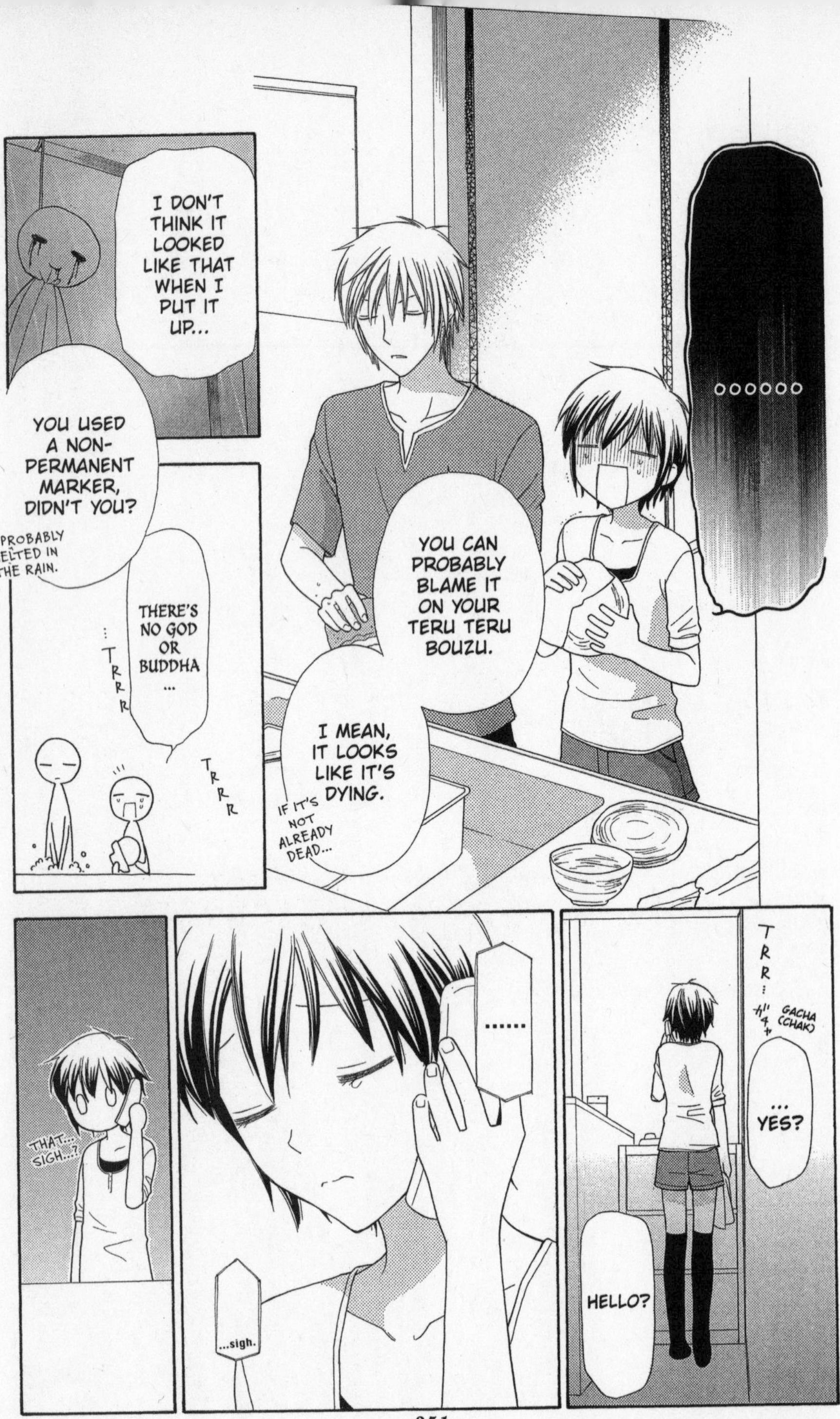
oooooo
YOU CAN PROBABLY BLAME IT ON YOUR TERU TERU BOUZU.
I MEAN, IT LOOKS LIKE IT'S DYING.
IF IT'S NOT ALREADY DEAD...
I DON'T THINK IT LOOKED LIKE THAT WHEN I PUT IT UP...
YOU USED A NON-PERMANENT MARKER, DIDN'T YOU?
IT PROBABLY MELTED IN THE RAIN.
THERE'S NO GOD OR BUDDHA...
...TRRR
TRRR
TRR...
GACHA (CHAK)
...YES?
HELLO?
......
...sigh.
THAT... SIGH...?

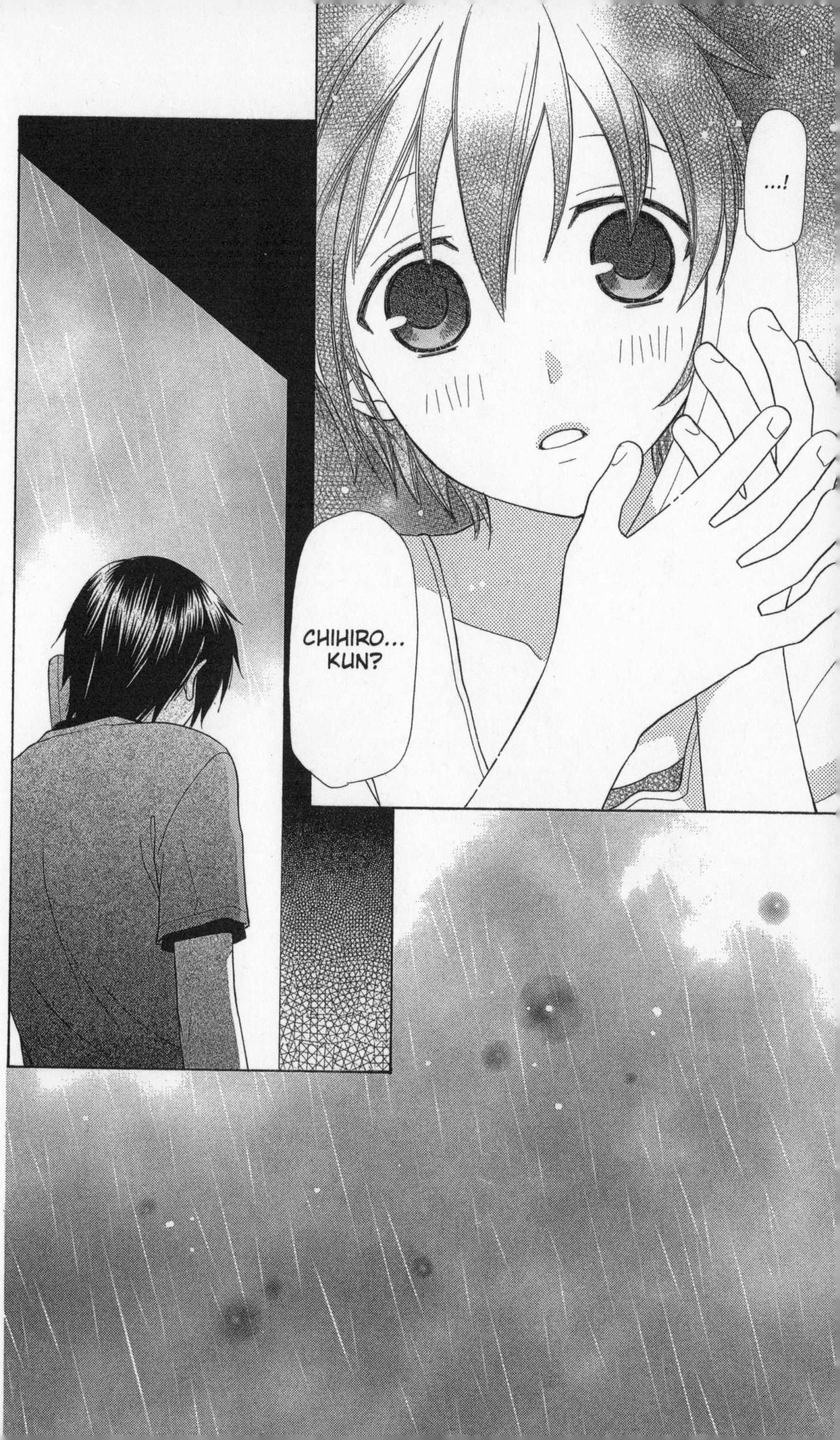
...!
CHIHIRO... KUN?

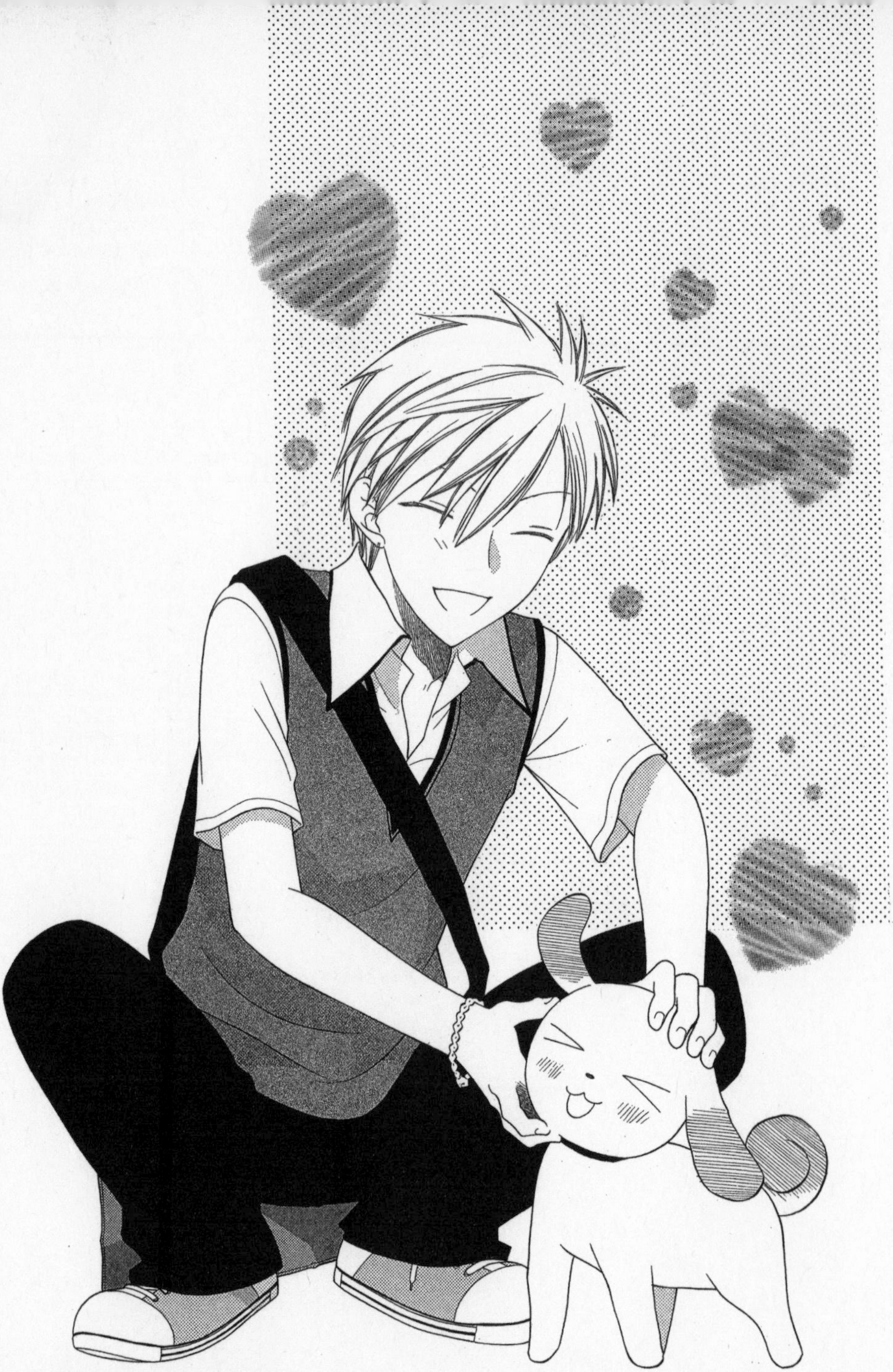

Chapter 11

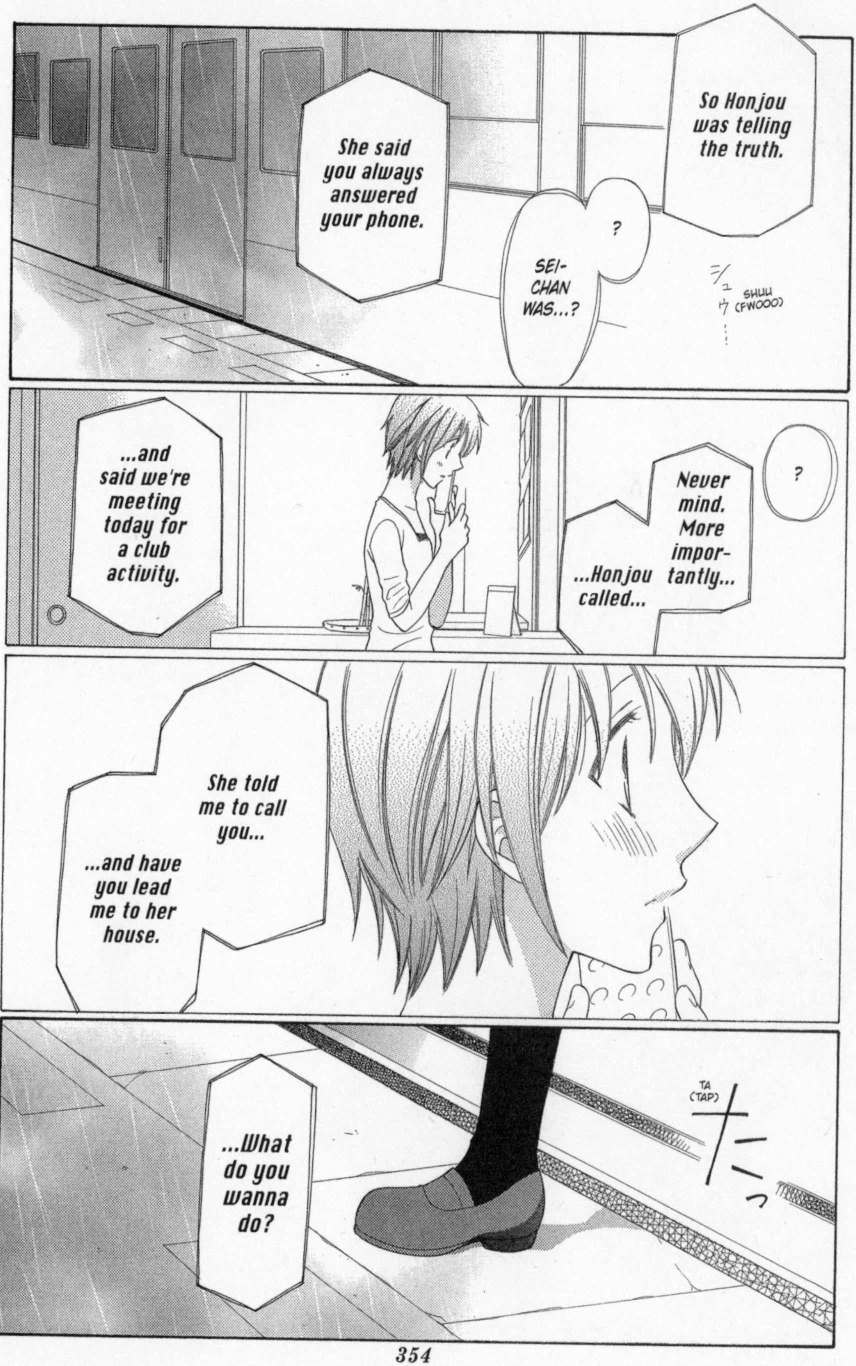
So Honjou was telling the truth.
SHUU (FWOOO)
?
SEI-CHAN WAS...?
She said you always answered your phone.
?
Never mind. More impor-tantly...
...Honjou called...
...and said we're meeting today for a club activity.
She told me to call you...
...and have you lead me to her house.
TA (TAP)
...What do you wanna do?

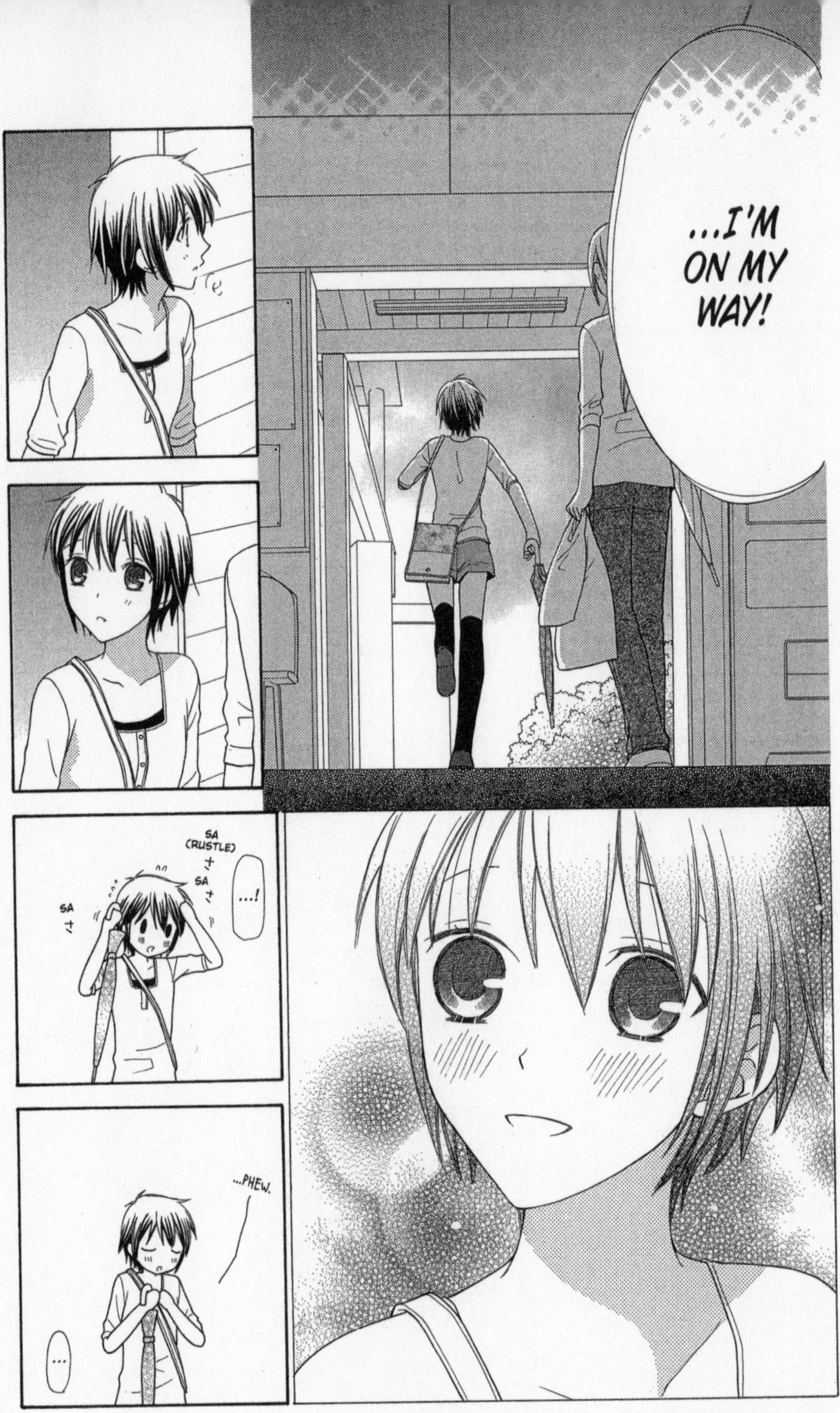
...I'M ON MY WAY!
...!
SA (RUSTLE) さ
SA さ
SA さ
...PHEW.
...

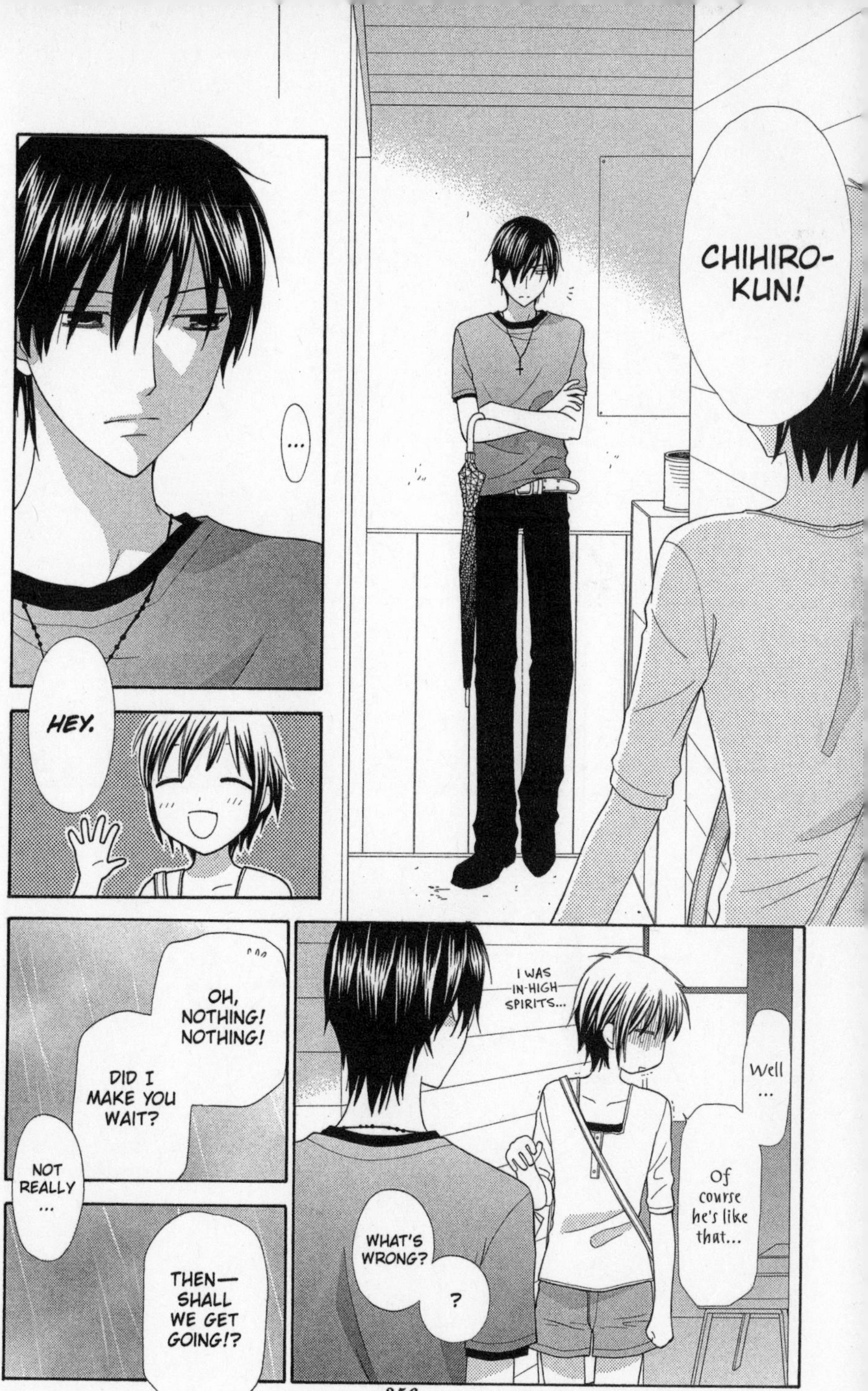
CHIHIRO-KUN!
...
HEY.
I WAS IN-HIGH SPIRITS...
Well ...
Of course he's like that...
WHAT'S WRONG?
?
OH, NOTHING! NOTHING!
DID I MAKE YOU WAIT?
NOT REALLY ...
THEN— SHALL WE GET GOING!?

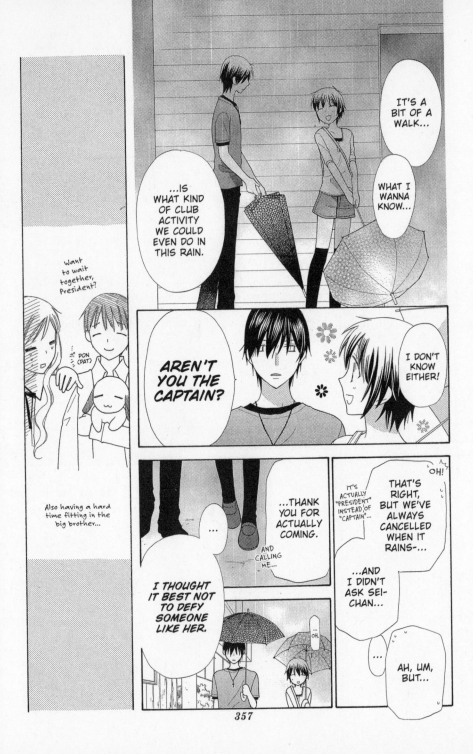

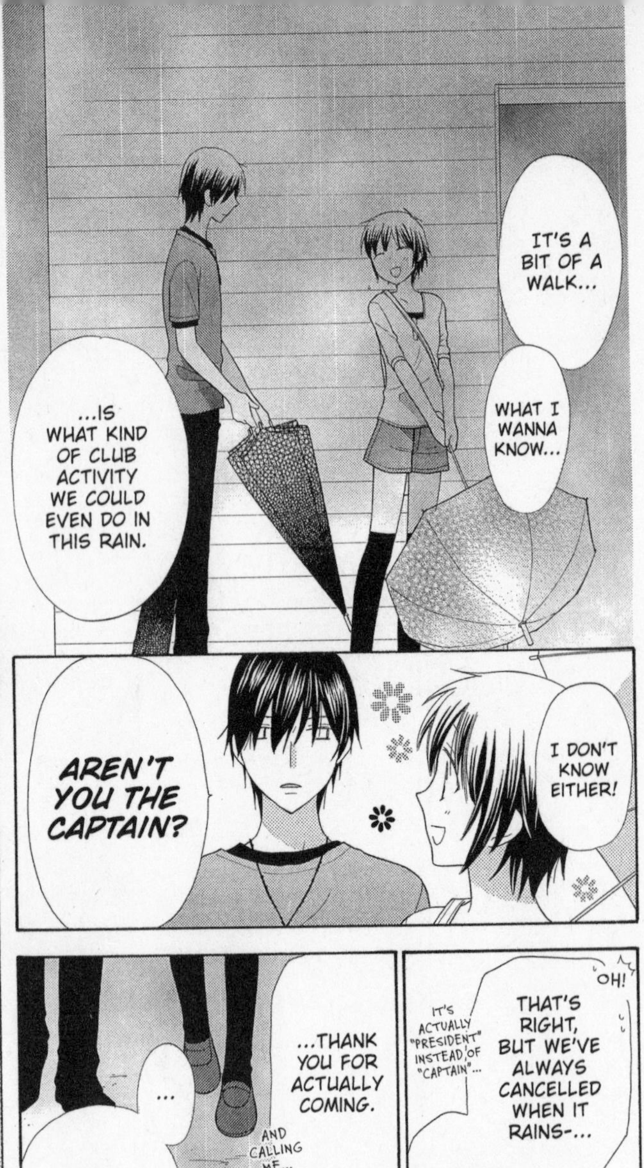
IT'S A BIT OF A WALK...
WHAT I WANNA KNOW...
...IS WHAT KIND OF CLUB ACTIVITY WE COULD EVEN DO IN THIS RAIN.
I DON'T KNOW EITHER!
AREN'T YOU THE CAPTAIN?
OH!
THAT'S RIGHT, BUT WE'VE ALWAYS CANCELLED WHEN IT RAINS-...
IT'S ACTUALLY "PRESIDENT" INSTEAD OF "CAPTAIN"...
...AND I DIDN'T ASK SEI-CHAN...
...
AH, UM, BUT...
...THANK YOU FOR ACTUALLY COMING.
AND CALLING ME...
...
...OH.
I THOUGHT IT BEST NOT TO DEFY SOMEONE LIKE HER.

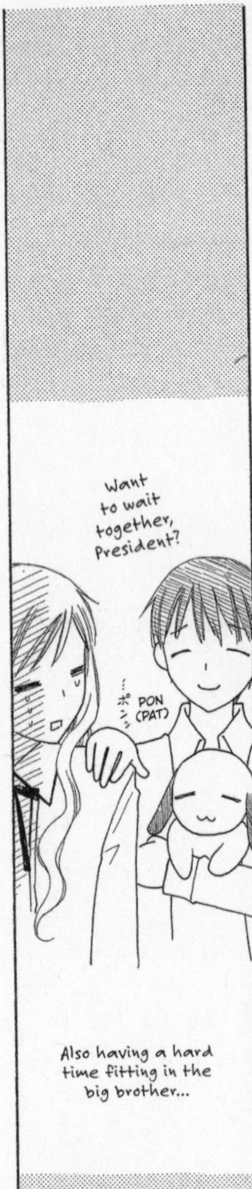
Want to wait together, President?
PON (PAT)
Also having a hard time fitting in the big brother...

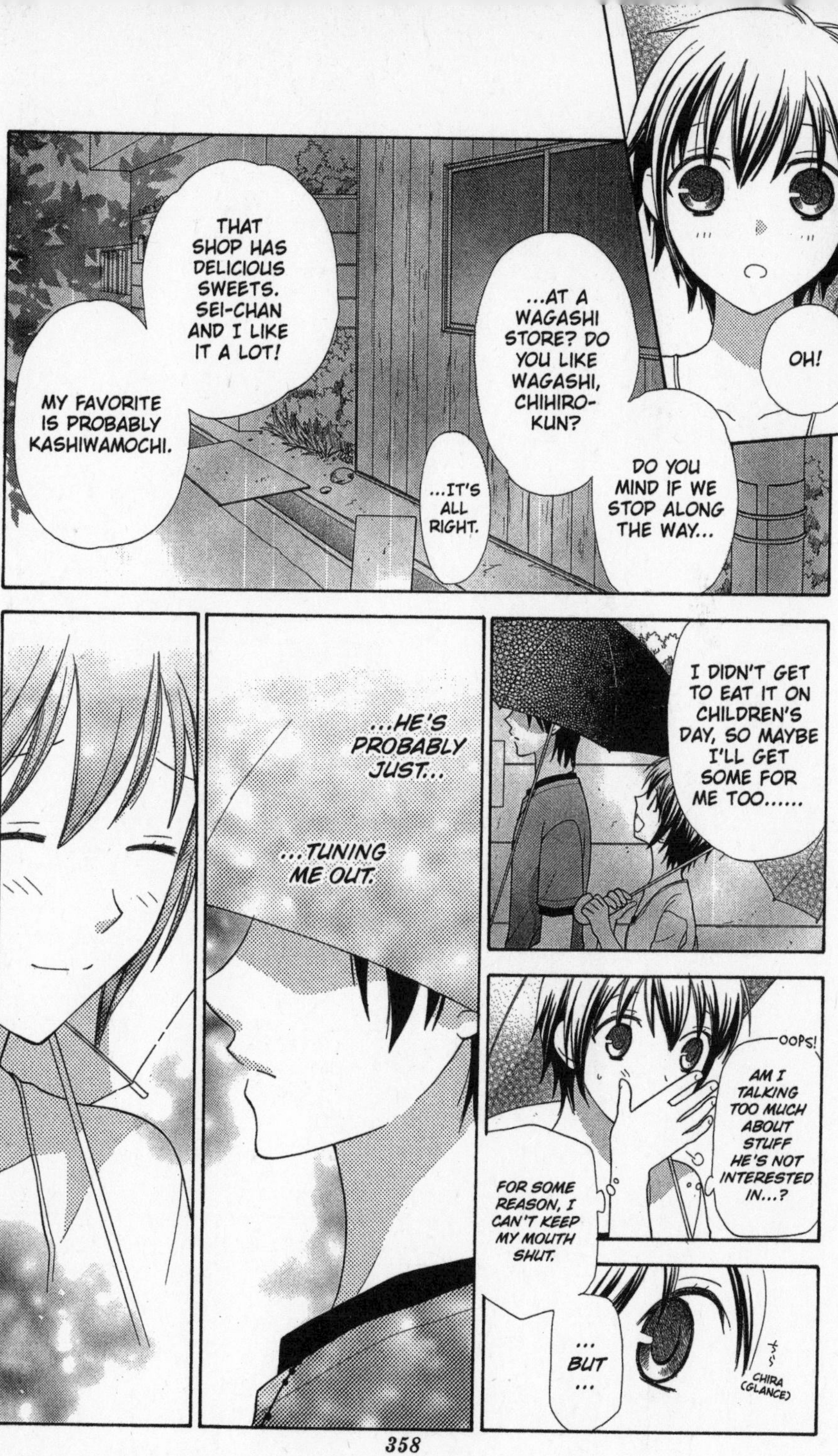
OH!
DO YOU MIND IF WE STOP ALONG THE WAY...
...AT A WAGASHI STORE? DO YOU LIKE WAGASHI, CHIHIRO-KUN?
...IT'S ALL RIGHT.
THAT SHOP HAS DELICIOUS SWEETS. SEI-CHAN AND I LIKE IT A LOT!
MY FAVORITE IS PROBABLY KASHIWAMOCHI.
I DIDN'T GET TO EAT IT ON CHILDREN'S DAY, SO MAYBE I'LL GET SOME FOR ME TOO......
OOPS!
AM I TALKING TOO MUCH ABOUT STUFF HE'S NOT INTERESTED IN...?
FOR SOME REASON, I CAN'T KEEP MY MOUTH SHUT.
CHIRA (GLANCE)
... BUT ...
...HE'S PROBABLY JUST...
...TUNING ME OUT.

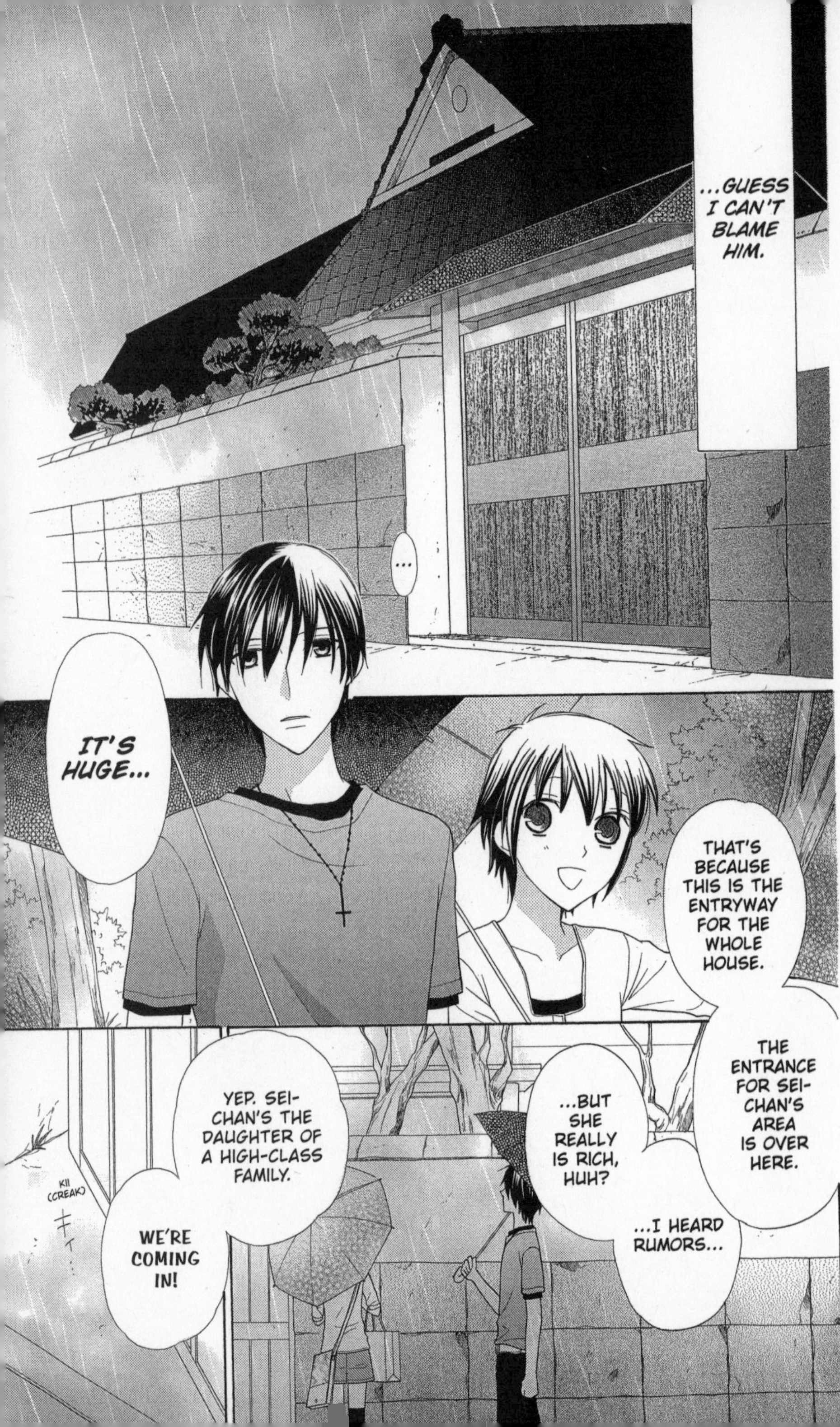
...GUESS I CAN'T BLAME HIM.
...
IT'S HUGE...
THAT'S BECAUSE THIS IS THE ENTRYWAY FOR THE WHOLE HOUSE.
THE ENTRANCE FOR SEI-CHAN'S AREA IS OVER HERE.
...BUT SHE REALLY IS RICH, HUH?
YEP. SEI-CHAN'S THE DAUGHTER OF A HIGH-CLASS FAMILY.
...I HEARD RUMORS...
WE'RE COMING IN!
KII (CREAK)

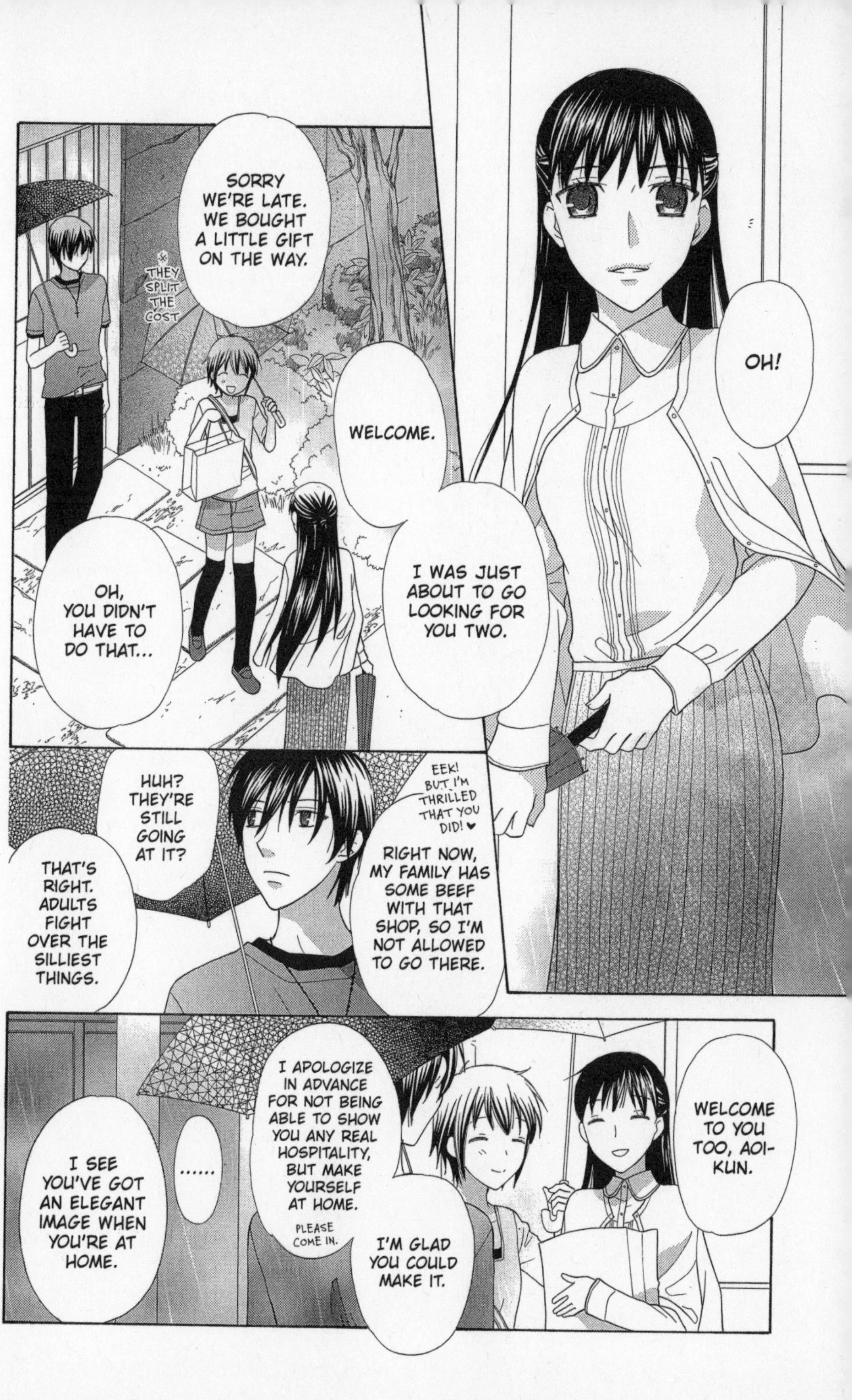
OH!
I WAS JUST ABOUT TO GO LOOKING FOR YOU TWO.
SORRY WE'RE LATE. WE BOUGHT A LITTLE GIFT ON THE WAY.
*THEY SPLIT THE COST
WELCOME.
OH, YOU DIDN'T HAVE TO DO THAT...
EEK! BUT I'M THRILLED THAT YOU DID! ♥
RIGHT NOW, MY FAMILY HAS SOME BEEF WITH THAT SHOP, SO I'M NOT ALLOWED TO GO THERE.
HUH? THEY'RE STILL GOING AT IT?
THAT'S RIGHT. ADULTS FIGHT OVER THE SILLIEST THINGS.
WELCOME TO YOU TOO, AOI-KUN.
I'M GLAD YOU COULD MAKE IT.
I APOLOGIZE IN ADVANCE FOR NOT BEING ABLE TO SHOW YOU ANY REAL HOSPITALITY, BUT MAKE YOURSELF AT HOME.
PLEASE COME IN.
......
I SEE YOU'VE GOT AN ELEGANT IMAGE WHEN YOU'RE AT HOME.

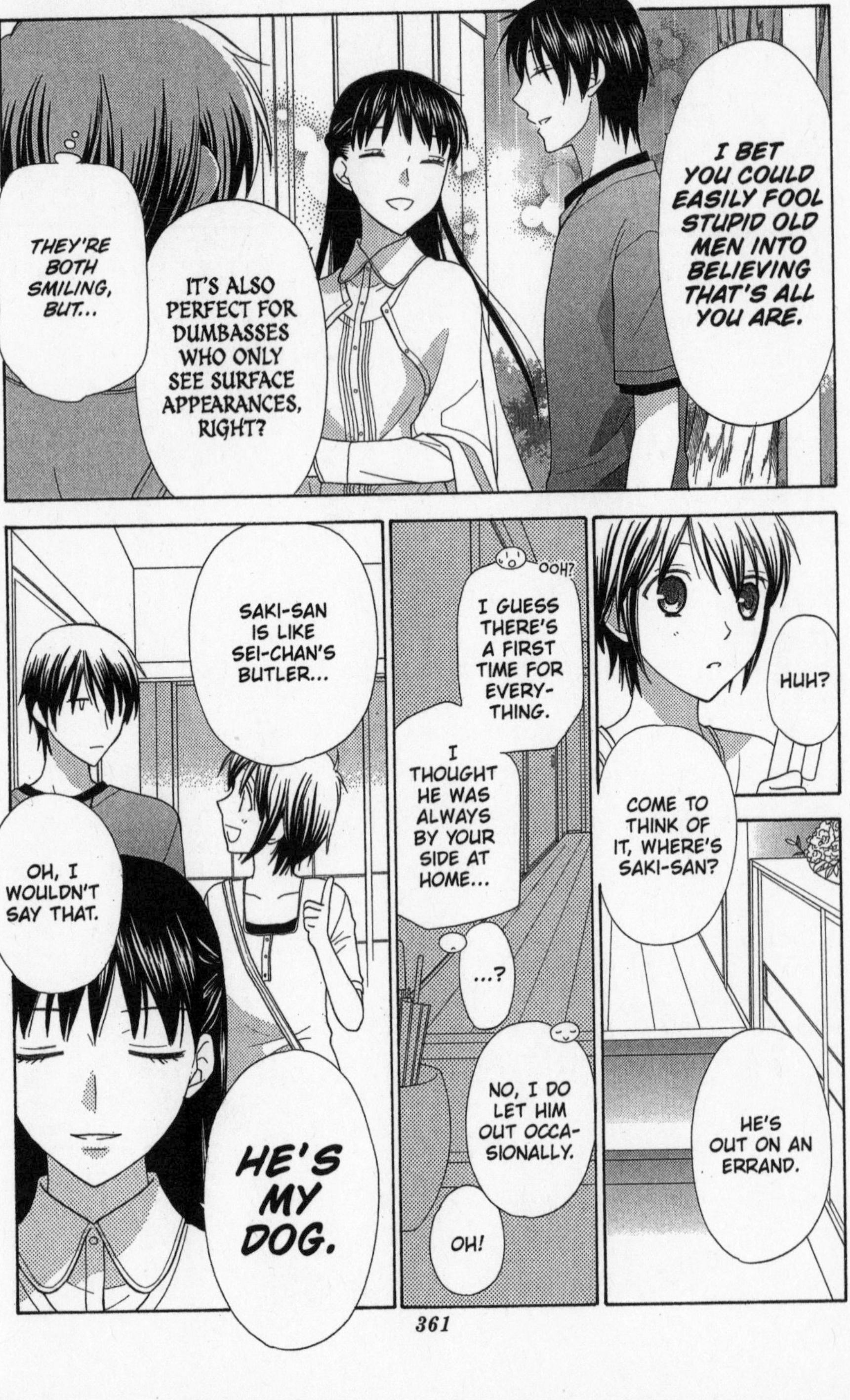
I BET YOU COULD EASILY FOOL STUPID OLD MEN INTO BELIEVING THAT'S ALL YOU ARE.
IT'S ALSO PERFECT FOR DUMBASSES WHO ONLY SEE SURFACE APPEARANCES, RIGHT?
THEY'RE BOTH SMILING, BUT...
HUH?
COME TO THINK OF IT, WHERE'S SAKI-SAN?
HE'S OUT ON AN ERRAND.
OOH?
I GUESS THERE'S A FIRST TIME FOR EVERY-THING.
I THOUGHT HE WAS ALWAYS BY YOUR SIDE AT HOME...
...?
NO, I DO LET HIM OUT OCCA-SIONALLY.
OH!
SAKI-SAN IS LIKE SEI-CHAN'S BUTLER...
OH, I WOULDN'T SAY THAT.
HE'S MY DOG.

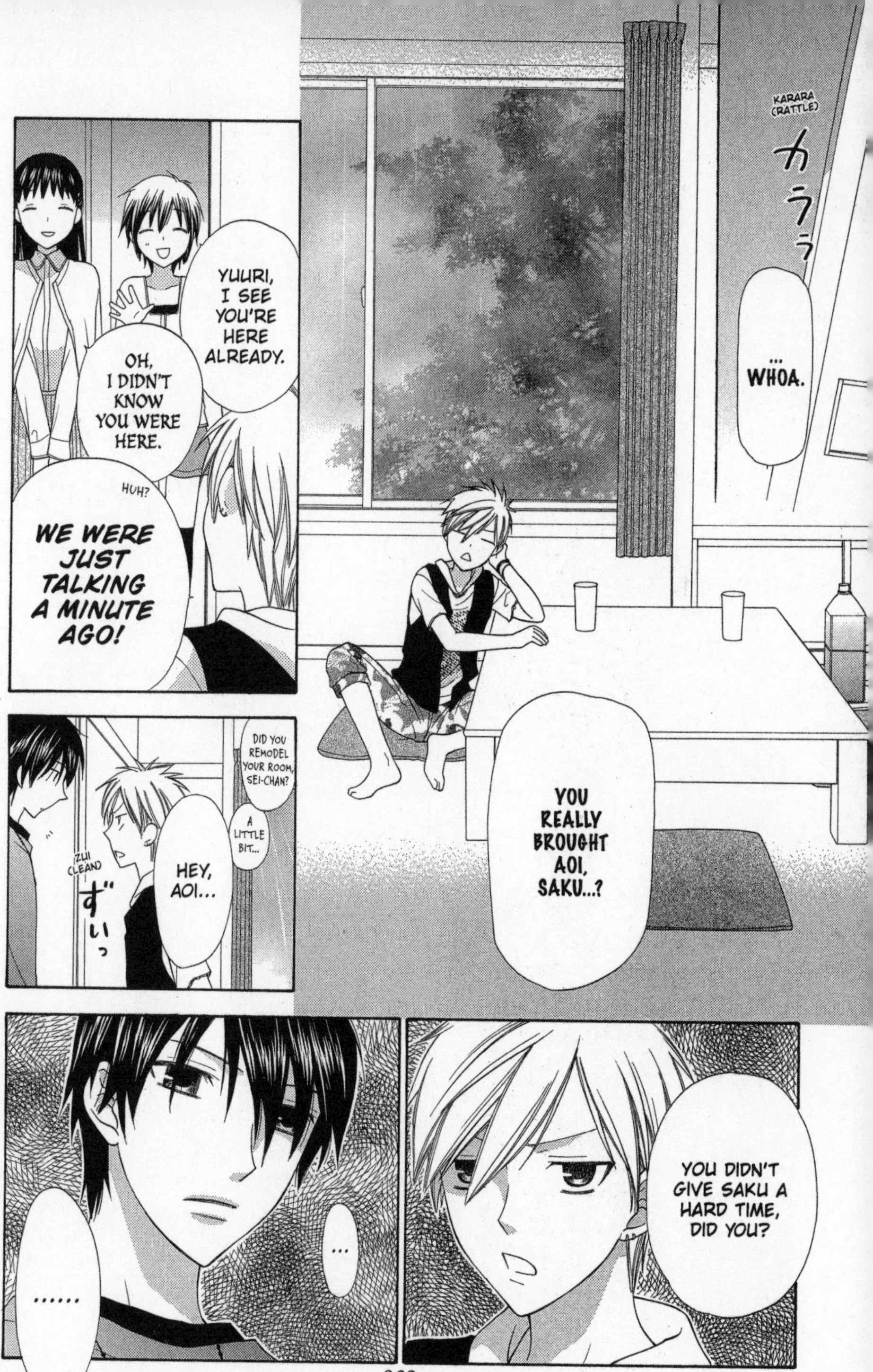
KARARA (RATTLE)
カララ
...WHOA.
YOU REALLY BROUGHT AOI, SAKU...?
YUURI, I SEE YOU'RE HERE ALREADY.
OH, I DIDN'T KNOW YOU WERE HERE.
HUH?
WE WERE JUST TALKING A MINUTE AGO!
DID YOU REMODEL YOUR ROOM, SEI-CHAN?
A LITTLE BIT...
HEY, AOI...
ZUI (LEAN)
ずいっ
YOU DIDN'T GIVE SAKU A HARD TIME, DID YOU?
...
......

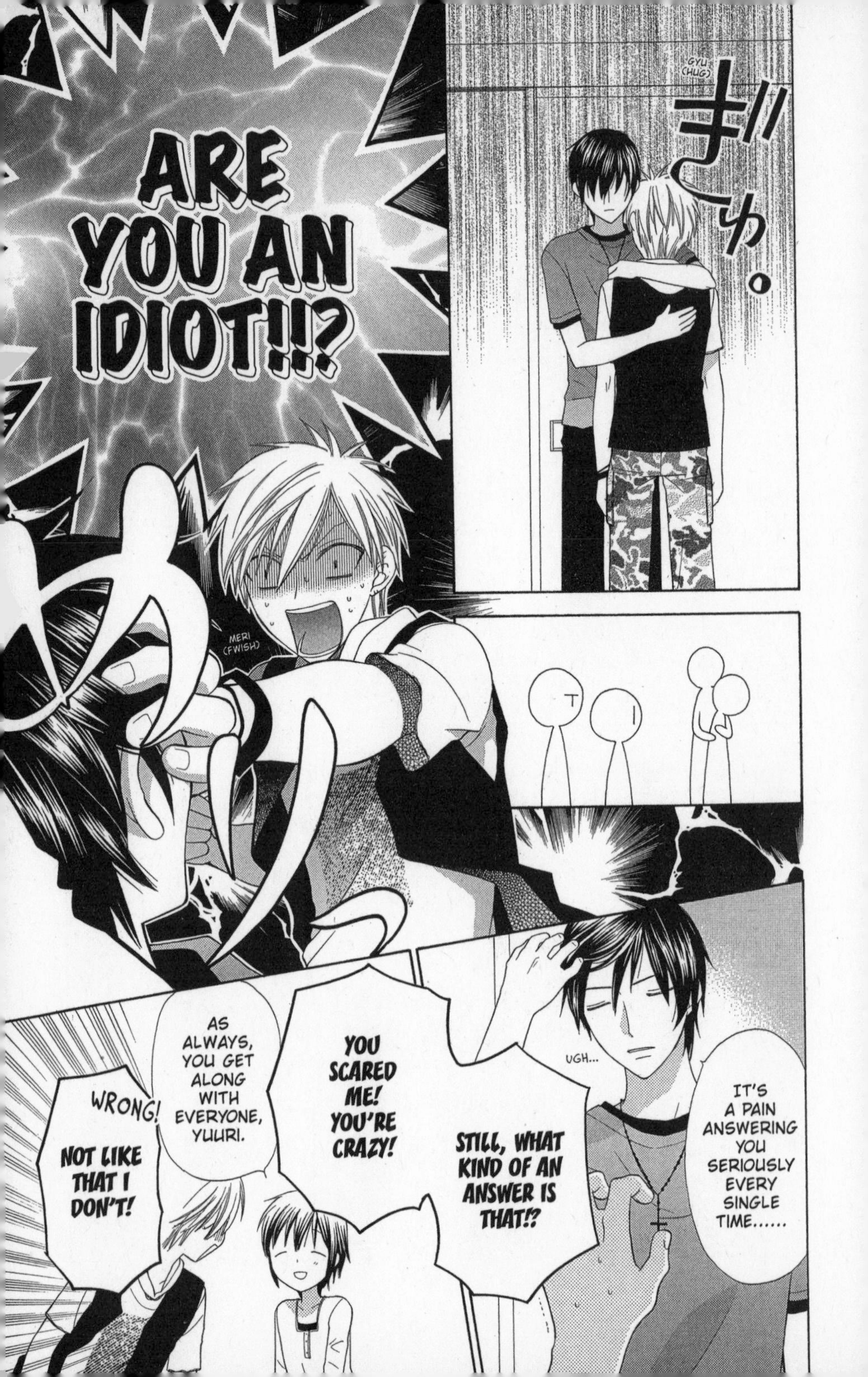
GYU (HUG)
ARE YOU AN IDIOT!!?
MERI (FWISH)
UGH...
IT'S A PAIN ANSWERING YOU SERIOUSLY EVERY SINGLE TIME......
STILL, WHAT KIND OF AN ANSWER IS THAT!?
YOU SCARED ME! YOU'RE CRAZY!
AS ALWAYS, YOU GET ALONG WITH EVERYONE, YUURI.
WRONG!
NOT LIKE THAT I DON'T!

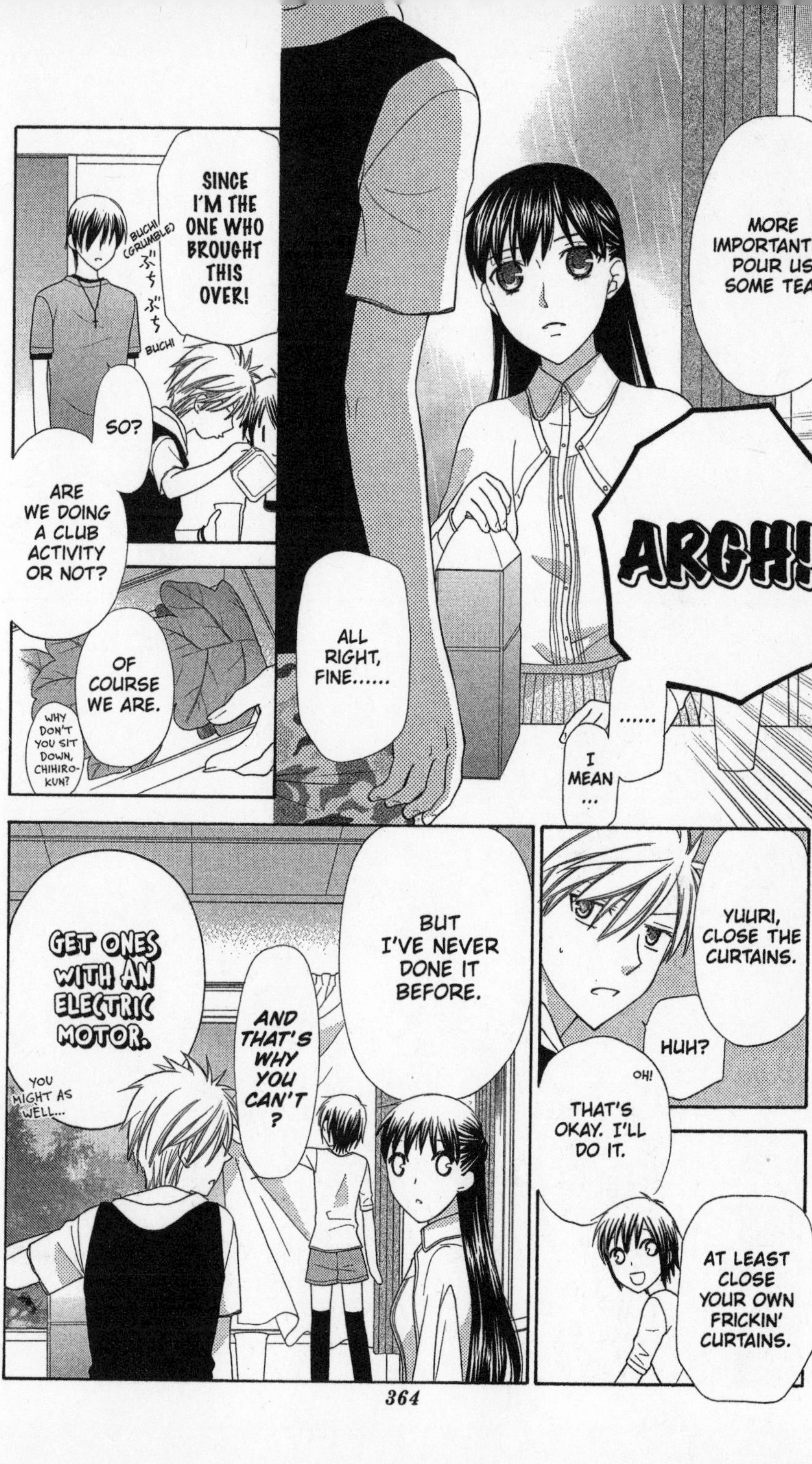
MORE IMPORTANTLY, POUR US SOME TEA.
ARGH!
......
I MEAN ...
ALL RIGHT, FINE......
SINCE I'M THE ONE WHO BROUGHT THIS OVER!
BUCHI (GRUMBLE) ぶち ぶち BUCHI
SO?
ARE WE DOING A CLUB ACTIVITY OR NOT?
OF COURSE WE ARE.
WHY DON'T YOU SIT DOWN, CHIHIRO-KUN?
YUURI, CLOSE THE CURTAINS.
HUH?
OH!
THAT'S OKAY. I'LL DO IT.
AT LEAST CLOSE YOUR OWN FRICKIN' CURTAINS.
BUT I'VE NEVER DONE IT BEFORE.
AND THAT'S WHY YOU CAN'T?
GET ONES WITH AN ELECTRIC MOTOR.
YOU MIGHT AS WELL...

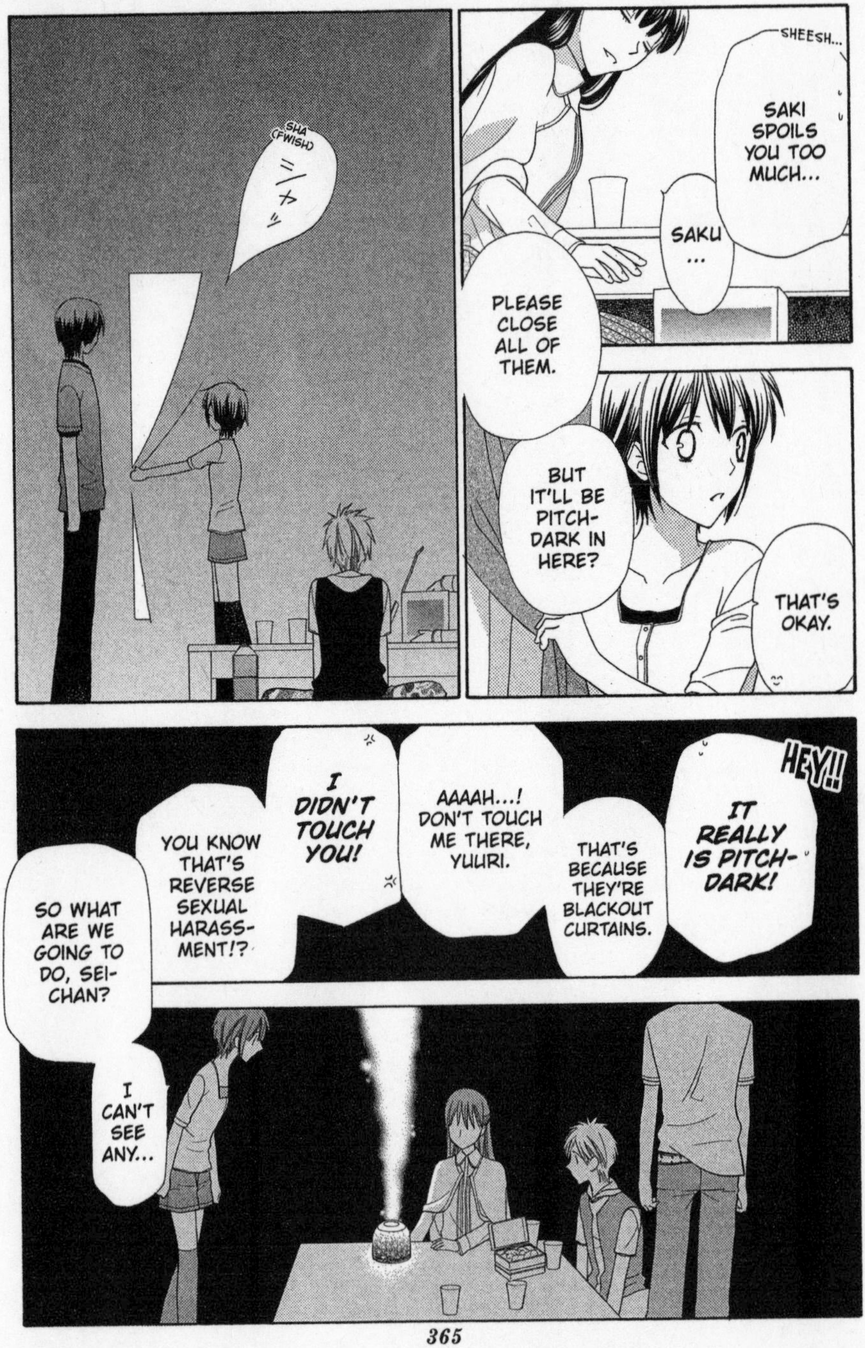

SHEESH...
SAKI SPOILS YOU TOO MUCH...
SAKU...
PLEASE CLOSE ALL OF THEM.
BUT IT'LL BE PITCH-DARK IN HERE?
THAT'S OKAY.
SHA (FWISH)
HEY!!
IT REALLY IS PITCH-DARK!
THAT'S BECAUSE THEY'RE BLACKOUT CURTAINS.
AAAAH...! DON'T TOUCH ME THERE, YUURI.
I DIDN'T TOUCH YOU!
YOU KNOW THAT'S REVERSE SEXUAL HARASSMENT!?
SO WHAT ARE WE GOING TO DO, SEI-CHAN?
I CAN'T SEE ANY...

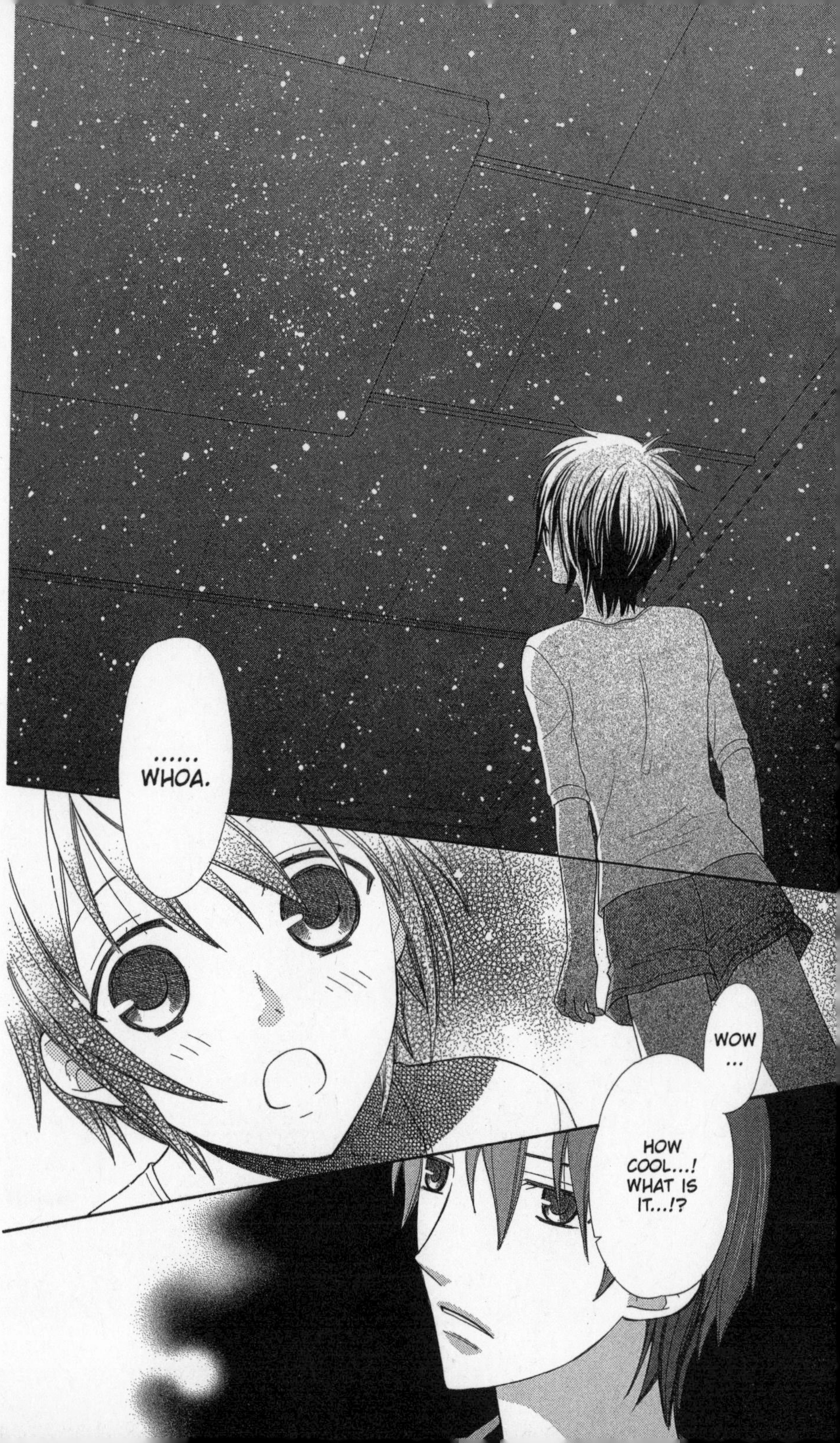
......
WHOA.
WOW
...
HOW
COOL...!
WHAT IS
IT...!?

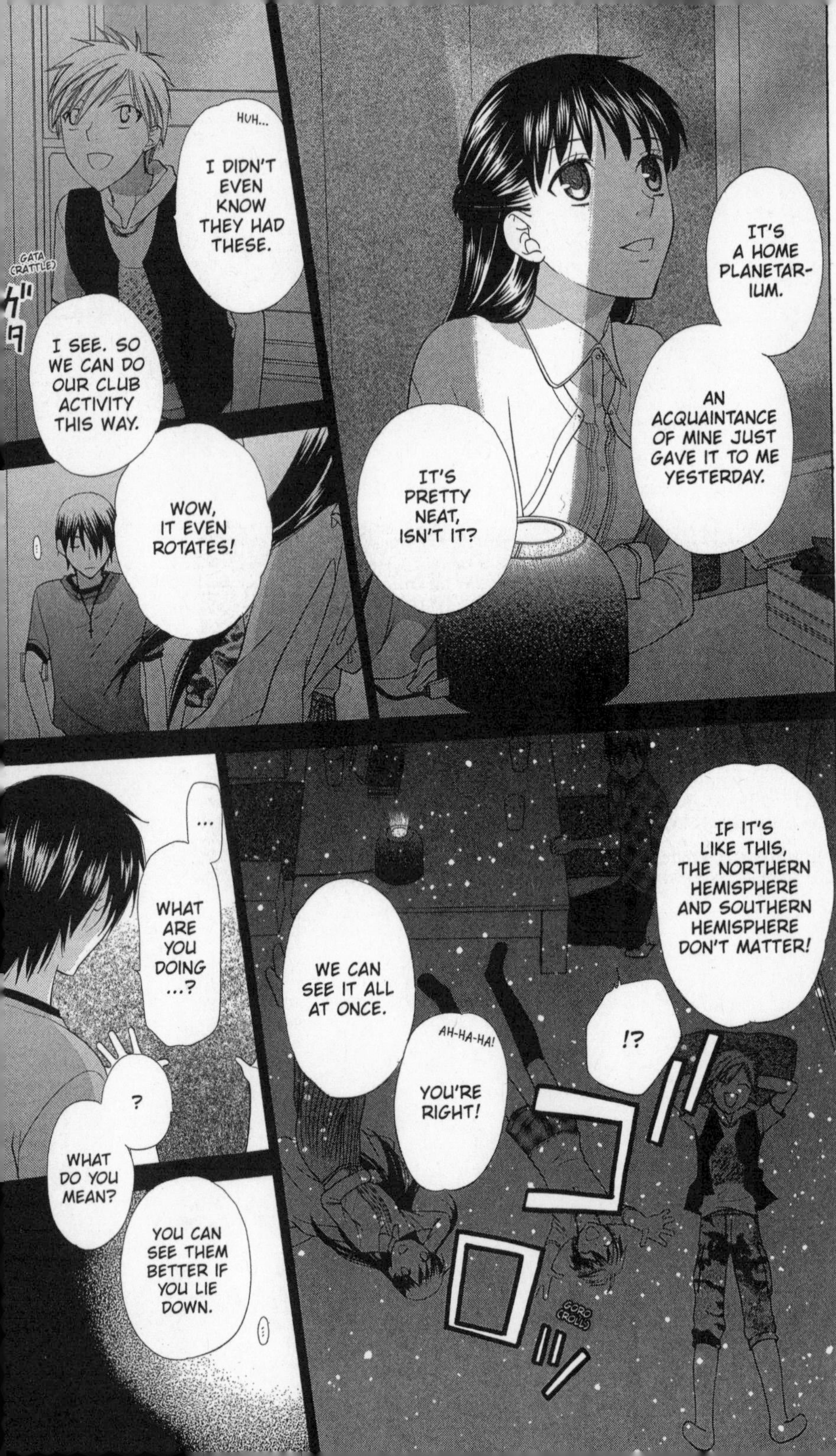
IT'S A HOME PLANETARIUM.
AN ACQUAINTANCE OF MINE JUST GAVE IT TO ME YESTERDAY.
IT'S PRETTY NEAT, ISN'T IT?
HUH...
I DIDN'T EVEN KNOW THEY HAD THESE.
GATA (RATTLE)
ガタ
I SEE. SO WE CAN DO OUR CLUB ACTIVITY THIS WAY.
WOW, IT EVEN ROTATES!
...
IF IT'S LIKE THIS, THE NORTHERN HEMISPHERE AND SOUTHERN HEMISPHERE DON'T MATTER!
!?
WE CAN SEE IT ALL AT ONCE.
AH-HA-HA!
YOU'RE RIGHT!
GORO (ROLL)
...
WHAT ARE YOU DOING ...?
?
WHAT DO YOU MEAN?
YOU CAN SEE THEM BETTER IF YOU LIE DOWN.
...

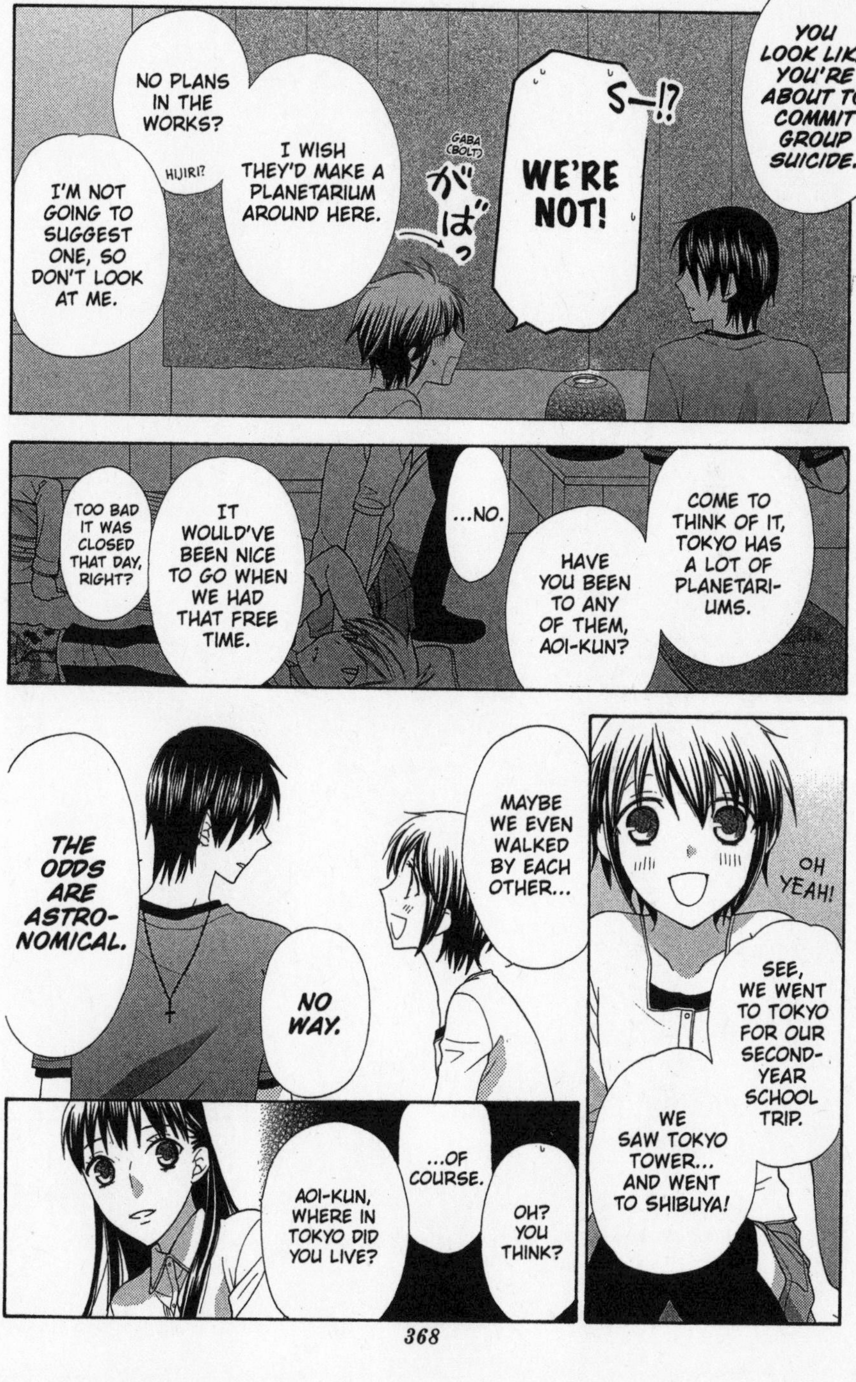
YOU LOOK LIKE YOU'RE ABOUT TO COMMIT GROUP SUICIDE.
S—!?
WE'RE NOT!
GABA (BOLT)
がばっ
I WISH THEY'D MAKE A PLANETARIUM AROUND HERE.
NO PLANS IN THE WORKS?
HIJIRI?
I'M NOT GOING TO SUGGEST ONE, SO DON'T LOOK AT ME.
COME TO THINK OF IT, TOKYO HAS A LOT OF PLANETARIUMS.
HAVE YOU BEEN TO ANY OF THEM, AOI-KUN?
...NO.
IT WOULD'VE BEEN NICE TO GO WHEN WE HAD THAT FREE TIME.
TOO BAD IT WAS CLOSED THAT DAY, RIGHT?
OH YEAH!
SEE, WE WENT TO TOKYO FOR OUR SECOND-YEAR SCHOOL TRIP.
WE SAW TOKYO TOWER... AND WENT TO SHIBUYA!
MAYBE WE EVEN WALKED BY EACH OTHER...
THE ODDS ARE ASTRONOMICAL.
NO WAY.
OH? YOU THINK?
...OF COURSE.
AOI-KUN, WHERE IN TOKYO DID YOU LIVE?

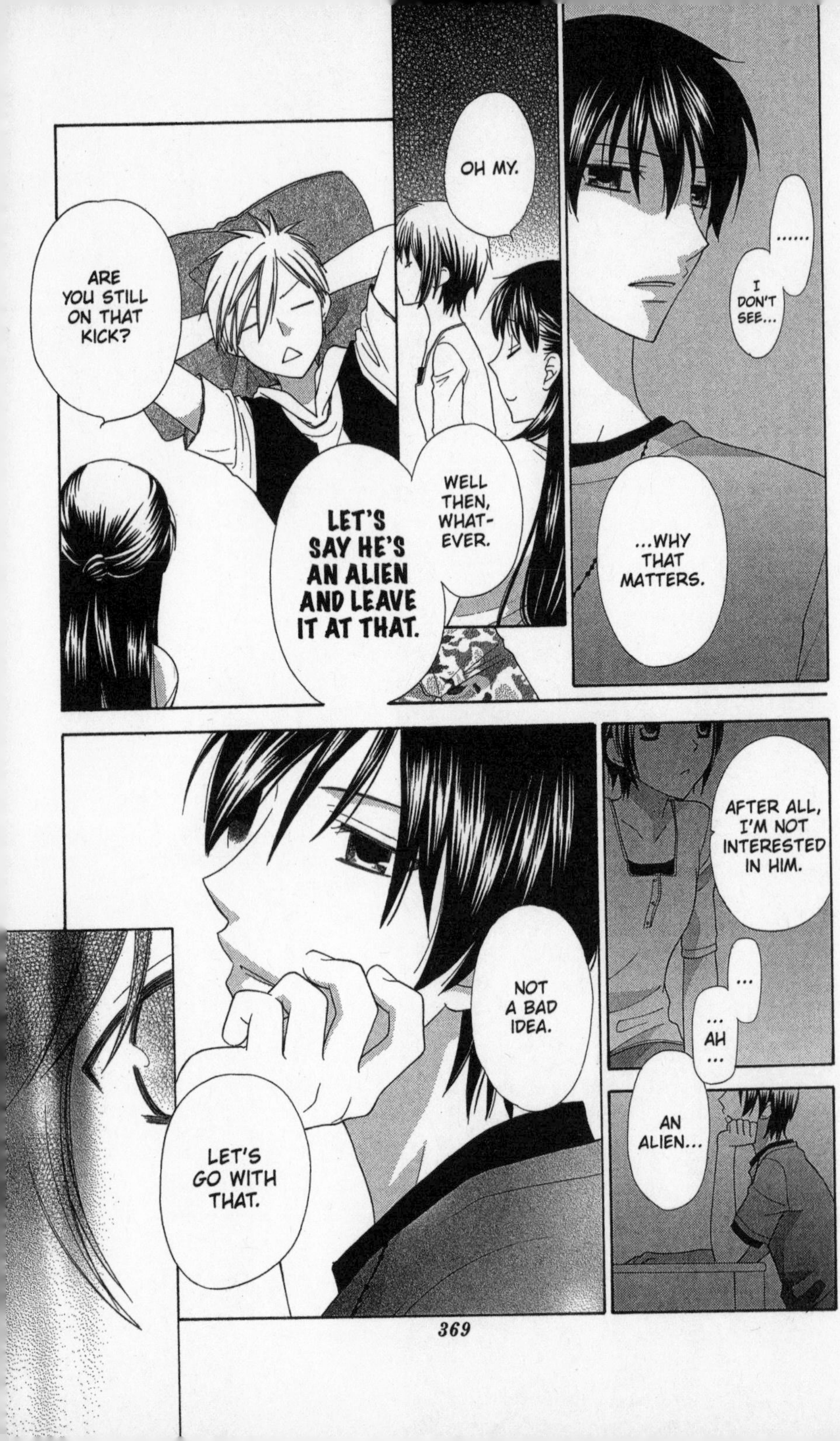
......
I DON'T SEE...
...WHY THAT MATTERS.
OH MY.
WELL THEN, WHATEVER.
ARE YOU STILL ON THAT KICK?
LET'S SAY HE'S AN ALIEN AND LEAVE IT AT THAT.
AFTER ALL, I'M NOT INTERESTED IN HIM.
...
... AH ...
AN ALIEN...
NOT A BAD IDEA.
LET'S GO WITH THAT.

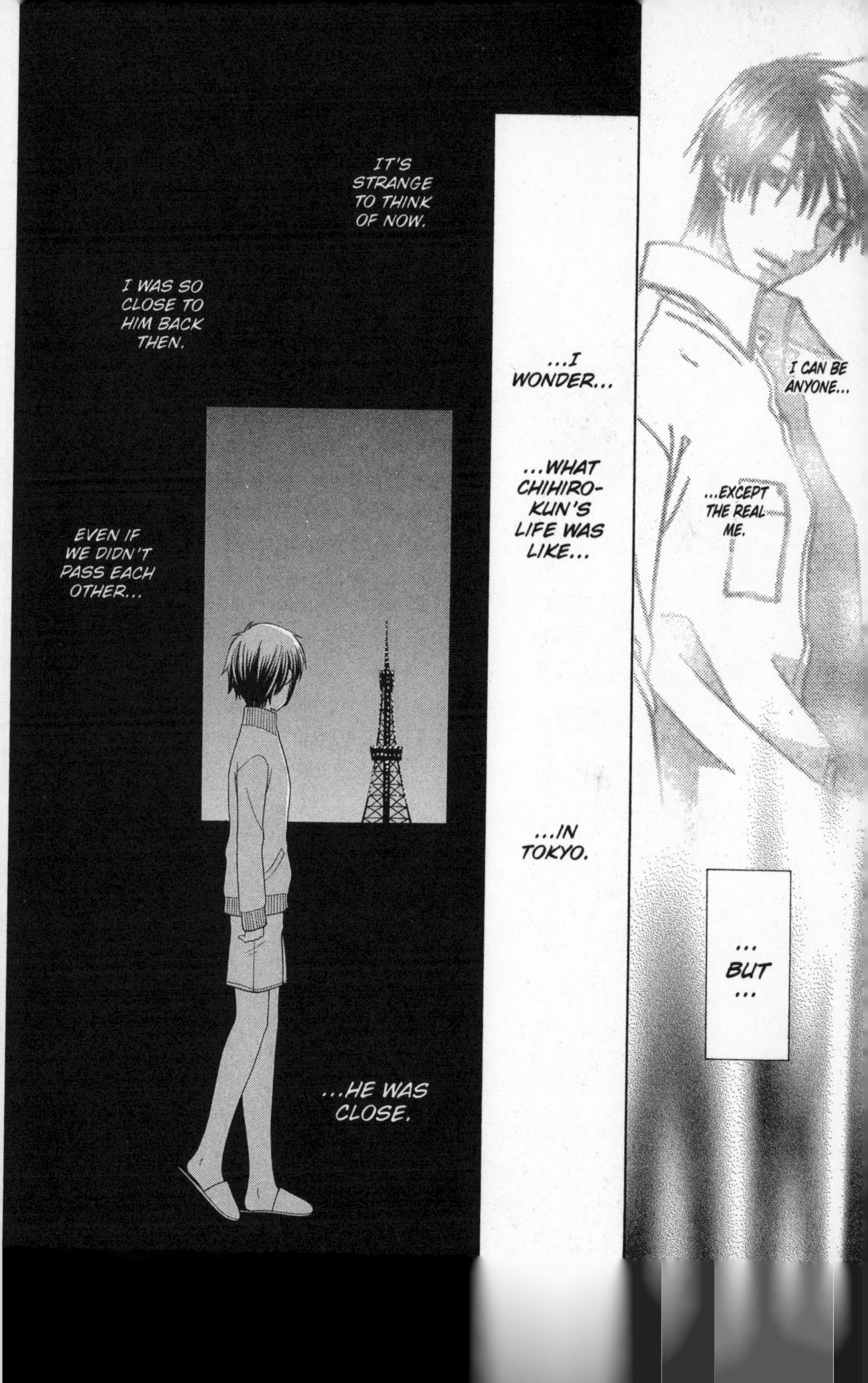
I CAN BE ANYONE...
...EXCEPT THE REAL ME.
... BUT ...
...I WONDER...
...WHAT CHIHIRO-KUN'S LIFE WAS LIKE...
...IN TOKYO.
IT'S STRANGE TO THINK OF NOW.
I WAS SO CLOSE TO HIM BACK THEN.
EVEN IF WE DIDN'T PASS EACH OTHER...
...HE WAS CLOSE.

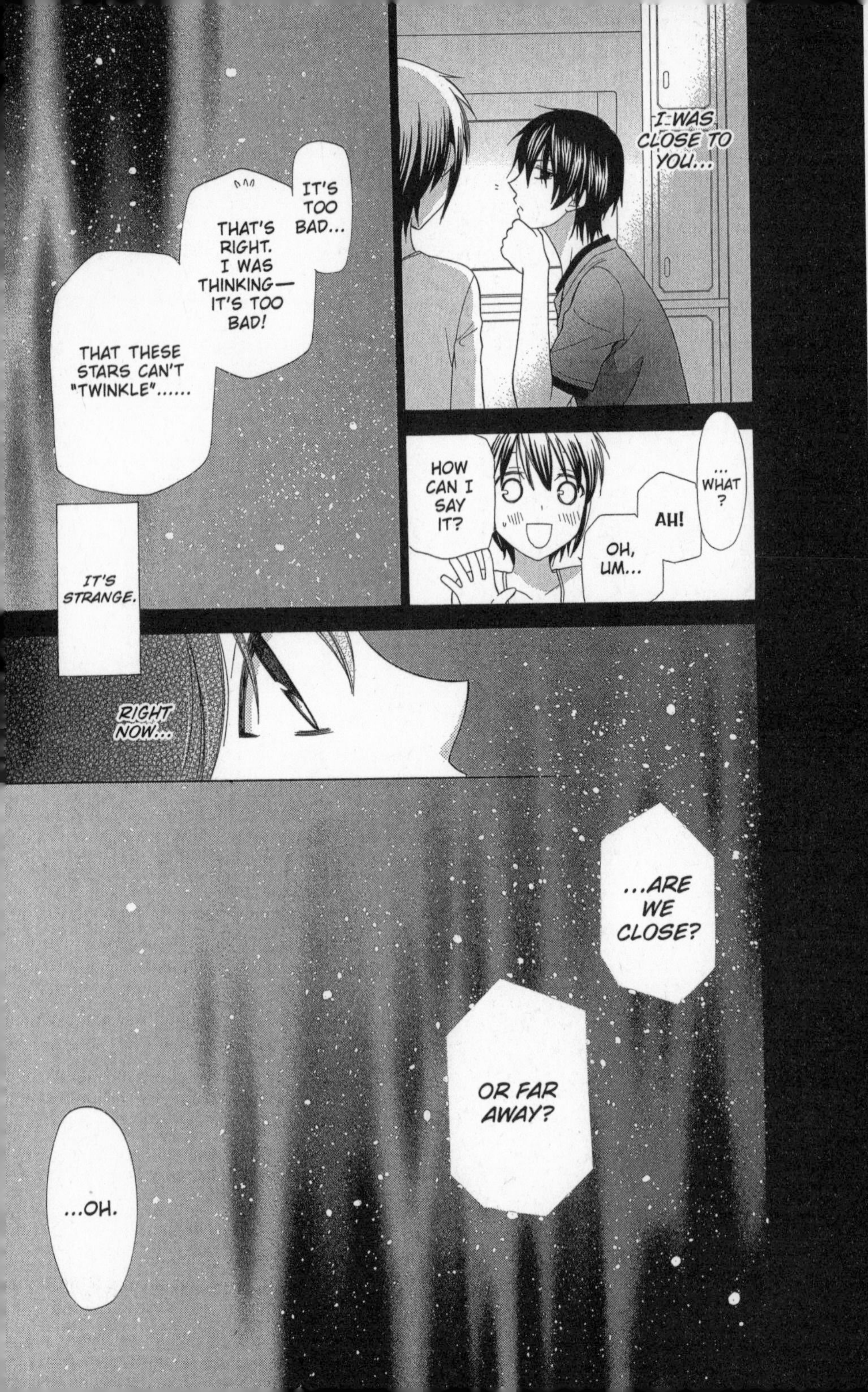
I WAS CLOSE TO YOU...
...WHAT?
AH!
OH, UM...
HOW CAN I SAY IT?
IT'S TOO BAD...
THAT'S RIGHT. I WAS THINKING— IT'S TOO BAD!
THAT THESE STARS CAN'T "TWINKLE"......
IT'S STRANGE.
RIGHT NOW...
...ARE WE CLOSE?
OR FAR AWAY?
...OH.

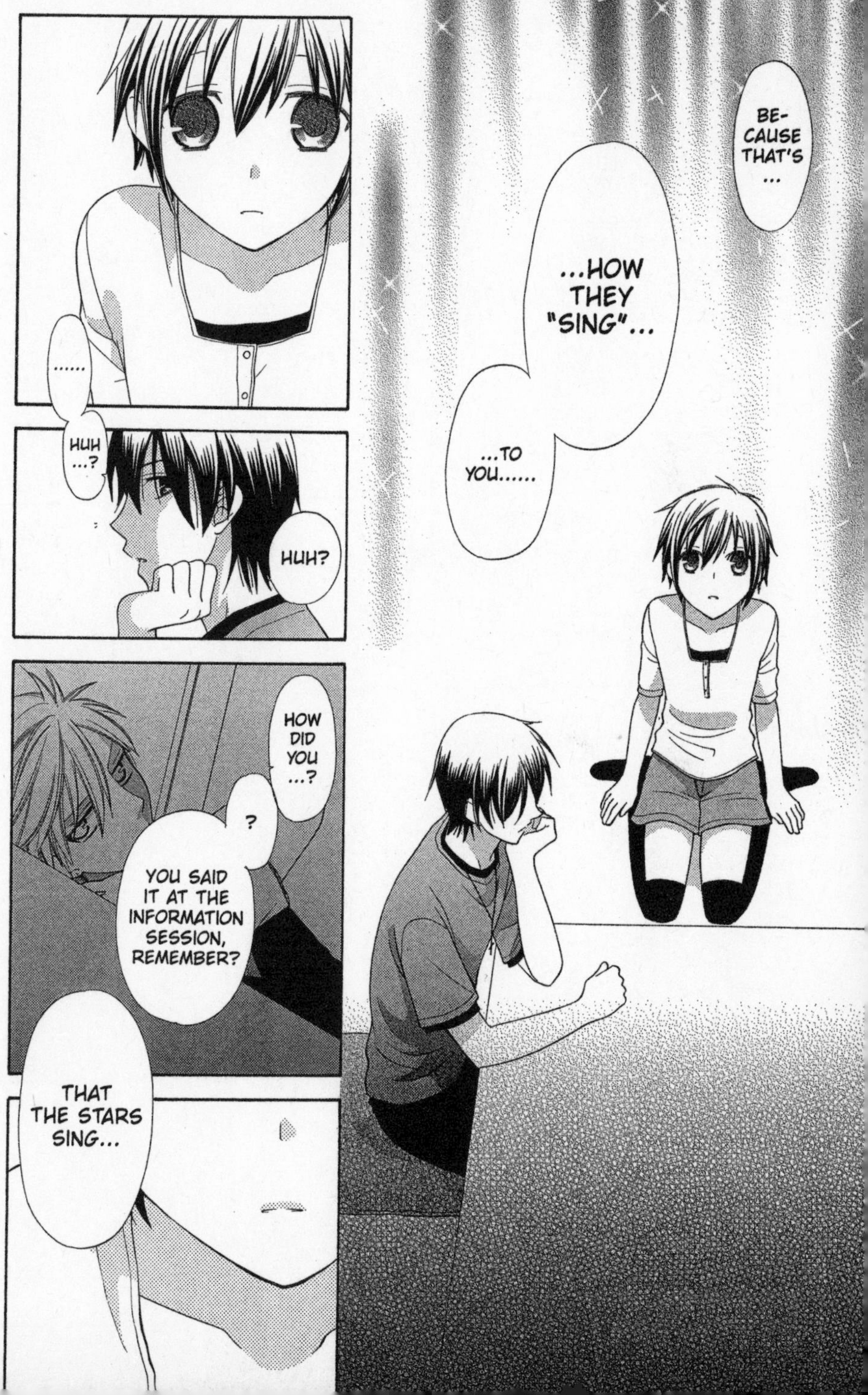
BE-CAUSE THAT'S ...
...HOW THEY "SING"...
...TO YOU......
......
HUH ...?
HUH?
HOW DID YOU ...?
?
YOU SAID IT AT THE INFORMATION SESSION, REMEMBER?
THAT THE STARS SING...

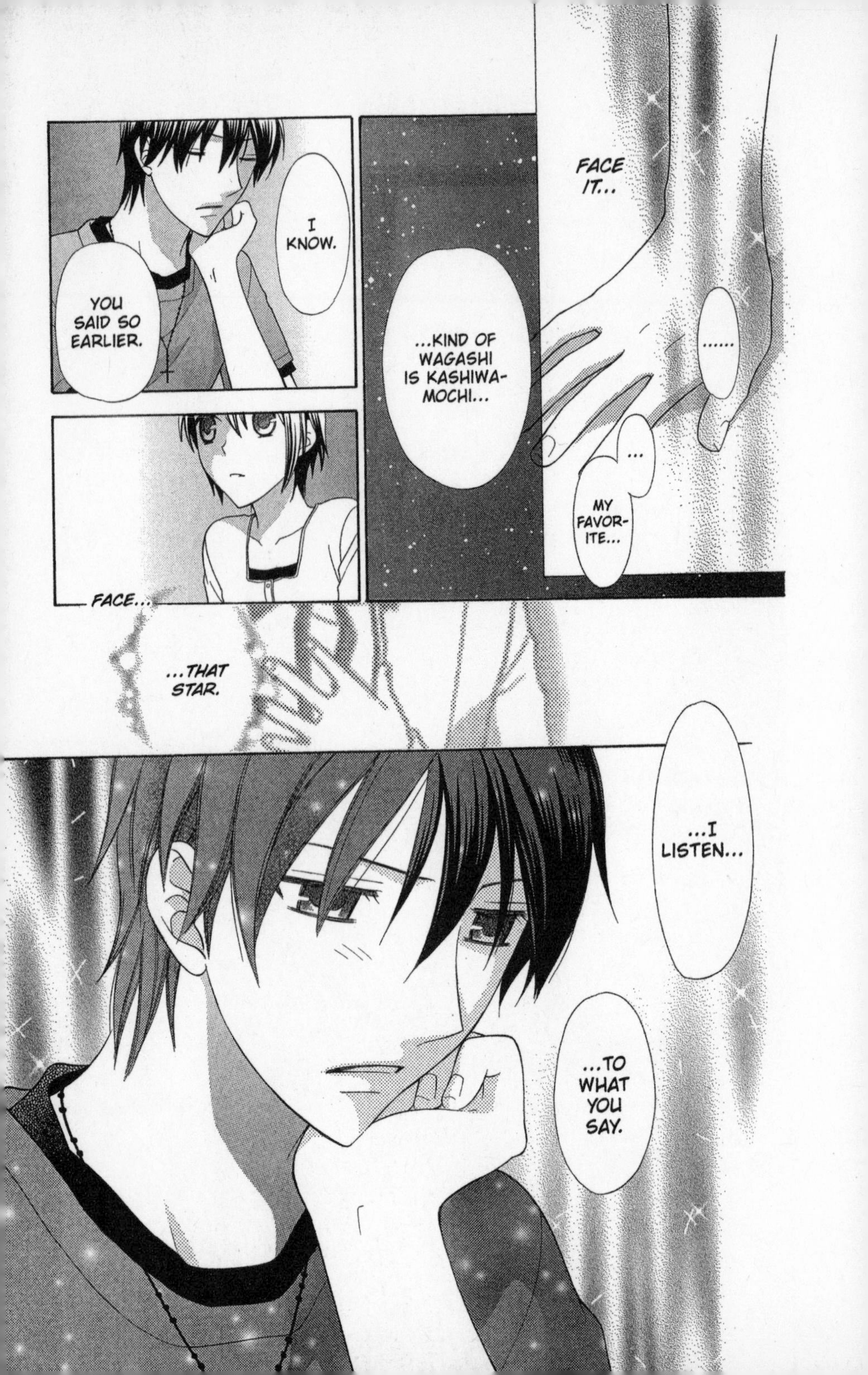
FACE IT...
......
...
MY FAVORITE...
...KIND OF WAGASHI IS KASHIWA-MOCHI...
I KNOW.
YOU SAID SO EARLIER.
FACE...
...THAT STAR.
...I LISTEN...
...TO WHAT YOU SAY.

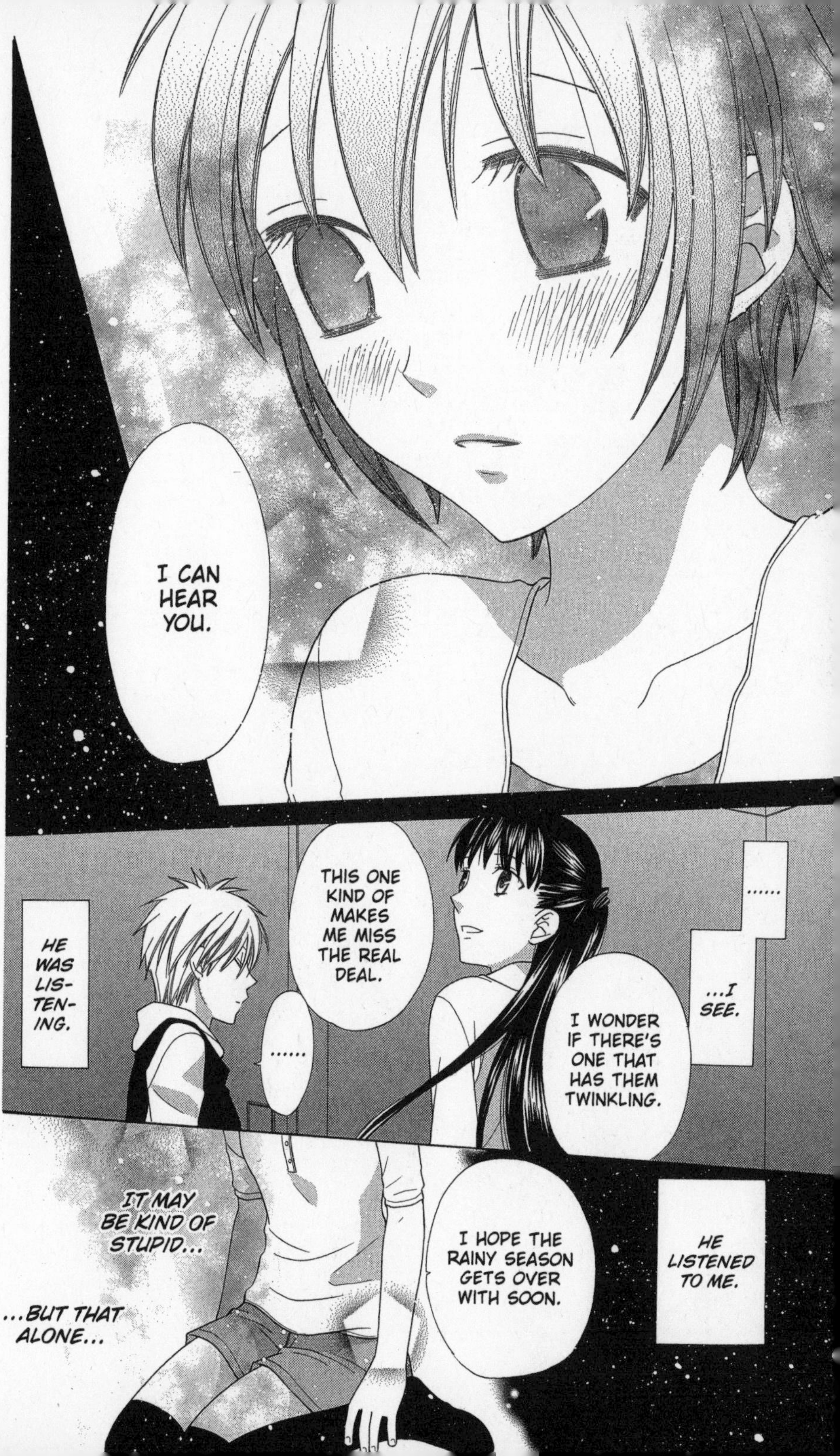
I CAN HEAR YOU.
......
THIS ONE KIND OF MAKES ME MISS THE REAL DEAL.
...I SEE.
I WONDER IF THERE'S ONE THAT HAS THEM TWINKLING.
......
HE WAS LIS-TEN-ING.
HE LISTENED TO ME.
I HOPE THE RAINY SEASON GETS OVER WITH SOON.
IT MAY BE KIND OF STUPID...
...BUT THAT ALONE...

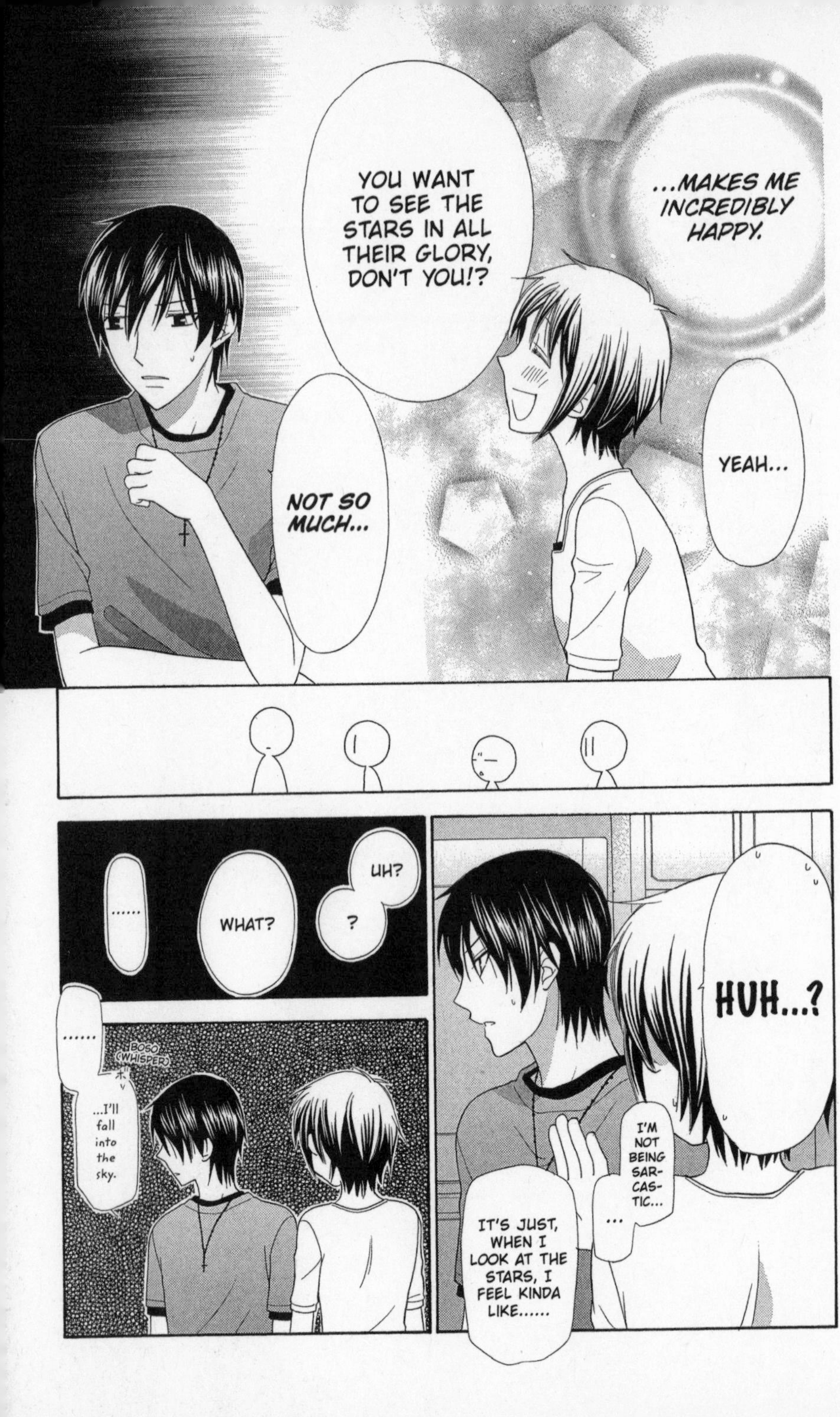
...MAKES ME INCREDIBLY HAPPY.
YOU WANT TO SEE THE STARS IN ALL THEIR GLORY, DON'T YOU!?
YEAH...
NOT SO MUCH...
HUH...?
I'M NOT BEING SAR-CAS-TIC...
...
IT'S JUST, WHEN I LOOK AT THE STARS, I FEEL KINDA LIKE......
UH?
?
WHAT?
......
......
BOSO (WHISPER)
...I'll fall into the sky.

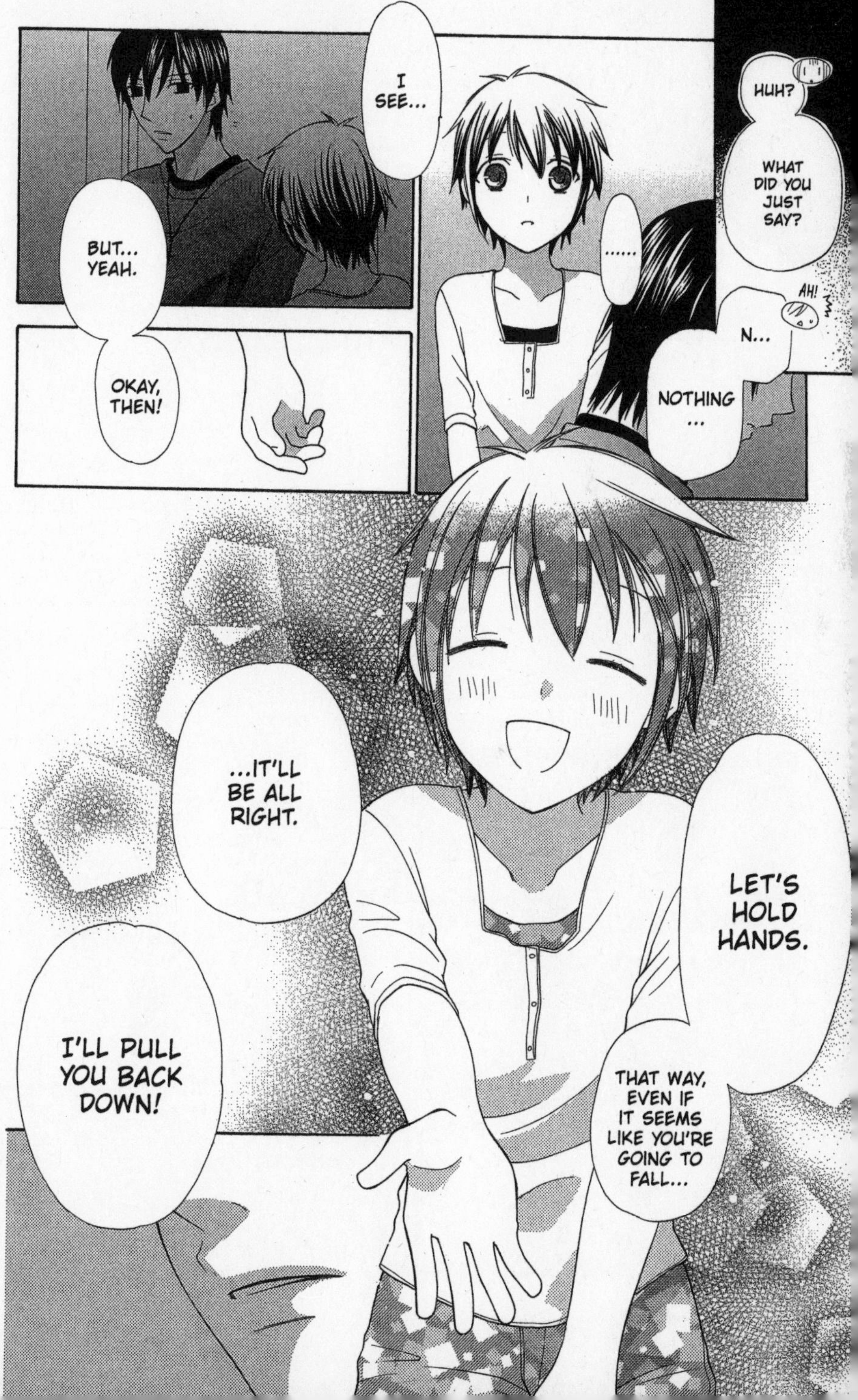

HUH?
WHAT DID YOU JUST SAY?
AH!
N...
NOTHING...
I SEE...
......
BUT... YEAH.
OKAY, THEN!
...IT'LL BE ALL RIGHT.
LET'S HOLD HANDS.
THAT WAY, EVEN IF IT SEEMS LIKE YOU'RE GOING TO FALL...
I'LL PULL YOU BACK DOWN!

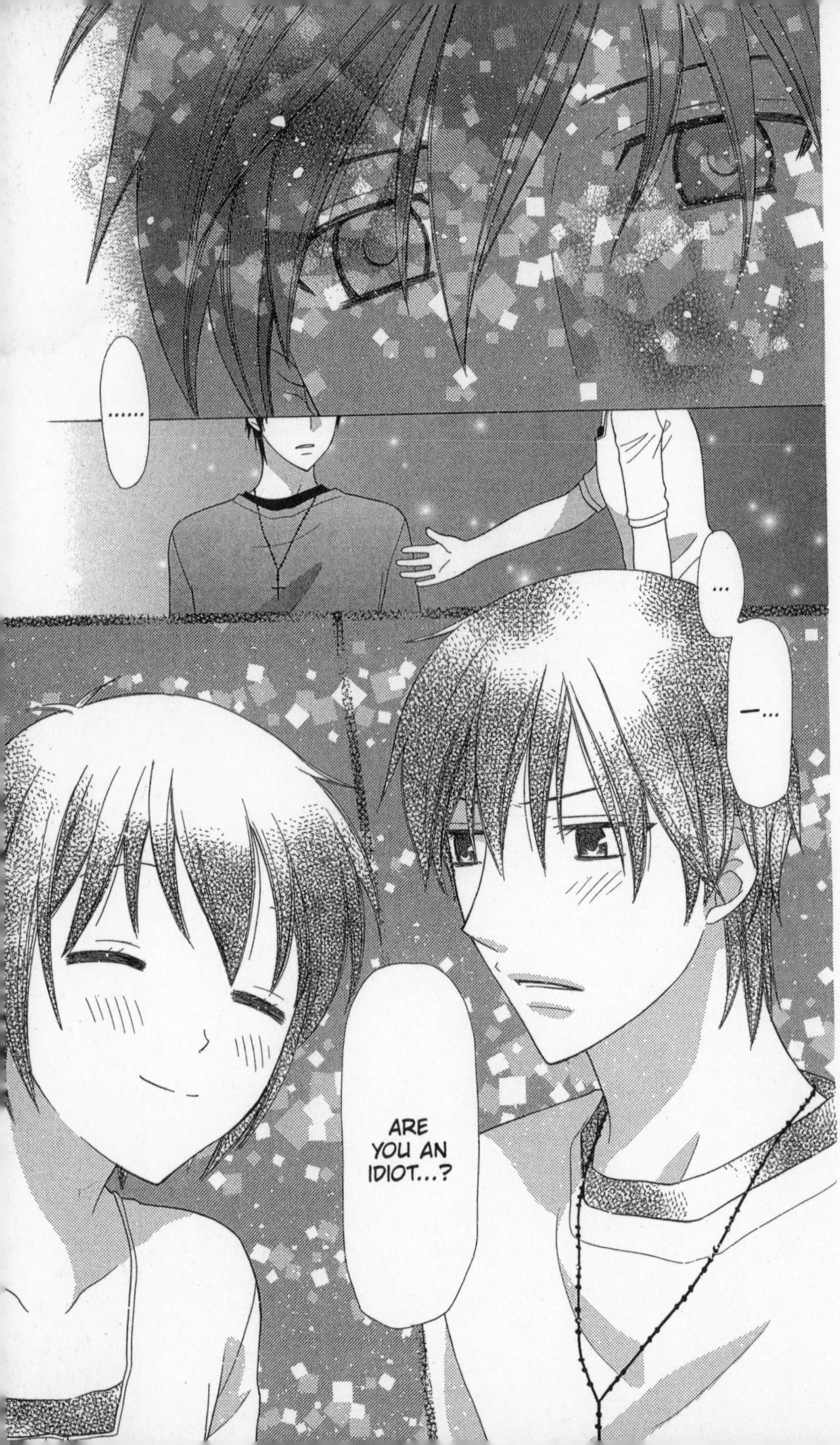
......
...
—...
ARE YOU AN IDIOT...?

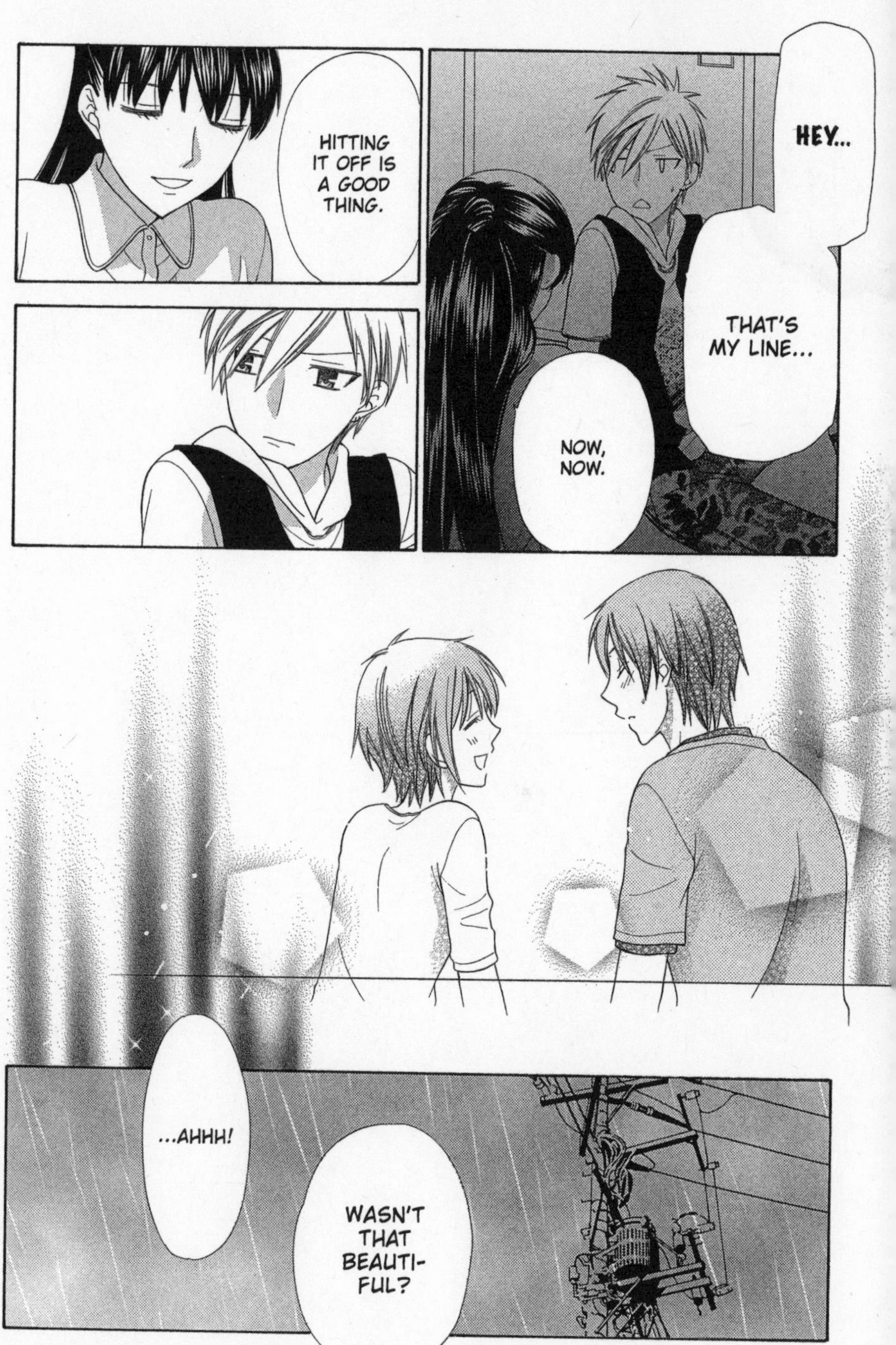
HEY...
THAT'S MY LINE...
NOW, NOW.
HITTING IT OFF IS A GOOD THING.
...AHHH!
WASN'T THAT BEAUTIFUL?

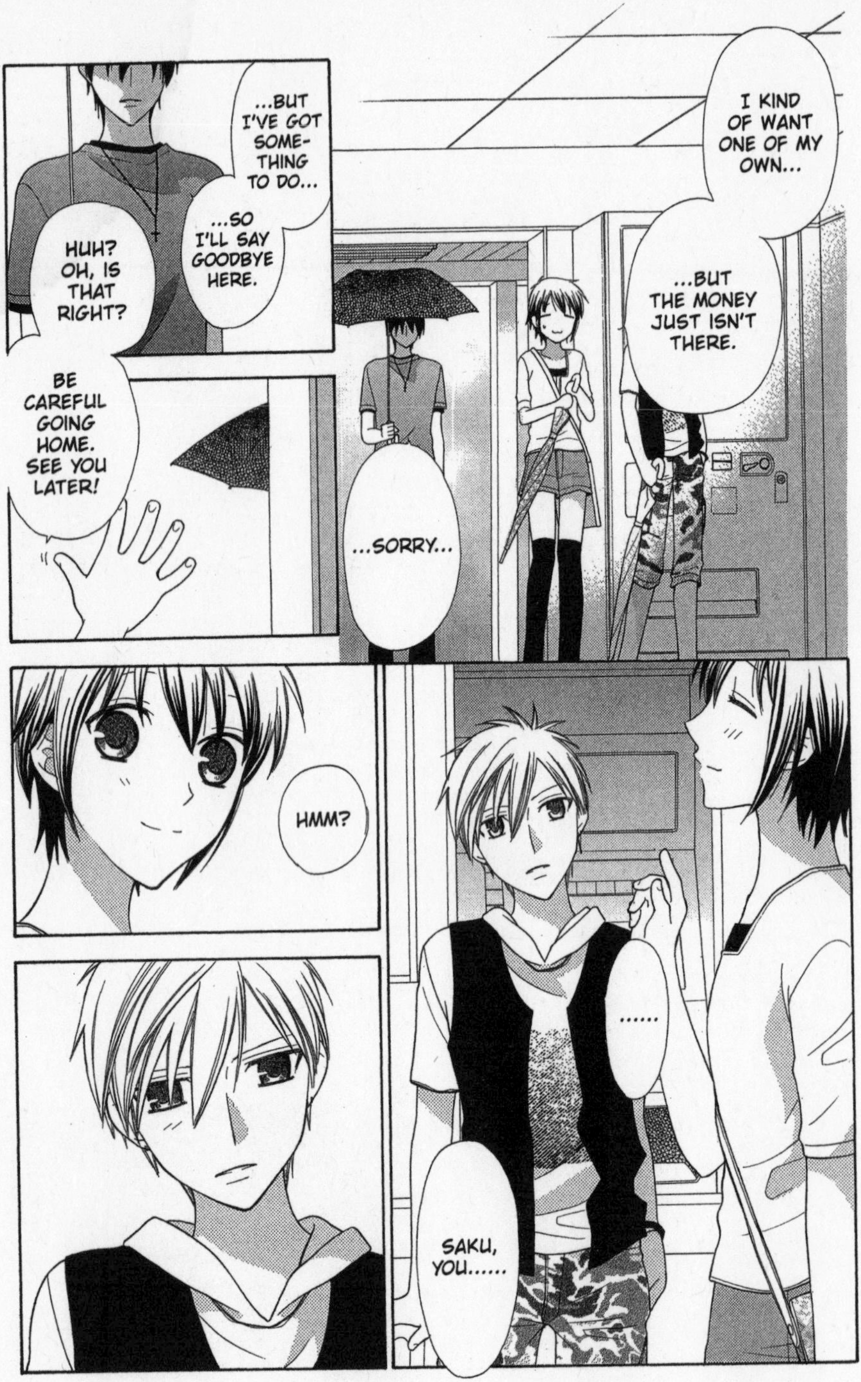
I KIND OF WANT ONE OF MY OWN...
...BUT THE MONEY JUST ISN'T THERE.
...SORRY...
...BUT I'VE GOT SOME-THING TO DO...
...SO I'LL SAY GOODBYE HERE.
HUH? OH, IS THAT RIGHT?
BE CAREFUL GOING HOME. SEE YOU LATER!
......
SAKU, YOU......
HMM?

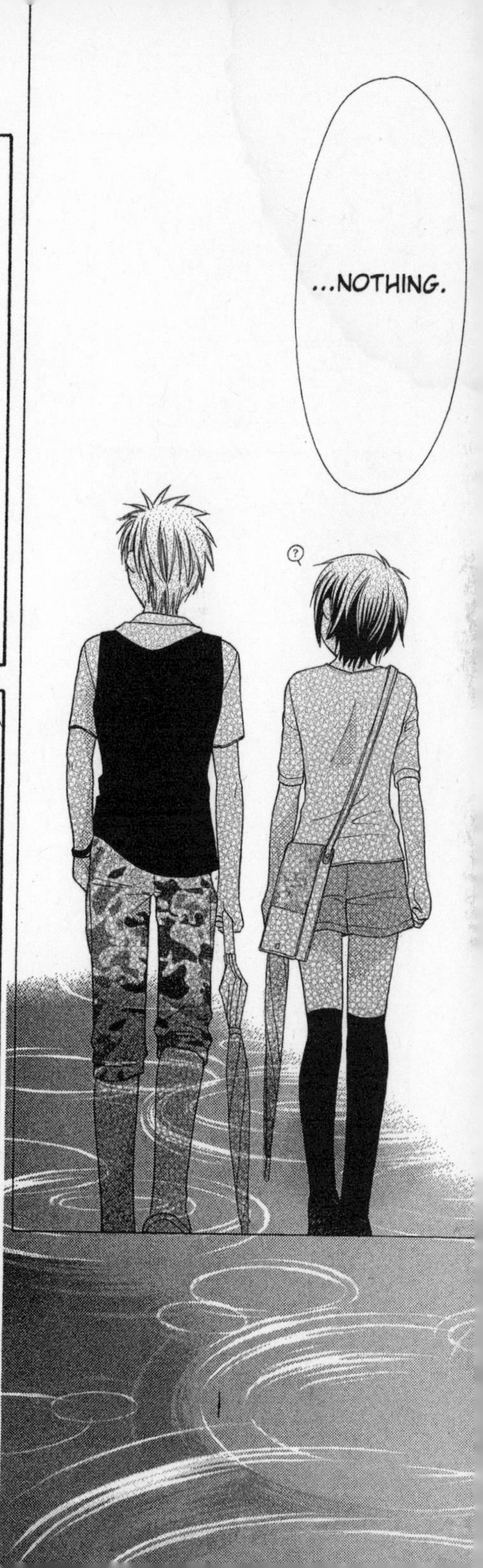
...NOTHING.

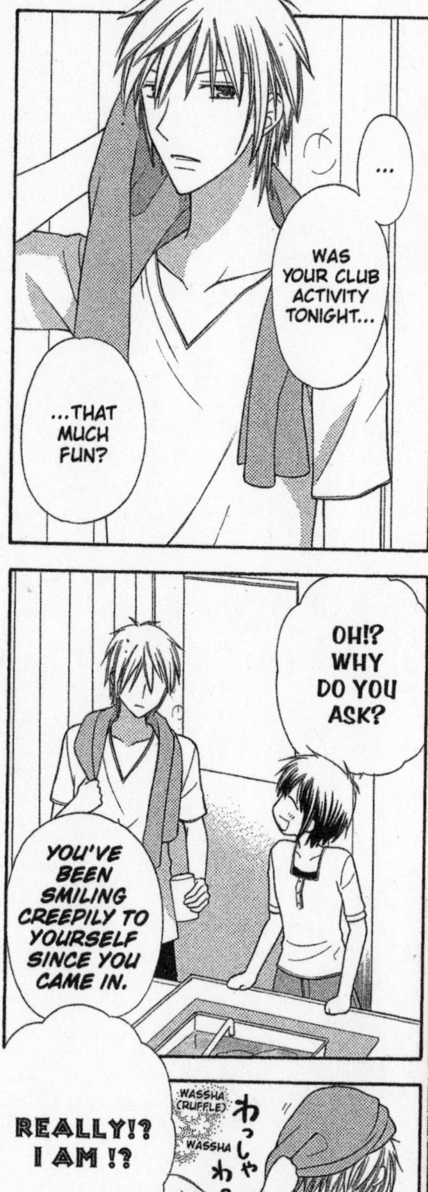
...
WAS YOUR CLUB ACTIVITY TONIGHT...
...THAT MUCH FUN?
OH!? WHY DO YOU ASK?
YOU'VE BEEN SMILING CREEPILY TO YOURSELF SINCE YOU CAME IN.
わっしゃ わっしゃ
WASSHA (RUFFLE) WASSHA
REALLY!? I AM!?

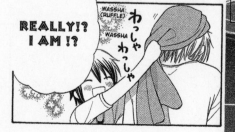

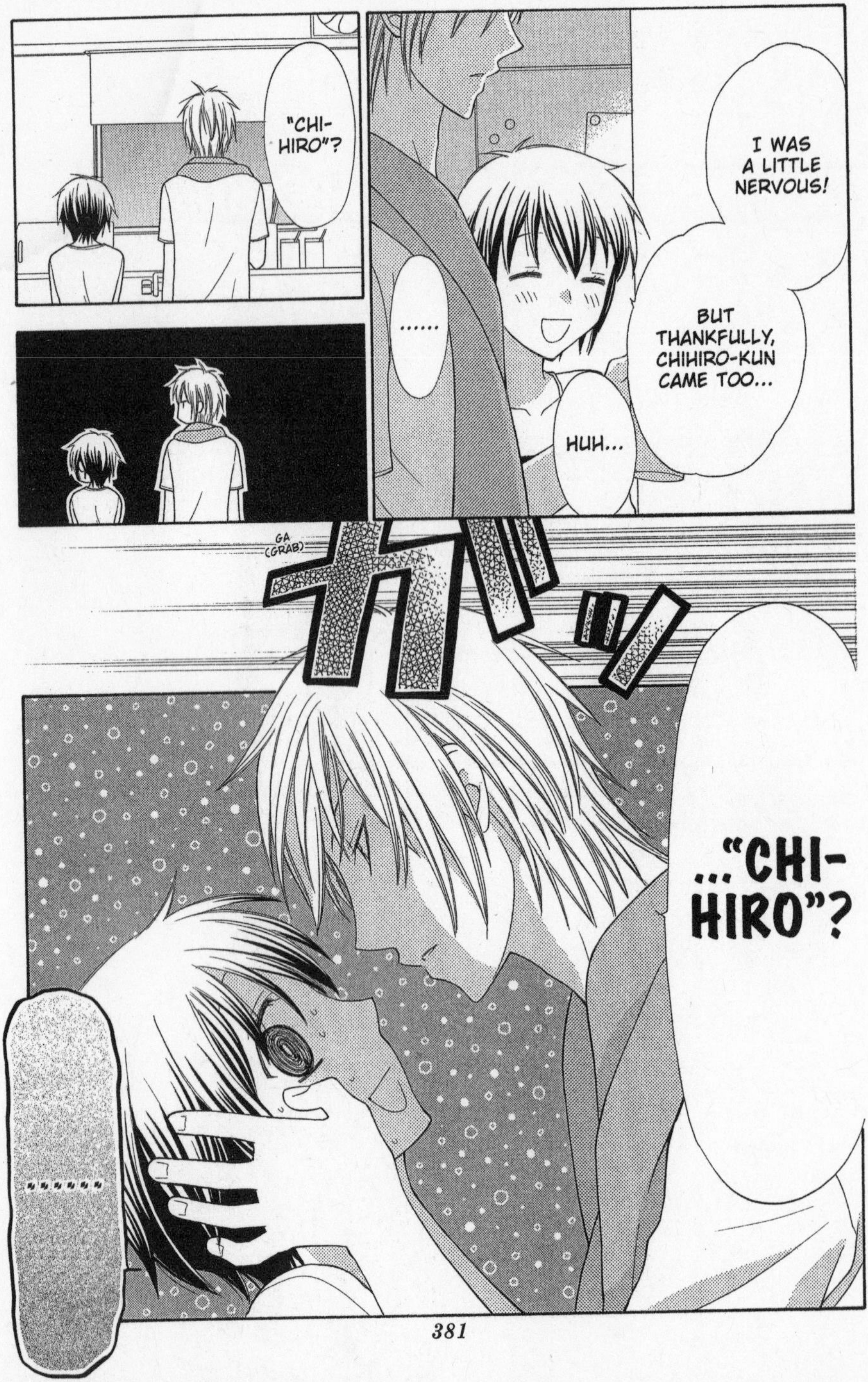
I WAS A LITTLE NERVOUS!
BUT THANKFULLY, CHIHIRO-KUN CAME TOO...
HUH...
......
"CHI-HIRO"?
GA (GRAB)
..."CHI-HIRO"?
......

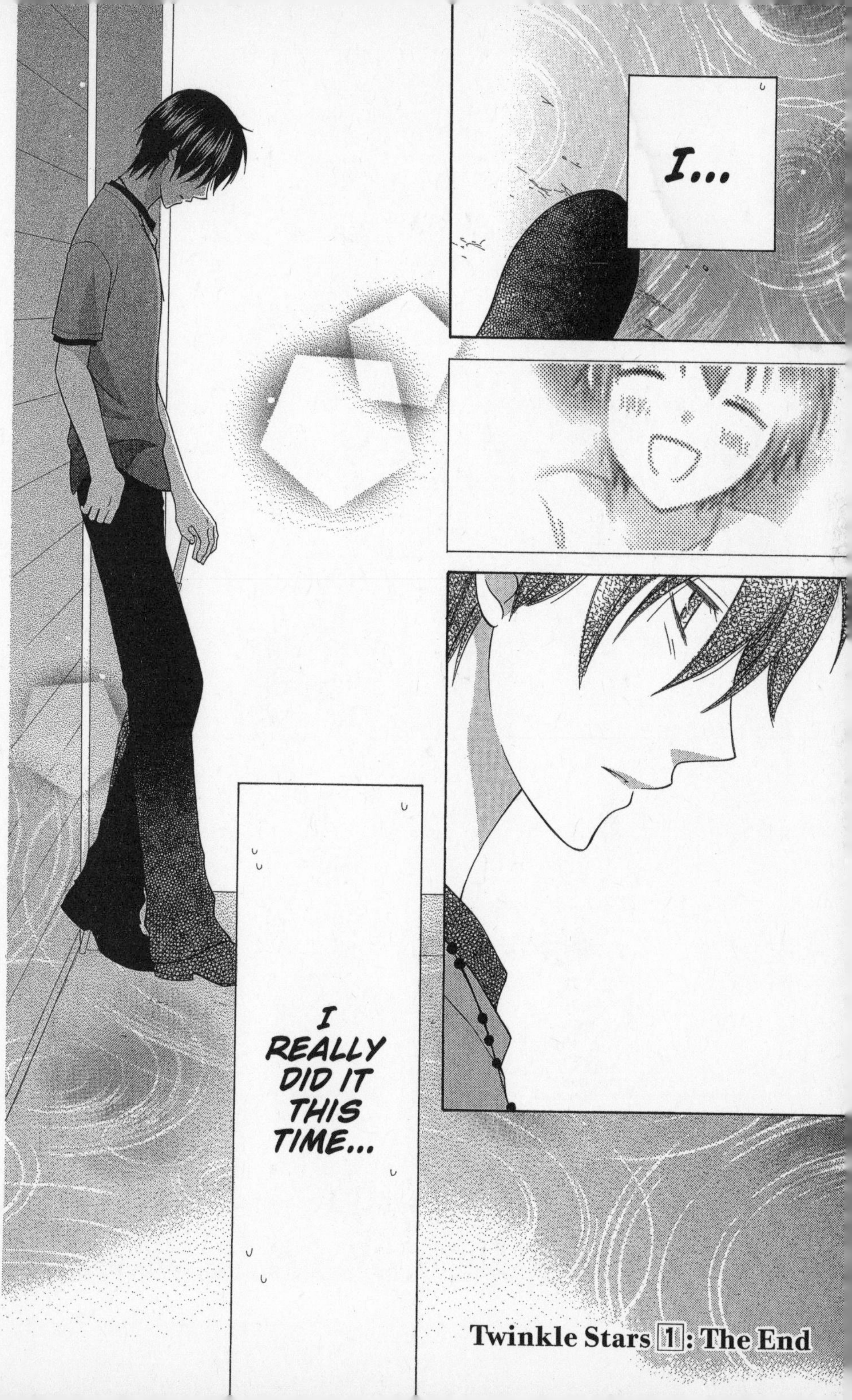
I...
I REALLY DID IT THIS TIME...
Twinkle Stars 1: The End

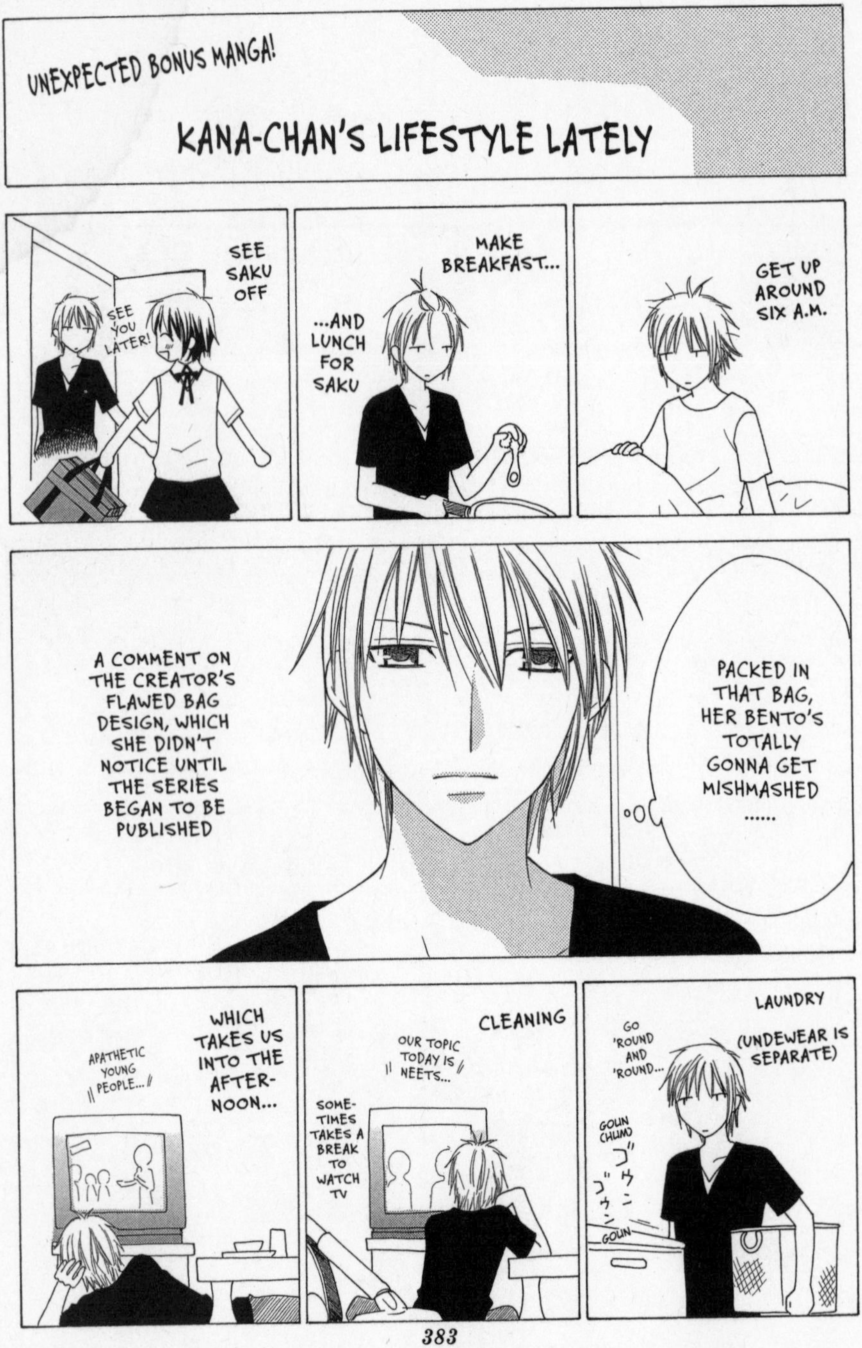

UNEXPECTED BONUS MANGA!
KANA-CHAN'S LIFESTYLE LATELY
GET UP AROUND SIX A.M.
MAKE BREAKFAST...
...AND LUNCH FOR SAKU
SEE SAKU OFF
SEE YOU LATER!
PACKED IN THAT BAG, HER BENTO'S TOTALLY GONNA GET MISHMASHED ......
A COMMENT ON THE CREATOR'S FLAWED BAG DESIGN, WHICH SHE DIDN'T NOTICE UNTIL THE SERIES BEGAN TO BE PUBLISHED
LAUNDRY
(UNDEWEAR IS SEPARATE)
GO 'ROUND AND 'ROUND...
GOUN
ゴウン
ゴウン
GOUN
CLEANING
OUR TOPIC TODAY IS NEETS...
SOME-TIMES TAKES A BREAK TO WATCH TV
WHICH TAKES US INTO THE AFTER-NOON...
APATHETIC YOUNG PEOPLE...

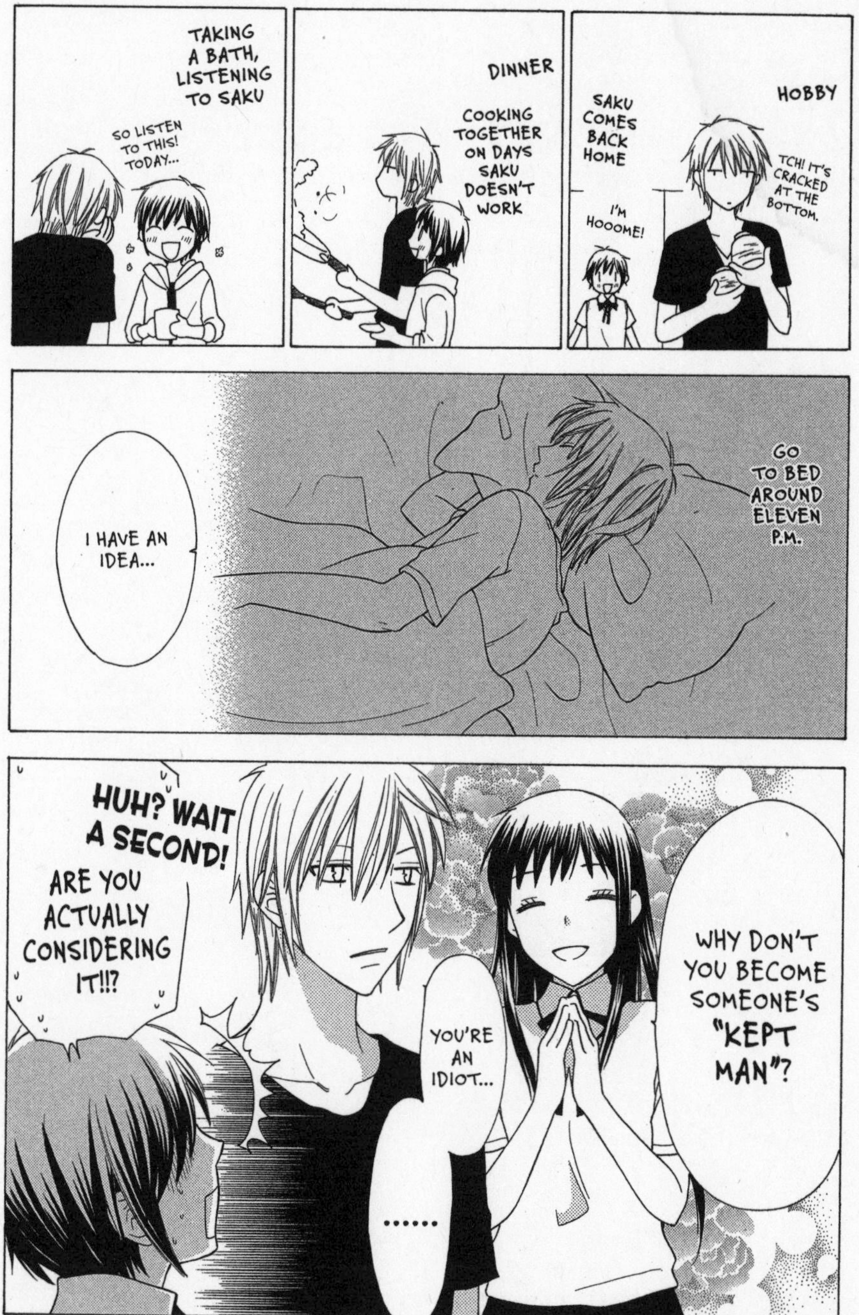
HOBBY
TCH! IT'S CRACKED AT THE BOTTOM.
SAKU COMES BACK HOME
I'M HOOOME!
DINNER
COOKING TOGETHER ON DAYS SAKU DOESN'T WORK
TAKING A BATH, LISTENING TO SAKU
SO LISTEN TO THIS! TODAY...
GO TO BED AROUND ELEVEN P.M.
I HAVE AN IDEA...
WHY DON'T YOU BECOME SOMEONE'S "KEPT MAN"?
YOU'RE AN IDIOT...
......
HUH? WAIT A SECOND!
ARE YOU ACTUALLY CONSIDERING IT!!?

THE END

Feeling of
Gratitude.

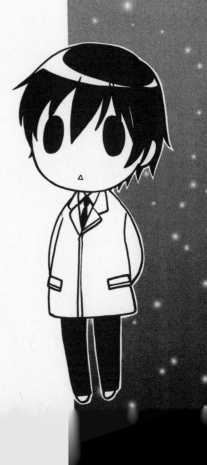

Harada-sama   Araki-sama

Mother   My editor

Everyone who supports me
and reads this series

高屋 奈月
Natsuki Takaya

TRANSLATION NOTES

COMMON HONORIFICS

no honorific: Indicates familiarity or closeness; if used without permission or reason, addressing someone in this manner would constitute an insult.

-san: The Japanese equivalent of Mr./Mrs./Miss. If a situation calls for politeness, this is the fail-safe honorific.

-sama: Conveys great respect; may also indicate that the social status of the speaker is lower than that of the addressee.

-kun: Used most often when referring to boys, this indicates affection or familiarity. Occasionally used by older men among their peers, but it may also be used by anyone referring to a person of lower standing.

-chan: An affectionate honorific indicating familiarity used mostly in reference to girls; also used in reference to cute persons or animals of either gender.

* * * * * * * * * *

Names

As with the main character in *Fruits Basket*, many of the characters in *Twinkle Stars* have names that play around with gender. "Sakuya" and "Yuuri" are gender-neutral names, while "Kanade," "Chihiro," and "Shizuka" (all men) have typically feminine names. Saku's best friend, Hijiri Honjou, has the masculine nickname "Sei."

Page 18

"Makes me think of 'sack'...": In Japanese, the name of their club is *hoshizora* ("starry sky/stars") *kanshou* ("appreciating a subject") *doukoukai* ("club/association/group"). The English name——Star Appreciation Club——is a direct translation, but our nickname is understandably a bit of an adaption. In Japanese, the nickname is *hokan*, a word with a number of possible meanings——none of which would lead you to think it's a stargazing club!

Page 23

Sei: Hijiri's nickname, derived from an alternate reading of the kanji for her name. Incidentally, that kanji has several meanings, including "saint," "sacred," and "emperor/empress"——very fitting for a character like her.

Page 85

Hoshigahara High School: Translated literally, the name of their school would be something like "Field of Stars" High School.

Page 87

Children's Day: A national holiday in Japan on May 5th. It was originally called Boys' Day, but the name was changed in 1948 to celebrate all children.

Page 91

Castor and Pollux: The "twin" stars in the Gemini constellation. Though they appear close together, the two stars are easily distinguishable. Pollux is brighter and more golden, while Castor is fainter and whiter. They were named after the twin brothers in Greek and Roman mythology who aided Jason on several quests, came to their downfall during the Trojan War, and subsequently transformed into the Gemini constellation so they could travel back and forth between Olympus and Hades.

Procyon: Procyon is the first star in the Canis Minor constellation. Technically, though, it's made up of two stars—one large white star (Procyon A) paired with a smaller white-drawf star (Procyon B). Procyon is the eighth brightest star in our night sky, but it owes that brightness to proximity, not because of any inherent luminocity—it's only 11.5 light-years away, making it one of Earth's closest neighbors.

Regulus: Like Procyon, Regulus is another "star" comprised of multiple stars (at least four!). It's the brightest piece of the Leo constellation and also one of the brighter stars in the night sky as a whole. Because of this brightness, many cultures around the world associate Regulus with royalty or noble power. Fittingly, the English name derives from the Latin word for "king."

Page 104

Carp streamers: Decorative wind socks designed as carp that are flown from high places from April to early May in celebration of Children's Day. The carp symbolize courage and tenacity for their ability to swim up even a waterfall.

Page 105

Iris leaves in the bath: The iris is a traditional flower for Children's Day. Bathing with its leaves on that day symbolically purifies and cleanses the child's body.

Page 109

First-magnitude star: The brightest stars in the night sky make up the first-magnitude stars, with the stars getting dimmer as the magnitude increases.

Page 104

"I can get a driver's license!": In Japan, the legal minimum age for most types of driver's licenses is eighteen.

Page 119

Alphard: The brightest star in the Hydra constellation. "Alphard" is derived from the star's Arabic name, *al-fard*, which means "the solitary one" (so named because there are no other bright stars in its proximity). Alphard is often seen as the red-orange heart of the water snake in the Hydra constellation.

Hydra constellation: The largest and longest constellation in the sky. Associated with the giant multiheaded snake that Hercules slew for his second labor.

Page 139

Spring Diamond: Otherwise known as the Great Diamond, it is an asterism (pattern of recognized stars) composed of Arcturus, Spica, Denebola, and Cor Caroli.

Arcturus: A giant orange star that is the brightest in the Boötes constellation and the fourth-brightest star in the night sky.

Spica: The brightest star in the Virgo constellation. Like Procyon, it's a binary star system, composed of a blue subgiant star and a smaller blue-dwarf star.

Page 140

Denebola: The second-brightest star in the Leo constellation. Its name means "tail of the lion" in Arabic. Denebola is a white star that is much brighter, hotter, and more immense than our sun.

Cor Caroli: A binary star, the brightest in the northern constellation Canes Venatici, the Hunting Dogs. The name is Latin and means "Charles's Heart." Historians disagree on whether it was named for King Charles I or King Charles II.

Page 184

Switching uniforms: Students in Japan usually have fall/winter and spring/summer school uniforms. Understandably, changing out of the heavier cold-weather uniforms is typically something students look forward to!

The rainy season: In most of Japan, the beginning of June through the middle of July means an unusually high amount of rain. Although it does not necessarily rain every day, it's often still cloudy and overcast, which would put a damper on most S.A.C. stargazing activities.

Page 191

Nihonshu: Japanese alcoholic beverages mostly made from rice. *Ponshu* is short for *nihonshu*. And from *ponshu* we get...

Ponta: The suffix -*ta* is often used for dog names in Japan, perhaps because of the kanji's general meaning, "big, plump, thick," which sounds cute for a dog.

Page 201

Kanji for "Chihiro": Most Japanese names have multiple spellings that sound the same but have different meanings depending on the kanji used. It's customary to explain which kanji make up your name when meeting someone for the first time. However, up until now, Saku has only heard Chihiro's name spoken aloud, so she hasn't actually known how to spell it——until she sees it written on the chalkboard. The first character read alone is pronounced *sen*, meaning "thousand" (in his name, this is *chi*!). The second character is *hiro*, which generally means "open" or "spacious."

Page 234
Ken-san: A reference to the late actor Ken Takakura (best known in the West as Michael Douglas's costar in 1989's *Black Rain*), noted for his brooding, stoic hero roles.

Page 260
"But you're a third-year student!": There are two reasons Chihiro's classmate is surprised he might be joining a club in his third year. For one, the last year of high school is typically the time when students *drop* club activities as they turn their focus toward college entrance exams (as Chihiro mentioned earlier to Saku & co.). Second, most students join clubs when they first enter school, so joining a club in one's last year seems a bit "too little, too late"——they'd hardly have time to form relationships before they have to say good-bye.

Page 298
Too many presidents: There are basically three "presidents" in this story——Saku, the president of the Star Appreciation Club; Sei, the class president; and the president of the Student Council. Three presidents, three very different personalities!

Page 331
Teru teru bouzu: A paper doll that is white and shaped like a Buddhist priest (but resembles a ghost to Western eyes), created and prayed to by Japanese children when they want good weather.

Page 358
Wagashi: Traditional Japanese confections that are often made with mochi (rice cakes), sweet red-bean paste, and fruit. Usually served with green tea.

Kashiwamochi: Mochi stuffed with sweet red-bean paste and wrapped in oak leaves.

Page 360
"We bought a little gift on the way.": In Japan, it's polite to bring a small gift when paying someone a visit (which is why Chihiro and Saku split the cost of the sweets, so that the present could be from both of them). Sei's reply of "Oh, you didn't have to..." is also customary.

Page 383
NEETs: An acronym that stands for "Not in Education, Employment, or Training." These people are typically looked down on and are viewed as a drain on society. Kanade is one of them, since he has graduated from college but doesn't have a "real" job.

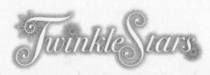

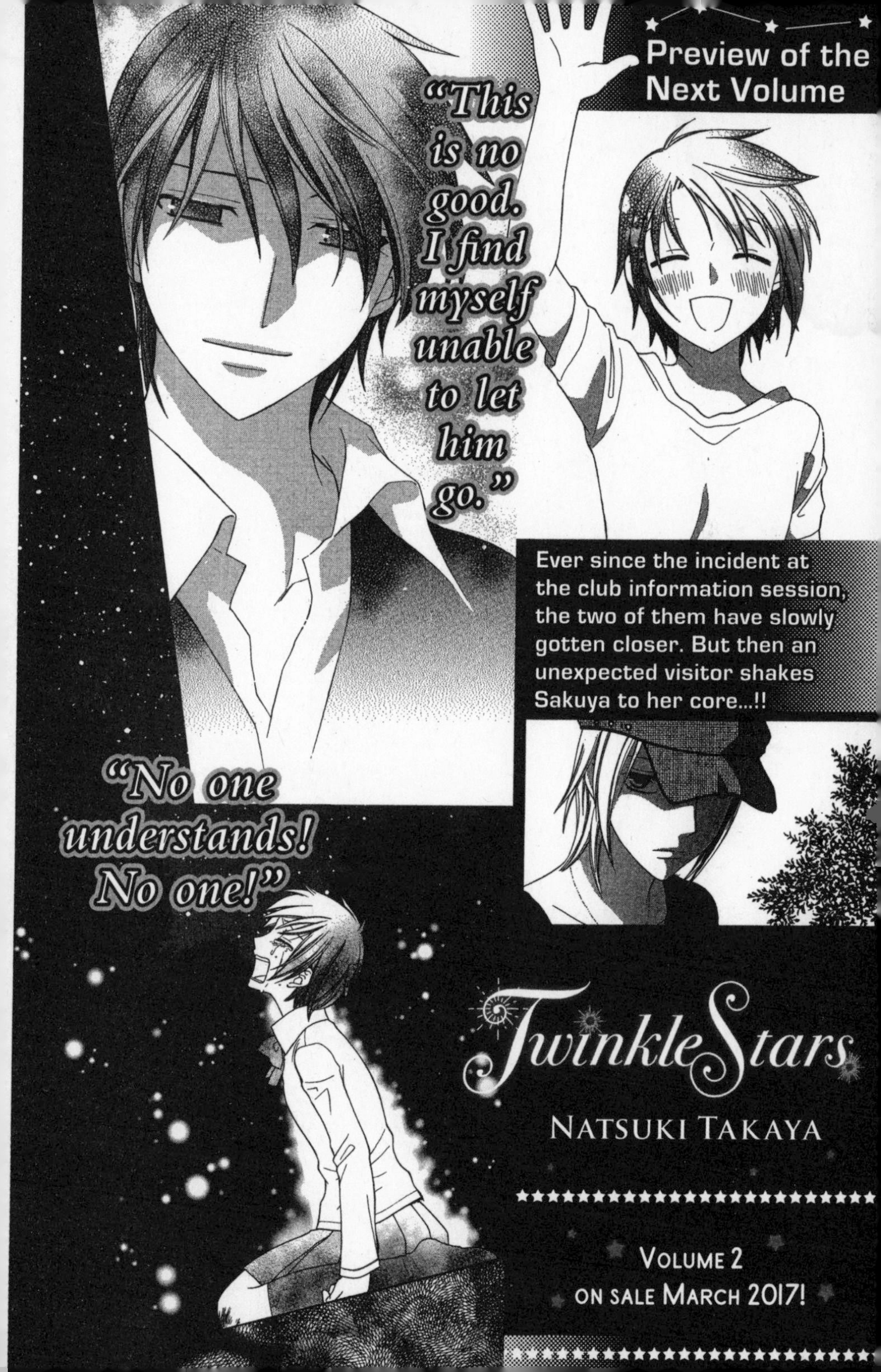
Preview of the Next Volume
"This is no good. I find myself unable to let him go."
Ever since the incident at the club information session, the two of them have slowly gotten closer. But then an unexpected visitor shakes Sakuya to her core...!!
"No one understands! No one!"
Twinkle Stars
NATSUKI TAKAYA
VOLUME 2 ON SALE MARCH 2017!

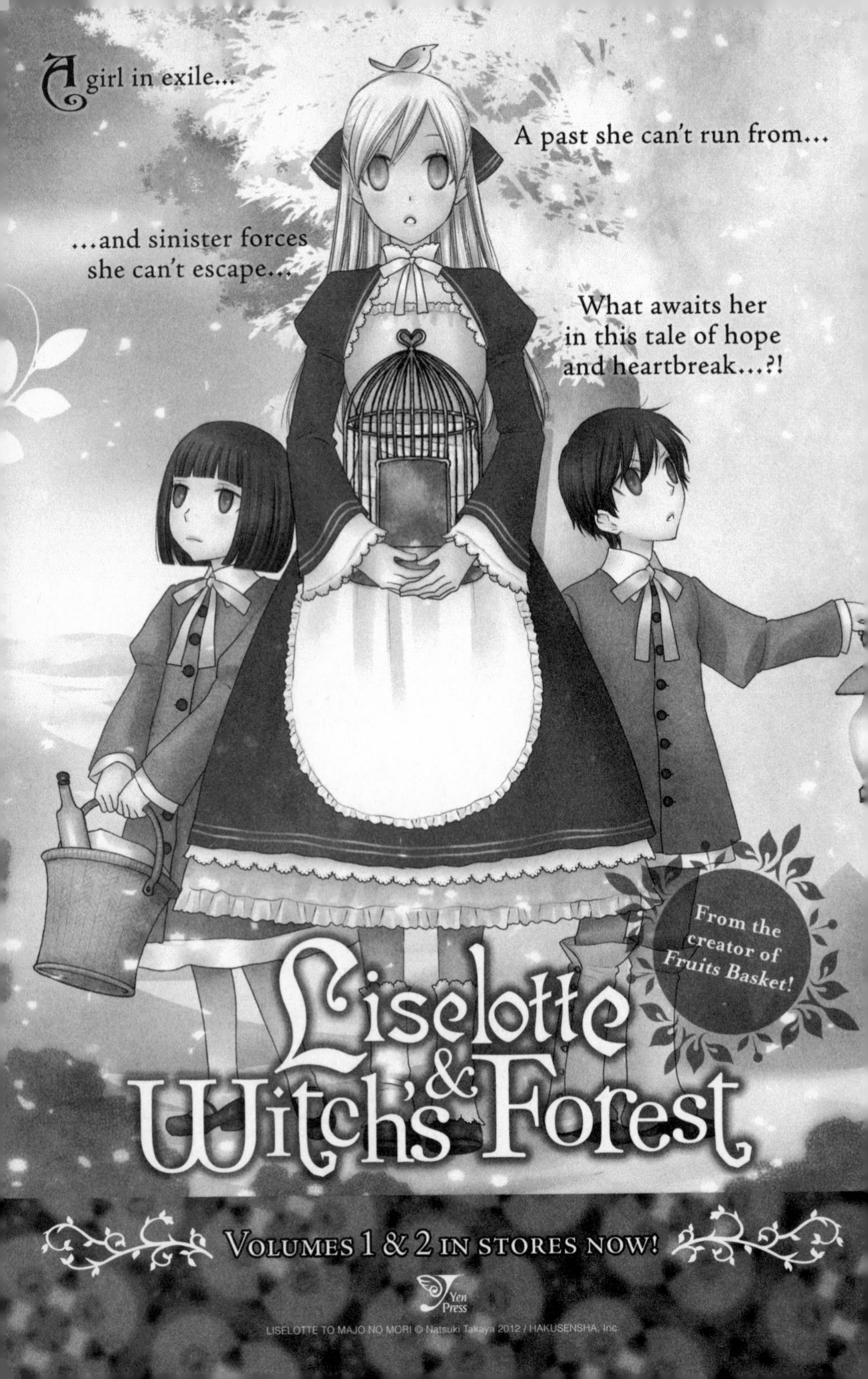
A girl in exile...
A past she can't run from...
...and sinister forces she can't escape...
What awaits her in this tale of hope and heartbreak...?!
From the creator of Fruits Basket!
Liselotte & Witch's Forest
VOLUMES 1 & 2 IN STORES NOW!
Yen Press
LISELOTTE TO MAJO NO MORI © Natsuki Takaya 2012 / HAKUSENSHA, Inc.

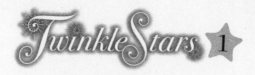

Twinkle Stars 1

Natsuki Takaya

Translation: Sheldon Drzka ★ Lettering: Lys Blakeslee

This book is a work of fiction. Names, characters, places, and incidents are the product of the author's imagination or are used fictitiously. Any resemblance to actual events, locales, or persons, living or dead, is coincidental.

HOSHI WA UTAU, Vol 1, 2 by Natsuki Takaya
© Natsuki Takaya 2008
All rights reserved.
First published in Japan in 2008 by HAKUSENSHA, Inc., Tokyo.
English language translation rights in U.S.A., Canada and U.K. arranged with HAKUSENSHA, Inc., Tokyo through Tuttle-Mori Agency, Inc., Tokyo.

English translation © 2016 by Yen Press, LLC

Yen Press, LLC supports the right to free expression and the value of copyright. The purpose of copyright is to encourage writers and artists to produce the creative works that enrich our culture.

The scanning, uploading, and distribution of this book without permission is a theft of the author's intellectual property. If you would like permission to use material from the book (other than for review purposes), please contact the publisher. Thank you for your support of the author's rights.

Yen Press
1290 Avenue of the Americas
New York, NY 10104

Visit us at yenpress.com
facebook.com/yenpress
twitter.com/yenpress
yenpress.tumblr.com
instagram.com/yenpress

First Yen Press Edition: November 2016

Yen Press is an imprint of Yen Press, LLC.
The Yen Press name and logo are trademarks of Yen Press, LLC.

The publisher is not responsible for websites (or their content) that are not owned by the publisher.

Library of Congress Control Number: 2016946117

ISBNs: 978-0-316-36023-4 (paperback)
978-0-316-36025-8 (ebook)

10 9 8 7 6 5 4 3 2 1

BVG

Printed in the United States of Ame

P9-AOI-083